I0787981

DISASTROUS VENTURES:

German and British Enterprises in East New Guinea up to 1914.

Hans-Jürgen Ohff

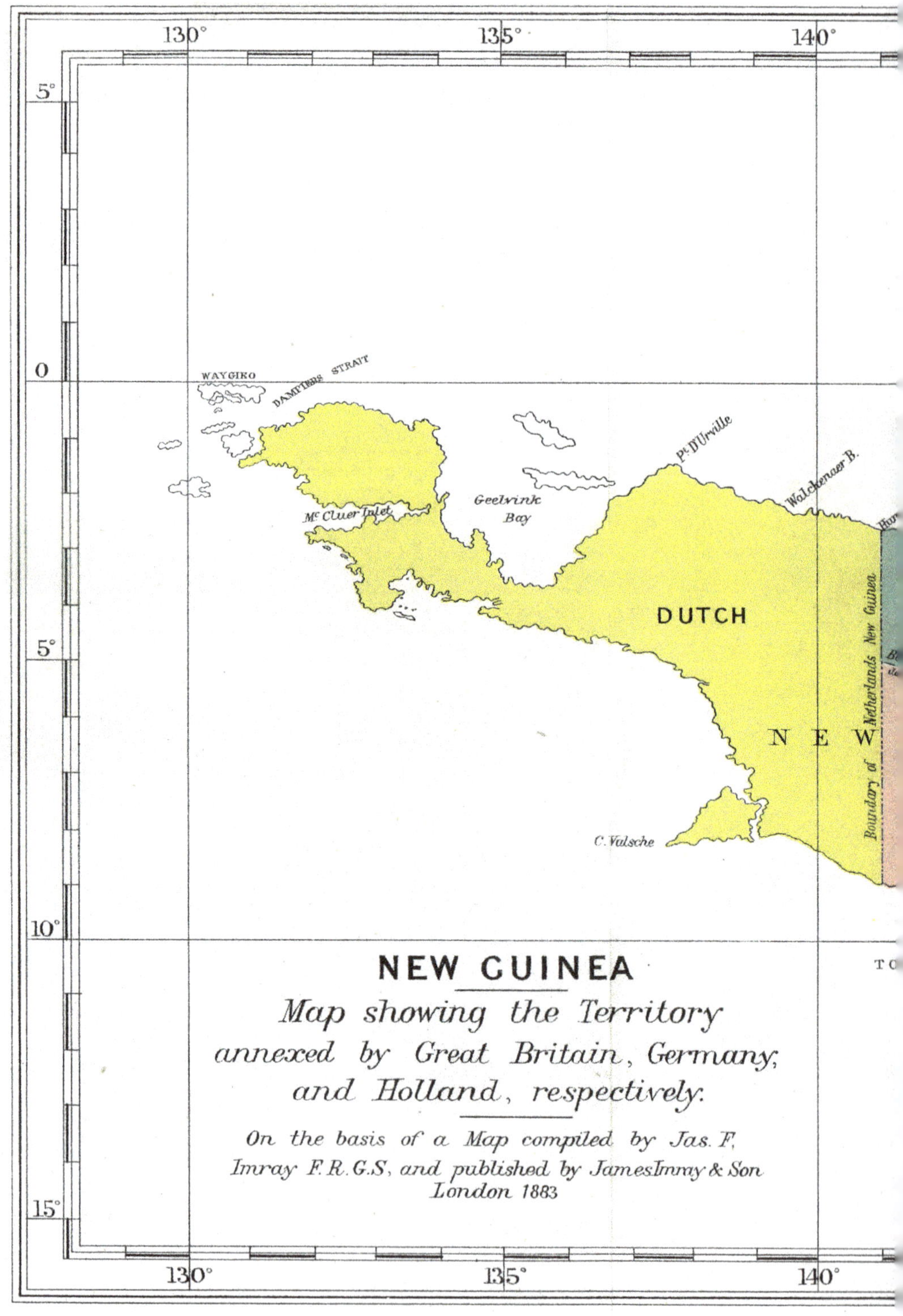

NEW GUINEA

*Map showing the Territory
annexed by Great Britain, Germany,
and Holland, respectively.*

*On the basis of a Map compiled by Jas. F.
Imray F.R.G.S, and published by James Imray & Son
London 1883*

145°
150°
155°
5°
0
5°
10°
15°
Commerson I. (P.D)
Anchorite Is (P.D)
The Monks (P.D)
Hermit Is (P.D)
St Mathias I. (P.D)
Squally I. (P.D)
Lyra Sh!
quier
vour
.I.
Boudeuse I. (P.D)
ADMIRALTY ISLES
La Vandola
C. Soloman Sweet
Byron Str!
Fisher I.
San Francisco
Gerrit Denys
rand I.
D'Urville Is
St Roissy I.
Jacquinot I.
Schouten Is
Lesson I.
Vulcan I.
Purdy Is
Admiralty I.
Elizabeth I.
Latent Rf.
Sydney Sh!
Sherburne Sh!
Circular Rf.
New Hanover
Sandwich I.
NEW IRELAND
D or York I.
Legelix Sh!
Caen Is
C. St Maria
al St John
AN
Albert Rf.
Gipps Rf.
French Isles
Father & Son
C. Lambert
Blosseville I.
C. St George
5°
Dampier Rich I.
Crown I.
Long I.
Lottin I.
Duportail Is
St George Chan!
C. Duperre
Astrolabe Gulf
Rook I.
Dampier Str. Willaumez I.
Raoul Is
Grequel I.
Wide B.
C. Orford
Fr. Iris
British
NEW BRITAIN
Jacquinot B.
& A German Territories
State for the Colonies dated 25th May 1885
Gracious Is
C. King William
Roos Is
South C.
P. Montague
TISH
ird R.
Huon Gulf
Riche I.
North I.
Tarten I.
Journey I.
Woodlark Id
Gulf of Papua
Albert Mts
Mt Yule
Mt Owen Stanley
S.E. Cape
Trobriand Is
Lagrandiere Is
Evans I.
Sharp I.
C. Stuckling
D'Entrecasteaux Is
10°
IT
Goschen Str!s
Blanchard
Deboyne Is
South Cape
St Aignan
Dochateau I.
Journet Is
LOUISIADE
South East ARCHIP!
Rossel I.
C. Deliverance
C. Sudest
15°

Disastrous Ventures

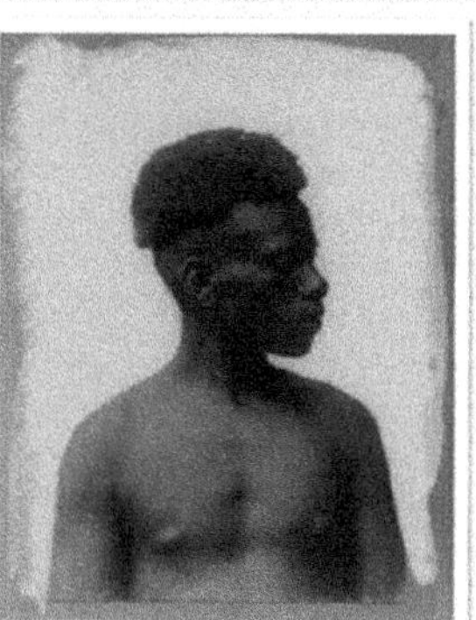

Buka Boys playing the flute, ca. 1885; **Tolai on the Gazelle Peninsula, New Britain,** ca. 1898; **Native of a Ralum River tribe,** ca. 1885; **Papuan warrior,** ca. 1889; **Son of Chief Makiri, Finschhafen,** ca. 1884; **Villagers on Siar,** ca. 1885. (Bildbestand der Deutschen Kolonialgesellschaft (Goethe University Frankfurt a. M. Nos. 044-4026-2, 002-0102-15; 043-4025-5; 042-0245-19; 043-4025-17, 001-0047-2)

In memory of those Islanders for whom the Papuan and Melanesian colonies were home, and not a resource for imperial governments.

Disastrous Ventures

Cover Image: William Hart, paradisea-augustae-victoriae (image courtesy Australian Museum)

First published in 2015 by Plenum Publishing Australia
http://www.plenumpublishing.com.au/
Revised edition in 2019

National Library of Australia Cataloguing-in-Publication Data

Author: Ohff, Hans-Jürgen
Title: Disastrous Ventures: German and British Enterprises in East New Guinea up to 1914

eISBN   978-0-9943045-4-4
ISBN   978-0-9943045-3-7 (paperback)
ISBN   978-0-9943045-2-0 (hardback)

Subjects: East New Guinea--Colonization
          Papua New Guinea--Economic conditions
          East New Guinea--History--19th century
          Germany--Colonies--Papua New Guinea
          Germany--Colonies--Administration
          Great Britain--Colonies--Papua New Guinea
          Great Britain--Colonies--Administration

Dewey Decimal Clasification notation: 995.302

Contents

MAPS

CHARTS

ILLUSTRATIONS

Acknowledgments

This book grew from a PhD thesis completed at the University of Adelaide, South Australia. I am grateful to all who have assisted me in this task. I am particularly indebted to Margaret Hosking, Peter Jacobs and Elise Benetto, research librarians at the Barr Smith Library at The University of Adelaide who provided me with invaluable assistance. In Sydney I made extensive use of the Mitchell Library at the State Library of New South Wales and the Fisher Library at The University of Sydney, and in Queensland of the John Oxley Library and the University of Queensland Library. The staff of the National Library of Australia and the National Archives of Australia in Canberra ably supported me in finding the manuscripts, rare books and archival records used in the manuscript. Similar assistance was also forthcoming from the library staff at The Australian National University and the Pacific Manuscripts Bureau. Peter Sack deserves special recognition for sharing his extensive knowledge and for giving me access to his large archival records on German New Guinea.

In Germany I received generous support from Edeltraud Wolff of the Bundesarchiv, Berlin-Lichterfelde and the staff of the Staatsbibliothek zu Berlin. In Frankfurt-am-Main I was given access to the Historische Institut of the Deutsche Bank AG by Reinhard Frost. In Hamburg Frau Becker and Herr Hoppe of the Hamburgisches Welt-Wirtschafts-Archiv provided trolleys laden with research material. Other archival material was examined in the Handelskammer and the Staatsarchiv in Hamburg and Bremen. Hermann Joseph Hiery, a fountain of knowledge on German New Guinea, was generous in his guidance on this German colony.

For advice in the research tasks I am indebted to Karl Baumann, Margit Davies, David Lewis, Peter Hempenstall, Peter Overlack, and Peter-Michael Pawlick. Adelle Howse assisted with the modelling of the financial data. Tony Santin and David Smithers offered advice on the presentation of the financial information. Sydney Hickman and Stephen Sasse read the entire manuscript. Their eyes for detail and editorial comments have been of considerable benefit.

Robert Dare, the former Head of School of History and Politics at The University of Adelaide, combined friendship with scholarship and academic control. I am grateful for all he has taught me. The many discussions I had with Roger Knight from the same School were inspirational, and I am appreciative for his pointed comments.

Marianne, my wife and best friend, deserves more credit than can be said. I thank all my friends for their tolerance and support.

Disastrous Ventures

Abstract

The colonies of German New Guinea (GNG) and British New Guinea (BNG) which from 1906 became the Territory of Papua, experienced different paths of development due to the colonial administrators' divergent commercial policies. The establishment of these colonies in the late 19th century, and all of the major events and decisions relating to them up to 1914, were based mainly on commercial imperatives. This book examines the circumstances leading to the founding of GNG and BNG. It analyses the impact of Government decisions and the growth of capitalist enterprises in East New Guinea during its first 30 years (1884–1914).

German and British Governments were reluctant to become involved in the colonisation of East New Guinea. In the context of the political pressures prevailing in Berlin and London, both Governments succumbed but insisted that the cost of administering and developing the colonies was not to be borne by the state. The establishment costs of GNG were accepted by the Neu Guinea Compagnie (NGC) until 1899. It was a haphazard and arbitrary undertaking which was expensive and costly in human life. When the German Government assumed administrative and financial control in 1899, the development of GNG had generally progressed in line with Chancellor Otto von Bismarck's view that Germany's colonies should be treated as economic enterprises. This was despite the bureaucratic form of Government NGC had established.

In contrast, there were claims that BNG was to be established to meet defence objectives, and to protect the Papuan population from non-British influences. This posturing by the Australian colonies hid their true objective of seeking to gain control over the entire eastern sector of New Guinea and adjacent islands. The Queensland sugar planters sought to procure cheap labour, and Queensland, New South Wales and Victoria were all opposed to the establishment of competitive agricultural industries. After Britain acquired southeast New Guinea and the recruitment of Papuan and Melanesian labour into Australia had been outlawed, BNG was left to the gold prospectors, with no meaningful plantation industry taking place until the Australian Federal Government assumed administrative control over the Territory in 1906.

Neither colony had any military significance. Both colonies shared a common European moral outlook in their administrations. By 1914 GNG had become a commercially viable enterprise, but BNG, now Papua, had failed to take advantage of the 1902–1912 boom in tropical agriculture. Given their comparable size and geography, the economic performance of the two colonies should have been similar. That this did not occur is beyond dispute, and the difference in commercial outcomes is explained by the divergent policy positions taken by the two administrations.

xii

Glossary

AA	Auswärtige Amt (Foreign Office)
AA	Auswärtige Amt (Foreign Office)
AA-KA	Kolonialabteilung (Colonial Dept of AA to 17 May 1907)
A-C	Astrolabe Compagnie
AG	Aktiengesellschaft (Shareholder Company)
AGM	Annual general meeting
AN&MEF	Australian Naval and Military Expeditionary Force
AJPH	Australian Journal of Politics and History
ANU	Australian National University
AR-BNG	Annual Report British New Guinea
A.R.M.	Assistant Resident Magistrate
AR-Papua	Annual Report Papua
ATP	Australian Territory of Papua-New Guinea
AWM	Australian War Memorial
BA	Bismarck Archipel (Bismarck Archipelago)
BAK/B	Bundesarchiv (German National Archives, Koblenz/Berlin)
BA/MA	Bundes/Militärarchiv (German National Archives–Freiburg)
BAG	Bismarck-Archipel-Gesellschaft (Company)
BNG	British New Guinea
BNGD	British New Guinea Development Company Limited
BP	Burns Philp Company Limited
BPP	British Parliamentary Papers
B & V	Blohm and Voss, Hamburg
CNA	Commissioner of Native Affairs and Control
CO	Colonial Office record (Public Records Office, London)
CPD	Commonwealth Parliamentary Debates (Australia)
CPL	Choiseul Plantation Limited Co.
CPP	Commonwealth Parliamentary Paper (Australia)
Capt	Captain
CSR	Colonial Sugar Refining Company
DB	Deutsche Bank AG
D-G	Disconto Gesellschaft
DHPG	Deutsche Handels und Plantagen-Gesellschaft der Südsee-Inseln.
D.K.G.	Deutsche Kolonialgesellschaft (Society for German Colonies)
DKG	Deutsche Kolonialgesetzgebung (German colonial legislation)
DKL	Deutsches Kolonial Lexikon
DM	Deutsche Mark
DOAG	Deutsch-Ostafrikanische-Gesellschaft

Disastrous Ventures

DR	Deutsche Rundschau
DSG	Deutsche Seehandels-Gesellschaft
DSP-AG	Deutsche Südseephosphat–Aktiengesellschaft
DZA	Deutsches Zentral Archiv Berlin
EBIT	Earnings before Interest and Tax
EGM	Extraordinary General Meeting
FO	Foreign Office (Britain)
FWH	Friedrich-Wilhelmshafen (Madang)
GmbH	Gesellschaft mit beschränkter Haftung (Pty. Ltd. Co.)
GNG	German New Guinea
GNG-IT	German New Guinea – Island Territory
HAPAG	Hamburg-Amerika Linie Aktien Gesellschaft
HASAG	Hamburgische Südsee-Aktiengesellschaft
HDW	Howaldtswerke Deutsche Werft
HWWA	Hamburgisches Welt-Wirtschafts-Archiv
Jb	Jahresbericht (Annual Reports NGC)
Jb A-C	Jahresbericht Astrolabe Compagnie
Jb J-G	Jahresbericht Jaluit Gesellschaft
J-G	Jaluit Gesellschaft
KA	Reichs-Kolonialamt (after 17 May 1907)
KAG	Kolonialbank, Berlin
KPM	Koninklijke Paketvaart Maatschappi (shipping company)
KR	Kolonialrath (Colonial Council)
KWK	Kolonial-Wirtschaftliches Komitee
KWL	Kaiser-Wilhelms-Land (mainland GNG)
KWLPG	KWL Plantagen-Gesellschaft
LLC	Limited Liability Company
LPPL	Lever's Pacific Plantations Limited
Lt.Cdr	Lieutenant Commander
MLC	Member of the Legislative Council
MSch	Manchester School of Economics
NAA	National Archives of Australia
NCO	Non-commissioned officer
NBAC	Noel Butlin Archive Centre – ANU, Canberra
NDB	Norddeutsche Bank
NDL	Norddeutscher Lloyd (German shipping company)
NGA	National Gallery Australia
NGC	Neu Guinea Compagnie (New Guinea Company)
NLC	Native Land Commission
NLA	National Library of Australian, Canberra
NSW	State or Colony of New South Wales
OK	Ost Karolinen (East Caroline Islands)
Papua	The Territory of Papua
P.R.P.	Papua Rubber Plantations Proprietary Limited

PIC	Pacific Island Company
P&L	Profit and Loss
PJ	Preußische Jahrbücher (Prussian Almanac)
PMB	Pacific Manuscripts Bureau
POW	Prisoner of War
PPC	Pacific Phosphate-Company Ltd
PR	Patrol Report
PRO	Public Record Office, London
PSH	Preußische Seehandlung (Prussian State Bank)
PV	Plenarversammlung (Board of Director Meeting)
Q (Qld)	State or Colony of Queensland
RGBl	Reichs Gesetzblatt
RKA	Reichskolonialamt (Colonial Office)
R&H	Robertson, Hernsheim & Company
R.M.	Resident Magistrate, (A.R.M.) Assistant Resident Magistrate
RT	Stenographische Berichte des Reichstags (German Hansard)
RTA	Reichstagakten (Parliamentary Records, Germany)
SA	State or Colony of South Australia
SAG	Deutsche Südseephosphat AG
SIDC	Solomon Islands Development Company
SJ	Statistisches Jahrbuch (Statistical yearbook 1894–1914)
StaL-Vic	State Library of Victoria
StaL-NSW	Mitchell Library, State Library of New South Wales
StaL-Q	John Oxley Library, State Library of Queensland
StaL-SA	State Library of South Australia
SPL	Shortland Plantation Limited
StaB	Staatsarchiv Bremen (State Archive, Bremen)
StaH	Staatsarchiv Hamburg (State Archive, Hamburg)
StaK	Stadtarchiv Kiel
VoBl.	Verodnungsblatt (NGC Gazette)
V&P	Votes and Proceedings Legislative Assembly
Vic	State or Colony of Victoria
WA	State of Colony of Western Australia
Wb	Weißbuch (Blue Book in the UK and in AUS)
WK	West Karolinen (West Caroline Islands)

German terminology:

Assessor	Fully qualified German Judge
Aufsichtsrath	Chairman of the Board of Directors
Behörde	Bureaucracy, Government Administration
Bestimmungen	Regulation
Bezirksgericht	District Court in GNG
Bundesrath	Federal Council of Parliament in Germany
Denkschrift	Promemoria, position paper, memorandum

Disastrous Ventures

Erlaß	Decree; declaration; ordinance; regulation
Etat	Government/NGC Budget
Faktorei	Trading station, warehouse, factory
Fiskus or Fiscus	Government Treasury
Geheimrat	Privy Council in Germany
Geheimer Kommerzienrat	Privy Councillor of Commerce' in Germany
Generalversammlung	Annual General Meeting (AGM)
Gesetz	Statute/law (Bürgerliches) Gesetzbuch, Civil Code
Gouverneur	Governor
Grundbuch	Land Register
Kadeh	Chinese community store
Kongsi	Chinese association, building
Kaiserlicher Richter	Imperial Judge
Kolonie/Schutzgebiet	Protectorate
Landeshauptmann	Chief Administrator
Landeshoheit	Sovereignty
Mandur	Javanese overseer
Reich	German Empire
Reichskanzler	Chancellor of the Reich
Reichstag	Parliament of the Reich
Referendar	German Articled Clerk
Schutzbrief	Charter
Stationsleiter	Station or Plantation Manager
Tandil	Chinese overseer
Vertrag	Agreement, contract, treaty; compact, indenture
Vize Gouverneur	Deputy Governor
Vorsitzender	Chairman

German Geographical Names:

<u>Islands:</u>

Admiralitäts-Inseln	Admiralty Islands (Manus Island)	2° 10' S 146°55' E
Bougainville Insel	Bougainville Island	6° 10' S 155°18' E
Hermit Inseln	Hermit Islands	1° 34' S 145°11' E
KWL	Mainland (German) New Guinea	
Kretin Insel	Cretin Island	6° 46' S 147°56' E
Neu-Pommern	New Britain	4° 45' S 150°30' E
Neu-Mecklenburg	New Ireland	3° 30' S 151°30' E
Neu-Lauenburg	Duke of York Islands	4° 10' S 152°28' E
Neu-Hannover	New Hanover	2° 29' S 150°13' E
Ost-Karolinen	E Caroline Islands (Ponape)	6° 57' S 158°13' E
Purdy Inseln	Purdy Islands	2° 53' S 146°24' E
Ritter Insel	Ritter Island	5° 36' S 147°56' E
Witu Inseln	French Islands	4° 45' S 149°18' E
Woodlark Insel	Woodlark (Murua) Island	9° 02' S 152°53' E

<u>Stations, Townships:</u>

Adolph-Hafen	Morobe	7° 45'32" S 147°35'38"
Alexishafen	North of Madang	2° 40' S 141°15' E
Angoram	Angoram	4° 03'55" S 144°04'00" E
Angriffshafen	Vanimo	2° 41'24" S 141°18'15" E
Konstantinhafen	Bibi (Enke Harbour)	5° 30' S 145°56' E
Dallmannhafen	north of Wewak	3° 33'26" S 143°36'48" E
Dregerhafen	Dreger H. (Cape Cretin)	6° 25' S 145°44' E
Eitape/Berlinhafen	Aitape	3° 08'31" S 142°20'46" E
Erima	Erima	5° 25' S 145°44' E
Finschhafen	Finschhafen	6° 35'54" S 147°51'10" E
Friedrich Wilhelmshafen	Madang	5° 13'58" S 145°47'18" E
Herbertshöhe	Herbertshöhe/Kokopo	4° 21'06" S 152°16'23" E
Hatzfeldthafen	Hatzfeldthafen	4° 23'57" S 145°12'39" E
Kap König Wilhelm	Cape King William	5° 55' S 147°20' E
Kävieng	Kavieng	2° 33'72" S 150°47'38" E
Kieta	Kieta	6° 12'51" S 155°37'23"E
Kronprinzhafen	Kronprinz Harbour	4° 27' S 145°21' E
Lae	Burgberg	6° 43'24" S 146°59'36" E
Peterhafen – Witu Inseln	Garowe/Deslacs Island	4° 54' S 149°09' E
Postsdamhafen	Awaro – Hansa Bay	4° 12' S 144°52' E
Prinz Albrechthafen	Bogia	4° 24' S 145°13' E
Rabaul	Rabaul	4°11'45" S 152°10'21" E
Ralum	Ralum	4° 21' S 152°16' E
Ramumünde	Station Ramu River	4° 02' S 144°42' E
Ramu Zwischenstation	Central Ramu Valley Station	4° 38' S 144°40' E
Samoahafen	Salamaua Station	7° 17'28" S 146°59'35" E
Simpsonhafen	Simpson/Rabaul Harbour	4° 16' S 151°58' E
Stephansort	Bogadjim	5° 26' S 145°45' E
Weberhafen	Weber Harbour	4° 15' S 145°13' E

<u>Rivers:</u>

Gogol Fluß	Gogol River	5° 13' S 145°48' E
Herkules Fluß	Waria River	7 °48' S 147°35' E
Kaiserin-Augusta Fluß	Sepik River	4° 11' S 143°31' E
Lehmfluß	Clay River	4° 43' S 144°08' E
Markham Fluß	Markham River	6° 44' S 146°58' E
Ottilie/Ramu Fluß	Ramu River	4° 02' S 144°41' E
Töpferfluß	Keram River	4° 27' S 144°13' E

<u>Mountains and Ranges:</u>

Bismarck Kette	Bismarck Range	
Finisterre Kette	Mount Sarawaket	6° 17' S 147°05' E

Disastrous Ventures

Hansemannberg	Mount Hansemann	5° 10' S 145°45' E
Hunstein Kette	Hunstein Range	4° 24' S 142°52 E
Oertzen Berge	Oertzen Range	5° 28' S 145°34' E
Sattelberg	Sattelberg	6° 28' S 147°44' E
Schraderberg	Schrader Range	4° 53' S 144°13' E
Torricelli Kette	Torricelli Range	3° 30' S 142°00' E
Wilhelmsberg	Mount Wilhelm	5° 47' S 145°01' E

Currencies:
(Rate of exchange: The Economist, 8 Aug. 1885, p. 974)

£Stg	Pound Sterling = 20 Shillings. 1s = 12d = RM20.48 = F25.15
A£	Pound Australian = Pound Stg for the period under review
s	shilling: 20s = £1
d	Pence: 12d = 1s
RM	Reichs Mark
Pf	Pfennig: 100 Pf = RM1
F	French Franc = RM1.25 = 10d
Hfl.	Dutch Gulden (Florin) = 100 cents = RM1.70
$	Dollar USA = 100 cents = RM4.75 = Peseta 5.60; Mex$
	Chilean/Mexican Dollar–price of silver = 2s 6d to 4s Stg
S$	Straits Dollar = RM2.04 in 1897; fixed at 2s 4d Stg in 1906
$	Gold Dollar = RM4.08, traded from 1895

Weights:

Catty	catty (kati) = 1.33 lb; 500 g
cwt	hundredweight = one twentieth of a ton dwt.
dwt	pennyweight (24 grains or one twentieth of an ounce troy)
DWT	total contents of ship in long tons (payload)
dz	Doppel Zentner = 100 kg
g	gram
gr.	grain = 0.0648 g
GRT or BRT	ship's internal volume, (1 GRT — 2.83m^3)
RT	100 cft or 2.8317 cbm; gross internal (ship) capacity
kg	kilogram = 1000 g (CL – Commerzlast [1 CL =3000 kg])
l	litre = 1000 cu. centimeters; 4.55 l = 1 imperial gallon = 8 pints
lb	metric pound = 500 g = 0.5 kg – weights for GNG are metric
lb	imperial pound = 0.4536 kg; 112 lb = one hundred weight
oz.	ounce = 28 g = a unit of one sixteenth of a pound avoirdupois
picul	one picul = 107 litres of grain = 8 picul = 1000 lbs
t	long ton = 2,240lb; freight ton = 1,016 kg or 40 cu. ft; tonne = 1000 kg
tahil	tahil (tael) = 1.33 oz
Troy	troy weight = 12 oz = 5,760 gr = 0.3732 kg

Other measurements:
Distance between 1° lat. and long. at the Equator is ~60 nmi =111.4 km

ac	acres
chain	66 ft
cm	centimeter = 0.01 m
dm	decimeter = 0.1 m
fathom	Faden = 6 ft = 1.8 m
ft (cu ft)	feet (cubic feet)
ha	hectare = 2.47 ac
km	kilometer = 1,000 m = 3,280 ft = 0.621 mile
knot	nautical mile per hour
mile	1.609 km = 1,609 m = 5,280 ft
League	league = ~3 miles = 4,812 m
m	meter
mm	millimeter = 0.001 m
nmi (n.m.)	Nautical mile (2025 yd = 1852 m = 10 cables)

Discovery Bay – New Guinea, ca. 1878 (*CAP J. Moresby, Discoveries & Surveys in New Guinea*, p. 216)

GERMAN, BRITISH AND AUSTRALIAN MOTIVATIONS

Part I

Disastrous Ventures

Bilibili people gathering at the Spirit House to perform ceremonial taboos; Tree House under construction on Milne Bay; Tattooed woman from Rogeia Island, and boy from Schering Peninsula dressed to impress (1884); Chieftain Makiri of Ssuam (Finschhafen); Madang Island; House of Tiár (Ali) Island; Elder at Parsi Point (1884). Images taken from Otto Finsch's *Samoa-Fahrten* (1888).

NEW GUINEA: A LAND OF GOLD AND RICHES

To find a land of gold and riches was the hope of the early explorers who ventured to the then largest known island in the world. The first person to suggest an association between the riches of Ophir—identified in the Old Testament—and New Guinea was Antonio Pigafetti in his account of Magellan's search for the Spice Islands (Moluccas) in 1521. Although Magellan never went as far south as New Guinea it is speculated that he had New Guinea in mind when he wrote: 'the king of those heathens, called Raya Papua, is exceedingly rich in gold, and lives in the interior of the island'. Before the Portuguese Jorge de Meneses set foot on New Guinea in 1527, the Spanish Alvaro de Saavedro gave the island the promising name *Isla del Oro* when he passed it in 1529 on his return voyage from the Moluccas to Mexico. The expedition by Pedro Fernández de Quirós from Peru in 1606 had more to do with the discovery of the 'great southern land' for Spain than searching for gold and silver in *Australia des Espiritus Santo* (New Hebrides). Yet in his account of the voyage to his patron, King Philip III, he used the words of the Portuguese Administrator of Tidore: New Guinea 'is a land of much gold, of which the natives make bracelets which the women wear on their neck and arms, and the men on pommels of their swords; and they have silver, and do not value it, and pearls to which they pay no heed'[1]

While the lure of gold and pearls tempted the fortune hunters to explore the unknown South Sea Island, the search for commercial opportunity was first seriously pursued by the expeditions of the Dutch and English East India companies.

Captain John Hayes of the English East India Company, with the private backing of three Calcutta merchants, established New Albion for the British Crown on 25 October 1793. The extent of his claim was from Waigero Island in the west to Rossel Island in the east, including the entire north coast of mainland New Guinea and its adjacent islands. Neither the British Government nor the East India Company showed any interest in spending money on a new settlement where the prospects for trade in spices or other riches were not immediately evident. The settlement was vacated after 21 months with considerable loss in European and Sepoy lives. Fearing the future plans of the British, Pieter Merkus claimed the southwest coast of West New Guinea on 28 August 1828 for The Netherlands with the establishment of Fort du Bus at Triton Bay. This settlement was abandoned in 1836 after more than 100 Dutch officials and Javanese soldiers had died there. Holland retained its territorial claim over West New Guinea to 141°1'47" east longitude, but it was not until 1898 that the first permanent Dutch administrative posts, Fakfak and Manokwari, were established on West New Guinea.

Disastrous Ventures

When European trade between the Australian colonies and East Asia grew, the need for accurate information on New Guinea waterways became vital. Captain Blackwood of HMS *Fly* led an expedition in 1845 to survey the Gulf of Papua, followed by Captain Owen Stanley's expedition on HMS *Rattlesnake* to the Louisades and the southeast coast of the mainland. In 1846 Commander C. B. Yule of HMS *Brambles* took possession of New Guinea for the British Crown at Cape Possession. Captain John Moresby on the HMS *Basilisk* surveyed the eastern cape of mainland New Guinea for the first time in 1873. This involved the charting of some 275 miles (475 kilometres) of virtually unknown waters from Hercules Bay on the north to Yule Island on the south coast of mainland New Guinea. In the course of his discoveries, Moresby ceremoniously took possession of a small part of New Guinea on 24 April 1873 by placing the islands Moresby, Hayter and Basilisk under British jurisdiction. In early 1878 Frank Jones and John Hanran formed the 'New Guinea Exploring Expedition' to examine prospective country on the south coast of East New Guinea. To begin with, their schooner *Colonist* landed in Port Moresby to install W. B. Ingham as Queensland Government Agent on 22 April. Thereafter the expedition traversed some 370 miles of rugged country drained by the Laloki and the Goldie Rivers without discovering 'half a grain of gold'.[2] Five years later the Queensland Government instructed Henry Chester to raise the British flag at Port Moresby. At a ceremony on 4 April 1883 Chester proclaimed East New Guinea a British possession, a claim the British Government did not ratify.[3]

The swindler Charles Bonaventure du Breuil, better known as the Marquis de Rays or Charles I, Emperor of Oceania, promised French and Italian investors a quick fortune without venturing from their porches. Between 1877 and 1881, the inventive Rays raised F9,000,000 (£356,000) by selling 600,000 ha on New Ireland and New Britain to some 3,000 backers of his idea. Without ever travelling to the South Pacific Rays sold a hectare of land on these Melanesian islands for five French francs. The transactions were carried out without provision of security of title or indeed description of the land other than generic pictures of South Sea Islands. The demand for his scheme became so large that by 1881 prospective pioneers paid him as much as F50/ha. All told some 700 settlers left Europe on three separate voyages between 1879 and April 1881 for Port Praslin on Tombara Island on the west coast of New Ireland to establish *Colonie Libre de Port-Breton*, or *Nouvelle-France* as the venture became known.[4] Rays could not have selected a worse location for his South Sea empire. Within a few months half of the settlers had perished at sea, fallen victim to cannibalism, or died of dysentery, fever, or starvation. The venture ended before the last vessel had arrived. Disillusioned and starving, some 70 of Rays' victims made it back to Europe and 200 settled in Australia. Only a few remained in the archipelago.[5]

The political origins of colonial development in East New Guinea

Australian and German interest in East New Guinea was economic from the beginning. The supply of cheap labour to the emerging sugar industry in Queensland dominated the political agenda in Brisbane. The desire for a British bulwark to the north of Australia was to safeguard all Australian commercial interests from foreign intrusions. German interests in Samoa competed for the same Melanesian labour, with the Hamburg merchants equally interested in the steady harvest of coconuts the New Guinea islands provided.

When Bismarck declared in his Kissinger Diktat of 15 June 1877 'Germany's extraterritorial ambitions were satiated', and that he was now interested in working towards equilibrium of European powers, few foresaw Germany harbouring ambitions to compete for an imperial presence overseas. However, only six years later Bismarck quickly assembled a portfolio of colonial territory that increased the size of the German empire five-fold. Africa was the fulcrum of the Reich's interest: Southwest Africa, the Cameroon and Togoland were all claimed within six months in 1884, followed by East Africa in 1885. Halfway around the world, the north eastern part of New Guinea together with the New Britain Archipelago was claimed in late 1884, followed by the Marshall Islands a year later. The attempt by Bismarck to acquire the Caroline, Mariana and Palau Islands from Spain in 1885 failed. It was left to *Reichskanzler* Fürst Hohenlohe-Schillingsfürst to conclude Germany's bidding for colonies in 1899. Kiaochow was leased for 99 years from China in 1898 and the Pacific Islands were finally purchased from Spain in June 1899 for RM17,250,000 (25,000,000 Peseta). An agreement with Britain in the same year for West Samoa in exchange for the Solomons—other than Bougainville and Buka Island—completed the division of the western Pacific between the two European powers.

Until 1884 Bismarck steadfastly opposed colonial engagement. He dismissed the political benefits of colonies as an illusion. In his view only private firms should engage in colonial ventures as taxpayers could not be expected to support a policy that may only accrue benefits for a few merchants. In geopolitical or strategic defence terms, Bismarck only saw disadvantages as he expressed to War Minister Albrecht von Roon in 1868:

> The advantages that many believe are to be gained for commerce and industry for the benefit of the motherland is largely illusory. Because the cost of establishment, the administration and in particular defence requirements for a colony exceeds quite often the benefit the motherland would receive in return. Quite apart from this, it would be difficult to raise considerable additional taxes for the benefit of a few traders and other businesses. England has given up the policy of colonial acquisition in view of the experience she has gained, and similarly, France seems to show little interest in establishing new colonies. Our navy is not yet sufficiently established to assume proper responsibility for the protection of faraway regions. Ultimately, the attempt to found colonies in regions which are also claimed by other countries—irrespective of whether lawful or unlawful—would lead to a great deal of undesirable conflict.[6]

A shift in Bismarck's extra-European policy occurred when he decided that German traders should no longer be pushed out of tropical markets in the southwest Pacific and on the African coast where they had been operating for decades. The change had its antecedents in the third period of world economic depression beginning in 1882. The German economy declined from 1815 to 1848 and 1873 to 1887; spectacular increases in industrial investments occurred from 1850 to 1873. During this period German production of semi-finished goods rose by 40%, coal by 100%, raw materials by 90% and durable goods by 50%. After 1873 the price index (1913 = 100) declined from 120 to 81 in 1879 for wholesale goods, from 116 to 49 for coal, from 181 to 76 for iron and steel and from 108 to 83 for textile materials. British industrial output mirrored some of the German trends. While the manufacture of goods in the United Kingdom increased by 40% from 1840 to 1850, by 90% from 1850 to 1860 and by 47% from 1860 to 1870, exports declined from 1872 to 1875 by some 25%. It took the British—and largely the world economy—until 1898 to return to a cycle of economic growth.[7]

In response to these trends German industry, trade and shipping campaigned increasingly for access to overseas markets. Thus, in early 1879, international trade became a firm plank in the platform of the Bismarckian interventionist state. It ushered in a period where a diverse group of politicians, estate owners, industrialists, bankers, merchants and ordinary people founded the *Deutscher Kolonialverein* in 1882 under Count Hermann zu Hohenlohe-Langenburg in Frankfurt.[8] The vocal members of this society, some 15,000 strong at the time, actively lobbied the *Reichstag* to support colonisation. One of their leading agitators, Wilhelm Hübbe-Schleiden claimed that 'only a new, huge, challenge in the far distance can save our national interest from ruin', and Friedrich Fabri and Ernst von Weber contended that 'the perilous situation of German industry and the resultant political radicalism of the proletariat would destroy the fabric of the German nation unless a relief valve in the form of colonies was created'. Hübbe-Schleiden concluded that these 'sentiments and ambitions inspired mainstream Germans into a pro-colonial mood.'[9]

Voter enthusiasm for colonies became Bismarck's theme for the 1884 *Reichstag* election. The aging emperor was 87 years old and frail. Bismarck had to consider his future with a university-educated, liberal-minded Crown Prince Friedrich Wilhelm and his self-assured English-born wife, Victoria. In early 1883, Dr. E. Schwenninger - the new personal physician of the Chancellor - uplifted the mood of the chronically ill 69-year-old, and the *Reichskanzler* again felt indispensable. Casting off any thoughts of retirement he now played the colonial card to cement and prolong his tenure of office.

Across the English Channel, Prime Minister Gladstone's impact on the rise of liberalism in Europe had been manifest when his Liberal Party was elected for the second time in 1880 with a large majority over the Conservatives. A similar trend had started in Germany where the conservative parties experienced major losses in the 1881 *Reichstag* election.

The similarities between Bismarck and Gladstone before 1878 were pronounced. Between 1867 and 1870 Bismarck pushed through the country's most progressive liberal laws; bills that echoed those of Gladstone's. Bismarck's foreign policy between 1871 and 1878 was also similar to that of Gladstone's Government from 1868 to 1874. Both avoided confrontation and each worked for appeasement in Europe. Gladstone found his support in the liberal Manchester School. The free traders of the Bismarck-friendly National Liberals determined liberal economic policy until 1878.

When Gladstonian liberalism increasingly influenced German mainstream political thinking the *Reichskanzler* adopted a distinct anti-British stance. Alarmed by Gladstone's electoral success and his acceptance as Europe's most influential politician, Bismarck berated the British Prime Minister's lack of understanding of foreign policy, taking the credit for pursuing *Realpolitik* as the basis of European stability.[10] Gladstone, in turn, started to regard Bismarck an unreliable partner in any European compact, a self-centered, dictatorial, blackmailing and unscrupulous person who often sent conflicting signals to confuse the issues.[11]

Crown Princess Victoria's sway over the future German king and her dislike for Bismarck became well known. Possessing the liberal views of her German-born father, Prince Albert of Saxe-Coburg and Gotha, she exercised her influence on Prussian political life.[12] Her British liberalism became the core of opposition to Bismarck who in turn drew on nationalism and protectionism to defend his Government.

France's quarrel with Britain over Egypt and the objections to German colonial acquisition by the Australian and Cape colonies provided Bismarck with the opportunity of re-establishing cordial relations with French Prime Minister Jules Ferry. A pursuit of German colonies should foster anti-English feelings in the minds of German voters who might otherwise have sympathised with the Liberal Left.

While there were few - if any - economic beliefs in Bismarck's colonial agenda, the ever-increasing lobbying by German industry for colonial acquisitions became central to his 1884 election platform. To win an election Bismarck was now prepared to accept the industrialists' argument that German economic activities in extra-European markets could be counter-cyclical. He had already intervened in offering government assistance to a German enterprise operating in the South Sea in 1880—albeit on strictly commercial terms—and had no difficulty in lecturing the *Reichstag* on its obligation to provide financial and political support to trading and plantation companies overseas. France and Italy had followed Germany in the implementation of high import tariffs and subsidies, and British overseas colonies were not accessible to German merchants due to the trading arrangements Britain had established with her dominions.

Again, responding to an impending election, the *Reichskanzler* became involved in supporting the proposals debated in the budget subcommittee of the *Reichstag* for subsidised German shipping services to Africa and the Far East.[13] Bismarck advocated a Prussian postal steamer service as early as 1866, while in 1872 the German diplomat and East Asia expert, Max von Brandt, saw merit in the payment of a subsidy for a German-operated shipping service to the Far East. In 1880 the Berlin banker, Adolph von Hansemann outlined the merits of a government-subsidised postal service to the Pacific region. Hansemann argued that European Governments had long provided shipping assistance to its industries. Since 1838 Britain had paid on average annual shipping subsidies of £800,000 and tacitly approved the predatory pricing by British shipping cartels. Between 1852 and 1881 France maintained subsidies to its trans-oceanic shipping worth £1,400,000, a policy that was followed by Russia, Austria, Italy, Holland and Belgium on a smaller scale.[14]

While Bismarck did not subscribe to the formal expansionist policies of Jules Ferry, 'It is the right and duty for the superior races to civilise the inferior races', he took some pleasure at the Gladstone administration's concerns with the Third Republic's newfound appetite for colonial expansion. While Ferry's real reason for colonial expansion was economic exploitation, Bismarck's motives in 1884 were entirely political. He also expected widespread resentment from the Colonial Office, the British dominions and British industry when Germany entered the race for overseas territory. He hoped the reaction would generate anti-British feeling in the electorate, thereby reducing the votes of the anti-colonialist, Left-Liberal Anglophiles in the *Reichstag* and, with it, the parliamentary support base for Crown Prince Friedrich Wilhelm and Princess Victoria.

That Bismarck was not genuine in his ambitions for German colonies was demonstrated by his confidence given to his Ambassador in London, Count Münster. 'The colonial question is for us, in the context of domestic politics, an issue of political survival ("*politische Lebensfrage*") … Public opinion in Germany currently favours pro-colonial politics so strongly that success of the Government's domestic politics largely depends on a successful colonial policy. Similarly, Bismarck remarked to his vice chancellor, Karl Heinrich von Bötticher, a few days before the election: 'The entire colonial idea is humbug; however, we need it to win the vote of the people'. Herbert Bismarck boasted later: 'When we started the politics of colonies, the Crown Prince was still healthy, and we could expect a long reign under which British influence would dominate German politics … We had to initiate colonial politics which is popular and can create conflict with England in no time at all'.[15]

Bismarck, the shrewd politician, was also an economic manager. Experience and the counsel of his personal banker, Gerson von Bleichröder, provided him with an understanding of how private enterprise worked; he possessed an understanding of the inability of the bureaucracy to apply sound commercial principles to government enterprises. Trade, whether domestic, European or overseas, was firmly on Bismarck's agenda. He was prepared to lend government support where he felt German commerce was disadvantaged. Quite unintentionally, it was this support for traders in Fiji and Samoa in the 1870s and the Lüderitz, Peters and Woermann affairs in Africa in 1884 that underpinned the political process of colonial acquisition by Germany.

Britain's move to an 'Informal Empire' in the mid-19th century assured the maintenance of an open-market economy. This provided German traders with ongoing access to British colonies. However, the annexation of the Fiji Islands by the Disraeli Government in October 1874 saw the free trade principle abandoned in the South Pacific.[16] In the same year Premier Julius Vogel of New Zealand—who sought to raise £1,000,000 through the New Zealand & Polynesian Co. to acquire all foreign interests in Polynesia—petitioned the Colonial Office to rid Polynesian islands of all German presence and influence.[17] The German colonial agitators in turn made the Fijian incident a case in point. They used the aggressive conduct by Britain and the Australasian colonies to appeal to the *Reichskanzler* for annexation of territory where German traders were dominant. To begin with Bismarck did not intend to oblige them. He believed that Britain had annexed Fiji to ensure the peaceful coexistence of tribal chiefs and that Britain would continue to adhere to free trade principles. When the German consul at Levuka advised his Foreign Office on 17 January 1874 about threats to German interests, Bismarck rejected the complaint. Taking the contrary view, he contended that the English occupation of Fiji would prove advantageous to the German settlers because it would provide the protection of a strong Government.[18] Even when the first British governor of Fiji, Sir Arthur Gordon, enacted the *Pacific Islanders' Protection Act, 1875* that made it a felony to retain natives by force, regulated business transactions between Europeans and natives, and forgave native debts incurred with Europeans before 1871, Bismarck remained cautious. The British move was in keeping with German law which ruled that illegal land purchases by Europeans were subject to repudiation by the state. The request for compensation for the loss of land, submitted on behalf of settlers by the German consul in Sydney, Carl L. Sahl, was set aside until the legality of the purchases was established. Bismarck held that diplomacy would ensure an equitable settlement.

The *Reichskanzler's* reaction to the Fijian claims was symptomatic of his lack of interest in extra-European affairs. When Heinrich von Kusserow, legation councillor in the Foreign Office, proposed the establishment of coaling stations on Tonga and Samoa in 1876, Bismarck remained unenthusiastic: 'we could not assess the consequences of such a move', he wrote in the margins of the report, 'because such a move would be akin to establishing an Imperial Colony'.[19] Instead, Bismarck favoured the leasing or buying of land rather than entering into formal agreements. On 13 December 1875 Georg von Schleinitz entered the port of Nuku'alofa on the Tongan Island Tongatapu to pay King Siaso (George) Tupou I (1845–1893) a (state) visit and investigate the possibility of establishing coaling stations on the islands.[20] Von Schleinitz had been given command of the imperial corvette *Gazelle* to carry out a voyage of circumnavigation to collect anthropological data, and chart sea currents and temperatures. He spent the summer of 1874 at the Kerguelen Islands in the southern Indian Ocean where astronomers observed the transit of Venus on 9 December. In mid-1875 von Schleinitz set course for New Guinea waters to collect Melanesian artefacts. It was on his way home that he called at Fiji, Tonga and again Samoa where he witnessed significant German commercial activities according to his report to the Foreign Office.

When the secretary of state for the Foreign Office, Bernhard Heinrich von Bülow, advised the Chief of the Admiralty, Albrecht von Stosch, to proceed discreetly in the South Sea so as not to provoke American and British interests, he seemed unaware of the encouragement von Kusserow gave Theodor Weber of the powerful Godeffroy trading house. Weber, also Hamburg consul in Samoa, Tonga and Fiji had followed up on von Schleinitz' visit to establish trading links with King George Tupou I via the influential missionary Shirley Baker of the Tongan Wesleyan Methodist Missionary Society. When Weber received instructions from Berlin in October 1876 to draft a Treaty to safeguard German interests in Tonga while also promoting friendly relations with the King and his people he foresaw his copra-trading empire expanding.

On 1 November 1876, Theodor Weber together with Captain Eduard Knorr, commanding officer of the corvette *Hertha,* signed a draft treaty with Tonga. The signing took place on the *Hertha* where the President of the Tongan legislative council, Uiliami Tugi, represented the king and where Shirley Baker acted as translator and witness. The Friendship Treaty embodied an undertaking by the *Kaiserliche Marine* to safeguard the ruler against usurpers and labour recruiters. It also provided German traders protection and commercial freedom and ceded the right to establish a naval coaling station in the safe harbour of Vava'u Island.

Three months later, Weber followed up by entering into similar agreements with 28 Samoan chiefs. Bismarck was annoyed about the precipitous action by the *Reichsmarine*. He considered the establishment of German naval and coaling stations in the South Sea as potential provocation to foreign Governments that could interfere with his politics of European stability. At the same time Bismarck was concerned that German trade in the South Sea could continue to develop without political interference by other nations. His instruction to his Ambassador in London, Count Münster von Derneburg was 'not to miss any opportunity to let it be known that the Imperial German Government has a vital interest to see its subjects treated fairly and equitably overseas,' formalised the trading arrangements entered into by the *Reichsmarine*. He did so with the caveat that his signature on the Tonga Friendship Treaty could not be construed as confirmation of a German Colony, 'an idea which he distinctly and particularly repudiate[d]'.[21]

Two years later, Theodor Weber and Captain Karl Bartholomäus von Werner of light cruiser *Ariadne* went on a west Pacific acquisition spree. Trading and coaling station agreements were signed with the king of the Gilbert and Ellice Islands, the tribal chiefs of the northern coast of New Britain, and the Marshall, Ralick and Duke of York Islands. In April 1879 the chiefs of the Society Islands were added to this catalogue of agreements.[22] By the time the *Reichstag* had ratified the treaties on 13 June 1879, Bismarck had become noticeably proactive on extra-European affairs. He was now satisfied that Britain had acted against the interest of German traders on Fiji and instructed the German ambassador in London to vigorously pursue compensation from the British Government. Within three years he had moved from a noninterventionist course of diplomatic guardianship via diplomatic objection against foreign interference to a protectionist policy of German trade. When the *Reichstag* applauded Bismarck for his vision on extra-European trade in the first 1880 session, he would have been pleased. It was this political support which encouraged him to take the next step and submit the 'Samoa Subsidy Bill' in April 1880.[23]

After nearly 11 years of German bickering and British delay, the German land claims in Fiji were settled for £10,000.[24] Much has been made of this compensation claim and London's dilatory treatment of the claims. M. von Hagen's argument that British political manoeuvring to keep Germany out of colonies was 'forcing Bismarck to move towards a formal colonial policy' overstates the evidence. In a note written on 7 March 1885, Herbert Bismarck advised his father: 'I think little of the claims in Fiji. A few of them are justifiable, but the majority are fictitious, and the German subjects concerned are several of them of doubtful existence'.[25] Equally debatable are Hagen's and Poschinger's arguments that von Kusserow deserves the credit for changing Bismarck's mind because his 'doggedness gradually overcame Bismarck's objection to colonies'. Herbert von Bismarck's low regard for Kusserow is demonstrated when he wrote to his brother Wilhelm: 'Kusserow has led us into a pile of goose shit in East Africa'. While the Chancellor relied to some extent on Kusserow and Lothar Bucher on overseas trade issues, he alone determined colonial policy. This was no more obvious than in the position he displayed during the West Africa Conference from November 1884 to February 1885. The gathering of European heads of state in Berlin carried Bismarck's proposal to create a free trading and shipping zone for all states in the Congo River basin. More importantly this prestigious conference benefited Bismarck's all-important election campaign. Herbert Bismarck confirmed as much when he told Friedrich von Holstein after the election: '[he] played the "Congo Card" for domestic political reasons before the outcome of the Conference was assured'.[26]

With the 1884 October election the Bismarck-friendly parties - DKP and NLP - were elected the largest bloc in the *Reichstag*. The threat of 'a German Gladstone Government' was no longer present and the resignation of the Gladstone Cabinet in early June 1885 was followed by the installation of a conservative Prime Minister. Lord Salisbury assured Bismarck that England was not pursuing Russia diplomatically at the expense of Germany which closed Bismarck's play with France over Egypt. German colonial policy was again reliant on private enterprise, managing and paying for their overseas initiatives.

Despite the signing of the first South Sea Treaty, the *Reichsmarine* coaling station on Tonga never materialised. During the ratification debate in the *Reichstag* Bismarck's visceral distrust of Admiral Albrecht von Stosch came to the surface. Von Stosch, the first chief of the newly created Imperial German Navy, was on the wrong side of Bismarckian conservatism. And when the treaty was finally ratified on 31 October 1877, it was indeed no more than a friendship compact that explicitly excluded coaling stations and garrisons and any installations that could be construed as an attempt at colonisation by Germany. While King George Tupou I expressed gratitude towards the *Reich* for signing the first treaty with his young state, he also entered into a treaty with Great Britain in 1879 and the United States of America in 1888. After George I was succeeded by his great grandson George II, Tonga became a British Protectorate in 1900. To discourage any German commercial advances, Tonga assented to a British request in 1905 to conduct all foreign affairs through a British consul, who had power of veto over Tonga's foreign policy and finances.

Notes

1   C. Kelly, 'Geographical Knowledge and Speculation in Regard to Spanish Pacific Voyages', *HS.ANZ* IX, 33 (1959) pp. 13 & 15; A.M. Healy, 'Ophir to Bulolo: the History of the Gold Search in New Guinea', *Historical Studies, Australia & New Zealand (=HS.ANZ)* XII, 45 (1965) p. 103.

2   *Brisbane Courier (BC)* (1878) 3 Jun., p. 3; *Nature (=N)*, vol. xix, 7 1878, Nov. p. 16.

3   J.L. Whittaker, et al., *Documents and Readings in New Guinea History, Prehistory to 1889.*

4   P. de Groote, *Nouvelle-France, Colonie Libre de Port-Breton (Océanie), passim*

5   A. Baudouin, *L'Aventure de Port-Breton et la Colonie Libre dite Novelle France*, P. Biskup, 'The New Guinea Memoirs of Jean Baptiste Octave Mouton', *JPH*, 7 (1974) pp. 6–20.

6   Bismarck to Roon, 9 Jan. 1868, in H. Spellmeyer, *Deutsche Kolonialpolitik im Reichstag*, p. 3

7   A.E. Musson, 'The Great Depression in Britain, 1873–96', *Journal of Economic History(=JEH)* 19 (1959) pp. 199–228; H-U. W.A. Lewis, 'World Production, Prices and Trade, 1870-1960', *Manchester School of Economic (=M.Sch)* 20 (1952) pp. 105–38 & 23 (1955) pp. 133–52; W.A. Lewis & P.J. O'Leary, 'Secular Swings in Production and Trade, 1870–1913'.

8   *Deutscher Kolonialverein* merged on 1 Jan. 1888 with the *Gesellschaft für deutsche Kolonisation* to promote migration, scientific expeditions, tropical research, and the economic evaluation of mineral discoveries. H. Schnee, ed., *Deutsches Kolonial-Lexikon (=DKL)* vol. i, pp. 311ff, vol ii, pp. 346f.

9   W. Hübbe-Schleiden, *Deutsche Colonisation*, Hamburg (1881); E. v. Weber, *Die Erweiterung des deutschen Wirtschaftsgebietes*, p. 50ff; F. Fabri, *Bedarf Deutschland der Kolonien?*, pp. 20, 23 & 136ff, and H.U. Wehler, *Bismarck und der Imperialismus*, pp. 142–55.

10 Taylor, *Germany's First Bid for Colonies*, p. 79.

11 M.R.D. Foot & H.C.G. Matthew, eds., *The Gladstone Diaries*; and Taylor, pp. 76, 79 & 99.

12 F. Pornsonby, *Letters of the Empress Frederick, passim.*

13 M. v. Hagen, *Bismarcks Kolonialpolitik*, pp. 97–114 and Wehler, pp. 205, 239-41 & 253–7.

14 R. Meeker, 'History of Shipping Subsidies', *American Economic Association* 6, 3 (1905).

15 Bismarck to Münster, 25 Jan. 1884 (J. Lepsius, et al, eds., *Die Große Politik Der Europäischen Kabinette,* vol. iv, p. 96); A. Riehl, *'Tanz um den Äquator'*, pp. 763ff; N. Rich & M.H. Fisher, eds., *Die geheimen Papiere Friedrich von Holsteins*, p. 174

16 Fiji had asked Britain and Germany for protection (W.H. Dawson, *The German Empire, 1867–1914 and the unity Movement* p. 175). J.D. Legge, *Australian Colonial Policy: A Survey of Native Administration and European Development in Papua*, pp. 10–11; E. Drus, 'The Colonial Office and the Annexation of Fiji', *The Royal Historical Society (=RHS)*4, XXXII (1950)

17 K.E. Jung, *Der Weltteil Australien*, vol. Iii, p. 121; T. Trood, *Island Reminiscences*, p. 55; K. Schmack, *J.C. Godeffroy*, pp. 186, 208, 229, 246 & 255.

18 Sahl to Bismarck, Wb. 1885, pp. 13ff; Hagen, 'Deutsche Land-Reklamation auf Fiji', p. 65.

19 Bismarck marginal note, RKA 1001:2809, pp. 140 ff, H. v. Poschinger, 'Aus der Denkwürdigkeit Heinrich von Kusserow', *Deutsche Revue der Gegenwart (=DRG)* I (1908); Hagen, pp. 61–2.

20 G. v. Schleinitz, *Die Forschungsreise S.M.S. „Gazelle" In den Jahren 1874–1876* (Berlin, 1888).

21 Tonga, RKA 1001:2810, pp. 143–6; Treaty, 1 Nov. 1876 (RT 3, Anlage 80, pp. 278–81); Hagen, pp. 58–61 & 67; H. v. Poschinger, *Stunden bei Bismarck*, p. 293; Townsend, pp. 65–75 & 104–5.

22 B. v. Werner, 'Die erste Kreuzung deutscher und amerikanischer Interessen auf Samoa', *Unsere Zeit, DR*, I, II (1889) pp. 162–76; G. Hoffmann, 'WIrtschaftsspionage in der Südsee', p. 107; P.G. Sack & B. Sack, eds., *Eduard Hernsheim: South Sea Merchant*, p. 48

23 Bismarck to Münster, 23 May 1879 in Hagen, p. 67; Townsend, pp. 71 & 76; Hagen, p. 69.

24 Britain accepted 517 of some 1,300 claims, dismissed 351, and deferred the balance, Schmack, p. 217, Hagen, pp. 95f; Taylor, *Germany's First Bid for Colonies*, p. 32

25 Hagen, pp. 90 & 571–5; E.T.S. Dugdale, ed., *Bismarck's Relations with England*, p. 191

26 S.E. Crowe, *The Berlin African Conference 1884–1885*, pp. 95–196; Rich & Fisher, p. 116

The signing of the (draft) German-Tonga Peace and Friendship Treaty on the Corvette SMS *Hertha* **on 1 November 1876. From left to right Uliami Tugi, Capt. Eduard von Knorr with his First Officer on his left, Consul Theodor Weber and Missionary Shirley Baker (G.A. Riemer,** *Die Reise SMS Hertha nach Ost-Asien und den Südsee Inseln 1874-1877*, p. 53, NLA, Canberra)

Clearing rainforest and tilling the soil for plantation land, ca. 1889, (Carl Ettling, *Unter Pflanzern* p. 32)

MONEY-MAKING MOTIVATIONS

Well before the last rush of colonial annexation in the 1880s, merchants and adventurers of the great Hanseatic trading cities of Hamburg and Bremen became interested in the trading opportunities in the south and west Pacific Ocean. The exploits of the companies and the characters outlined in this chapter provided the economic context that led to the annexation of East New Guinea in 1884/5.

During that time Honolulu was a favoured geographical location for British and French whalers and traders. The Hamburg firm of Stapenhorst & Hoffschläger also established their base in Honolulu in the 1860s. Trading for sandalwood and servicing their whaling fleet, they had established stations on Ebon Atoll in the Marshall Islands, some 4,000 km west of Hawaii. The brothers Frederic, Gustav and William Hennings from Bremen started the Fiji branch of the region's leading trader and plantation owner, Johann Cesar Godeffroy & Sohn, in 1860. Three years later, two of the brothers branched out and founded F&W Hennings. The Hamburg traders Ruge & Hedemann tried their luck in the South Sea ten years later. They sought the backing of the Hamburg shipping firm Wachsmuth & Krogmann to establish Ruge, Hedemann & Co. of Apia in 1875. The company operated a network of trading stations throughout Polynesia with stations on the Fiji and Tonga islands. Wilkens & Co. and Kost & Brander cooperated with the Apia-based Joh. C. Godeffroy & Sohn on Tahiti from 1876, while Hachtfeldt & Co. and A. Capelle & Milne were independent traders until Adolph Capelle became the agent for the Godeffroy successor company, the Deutsche Handels und Plantagen-Gesellschaft der Südsee Inseln (DHPG). The Hernsheim brothers—who started trading in the Pacific region in 1874—joined their west Pacific interest in Robertson & Hernsheim (R&H) with DHPG to found Jaluit-Gesellschaft in 1887. The redoubtable Emma Coe-Forsayth created a highly profitable South Sea business in Forsayth & Co before selling it to Hamburg Senator Heinrich Rudolf Wahlen in 1911.[1]

From 1868 to 1871 English imports of goods to Samoa declined from 8,038 tons to 4,856 tons while German goods shipped to Apia grew from 3,875 t to 8,696 t. The number of German traders calling on Samoa reached a peak when German ships totalling 31,000 BRT called on Apia in 1875. The future administrator of GNG, Captain G. von Schleinitz, reported from SMS *Gazelle* in 1876: 'German trade and German ships are encountered everywhere, almost at the exclusion of any other nation'. The *Bundesrath* in Berlin learnt of German firms exporting RM7,021,000 worth of goods in 1878 from the Tongan, Samoan, Fiji, and Gilbert & Ellice (Tuvalu and Kiribati) islands, the Society archipelago in French Polynesia, the Micronesian atolls (Caroline and Palau), from many of the coral islands making up the Marshall atoll, and from New Britain and Duke of York Islands (Bismarck Archipelago).[2]

Disastrous Ventures

Coconut oil was introduced in Prussia in the 1860s as a source of edible fat. An imbalance in supply and demand in Europe drove copra (from which the oil was extracted) to record prices in 1878 and 1879. With landed copra fetching RM480 in Hamburg and Bremen and £26 in London, South Sea trade was extraordinarily profitable during this period.[3]

By the late 1880s the South Pacific map of German commerce had changed. The colonisation of Fiji by Britain in 1874 saw to it that German traders were all but excluded from these islands. Fijian sugar boosted that colony's exports by nearly 75%, from £59,000 in 1882 to £176,000 in 1883. From then on its economy outperformed all other colonies in the region. While the German share of exports from Samoa was never less than 82%, Britain's annexation of the Gilbert and Ellice Group in 1892, and her sway in Tonga reduced German activities in that region to 25% of total exports by 1897.[4] Apart from the demand for Melanesian workers for DHPG's Samoan plantations, Britain's plantation activity on Fiji helped drive the formation of a major German company, the Neu Guinea Compagnie (NGC), in East New Guinea.

J. C. Godeffroy VI, ca 1880

Johann Cesar Godeffroy VI: King of the South Sea.

No company shaped the mid-19th Century business history of the West, Central and South Pacific more than Johann Cesar Godeffroy & Sohn of Hamburg. The Godeffroys escaped the religious persecution in La Rochelle at the turn of the 18th century to settle in Hamburg in 1758. Of Huguenot descent, their industriousness and entrepreneurship elevated them to the patriciate of Hamburg inside three generations. During this time they gained and lost unparalleled wealth and power from trading, shipping and shipbuilding. When their businesses crumbled in the 1870s, their survival was a matter of concern to the governments in Berlin and Hamburg.

In the 1830s Godeffroy expanded trading and shipping activities across the North Atlantic to Mexico, New Orleans and the Caribbean Islands. By 1844 the Valparaiso trading station in Chile serviced the west coast of South America. In the late 1840s the company became a shareholder in South Australia's Burra-Burra Mine which produced 5% of the world's copper concentrate up to 1860. At that time, the Godeffroy fleet, comprising the extreme clipper *Sovereign of the Seas*,[5] 26 California or Canada–type clippers, and many barques and brigs of various sizes, sailed the North Atlantic and the Pacific Oceans, taking migrants, muskets, gunpowder, lead for bullets, machetes, knives, axes, and all manner of tradable goods to the British colonies of Australia, the Cape Province, the Indian Sub-Continent, Southeast Asia, China, and across the Pacific to Chile and California.

In 1851 some 11,798 emigrants left Hamburg for Australia and in 1852 a further 23,449. Godeffroy shared this traffic with Hamburg's prominent emigrant carrier R. M. Sloman. Gabriele Hoffmann writes that the Governor of the British Cape Province Kaffraria, Sir George Grey—previously governor of New Zealand and South

Australia—placed an order with Godeffroy for 15,000 'respectable persons, of sound character, healthy, vaccinated, not over 45 years old' for the British Cape Colony.[6] Gold prospectors embarked on Godeffroy ships to try their luck in California and in Australia. On their journey home, the vessels back-loaded South Australian copper ore for the Godeffroy Elbhütten-Affinir smelter in Hamburg-Harburg, tropical goods from the South Sea Islands, hides, saltpetre, cotton, latex, guano, timber and tobacco from America for the Liverpool, Bremen and Hamburg markets.[7]

In quick succession, beginning in the 1850s, the company expanded its network in the South Sea through the Penrhyn and Cook Islands and onwards to Samoa, Tonga and Fiji, trading for coconut oil, pearl shell and bêche-de-mer (trepang). The first trading station in the region was set up by the Valparaiso manager, August Unshelm, in 1857 at Apia Bay on the West Samoan island of Upolu. When Unshelm lost his life at sea in March 1864, the firm was fortunate to have a man on the spot—to take the reins of Godeffroy's South Pacific trading empire, thriving by then on profits from trading in guns, black powder, machetes and other metal wares, and from coconut oil. In 1861, Cesar Godeffroy had sent his 18-year-old junior accountant Theodore Weber—a chubby faced Rheinlander—to Apia. Three years later Weber succeeded Unshelm to quickly grow the South Sea enterprise into Godeffroy's most valuable asset. He drove the company with foresight, measured risk and iron-willed determination that belied his age. Appointed in 1865 as Hamburg's consul for Samoa, Fiji and Tonga, and in 1868 elevated to consul for the *Norddeutscher Bund* (North German Confederation) he was, according to R. L. Stevenson, 'an artful and commanding character; in the smallest thing or in the greatest, without fear or scruple'.[8]

Weber was quick to take up the idea of sending dried coconut meat in sacks to Hamburg for reconstitution rather than palm oil in leaking vats. First proposed to Unshelm by Cesar Godeffroy junior, who knew of 'Copprah' making in Ceylon, Weber followed the method of de-husking the nut, cutting the meat into strips and drying it in the sun. This was less labour intensive than pressing the nuts for oil. The dried meat (copra) containing 4–5% water and 63–70% oil compared to 50% water and 35% oil in the raw fruit provided benefits through increased shipping space. Copra was shipped in hessian sacks and the elimination of expensive oil vats, the higher prices attained for the clean, mechanically extracted oil from reconstituted copra, and the sale of the fibre *(taur)* for cattle and pig feed were additional benefits.[9]

Weber successfully grew coconut and cotton near Apia, enjoying the cotton boom caused by the American Civil War. Apart from the high-quality plantation product, the abundance of wild South Sea coconuts made Godeffroy the foremost trader in the region by 1870. Under the leadership of missionary Shirley Waldemar Baker, the Tongan Wesleyan Methodist Missionary Society became large contributors to this success. Contracted by Weber in 1869, Baker orchestrated the islanders to gather nuts. Paying partly with pieces of ironware and partly in silver dollars, its supply became a most profitable and reliable source of trade-copra for Weber.[10] By introducing an overvalued Chilean, Mexican or Bolivian silver dollar as its principal medium of financial transactions in the region, profits increased further. The currency had an intrinsic value in silver but was circulated as though equivalent to the United States dollar. Weber entered into an agreement with Baker that provided money to Tongans at collection time in return for a lien on the harvest. Through this missionary Baker—the middle man—became the islands' preeminent banker, lining his pockets, and the Missions and King Georg Tupou I of Tonga treasuries. It also filled the coffers of the Godeffroy enterprise, albeit at the expense of the indigenous population.[11]

Weber was innovative. To provide shade for fragile palm seedlings he planted coconuts between the rows of cotton. When the cotton boom abated, plantation coconut started to fill the revenue gap. By 1870 some 10,000 ha had been requisitioned—more or less legally—from the villagers on the coastal fringes of western Upolu (Samoa) and on the northern coast at Apia, with about 160 ha under cultivation.[12] Nine years later this land yielded high returns for the DHPG—the successor Company to Godeffroy—with quality plantation copra making RM440/t (£22/t) in Hamburg and London, while the cost of production barely exceeded RM6/t.[13]

The industrious Weber established a far-reaching network of trading stations, plantations and copra factories throughout much of the Pacific region. From Apia he oversaw Godeffroy's activities in distant New Britain to the Tongatabu Group (Tonga) in the south, along the 1,600 mile chain of Line Islands atolls in the central Pacific, and to Micronesia and the Marshall Islands. When, by the end of the 1860s, the novelty of picking cotton had worn off for the Polynesian people, and they started to reveal much loathing for the 'white man', Weber's recruiters ventured into what became known the Bismarck Archipelago in search of workers. Here a labour depôt on the Duke of York Group gathered Melanesians for his Samoan plantations.[14]

In collaboration with Wilkens & Co., Godeffroy founded the company Société Commerciale de l'Oceanie to give their trading activities on Tahiti and the other Society Islands a French appearance. This joint shareholder company, capitalised at RM1,050,000, operated trading stations, plantations and factories (*Faktoreien*) in Papeete and Raiatea (French Polynesia), and Rarotonga (Cook Islands).

Cesar Godeffroy earned the respect of the German scientific community. Eduard Graeffe, Amalie Dietrich, Andrew Garrett, Johann Stanislaus Kubary, Franz Hübner, Theodor Kleinschmidt, Alfred Tetens and others collected for him in Australia, the Dutch East Indies and in the Pacific. They sent ethnographic artefacts to the Godeffroy Museum in Hamburg by the shipload. Founded in 1861, the museum published its findings in the *Journal des Museums Godeffroy* from 1871 to 1878. Captain Tetens, who in 1866 established Godeffroy's first trading station on Yap, discovered the unique stone money the Yapese used as traditional currency. While this westernmost part of the Caroline Islands was rich in coconuts, the 'rock-money' of many shapes and weights—but generally with a hole in the middle—prompted German interest in the South Sea, as did the many other curiosities Tetens unloaded from his brig, the *Vesta,* when he returned to Hamburg in 1868.[15]

The eventual decline of the Godeffroy firm resulted from financial overextension. In 1867 the family began the construction near Osnabrück of Germany's first large-scale steel plant based on the Bessemer converter. In connection with this plant, they made considerable investments in coal mines and railways in the Rhine-Ruhr region. This Hanseatic merchant knew much about sailing ships and he built and managed one of Germany's most successful trading-houses, but he knew little about steel mills. Plagued by delays and high completion costs, the mill never showed an acceptable return on its investment, and when the collapsing commodity market showed no sign of abating, Cesar Godeffroy became insolvent in 1877. In order to protect the family's most productive asset Godeffroy established the Deutsche Handels-und Plantagen-Gesellschaft der Südsee-Inseln zu Hamburg (DHPG) on 16 March 1878 to purchase the South Sea businesses of Joh. C. Godeffroy & Sohn for RM4,000,000.

But the cash raised via an equity issue was nowhere near sufficient to meet the lenders' demands. A proposed involvement by the Reichsbank and/or the Preußische Seehandlung (PSH) to take up a tranche of DHPG shares and to provide immediate liquidity of RM2,000,000 failed. Unable to sell any of his 880 shares in DHPG, Cesar pledged them to Baring Bros & Co. of London and raised RM3,500,000 to settle in part an overdue loan with J. Henry Schröder Co. of London (£87,000) and with Nordeutsche Bank (NDB) of Hamburg (RM2,400,000).[16]

In March 1879, Adolph von Hansemann of Disconto-Gesellschaft (D-C) and Bismarck's private banker, Gerson von Bleichröder of S. Bleichröder Private Bank, offered to underwrite DHPG provided the *Auswärtige Amt* (AA) guaranteed the loan. Bismarck instructed his department to investigate the purchase of DHPG or the granting of a government subsidy. In the meantime DHPG was running out of money. The 1879 copra harvest was poor and neither DHPG nor Godeffroy were able to pay creditors while Baring Bros refused to honour a draft presented on the firm. When other creditors followed suit the enterprise was bankrupted on 1 December 1879.[17]

The publicity surrounding Godeffroy in 1879 focused Bismarck's mind on Samoa. The enterprise was too significant, in particular in the southwest Pacific, and it could not be ignored because the company had run into difficulties. Not surprisingly therefore, on 1 January 1880 the *Reichskanzler* requested the Under Secretary of the Treasury, Adolf von Scholz, to instruct PSH to provide funds to DHPG:

> Not connected with its South Sea trade [Bismarck reasoned] the company has encountered financial difficulties which threaten the loss of all its possessions and business … In the interest of overseas trade, I am of the view the Imperial Government should introduce an appropriation Bill in order to supply the means necessary to avert this threat.[18]

The state-owned bank was reluctant to act on its own, however, and approached the Berlin bankers, Bleichröder and Hansemann, and Hermann Wallich of Deutsche Bank (DB) also of Berlin to work on a solution. On 13 February 1880 DB, D-C and Bleichröder Private Bank agreed to establish the Deutsche Seehandels-Gesellschaft (DSG). The company issued a prospectus outlining the purchase of DHPG shares from Baring Bros, the immediate injection of RM1,200,000 and flagged its intention to take control of business in the South Sea. The nominal capital of DSG was RM10,000,000 of which RM8,000,000 was to be issued as a first tranche. Bismarck's endorsement and the impressive business records of Hansemann, Bleichröder and Wallich ensured that the offer was oversubscribed.[19] Immediately after the business of

DSG was formalised on 23 February 188. it transmitted RM1,200,000 to Preußische Seehandlung for bridging finance. The money was extended on the basis that it would be refunded should negotiations with the Reich prove unsuccessful. Discussions with DHPG and Baring Bros advanced quickly to agreement. DSG would receive security over the assets of DHPG in exchange for providing liquidity, with Baring Bros extending a RM2,000,000 (£100,000) promissory note secured by Hansemann and Bleichröder via their banks.

An application was submitted to the Treasury, requesting the government to subsidise annual dividend payments for the next 20 years. Hansemann projected annual profits of at least 4.5% calculated on the issued DSG capital of RM10,000,000. In the event of RM450,000 in a particular year not being earned Hansemann proposed that the government guarantee a dividend payment of RM300,000. When annual earnings exceeded RM450,000 any government advanced dividends were to be refunded. Under the agreement the dividend subsidy lapsed when payment was not required for five consecutive years. Notwithstanding that Apia's newly appointed Consul, Captain Zembsch, provided Berlin with a much reduced estimate of the company's assets (RM4,800,000), Bismarck accepted the proposal by sponsoring a Bill in the *Reichstag* on 21 April 1880 in support for DSG.[20]

The government expected the Bill to pass without much opposition. But in the absence of Bismarck—who apparently did not participate in the debate because of ill health—strong opposition came from Godeffroy's major competitor, the Bremer banker, merchant and principal of *Norddeutsche Lloyd*, Hermann Heinrich Meier: 'Why should the Reich assume the liabilities of a bankrupt private company?' Meier demanded to know. Picking up on Consul Zembsch's allegation of DHPG's 'legally and morally obnoxious' labour recruiting schemes noting that a transfer of DHPG plantations to foreign interests would not interfere with the security of the Reich, the parliamentary leader of the Liberal Left *Deutsche Freisinnige Partei*, Ludwig Bamberger, attacked the Bill as an illusion of 'national glory'.[21]

After several days' debate the Bill was defeated (122 for and 128 against). Many *Reichstag* members abstained from voting as they may have felt uneasy at the prospect of the government guaranteeing dividend payments to the three most influential German bankers. H. H. Meier (Bremen) joined the Liberal Left to defeat the Bill, thereby confirming his ascendancy over his Hamburg rival Godeffroy. Robertson & Hernsheim, and other Hanseatic merchants would not have shed too many tears over the demise of Johann Cesar Godeffroy & Sohn. His enterprises had dominated the South Pacific trade for 25 years, leaving little room for rival businesses.

The defeat of the Bill left Hansemann, Bleichröder and Wallich free to withdraw the prospectus for DSG. The company was dissolved, but the consortium remained alive because the *Reichskanzler* conveyed to Hansemann and Bleichröder his satisfaction that the board of DSG had not been discouraged by the negative public sentiments. 'In the national interest', he told Hansemann, 'the banks demonstrated confidence by getting involved in trade and shipping in the South Sea at their expense [these] activities in the South Sea will not be lost to others'.[22]

Buoyed by Bismarck's interest, Hansemann negotiated a capital restructure with Cesar Godeffroy and the major creditors of DHPG. The debt of RM1,200,000 owed to DSG was converted into 10 year debentures with annual interest of 5%.

After several additional capital restructures, including impairment of assets, issuing of new shares and RM2,500,000 in debenture notes, DHPG became profitable. When copra climbed above RM360/t cif at European ports in 1884, Hansemann bought Baring Bros' £Stg100,000 holding in DHPG for £19,000, and subsequently had Directors declare a 4% maiden dividend. In line with increasing demand for copra, DHPG's coconut plantations grew with total land holding on Samoa (Upolu Island) nearing 30,000 ha in 1890. Notwithstanding that the driver of the Godeffroy/DHPG South Sea enterprise—Theodor Weber—returned to Hamburg in 1888 because of ill health the company continued to grow strongly. By 1900 DHPG harvested a record 11,050 t of copra from its Samoan plantations and trade copra from the Bismarck Archipelago and Tonga. That year's return exceeded the annual copra harvest for the entire 'Old Protectorate' of GNG until 1912. Off-market trading in DHPG shares touched 345% above par value in 1909. DHPG's earnings after interest and tax totalled RM10,000,000 for the period 1898 to 1913. The average annual dividend payment during this period was 30.5% on the issued capital.[23]

The performance of DHPG backed the Berlin bankers' judgement to invest in the company. It also vindicated Bismarck's backing of the Samoa Bill. For Hansemann and Bleichröder, the Godeffroy story was a two-edged sword. It was a very profitable investment for the two Berlin bankers that in turn led to the formation of NGC, which turned out to be a disastrous undertaking.

Eduard and Franz Hernsheim

Eduard and Franz Hernsheim (*Illustrirte Zeitung* Leipzig, 14 March 1885)

Godeffroy & Sohn was not the only prominent German firm in the Pacific. The audacious Eduard Ludwig Hernsheim (1847–1917) established arguably the most profitable German enterprises in the Pacific region in Robertson & Hernsheim, Hernsheim & Co, and in Jaluit-Gesellschaft. Eduard Hernsheim did not fit the mould of a Hanseatic merchant. In fact he had a profound dislike for anything Prussian. Born in Mainz on the River Rhine, rather than on the Elbe or Weser, in Hamburg or Bremen, he did not follow in his father's footsteps to become a lawyer. Nor did he finish his studies in chemistry at a technical college in Darmstadt. Of strong build and outgoing personality Eduard Hernsheim had inherited his mother's Portuguese dark complexion and an adventurous spirit, most likely passed on by his Dutch grandfather. His father died in 1863—his mother had passed away giving birth to her fourth son, Eduard—and in 1865 he skipped formal studies altogether to sign on as a deckhand on the 400 ton clipper *Ceres*. Eduard's first voyage took him from

Hamburg to Singapore and Hong Kong, across the Pacific Ocean to San Francisco, back to Auckland and back again to Valparaiso, then to Port Elizabeth, Cape Town and around Cape Horn to arrive back in Hamburg in the winter of 1866.

Never one to waste time in a class room Eduard Hernsheim took a short course with a master sailmaker in Hamburg-Altona, and, when offered a berth as an unpaid sailmaker on the *Johanna Brodersen,* sailed from the northern German Baltic town of Flensburg to the West Indies.

Returning a short 12 months later Eduard now believed he knew everything required for a mate's examination, but could not gain admission to the *Seefahrtschule* (maritime school) in Hamburg, as he did not have the requisite six years of studies and experience at sea. So, he went to the less stringent maritime school in Kiel where, after a short preparation, he passed his mate's and master's examination in November 1867. Now qualified for *Grosse Fahrt,* taking ships of any size across all oceans, and with his father's inheritance of RM30,000 in his pocket, Eduard Hernsheim bought a schooner to set out and become a trader in goods of any type in the Pacific region.

Initially based in Hong Kong, Eduard Hernsheim set up his first trading station in 1874 on Malakal, a small volcanic island off Palau. A year later Eduard's older brother, Franz Hernsheim, joined him with a cash injection of DM50,000, and the company was named Hernsheim & Co. Capitalised at RM100,000 the young enterprise remained critically short of working funds, and the partnership was kept afloat by a credit line provided by their uncle, the Hamburg merchant, R.I. Robertson.

The two brothers organised their Pacific business geographically. Eduard Hernsheim headed southeast to establish a trading station at Port Hunter in the Duke of York Islands in October 1875. He moved the factory to nearby Makada Island in July 1876 and a year later to Matupi Island at the mouth of Blanche Bay. The brothers bartered Hong Kong trinkets for South Sea pearls, trepang and coco-nuts. They taught the islanders to make copra and engaged in labour recruitment for the Godeffroy Samoan plantations and for their factories in the New Britain Archipelago and on the Marshall Islands. Franz Hernsheim was running the Pacific islands business together with Robertson's son Henry—who had joined the company in late 1878—from the geographically central Jaluit Island. Another factory was set up on Ebon Atoll, one of the twelve southernmost islands of the Marshall Islands. By the late 1870s Hernsheim & Co. shipped goods to Hong Kong on their steamers the *Freya* and the *Pacific* and sent copra directly to Hamburg on the large German charter barque, the *Adolf.* The rapid expansion meant a considerable increase in debt. While the record shipments of 900 t copra realised profits of nearly RM100,000 in Hamburg, most of it was disbursed in interest payments to uncle Robertson, creditors and vessel charter.

In 1881 R. I. Robertson severed his business relationship with Hernsheim & Co. on the condition that his son Henry become managing partner in the firm with a capital injection of RM600,000, and that the company be renamed Robertson & Hernsheim (R&H).[24]

When Eduard expanded his trading activities to the Duke of York Group—situated roughly halfway between New Ireland and the Gazelle Peninsula of New Britain—he was unable to barter for commercial quantities of exportable goods. He grumbled

> the natives had nothing to sell except perhaps a few pieces of half-burnt tortoise shell. They
> were too lazy and timid to bring us the coconuts growing wild in the bush. Unlike the natives
> in the Carolines, who were skilled in all types of work, these savages were almost completely
> useless.[25]

But seven years later, in April 1884, after Hernsheim had moved his main operations from Jaluit to Matupi, he offered a revised view on trading possibilities. Boastfully, he recalled:

> Within a few months these people, who in the beginning brought us human flesh for sale and in
> many other ways had shown that they were complete savages, had become sufficiently familiar
> with our ways of requirement … They soon learned to bring not only coconuts but ready-cut
> coconut kernels. … In the complete absence of competition, we could dictate our own price.
> The most highly prized trade goods were beads and ironware. The tobacco habit first had to be
> inculcated in the natives in order to create a constant demand for a quickly consumed commodity.

Eduard Hernsheim recalled with satisfaction how he had set up smoking schools with the traders as instructors, 'so that in a few years tobacco was the most coveted and indispensable commodity among the natives'. Thus, they dictated the prices in a two-way barter exchange.[26]

Between 1882 and 1885 R&H took possession of 1,640 ha (2,050 ac) on New Britain and the Duke of York Islands and 780 ha (1,927 ac) in the Hermit Group. In all, approximately 30,000 ha (74,130 ac) of claims were forwarded to the German government for registration. The ownership of native land was difficult to establish. But for Hernsheim, like any other European trader at the time, possession equalled tenure until proven otherwise.[27]

Eduard Hernsheim welcomed the Reich's decision to take possession of the north coast of mainland New Guinea and adjacent islands in November 1884.[28] He was, however, unsupportive of the Imperial Charter the government offered Adolph von Hansemann's NGC on 17 May 1885. Strongly critical of the proposal, Hernsheim believed that 'a syndicate of German capitalists had influenced the *Reichskanzler* with excessive enthusiasm entirely in conflict with sober commercial considerations'. He feared that NGC would crowd out his operations in the Bismarck Archipelago. Similarly, R&H and DHPG were concerned about losing market share in the northwest Pacific if the government would not place the Caroline and the Marshall Islands under imperial protection.[29]

After meetings with officials in Berlin, E. Hernsheim saw little likelihood of accommodating NGC in his plans. After meeting with Hansemann in Berlin he told his brother Franz 'we have to decide whether it was better to go into liquidation or to continue to operate on a reduced scale'. The crafty South Sea trader did neither; instead he decided on expanding the business.[30]

The Jaluit Gesellschaft

Agreement between the German government and Marshall Island Chiefs on 15 October 1885—facilitated by Hernsheim with the help of the German navy—set Eduard Hernsheim on the path of prosperity.

Consistent with the New Guinea model, Bismarck insisted that the Marshall

DHPG factory on Mioko, ca. 1887 (Goethe University F. a. M., No. 044-4026-16; M. v. Hein, Mitschell Library, FM3/846)

Islands also be administered under an Imperial Charter. In a two-pronged attack, Hernsheim reached agreement with the Godeffroy creditors to merge the interests of DHPG in the Marshall, Caroline and Gilbert Islands with the Micronesian business of Robertson & Hernsheim (R&H). The result was the formation of the Jaluit Gesellschaft (J-G). Excluded from this deal were DHPG's Melanesian labour recruiting activities for its Samoan plantations. R&H retained its factories (trading stations and land) in the Duke of York (2) on New Britain (14) and New Ireland (9), with the stations on the Hermit (4) and Anchoret (2) Islands in the Admiralty Group and Hernsheim's activities on the Marshall (6) and Kingsmill (Gilbert) Islands (2) also excluded from the deal. Here he entered into a term purchase agreement with his brother Franz and Henry Robertson and renamed his company Hernsheim & Co.[31]

It took R&H and DHPG two years before Jaluit Gesellschaft (J-G) was incorporated on 21 December 1887. The issue of 240 fully paid shares, raising RM1,200,000, assisted J-G to acquire the R&H and DHPG Micronesian assets, comprising 60 trading stations, plantations, equipment and ships, valued at RM360,000; stock, debtors and cash, valued at RM660,000, for RM1,020,000. Each company owned approximately the same number of shares in the new company with only 40 shares issued to non-related parties. F. Hernsheim and F. Gerdzen were appointed joint Managing Directors, with H. Robertson (chairman) J. C. Godeffroy (deputy chairman) H. E. Bense, R. Böker and T. Weber (replaced by H. Meyer-Delius after Weber had passed away on 7 July 1889) appointed to the Supervisory Board.[32]

Under a charter entered into with the Reich on 21 January 1888 J-G accepted responsible for administrating the Marshall Islands at a budgeted cost of RM37,000 per annum. For its efforts, J-G earned the privilege to raise taxes, fees and fines, take 'ownerless' land into its possession and exploit the maritime and land resources of the estimated 1200 islands that make up the Marshalls. J-G was responsible for submitting an annual administration budget to the colonial administration in Berlin for the approval of the Chancellor. The company had some influence on the appointment of government officers, but was solely responsible for their salaries, posting allowance, holiday payments, pension fund, sick leave, accommodation and travelling expenses. Under the administration plan between the government and the company, provision was made for one governor, one secretary, five local policemen and a crew for a small sailing boat. Apart from providing housing for government employees, J-G was responsible for building and maintaining appropriate infrastructure on Jaluit. After balancing revenue with expenditure, the company budgeted for positive cash-flow of RM11,500 during the first year of operation. Non-recurring expenditures were costed at RM40,000 of which RM31,000 was delivered in existing infrastructure. J-G estimated income for the first year at RM18,000. This amount was to be achieved from ship registration fees (RM800), registration and court fees (RM800), court fines (RM800), harbour entry fees (RM400); pilot fees (RM2,800), trading licence fees (RM800), hotel licence fees (RM800), customs duty (RM1,600), poll tax on Europeans and Japanese (RM1,200) and on the local population (RM13,500), less RM5,500 to village Chiefs for overseeing the collection of copra.[33]

J-G had land tenure and set import duty and harbour fees which gave it effective control over its competitors. The San Francisco based A. Crawford & Co. saw it differently. By providing free medical care to the Jaluit islanders and valuing the Chilean dollar higher than J-G did, Crawford received the maximum supply of copra from the locals. It took the Germans until 1892, after the death of Crawford, to gain dominance on the Marshall Islands. At that time J-G purchased the assets of A. Crawford & Co in the central Pacific.[34]

More friendly was the arrangement between J-G and DHPG's former agent Cesar von Capelle who owned a productive coconut plantation on Likieb (Marshalls). In a transaction which involved a hotel and warehouses in Jaluit and a 33% stake in the Likieb plantation Capelle received RM75,000 from the Hamburg firm.[35] Whiteman Brothers on the Buratirari Atoll (Kiribati) and the small German trader Eckfort had no desire to compete with J-G and sold their holdings to the company in 1893. The New Zealand trading interests of Henderson & MacFarlane were all but dissolved with the acquisition of its Nauru activities in 1898 by the Pacific Islands Co. Ltd (PIC). The latter entered into an agreement with J-G in August 1901 to form the Anglo-German Pacific Phosphate-Company (PPC) in London. The formation of PPC included the sale of Henderson & MacFarlane in the Marshall Islands and Nauru to J-G for an undisclosed sum.[36]

When the Reich merged the administration of the tiny atoll of Nauru (21.3 km^2) with the Marshall Islands on 2 October 1888, J-G first thought this to be a liability. Barely ten tons of copra had been exported annually from Nauru till then. All this changed when New Zealand-born prospector Albert Ellis confirmed the presence of quality guano on Ocean Island and Nauru between May and October 1900.

Mindful of the commercial value of his find, Ellis persuaded the two Chiefs on

Ocean Island to put their marks on a document giving PIC the right to mine phosphate for 999 years for the sum of £50 per year.[37] J. T. Arundel, the founder of PIC, convinced the British government to annex this coral atoll to the Crown colony of the Gilbert and Ellice Group in 1901 and issue an exclusive licence to PIC.[38] In exchange the Exchequer received 6 d (RM0.50) for every ton of phosphate shipped from the island. To make the smaller deposits on Ocean Island more economically viable, Arundel needed the cooperation of J-G. On the German side, Eduard Hernsheim knew all about South Sea trading and running copra plantations but the mining of phosphate rock was not his forte. It was, therefore, no surprise that J-G entered into a management arrangement with PIC on 1 March 1901 with the objective of exploiting the deposits on Ocean Island and Nauru.

Under the chairmanship of A. H. Gordon, former British High Commissioner for the Western Pacific, the newly founded PPC listed 125,000 £1 ordinary shares and 125,000 £1 debentures with an annual coupon value of 7% on the London Stock Exchange on 18 May 1902. The mining rights conferred to PIC for Nauru were transferred to PPC. In return J-G received £25,000 in goodwill, a royalty of 1s (RM1) per ton of exported guano and 12,500 (10%) free issued PPC shares. Under the shareholder agreement J-G was prevented from selling more than 50% of its holding. Another German company (UFCP) bought 16% equity in PPC which gave it a seat on the Board of Directors and secured feedstock for its chemical plant in Stettin.[39]

Containing 86.76% tricalcic phosphate and 39.66% phosphoric anhydrite, a little fluorite, alumina and ferrite, Naurite became the most sought after organic fertilizer on the world market. The Ocean Island mine was operational within a year of the agreement being signed. In 1903 PPC paid a maiden dividend of 25 per cent.[40]

The high dividend payments from PPC enabled J-G to expand its plantation and trading business without having to call on shareholders for funding. In an effort to pry trade from competitors, J-G matched new setups by opening larger stations nearby, and where competitors' pacts with the local Chiefs needed to be overturned J-G contested the agreements by gazumping the opposition with a higher price for the copra. The vast cash reserves of J-G enabled it to prevent new companies from gaining a foothold or existing ones to expand.[41]

When Burns Philp & Co. (BP) decided in 1904 to send a steamship to open trade in the Marshall Islands, J-G responded by invoking unreasonably high harbour and trading licence fees. Complaints from the Australian firm that J-G was in breach of the free trade provisions of the Anglo–German Declaration of 10 April 1886 led to the termination of the charter with the German government on 31 March 1906.[42] Although no longer obligated to pay for the administration of the Marshall Islands and Nauru, J-G had to give up its land and trading privileges. In exchange, the company received a 94-year phosphate concession for Nauru from the German government on 21 November 1905. It became J-G's most valuable asset. The company obtained government approval to transfer its mining right to PPC on 12 Dec. 1905 and, after lengthy site preparation, mining of phosphate on Nauru commenced in 1907.

To bring the agreement into line with the arrangement the British government had with PPC for Ocean Island, J-G was obliged to pay a RM25,000 annual royalty to the GNG government. On 1 April 1906, the Friedrich Wilhelmshafen administration imposed a super-tax of RM0.50/t for exports over 50,000 tons per annum. Nauruans received a paltry halfpenny per ton for land degradation and the relocation of houses.[43]

Setting aside the royalties J-G paid the GNG government, it pocketed customs excise, recruitment fees and reimbursement for maintaining a local police force. This, in the view of GNG Governor Albert Hahl and Colonial Secretary Dernburg, was far too generous and a threefold increase in royalty would have been more equitable.[44] Notwithstanding Berlin's disquiet about the low impost PPC commenced with the building on Nauru of worker and staff housing, a rail track and funicular system, pre-drying sheds, dehydrators, warehouses, transit barges, power generators and an 18 ton per day desalination plant. Some RM1,500,000 was spent before the first consigment of guano (11,630 t) was shipped in 1907.[45]

J-G was responsible for the recruitment of workers, and when Nauruans found working for PPC not to their liking, J-G indentured some 600 Chinese. The operational cost of the mine was passed on to PPC, and J-G was soon in a position to reward its shareholders with the biggest dividends ever paid by a plantation company. Reaping high returns from increasing sales in copra, J-G benefited from guano exports from Nauru of 55,019 t in 1908 and up to 138,086 t in 1912.[46] On the strength of this the company participated in several share issues by PPC. A one £-Stg PPC share, partly paid to 6s 8d, was quoted at £2 10s on the London Stock Exchange in November 1911. This translated to a seven-fold paper profit for J-G's shareholders.[47]

In 1907 J-G prepared for its listing on the Hamburg Stock Exchange by splitting the RM5,000 ordinary shares into five RM1,000 new shares. In addition, 2,400 none-voting bonus shares were issued which had equal dividend rights. J-G was listed on 20 July 1909 at a 45% premium and the profit certificates (bonus shares) were offered at RM1,345 each. Two years later J-G shares attracted a 296% premium on the float issue. The company's dividend policy of 10% in 1907, rising to 25% two years later drove the price to a high of RM4,000 for each J-G share in 1912.[48]

Guano was also mined on Angaur Island, albeit with less spectacular rewards. After its discovery in 1905, Governor Hahl offered the mining rights of this tiny island 35 nautical miles southwest of Palau to a German-Australian fertilizer manufacturer in Melbourne. When the firm was unable to form a consortium with the required German majority the mining opportunity was offered to Norddeutsche Lloyd (NDL) of Bremen in 1906.[49] After exploration and delineation work was carried out in the West Carolines by a consortium led by the Bremer Deutsche Nationalbank (DNB), Deutsche Südseephosphat A.G. (SAG) was established on 20 May 1908 with an authorised capital of RM4,500,000.[50] The 35-year Angaur mining concession awarded to SAG was much stricter than that imposed on J-G for Nauru. Under the terms of the agreement SAG was obliged to pay the GNG administration RM1.25 for every ton of phosphate exported from Angaur, but not less than RM30,000 after the first four years of operations had been completed. When profit returns exceeded 8% of the share capital, the government was entitled to a 40% share in the retained earnings. This

Phosphate loading at Angaur Island, and the SS *Mai Rickmers* laods guano at Nauru (Kololonial Lexikon Bd. ii, plate 149

formula was applicable for the first 25 years of the concession. Thereafter payments to government increased to 50% for years 26 to 30 and to 60% thereafter.

The Rabaul government awarded a concession for phosphate extraction on Fais (Feis) Island (approximately 230 km northeast of Yap) to SAG subsidiary Hanseatisches Südsee–Syndikat. Except for a RM1.50/t export royalty the agreement reflected the Angaur agreement.[51]

The first Fais guano shipments left the island in the second half of 1909. Before SAG was listed on the Berlin Börse in 1910 the shares traded at around 230% of the par value.[52] The maiden dividend (6%) was paid in 1912, increasing to 11% when the company recorded a gross profit of RM1,364,280 in 1913. This increase triggered the 40% appropriation to the government, comprising its share of the retained earnings. The deposits on Nauru were estimated to contain 40,000,000 tonnes of guano, Angaur 3,500,000 t and Fais 600,000 t. From 1907 to August 1914 guano exported from the German possessions amounted to 1,088,100 t. At a production cost of RM9/t and a mean selling price of RM30/t (fob Angaur), guano mining was very profitable.[53] When the German Island Territories and GNG became a monetary union in 1909 the Old Protectorate benefited the most. While only 236,087 t of guano were exported from Angaur between 1909 and 1913 compared to 648,157 t from Nauru for the same period, the SAG filled the coffers of the Rabaul government to the tune of RM383,900 in royalties and approximately RM140,000 in tax until early 1914. This compares to RM390,500 in royalties collected from the Nauru enterprise and RM200,000 in concession fees. For GNG the return from 5 years of phosphate mining were greater than the gross income from agriculture and trade over 30 years.

Eduard Hernsheim had bought R&H to re-launch Hernsheim & Co. in 1908. The company continued developing copra plantations on New Ireland, Bougainville and the Admiralty Group while generating income from trade copra. On 29 October 1909 Hernsheim & Co. became a shareholder company (*Aktiengesellschaft*) with an issue of 1,200 shares at RM1,000 each. E. Hernsheim retained 770 shares in the new company. As Chairman he authorised a maiden dividend of 8% in the year of incorporation.[54] For 1910 and 1911 Hernsheim & Co paid 11%, which also applied to the increased capital of RM1,800,000 for 1912. The main station on Matupi relocated to Rabaul in 1912 with the district offices in Kavieng, Kieta and on Komuli responsible for developing plantations on New Ireland and the Solomons. Hernsheim & Co retained the lucrative coal depot on Matupi for the *Reichsmarine* and the government steamers. Plantation area in 1912 was about 3,000 ha with some 160,000 palm trees planted. At that time the company employed 40 Europeans, 20 Chinese and 750 Melanesians. The profitability of Hernsheim & Co is best illustrated by the dividends of nearly RM1,000,000 paid from 1908 to 1914.[55]

Non-German trading and plantation interests in North-East New Guinea

Germans were in a minority among Europeans in the Bismarck Archipelago and in the German Solomons. At the turn of the century Australians, French, Dutch, Scandinavians, Belgians outnumbered the Germans by more than four to one. Australians and Fijians staffed the Methodist Mission; the head of the Sacred Heart Mission from 1889 was the Frenchman Ludovicus Couppé; and, by setting up a significant shipyard on Matupi in 1903, a Chinese, Ah Tam, became the first major shipbuilder in GNG. The Belgian Jean Maximillian Mouton and his 18-year-old son, Octave, arrived in Port Breton (west coast New Ireland) in August 1881. They had paid the swindler Rays 1,000 French Francs to work as plantation labourers in the hope of owning their own small plantation after a five-year indenture. The Moutons remained near Port Breton until food rations ran out and the place was evacuated. Unlike most of their compatriots, they moved to Mioko in February 1882 to work for E. E. Forsayth Co., R&H and DHPG. In 1883 M. Mouton bought some 2,000 ha in the Kinigunan district to set up his first small coconut plantation. After the death of his father in 1888 Octave sought independence with the financial backing of the Sacred Heart Mission. Apart from working as a labour recruiter for NGC, he expanded his trading activities by setting up stations at Balgai near Nusa, Kabakaul, Garden Island (Simberi), Biritanai on the northern coast of New Ireland and on Ontong Java.

The formation of O. Mouton & Co. in 1897 brought into partnership the Swede Johann Rondahl and the Dane Axel Monrad. The company's copra schooners *Minna, Muruna, Monantha* and *Takubar* flew the German flag which required taking out

Disastrous Ventures

German citizenship. In 1906 the company owned 12 trade stations, the same number Hernsheim operated and five more than DHPG. The income from 350 ha of fully matured coconut palms standing on Kinigunan and from trading activities was reflected in the RM2,000 tax the company paid in 1912. This was approximately the same amount of tax paid by DHPG, but only half of what Hernsheim paid the Rabaul government for his company's activities in the region.

Queen Emma

Emma Coe-Forsayth, ca. 1884

Arguably the largest contributor to the early development of German New Guinea (GNG) was Samoan-American, Eliza Emma Coe. Born in 1850 to Jonas Coe, American trader and Consul at Apia, and his wife Jo(h)ana or Le'utu, daughter of a respected Samoan Chief from the ruling Malietoa tribe, Emma Coe enjoyed an unparalleled upbringing in mid-nineteenth century Samoa. The second child of her father's first marriage—apparently Jonas had six wives and untold affairs producing at least 18 children—Emma began life in Apia surrounded by a large family. At age eleven her father sent her to Sydney for private schooling and two years later to her uncle and aunt, Edward and Elizabeth Coe, in San Francisco. The teenager found hours of imposed chores and piano practice boring, She managed to escape the watchful eyes of the Edward Coe household to enjoy the many trappings California's gold rush brought to San Francisco. But after four years of discipline in a traditional American home Emma longed for Samoa and family. She booked a passage on the *Emilie Ann* to arrive back in Apia in 1869.

Also disembarking the brigantine was second mate James Forsayth who had fallen in love with the flirtatious Emma on the voyage to Apia. The Edinburgh-educated James Forsayth was, in the eyes of Emma's father, a suitable match for a nineteen-year-old flamboyant Samoan girl with European roots. Thus James Forsayth and Emma Coe married in October 1869, and father Jonas was happy to help his new son-in-law to acquire a schooner and become a trader.

Emma's part-time work with her new husband on board the little two-masted trader, calling on Polynesian islands, including New Zealand, came to a sudden halt in mid-1873 when James Forsayth disappeared, presumed lost at sea. Two children, a girl who died when her father was at sea and a son, James, who, born in 1873, was never to see his father, did not restrain Emma for long. Continuing to run the business more or less successfully, she also got involved in numerous affairs, including a scandalous relationship with US President Grant's special agent to Samoa, Colonel A. B. Steinberger. But for reasons of meddling in Samoa's political affairs the Colonel and Emma's father, Jonas Coe, were deported from Samoa in 1876. And Emma, whose new lover and business partner was the Irish-New Zealander Thomas Farrell, moved to the Marshall Islands to trade around Majuro and Ebon.

Competing with the Hernsheim brothers and Adolph Capelle over the same space was bound to end in failure. Emma Coe-Forsayth, who Capelle facetiously called the

'Princess of the South Sea', and Thomas Farrell went bankrupt leaving their creditors behind—mainly New Zealanders—to move to Mioko in the Duke of York Group and work for Deutsche Handels und Plantagen-Gesellschaft (DHPG) in March 1878.[56]

Starting afresh as independent labour recruiters for DHPG on New Britain and New Ireland Farrell and Coe soon established a substantial trading business in the New Britain Archipelago. With European business acumen and ruthlessness, good looks and Samoan charm, and a store full of DHPG trade-goods in Mioko, Emma took advantage of a demand among the Tolai for knives and firearms. Trading profits were invested in land and by 1879 the two had acquired large tracts from the Tolai people on the Gazelle Peninsula, New Britain Island. Before the German colonisers gained a foothold on the Peninsula Emma travelled to Australia to register title over the most valuable land at the American Consulate in Sydney to safeguard the 'integrity' of the acquisitions.

Profiteering and overcharging DHPG for goods traded, and seizing most of the stranded cargo and the ships of the failed Marquis de Rays expedition,[57] underpinned Emma Coe-Forsayth's spectacular career as a plantation owner and trader in GNG. But she also needed expertise to establish her new plantations.

The answer was Richard Parkinson, the lanky Danish plantation manager, who joined Godeffroy & Sohn at Apia in 1876 to be responsible for all plantations on Upolu before joining DHPG in 1879. Parkinson was family. Married to Emma's youngest sister Phoebe, he left Samoa in 1882 to be reunited with his wife, daughter and niece who had joined Emma on Mioko 12 months earlier.

While Farrell was hungrily developing his trading interests Emma was more interested in real-estate, that is land acquisition for her, and now also Parkinson's plantation project on Ralum Point on the northern shores of the Gazelle Peninsula.

Adopting the planting practice he had successfully applied to the Godeffroy estate on Samoa, Parkinson planted cotton with coconut palms. This method gave the young palms shade from the harsh tropical sun during the first few years and provided a cash crop from cotton during the first eight years before the palms came into bearing. Clearing the land while dealing with contending Tolai tribesmen was no easy task, and it took him until 1885 to establish the first major plantation in GNG. During the first year of this harvest Ralum produced cereals, cotton, coconut palms and coffee shrubs on 85 ha. In 1887 the *Deutsche Kolonial Zeitung (DKZ)* reported that an Australian company in the Bismarck Archipelago was very profitable 'by selling sorghum into the Australian market at above RM1,000/t landed in Sydney'.[58]

When Farrell died in March 1888 of tuberculosis in a Brisbane hospital Coe bought his estate for a fraction of the money owed to his creditors and changed the trading name of Farrell-Forsayth-Parkinson Plantagen-Gesellschaft to E. E. Forsayth & Co. Richard Parkinson was unimpressed with his treatment by his sister in law. The loan for his labour was too low, and being excluded from the estate made him quit his work with Emma to join in June 1889 the omnipresent Neu Guinea Compagnie (NGC) to establish Kokopo, named Herbertshöhe, a few miles east of Ralum.

By 1889 Emma's plantations, Kuradui, Malapau and Ralum produced 35,000 lb

(16 t) of cotton, four times as much as the Neu Guinea Compagnie (NGC) plantations. With the engagement in 1890 of nearly 1200 Melanesians and 50 overseers the two main stations at Ralum and Malapau grew 235 ha (580 ac) of cotton and 350 ha (860 ac) of coconuts.[59] The trading results of Emma Coe—by now known as Queen Emma—were brought to the attention of NGC shareholders. The 1892/93 report stated that NGC exported RM103,000 worth of goods compared to approximately RM306,550 worth of produce shipped by Forsayth & Co. for the period from January 1892 to June 1893.[60]

In 1894 Coe-Forsayth added a German to her collection spouses by marrying the 15-year-younger Paul Kolbe. They believed they were in love—both for their own reasons. It was a hopeless union. Both went on to have affairs, Kolbe with Grace Rondahl in GNG—Emma's half-sister—and Queen Emma with whoever took her fancy, including Tolai Chiefs if scuttlebutts are to be trusted.[61] But, notwithstanding the Kolbes' love-life and the lavish champagne parties at Queen Emma's luxurious residence 'Gunantambu' or the partying at her Fürst Bismarck Hotel in Herbertshöhe, the palm trees continued to grow delivering healthy profits. And Queen Emma soon rose to become the wealthiest plantation owner in New Guinea.[62]

The success of Forsayth & Co. had long been a thorn in the side of Hansemann. NGC contested the legality of Coe's claims to 50,000 ha on Gazelle Peninsula and 14,150 ha on New Ireland, Bougainville and the Admiralty Group.[63] But even without this landholding Forsayth & Co owned an uncontested 28,484 ha of which 2,993 ha was planted with 333,300 coconut palms, 385 ha with India rubber and

Queen Emma arriving at Gunantambu, ca. 1910 (Goethe University Frankfurt a.M., No. 043-4006-04)

50 ha with coffee in 1907/08. With assets of RM4,905,050 and annual profits of about RM200,000 it was then by far the most profitable enterprise in GNG.[64]

In 1906, and nearly 60 years old, Queen Emma sought to sell her company to anyone coming up with the right amount of cash. After fruitless negotiations with American, Australian and English interests she entered into an option agreement with the Bismarck-Archipel-Gesellschaft GmbH (BAG) of Hamburg. BAG, formed in 1907 with an authorised capital of RM650,000, offered to buy the assets of Forsayth & Co. for RM3,200,000. But the deal fell through because BAG offered to buy the assets of the company in share capital rather than paying Queen Emma in cash.[65]

In November 1910 Queen Emma founded Forsayth, Kirchner & Co (F.K & C). The company issued Forsayth & Co. with RM2,750,000 in equity. Coe-Kolbe received RM1,750,000 in cash. The balance owed was secured by a first mortgage over the assets of the company. When Hamburg Senator Heinrich Rudolf Whalen became a major shareholder and the Managing Director of F. K & C on 11 February 1911 Berlin announced 'the transfer of ownership to a German company of the Forsayth plantation enterprise, the second largest in the Protectorate, till then in British hands' as an event of national importance. It was a good deal for all concerned. The first 10 months' result under Wahlen showed a profit of RM262,445 less overhead, bank interest of RM11,643 and formation costs of RM67,213. The export of 2,065 t of copra paid shareholders a maiden dividend of 7% (RM140,000) for 1911 with directors and management receiving additional benefits of RM6,030 and RM14,675 respectively. In the following year F. K & C exported 3,633 t of copra worth RM404,230, allowing Directors to declare a 13% dividend (RM260,000) for 1912.[66]

Swedish-born Wahlen had joined Hernsheim & Co. as plantation manager in 1895. He left the company in 1903 to trade on his own account. Within a few years he built a flourishing plantation business in the northwest Bismarck Archipelago. By 1906 Wahlen GmbH had acquired much of the Hermit Islands and atolls in the Admiralty Group, 56 islands in all. When he extended his plantation interests throughout the archipelago by acquiring Coe-Kolbe's interests, he became next to NGC the largest operator in GNG. On 13 November 1913 Wahlen merged Forsayth, Kirchner & Co. GmbH with the Hamburgische Südsee-A.G. (HASAG). Apart from himself, the Hamburg banking and trading houses of M. M. Warburg and F. Rosenstern, O. Thiemer and C. E. Scharf became the major shareholders in HASAG.[67] In addition to expanding the rubber, cacao, coffee, and the coconut plantation MATANAR at Ralum, the company invested in the extraction of guano.

In 1909 Queen Emma transferred her Shortland Islands landholdings to her son Jonas Forsayth. These assets together with land owned by Burns, Philp (BP) in the Solomons were sold to BP's subsidiary, Shortland Plantation Ltd (SPL) in 1911. Upon the Kolbe's death in Monte Carlo in July 1913, Jonas Forsayth inherited most of his mother's wealth. As the Managing Director for SPL he proved to be inapt though. Unable to develop SPL as the new Forsayth enterprise. R. Wahlen and F. Hernsheim became the most influential and wealthiest owner-managers in GNG.

Disastrous Ventures

David O'Keefe: The buccaneer who converted limestone to sovereigns

Thomas Farrell was not the only Irishman who became a headache for the Hernsheim brothers and the Godeffroy firm. The tall, broad shouldered, David Dean O'Keefe (1843–1901), a firebrand with flaming hair, whose good looks, luck and ingenuity made him a fortune that his German competitor in the West Pacific found difficult to stomach. The Irish-born O'Keefe did not need support from the German or Spanish governments or traders. He had worked it all out when the Palauan people gave him access to the limestone deposits that provided the material for stone-money the Yapese used as barter currency. Of similar ilk to Eduard Hernsheim, O'Keefe established his presence on Yap in 1872 or early 1873.

Driven from his home country by the Irish potato famine, O'Keefe came ashore in Savannah, Georgia, in 1856. Working on the rail road, and as a deckhand, he apparently managed to get his master's certificate at the young age of 21 by running blockades during the American Civil War.[68] In 1869 he married Catherine Masters, whose temperament was as fiery as his. Shortly after the birth of the couple's first daughter, Louisa Victoria, O'Keefe left his young family and signed up as a first mate on the *Belvidere* that took him back to Liverpool. From England he sailed to Manila in the Philippines where he jumped ship to catch a vessel bound for Hong Kong where he arrived in September 1871. Employed initially by a certain Mr Field of Hong Kong, his new employer soon financed O'Keefe's first vessel, the junk *Catherine,* named after his wife who was still waiting in Savannah for his return.[69]

Making trade-runs with cargos of tea and silk, David O'Keefe inexplicably washed up on Yap or Uāā in the Carolines about December 1872. Just how the incident happened is not clear. It is known, however, that at the time of his arrival on Yap he had dumped his employer, Mr Field, and had the *Catherine* now on charter for the Hong Kong-based Celebes South Sea Trading Company. The Carolines, particularly Yap, were abundant in quality coconuts, and the trading of hoop iron, a few sticks of tobacco or a shot of spirits for tortoise shell, bêche-de-mer or copra was profitable business. This arrangement held firm until Mr Webster—a partner in the Company who skippered his own trader, the *Seabird*—died from an axe blow during a fight on Palau in 1875.

In mysterious—more likely fraudulent—circumstances O'Keefe 'inherited' Weber's ship, trading stations and trading connections. Notwithstanding stiff competition from Robertson & Hernsheim and Crayton Holcomb, an American trader who arrived on Yap around 1870, he established a web of trade stations on Yap and Palau.[70] By 1880 O'Keefe operated the traders *Seabird, Wrecker, Queen* and *Lilla,* collecting more than his fair share of high quality copra. He motivated the Yapese who would normally object to gather coconuts for the European intruder.

As O'Keefe got to know Yap better, he became aware that the local people coveted stone-money they called 'Fei'. The Yapese quarried their 'hard currency' in an aragonite limestone deposit in shallow water off the Palauan coast some 250 n.m. south-west of Yap. Varying in size from a few centimetres to over two meters in diameter, and weighing from a few grams to several tons, the hard crystalline structure of aragonite was difficult to manufacture with stone and shell tools and equally difficult to transport on small outriggers across an often treacherous sea from Palau to Yap.[71] Under his get-rich-quick scheme O'Keefe provided the Yapese with steel tools and taught them a speedy method to cut the large stones into circular shape with an undulating surface, and how to grind the important hole in the middle efficiently. He taught the people how to move the rock to the carving site and on to his boat for shipping to Yap. To make himself the revered white Chief in the Carolines he offered to transport the semi-finished rocks on his ships, thus avoiding loss of goods and lives that occurred frequently when the material was transport on the local outriggers.

By 1882 some 400 Yapese quarried aragonite on Palau producing Fei on an inflationary scale. The money was, however, also of intrinsic value, determined by the crystal structure of the rock, the design and the execution by the craftsman of a piece, and how many lives were lost in producing the finished product. All this was of little importance in the Irishman's scheme, of course. In return for his smart advice and transportation services O'Keefe reaped the benefit from several hundred islanders who harvested and husked coconuts, cutting the white meat into strips to sun-dry it. By releasing the stone money only after payment was made in copra O'Keefe started an enterprise that expanded across the West Pacific.

Setting up trading stations on Yap, Palau and elsewhere in the western Pacific, and establishing copra plantations on the tiny Mapia Atoll, David O'Keefe's share of the 1500 tons annual copra production was somewhere around 60 per cent. By mid-1880 he was rich enough to move into a red brick home on Tarang, the island in the middle of Yap harbour. Aside from a large library he imported a piano, silver utensils and valuable antiques, and his property included four warehouses, a dormitory for his employees, a wharf with moorings for four ships, and a store known as O'Keefe's Canteen that sold the locals rum at 5 cents a measure. O'Keefe enjoyed his wealth and king-like status on Yap, raising his flag with the letters OK in black on a white background at Tarang every morning.[72]

When O'Keefe ventured as far south as the Hermit Group in the Bismarck Archipelago to trade copra for guns and spirits, Franz Hernsheim called the Irishman a most ruthless competitor, a perception that had not changed when the Jaluit-Gesellschaft (J-G) took over the reins. An offer by J-G's joint Managing Director, H. Grösser, to purchase O'Keefe's business was rejected in the same manner that previous overtures by Franz Hernsheim had been dismissed. Also in vain was Grösser's trip to Yap in 1897 to convince O'Keefe of the advantage in dividing the Carolines into two trading zones. Under this proposal O'Keefe would retain the exclusive trading rights to the western and J-G to the eastern part of the Carolines.[73] There was no need for him to acquiesce. His business continued to grow. Thirty smaller vessels picked up copra from his factories on and around Yap and his schooners *Jenny* and *Santa Cruz* delivered the goods to Hong Kong, Singapore and Manila. In Francis Hezel's words David O'Keefe had earned his reputation as 'The King of Yap.'

On 30 June 1899, following Spain's loss of her Philippine territory to the USA, and her selling the Carolines, together with Palau and the Marianas (except Guam), to Germany for 25 million Pesetas (RM17.25 million), the good luck ran out for O'Keefe. The turn of fortune started in 1895 when a palm leaf disease began to infest Yap's plantations, cutting production of copra to as little as 100 tons a year.

In April 1901 O'Keefe left Yap for Hong Kong on his schooner *Santa Cruz* with his two sons and his agent Georg Hoff. Lost at sea, they never returned to Yap.

David Dean O'Keefe left an impressive legacy. He never divorced his first wife, supporting her and his daughter with generous annual payments. But he also married a local girl on Yap and on Mapia, and enjoyed the company of several mistresses, producing 12 or more children. His estate was estimated to be worth anywhere between 1 and 10 million American Dollars. His wives, Dolibu on Terang and Charlotte on Mapia, and his first wife and daughter in Savannah, shared in some of the receipts when assets were sold in 1904. His oldest local daughter, Euginia, and her husband continued with the trading stations until December 1911 when they sold the business into the Westkarolinen-Gesellschaft. J-G took up 75% of the RM400,000 share capital with the O'Keefe family retaining the balance.[74]

The exploits of Theodor Weber, David O'Keefe, Emma Coe, and the Hernsheim brothers set the mood in Germany, England and Australia for seizing control of those Pacific Islands straddling the equator. Their successes had much to do with grasping the opportunity for the fraudulent exploitation of people with no previous experience of European culture and products. Their modus operandi was to exchange cheap European goods for copra and land. Storytellers glamorized the Kings and the Queen of the Pacific Islands. But they were simply robber barons, living and acting in accordance with their own dubious rules, answerable to no one but themselves. Their successes were personal achievements and ended with their departures. The shareholder companies that followed them in the 1880s did not—as we shall find out in the following chapters—conduct their businesses in the same laissez-faire manner and neither did they reap the commercial successes enjoyed by these early buccaneers of the central Pacific.

Fei money on Yap ca. 1910 (Goethe University Frankfurt a. M. Nos. 043–4012–3 & 7)

Notes

1   K. Schmack, *J.C. Godeffroy*, pp. 127, 140, 184, 228 & 237; Wachsmuth & Krogmann, *Jubiläumsschrift*; see S. G. Firth 'German Firms in the Western Pacific', *JPH*, 8 (1972) p. 5.

2   *Bundesrath*, 1879, vol. 2, *Denkschrift*, xxiv–xxvii, p. 96. *Deutsche Kolonial Zeitung (=DKZ)*, 17 (1887) p. 524. Masterman, S., The Origins of International Rivalry in Samoa, 1845–1884, p. 65; Schleinitz to Admiralty, 28 Dec. 1875, *Drucksache zu den Verhandlungen des Bundesrath*, 1879, vol. i *Denkschrift*, xxiv–xxvii, p. 3.Schmack, p. 185.

3   H. Wolff to H.H. Meier & Co., Sydney, 18 Oct. 1878 (Staatsarchiv Bremen (=StaB) Nachlaß H.H. Meier, vol. 32/7 – xxvi); *Bundesrath*, 1879, vol. 2. *Denkschrift*, xxiv–vi.

4   'Südsee Handel und Verkehr mit England 1886–1908'. Minutes of DHPG Board Meeting, 20 Jan. 1891 (RKA 1001:2560; StaH, DHPG Folder).

5   Built by Donald McKay of Boston, USA, in 1851-52, the *Sovereign of the Seas* (2421 BRT) was acquired by Godeffroy in May 1854 and sold to Balls & Eggers of Liverpool in Aug. 1859.

6   Hoffmann, *Das Haus an der Elbchaussee*, pp. 197ff, plate 11.

7   Schmack, pp. 88–96 & 98–107; G.J. Drew, 'Discovering Historic Burra', ed., Adelaide (1988)

8   R.L. Stevenson, *A Footnote to History: Eight Years of Trouble in Samoa*, p. 89.

9   Schmack, pp. 146–7; F. Hernsheim, „Die Marshall Inseln," *Geographische Gesellschaft*, p. 307.

10   E. Suchan-Galow, 'Die Deutsche Wirtschaftätigkeit in der Südsee vor der ersten Besitzergreifung 1884', pp. 73–5; D. Scarr, *Fragments of Empire*, p. 88.

11   The Germans set the value of one Chile dollar at RM4.00. After 1888 the currency traded to a low of RM2.50 (W. Hintze, *Das Geldwesen in Den Deutschen Schutzgebieten*, p. 47). See also J.H. Voigt, 'Tonga und die Deutschen' in H.J. Hiery (ed.) *Die Deutsche Südsee*, pp. 712ff, and N. Rutherford, 'Shirley Waldemar Baker', *Australian Dictionary Biography*, vol. 3.

12   H.S. Cooper, *The Coral Lands of the Pacific*, p. 232.

13   H. Blum, *Neu Guinea und der Bismarck Archipel*, p.169.

14   P.G. Sack, *Eduard Hernsheim*, pp. 16–17, 19 & 28–35.

15   StaH, Family Archive Tetens, mfm84/07, deposit 622–1/103

16   StaH, 621, pp. 1–5, DHPG, p. 878, 'Balance Sheet'; Firmenarchiv: DHPG. Minutes of Meetings, 1878–91, folio Godeffroy in StaH, Hanseatische Gesandtschaft in Berlin Nr. 132–5/2, N 1; Hamburgische-Weltwirtschafts-Archiv (=HWWA) A9 D8-y. Iii 2425; Godeffroy to Bülow, 25 Jan. 1879, StaH, vol. 132-5/2 anseatische Gesandtschaft Berlin. Schmack, p. 206; R. Hertz, *Das Hamburger Seehandelshaus J. C. Godeffroy & Sohn 1766–1879*, p. 60.

17   H. Münch, *Adolph von Hansemann*, pp. 258–9; M.J. Wolff, *Die Disconto-Gesellschaft*, pp. 27–43. Godeffroy to Bülow, 18 Mar. 1879, Schmack, pp. 252 & 257.

18   RT 4. Anlage 101, pp. 720–49 & 747–49.

19   L. Gall et al., *Die Deutsche Bank 1870–1995*, pp. 16–17; Stern, p. 398; Schmack, p. 268..

20   Zembsch to Bismarck, 26 Jan. 1880. M. Hagen, *Bismarcks Kolonialpolitik*, pp. 75 & 78–97; P.M. Kennedy, "Bismarck's Imperialism: The Case of Samoa, 1880-1890," *Historical Journal (=HJ)* xv, 2, pp. 264ff; Schmack, pp. 267–76; H.U. Wehler, 'Bismarck's Imperialism', *Past & Present* (1970) pp. 215–23; Münch, pp. 224–5; S. Firth, *New Guinea under the Germans*, p. 11.

21   Zembsch to AA, Report vol. 13112, 29 April, p. 30, 23 May, p. 39; 3 Jun., p. 40; Hoffmann, 'Wirtschaftsspionage', pp. 101–14; Schmack, p. 79.

22   Bismarck to Hansemann, 7 May 1880 (Smith, *German Interests*, Weissbuch (=Wb). no. 1, p. 25; Münch, p. 225. Hagen, p. 84; Schmack, pp. 273–75; Washausen, pp. 29–32, n. 39; Sack, *Eduard Hernsheim*, p. 88.

23   DHPG, Prospectus 1889, HWWA, A9, D8. Jb-DHPG 1898 – 1913 (StaH, 601); Schmack, p. 291; Heydt'sches Kolonialkontor, *Deutsches Kolonialblatt (=DKBl)* (1909) pp. 1164; (1911) p. 918.

24   Hernsheim agreed to pay R.I. Robertson RM200,000 annually until his uncle's investment in the firm was annulled, P.G. Sack, *Eduard Hernsheim*, pp. vi–viii, 9, 30, 34, 58–9, 70 & 72

25   E. Hernsheim, 'Der Bismarck-Archipel und seine Zukunft als Deutsche Colonie' in *Hamburgischer Correspondent (=HC)* (1886) p. 46 ff, StaH, 622-1; Sack, *Hernsheim*, pp. 30–1 & 47–8.

26   Sack, *Hernsheim*, p. 60. Firth, 'German Firms in the Western Pacific Islands', *JPH*, 8 (1972) p. 6.

27   Sack, *Hernsheim*, pp. 81 & 154–5; Hernsheim, StaH, 622-1, 2; P. Sack, 'Traditional Land Tenure', p. 179; P.J. Hempenstall, *Pacific Islanders under German Rule*, pp. 124–5.

28   Hagen p. 562.

29   E. Hernsheim to Bismarck, 23 Jan. 1885 (RKA 1001:3701).

30   Sack, *Eduard Hernsheim*, pp. 87, 101, 110 & 205; Hagen p. 202.

31   StaH, Hernsheim stationen, vol. 43, 1885, no. 8340; RKA 1001:2954; see Washausen, pp. 627.

32   Jb. J-G (1889); W. Treue, 'Die Jaluit-Gesellschaft', *Tradition Zeitschrift für Firmengeschichte und Unternehmer,* vii (1962), pp. 55–78.

33   Treue, pp. 58, 62 & 114–120.

34   *DKBl* (1893) pp. 383–6.

35   Treue, pp. 108–9; Schmack, pp. 228 & 237.

36   Treue, p. 108; J-G to AA, 4 Feb. 1892,

37   A.F. Ellis, *Ocean Island and Nauru,* pp. 55–62.

38   Ocean Island (Banaba) lies 400 km west of its neighbour Gilbert Island (Kiribati) in the west central Pacific. Arundel mined guano in the Central Pacific since 1886. J.T. Arundel & Co. merged with other trading entities in 1897 to form the PIC.

39   The London Stock Exchange, Year Book 1905; H. Haller, *Die Phosphat-Gesellschaften der Südsee*, p. 13; C. Elschner, *Korallogene Phosphatinseln Austral-Ozeaniens und ihre Produkte*, p. 68. (UFCP stands for German Superphosphate Manufacturer Union, Fabrik Chemischer Produkte).

40   Jb. J-G (1901) p. 1.

41   F.X. Hezel, *Strangers in their own Land* (Hawaii, 1995) pp. 70–1.

42   K. Buckley & K. Klugman, *The History of Burns Philp*, pp. 150–1 & 176.

43   Deutsche Kolonialgesetzgebung (=*DKG)* vol. 11, p. 121. 'Bergverordnung 1906' (German Mining Act) Section 76–85.

44   Hahl, p. 40; H. Linckens, *Auf den Marshall–Inseln*, p. 67.

45   RKA 100:6526; Jb. Marshalls 1906/07, p. 17; *DKZ* (1906) Nr. 45, p. 529; *DKBl* (1907) p. 1059;

46   S.G. Firth, 'German Labour Policy in Nauru and Angaur, 1906–1914', *JPH*, 13,   pp. 36-52, Treue, p. 117-20 & 147; Chart 39

47   J-G shareholder notice, *Berliner Börsen Courier (=BBC)*, 22 Aug. 1910.

48   *BBC* 17 and 18 Sep. 1907; Heydt'sches Kolonialkontor, 11 Dec. 1909. *DKBl* (1909) p. 1164. J-G issued 3,600 bonus shares in 1913. *BBC*, 8 Oct. 1910; 25; Kolonialbank, *DKBl* (25 July 1914). Heydt'sches Kolonialkontor, *DKBl.* (1911) p. 918; Jb. J-G (1889 to 1913), chart 39

49   The coral island Angaur has an area of 8km^2, with an estimated local population in 1908 of 150. A. Hahl, *Gouverneursjahre in Neu Guinea*, pp.191–2; P. Sack & D. Clark, eds., *Albert Hahl*, p. 117.

50   The authorised capital of 4,500 shares at RM1,000 each was divided into a series A to I (NDL: 2000, DNB: 2000, H. Müller & Co., Rotterdam: 2000, Tellus AG: 1500, Beer, Sondheimer & Co: 500 shares). The lead bank, DNB, received 1000 fully paid shares gratis at formation. In Oct. 1908 DB acquired 800 shares from DNB at 170%. (DB, file note, 4 Sep. 1926).

51   A. Scharpenberg, 'Die Bedeutung des Norddeutschen Lloyd', p. 103.

52   Heydt'sches Kolonialkontor, *DKBl*, (1909), p. 854. H. Haller, *Die Phosphat-Gesellschaften Der Südsee*, p. 25; Kolonialbank, 25 Jul., 1914; 'Geschäftsbericht der SAG 1913' (RKA 1001:2465).

53   P. Preuß, „Wirtschaftliche Werte in Den Deutschen Südseekolonien," *Der Tropenpflanzer (=TP)* 8 & 10, pp. 511–17; A. Hahl, *Deutsch-Neuguinea*, 2nd ed. p. 54; Scharpenberg, pp. 127 & 130; The British Foreign Office, *Pacific Islands*, p. 66, charts 26 & 28

54   *DKBL* (1910) Announcement

55   Hernsheim & Co, Jb. 1909–1913, HWWA & StaH, vol. 43, 1885, Nr. 8340; *DKBL* (1912) pp. 617.

56   R.W. Robson, 'Steinberger in Command', *Queen Emma*, pp. 62–88; K. Baumann, *The Parkinson Family Queen Emma and Relations in New Guinea*, p. 22, *The Australasian*, 'A Chapter in the Histories of the South Sea', 21 Nov. 1885, p. 5.

57   R.W. Robson, pp. 116–22.

58   Parkinson', *DKZ*, (1887), Nr. 18, pp. 694 & p. 695.

59   M. Krieger, 'Handelsunternehmungen in unseren Südseekolonien', *DKZ* (1899) Nr. 31, pp. 277–8.

60   Jb (1892/93) p.17; Sack & Clark (1892–93) p. 83; *Nachrichten über Kaiser Wilhelmsland und dem Bismarck Archipel (=NKWL)* 1894, p. 20; (1896) p. 30.

61   K. Neumann, *Not the Way it Really was: Constructing the Tolai Past*, p. 231

62   A demonstration of Coe-Kolbe's progressive thinking was the installation of a telephone, connecting Ralum plantations with her residence Gunantambu in 1895.

63   Hahl to AA, 21 Feb. 1899, RKA 1001:2278; see P.G. Sack, *Traditional Land Tenure*, pp. 239–40.

64   Jb. Forsayth (RKA 1001: 2431); Jb. (1907/08) pp. 9–10.

65   Buckley & Klugman, p. 176. BAG *Denkschrift*, Feb. 1909, pp. 1–55; Robson, pp. 204–7; Schnee, vol. i, pp. 216–17. BAG, *Denkschrift*, pp. 33–4.

66   *DKBL* (1912) pp. 869 & 1039–40; Sack & Clark (1910–11) p. 320; Jb. Forsayth (RKA 1001:2431).

67   Schnee, vol. iii, p. 656, vol. ii, p. 13.

68   Many details of O'Keefe's life remain obscure or are half-truths. See F.X., Hezel, 'The Man who was reputed to be King: David Dean O'Keefe.' *JPH* No. 43, issue 2 (2008) pp. 239–52

69   Ibid., p. 242

70   P.G & B Sack, eds., *Eduard Hernsheim: South Sea Merchant* (Boroko, 1983) p. 28. F.X Hexel, 'A Yankee Trader in Yap' in D. Scarr, ed., *More Pacific Island Portraits*, (Canberra, 1978) pp. 59–74

71   Furness, W.H., *The Island of Stone Money—Uap of the Carolines* (London, 1910) pp. 94–7 Berg, M.L., 'Yapese politics, Yapese money and the *Sawel* tribute network before World War I.' *JPH* No. 27 Issue 2 (1992) p. 150.

72   Hezel, p. 248.

73   Hernsheim, 'Die Marshall Inseln', p. 129; Treue, pp. 110–11.

74   Hezel, p. 251; Heydt's 'Jahrbuch der deutschen Kolonial- und Überseeunternehmungen', 6 (1912).

Begrüßung des Dr. Finsch in Dallmannshafen, ca 1884 (Painting by Moritz Hoffmann (1885) courtesy Übersee-Museum Bremen, Inv. No. D15.393).

ANNEXATION OF EAST NEW GUINEA

3

The enthusiasm for colonies by a sector of the German community matched the commitment by German commercial interests in the Pacific. This eagerness galvanised the Australasian colonies and Fiji into pressuring the British government to prevent Germany from gaining further foothold in the region. When Queensland gained independence from New South Wales in 1859 the new colony looked north to meet its economic needs with South Sea labour. Convict labour was no longer available, and to develop plantations profitably Queensland required access to cheap workers. Competition for South Sea labour between the German plantation owners in Samoa and the Australian sugar planters played a role in the development of Queensland agriculture; it hastened decisively the colonization of East New Guinea.

Competition for indentured labour

The pastoralist Benjamin Boyd became the first New South Welshman to employ South Sea islanders on his Riverina property in 1847.[1] Fourteen years later, Robert Towns, the New South Wales (NSW) parliamentarian, Sydney merchant and plantation owner, recruited 67 South Sea islanders for his cotton plantation on the Logan River in SE Queensland. Towns may not have realised in 1861 that he was starting a 'deluge of kanaks' from the Melanesian islands to NSW and Queensland; indeed he could not have known that by his action he would start a race for the annexation of East New Guinea.[2] By the time Harold Finch-Hatton, fourth son of the Earl of Winchilsea and Nottingham, took up land on the central Queensland coast around 1875, the search for South Sea labour had become a matter of economic survival. Yet the arrival of Melanesian workers in the Queensland cane fields in 1863 was not readily supported by British Prime Ministers, Palmerston (1859–65) and the profoundly humanitarian William Ewart Gladstone (1868–74). By the end of the 1870s Finch-Hatton had become convinced that North Queensland would only prosper after seceding from metropolitan Brisbane because 'the sugar industry is entirely dependent upon coloured labour (when) white men cannot and will not do work done by niggers in the field, and (if) white labour were available, it would only be at wages which the planters could never afford to pay.'[3]

The opening up of tropical north Queensland started in the early 1860s. Successful plantation industry depended on three factors: cheap fertile land, cheap labour and reliable rainfall. European labour was scarce and expensive and the white man was susceptible to tropical diseases. In 1862 the Queensland Parliament permitted the importing of indentured labour from India for the emerging sugar-cane industry on the Brisbane, Maryborough, Bundaberg, Mackay, Bowen and Cairns river plains.[4]

Disastrous Ventures

Because of the high transportation cost and the Queensland government's refusal to provide a shipping subsidy, the scheme lapsed. Convict labour sent by New South Wales to Queensland went no further than Moreton Bay and by the time settlers tried their luck further north, convict transportation to Australia had come to an end.

The conscription of 'kanakas' from Melanesia was the subject of strong protest by the London Aborigines' Protection Society, the Christian Missions and the humanitarian factions in Prime Minister Gladstone's administration. In their quest for labour the Queensland planters ignored the moralists in faraway London. They felt much more threatened by the ubiquitous German traders and planters on Samoa, Fiji and Tonga who drew their labour needs from these nearby Pacific Islands.[5]

The labour requirements of the Godeffroy plantations on Samoa were initially met with Cook Islanders and after 1864 from other Polynesian islands. Micronesia, in particular the Gilbert Islands, was the preferred recruiting area for the Hamburg firm from 1867 until the early 1880s. The Melanesian islands of Bougainville and Buka, New Ireland and New Hanover, delivered most of the workers for the Godeffroy successor DHPG. When NGC started to draw labour from this area in 1885–86, DHPG continued to exercise its right to take men from the region until the outbreak of World War I. Godeffroy and DHPG recruited 4,345 Melanesians from 1867 to 1884 and 5,746 during 1885 to 1913 for their Samoan plantations. German recruiters took an estimated 12,500 Pacific Islanders to Samoa.[6] By comparison, Britain moved over 27,000 Pacific Islanders and 61,000 Indians from her Dominions to Fiji from 1874 to 1913. The Queensland planters recruited about 30,400 people from the New Hebrides, Torres Strait Islands, and some 13,300 from the Solomons and Santa Cruz. The Bismarck Archipelago provided approximately 14,300 workers for Queensland until NGC shut this source for the Australian colonies in 1885.[7]

With the annexation of Fiji by Britain in 1874, the Western Pacific High Commission outlawed labour crimping and invoked regulations that prohibited the transportation of indigenous people within the same island group. The amended *Pacific Island Labourers Act, 1880* came into force in 1884. It proved mostly ineffective against the Queensland recruiters. The Griffith administration's amendment in November 1885 provided for the importation of South Sea Islanders until 31 December 1890. By supplying axes, guns and ammunition recruiters continued conscripting Melanesian workers for the northern Australian plantations. Bismarck's decree of 8 June 1885 paralleled the British labour law applicable to Pacific Islanders. It restricted Europeans' right to acquire land in GNG and prohibited trading in guns, ammunition and spirits; it outlawed the export of labour from Northeast New Guinea and the Bismarck Archipelago other than to West-Samoa. The immediate effect was lessened as islanders arriving up to 31 December 1890 could stay in Queensland for up to three years to complete their indenture, and a prolonged depression in the sugar industry permitted the importation of Melanesian labour until December 1892.

Coloured labour recruitment to Australia was brought to a complete end on 31 March 1904, the day when the Australian *Pacific Island Labourers Act, 1901* and *Immigration Restriction Act* of the same year came into force.[8]

The labour issue played an important role in the annexation by Germany of northeast New Guinea. The German trader, Eduard Hernsheim of R&H, relied on the local people to collect coconuts and prepare copra, and Theodor Weber, the head of DHPG, needed labour for his Samoan plantations. When the Queensland labour boats competed for this scarce resource in the archipelago and the Solomons in an increasingly belligerent manner, Hernsheim and the German consul in Apia, Oscar Stübel, raised the issue with the Colonial Department of the Foreign Office (AA-RKA) in Berlin. In a 29 May 1883 submission Hernsheim implored the stationing of a light cruiser at Matupi to counter 'the aggressive recruiting tactics employed by British labour ships' while Stübel requested the permanent deployment of a German man-of-war in the archipelago to serve the interests of R&H and DHPG. With a measure of self-righteousness, Hernsheim wrote to Bismarck in 1883:

> The labour traffic, as carried out here, differs altogether from what is done in other South Sea Islands, and if the facts were known, would no doubt be stopped by the English colonial authorities … Slavery is an ancient institution of these islands, and a chief, desirous of procuring arms, will sell his own people … Fire-arms and ammunition, at the rate of three muskets to two labourers, are the usual means of payment.[9]

In reference to the demand by Captain Kärcher of the German light cruiser the *Carola* that the trade in firearms be stopped in the interest of peaceable commerce,[10] Hernsheim let it be known, 'one-sided German measures would not achieve the desired results'. Rather, he urged for government representations to London 'to protect German property against the arrogant conduct of the crews of English labour vessels in their attacks on the natives'.[11]

Inaction by the German government led Hernsheim's agent on the Laughlan Islands, Karl Tetzlaff (alias Charlie Fitzloff), to intervene in a labour trade. Captain Davis and the government agent, W. McMurdo, both of the Queensland recruiting schooner the *Stanley,* had a deal with Island Chief Tomin for the supply of workers in exchange for merchandise. Tetzlaff's suggestion to Tomin that the recruited men would suffer mistreatment at the hands of the Queenslanders and would never return to their islands incurred Davis' wrath. The *Stanley* crew burned the station and twenty tonnes of copra. Intervention by the German government in London resulted in the Queensland government awarding Hernsheim £550 in damages.[12] The High Commissioner in Suva found Davis and McMurdo guilty 'under extenuating circumstances', sentencing them to three months' incarceration on 7 August 1884, but giving the two culprits parole after one week.[13]

Precursors to a German colonial presence in the southwest Pacific

Ludwig Bamberger's concern that passing the Samoa Subsidy Bill would open the gate for overseas annexations proved partly groundless. Initially only von Hansemann, head of the Berlin Disconto Gesellschaft, launched a foray into colonial acquisition. After the *Reichstag* had rejected a rescue package for the distressed Godeffroy enterprise Hansemann drafted a memorandum on a German colony in the South Sea. In his plan, submitted to *Wilhelmstrasse* (the Foreign Office) on 9 November 1880 for consideration, he expressed concern that Germany would lose its foothold in the region if Britain annexed East New Guinea, Tonga and Samoa. He reasoned that on geo-economical grounds alone 'Samoa should be annexed forthwith because the [islands] are situated approximately half-way between the American and Australian continents, with the latter becoming an increasingly important market for Germany'.[14] The kernel of Hansemann's submission related to his considerable interest in northeast New Guinea. The opening of the Suez Canal had increased trade, with volume to grow substantially after the completion of the Panama Canal. Hansemann argued that in such an expanding economy overseas possession are increasingly attractive to private enterprise and would improve Germany's trade balance.[15]

Because of the considerable market opportunities in Australia, his report identified the New Guinea coast with its enormous hinterland offering the best opportunity for the establishment of such a colonial enterprise. Hansemann proposed:

> Mioko, a coaling station of the German navy in the Duke of York Island, be made the centre of future colonial efforts. An Imperial subsidy be granted for a shipping service, which a consortium of present commercial firms were prepared to start to connect Mioko and Apia, Tongatabu and the other places with German factories. Coaling stations are secured along the northeast coast of New Guinea, between the East Cape and 141° E, where interested commercial firms would establish factories.[16]

Bismarck's adviser on overseas trade, Heinrich von Kusserow, supported the submission. Alluding to the *Reichskanzler's* concern on British Imperial Preference and protective duties maintained by France, Kusserow advocated the acquisition of colonies as an important step in providing German industry with large and secure markets:

> It is fortunate that the financial capacity that stood behind the Deutsche Seehandels-Gesellschaft was not discouraged by the defeat of the Samoa Subsidy Bill and is prepared to invest funds in the development of German colonies. The initial proposal of this consortium is to establish a shipping service in the South Sea to open up the region for German trade.[17]

Bismarck was not moved by his counsellor's enthusiastic support for the scheme. What was now proposed would inevitably lead to considerable financial and political intervention by the *Reich*. 'This is unthinkable', Bismarck reminded his bureaucrats.

> The Government does not have the personnel or expertise to run a colony. The English enter the colonial service at the age of sixteen, without tertiary education. Our civil servants are ill prepared for the task. Any involvement would have to be initiated by the German business organizations. But, the colonialists do not front up, except for the Hanseatic merchants, and they have their own ideas. Occupation and annexation of South Sea Islands is out of the question.[18]

Yet the briefing on 15 February 1881 by the Acting Foreign Secretary von Limburg-Stirum would not have disappointed Hansemann. While the grounds given for rejecting his proposal were predictable Bismarck left the door ajar for the next step to be taken. The *Reichskanzler* determined that 'the government could not occupy territory in the South Sea … this was to be left to private enterprise'. Importantly, Bismarck now sanctioned naval and consular protection 'to property in land acquired by private ventures'. Hansemann considered this shift an opportunity to procure land in the South Sea under the legal umbrella of the *Reich*.

British and Australian interests in the southwest Pacific

The constant in Australia's interest in the southwest Pacific was its concern with developing trade. Whereas the region did not rate highly in Britain's policy making, the Queensland labour trade, mostly conducted by New South Wales, were factors leading to Britain's annexation of Fiji and southeast New Guinea. [19]

Thus t1he statement in 1850 by Sydney's consul-general in Hawaii, Charles St Julian, 'the islands of the Pacific afford an almost unlimited field for enterprise, which as yet has been but little touched by the Australian merchants' was significant for the attention it drew to the commercial potential of the region. Based on mistaken assumptions, St Julian believed that 'the islands afford an incalculable extent of the most fruitful soil, with an unlimited supply upon the spot of the cheapest possible labour for its tillage'. Then in 1858 the governor of New South Wales, General W. T. Denison, pointed to 'a trade, of an extent almost unequalled in any group of colonies', when he referred to the commercial opportunities for Australia. And the traveller John MacGillivray reported in 1852:

> [The] specimen of pottery procured at Redscar Bay contained a few laminar grams of gold. The clay in which this precious metal is imbedded was probably part of the great alluvial deposit on the banks of the rivers the mouths of which we saw in that neighbourhood, doubtless originating in the high mountains behind, part of the Owen Stanley Range. [20]

Despite these early 'noises', intercourse between Australia and the Pacific region remained insignificant until the end of the 19th century. NSW recorded the highest activity with a meagre 2.39% of total imports in 1850, declining to 0.15% in 1870. The export activities were even less impressive with only 1.27% of goods shipped from NSW to the region in 1850. After Fiji became a British colony, NSW increased its overall exports to the region to 2.69% of total exports in 1883, declining again to 1.73% in 1899. Trade between the Pacific region and Queensland or Victoria never exceeded 1% of total trade.

Imports and exports (£) by Australian-based firms with the Pacific region. [21]

	New South Wales		Victoria		Queensland	
	New Guinea, Guam, Fiji, Marshall, New Britain, New Caledonia, Norfolk, New Hebrides, Solomons		New Guinea, Fiji, Guam, New Britain, Malden, Tonga New Caledonia, Marshall, Samoa,		New Guinea, Fiji, Guam, New Britain, Malden, Tonga New Caledonia, Marshall, Samoa,	
Year	Import	Export	Import	Export	Import	Export
1850–59	382,234	355,100	No data	No data	No data	No data
1860–69	361,754	645,804	No data	No data	No data	No data
1870–79	1,936,602	2,480,704	162,455	110,647	11,709	93,297
1880–89	2,762,629	3,746,123	407,833	258,579	110,411	165,824
1890–99	1,794,917	3,438,949	442,282	110,026	177,256	217,582

Disastrous Ventures

The lure of Polynesia

Rather than concentrating on New Guinea, a short sailing distance from north Queensland, Australian and New Zealand interests started their commercial exploits by competing with the European, British and American traders for favours with the chiefs of Fiji, Tonga, Samoa and Tahiti. Melbourne business interests formed the Polynesian Company during the 1860s to take advantage of inter-tribal warfare on Fiji. In exchange for protection and sham political support, the company tried to secure 200,000 ac (80,940 ha) of land from Chief Thakombau who angled for a deal over land that belonged to another tribe.[22] Acting British Consul for Fiji and Tonga, Sir John Thurston, advised against investing in Fijian enterprises. He informed the Earl of Bellmore (governor of NSW): 'the great interest manifested in this group of islands by the commercial community in the colony and the probable disappointment and pecuniary losses that may accrue from the action [are] based on incorrect or insufficient information as to the social and political condition of Fiji'.[23]

Notwithstanding Thurston's caution, Australian trade interests in the Pacific drove the agenda of the 1870 Intercolonial Conference in Melbourne. The New South Wales parliament had received petitions from 23 Sydney merchants seeking greater involvement in the Pacific region, particularly Fiji, which already had an established trading relationship with Sydney'. The outspoken Rev Dr John Dunmore Lang articulated the merchants' claim that other colonists were becoming increasingly interested in developing the resources of the region and that Sydney's role as an entrepôt would benefit from such a move. The conference resolved to urge the establishment of a British protectorate over the Fiji Islands.[24]

The first Gladstone government rejected the Melbourne resolution. The issue became again the focus of the 1873 Intercolonial Conference, with the mood of the delegates conveyed to the colonial secretary Lord (Henry) Carnarvon:

> Britain must give attention to the anarchic conditions prevailing in Fiji in the interest of the Australian colonies, as well as the rest of the Empire … Ministers of this Colony supported by leading merchants, urge the annexation and colonization of these islands because they form the most important settlement on the line of communication between Australia and America; have been chiefly settled by British subjects from these colonies; are rich fields for the commercial enterprise of Great Britain.[25]

The newly elected Conservative Party of Benjamin Disraeli—formed in early 1874—was more in tune with the Australian premiers provided the Australian Colonial governments were prepared to share in the cost of Fiji's administration. With Premier Henry Parkes the first to agree to Carnarvon's proposal, Victoria and Queensland soon agreed to follow the New South Wales lead by contributing £4,000 annually towards the cost of government of the new Colony. Thus the colonization of Fiji by Britain on 10 October 1874 started a chain of events that led to the annexation of East New Guinea by Britain and by Germany ten years later.[26]

East New Guinea, the pivot of an Australian Monroe doctrine

It was highly likely that British traders had visited New Guinea in the early 19th century. Their commercial interests would have followed the explorers with bêche-de-mer (trepang), pearls, tortoise-shell and sandalwood being the main attractions. The first serious attempt to extract the imagined riches of New Guinea was in June 1867 with the founding in Sydney of The New Guinea Co. (Ltd). Rev. Lang promoted eastern New Guinea and the Melanesian islands as an 'immense field for industry and enterprise [which] shall become one vast plantation, unequalled by any other country of the world'. Lang sought shareholder interest to occupy the land, develop it with European skill and knowledge, and cultivate it with the 'native population [as] willing labourers in the cause of peaceful prosperity'.[27] While the project had political support from Parkes, it collapsed for lack of funds and a profound lack of interest in New Guinea by the newly installed Gladstone government in Britain.

The next big idea was concocted in 1871 when a prospecting company was formed in Sydney to search for gold in southeast New Guinea. A year earlier, Queensland government geologist, Richard Daintree, reported that the gold-bearing rock formation, the Peak Downs and a portion of the Gilbert in north Queensland were largely represented at the southeastern extremity of New Guinea.[28] This statement provided enough reason for the more than 150 fortune hunters who assembled in Sydney on 1 December 1871 to found the New Guinea Prospecting Expedition (NGPE). Lang became a chief supporter of NGPE. He regarded the undertaking as the most important event that had ever taken place in the colony. Continuing to promote New Guinea as being of immense strategic and economic importance to Australia, he had no doubts that the expedition would come up with significant discoveries.

Lang's oratorical power got the venture started. However, with a signing-on fee of £1 and a further £9 for full membership, only 69 men joined NGPE. It was not cheap for a prospector who, on top of these fees, was required to provide his own tools, firearms, tents and cooking utensils. Also, while given free passage to and from New Guinea, he would not earn a wage; the rewards were to come from the equal shares in profits from the sale of gold, land and trade of any kind.[29]

When the organising committee failed in stimulating interest from merchants and the Colony's government the expedition proceeded on £600. It was enough to charter a laid-up collier, the brig *Maria,* with only a few Pounds left to get her sea ready. The venture commenced on 25 January when the 156-ton brig left Sydney for southeast New Guinea. It lasted 33 days. On 8 March 1872 the *Sydney Morning Herald* reported: 'the *Maria,* with her freight of hopeful adventurers, bound upon an enterprise which promised to have no inconsiderable influence upon the future commerce of Australia, struck upon the Bramble Reef on the morning of February 26'.[30] Instead of striking a gold reef in New Guinea, the old collier struck a reef off Cardwell in north Queensland and foundered. This also buried the first commercial enterprise leaving Australian shores for New Guinea. En route to survey the southeast and northeast coast of New Guinea, Captain John Moresby of the Royal Navy survey ship *Basilisk* rescued eight survivors; 37 hopefuls were either lost at sea or clubbed to death by the local people when they reached land.[31] As luck would have it, the crew of the *Basilisk* picked up pieces of auriferous quartz on the shore of Fairfax harbour. While this discovery was of no commercial value, the British government regarded the harbour location suitable for the first settlement and named it Port Moresby.[32]

Undaunted by the *Maria* disaster London-based, Melbourne-born barrister, Francis Peter Labilliere, submitted a petition in 1875 to try and convince Colonial Secretary Earl Carnarvon of the merits of annexation. An advocate of imperial federation, Labilliere believed that New Guinea formed the natural extension to North Queensland. And like Rev. Lang, he argued for annexation because of the growing interest by European countries in this area. 'In a very few years', he claimed', they will swarm in the island' and, if Britain did not act, 'another power would acquire New Guinea, and thus threaten the security of Australia'.[33] A fellow of the Royal Colonial Institute, Labilliere mixed economic and humanitarian activities by claiming that the New Guineans had to be protected from diggers, land grabbers and labour recruiters when the inevitable gold discoveries would become widely known in Australia.[34]

While Carnarvon believed that no other power threatened the acquisition of East New Guinea, he was not opposed to acquiring East New Guinea provided the costs involved were largely borne by the Australian governments. Based on the experience with Fiji, he advised cabinet that Britain should not shoulder any further burden of colonization without financial assistance from the Australian colonies. Secretary of the Colonies, Lord Derby, expressed his support when the French government sanctioned an expedition to New Guinea, exclaimed Britain's interest in New Guinea as being 'prior to that of any other European power'.[35]

On the back of Labilliere's petition, Lieutenant R. H. Armit and Edward Schubert founded the New Guinea Colonizing Association in London in 1875. Armit claimed to have visited New Guinea in 1872 and intended to raise funds for a trading expedition to the island: 'gentlemen wishing to join were welcome provided they contributed 250 guineas to the fund'.[36] The association petitioned the British government for a Royal Charter with exclusive rights for the exploitation of the land and mineral resources. Because Armit and Schubert had planned to import labour from East Asia, opposition to the idea by the London Missionary Society and the British and Foreign Anti-Slavery Society put a halt to the scheme before it got started.

Some Australian colonies devised similar schemes. For instance, Queensland and NSW provided support for reconnaissance expeditions on the Fly River by Luigi d'Albertis whose report in 1877 of 'the riches of the land we visited, its vegetable and probably mineral production, the soil suitable for the cultivation of many of the most valuable plants, as coffee, sugar, India-rubber, sago, tobacco, nutmeg, ought to attract the capital of the colony to open up the country' stoked the fires of the Australian colonial expansionists more than ever.[37]

Lawrence Hargrave, who survived the NGPE voyage on the *Marie*, ventured to New Guinea on four further occasions. Cofounder of the Royal Geographical Society of Australasia, he drew attention to this *terra incognita* like few others before him. 'Our new found society cannot do a better thing to inaugurate its birth', he told Society members, 'than by dispatching a party to thoroughly investigate that large island that must eventually prove of immense value to the British Empire'.[38] In 1876 he joined d'Albertis to navigate 840 km up the Fly River in the steam-launch *Neva*, provided by the NSW government. At the upper most point of their expedition, immediately above the junction where the Ok Tedi River meets the Fly (D'Albertis junction), Hargrave collected a speck of gold and some copper specimens.[39]

The magic word 'gold' brought hundreds of Australians rushing to New Guinea where, in early October 1877, Andrew Goldie (a naturalist, storekeeper and trader from Port Moresby) and the Rev. W. G. Lawes (New Guinea Mission) panned gold from the Laloki River near Port Moresby. The specimens they took to C. S. Wilkinson (NSW government geologist) for assaying 'were neither particularly rich nor particularly attractive' according to the *Sydney Mail*,[40] but it contained some gold. On 24 January 1878 the New South Wales New Guinea Prospecting Expedition was set up to raise £3,600 for the purchase of two boats and six months rations for 100 prospectors.[41] They followed the rush of men to the Laloki and Goldie Rivers from all over Australia and New Zealand. By December the wet season, increasing bouts of malaria and dysentery forced even the most hardened diggers to abandon prospecting. After eight months and untold deaths, the Goldie claim was abandoned although many remained convinced that New Guinea's rivers contained much gold.[42]

News of a New Guinea 'gold rush' did not change the Colonial Office's attitude towards annexation. With payments towards the cost of administrating Fiji not forthcoming, Carnarvon sent a dispatch to the Australian governors, advising them that there would be no further annexation in the Western Pacific unless the costs

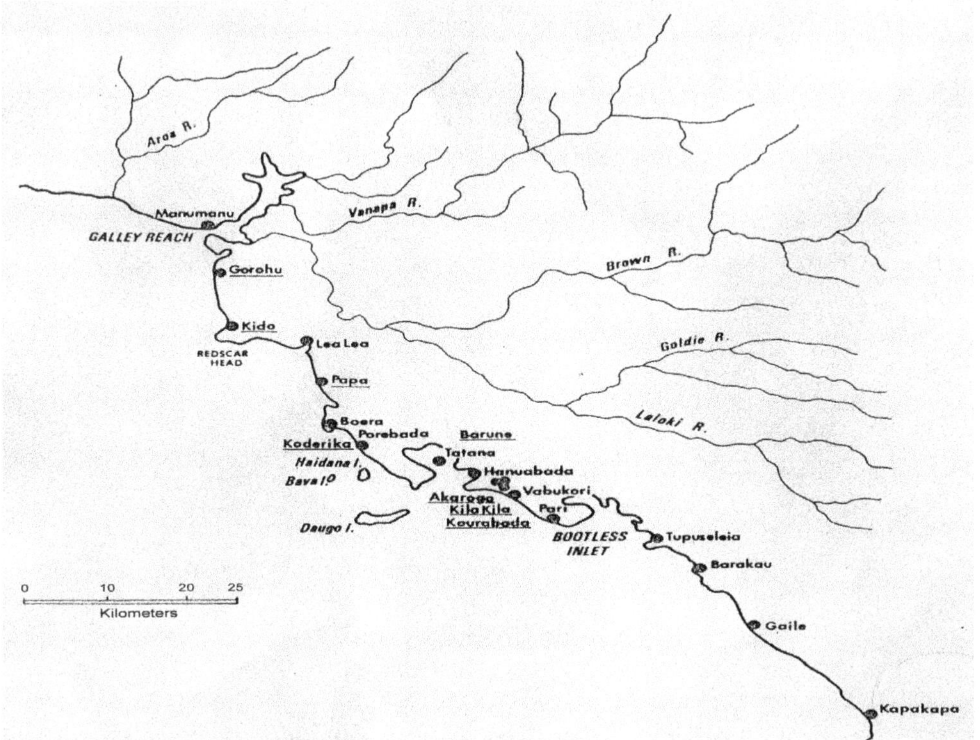

Map 2: **The Laloki and Goldie River district**

involved were substantially borne by the Australian governments pressing for British intervention in the area.[43] Also, the Disraeli government continued the course of its liberal predecessors. Agreeing with Gladstone in little else, Benjamin Disraeli told Lord Malmesbury as early as 1852: 'these wretched Colonies will all be independent in a few years, and are millstones around our necks'.[44] Since the Congress of Berlin in 1878, the now Earl of Beaconsfield had struck up a friendship with Bismarck, but their attention concerned Europe, not the acquisition of far-flung places.

Other New Guinea hopefuls were the shareholders in the New Guinea colonization Company. Formed in Melbourne in 1878 under the chairmanship of N. F. Dixon, the company made application to 'His Excellency the Governor General of Netherlands India for permission to lease for 99 years 150,000 acres of land on the north-western side of the island of New Guinea, between Humboldt Bay and the harbour of Dory'. The company sought the right to 'lay out and build towns and villages, to cultivate, graze, and mine upon such lands for gold, silver, copper, tin, lead, iron, coal or other metals or minerals'. The company advised that the north-eastern coast of New Guinea was far more suitable to its purpose than the Port Moresby region. But it will also present 'a petition to Parliament, praying for the annexation of New Guinea by Victoria'. The Queensland Morning Bulletin regarded the scheme 'the most impracticable of all the crack-brained projects of this kind which have recently set foot by ambitious Victorians'.[45]

Wilfred Powell, who visited the South Pacific on his ketch *Star of the East,* returned to explore the New Britain Archipelago from 1877 to 1880. He released a prospectus to raise funds 'for the purpose of opening up a trade with, and developing the resources of the Islands of New Guinea, New Britain and the adjacent groups'. To attract investors Powell undertook to conduct the operations personally, and provide potential investors with a detailed list of items for which he claimed a ready market in London and China. He submitted an income and expenditure budget, identifying potential goods of sale such as ebony wood, camphor, sago, tannin bark, gum and animal skins. While he did not specify the year in which his company could be profitable, Powell forecast positive cash-flow and a 25% return on funds invested.[46] But the London merchants were not attracted to the scheme. And Powell, unable to raise the required capital, accepted the position of Deputy Commissioner of the Western Pacific and Consul-General for the Navigator Islands (Samoa).

Australian interest in the Pacific culminated when the 1881 Intercolonial Conference in Sydney carried a motion that it was desirable that

> a representation be made to Her Majesty the Queen calling her attention to the lamentable state of affairs existing between the natives of many of the islands in the Pacific and the subjects of Her Majesty trading in these seas, more particularly since the appointment of a High Commissioner for the Pacific, and praying that Her Majesty will cause such action to be taken as will prevent the recurrence of such outrage against life and property as have lately prevailed.

This thinly veiled attack by the Colonial governments on the Suva-based High Commissioner Sir Arthur Gordon created tensions between the parties with long-lasting effects.[47] Gordon answered the charges by putting the interests of the indigenous people above the trading interests of the white man.[48] However, when Captain Ferguson of the HMS *Sandfly* and five of his seamen were murdered by

Solomon Islanders, Sydney merchants complained that traders in the South Sea Islands were not afforded sufficient protection. 'As long as British subjects are engaged in legitimate trade,' the *Sydney Morning Herald* wrote in September 1880,

> [T]hey are working for the benefit, and are entitled to the protection of their country. These colonies reap no small advantage from the South Sea Island trade, and they expect to reap larger advantages hereafter. … Where we push our trade we should have some legal machinery for protecting our interests… Colonial Governments have not begun to consider it a part of their duty to protect the traders of the South Seas, but the subject is one which they might conveniently consider, and which they might impress upon the attention of the authorities in Downing Street.[49]

Labilliere weighed into the annexation question again towards the end of 1882. Stirred to action by the German expansionist campaigner, Emil Deckert, he implored the Colonial Office to pre-empt any German intentions. Deckert argued for immediate German annexation of New Guinea in the *Augsburger Allgemeine Zeitung* on 27 November 1882.[50] The translation of the article in the *SMH* on 7 February 1883 caused much alarm in Australia. While the editorial reasoned: 'if the place is to be annexed by any other power than England, we should be glad to see it in the hands of Germany',[51] the *Queenslander* urged for the immediate annexation of New Guinea by Britain, as 'for our Parliament to remain longer inactive would involve almost criminal neglect'.[52] Writing on behalf of the Royal Colonial Institute, Labilliere drew the attention of Lord Derby, but was advised that the Colonial Office 'has no reason for supposing that the German government contemplate any scheme of colonization in the direction indicated by the *Norddeutsche Allgemeine Zeitung*'.[53]

Unconvinced, Premier Thomas McIlwraith instructed Queensland's Agent-General in London, Thomas Archer, to inform the Colonial Office that Queensland would assist in taking formal possession of New Guinea and would carry the cost of government. While Derby told Archer that 'if New Guinea should become a *place d'armes* of some foreign state it would be a perpetual menace to the continent, and would call for great military preparation on the part of the Australian people', he also doubted whether Queensland could afford the cost of annexation. Before submitting his recommendation to the cabinet he asked for assurance that Queensland would carry the entire financial burden save that of protection from foreign aggression.[54] Derby received an unexpected answer. While the Colonial Office was equivocating McIlwraith instructed the Police Magistrate on Thursday Island, Henry Chester, to travel to Port Moresby and claim 'all that portion of New Guinea and the islands and islets adjacent thereto, lying between the 141st and 155th meridians of east longitude in the name and on behalf of Her Most Gracious Majesty, Her heirs and successors'.[55] Chester hoisted the British flag in Port Moresby on 4 April 1883, an event reported 12 days later in *The Times,* wherein Gladstone learnt of Britain's new dependency. McIlwraith's resolute deed was generally applauded by newspapers in Britain and Australia, although one, the *Spectator*, was aghast at the prospect of colonies conducting annexationist policies.[56] Bismarck learnt of the event from his Consul in Brisbane, Carl Sahl, who cabled on 16 April 1883: 'a telegram from Cooktown, published this day, announced that New Guinea was formally annexed on the 4th inst., by Mr. H.M. Chester, Police Magistrate of Thursday Island'.[57]

Disastrous Ventures

Gladstone, Prime Minister again, remained opposed to imperial expansion. His concern for the well being of the indigenous population was in tune with that of the Aborigines' Protection Society which urged the government not to accede to the annexation because of Queensland's record in the Kanaka trade.[58] The issue of native subjugation was also addressed in a letter from Sir Arthur Gordon to Gladstone. Unaware of the sparsely populated island, Gordon was particularly concerned because Queenslanders regarded 'natives as vermin' and if 'New Guinea becomes a part of Queensland its vast population will become available for recruiting without any other restrictions than those the Parliament of Queensland chooses to impose'.[59]

Gordon's central point that Queensland was not overly concerned with the defence of its northern border but wanted to secure cheap labour for its sugar industry was a conclusion also reached by a Royal Commission in Britain in October 1883. Appointed to enquire into the workings of the Western Pacific Orders, the Commissioners commented specifically on the undesirability of giving Queensland any special voice in New Guinea matters because 'its vast regions will be available as recruiting ground for labour, without any restrictions'.[60]

When Gladstone informed Queen Victoria of the cabinet's decision not to ratify Queensland's provisional annexation,[61] he did not shut the door on future annexation of some parts of New Guinea. In a May 1883 memorandum he suggested to Derby that the Australian colonies should combine into some kind of political union, which would then provide a better approach to annexation.[62]

Henry Chester raises the Union Jack at Port Moresby (*The Australasian Sketcher* 4 July 1883)

Carried along by public opinion, Australia's role in the southwest Pacific was again an agenda item at the 1883 Intercolonial Convention in Sydney. The prevaricating attitude of the British government drove Victoria's Premier James Service to advocate an Australasian Monroe doctrine over all islands south of the equator. Service's Protestant Christianity and his close connections with the Rev. John Paton gave him a personal interest in the area. In addition to New Guinea, the New Britain Archipelago and the Solomons, he insisted on the New Hebrides being included in any settlement. Premier Alexander Stuart (NSW) concurred on New Guinea, but cautioned against unfettered expansion in the Pacific on the grounds of cost.[63] Unlike the people of Melbourne and Brisbane, Stuart's Sydney constituents were not overly excited about annexing Pacific Islands. They were more interested in economic outcomes. What was in it for them? And, because most of the southwest Pacific trade was routed through Sydney, why disturb a beneficial commercial arrangement? Stuart believed that a declining population would make New Guinea 'as useless to Australia as if they were in the other hemisphere'. Instead, Stuart believed in the benefit of sending more missionaries and traders to New Guinea to inculcate European habits, which 'might in no long time render them of immeasurably greater value to Australia than they are now'. It formed the view that 'such steps should be immediately taken as will most conveniently and effectively secure the incorporation within the British Empire of so much of New Guinea, and the small islands adjacent thereto, as is not claimed by the government of the Netherlands'.[64]

To play to Gladstone's tune, delegates demanded that immediate steps be taken to protect the indigenous population against the ravages of fortune hunters. As regards cost, the council agreed to recommend to their respective governments that the expenditure for administration would be shared equitably with the British government.

Twelve months later, on 9 May 1884, Derby submitted the figure of £15,000 as the likely annual cost of administration.[65] Without specifically identifying which part of New Guinea the British government was intending to annex, he invited the governors of the Australasian colonies to contribute towards the cost of establishing a High Commission in Port Moresby.[66] S. W. Griffith, Queensland's premier since November 1883, agreed immediately. In his letter to Derby and copied to the other colonies, he accepted the British proposal on the proviso that parliament would appoint a High or Deputy Commissioner with large powers of independent action. Service confirmed on 27 July 1883 that, Victoria, Queensland and New Zealand had committed to the contribution of costs for British intervention in New Guinea. Governor, A.E. Kennedy (Qld) advised: 'I have only to express my entire satisfaction with the action of my Government [and] I do not anticipate any difficulty in providing for the cost of maintaining our authority'. Believing a colony would be established over all of eastern New Guinea, the Queensland Parliament passed *The New Guinea and Pacific Jurisdiction Contribution Act* on 21 August 1884.[67]

Meanwhile, German attention towards New Guinea was increasing. On 24 April 1884 Bismarck placed land acquisitions by the Bremer trader Lüderitz in southwest

Africa under the protection of the *Reich*. The *Reichskanzler* used the debate on the Mail-Steamer Subsidy Bill to deliver a landmark statement on 23 June on his new colonial policy. Bismarck now intended to proceed with annexations 'by granting charters to private companies'.[68] This shift in policy encouraged the two bankers, Hansemann and Bleichröder, to revisit their ideas of 1880. They were now certain that the *Reich* could be persuaded to annex northeast New Guinea. They believed that if they could get there quickly, the territory was theirs for the taking.

The plan to send an expedition to northeast New Guinea was underway even before Hansemann's consortium raised RM1,000,000 in start-up capital. When the Berlin banker became aware that Britain intended to appoint a Commissioner in Port Moresby, immediate action became essential if he wanted to see his long-held wish of establishing a German New Guinea realised. In order not to alert the anti-colonialists in the *Reichstag* or indeed speed up Australian designs on the territory, he commissioned the South Sea veterans Otto Finsch and Captain Eduard Dallmann to undertake hydrography as well as procure large tracts of land along the north coast of New Guinea and the adjacent islands surreptitiously. The Hansemann-controlled DHPG had been instructed to purchase and refit a steamship for the expedition while the two explorers, first mate Hinrich Sechstroh and marine engineer Lars Nielsen travelled to Sydney on the SS *Chimborazo*. The remaining crew was hired in Australian, and on 11 September 1884 Finsch and Dallmann set course for northeast New Guinea.

Hansemann did not realise that his 'secret' New Guinea plan motivated Eduard Hernsheim. Keen to foil competition for labour and copra, the South Sea veteran informed the inveterate critic of German colonialism, Ludwig Bamberger, and Cesar Godeffroy's erstwhile business foe, Hermann Heinrich Meier of Bremen, of Hansemann's plans. Bamberger, who was a member of the subcommittee enquiring into the Pacific Mail-Steamer Subsidy Bill, accused von Kusserow of complicity with Hansemann, who he claimed would benefit from a subsidised steamer service in the South Sea. To check the damage, Hansemann and Bleichröder informed Bismarck of their intentions to establish a consortium for exploring northeast New Guinea and 'look for the best harbours, purchase land and establish friendly relations with the natives'. Kusserow also jumped to the defence of his brother-in-law, Hansemann, by advising Bismarck:

> [T]he English experience tells us to place territory under the protection of the *Reich* where German commerce and trade are predominant and where expensive German expeditions have established land ownership. Whereas the Australians cannot be denied right of occupation on the south coast of New Guinea, the north coast is a different matter altogether; in this region it should be entirely possible for the *Reich* to assume sovereignty. [69]

The German consul-general in Sydney, Richard Krauel, supported Kusserow's submission: 'New Guinea is of no commercial importance to Australian commerce', he informed the Chancellor', Queensland's annual export to the island was worth £20,000 and it 'merely consisted of goods intended as payment for labour engaged there to work on the Queensland sugar plantations'. The only bona fide trading activities were those of Sydney and Auckland. 'These two entrepôts', Krauel continued, 'have monopolised the Australian trade with the South Sea Islands, much of which is carried out with Fiji and New Caledonia'.[70]

On 20 August 1884 Hansemann's dream of owning a colony edged closer to realization. Bismarck announced on that day: 'the *Reichsmarine* will provide protection to the Hansemann consortium to the same extent the enterprises enjoy in Africa'.[71] Bismarck approved the hoisting of the German flag on unoccupied land 'as long as it was understood that government-sponsored colonies, along the lines of the French system, would not be supported by him'.[72] As regards the Australian colonies' initiative to annex all of East New Guinea Bismarck noted on a draft from his Foreign Secretary, Paul von Hatzfeldt:

> [I]t cannot be a matter of indifference to us when we find that regions of the South Sea, within which German commercial enterprise had hitherto free scope for development are all at once declared natural domains of Australia, and if, with a view to a proposed occupation, all acquisitions made thereby others are declared null and void.[73]

The German government recognised British interests in southeast New Guinea while outlining its interests in the north and the adjacent islands. Before the instruction to hoist the German flag was cabled to Consul Oertzen in Matupi and the commanders of the two German war ships sent there for this purpose, Bismarck wrote to the British Foreign Secretary Granville: 'in the interests of our respective subjects and to avoid frictions between them we wish to reach in advance agreement with Britain about the boundaries of our respective areas of protection'. [74]

The Gladstone cabinet responded on 6 August by annexing East New Guinea. This decision, according to the German Ambassador in London, Count Münster, was not conveyed to him when meeting with Granville two days later.[75] The degree of British authority in New Guinea, further discussed in cabinet on 9 August, led to the reversal of the decision. This time the Foreign Office informed Hatzfeldt of the meeting that had taken place between Granville and Münster.[76] It noted that 'the extension of some form of British authority in New Guinea, which … will only embrace that part of the island which especially interests the Australian colonies, without any prejudice to any territorial questions beyond those limits'. Granville also informed Münster that 'Her Majesty's Government is earnestly desirous of settling these territorial questions as proposed by the [German] Imperial Government'. Bismarck surmised that the British communiqué excluded the north coast of the mainland. Without seeking clarification, he proceeded to formalise a German presence in the South Sea. On 19 August he cabled Consul Krauel in Sydney:

> Inform Imperial Commissioner von Oertzen in New Britain it is intended to hoist the German flag in the archipelago of New Britain and along that part of the northeast coast of New Guinea which lies outside the sphere of Holland and England, where German settlements already exist.[77]

Bismarck advised Hansemann and Bleichröder a day later: 'Instructions have been given to support your undertaking. The acquisition made by you will be placed under the protection of the Empire, on the same conditions as in southwest Africa'.[78]

British annexation of southeast New Guinea

The British Foreign Office obstructed Bismarck's intention to raise the German flag in East New Guinea. On 19 September 1884 Granville advised Berlin: 'Her Majesty's Government proposed to proclaim and establish the Queen's prerogative over all the coast of New Guinea not occupied by the Netherlands Government'.[79] Bismarck's response to Granville a week later was carefully worded:

> The intended extension of the British Protectorate in the north and northeast of New Guinea after the previous declaration of your Excellency comes unexpectedly to the Imperial Government. [In] the view of the Imperial Government, the delimitation of the areas which interest both sides on that stretch of coast should be the subject of a friendly understanding by means of a commission.[80]

The British Foreign Secretary communicated six weeks later that he was not in favour of a 'Border Commission', and that Her Majesty's Government

> shall limit the British Protectorate to the whole of the south coast, including the islands contiguous to it, instead of that they had at first proposed. This will be done without prejudice to any territorial questions beyond these limits. It is with great satisfaction that Her Majesty's Government has come to an agreement in which they find themselves in perfect accordance with Germany. In case any questions should arise as to those districts which lie beyond the limits described, Her Majesty's Government is of opinion that it would be better to deal with them diplomatically.[81]

To forestall any further negotiations, Commodore James Erskine was instructed by the British Admiralty on 8 October to proceed to New Guinea and hoist the British flag on the south coast eastward of the 141st meridian. A day later Derby cabled Acting Commissioner of the Western Pacific H. H. Romilly to declare 'British Protectorate, New Guinea, from Dutch boundary to East Cape and Islands to Kosman Island. Notify settlement and purchase land forbidden'.[82]

While the *Norddeutsche Allgemeine Zeitung* claimed that a limited British Protectorate over New Guinea was the result of an agreement between Great Britain and Germany, Romilly hastened from Cooktown to Port Moresby to declare most of East New Guinea a British Protectorate before the Royal Navy had arrived. On 6 November Erskine repeated the official ceremony and thereafter the Royal Navy ships *Nelson, Espiegle, Raven, Swinger* and *Harrier* completed the mission by occupying eight strategic locations from 141° E to East Cape, with adjacent islands to Cape Kosman and the islands in the Goschen Straits and the D'Entrecasteaux Group.[83]

Berlin was not aware of the exploratory voyage to southeast New Guinea in June/July 1884 by Police Magistrate H. Milman, and the Rev. S. MacFarlane on the London Missionary Society schooner *Eilangown*. And the British government was not aware that Finsch and Dallmann had raised the German flag on land they had acquired during October and November. The British were also not aware that the *Reichsmarine* had deployed her warships, the SMS *Elisabeth* and *Hyäne,* to Matupi where Captain Schering and Captain Langemak were to proclaim the future intention of the *Reich* on 3 November; repeating the ceremony the following day in the Duke of York Group and at Nodup, Kinigunan, Raluana, Kabakada and Kabiara on New Britain, and at Nusa and Kapsu on New Ireland on 11 and 12 November. The *Reichsmarine* then proceeded to raise the German flag on the Schering Peninsula (Friedrich Wilhelmshafen) and Finschhafen on 20 and 27 November. Effective from

HMS *Raven*, **ca. 1898**
(NLA Canberra H91.325/2245)

HMS *Nelson,* **ca 1884**
(StatL. South Australia B12404)

SMS *Hertha* at anchor off Apia
Harbour, **ca 1882**
(Bundesarchiv no. 134 B0677)

SMS *Hyäne*, **ca. 1884**
(Bundesarchiv no. 134 B0327)

those dates, Bismarck placed German settlements in northeast New Guinea—from 141°E to the region of the Huon Gulf—under the protection of the *Reich*.[84]

The German actions were kept secret until Oertzen asked Commander Marx of HMS *Swinger*—who had repatriated indentured labour from Queensland to Matupi— to deliver a telegram to Cooktown from where Bismarck was to be advised of the successful flag-hoisting ceremonies. Oertzen's message was in plain text so Britain would have received the news of the German annexation from the Royal Navy since Bismarck only advised Sir Edward Malet, the British Ambassador in Berlin, of the German actions in New Guinea on 19 December. Mindful of not causing a diplomatic incident Bismarck had only advised Granville shortly after he had spoken to Malet that Germany remained open to negotiations on New Guinea.[85]

Without referring to the German proclamation, Granville informed Queen Victoria on 3 January that the Royal Navy had been instructed to proclaim the New Guinea north coast from East Cape to the Gulf of Huon, including the Louisiade and Woodlark Islands as British territory. The British action was demanded, Granville added, 'by the desire to obviate all the inconveniences that might arise from an absence of jurisdiction on the coast'.[86]

Without mentioning the action taken by Britain, Granville expressed surprised in his communiqué to Bismarck. 'Recent negotiations with the German Government', he proffered, 'had led him believe that a friendly understanding had been arrived at between the two governments, in virtue of which neither Power would make fresh acquisitions in the Pacific Ocean pending a meeting of the Anglo-German Commission which had been agreed upon'.[87] Not one for letting diplomacy derail his objectives the *Reichskanzler* responded bluntly on 20 January 1885:

Raising the Imperial Flag at Mioko on 4 November 1884 (Goethe University Frankfurt, No. 043–4012–3&7)

> If the British Government did not know that Germany was planning further annexations east of Huon Gulf this could only be attributed to the fact that our communications in this matter did not receive the degree of attention we expect.[88]

London's tit-for-tat reply on 27 January advised Berlin that Britain had also acted to extend the boundaries of its New Guinea Protectorate.

Gladstone, however, more interested to have an ally in Germany on his disagreement with France over Egypt than a prolonged disagreement over New Guinea, urged Granville to seek a solution with the German government.[89] On 7 February 1885 the Foreign Secretary informed the German Ambassador that the British government now sought a friendly examination of the boundary in New Guinea. After Derby communicated the decision to the Australian colonies he told Granville: 'we accept the line of 8° [longitude]. I am sorry we can do no more for Australia, but agree that the question of Egypt overrides all others'.[90] Bismarck was pleased with the outcome. New Guinea played no part in European politics and in light of France's reluctance to enter into a strategic alliance with Germany, good relations with Britain were now important.[91]

The British–German accords were signed on 6 and 10 April 1886. The Australian colonies were displeased with the outcome. They looked for the whole of East New Guinea and were annoyed that Germany had been allowed any of the islands.[92]

Granville proposed a general basis for the demarcation of the boundaries between the two protectorates in a note to Münster on 25 April. By then Bismarck's interest in colonial possessions had waned. The *Reichstag* election in October of the previous year had installed a largely Bismarck-friendly majority; and when the boundary negotiations over New Guinea did not proceed as quickly as expected, he commented laconically: 'we already have more land than we can make use of'.[93] The accord with Britain suited him. It included an agreement concerning reciprocal freedom of trade and commerce in the Western Pacific. Hansemann opposed the free trade agreement because of the competitive advantage the Australian colonies would have in the region. He advised Bismarck 'her geographical proximity and her strongly developing industrial base will make it very difficult to compete with Australia in the region'.[94]

The formation of GNG is related to the insolvency of Godeffroy with a considerable measure of assistance from the Australian colonies. It is linked with the attempt by Queensland on 4 April 1883 to annex all of East New Guinea. The proclamation by the Australian colonies: 'the acquisition of territory south of the equator by any foreign power would be highly detrimental to the safety and well-being of Australia', spurred Hansemann to acquire northeast New Guinea.[95] Bismarck would not have engaged in colonialism had England, France and Portugal guaranteed German traders safe access to the African markets, and had the Australian colonies not been so noisy about New Guinea. He told parliamentarians on 12 May 1885, 'Gentlemen, colonising is not the forte of Generals or Privy Councillors, it depends on the expertise of the trading houses.'[96] And Herbert von Bismarck dismissed the New Guinea acquisition altogether when he wrote to his father on March 1885:

Disastrous Ventures

> About New Guinea there is evidently a misunderstanding on both sides. I myself should have wished we had let New Guinea go altogether. This was prevented by the aggressive position Australia has taken. Nevertheless, I think that annexation by Germany is a mistake, and that you will have a great deal of trouble there in the future. Australia is expanding in strength and population. In a generation or two, when perhaps she may have broken away from us, she will feel strong enough to wage war, like the old European Powers, and will clear out all foreigners from her neighbourhood. The great distance will make it difficult for Germany to fight Australia and she will be forced in the awkward situation of having to evacuate New Guinea.[97]

As for BNG, Gladstone told Granville that he would not have agreed for southeast New Guinea to become a British Protectorate if he had not felt the need 'to act in the face of great colonial communities'. When he finally put up with the demands of the Australian colonies he could have hoped for another Fiji where private enterprise was well on the way to commercial success. Here the optimistic trading projections by the Australians were borne out in time. The Sydney-based Colonial Sugar Refining Company opened its first mill in Fiji soon after annexation, and exports began in 1898. However, as soon as southeast New Guinea was declared a British Protectorate, the Australian colonies lost interest. While Queensland, NSW and Victoria bore the cost of administration for the first ten years, they did little to advance the economic development of the young British colony or the well-being of the Papuan people.

The Proclamation at Port Moresby, 6 November 1884 (StaL-Vic. No. 03113/793

Notes

1   B.H. Molesworth, 'Kanaka Labour in Queensland', Royal Historical Society of Queensland, 1916 '.

2   R. Evans, K. Sauders, & K. Cronin, *Race Relations in Colonial Queensland*, p. 149; E.W. Docker, *The Blackbirders: A Brutal Story of the Kanaka Slave-Trade*; C. Moore, J. Leckie, & D. Munro, *Labour in the South Pacific*; O.W. Parnaby, 'Britain and the Labour Trade in Southwest Pacific', *Journal of South Pacific Law (=JSPL)*.

3   R. Evans, K. Saunders & K Cronin, 'A Queensland plantation owner', in *Race Relations in Colonial Queensland*, p. 158. H. Finch-Hatton, *Advance Australia*.

4   Indian Labourers Act 1862, Section 1, (R. Mortensen, 'Slaving in Australian Courts: Blackbirding Cases, 1869–1871', *Journal of South Pacific Law*, 4 p. 2, n. 4).

5   Parnaby, pp. 29–32 & 51–4.

6   Stübel to Bismarck, 27 Jan. 1886, Hahl to RKA, 16 Nov. 1913, (RKA 1001:2316, pp. 50–1)

7   Parnaby, pp. 201 & 203. See also A.G. Davies, 'The Pacific Islands – Their Glamour & Tragedies', Historical Society of Queensland 22 April 1943.

8   K. Buckley, & K. Klugman, *The History of Burns Philp*, pp. 23–8 & 60–4. R. Mortensen, 'Slaving in Australian Courts', JSPL, 4, (2000) pp. 1–13. The Argus, (1884) 1 Oct., pp. 4–5; *BC* (1885) 28 July, *SMH*, (1885) 29 July (RKA R1001:2298-97, pp. 1ff).

9   E. Hernsheim to Bismarck, 29 May 1883; R.M. Smith, (tr.) 'German Interests in the South Sea', Abstracts of the White Book (Wb) 1883, no. 8, p. 29. Deutscher Reichstag, 1 Session, 6 Legislaturperiode, Deutsches Interesse in Der Südsee, Land-Reklamation Auf Fiji, 1885. Drucksache Nr. 167.

10   Kärcher to the Chief to Admiralty, Berlin, Batavia, 6 July 1883, German Embassy, London, to AA, 4 Sep. 1883, Smith, Wb 1884, no. 8, p. 29, pp. 31–2. Mitchell Library, Sydney, vol. 16, no. FM4/1658.

11   Hernsheim to Bismarck, 29 May 1883, Smith, Wb 1884, no. 8, pp. 29–31.

12   Granville to Münster, June 1884, Smith, Wb 1884, no. 16, p. 36.

13   Hernsheim to Bismarck, 26, Aug. 1883; Stübel to Bismarck, 15 Dec. 1883; Busch to Münster 5 Jan. 1884, Granville to Münster, 6 Feb., 9 June 1884; Krauel to Bismarck 23 May 1884; (Smith, Wb 1884, no. 11, pp. 33–4, no. 14, pp. 35-6, no. 17, pp. 36–7; V&P (Vic), 1884, ii, no. 25, p. 70; CO 422-1, mf 2685. BC (1884) 11 Sep., p. 3.

14   Denkschrift Hansemann, 9 Sep. 1880 (RKA 1001:2927, pp. 9–34)

15   H. Münch, *Adolph von Hansemann*, pp. 226–7. (RKA 1001:2927, pp. 2–7)

16   Münch, p. 226; M.J Wolff, *Die Disconto-Gesellschaft*, p. 64; H. Wehler, *Bismarck und der Imperialismus*, pp. 223–4; Jacobs, 'The Colonial Office and New Guinea 1874–84', *HS.ANZ*, (1952) vol. 5.

17   Kusserow Memorandum, 21 Dec. 1880 (RKA 1001:2927, pp. 203–57). H. v. Kusserow, 'Fürst Bismarck und die Kolonialpolitik', (*DKZ*, [1898] no. 15, p. 297).

18   Smith, Wb 1883, no. 2, p. 25.

19   R.C. Thompson, *Australian Imperialism in the Pacific: The Expansionist Era 1820–1920*.

20   J. MacGillivray, *Narrative of the Voyage of H.M.S. Rattlesnake*, vol. ii, p. 69.

21   Krauel to Bismarck, 20 Aug. 1884 (Smith, 1884, Wb no. 7, pp. 26–8).

22   Different spellings of 'Cakobau', 'Thakombauor' or 'Tackombau' (NLA, mfm G22814).

23   V&P (NSW), 1868–69 vol. 1.

24   Lang petition to the NSW Legislative Assembly, 27 Oct. 1869. V&P (NSW), 1871–72, vol. 2, John Dunmore Lang founded the Scottish-Australian Presbyterian Church. While championing emigration of Scottish and English working families, he also promoted the immigration of German Lutheran missionaries to Australia. He promoted the expansion of New South Wales interest in the South Pacific.

25   V&P (NSW), 1894, vol. 1, NSW government to the Secretary for the Colonies, 14 Oct. 1873.

26   Parkes to Carnarvon 20 Jul. 1874, V&P (NSW), 1874, vol. 2. Carnarvon to Robinson, 7 Aug. 1874.

27   NLA, Lang pamphlets vol. 5. The Goulburn Herald and Chronicle (1867) 1.May, p. 4

28   R. Daintree, 'General Report upon the Northern District' (V&P [Qld] 1870, vol. 1)

29   L. Hargrave papers' (PRO, London, no. 3545).

30   *SMH*, (1872), 8 March, p. 5, 24 May, p. 4

31   L. Lett, Papuan Gold, pp. 1–4; P. Maiden, 'The Tragedy of the New Guinea Prospecting Expedition,' *Australian Heritage*, pp. 56–60. Hargrave (PRO, London, no. 3545).

32   J. Moresby, 'Recent Discoveries', Royal Geographical Society, vol. XLIV, 1873–4.

33   'The New Guinea Colonising Association', *Townsville Daily Bulletin* (1946) 30 Aug., p. 7. Legge, p. 16; Jacobs, 'The Colonial Office and New Guinea', pp. 106–18.

34   Royal Colonial Institute, vol. VI, 1874, pp. 191–3; W.P Morrell, *Britain in the Pacific Islands*, p. 238

35   Carnarvon to Robinson, 8 Dec. 1875 & to the governors of the Australasian colonies, 13 Jan. 1876 (BPP, C-1566). Herbert to Tenterden, 3 July 1876 & Lyons to Derby, 14 July 1876 (CO 201/582).

36   V&P (NSW),1875-76 vol. 2; J.D. Legge, 'Australia & New Guinea to the Establishment of the British Protectorate, 1884', *HS.ANZ*, (1950) vol. 4, p. 36. See Whitaker et al (p. 271).

37   V&P (NSW), 1876–77 vol. v; L.M. D'Albertis, 'New Guinea: Its Fitness for Colonization,' Royal Colonial institute, Proceedings Royal Colonial Institute.

38   Mitchell Library FM4/1060. J.L. Whittaker et al., pp. 272–3.

39   Hargrave papers, Mitchell Library FM4/1060. The find was 90 km south of the present Ok Tedi mine (T. Neal, 'Historical Overview of Mining in PNG', New Guinea Gold Corporation of Canada).

40   *Sydney Mail* (1878) 19 Jan., p. 47.

41   *Australian Town & Country Journal* (1878) 26 Jan. (=*AT&CJ*)

42   H. Nelson, 'The Swinging Index: Capital Punishment & British & Australian Administration in Papua New Guinea, 1888–1945,' *JPH*, 13, pp. 76–80; S. v. Gnielinskie, 'Struktur und Entwicklung Papuas', Dissertation (Hamburg, 1957) p. 78.

43   BPP, 'Correspondence Respecting New Guinea' (C-1566, pp. 85–6).

44   Disraeli to Malmesbury, in Leo Maxse, 'British Foreign Policy', *The National Review*, Nov. 1901.

45   Argus (1878) 9 Aug., p. 10; *The Queenslander* (=*Q*) (1878) 24 Aug., p. 672; *Morning Bulletin* Rockhampton (1878) 31 Aug., p. 2

46   W. Powell, *Wandering in a Wild Country*. 'Prospectus', NLA, mf 1688.

47   A.C.H. Gordon (1829–1912) private secretary to Gladstone in 1858. He entered the colonial service in 1861, was Lieutenant-Governor of New Brunswick (1861–66), Trinidad (1866–70), Mauritius (1871–74), Fiji (1875–80), New Zeal (1880–82), Ceylon (1888–90). Gordon was British High Commissioner for the Western Pacific from 1877 to 1883. He was created Baron Stanmore in 1893.

48   Gordon memorandum 28 Feb. 1881, Intercolonial Conference Dispatch, Melbourne/Sydney 1881.

49   *SMH* (1880) 29 Sep., pp. 4–5, (1880) 30 Nov., pp. 4–5.

50   Krauel to Bismarck 13 March 1883 (Smith, Wb 1883, no. 3, p. 26).

51   *SMH*, (1883) 7 Feb., p. 4, 10 Feb, p. 4 & 6 and 9 June., p. 12; (Smith, Wb 1883, no. 3, p. 25).

52   *Q* (1883), 17 Feb., p. 257; (Smith, Wb 1883, no. 7, pp. 26–7).

53   Labilliere to Colonial Office, 11 Dec. 1882 (BBP, C-3617, 1883, p. 118).

54   McIlwraith to Archer, 26 Feb. 1883 (V&P, [Qld] 1883, vol. 1, pp. 773–76). *SMH*, (1883) 6 Jun., p. 4

55   V&P (Qld), 1883, vol.1, p. 780.

56   Gordon, *Australian Frontier in New Guinea*, pp. 159–61; Legge, *Australian Colonial Policy*, p. 25.

57   Sahl to Bismarck 16 April 1883 (Smith, Wb 1883, no. 5, p. 26).

58   Letter from the Society to Derby, 14 May 1883, (BPP, C–3617, pp. 140–1). 'The Refusal to Annex New Guinea', *Q* (1883) 7 July, p. 17.

59   P. Knaplund, 'Sir Arthur Gordon on the New Guinea Question, 1883', *HSANZ*, 7 (1956) pp. 328–35.

60   BPP, 1884`, vol. Lv, p. 793.

61   V&P (Qld), 1883, vol. 1, pp. 781 & 786–7.

62   BPP series iii, vol. 281, p. 18; Gladstone to Derby 19 May 1883. Derby to Administrator of Queensland, 11 Jul. 1883 (BPP, 1883, C-3691, pp. 22–4; V&P (Vic), 1884, vol. Li, paper no. 25, pp. 78–9; 'Correspondence Respecting New Guinea', BPP, C-3839, 1884, pp. 34–5).

63   Service to McIlwraith, 31 July 1883, *SMH*, (1883), 6 Aug., p. 6. Jacobs, p. 114, n. 52 & 54.

64   Report of the Inter-Colonial Conference, Sydney, Nov.-Dec. 1883 (V&P (NSW) vol. 9, pp. 83–91).

65   BPP, C-3839 (1884), pp. 34–5.

66   Derby to Governors, 9 May 1884 (BPP, C-3839, 1884). Krauel to Bismarck 26 June 1884.

67   BPP, C-3863 (1884), pp. 9–11; C-4217 (1884), pp. 2–3 & 47–8 & C-4273, pp. 11–15.

68   Smith, Wb, 1884, .no. 19, p. 37; 'German Colonial Policy', *The Times* (1884), 25 June pp. 10–13. Mail-Steamer Subsidy Bill in Hagen, pp. 97–114

69   Hansemann & Bleichröder to Bismarck, 27 Jun. 1884, (Smith, Wb 1884, no. 19, p. 37; RKA 1001:2789, pp. 100–04); Kusserow to Bamberger, 28 June 1884, Kusserow to Bismarck, 30 July 1884; Sack, Eduard Hernsheim, p. 87.(Wehler, pp. 393–4. (RKA 1001:2789, pp. 201–07).

70   (RKA 1001:2789, pp. 201–07).

71   Bismarck to Hansemann, 20 Aug. 1884 (Smith, Wb 1884, no. 25, p. 42; RKA 1001:2790, pp. 95–8).

72   RKA 1001:2790, pp. 95–8); see Wehler, p. 394; Münch, p. 227.

73   Hatzfeldt to Münster, 2 Aug. 1884 (Smith, Wb 1884, no. 20, p. 38; RKA 1001:2790, pp. 10–13).

74   (RKA 1001:2790, pp. 10–13)

75   (BBP, C-4273, (1885) p. 4; Smith, Wb 1884, no. 21, pp. 41 & 47–54; (RKA 1001:2296, pp.10–3).

76   Granville to Ampthill in Berlin, 9 Aug. 1884 (FO 64/1144 in BPP, C-4273); Granville to Münster (RKA 1001:2791), Münster to Bismarck 9 Aug. 1884 (Smith, Wb 1884, no. 23, p. 41). Confirmation of discussion Granville and Münster, Scott (Chargé d'Affaires British Embassy, Berlin) to Hatzfeldt, 19 Sep. 1884 (BPP, C-4273, pp.10–13); see Jacobs, 'Bismarck and the Annexation of New Guinea', *HS.ANZ*, (1952) vol. 5, pp.16 & 24, n. 40; P.G. Sack, *Protectorates & Twists*, p. 36.

77   Bismarck to Krauel, 19 Aug. 1884 (Smith, Wb 1884, no. 24, p. 42).

78   Bismarck to Hansemann & Bleichröder, 20 Aug. 1884 (Smith, Wb 1884, no. 25, p. 42.

79   Granville & Scott to Hatzfeldt, 19 Sep. 1884 (Smith, Wb 1884, no. 28, p. 43; BPP, C-4273, p. 11).

80   Hatzfeldt to Chargé d'Affaires in London; Plessen to Granville, 27 Sep. 1884, Smith, Wb 1884, no. 30, p. 43; (BPP, C-4273 (1884), p. 12).

81   British Embassy in Berlin to German Foreign Office, 9 Oct. 1884 (BPP, C-4273, p. 13).

82   Appointment of Romilly, *SMH*, (1884) 15 Oct., p. 10, (BPP, C-4217 [1884], p. 36.]

83   Romilly Proclamation 23 Oct. 1884 (BPP, C-4217, pp. 32–45, 134 &148) *Norddeutsche Allgemeine Zeitung*, (1884) 14 Oct., *SMH*, (1884) 15 Oct., p. 10. *The Brisbane Courier* (=*BC*), (1884) 17 Dec., p. 5. German consulate at Sydney to Bismarck on 18 Nov. 1884 (Smith, Wb 1884, no. 35, p. 44).

84   *NKWL* (1885) Heft ii, pp. 5f. Heft iii, p. 5; *Q* (1884) 5 Jul., p. 1; *BC* (1884) 11 Sep., p. 3.

85   Malet to Colonial Office (BPP, C-4273, pp. 72 & 75; RKA 1001:2794, pp. 6–7). Bismarck to Münster to Granville 23 Dec. 1884 (Smith, Wb 1884, no. 37, p. 45).

86   (BPP, C-4273 (1884), pp. 140–4, 147 & 150).

87   Granville to Queen Victoria, 3 Jan. 1885, (PRO, London, 30/29/45; BPP, C-4273, p. 131).

88   Bismarck to Gladstone, 20 Jan. 1885 (BPP, C-4273, pp. 91 & 100-03).

89   Gladstone to Granville, 31` Jan. 1885, Granville Papers (PRO, London, 30/29/179).

90   Derby to Granville, 6 March 1885, Granville Papers (PRO, London, 30/29/120; BPP, C-4273, pp. 157–60 & 178). Hagen, pp. 460–8; Jacobs, 'Bismarck and the Annexation of New Guinea', p. 25.

91   Smith, Wb 1884, no. 29, p. 43, nos. 38–9, pp. 45–8, nos. 40–1, pp. 48–9, nos. 44–7, pp. 50–5. Granville to Münster, 16 March 1885 (PRO, London, 64/1149; BPP, C-4584 [1884], pp. 84 & 87).

92   *NKWL* (1886), Heft ii, pp. 49–54; BPP, C-4656 (1886).

93   BPP, C-4441 (1885) p. 1. 'Grenzverhandlungen mit England', (RKA 1001:2518, pp. 54–9 & 73ff).

94   Hansemann to Bismarck, H. Bismarck to Hansemann, 8, 19 Apr. 1886 (RKA 1001:2559, pp. 46ff).

95   Inter-Colonial Conference, Sydney, 1883 (V&P [NSW] 1883 vol. 9; CO 422-1, mf 2685 at 553). 'The Refusal to Annex New Guinea', TQ (1883) 7. July., p. 17

96   H. v. Poschinger, *Fürst Bismarck und die Parlamentarier*, p. 279.

97   E.T.S. Dugdale, ed., *German Diplomatic Documents*, 1871–1914, p. 191.

Disastrous Ventures

Proposed German New Guinea
Coat of Arms (1913)

Flag of the New Guinea Company (1885-1921)

German Foreign Office Emblem

Proposed German New Guinea Flagg (1913)

Proposed Insignia for German
New Guinea

Flag of the German Colonial Office used in New Guine
(1899–1914)

GERMAN COLONIAL INTENTIONS AND PRACTICES IN NORTH-EAST NEW GUINEA

Part II

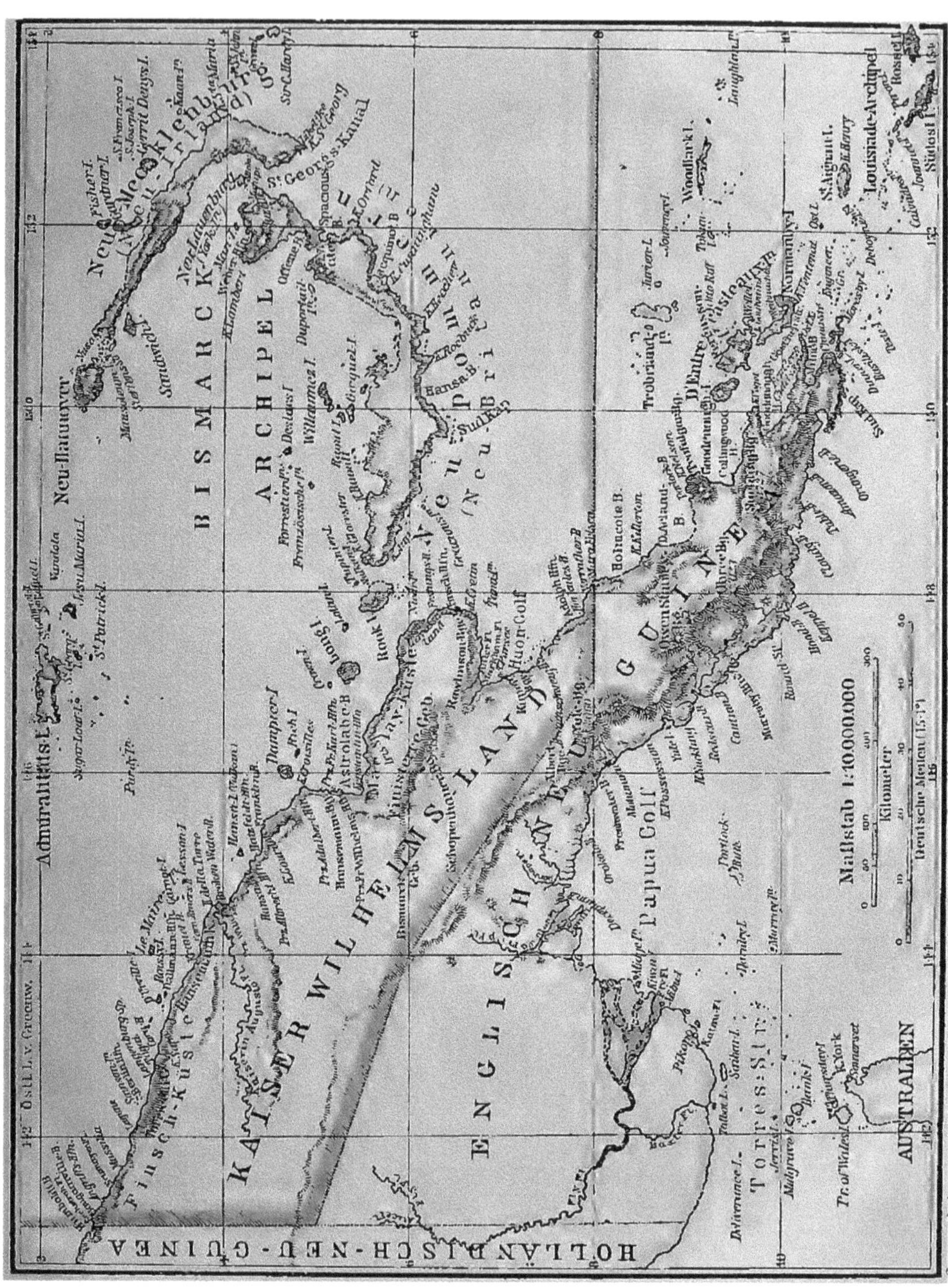

Map 3: **East New Guinea as seen by Dr Otto Finsch in 1885** *(Samoafahrten, 1888)*

A RICH MAN'S PROJECT: BERLIN BANKER ADOLPH VON HANSEMANN

4

Adolph von Hansemann, ca. 1898

Adolph von Hansemann was nearly 60 years old when he embarked on his New Guinea venture in 1884. He was determined to acquire as much land as possible in New Guinea prior to the *Reich* declaring sovereignty over northeast New Guinea and the New Britain Archipelago. By establishing a footprint in the country, his objective was to prevent another Samoa debacle in the *Reichstag* and to pre-empt any third party competing for ownership.

Before signing an Imperial Charter, Hansemann needed to be clear on what type of business the New Guinea venture was going to be. The onerous task of managing a colony—ordinarily carried out by the government—in parallel with a company's commercial activities required diligent planning. A business and operational plan, outlining funding requirements and cash-flow projections had to be prepared. Hansemann's preferred option of acquiring land for little or no cost and selling it to settlers at a profit was attractive but its feasibility had to be investigated. The establishment of a plantation industry, requiring large amounts of capital without generating early returns, needed to be carefully considered. The funding prospects for mining, timber and fishing ventures had to be assessed and given effect in a practical operational plan. The value of barter and projections for selling European goods locally had to be addressed. Procedures for hiring staff, requisitioning materials, provisions, fuel and equipment needed to be identified in the plan. If Hansemann was to see his dream of a South Sea colony realised these issues had to be resolved before NGC would seek authorisation to commence business in East New Guinea. The Berlin banker was intent on making the best of a 12 month window available for negotiating an Imperial Charter with the Auswärtige Amt (AA).[1]

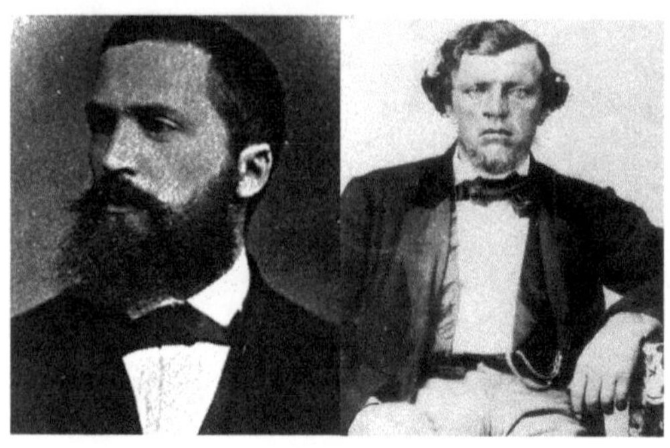

Otto Finsch and Eduard Dallmann, ca. 1885.

The Finsch and Dallmann expeditions
The ornithologist Dr. Otto Finsch and Captain Eduard Dallmann arrived on Mioko Island in the Duke of York Group on 26 September 1884. Hansemann hired the two veteran explorers to gather information on the geography and environment of northeast New Guinea. His directions included identification of natural harbours and the establishment of friendly relations with the indigenous population. It also included the acquisition of land for a future German colony.

From 7 October 1884 to 28 May 1885 Finsch and Dallmann made five voyages around northeast New Guinea and adjacent archipelagos on their exploration vessel, the *Samoa*.[2] They compared the coastline from East Cape to Humboldt Bay on the Dutch New Guinea (DNG) border with British Admiralty charts and had their findings published by Paul Langhans in the *Deutsche Kolonialatlas* (1897) and by Richard Kiepert in the geographical periodical *Globus*. The discoveries of bays, estuaries, rivers, coastlines and mountain ranges were entered into Finsch's journal in numerical order. 'Only after I was given permission by Berlin did I replace the numbers with names', Finsch explained in a 1902 article.[3] To establish safe shipping lanes and to identify harbours for future stations, Dallmann and his first mate Sechstroh carried out hydrographical surveys. Finsch also continued the extensive meteorological observations of his 1879 and 1882 voyages. Air and sea temperatures, cloud cover, rainfall, wind direction and strength were recorded daily at 07:00, 13:00 and 19:00 hours.[4]

The distinctive formation of the Oertzen Range became visible a long distance from shore. Because of its clear separation from other mountain peaks, it provided Finsch and Dallmann with a perfect beacon for their voyage.[5] Dallmann took the *Samoa,* towards this landmark on the first voyage to make landfall in Astrolabe Bay on 11 October 1884 signifying German political presence on mainland New Guinea for the first time. Subject to imperial approval northeast New Guinea was henceforth called Kaiser Wilhelms-Land (KWL).[6]

In KWL the explorers made contact with the local people and purchased roughly 100 ha near the village Bongu for RM150 in glass pearls, tobacco and hoop iron.[7] Finsch and Dallmann had landed near where the Russian naturalist and anthropologist, Nikolaj Nikolajewitsch Mikloucho-Maclay, explored the rai coastal region around Astrolabe Bay from September 1871 to December 1872, and Bilbil village from June 1876 to November 1877.[8] In the belief that the Russian explorer had returned to give the people iron tools to cut wood and build huts, the indigenous communities shouted 'Maclay' everywhere the party landed along this stretch of the Rai or Maclay Coast.

It was on 17 October 1884 at Bongu village that Finsch raised the German flag to mark the first German station on mainland New Guinea. Respecting the earlier

The SS *Samoa,* ca. 1884 (O. Finsch, *Samoafahrten*, 1888)

Russian presence, he proposed that the place be named Konstantinhafen.

A few miles due north of Astrolabe Bay, on 19 October, Dallmann discovered a second harbour in the protected waters of the Schering Peninsula. Although they recognised the location as probably the best and safest harbour on the entire north coast, they decided not to establish a sation immediately because of thick mangrove everywhere. However, when Captain Schering of the light cruiser SMS *Elisabeth* arrived to raise the *Reichsflagge* a month later, the natural advantage of the harbour outweighed the coastal swamp and the future location for Friedrich Wilhelmshafen was agreed.

On the second voyage Dallmann took the *Samoa* due south to Mitre Rock. Then, turning north on 18 November, he sailed into Morobe Bay on the Huon Gulf where they identified Adolph-Hafen in Hansemann's honour. 'This area was safe with a good seabed for anchoring and a brook providing drinking water'. Finsch assessed the swampy foreshore and the heavily timbered mountains as being of low commercial value and, with no prospect of engaging labour as he only 'saw seven naked natives'.[9]

Continuing in a north-westerly direction, Finsch reported on 23 November 1885: 'our endeavour to find safe anchorage before the warships arrived was rewarded with the investigation of a creek north-west of Cape Cretin. A basin provided all-weather sanctuary for smaller vessels, while the outer harbour was suitable for large ships in most weather conditions. Finsch was so impressed with this natural harbour and the lushness of the shoreline that he chose the name Deutschland-Hafen for what he believed was worthy of becoming the capital of GNG. In his report to Hansemann he praised 'this wonderful, fertile district, reminding us of a European estate, stretching from Cape Cretin to Fortification Point. [It] is comparable to that in Blanche Bay but with the added advantage that this area is more densely populated'. Finsch

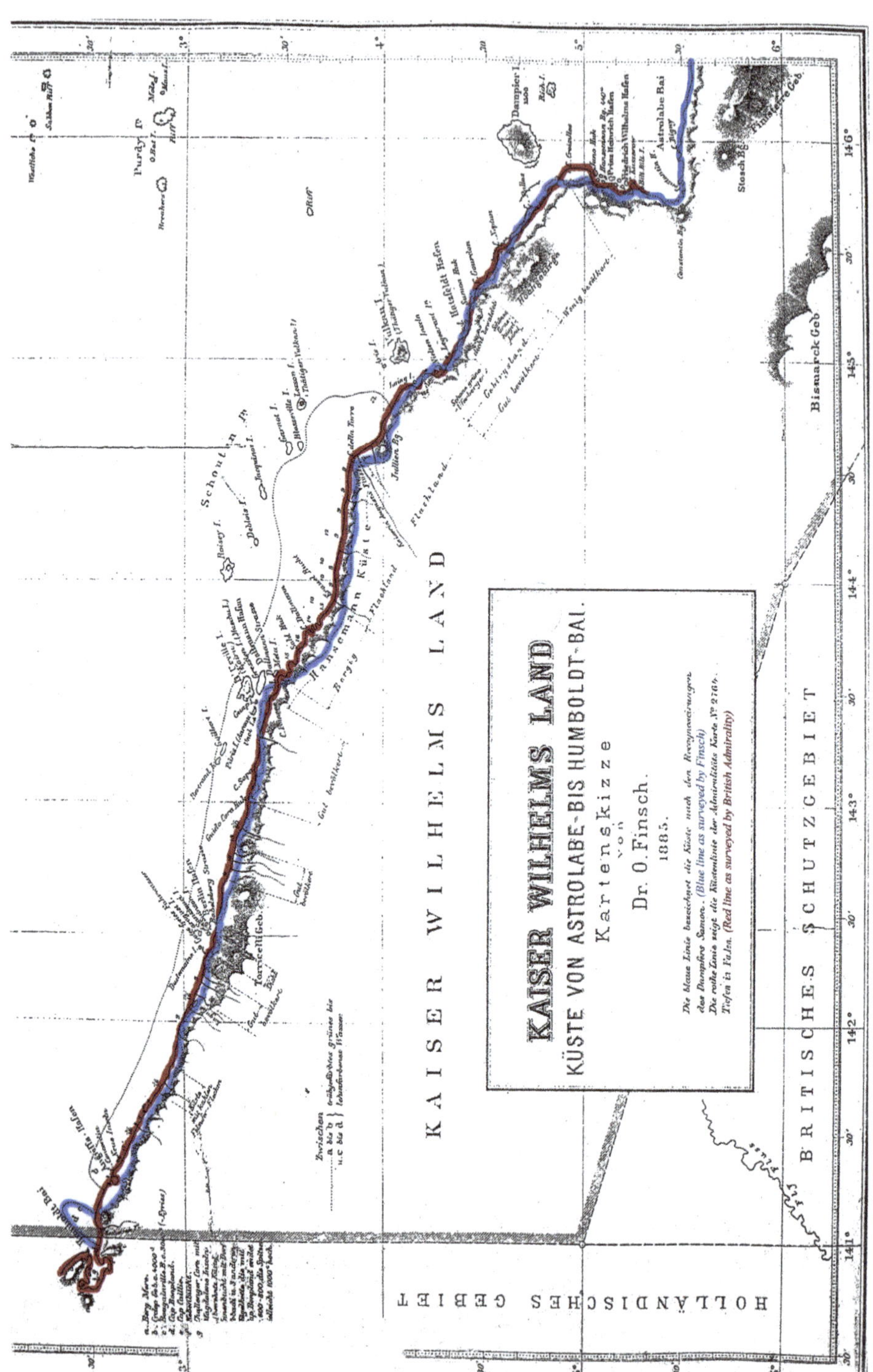

Map 4: **Survey by Otto Finsch & E. Dallmann: North-East Coast of GNG from Astrolabe Bay to Humboldt Bay** (*NKWL*, 1885)

believed that small villages nestle around the harbour and in the wooded hills. The *Reichsmarine* agreed with Finsch and honoured the inveterate explorer by renaming the place Finschhafen at its flag-raising ceremony on 27 November 1884.

The fourth voyage lasted from 23 March to 18 April 1885. It was largely a repeat of the third expedition. When Hansemann learnt that Britain had extended its protectorate of New Guinea no further than East Cape, exclusive of the Louisiade Archipelago and the islands Woodlark, Trobriand and D'Entrecasteaux, he became interested in this 'particularly fertile' region. Even before Hansemann's direction of 11 November 1884 to 'gain foothold on D'Entrecasteaux and all land north of East Cape' reached the explorers, Dallmann had set the *Samoa* on course to East Cape.[10] On the southern shore of Goodenough Bay, 20 miles west of East Cape, he found good anchorage in Bentley Bay. Here Finsch took the opportunity to buy land from the Hihiaura people to establish NGC's most eastern Station Blumenthal. The New Guinea-experienced Carl Hunstein—hired in Cooktown by Finsch—and Danish seaman Peter Hansen stayed behind to build houses and make their presence felt. But Hansemann's intention to extend GNG to East Cape, the most south-eastern tip of mainland New Guinea, was short-lived. The British–German Boundary accord of 16 March 1885 determined Bentley Bay British territory. Subsequently, Hunstein and Hansen transferred to Killerton Island on the northern side of Milne Bay where missionaries provided a 'safe haven'. En route to GNG on her maiden voyage from Germany, NGC's new steamer, the *Papua,* stopped in Killerton Island to take the two 'colonizers' to Finschhafen where they arrived safely on 1 November 1885.[11]

By the end of the fifth and final voyage on 28 May 1885 the *Samoa* had voyaged more than 5,000 nautical miles. While Finsch and Dallmann were well satisfied with their geographical study, their land acquisitions were less successful. Only small parcels had been acquired in Astrolabe Bay and near East Cape, with the latter returned to Britain. Imperial Commissioner von Oertzen made the only other recorded agreement for land purchases at the time by entering into a deed of occupation with the Kranket, Tebog and Belialo tribes during his visit to Schering Cape on 15 November 1884. Finsch believed he had acquired northeast New Guinea in one fell swoop. His negotiations with tribal elders—from Humboldt Bay to the Huon Gulf—led to his claim that all land along this coastal strip now belonged to NGC.[12]

Commissioner Oertzen was not prepared to recognise Finsch's claims, though. He advised Bismarck on 15 December 1884 that the land obtained by Dr Finsch and Captain Dallmann may not have been procured from the rightful owners and the action should therefore be regarded as a political demonstration rather than the legal transfer of land ownership. It took fourteen years until Imperial Judge Hahl examined the legality of the claims in 1898. Without having the land in question surveyed, he determined an arbitrary area of 5,000 ha for each NGC station on mainland New Guinea other than Konstantinhafen. But NGC never applied for registration of the land and subsequently withdrew the claims. Hahl also recognised claims of approximately 40,000 ha by DHPG on behalf of NGC on New Hanover, 7,000 ha on New Ireland and the Duke of York and 4,000 ha at Blanche Bay as legally binding.[13]

Disastrous Ventures

So, while Finsch may have thought he had acquired land similar in size to Prussia, the government rejected most of his claims. NGC was unable to demonstrate that the land was obtained in a fair manner at a time when northeast New Guinea was not even a German Protectorate. Arguably 35,100 ha were 'purchased' by Finsch on the mainland. But even this so-called entitlement was withdrawn by Hansemann in his 1898 settlement with the government on administrative responsibility for GNG.[14]

Instructions to the Administrator

Hansemann saw to it that, in parallel with the Finsch mission, management procedures and instructions for future NGC employees were drafted and promulgated. On 18 August 1885 he released a manual 'Instruction to the Administrator'. Two months later 'Instructions to Scientific Expeditions' and the lesser 'Policy for the Establishment of Christian Missions' was issued.[15] The two main documents, comprising 51 lengthy paragraphs, provided insight into Hansemann's vision for German New Guinea. A trained banker, he understood and believed in the necessity for management transparency. The personnel to be employed in Hansemann's colony required skills in the disciplines of administration, medicine, geology, botany, agriculture, forestry, engineering, mining, shipping and carpentry. He was intent on employing young men with experience who were decisive yet followed instructions obediently. Hansemann wanted to reconcile these antithetical characteristics by devising a management plan that gave employees maximum ownership of their actions without him losing control. 'As long as circumstances permit', the instructions read, 'it is intended that the Board shall issue only general guidance, with managerial responsibilities to be left to the person held accountable for the running of the business'. But, in the same paragraph, the company's representative in New Guinea (the Administrator), was advised that 'departure from the laid down instructions is only permitted in urgent situations and a request stating the reasons, shall be submitted to the Board for retrospective approval'. Whereas the instructions appeared logical, it was a very prescriptive manual for the Administrator and Station Managers.

In addressing the executive powers of NGC Hansemann articulated his understanding of the local sovereign rights transferred to NGC by the AA. Other than the judiciary and foreign affairs, which remained expressly the responsibility of the government, he emphasized that all other powers, within the context of local sovereignty, were powers to be exercised by NGC.

By no means did Hansemann regard the exclusive acquisition of land as the only privilege of NGC. The exclusive exploitation of natural resources and the concession on tradable goods (such as bird plumes, pearls, trochus and guano) ranked of equal importance in his business model. Further, he regarded the implementation and collection of business and poll taxes, licence, customs and harbour fees and legal fines necessary to pay for the cost of administration. In the last paragraph of the manual to the Administrator, Hansemann mandated that 'artefacts and other objects of ethnological or scientific value, whether attained by barter with the natives or in any other manner, were acquired on behalf of the company'. The goods 'must be handed over unless the company renounces its right', he insisted.[16]

While drawing up the instructions, Hansemann kept an eye on the legislators. The drafting of the 'Protectorate Act' in the Foreign Office included the important section of land ownership before November 1884.[17]

But Hansemann had no intention of waiting for the outcome. Well before the Act was proclaimed he informed Finsch and Dallmann that no other foreign power, person or company had any rights to land in Kaiser Wilhelms Land (KWL).[18]

In the Bismarck Archipelago, Hansemann readily acknowledged the 820 ha claimed by DHPG on the Duke of York islands. He was a shareholder in the company and had commissioned it to procure land on behalf of his 'Consortium'. In contrast, the relationship between Hansemann and the South Sea veteran, Eduard Hernsheim, was less than cordial. Claims to 1,640 ha on the Gazelle Peninsula and in the Duke of York islands and 780 ha in the Hermit Group, eight square miles on New Ireland and smaller acreage acquired by Hernsheim for his trading stations, did not please Hansemann. Equally, Hernsheim was not enthused by Hansemann's foray into New Guinea. He regarded the Berlin banker's approach to colonising GNG 'based on Utopian plans with the same aims as those of the Marquis de Rays' colony'.[19]

The 52,000 ha claimed by E.E. Forsayth on the Gazelle Peninsula, New Ireland and Admiralty Islands, and 100,000 ha in the Solomons were registered in Australia. However, Hansemann did not recognise British jurisdiction over past land claims in GNG and referred them to *Wilhelmstrasse* for assessment.[20] Other claimants included R & H, Richard Parkinson, Auguste Dupré, Friedrich Schulle and John MacDonald. Jean Maximillian Mouton and his son Octave, survivors of the infamous Marquis de Rays expedition, claimed ownership of 2,050 ha around the Vunmami district on the north coast of the peninsula.[21] In total, Hansemann estimated that the eight claimants would not have acquired more than 30,000 ha. The Rev. G. Brown established the first mission of the Australian Wesleyan Methodist Missionary Society in Hunter Harbour in the Duke of York Group on 15 Aug. 1875. According to Hansemann only the Wesley Mission with claims of about 400 ha was present in New Guinea and adjacent islands in 1884.

By 1886 various parties had claimed an estimated 288,400 ha, including 76,000 ha by NGC. Where claims were deemed spurious NGC lodged its own entitlement with the government. Hansemann wanted to discourage unwanted settlers and directed that 'no settlements and no land acquisition must occur in the Protectorate without [the board's] prior approval'. The registration of title in the 'ground book' (Grundbuch) was a pedestrian process, and in 1889 NGC advised shareholders:

> The settlement of land claims were progressing, albeit slowly. Three hundred and twenty-seven titles had been entered in the Register compiled by the former Imperial Commissioner von Oertzen. A further 167 notification of claims had been received within the statutory time limit of 1 March 1888. Only 23 claims had been accepted as valid by von Oertzen thus far.[22]

Establishing the main Stations

The topography of Kaiser Wilhelms Land and the many islands in the archipelago as much as the cooperation of the local people determined the speed of colonisation. It was a haphazard start for NGC. A military presence was not planned. And like any other business, the core of colonisation was financial resources. Hansemann decided therefore to establish stations on the coast gradually, in accordance with available funds, and subject to locating suitable sites.

While prescriptive, Hansemann's instruction manual served as a guide. The establishment of a station was a matter of judgement, requiring a safe anchorage, drinking water, clean air, fertile soil and friendly natives.

Initially three stations were considered for KWL with Finschhafen intended as the capital of GNG. The second station was to be established between Friedrich Wilhelmshafen and Heinrichs-Hafen. While Hansemann left the decision on the location of the third station to his managers, he visualised the station to be further westward at approximately the midpoint of the coast of KWL.

To attain a European standard of comfort, Hansemann (wrongly) considered that 'Swedish' houses—prefabricated in Germany and assembled on site—would provide suitable accommodation for staff. Workers' housing, storerooms and sheds for domestic animals were built on stilts in accordance with local custom, with timber frames and eaves held together by rattan and the roof covered with ataps. Finschhafen was nominated as the administration centre. Here the building of a labour camp would centralise the distribution of indentured workmen. The distribution of goods to all parts of the Protectorate would be serviced via a central warehouse. Hansemann's plan also included a church and a school for the local children who were 'to be taught scripture in the German language by the missionaries'.[23]

Nearly 12 months before the company was assured of its legal rights, Hansemann engaged the retired Army Officers, Richard Mentzel and Rudolph von Oppen, the Borneo-experienced Fritz Grabowsky, and Ernst Schollenbruch to consolidate Finsch's work in setting up NGC's first settlements. The expedition left Germany for the Queensland port of Cooktown by commercial steamer on 29 June 1885. Provisions, Swedish-type houses and other construction materials were taken to Finschhafen by the brig *J.H. Lübcken*. Before travelling on to GNG, Grabowsky stayed over in Batavia to enquire about Dutch plantation methods, and how to model GNG on the Java and Sumatra sugar, rice, tobacco, coffee and tea plantations.[24]

Grabowsky investigated the means of clearing the jungle in preparation for plantations, and the plants and livestock that would thrive in KWL before embarking on his new assignment. Because the availability of suitable local workers was unknown, he intended to recruit Malays (Javanese and Chinese) as the core of his workforce. Captain Pfeiffer picked up Grabowsky, his colleagues Oppen and Schollenbruch, 37 Malays, three horses and provisions in Surabaya in early October 1885 on NGC's most recent acquisition, the steamer *Papua*. The party joined Mentzel in Cooktown: he had arrived there from Sydney on the SS *Samoa* under Captain Dallmann. The course of the two steamers was set for Finschhafen on 28 October where they cast anchor in the first week of November 1885.

The day following his arrival, Mentzel went into action. He determined that the small island at the north end of the harbour was best suited to establish a town. Aptly named Madang Island (Timber Island) by the local people because of the

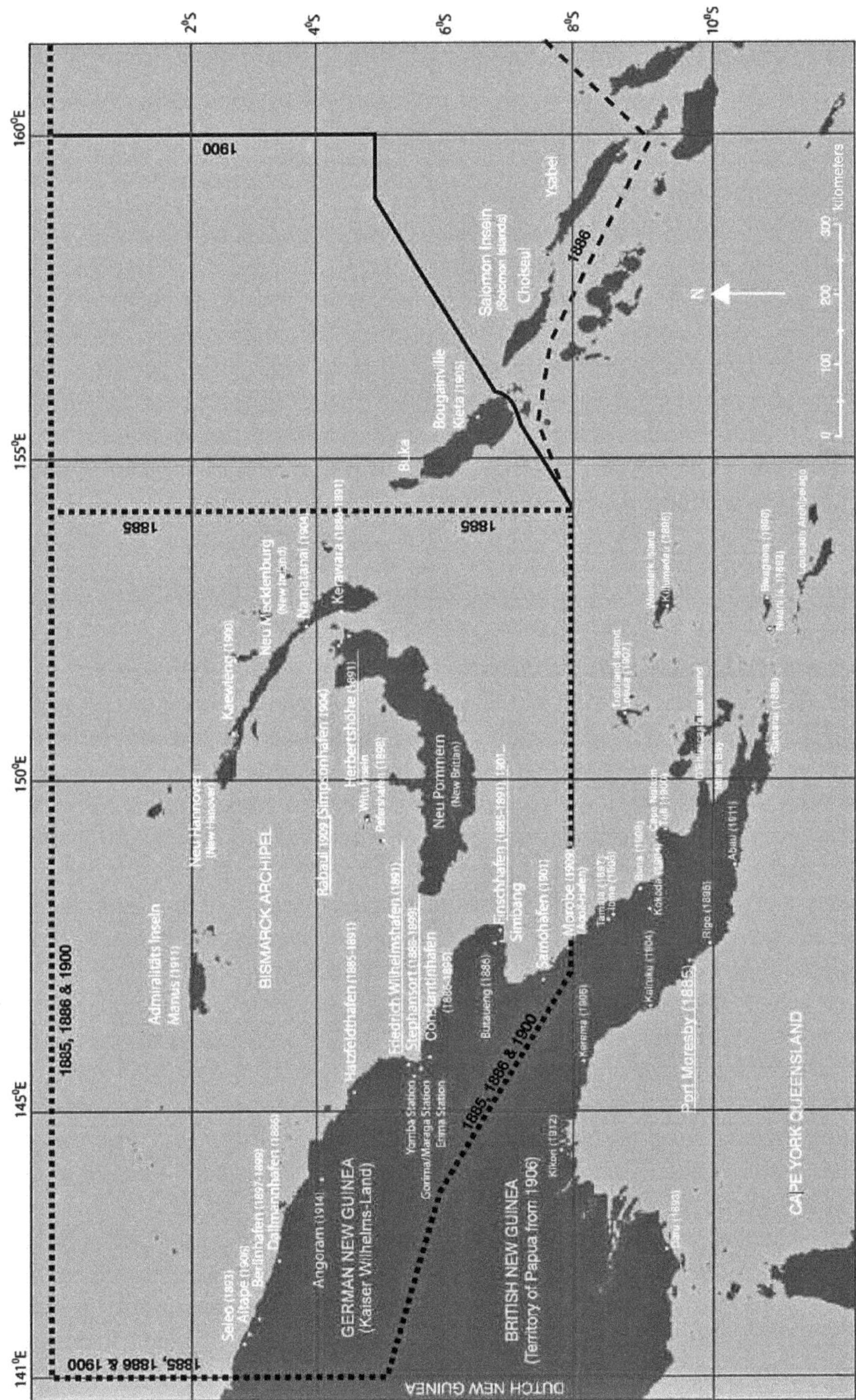

Map 5: **North-East New Guinea boundaries and government stations** (HJ Ohff)

densely timbered land, Mentzel wrote: 'already in the afternoon, immediately after our arrival in Finschhafen we entered into an agreement with the natives Jeffari and Aru and bought the island, including all trees and plants, from them'.[25] Compliant with company procedure Mentzel assured Hansemann that 'the forms provided for a contract of sale with natives were used', [with] a certified copy of the sales contracts for the land kept safely in a fire-proof room'.[26]

Mentzel justified the purchase of the island on the grounds that the soil was 'calcium rich, permeable and dry', and that the timber provided excellent feedstock for the company's steamers. He also claimed that Madang was safe from 'any attack [and] can be easily defended due to an uninterrupted view in all directions'. A sandbank connected the island with the mainland at low tide, 'allowing easy construction of a dam to connect the island with the mainland'. Another important factor for Mentzel's choice was 'the prevailing breeze from the south, southeast and southwest [which] made the tropical climate less debilitating [with the] ambient temperature three to four degrees Centigrade lower than on the mainland'.[27]

But Finschhafen was established too hastily, and the preassembled Swedish houses proved unsuitable for tropical conditions. The imminent arrival of the Administrator, Vice-Admiral (ret.) Baron Georg von Schleinitz with his family and staff, demanded a timetable that took away any opportunity for reassessing the approach for building Finschhafen.[28] Mentzel cleared an area of jungle and, within a few days, he started erecting the first houses. To secure good quality drinking water the retired army officer designed the causeway from the mainland to the island to also channel pristine creek water along this access road. It took less than 3 weeks to see the site and the first houses completed. Although a Herculean achievement, it took too long for Mentzel who described logging, digging post-holes into stony dirt and fastening iron bark to building frames as arduous tasks. Also completed within weeks was the out-station Butaueng, a few kilometres south of Finschhafen at the mouth of the Bubui River on Langemak Bay. From here the planting of maize, sweet potatoes, sorghum, tropical fruits and coffee was to ensure fresh supplies for Finschhafen.[29]

During the following 3 years a steam-powered sawmill delivered building timber for the construction requirements at Finschhafen and other NGC locations in KWL. Philip Schmidt had ariived on the maiden voyage of the *Ysabel* on 14 January 1887 to oversee construction of a pier, sheds, and moorings for naval and large merchant ships. A European hospital was built as were sickbays for the local workers. The Administrator's residence and various other buildings, the causeway connecting Madang Island and the mainland, were acompleted by early 1887.[30]

While Mentzel set up Finschhafen, Dallmann, Fritz Grabowsky and a Scottish carpenter continued the voyage to Dallmannhafen (Wewak) some 380 nautical miles northwest from Finschhafen. Contrary to Hansemann's instructions, they considered this location too far north for the second station. Instead they travelled 120 nautical miles down the coast towards Finschhafen to cast anchor on 19 December 1885 at a place which became Hatzfeldthafen. Here, a Malay overseer, nine Malays and five Malay women (with children), all hired for NGC's second station, unloaded the building materials stowed in the steamer.

Establishing this station proved a challenge for the experienced Grabowsky. After the departure of the *Samoa*, he and his carpenter were the only Europeans in an unfriendly region. The support hoped for from the Dugumor and Tombenam people was not forthcoming. The villagers were aggressive, reluctant to work and only 'interested in trading for hoop-iron', according to Grabowsky. Considering the circumstances the two pioneers had to weigh up the risks of building the Station on the fertile soil of the mainland or on nearby Tschirimotsch (Mahde Island). For better security they chose the latter.[31]

With no time to waste Grabowsky and his men erected the first houses on the island. By the time von Oppen, Hunstein, and Heidemann arrived much of the preliminary work was done. Within a few months a fruit and vegetable garden, living quarters, including a kitchen and stores, had been completed for permanent occupancy.[32]

Seemingly improving relations with the local people encouraged Grabowsky to start with plantation work on the mainland in the latter part of 1886. Returning to Java to recruit 50 coolies who were regarded as indispensable for tobacco farming, the rich soil around Hatzfeldthafen produced plantation tobacco for the first time in GNG in 1887. While ongoing tribal unrest lead to Grabowsky's resignation in late 1887, a small quantity of tobacco was harvested by Grabowsky's successors, the former German East African farmer Adolf Hermes and Philip Schmidt in May 1888.[33]

Over the following 3 years a stream of managers (E. Schollenbruch, W. v. Puttkamer, J. Schoevers) developed Hatzfeldthafen into a commercial tobacco-growing Station.[34] A five-meter-wide bridge across the Daigon River and a 7 km road accessed new fertile land. A shortage of quality drinking water was overcome by digging wells; a network of tracks, two meters wide, were built to better manage the fields; five drying and fermentation sheds were completed; and a hospital built.[35] All this came to a sudden end on 26 and 27 May 1891 when tribesmen slew the missionaries Friedrich Wilhelm Scheidt and Friedrich Bösch, NGC employee Bodo von Moisy, and 14 labourers in nearby Franklin Bay. A large punitive expedition was mounted, led by Acting Administrator and Imperial Commissioner, Fritz Rose, comprising 14 NGC employees and some 130 plantation workers. The party killed 27 local people and destroyed several villages, gardens and coconut palms. The local offenders most likely escaped into the deep jungle. Powerless to control the situation Rose recommended to Hansemann that the Station be closed.[36] When Hatzfeldthafen overseer Ludwig Müller and five local workers disappeared six weeks later, on 14 August 1891, and the subsequent search party was attacked, Hansemann acted. Hatzfeldthafen Station was shut down the following month, with buildings, stores and livestock shipped to Friedrich Wilhelmshafen.[37]

Hatzfeldthafen was the only plantation in KWL that had to be evacuated because of conflict;[38] it was, however, not the only establishment vacated by NGC. A particularly virulent influenza epidemic in Finschhafen in conjunction with malaria took the lives of the acting Administrator, Hans Arnold, on 31 January 1890, his replacement, Eduard Wißmann, on 28 February 1891, and the company doctor, Carl Weinland, on

12 March. These casualties and those of 10 other NGC staff (C. Apell, H. Christer, A. Hildebrandt, F. Jäger, C. Ludwig, L. Ludwig, H. Langmaak, Hr. Lutz, C. May, and C. Ritzer) spelled the end of Finschhafen. Rose had suggested in 1889 that the 'capital of GNG' be relocated to Astrolabe Bay, with Finschhafen and Butaueng to be retained as plantations. Now, save for three officers and some workers left behind for dismantling work, Rose ordered the immediate evacuation to makeshift facilities in Stephansort, with buildings and livestock moved to Friedrich Wilhelmshafen where NGC's new central Station opened in September 1892.[39]

The other Station established before NGC became legally incorporated was Konstantinhafen. The discovery by Friedrich Drees and Otto Elle of good quality water and an expanse of fertile land 64 km south of Friedrich Wilhelmshafen made setting up the third Station an easy decision. During Drees' time in Finschhafen, where he was responsible for the construction of the causeway to the mainland, Elle and Rücker, plus seamen Theel and Scholz from the barque *Norma,* and eight Malays commenced the establishment on 30 May 1886 of Konstantinhafen. The importance of this Station was seen in its potential for cotton and tobacco plantations on the Astrolabe and Jomba Plains. But, as had to be expected by now, the setting up of a new Station in GNG never proceeded as planned. Manager Elle's attempt to purchase land from the Gorendu and Bongu people was answered with considerable resistance by them; in fact, the villagers tried to take back what they had sold NGC months earlier. In the absence of local cooperation, and to get work underway, Elle sent for Yabim people from Finschhafen. But again malaria and dysentery got the better of the Malays and Europeans, and even the hardened Yabim people were not spared from these debilitating diseases, and it took some 3 months before real work could be started. For the first year, staff and workers alike made do with what little was available. Maize, vegetables and tropical fruits grew inside the fenced-off Station and provided staples for all. Tobacco seeds, growing into 2-m high flowering shrubs inside 2 months, provided the seeds for future tobacco fields.[40]

Like most of his staff, Elle was only able to perform his job for a few short months. When he went on sick leave to Australia, the scientific explorer Dr Carl Schneider, who had arrived in Konstantinhafen on 16 August 1886, took on the role of manager. With Elle too sick to return, Hunstein relieved Schneider later that year, with Johann Kubary joining him 9 months later in July 1887. The two experienced New Guinea hands, Hunstein and Kubary, finally made progress. With the additional crew of 12 Mioko people, station buildings, including the now mandatory prison, were quickly completed. By 1888 Kubary had established experimental tobacco and cotton fields with coconuts planted intermittently.[41]

Johann Kubary's influence on the development of the NGC Protectorate and of Konstantinhafen in particular was profound. His work in Micronesia between 1871 and 1885 for Godeffroys, Eduard Hernsheim, O'Keefe, and the East Asian Squadron of the *Reichsmarine*, qualified the Polish-born Kubary more than any other manager engaged by NGC during the early stage of colonial development. Making good Finsch's failed attempt to acquire plantation land on Astrolabe Bay,

Kubary acquired valuable tracts along the central coastline of KWL His success in securing some 13 km^2 around Konstantinhafen for a few pieces of hoop iron and 'Kubary-Wasser'—a mix of rum and cognac—delighted Hansemann. Clearly elated with Kubary's approach to land acquisition he instructed the acquisition of a land corridor between Konstantinhafen and Friedrich Wilhelmshafen.[42] Kubary did obtain 32,780 ha along the coastline but he did not support Hansemann's eagerness to buy land indiscriminately. On 7 October 1889 he informed NGC's chairman that 'further acquisitions of useful land, in a way consistent with the friendly understanding with the natives [is] not possible'. Kubary was only too aware that Papuans had no understanding of what a sales contract meant, and he first sought their understanding and goodwill before acquiring the land. Judge Phillips shared this view. He found 45 years later: 'the Bilibili and the Jabob (people), both groups of potters living on their small offshore islands, did not own any of the land they sold and that they probably did not understand that they were supposed to have sold land at all'.[43]

Alcoholism and subsequent self-aggrandisement, leading to statements like: 'I am the Lord of Astrolabe Bay' and the destruction of a native village led to the dismissal of Kubary in 1894. Setting aside his often dubious land purchases, Kubary's actions formed the foundation of the plantation industry that NGC started on the Jomba Plains in 1890. In order not to forego the purchases, Hansemann pressed his administration in Finschhafen to have all documentation relating to the Kubary purchases completed on the proper company forms so that the land titles could be duly entered into the 'ground book'.[44] Although it took six years of negotiations with the government before Acting Administrator, H. Rüdiger, certified NGC as the landowner in March 1896, it did not prevent Hansemann from immediately starting a most ambitious, ultimately unsuccessful, tobacco plantation industry on Astrolabe Bay.

Roads, land and settlers

Hansemann made road building a priority. His bank was a major investor in the construction of a railroads that had facilitated the industrialisation of Germany. And he planned on developing roads to open up the interior of GNG by connecting future stations and mine sites.[45] In GNG, however, topographical surveys put a halt to this idea. The 800 km coastline was demanding road-building terrain. The interior was even more difficult. The plans were put on hold and development of GNG was restricted to the coast where fertile land was accessible by sea and rivers.

It is not clear whether Hansemann intended to expand into coconut plantations from the start. On the one hand he instructed staff to study the coconut planter's manual in depth; on the other he declared that 'it was not the intention of the company to undertake large-scale farming on its own account but rather leave it to the livestock companies … after they have purchased the land [from NGC]. To acquire land and sell it to corporations or settlers was considered easier to promote to his fellow investors in any event. When speaking of the viability of his New Guinea enterprise, Hansemann convinced Albert von Oppenheim, for instance, that 'the extensive coastland in KWL could be sold for sheep and cattle grazing as soon as the company had built stations and established shipping connections with Australia'. In the eyes of many—not least NGC's staff—this left the impression that Hansemann was solely interested in acquiring part of the 'largest' island on earth as a massive land speculation. While such a proposition would have been attractive to an investment banker, the reality proved to be quite different. [46]

To become successful commercially NGC needed to create an economy of scale. This, in Hansemann's view, was only possible through large-scale European migration. Of the estimated 76,000 Germans living in Australia, those living in Queensland were regarded as the best-suited migrants for GNG. Used to the tropics and equipped with a pioneering spirit, German-Australians, he believed, would contribute strongly.[47] It was not until 1888, however, that an attempt was made to attract this important resource to the Protectorate. Following an announcement in the February issue of the company's publication, *NKWL*, the sale of land in GNG was advertised in the *Nord-Australische-Zeitung*.[48] Urban blocks and rural land were offered for outright purchase or on 5-year leases with an option to buy at a pre-determined price. Leaseholdings were also available. The advertisements showed maps of the allotments in Finschhafen, Konstantinhafen and Hatzfeldthafen where broad-acre plantation and grazing land was offered. The lure for German-Australians was the promise that 'the size of the individual blocks of land in all the districts could be subdivided in a manner so that settlers with lesser means could acquire property'. NGC remained vague on pricing, though. The scale of RM20–100 for a 0.10–0.25 ha town allotment was also applicable to 1 ha of agricultural land. Interested buyers learnt that the general conditions of sale or lease were modelled on those of the British North Borneo Company.[49] To induce wavering settlers to reach a decision, NGC advertised entitlements to temporary accommodation and provisions in Finschhafen at low cost.

NGC's meager assistance to German-Australians with travelling and establishment costs proved a miscalculation. Land in GNG was too expensive compared to leasehold land in Australia, and the rush to GNG by German-Australians did not materialise. The Colonial Society in Germany cited a report that appeared in Australian newspapers: 'Germans living in Australia would not be attracted to German New Guinea because of the bureaucratic administration and the high price of land.[50] With massive tracts of cheap leasehold land available in Queensland, this was an accurate assessment. Already in February 1887, when a German and an Englishmen arrived on their cutter in GNG with the intention of setting up a small plantation and panning for gold, the NGC administration demonstrated their lack of interest by denying their request. Otto Schellong was disgusted with this bureaucratic bungle: 'they should have been given land, gratis … wherever and for whatever purpose', NGC's first medical doctor exclaimed, 'the company would reap the benefit' from every hand lent to establish the place, 'since each tree felled will be additional profit' for NGC.[51]

From the beginning, the administration in Finschhafen did not share Hansemann's optimism as to early land sales. Schleinitz cautioned prospective buyers to advise that

[At] present it is still not possible to open up the whole *Schutzgebiet* for the purpose of development. Land can be leased in designated areas; however, it will only be made available to settlers with sufficient capital. No land will be sold for the time being. The tenure of lease will befor five years with the possibility of taking out an option for purchase. Settlers have to cater for all of their needs, including workers as these are not available in KWL. The NGC is only equipped to supply small rations of food as it imports supplies for its own needs and does not offer it for sale to the public. No employment is available to unskilled workers or tradesmen.[52]

However, when Bismarck granted Post Office Inspector-General Reinhold Kraetke leave of absence to relieve Schleinitz in March 1888, a new importance was attached to the opportunities in GNG. Within 6 months of his arrival, Kraetke invited interested persons to apply for the purchase of land in KWL:

The administrative and economic condition in the colony of the Neu Guinea Compagnie has now sufficiently progressed to open up the territory to settlers. The construction of all-weather roads and bridges has progressed. The soil has been thoroughly tested by competent institutions and verified in garden plantations, and found to be extremely fertile and particularly suited for vegetables and tropical plants.[53]

The public learnt that European foodstuffs were exempt from tariffs and that company steamers provided regular connection with Australia, while Kraetke appealed to families with children by advising them of the construction of a school in Finschhafen. When this campaign proved equally unsuccessful Hansemann's office manager in Berlin, Hans Arnold, replaced Kraetke on 1 November 1888. Arnold was known in Berlin for his optimistic sales pitch to staff and interested parties who enquired about settling in the Protectorate. Like some of his predecessors, he had little opportunity to make a difference. He died of malaria within 3 months of arriving in Finschhafen.

The discontinuation by NGC of the shipping service between Finschhafen and Cooktown in 1889 closed the option for prospective German-Australian settlers. GNG was no longer in easy reach of European workers and the company stopped pursuing settlers from Australia.[54] As was the case with the promotion in Australia, very few Germans applied for land. With no financial assistance and the costs of travelling, land and establishment too high, Germans might dream about a place in the sun, but GNG was an unknown and the risks too high.

Race relations

The importance of an indigenous labour force in the context of economic development was as big an issue as European migration. Hansemann recognised that friendly relations with the indigenous people were a priority. He addressed the matter by including a code of conduct in his 'Instruction Manual for Employees'. The first requirement was not to get embroiled in any violence. Only in circumstances of self-defence or 'where it was unavoidable that a lesson be taught' were NGC employees permitted to use force against the local people. The imperial regulation that prevented the indigenous population from acquiring guns and spirits was to be strictly adhered to by the company staff. The objective, Hansemann stated, was to win them over peacefully. He understood the competing factors of subjugation and a cooperative workforce. By reminding his employees 'not to steal from them or worse still, to commit cannibalisation', he seemed concerned that his employees may adopt some of the local habits.[55]

Apart from some policing to maintain law and order NGC did not intend to establish an armed force: the cost was prohibitive and in any event, under the Imperial Charter the *Reich* guaranteed the safety of its citizens in GNG. Yet Hansemann was concerned by the ongoing belligerence of the tribal warriors and the passive resistance of many villagers. He saw value for the social associations—commune and tribes—remaining in their present form and that the leaders of the tribes were brought onside. All this, he demanded, required staff to act with patience, level headedness and friendliness.

Hansemann prefaced the section on land acquisitions: 'Native ownership of land must be respected universally'. He drew on Finsch's advice that the natives had little understanding of property ownership and that they lay no claim to land they could not cultivate or was not within their settlement. In this regard he directed that any land not claimed by the natives by way of physical occupation is to be taken into possession.

Until the issue of a NGC currency, all trade with the indigenous people was conducted by bartering. Barter trade was a key to the pacification process. Interaction would provide the local people with the opportunity to become acquainted with the company's peaceful intentions. Whereas peaceful contacts were regarded first and foremost the responsibility of the Christian missions, Hansemann insisted on his own brand of pacification. By marrying his 'altruism' with commercialism, he declared that the locals should develop a gradual preference for goods that are not just gimmicky or serve pleasurable consumption, but instead bring elevated values into their lives which, at the same time, would benefit German industry. Once the people had become economically dependent he was certain they would be willing to work.

ADM G. von Schleinitz, ca, 1885

The mobilisation of NGC staff

NGC's first doctor, Otto Schellong and NGC's first engineer, Friedrich Drees, stepped ashore in Finschhafen with the professional huntsmen Heidemann and Rücker on 26 January 1886. Others followed (and went) in rapid succession. Viennese Conrad Götz arrived with his wife Emma in Finschhafen in April to start at his expense the staff canteen. NGC supplied the land and the workers for the establishment of a market garden, the Götz family brought with them poultry and dairy cattle to provide for the catering. The good diet of fresh vegetables, eggs and milk lasted for almost three years when the Götz left GNG to try their luck in Paraguay.

Hansemann appointed a retired Vice Admiral of the *Kaiserliche Marine*, Georg von Schleinitz, the first Administrator of GNG, in February 1886. Confident in his future, Schleinitz bought six first-class tickets from the British Indian Steam Navigation Co. for himself, his wife Margot and their four children, Gretchen and Lorche, 14 and 9 years old, and two younger boys, Heinrich and Siegmund. The tutor for the children, Paul Ehmann, the servant (Nell) and his wife made up the group. The party of nine embarked on SS *Dorunda* in London on 7 April 1886 and arrived in Cooktown on 26 May. Cooktown's councillors honoured Schleinitz with a banquet. Special Commissioner for BNG, John Douglas, and the New Guinea explorer, Henry

Forbes, along with 50 guests toasted the successful beginning of the new German colony, expressing the hope and desire of close co-operation between Cooktown and Finschhafen.

Schleinitz and his entourage arrived in Finschhafen on 10 June to be greeted by his staff in full dress (long white trousers, white coat and stiff upright white collar). That the event occurred 11 days before NGC became a legally constituted corporation would have pleased Hansemann. His plan of concurrent activities had worked. By contrast, the Schleinitz family was not pleased. Their furniture and utensils were still in transit from Germany with the *Ottilie* only scheduled to arrive in a month's time. Ignoring the recommendation by Finschafen manager Richard Mentzel for Frau Schleinitz and the children to stay in Cooktown until the residence was completed the family took up temporary accommodation on the barque *Norma*, a vessel not built for luxury. Purchased second hand in 1885 for the transport of personnel, building material and then storing coal, the cabins of the old hulk provided little comfort. Otto Schellong, who lived on the hulk for the first few months after his arrival regarded the conditions on the vessel bearable: 'On the *Norma*, riding in a steady breeze, no person had been struck by malaria fever', he claimed. 'This was in stark contrast to the crowded Swedish houses leeward of the mountains, which were absolute 'fever-ridden holes'.[56]

Vice Consul Knappe was more strident in his criticism of Finschhafen. En route from Apia to Jaluit, he filed a report expressing distress about the atrocious conditions of the place. He considered the Swedish houses rat holes, where 1.8 x 3m cells with beds and furniture made from wooden boxes served as accommodation.

The first frontier town of GNG was a place for bachelors at best. Mosquito infested, rough and filthy, where the daily monsoon washed away the excrement in open drains. The Schleinitz children were down with fever within a few weeks of their arrival, with Frau von Schleinitz finding the conditions atrocious when compared to her long stay in Cuba. On 18 January 1887 Administrator von Schleinitz lost his wife to diphtheria or tuberculosis; his servant, Nell, died 3 months later of malaria. He spent little time in Finschhafen himself and was spared the 'miasmic air and generally unhealthy conditions of the place'. Hardly ever in one location for a long time, according to Schellong he was more intent on exploring his new colony.[57]

Unlike his successors, von Schleinitz had multiple responsibilities. When given judicial powers by the Chancellor on 24 June 1886 he was effectively accountable to both Hansemann and the imperial government. The appointment of George Schmiele as the imperial judge for the Bismarck Archipelago on 14 July 1886 did not make it any easier for Schleinitz. Infrastructure development, commerce and government administration were NGC's obligations while the judiciary remained within the authority of Berlin. Schmiele was on the payroll of NGC but remained responsible to Schleinitz. And much to the annoyance of the Administrator, he freely used his line to the Colonial Department of the Foreign Office.[58]

On an expedition to the Bismarck Archipelago Schleinitz initiated the first of several moves to relocate the principal Station in the archipelago. In October 1887 he instructed the relocation of Mioko Station to nearby Kerawara Island, also in the Duke of York Group, because of the harbour's capacity to take ships of 6 m draught. The building of a 12 m wide, 6 km long road across the island from north to south became GNG's first major road-building project. Under the supervision of surveyor August Rocholl, the work was completed through heavily timbered country within 12 months.[59]

When the health of Schleinitz's children did not improve he applied for home leave. His relief, Reinhold Kraetke, arrived in Finschhafen in February 1888, and the Administrator left the Protectorate with his children a month later, on 19 March 1888. His subsequent discussions in Berlin with Hansemann crystallized strong disagreements concerning the management of NGC and the level of expenditures required. Schleinitz also expressed unease with the excessively aggressive policy towards the indigenous population. The Directors did not accept Schleinitz's views, and they terminated his contract on the grounds of irreconcilable differences.[60]

Three years after NGC had commenced business, the number of European staff had grown to 46 and marine personnel to 74. This was the highest number NGC ever employed in GNG. Between 1886 and 1913 the average number, including ships' personnel, was 66. This was attained with one in three employees either dying or leaving after only a short stay with the company. The high staff turnover was worrisome and impeded the speedy development of GNG as envisaged by Hansemann. Notwithstanding the travelling costs home employees incurred when breaking their employment contract, for every person completing the 3-year indenture two chose not to do so. Up to 1891, one in four Europeans who arrived died, and NGC had a massive problem on its hands; a problem aggravated by the high number of absences due to sickness and recuperation leave. NGC did not shy away from reporting employment movements, including early retirements, dismissals and mortalities in its publication. Hansemann tried to lessen the problem by having hospitals built and by sending successively seven doctors to KWL in the first seven years.[61]

Kraetke drew on the assistance of a former colleague, Eugen Ewerlien, who, together with Victor Schmidt-Ernsthausen and Richard Jordan, was responsible for postal services and financial accounting in Finschhafen. Dr Lukowicz replaced Dr Schellong as the company physician in April 1888, and the agriculturalist, Dr R. Hindorf, was the registrar, harbour master and Station Manager. Butaueng, Dr Marnow was Magistrate and Secretary to the Administrator. J. Kubary was in charge at Konstantinhafen, A. Hermes at Stephansort, and E. Schollenbruch managed Hatzfeldthafen. In the Bismarck Archipelago Graf Pfeil and B. von Mengden managed Kerawara, while Judge Schmiele, Oskar Hering (judicial clerk) and H.J. Langmaak (bailiff) carried out government business. Retired army officer Robert Steinhäuser and two petty officers were engaged to train a small police force from indigenous recruits. Sechstroh was now in command of SS *Samoa,* Rasch of the *Ottilie,* Dallmann of the *Ysabel;* Dücker, later Weller, of the barque *Esmeralda* and Hutter of the barque *Florence-Denver.* The Australian Fossgreen acted as relief captain.[62]

Finschhafen, Madang Island, ca. 1890 (Hiery, *Die Deutsche Südsee*, no. 24; **Residence of Administrator Georg von Schleinitz at Finschhafen** (*NKWL*, 1888), **Celebration of peace accord at FWH**, ca. 1894 (M. v. Hein, Mitchell Library, FM 3/846)

Other than the Schleinitz and Götz families, GNG was a bachelor colony. NGC staff had time to drink and to complain. They grumbled about the houses, the low pay, the high cost of living and the poor standard of food. The explorer Ernst Tappenbeck, who joined NGC shortly before the closure of Finschhafen regarded the place as unproductive: 'a meeting place where an army of company officers congregated to keep the slow wheel of a bureaucracy moving along'. Finsch was unhappy that he was not given the position of Administrator; Schleinitz was not happy with the general conditions in GNG. Dallmann regarded the Colony a mad-house, believing that NGC would pack up and leave KWL inside three years. Schellong identified the high morbidity and mortality as the biggest obstacles for a successful start in GNG.[63]

The start-up problems of NGC attracted attention in Germany and in Australia alike. *The Queenslander* picked up the story of NGC mismanagement from the *Münchner Neuesten Nachrichten*. In its 9 March 1889 edition the Brisbane paper informed its readers:

To our regret the management of the NGC is not what it should be....The Company has made worse mistakes than the East African one, and it is only due to the much more favourable condition of its territory for colonisation that the evil consequences are not yet so prominent. The blunders committed Firstly, the action of the Berlin Directors, who do not simply give general instructions for the administration of the company, but wish to conduct the whole management from Berlin. Secondly, opening the country to large capitalists and excluding as much as possible small enterprises. Thirdly, the continual postponement from one half-year to another of the opening up of the country, and the conditions imposed on settlers, which are well qualified to prevent a large immigration. Fourthly, the squandering of money. It is rumoured that the company has offered its territories to the Empire for 4,000,000 marks.[64]

Hansemann pointed the finger at everyone except himself. The decision to experiment with cotton and tobacco without first establishing good race relations, observing weather patterns and dealing effectively with malaria and dysentery were costly errors. To plant tobacco at Hatzfeldthafen only to abandon the place a few months later demonstrated ineptitude at senior levels both in Berlin and in the Protectorate.

The establishment and running costs from 1885 to 1891 of Finschhafen, Butaueng and the guano loading facilities on the Purdy Islands amounted to RM3,650,013. Establishing and operating Hatzfeldthafen from 1885 to 1891 came to RM395,204, with the costs for Konstantinhafen amounting to RM388,693 before the plantations were given up in 1895. NGC was obviously not equipped to manage three plantation stations over a distance of 500 km during the founding years of GNG.[65]

Notes

1   Hansemann's vision, *DKZ* (1885) p. 376.

2   *NKWL* (1885) Heft ii, pp. 3–9, Heft iii, pp. 2–10, Heft iv, pp. 3–19; O. Finsch, *Samoa-Fahrten: Reisen in Kaiser Wilhelmsland und Englisch-Neu-Guinea in den Jahren 1884 und 1885 an Bord des deutschen Dampfers "Samoa"*, O. Finsch, *Systematische Übersicht der Ergebnisse seiner Reisen und Schriftstellerischen Thätigkeiten (1859-91)*, O. Finsch, 'Wie ich Kaiser Wilhelms-Land erwarb. Mein Anteil an der Gründung der Neu-Guinea-Compagnie', *Deutsche Monatsschrift für das Gesamte Leben der Gegenwart 1* (1902), pp. 406–24, 570–84, 728–43 and 875–89

3   O. Finsch, 'Deutsche Namensgebung in der Südsee', *Deutsche Erdkunde*, 1 (1902) pp. 42–5

4   *NKWL* (1885) Heft iv, pp. 23–9

5   *NKWL* (1891) Heft i, p. 3. Mt Wilhelm (4,509 m) was an unlikely navigation beacon because of regular cloud cover, NKWL (1885) Heft iv, pp. 17–8; (1889) Heft ii, p. 49

6   The Emperor granted the application by NGC to have northeast New Guinea renamed to Kaiser Wilhelms-Land and New Britain Archipelago to Bismarck-Archipel on 17 May 1886 (*NKWL* [1885] Heft iv, p. 6; H. Schnee, ed., *Deutsches Kolonial-Lexikon*, vol. i, p. 213)

7   *NKWL* (1885) Heft ii, pp. 4–5

8   Finsch, *Samoa-Fahrten*, pp. 28–53; Jb (1887) p. 4; Sack & Clark (1886–87) p. 6. Mikloucho-Maclay (1846–88) studied natural science and medicine at St Petersburg. Maclay travelled to North America, the Philippines, New Guinea, Java and India. In 1883 and 1884 he protested against Australian, British and German colonisation intentions. Konstantinhafen was named after the Minister for the Russian Navy, Grand Duke Konstantin Nikolajewitsch and Alexishafen after his brother Tzar Alexander II (N.N. Mikloucho-Macklay, *New Guinea Diaries* 1871–1883, translated by C.L. Sentinella)

9   *NKWL* (1885) Heft i, pp. 10, 49, ii, pp. 3–10, iii, pp. 3–4; (1886) Heft i, pp. 13, 15 & 83; (1891) Heft i, p. 8; (1892) p. 22

10   Hansemann to Bismarck, 20 Dec. 1884 (RKA 1001:2794). O. Finsch, 'Wie ich Kaiser Wilhelms-Land erwarb', *Deutsche Monatsschrift* (1902) p. 584

11   W.C. Groves, 'Peter the Island King', NLA mfm PMB MS 612. Finsch writes of a Scottish carpenter—not Hansen—who he hired in Cooktown; *NKWL* (1885) Heft iv, pp. 3–4, (1886) Heft ii, p. 66); 'The German Station at Bentley Bay', *The Mercury* (1885) 13 July

12   Oertzen to Bismarck, 15 Dec. 1884 (RKA 1001: 2778 & 2297); *NKWL* (1885) Heft i, pp. 4–5; P.G. Sack, 'Traditional Land Tenure', pp. 174–6

13   Hahl to AA-KA, 21 Feb. 1899 (RKA 1001:2278 & 2797). See P.J. Hempenstall, *Pacific Islanders under German Rule*, p. 164; P.G. Sack, *Land between Two Laws*, p. 122

14   RKA 1001:2278. NGC to AA-KA, 24 Feb. 1899, (RKA 1001:2943)

15   NGC, 'Instruction für den Landeshauptmann 1885', (RKA 1001:2408) pp. 1–33. (Landeshauptmann and Administrator is interchangeable); NGC, 'Instruktion für die wissenschaftliche rschungsexpedition' (R K A 1001:2408, pp. 1–14). NGC, 'Grundsätze für die Niederlassungen von Missionaren 1886' (RKA 1001:2409, pp. 1–3

16   Jb (1888) pp. 8–9; Sack & Clark (1887–88) pp. 27–30. von Kotze, *Aus Papuas Kulturmorgen*, pp. 24ff

17   Until the 'Protectorate Act' was proclaimed by the emperor on 17 April 1886 German colonial law was based on the Act for Consular Jurisdiction of 10 July 1879 (DKG vol. 1, pp. 28–36; Schnee, vol. ii, p. 339 and vol. iii, pp. 317–18). Application of the law in GNG was by 'Imperial Ordinance regarding the Laws in the Protectorate of NGC' of 5 June 1886, implemented on 1 Sep. 1886. Ordinances were based on German and Prussia metropolitan law. Metropolitan law did not apply to the indigenous population unless specifically directed. Ordinances were submitted to the Bundesrath and Reichstag for information only (Sack, *Land between Two Laws*, pp. 127–36)

18   Sack, 'Traditional Land Tenure', pp. 192–6; Hempenstall, *Pacific Islanders*, pp. 124–5

19   P.G. Sack & B. Sack, eds., *Eduard Hernsheim*, pp. 87-8, 101-2 & 111, E. Hernsheim diaries.

20   (RKA 1001:2791); C. Ribbe, *Zwei Jahre unter den Kanibalen der Salomons-Inseln*, pp. 56–8

21   B. Jinks, P. Biskup, & H.N. Nelson, eds., *Readings in New Guinea History*, p. 24

22   NGC, 'Instructions', §15, pp. 11 &17; Hahl to AA, 21 Feb. 1899, (RKA 1001:2278Jb (1889) p. 10; Sack & Clark (1888-89) p. 41; Sack, 'Traditional Land Tenure', pp. 177–80

23   NGC, 'Instructions', '§12, p. 9; *NKWL* (1885) Heft i, pp. 6 & 8, Heft ii, pp. 61-2. NGC, 'Grundsätze für die Niederlassungen von Missionaren' (RKA 1001:2409, pp. 1–3)

24   *NKWL* (1886) Heft i, pp. 6–7 (1887) Heft v, p. 163 (Cooktown was serviced by steamers from Brisbane and Sydney. The town was founded in 1873 during the Palmer River gold rush. During the rush it reached a population of 30,000 which declined with the drop of gold production in 1885)

25   O. Schellong, *Alte Dokumente aus der Südsee*, pp. 37–8

26   NGC, 'Instructions', §15, p. 11; §17, pp. 11-12 & §20 p. 13

27   O. Schellong, p. 201 n. 64

28   G. von Schleinitz (1834–1910) joined the Navy in 1849. He participated in the first Prussian expedition to Siam and China (1859–62) and commanded the SMS *Arkon* around the world (1869–71). Commanding the corvette SMS Gazelle, he repeated the Venus transition observed by James Cook 100 years earlier while also carrying out hydrographic work in Melanesia and Micronesia. (G. von Schleinitz, Die Forschungsreise SMS "Gazelle" in den Jahren 1874–1876)

29   *NKWL* (1888) Heft i, p. 8; Heft ii, pp. 58ff; Heft iii, p. 151; Heft iv, p. 181; (1890) Heft i, p. 10; Heft ii, p. 68

30   *NKWL* (1887) Heft iii, p. 81; (1888) Heft i, p. 58.

31   *NKWL* (1886) Heft II, pp. 61–9, 82; Jb (1887) pp. 3–4; Sack & Clark (1886–87) p. 5

32   F. Grabowsky, 'Erinnerungen an Neu-Guinea', *Das Ausland* 63 (1889) pp. 121–3, (1890) pp. 91ff.

33   *NKWL* (1886) Heft iv, pp. 113–14, (1887) Heft v, p. 163; Jb (1887) pp. 4 &16–17; Sack & Clark (1886–87) pp. 5 &16–17

34   *NKWL* (1889) Heft i, p. 25–6; (1890) Heft i, p. 14; (1891) Heft i, pp. 12–14

35   *NKWL* (1888) Heft iii, p. 82

36   'Die Bluttat von Malala', G. Kunze, Im Dienst des Kreuzes auf Ungebahnten Pfaden; *NKWL* (1891) Heft I, p. 13. Compare Firth, *New Guinea under the Germans*, p. 32

37   *NKWL* (1891) Heft I, pp. 13–14; (1892) Heft i, p. 21

38   *NKWL* (1887) Heft v, p. 192; (1888) Heft iv, p. 179; 1890, Heft i, p. 15; 1891, Heft I; p. 14, 1892 Heft i, pp. 21–2; Rose to Caprivi, 1 & 9 Sep & 27 Nov. 1891, memo 23 Sept. 1891 (RKA 1001:2980, pp. 90 & 167–68); Jb (1890/91) pp. 6–7; Sack & Clark (1890–91) pp. 60–61. F. Grabowsky, 'Der Bezirk von Hatzfeldthafen und seine Bewohner', *Petermanns Geographische Mitteilungen* (=*PGM*) 41 [1895]. See 'A Short and Brutal Life' in Sack, *Phantom History*,p. 116–8, v, p. 194–5; (1888) Heft i, p. 20

41   Jb (1888) p. 12; Sack & Clark (1887–88) p. 32

42   *NKWL* (1888) Heft i, pp. 20–2, F. Thiel, 'Johann Stanislaus Kubary', *DKZ Beilage*, 31 (1899). 'Land-Verwaltung' (RKA 1001:2942). Hempenstall, *Pacific Islanders under German Rule*, pp. 167f; 43   Justice Phillips annulled the purchases on 25 May 1932 (Sack, 'Traditional Land Tenure', pp. 209f)

44   NGC to Rose, 14 Jan. 1890 (RKA 1001:2942)

45   NGC, 'Instruction für den Landeshauptmann' §23, p. 15

46   NGC, 'Instruction', §18, pp. 12-13. See J. Ferguson, *All about the Coconut Palm*; Schellong, pp. 32 & 85; Sal. Oppenheim & Cie., Köln, vol. 112, Committee of NGC, 25 July 1885

47   *NKWL* 1885, Heft i, p. 34; Jb (1887) p. 22; Sack & Clark (1886–87) p. 21

48   *NKWL* (1888) Heft i, pp. 2–14; (1889) Heft i, p. 1 & 30; (RKA 1001:2997, pp. 8–9)

49   Jb (1888) pp. 11–12; Sack & Clark (1887–88) p. 31; *'Allgemeine Bedingungen für die Überlassung von Grundstücken an Ansiedler im Schutzgebiet der NGC'*, DKG, vol. i, pp. 472–5

50   Deutsche Kolonial Gesellschaft, ed. *Koloniales Jahrbuch*, vol. ii, 1889, p. 281

51   Schellong, p. 113. The unannounced arrivals were escaped prisoners from New Caledonia (German New Guinea: Correspondence (NAA G255/4 [1 Jan. 1885–31.Dec.1914])

52   *DKZ* (1888) 12 Jan. p. 8

53   *DKZ* (1888) 18 Sep. 7

54   *NKWL* (1890), Heft i, p. 9; Jb (1889) p. 11, (1890) p. 1; Sack & Clark (1888–89) pp. 22, 42 & 46

55   'Es ist die Aufgabe, sie friedlich der menschlichen Kultur zu gewinnen, nicht zu unterdrücken, zu berauben oder gar zu vertilgen', *NKWL* (1885) Heft i, p. 5

56   Knappe to Bismarck, 4 Sep. 1886, (RKA 1001:2977, pp. 11–32). *NKWL* (1886) Heft i, pp. 2–4; ii, pp. 60–1, pp. 79 & 80; Schellong, pp. 72, 93 & 175.

57   *NKWL* (1887) Heft iii, p. 79; Schellong, pp. 83ff.; O. Schellong, D*eutsche Medizinische Wochenschrift*, Nr. 23–4 (1887); S.C. Wigley, 'Tuberculosis & New Guinea, 1871–1971'(RMB 1182/4-5)

58   Colonial Protectorate Act, 1886; *NKWL* (1886) Heft iii, pp. 74–5 & 77–8

59   *NKWL* (1888) Heft i, pp. 17–8; (1890), i, p. 16

60   Jb (1888) p. 1; Sack & Clark (1887–88) p. 22; *NKWL* (1888), Heft ii, p. 57. Schellong, pp. 140ff. G. von Schleinitz: 'Was gibt uns der Fall Wehlan zu denken und zu lernen' (*DKZ* (1896) pp. 65–6)

61   M. Davies, *Public Health and Colonialism*, pp 54 & 202–6, chart 10

62   Jb (1888) p. 7; Sack & Clark (1887–88) p. 27

63   *NKWL* (1891) Heft i, pp. 5–11 & 21; Jb (1891/92) pp. 5–7. Sack & Clark (1890–91) pp. 59 & 62. Dallmann to von Oppen 2 Mar. 1887 (Pawlik, pp.126–7)

64   *Q* (1889) 9 Mar. p. 468

65   *NKWL* (1890) Heft i, p. 10, ii, pp. 66–70; (1891) Heft i, pp. 12 & 14. (1896) p. 15

THE NEU GUINEA COMPAGNIE

The Agreement entered into by Britain and Germany on 6 April 1885 gave Germany control over the north-eastern quadrant of mainland New Guinea and the New Britain Archipelago. Britain asserted control over the south-eastern quadrant of New Guinea inclusive of all adjacent islands. On 17 May 1885 the German emperor offered Hansemann, as principal of the Neu Guinea Compagnie (NGC), protection under an imperial charter for the area under the *Reich's* control. Subsequent to the 'Declaration relating to the Demarcation of the German and British Spheres of Influence in the Western Pacific' of 6 April 1886, this charter was amended on 13 December 1886. The Solomon Islands of Bougainville, Buka, Shortland Choiseul and Santa Isabel became part the Protectorate of German New Guinea in 1899.[1]

Bismarck intended to limit government involvement in German protectorates to diplomatic and—if needed—military protection of German Christian missions and commercial enterprises. The 'Declaration between Great Britain and Germany relating to the reciprocal Freedom of Trade and Commerce in the British and German Possessions and Protectorates in the Western Pacific' of 10 April 1886 reflected this.

Adolph von Hansemann, Germany's pre-eminent banker, was a man on a mission. He was prepared to accept a charter that transferred the privileges of local sovereignty over GNG to his company in exchange for meeting the costs of establishing and running the Protectorate. Specifically, he was willing to agree to the promotion

> of trade and the economic development of arable land, for the establishment and cementation of peaceful relations with the natives, and for their civilisation, to establish and maintain at [his] expense an administration in the Protectorate, on conditions that the *Reich* grant his consortium the exclusive right to exercise local sovereignty.

And, subject to government supervision, be given the exclusive right to

> take possession of ownerless land, to dispose of it, and to enter into binding agreements with the natives for land purchases and over land rights, all under the supervision of the *Reich* which will enact the regulations necessary to safeguard property rights, and to protect the natives.[2]

The regulation and conduct of relations between GNG and foreign governments, and the judiciary remained the responsibility of the *Reich*, albeit at the expense of NGC.[3]

Establishing a corporate structure

On 25 May 1884 Hansemann convinced 12 business friends and associates to join his Neu Guinea Consortium. Well before investors could be assured control of GNG they paid a total of RM1,000,000 into a consortium to start the colonisation process of the new German Protectorate in the South Sea. Bismarck demanded that the Protectorate be governed by imperial decree and not by parliamentary legislation. He achieved his aims by appointing Adolph von Hansemann an executive of the *Reich,* thus bypassing the government's budget process.[4] Hansemann, in turn, was keen to minimise government meddling to gain maximum flexibility in the running of NGC.

The foreign office and Hansemann rejected the idea of incorporating the Consortium as a limited liability company (LLC). Both parties deemed the law of the LLC, with its tight and prescriptive regulations, inappropriate. For Hansemann, the share register of an LLC was too open and the extensive disclosure requirements would undermine the commercial position of NGC. Neither he nor the government were happy to disclose their intentions in New Guinea while negotiations with Britain over the final boundaries remained open. Also, the highly speculative nature of the New Guinea venture would have been detrimental to the reputation of Hansemann's bank, the Berlin Disconto Gesellschaft (D-G), and Hansemann himself if calls for new equity had to be made repeatedly or worse, if a total loss of shareholders' funds were to occur. For Bismarck the LLC was even less desirable. Under German law, the emperor could not transfer government business to an LLC nor was he empowered to award privileges to such a company without approval from the *Reichstag*.[5]

Surprisingly, Hansemann opted for the *General Prussian Landrecht* (Prussian Civil Code) for the legal framework for his new enterprise on the grounds of the

    a) legal structure of the 'Corporation' was equivalent to that of a person;
    b) publication of a balance sheet was not required;
    c) Directors were not personally liable to the shareholders;
    d) new capital could be raised by a simple share-holder majority.

It must have particularly suited the government because the Directors of a corporation required approval by the government for the

    a) statute and amendments to the statute;
    b) issue of old and new share capital;
    c) identity of shareholders;
    d) appointment and retirement of Directors;
    e) appointment and retirement of senior employees;
    f) sale of fixed assets; and
    g) liquidation of the corporation.

Further, the government was empowered to hold the Directors personally liable for misappropriation and gross negligence.[6]

In accordance with the requirements of German corporate law the business was defined in the statute of the company. In the first paragraph the obligation of establishing government institutions in GNG were identified, as were the rights by NGC to acquire 'ownerless' land for agricultural and mineral exploitation, the establishment of infrastructure for prospective settlers, the establishment and operation of agricultural, trade and commercial enterprises, to the extent deemed necessary for the development of the company or for the stimulation and sponsorship of private enterprises. The statute outlined the rights of the government:

    a) The *Reichskanzler* appoints the Imperial Commissioner;
    b) The Commissioner is empowered to attend Board and the Shareholder Meetings;
    c) The Commissioner is authorised to inspect the books of NGC;
    d) The Government can call an EGM if the Board ignores shareholders or auditors requests;
    e) Government control is to ensure that management complies in accordance with the law.

In particular, NGC had to seek government approval for the

a) Rights and obligations under which the company carries out the conferred local sovereignty;
b) Implementation of ordinances;
c) Rules of conduct under which ownerless land can be acquired and disposed of;
d) Election of the chairman and his nominated representatives
e) Issue of equity and intentions of borrowing; and
f) Any changes to the statues, return of capital, liquidate the company.

Ten Directors were elected at a general meeting by shareholders. Each Director had to be a German national; at least six had to be shareholders in NGC; and no fewer than five had to have their place of residence in Berlin. Similarly, only German nationals with a permanent residential address in Germany were allowed on the share register. This ruling also applied to mining and trading companies. Initially, 800 partly paid shares were issued at RM1,250 each to raise RM1,000,000. Subject to three weeks' written notice given to shareholders and for total calls not to exceed RM5,000 the Board was authorised to make calls of up to RM500 per share at a time. In the event of payment on calls not being received on the due date, the company was entitled to recover the debt (including interest) through the courts.

The authorised share capital was RM4,000,000. Additionally, 20 bonus shares with a face value of RM5,000 each were issued for services rendered. The bonus shares ranked *pari passu* with fully paid ordinary shares. A minimum of 10% and a maximum of 15% of net profits had to be booked to a Reserve Fund. Dividends could be declared when RM500,000 was provisioned in the accounts.[7]

Shareholders and the Board of Directors

The statute was submitted to the emperor on 29 March 1886 and was approved on 12 May 1886 – five days before the provisional charter was due to expire. NGC became a legally compliant company when shareholders confirmed the statute at the 21 June 1886 inaugural general meeting. The meeting voted on a 10-member Board and appointed the external auditors. Hansemann was elected chairman and managing Director; the former State Secretary, E. Herzog, deputy chairman; and Consul-General E. Russell, deputy managing Director. Other executive Directors appointed were A. Lent and A. Siemens. Hansemann was the major shareholder with 23% of the issued capital. The second largest shareholder was Bleichröder with 12% of the issued capital. Hansemann's bank took up 10%, with three of his executives (A. Salomonsohn, E. Russell and A. Lent) collectively acquiring 3%. The only other substantial shareholder was the industrialist and estate owner, Baron von Eckardstein-Prötzel, who had acquired 8% of the issued shares. In addition to the major shareholders, Dr F. Hammacher, Count Henckel von Donnersmarck (industrialist and close business associate of Bleichröder) and A. Woermann (East Africa Shipping Line owner) were elected to the Board. The list of elected Board members was submitted to Bismarck for approval on 4 April 1887. Notable omissions from the list were Albert von Oppenheim, Herzog von Ujest and Kraft Friedrich Prinz zu Hohenlohe-Öhringen.

Management and supervisory Boards were united under Hansemann until March 1903. His retirement from executive duties on 14 March 1900 saw the promotion of D-G's Carl von Beck and Dr Carl Lauterbach to the position of joint managing

Directors. Hansemann remained chairman of the supervisory Board until he died on 9 December 1903. When Lauterbach retired in 1903 to join the NGC supervisory Board, African specialist Dr Paul Preuß was appointed joint managing Director on 1 June 1903. Alexander Schoeller of D-G was NGC's chairman until his death on 22 November 1911. Arthur Salomonsohn, also managing Director of D-G, was chairman from 1912 until his death on 15 June 1930. While Hansemann's shares would have remained with D-G until the bank merged with Deutsche Bank (DB) in 1929, the whereabouts of Bleichröder's and Eckardstein-Prötzel's shares in NGC after their deaths in 1893 and 1898 respectively have not been identified.[8]

Financial performance

Hansemann established the NGC venture without first developing a comprehensive business plan – including forward estimates of income and expenditures.[9] While allocating considerable time to the drafting of management procedures, his unstructured approach to business planning was not at all characteristic of a banker. The result was financial disaster while the company was under his control. Over a period of 28 years, shareholders invested RM20,266,887 in NGC and RM2,400,000 in the subsidiary Astrolabe-Compagnie (A-C).[10] Hansemann never generated a financial return from his investment and it would seem that he found little enjoyment in directing the company from the other side of the globe. After the company was relieved of the government burden in 1899, shareholders could only hope that their long-term investment would finally pay off. They had to wait another 12 years before NGC paid its first dividend. However, their ultimate disappointment came when World War I prevented the company from enjoying a buoyant copra market.[11]

A more detailed analysis reveals that the first RM1,000,000 was raised with the placement of the 800 partly paid shares. The money was spent by the time the first trial balance was presented to the Directors on 31 December 1886. The costs incurred by the Finsch and Schrader expeditions and the acquisition of the steamer *Samoa* amounted to RM447,443.[12] Combined with the acquisition cost of three steamers and three sailing ships between 1884 and 1886 (approximately RM714,000) and the costs for mobilisation of staff and equipment, share capital was exceeded almost twofold. Three calls on shareholders made before the first annual general meeting on 13 December 1887 raised RM1,200,000. This injection of funds paid for the operations until 1889 when the authorised capital of RM4,000,000 was fully utilised. The planned issue of 800 new shares at the 12 May 1887 EGM was unsuccessful with only 14 new shares placed.[13]

On 30 April 1889 the nominal value of the ordinary share was raised to RM6,500. This time shareholders were advised that the company would no longer perform government duties, thus freeing management to pay undivided attention to the cultivation of tobacco and cotton.[14]

As shown in Chart 5.1 the capital-raising of NGC changed in 1890. To reduce operational costs and to quickly generate income the Kaiser Wilhelms-Land-Plantagen-Gesellschaft (KWLPG) issued a prospectus in June to raise funds to establish cacao and coffee plantations in GNG. In exchange for 12.5% equity NGC sold KWLPG land in the new enterprise. However, this did not transfer the risk. The RM500,000 share capital issued by KWLPG was substantially raised from NGC shareholders, with Hansemann the largest shareholder (subscribing to 24%).[15]

The venture failed within a year. Rather than coffee and cacao, Hansemann now decided on setting up tobacco plantations modelled on Deli in Sumatra. Potential investors received a prospectus of A-C in early 1891 and on 22 December 1891 the tobacco plantation company was formed with an authorised capital of RM2,400,000. This time NGC transferred 14,000 ha it valued at RM300,000 in exchange for 12.5% equity in A-C. Hansemann effectively controlled the enterprise by subscribing to 24% of the share capital and by NGC taking up a 25% stake in A-C. NGC recognised RM300,000 in its 1891/92 profit and loss statement for the sale of the land. The company also generated an ongoing benefit for services rendered in head office support and the supply of the labour by charging A-C an on-cost management fee of 10%.[16] The authorised capital of A-C was called upon over 3 years and with RM900,000 was fully recognised in the 1893/94 NGC balance sheet.

A-C was bankrupt within 3 years. Accumulated losses stood at RM1,696,426 of which NGC was owed RM1,241,447. In order to keep the company afloat NGC received shareholder approval to acquire the shares in A-C on 1 October 1895.[17] In the 1896/97 accounts NGC wrote off its RM900,000 equity investment in A-C and revalued the repossessed land at RM300,040.[18] Since the cultivation of tobacco was to continue, amounts owed for services rendered by NGC were capitalised in the accounts. Hansemann and the other A-C shareholders converted their holdings into 150 NGC preference shares with a nominal value of RM10,000 each.[19]

Chart 5.1: **Major shareholders in NGC and its subsidiaries**

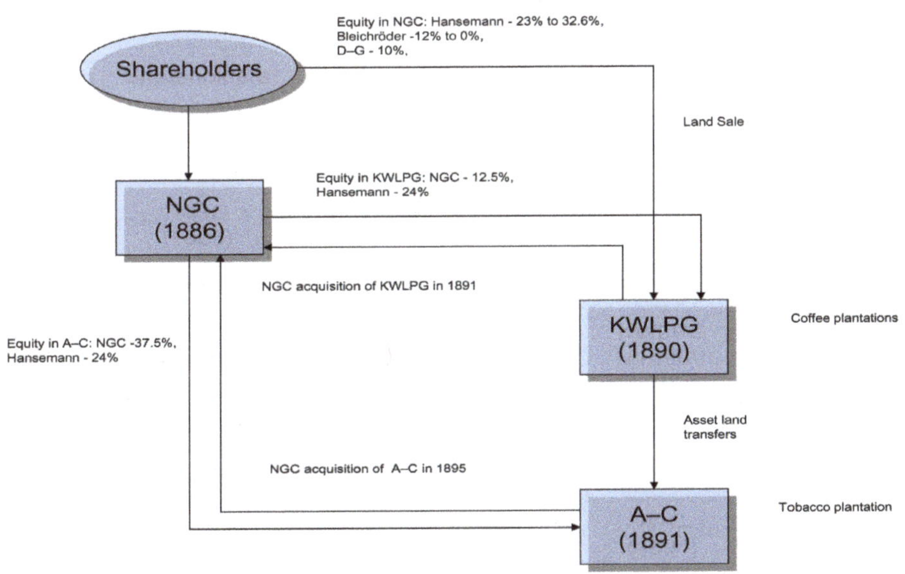

Disastrous Ventures

The transaction ensured that there was no paper loss; in fact, at face value, it was a better investment because the preference shares attracted a 5% cumulative dividend payable before the ordinary shares qualified for distributions.

Concurrent with the equity raising for A-C, NGC shareholders voted at an EGM on 29 December 1892 to increase the par value of ordinary shares by RM1,500. Shareholders agreed on 28 November 1896 to provide further capital into NGC by approving an increase in the nominal capital of RM3,000. The nominal value of each ordinary share in NGC had now reached RM10,000.

Transfer of administration responsibility to the *Reich*

Separate from the activity of A-C, the Board concluded in 1892 that NGC would not become profitable unless it was relieved of its political administration and infrastructure development burdens. The resolution to transfer the administration of the Protectorate to an Imperial Officer in November 1889 had proven unworkable and was reversed on 15 June 1892.[20] It took another 2 years before Hansemann sent an unequivocal memorandum to *Reichskanzler* Caprivi that NGC was no longer in a position to carry the dual responsibilities because

> the experience of the Administration of the Protectorate has … increasingly confirmed the fears expressed in the last report, that it would prove impossible to combine the responsibility of political administration with the profitable management of commercial business activities … By combining the two functions in one body not only are the financial resources and the staff of a private company overstrained— no matter how many sacrifices its shareholders are prepared to make—but due to intrinsic conflicts of interest, obstacles are placed in the way of fulfilling both functions, making their achievement much more difficult—in fact, impossible in the long run.[21]

Negotiations between the *Reich* and NGC on the handover of responsibilities started in November 1894. Surprisingly, an in-principle agreement was in place shortly thereafter.[22] Subject to budget approval by the *Reichstag*, the new chancellor, Hohenlohe-Schillingsfürst, agreed to release NGC from administration services by assuming full sovereignty over GNG on 1 April 1895. In recognition for establishing the Protectorate, NGC was to retain the land and mining monopolies on the mainland, New Britain (exclusive of the Gazelle Peninsula) and all GNG islands west of 149° longitude for 75 years. The harvesting of coconuts not owned by local people in KWL and the exploitation of timber resources was to remain the exclusive right of NGC. The company was also to retain exclusive labour recruiting rights for its economic zone for 20 years, and was exempt from government taxes for 5 years. Apart from assuming control over New Britain and taking over the administration centre (Herbertshöhe) the government would take administrative responsibility for the Duke of York Group, New Ireland, New Hanover, Bougainville and Buka Islands and all smaller ones east of 149° longitude. The privilege of NGC to raise and collect taxes, fines and fees was to be transferred to the government, as would the fishing rights for the Protectorate. To facilitate a smooth and speedy transition, NGC would transfer land, buildings and inventory in Friedrich Wilhelmshafen and Herbertshöhe to a value not exceeding RM71,000 and other installations (including harbours) for a value not exceeding RM30,000. Under the agreement, the government was entitled to redeem the company's privileges by 1 April 1905. If these rights were bought back on or before 1 April 1900, NGC would receive RM4,000,000 in compensation. If activated after 1 April 1900 the company would receive RM120,000 p.a., not exceeding RM600,000 in total. Under this arrangement, all improved land, including 14,000 ha belonging to A-C, would remain the property of the two companies.[23]

NGC's petition was tabled in the *Reichstag* on 2 and 15 June 1896 together with an appropriations bill for GNG. The debate centred on the Hohenlohe–Hansemann agreement, rather than on supplementary budget approvals for a colony which was not the financial responsibility of the *Reich*. The free traders and Members from the liberal left ridiculed the *Reichskanzler* for signing a one-sided contract *(Löwenvertrag)*, where the *Reich* was burdened with the legacies of the company while 'the Neu Guinea Compagnie would retain absolutely everything that was of economic value'. Other speakers rejected flatly any increased government involvement in GNG by advocating the return of KWL to the local people as it had no commercial value. The Social Democrats raised the issues of native mistreatment and the huge loss of European life in the Protectorate. One speaker cited a letter from a former A-C employee who alleged that at least one of the 60 Europeans in KWL in 1891 had died each month. The informant also charged the Directors of NGC with kidnapping, slavery and having carried out 'mass murder'. After two days of acrimonious debate, the Bill was referred to the Budget Committee which, without mentioning the agreement, recommended against any expenditure for GNG.

NGC's Board replied with an open letter to its shareholders. Taking umbrage at the allegations of kidnapping, slavery and mistreatment of its labour force, NGC identified seven deaths in the European population in 1891, with fatalities amongst the coolie and native population mainly a result of influenza transmitted to GNG from Europe. The Directors pointed out that A-C had spent in excess of RM200,000 for labour accommodation, medical care and improved provisions during the period from 27 Oct. 1891 to 5 Feb. 1892. Further, NGC drew attention to the unacceptably high costs it incurred on government-related work: between 1 November 1889 and 31 March 1893 RM105,216 had been spent annually on judicial and other government-related activities. Rather than being the lion, by persisting with the development of KWL it had entered the 'den of the lion', according to Hansemann. Directors insisted that expenditure should balance the income from business tax and import/export duties. However, only RM30,816 was received for the period from 1 April 1890 to 31 March 1896 for these activities, which, according to Hansemann, covered only a fraction of the costs NGC had incurred since commencing government work on 16 May 1886. Directors explained:

NGC raised RM8,140,000 and A-C RM2,400,000 in shareholder equity. More than fifty per cent of the total sum was expended on establishing the business in GNG. The company paid RM447,443 for the acquisition of the SS *Samoa* and the scientific expeditions. The costs incurred for maintaining shipping connections between Europe and the Protectorate until May 1893, amounted to RM2,450,531 and the cost for providing Government related services up to 1896 amounted to approximately RM1,200,000.

Hansemann forewarned NGC shareholders that operational costs, bank interest and corporate overheads could not be reduced to a level where the company would become profitable unless the government took up its responsibilities in GNG.

In KWL land had only been sold to A-C and the Christian missions with settlers and traders taking up small parcels. Minor proceeds had been received for fishing and bêche-de-mer licences. Minerals had been found but not delineated. On gold discoveries by 'Australian Diggers' on the Louisiade and in the northern sector of the Huon Gulf Hansemann cautioned: 'a great deal of work is required before traces [of gold in the Upper Ramu] can be confirmed, and this can only be done by calling on shareholders for additional funds'.

Referring to the government's desire to change from bimetallism to the gold standard, Hansemann had proposed to explore for gold in a joint venture with the government. 'But', he went on, 'the risk-averse gentlemen in the Government made it known to us that they could not accept such a proposal and instead preferred to receive a benefit from the introduction of a royalty which was applicable to all mining ventures in the Protectorate'. In the end, Hansemann offered to give up all privileges under the charter provided NGC was properly recompensed.

The comparison with BNG which, according to one speaker in the *Reichstag,* was much further developed than the NGC Protectorate brought the following response from Directors:

> BNG has adopted the high customs tariff of Australia, averaging 10% on all imported goods. The expenditures of the Colony—amounting to RM470,000 [£23,180] in 1894/95—was mainly incurred on administration and was funded from tariff receipts amounting to RM94,751 [£4,644].

Contrasting NGC's performance with that in BNG, Hansemann pointed out that tariffs and taxes in GNG had been kept to a minimum. The revenue-raising measures introduced on 30 June 1888 exempted agricultural activities other than a RM4/t levy on copra export, 'a mere 1.6% of its value', according to the Chairman. Customs duties imposed on the importation of wine and spirits (13.3 to 80 *Pfennig* per litre by volume of alcohol) were implemented to control consumption and raise revenue. While BNG did not have a business tax—activities were virtually nonexistent—the RM6 applicable to earnings from RM1,000 and RM1,500 p.a. and the annual flat rate of 2% on earnings above RM1,500, applicable to GNG, was insignificant in the opinion of Directors.[24]

Surprisingly, Hansemann claimed that NGC had not sought the privilege of local sovereignty. Renouncing his original company model, he now claimed 'the *Reich* has taken possession of the Protectorate in ceremonial procession, and therefore is the legal owner'. NGC, he asserted, was acting as the agent of the government until it became obvious that GNG would be better served by a government administration and 'if the *Reich* did not take up its responsibility the Protectorate would suffer [and] if NGC was not compensated equitably, the action would be deemed enrichment by the *Reich* at the expense of NGC'.[25]

The government referred the matter to the *Kolonialrath* (KR) for advice.[26] This gave the Board some respite since the foreign office had recently appointed former NGC Acting Administrator Reinhold Kraetke, Dr Richard Hindorf (a former NGC adviser and employee) and Hansemann himself to the KA.[27] Not surprisingly the KR recommended unanimously on October 1896 that the *Reich* assume full responsibility for the Protectorate and, in return for commensurate compensation, that NGC be required to surrender all privileges under its charter to the *Reich*.[28]

Negotiations with the government resumed in July 1898. The 7 October 1898 agreement was again subject to *Reichstag* approval. Now the land acquisition monopoly of NGC would devolve to the *Fiscus* of GNG as would all other privileges the company had received under the 15 May 1885 and 13 December 1886 imperial charters. In essence, the parties agreed to NGC receiving 10 interest-free annual instalments of RM400,000 from 1 April 1899. Each payment was conditional on NGC spending the money on capital works in the Protectorate within 4 years of each instalment. Since NGC would no longer enjoy the privilege of exclusive labour recruitment, the foreign office would facilitate the hiring of labourers to carry out such work. Further, NGC would retain all land legally acquired on or before 1 April 1899. The company was obliged to complete a sales agreement for 400 ha with the Catholic mission in Weberhafen. Administrative establishments in Friedrich Wilhelmshafen (residences of the Administrator and the secretary, office buildings, harbour installations and three boats, guns and ammunition for the police force, land register and court library) and Herbertshöhe (the courthouse, jail, residences of the Imperial Judge, court clerk and police sergeant, native police station, harbour installations including a whaleboat, a gig, pontoons, gangway and beacons), were to become the property of the *Reich*. Other salient points were the acquisition by NGC within 10 years of an additional 50,000 ha in KWL and/or New Britain, a reduction of 50 per cent compared to the 13 March 1996 agreement. The offered land was now not to exceed a continuing coastal strip 100 km long and no further than 1 km inland. In recognition of the exploration work NGC had carried out in the Ramu Valley, it was awarded mining concessions for precious metals and coal in this district for which the government was to receive a royalty of 10% on exports; alternatively, the government had the option to participate in mining ventures of its choosing, subject to participating equally in the expenditure.[29]

The agreement became effective on 1 April 1899. Two amendments: the right to acquire the additional 50,000 ha was restricted to KWL and the reduction of the acquisition period from 10 to 3 years, were then invoked.[30] An amendment to the agreement on 3 February 1900 gave NGC an exclusive 5-year licence to mine guano on the Purdy and the Admiralty Islands. In return, the government received entitlement to a 15% royalty on the net earnings achieved by NGC.[31]

Restructure and refinancing

The transfer of colonial responsibilities resulted in a restructured and refinanced NGC. The failure of A-C forced the Directors to make three further calls on shareholders while negotiations with the foreign office were ongoing. By 1 April 1899 the par value of the ordinary NGC share had increased from RM1,2500 in 1886 to RM12,000. Despite 14 capital raising in as many years liquidity remained tight, plantations were overvalued and additional funds were needed for the planned explorations for precious metals in the Ramu Valley, the Huon Gulf and the Purdy Islands.[32]

The Board called an EGM for 30 May 1899 to seek authority to amend NGC's statute. The changing role of NGC in the Protectorate made it necessary to alter the legal status of the company to that of a colonial company as prescribed in the German statute of 15 March 1888.[33] The meeting also sought approval for the capital restructure of the company and the implementation of management changes.

Because infrastructure establishment costs had blown out to RM9,768,000 worth of non-performing assets the Board of Directors submitted to the shareholders:

    a)   to make a call of RM2,500 per share thereby raising the par value to RM14,500;
    b)   the NGC assets be written down by 73.5% to RM2,235,900;
    c)   the par value of each RM14,500 share be reduced to RM4,350;
    d)   a new RM500 share be created by converting 8.7 old shares into one new share.[34]

The Board requested approval to issue 12,000 new shares with a face value of RM500. The old issue of 814 shares, the 20 bonus shares and the 150 preference shares were to be converted to 8042 ordinary shares. Further, the Board sought authority from the shareholders to issue RM6,000,000 in new equity.

The asset write down of RM7,532,100 in the 1898/99 accounts should not have surprised shareholders. The share capital of RM11,803,000 did not reflect the tangible assets which were RM2,035,000, and the resolution was passed on 30 May 1899. The capital of NGC was now RM4,021,000. While at the helm of NGC Hansemann incurred personal investment losses of RM3,760,368 (NGC RM3,184,368 and A-C RM576,000). Nevertheless, Hansemann backed his judgement, or rather obsession with GNG, by increasing his holding in 1899 to 32.6%. It was his last capital injection; he died on 9 December 1903, aged 77.

Post-restructure

NGC became profitable after 1 April 1899 because of the infrastructure in place and the transfer of administrative responsibilities to the *Reich*. While many *Reichstag* members regarded RM4,000,000 compensation for a mismanaged undertaking overly generous, Hansemann considered it inadequate reward for the work his company had performed. Compared to the RM6,500,000 the *Reich* paid to DOAG for establishing German East Africa from 1885 to 1889, Hansemann's grievance was understandable.

When Dr Paul Preuß was appointed Managing Director of the NGC in 1903, he prioritised regular visits to GNG. Determined to clean up the balance sheet he decided to discontinue exploration and expedition activities after his first inspection visit in January 1904. The minor gold discoveries during the 1900 to 1902 Ramu River expedition required extensive delineation before mining could be justified. Preuß recommended to the Board that a lack of labour resources and the requirement for substantial additional funding made it necessary to defer the project. Consequently, the Directors agreed to write off both the carrying amount of RM475,538 in the Ramu expedition in the 1903/04 accounts and the investment of RM187,500 in the Huon Golf Syndikat. The gold discovered in 2 years of exploration was insufficient to justify continuing the venture and the syndicate comprising NGC, Deutsche Bank and the Berliner Handels-Gesellschaft, was dissolved in 1903. The expensive cotton and tobacco cultivation ventures had been discontinued in 1900 and 1902 respectively with the remaining inventory of RM246,799 written off in the 1903 accounts.

The new direction set by Preuß concentrated on the most profitable cultivations of copra, gutta-percha and cacao. He determined to

a) Expand crops in suitable locations subject to the availability of workers and funds.
b) Continue with existing coffee plantations at the present level (no expansion).
c) Phase out kapok in favour of coconut palms and gutta-percha.
d) Avoid setting up of plantations in new regions.
e) Continue with food, tobacco, lemon grass, Javanese pepper and crops for home consumption.
f) Energetically develop plantations and trade on the French Islands.[35]

A strengthening of the balance sheet required additional funds. Whereas the total RM909,837 write-off in the 1903/04 accounts did not affect the cash position, when combined with a trading loss of RM514,009 for creditors amounting to RM2,247,526, it made for a weak balance sheet and, thus, expensive borrowing. While the Board could issue 3,958 shares without seeking shareholder approval, without Hansemann the Directors could no longer be assured of the same loyal response from shareholders. The Board decided therefore to call an extraordinary shareholder meeting for 27 June 1904 to seek approval for issuing 12,000,000 preference and 12,000 bonus shares. Because the preference shares carried 5% cumulative interest, ranking ahead of dividends, the meeting accepted the motion. Of the 3,958 preference shares issued 3,077 were taken up.[36]

Poor liquidity and high interest payments resulted in a further issue in 1908 of 3,000 cumulative preference shares of 5%, raising RM1,500,000. Following the Directors' assurance that the accumulated interests from the 1904 preference share issue —now 20%—would remain valid, the outstanding sum of RM354,000 for 708 preference shares was also paid. In 1910 shareholders were given the opportunity to convert their 8042 ordinary stock into preference shares by paying RM200 on each share held: they responded by converting 7,375 ordinary shares, realising RM1,475,000, less administration costs of RM74,534. An amount of RM1,400,466 was booked to a special reserve account. The number of preference shares had now increased to 14,333 with a nominal value of RM7,166,500. The conversion of 667 ordinary shares with an aggregate value of RM333,500 was still outstanding.[37]

The mean copra price had risen to RM550/t cif to European ports, helping to produce record profits in 1913 and early 1914. At that time Preuß assessed NGC plantation assets as undervalued.[38] Of the 8381 ha under cultivation at December 1913, palm plantations combined 85%, producing 75 to 80% of annual revenue. In the best financial position since NGC's formation, the Directors forecast a 7% dividend for the 1913/14 financial year and higher future dividend payments. Apart from minor receipts from gutta-percha, cacao and sisal, the profit of RM912,259 was primarily achieved on 2647 t plantation and 1392 t trade copra. Of the 794,400 plantation trees only 29% were at or near full production. With more trees maturing, the company forecast 8,000 t of plantation copra annually over the next eight years. The *Koloniale Rundschau* agreed with Preuß's review. Provided copra prices remained firm 'the NGC can expect considerable increases in future earnings', the paper predicted.

To reduce debt and take advantage of the buoyant copra market, shareholders approved the public listing of 7,000 new shares on the Berlin Börse on 16 February 1914. The company's common shareholders were given the opportunity to purchase two new shares at RM510 each for every five old shares they held. The capital raising of RM3,500,000 was for debt reduction and liquidity; although, bank debt in 1914 remained high at nearly RM4,000,000. Shareholders also voted on a company buy-back of the 15,000 NGC bonus shares at one Reichs Mark each, and agreed on the conversion of the remaining 62 ordinary shares into preference shares.[39]

The Berlin-based Kolonialbank and the Hydt'sches Kolonialkontor traded in NGC debentures from 1908. Notwithstanding the fixed 5% cumulative interest coupon, the shares hardly ever traded above par. Shortly before the listing on the Berlin Börse, the Kolonialbank pushed NGC debentures to a high of 143% by advising its clients 'we take the liberty to recommend the debentures of NGC and point out that the 1912/13 result will be published in a few days and is likely to produce favourable results'.[40]

In February 1914 the *Koloniale Rundschau* reported—prematurely—the listing of the largest plantation company in the world on the *Berlin Bourse*. With this listing NGC would have joined the Deutsch-Ostafrikanische Gesellschaft as the only other colonial plantation company on the German Stock Exchange.[41] However, shortly after shareholders had approved the issue, the debentures fell to 110% with the new issue barely trading at par. A dividend of 7% forecast for 1914 did not lift the share price. When the dividend payment was cancelled because of the outbreak of World War I, NGC's listing on the Berlin Bourse was also cancelled.[42]

Financial overview

In summary, NGC suffered significant financial losses until the turn of the century. The level of expenditure required to establish an organisation, infrastructure, and the cost of administration while acting as the government's agent were the primary cause for the negative cash-flow. After 1899 the *Reich* relieved the company from all government-related responsibilities Under the agreement NGC transferred land and inventory to the *Reich* for a consideration of RM4,000,000, payable in 10 equal annual instalments. NGC was obliged to expend the receipts inside four years on infrastructure in GNG. The company also agreed to renounced its land acquisition monopoly and other economic privileges. In return it received an allocation for additional 50,000 ha freehold in KWL and mining rights in the Ramu Valley.

Following the implementation of the agreement with the government NGC cleaned up its balance sheet. The write off in the value of infrastructure assets (RM7,532,100) corresponded with the reduction in equity. For the period 1 April 1889 to 31 March 1899, the cost of governing GNG amounted to RM1,467,029 in salaries and allowances (bureaucrats, judiciary, collection of taxes and duties, postal services, policing and harbour master expenditures). This was partly offset by income from customs duty, business tax, land registration, licence and harbour fees, court fines and income from labour hire (RM1053.530), resulting in a net cost to NGC of RM413,499. It was immaterial compared to the significant opportunity cost for not concentrating on the commercial development of the NGC. From 1885 to 1899 NGC spent RM14,971,962 against revenue of RM4,414,003. Added to the negative cash flow were capital expenditures for ships (RM595,550), machinery and other assets (RM261,290) and a capital loss of RM900,000 resulting from the investment in Astrolabe Compagnie.

Contrasting this, the BNG administration did not develop its protectorate into a colonial enterprise, nor did the British incur a funding shortfall. Rather, BNG accumulated £43,848 (RM876,960) in savings until Britain handed responsibility for the protectorate to the new Australian federal government on 1 January 1901. The surplus was attained through guaranteed annual funding by the Victorian, New South Wales and Queensland colonies and by the British government, and significantly through under-spending in infrastructure development and healthcare services.[43]

Share capitalisation of NGC as recorded in the balance sheet (value in RM)

Year	Ordinary Shares		Preference Shares		Bonus Shares		
	Issued	Par value	Issued	Value	Gratis	Bonus	Value
1886	800	1,250			20		5,000
1887	800	2,750			20		5,000
1888	806	3,750			20		5,000
1889	811	4,750			20		5,000
1890	814	5,750			20		5,000
1891	814	6,250			20		5,000
1892	814	7,000			20		5,000
1893	814	8,000			20		5,000
1894	814	8,750			20		5,000
1895	814	9,500			20		5,000
1896	814	10,000			20+15		5,000
1897	814	10,500			20+15		5,000
1898	814	11,500			20+15		5,000
1899	814	12,000			20+15		5,000
1899	8,042	500			6+3	9+8,042	500
1904	8,042	500	3,958	500	6+3	9+3,958+8,042	500
1908	8,042	500	3,000+3,958	500	6+3	9+3,958+8,042	500
1911	667	500	7,375+6,958	500	6+3	15,000	500
1912	663	500	7,379+6,958	500	6+3	15,000	500
1913	663	500	7,379+6,958	500	6+3	15,000	500
1914	7,000	500	15,000	500	6+3	Nil	500

Disastrous Ventures

Notes

1   Until Germany assumed full administrative responsibility for GNG on 1 April 1899, this German sphere of interest was called Schutzgebiet der Neu Guinea Compagnie (Protectorate of the NGC). Germany annexed the Marshall Islands in 1885 and, under the 1886 convention with Britain, the phosphate-rich island of Nauru. In 1899 Germany ceded to Britain the Solomon Islands—other than Buka and Bougainville—under the Samoa agreement of 1899, and bought the Micronesian Islands of Palau and the Marianas (excepting Guam) from Spain

2   H. Münch, *Adolph von Hansemann*, pp. 229–31; *NKWL* (1885) Heft i, pp. 2–4

3   P.G. Sack, *Land between Two Laws*, pp. 127–8

4   The founding members of NGC were: G. von Bleichröder, Albert von Oppenheim, Dr F. Hammacher (*Reichstag* members), Henckel v. Donnersmarck, Kraft Friedrich Prinz zu Hohenlohe-Öhringen, Prince Hatzfeldt zu Trachenberg, Count Stolberg-Wernigerode, Herzog von Ujest, E.W. von Siemens, L. Ravené, Senator Achelis from Bremen and the Consul-General of Sydney C.L. Sahl in Sydney (*Die Disconto Gesellschaft, Denkschrift zum 50 jährigen Jubiläum 1851-1901*, p. 231; O. Finsch, 'Deutsche Namensgebung in der Südsee', *Deutsche Erdkunde*, (1902) Nr. 1, p. 45). By drawing on German constitutional law, Article 11 all powers of the *Reich* outside its borders are vested in the Emperor (P.G. Sack, *Phantom History*, pp. 275–87)

5   'Limited Liability Act of 11 June 1870', W. Oechelhäuser, *Die Nachteile des Aktienwesens und die Reform der Aktiengesetzgebung*. Hansemann to Bismarck 15 Feb. 1885 (RKA 1001:2395, pp. 1–4 and 26ff); Hansemann to Bismarck, 17 Dec. 1885 (RKA 1001:2396, pp. 1–3); Hansemann to Albert von Oppenheim, 25 Jul. 1885

6   *Prussian Landrecht* is the law of the Prussian State invoked by Frederick William II in 1794; the law was enforced where it did not conflict with local custom. It remained in force until 1900

7   'Statute of the Neu Guinea Compagnie', 26 Mar. 1886, §§ 1. 5, 7, 8, 10, 11, 12, 18 & 19 (*NKWL*, [1886] Heft. ii, pp. 31–49)

8   Münch, pp. 228-9; NGC shareholders list EGM on 29 Dec. 1887 (RKA 1001:2402, pp. 9 & 44-3). *NKWL* (1886) Heft. ii, pp. 30–49, iii, pp. 78–9; Jb (1887), p. 2; Sack & Clark (1886–87) p. 3–4

Jb (1929/30) p. 1; C. Beck, 'Neu Guinea Compagnie', *Südseebote* (1918) p. 52. P. von Schwabach, senior partner in S. Bleichröder Privat Bank, joined NGC's supervisory Board in 1904. E.R. Stern, *Gold and Iron: Bismarck, Bleichröder, and the Building of the German Empire*, pp. 542–3; Münch, p. 229; Sal. Oppenheim Jr & Cie, 'Die Kolonialen Unternehmungen', *Archiv des Bankhauses Oppenheim*, vol. 112. L. Gall, D.D. Feldman, et al., *Die Deutsche Bank 1870–1995*, pp. 259–70

Carl Lauterbach (1864–1937) received his doctorate in botany from the University of Heidelberg in 1889. From 1889 to 1891 he study and collect flora and fauna specimens around the globe. The taxonomy of his discovered genera comprised 300 plants of the phanerogamous, 100 plants of the cryptogamous group, numerous geological samples and some 100 arthropodan species

Friedrich Hammacher (1824–1904) was foundation member and president of the *Deutsche Kolonialverein* and *Reichstag* member in 1885 (Schnee, vol. ii, p. 15)

Paul Preuß (1861–1926) received a doctorate in natural science from the Humboldt University in Berlin. He participated in scientific expeditions in Cameroon between 1886 and 1898, and in West Africa he also worked as Station Manager. From 1898 to 1900 he travelled South America for the *Kolonial Wirtschaftliches Komitee* (Committee for Economic Development in the Colonies) to study tropical agriculture on the American continent (Schnee, vol. iii, p. 101)

9   J. Loag and O. Häsner prepared the business plan the years 1902 to 1912 (Jb [1901/02] p. 1)

10   The German government paid NGC in 1927 RM5,350,952 in restoration (*Liquidationsschaden*), NGC Jb (1927/28) p. 5

11   *DKBl.* (1915) pp. 288–9

12   (RKA, 1001:2941, p. 74)

13   Jb (1887) pp. 7 & 30–1, (1890) p. 39; Sack & Clark (1886–87) p. 8; *NKWL* (1887) Heft ii, pp. 93–4.

14   Jb (1889) p. 3; Sack & Clark (1888–89) p. 35.

15   KWLPG share register, 6 Feb. 1892 (R1001:2425, pp. 51–2)

16   Prospectus, pp. i–iv, share register A-C, 27 Oct. 1891 (R1001:2427, pp. 64–5)

17   Jb (1895/96) pp. 3 and financial accounts (Sack & Clark [1895–96] p. 117; *NKWL,* 1896, p. 4)

18   Jb (1896/97) p. 28

19   'Geschäftsreglement für die Vereinigte Verwaltung im Schutzgebiet der Neu Guinea Compagnie und Astrolabe Compagnie' (RKA 1001:2422, pp. 17ff; *NKWL* (1896) pp. 4–6, 1897, pp. 12–13)

20   Jb (1892/93) p. 3; Sack & Clark (1892–93) p. 71. S.G. Firth, *New Guinea under the Germans,* p. 31

21   Jb (1893/94) p. 5; Sack & Clark (1893–94) p. 89

22   Jb (1894/95) pp. 2–3; Sack & Clark (1894–95) p. 105. 'Vertragsabschluß zwischen dem Reichskanzler und NGC', 13 Mar. 1896 (RKA, 1001:2944, pp. 10–14 & 119–30)

23   'Agreement' §§1–11, pp. 1–6, assets and inventory schedules A and B, pp. 7–9. (RKA 1001: 2941, pp. 119–32). Compare Sack (*Land Between Two Laws,* p. 100, and Firth, p. 40)

24   Letter to NGC shareholders (15 Sep. 1896, p. 10-30). The information in the P & L accounts does not correspond with the statement in the letter. The amount was RM359,482 for 41 months. BNG's 1894/95 accounts showed revenue of £5,110, expenditure of £21,563, compared to NGC's revenue of RM520,878 (£26,044),expenditure of RM1,055,887 (£52,794) (AR-BNG, pp. 33–35; Jb [1894/95] pp. 18–30)

25   (RT, 1895–96, Anlageband, No. 378); AA-RKA- to Kolonialrath, 25 Sep. 1896 (RKA 1001:2941)

26   The government set up the Colonial Counsel (KR) on 10 Oct. 1890 (*Reichs Gesetzblatt (=RGbl*) p. 179). Members were appointed for three years. The presiding member was the RKA Director. The KR provided advice on issues referred to it by the RKA. The advice given by the KR was not binding on the government (Schnee, vol. ii, p. 338)

27   The government appointed NGC shareholder and Board member, Simon Alfred von Oppenheim, to the KR in 1897 (Sal. Oppenheim Jr & Cie, 'Die Kolonialen Unternehmungen').

28   Jb (1895/96) p. 2; Sack & Clark (1895–96) p. 117; *NKWL,* (1896), Heft i, pp. 7–8

29   *NKWL,* (1898), pp. 75–81

30   Bundesrath, 8 Feb. 1900 (*DKBl,* (1900), pp. 275ff; DKG, vol. 5, pp. 22–30; Jb (1898/99) p. 1, Sack & Clark (1898–99) p. 147)

31   RKA 1001:2941, p. 148. The agreement became effective on 1 July 1900

32   Jb (1898/99) pp. 1 & 25; Sack & Clark (1898–99) pp. 147 & 165

33   Schnee, pp. 329–31

34   The issue should have been 8,200 shares. An audit of the original shares revealed that RM79,000 was unaccounted for (Jb [1898/99] pp. 2–3; Sack & Clark [1898–99] p. 148)

35   Jb (1901/02) p. 9, Jb (1902/03) p. 26 (The Government withdrew the licence on 7 Feb. 1908, *DKBl* (1908), p. 209), Jb (1903/04) p. 6 & P & L statement

36   *DKBl.* (1904) 15 Aug., p. 515; Jb (1903/04) p. 11, (1904/05) pp. 11–12

37   AGM 27 Mar. 1908, Jb (1907/08) pp. 7–8; Jb (1910/11) pp. 8 & 15

38   Jb (1913/14) pp. 3-5 & 13. Preuß, *Die Kokuspalme und ihre Kultur,* p. 541

39   The issue price was 107.5% of the par value. (Jb [1912/13] pp. 20–1; *DKZ,* Nr. 10, 1914, pp. 187–8; *DKBl,* 11, June 1, 1914& 1915, p. 288). ' NGC Satzung Änderungen' (*DKB.* 1914, pp. 485–6)

40   Kolonialbank leaflet, 26 Jan. 1914

41   KR, (1914), pp. 185–6 & 376

42   Kolonialbank, 25 July 1914, A. Neumann, *Kurs-Tabellen der Berliner Fond-Börse* (1918)

43   1BNG revenue—other than government funding— from 1 July 1888 to 30 June 1899: £67,949 (RM1,358,980); expenditure for the same period: £270,785 (RM5,415,700)

CONTENTIOUS EMPLOYMENT POLICIES

> Whatever policy may be laid down by the Imperial Government or even by the Colonial Government, the average African will be much, perhaps most, affected by his European rulers on the spot, by the sort of men his District Commissioner and his several technical officials are. That is to say, you cannot discuss colonial policy and administration without giving a good deal of attention to colonial officials. Their quality and their morale are primordial.[1]

The eminent Australian statesman, Sir Walter Crocker, was well qualified to pass this judgment on the importance of the 'men on the ground' in colonial Africa. Of course, it did not matter in which continent the colonial enterprise was, nor did the level of funding matter as much as the colonial Governors and commissioners believed. If the quality of personnel did not meet the demands of the situation, failure was inevitable. On the German side, eyewitness reports hailed the soundness and experience of the British administration under Lieutenant-Governor William MacGregor while deriding their own. Hans Blum wrote of his experience in GNG in 1897–98 and compared the 'disastrous fifteen years' of administration by NGC with that of BNG under MacGregor. GNG 'consumed' 11 Administrators, four of whom died during the administrative control of NGC. While BNG had its share of administrative changes, MacGregor had the leading role from the founding of the Colony in 1888 until the end of 1897. With the exception of the Queensland sugar-cane growers who labelled MacGregor a 'nigger lover [who stifles] the legitimate trade of the white man', there was almost universal acceptance and praise for this extraordinary man. Magistrate Monckton regarded him 'as the most formidable man he had ever met'. Comparing him to the likes of 'Cromwell, Drake, Caesar or Napoleon', he noted that 'only once in my life, have I felt that a man was my master in every way, and that was when I met Sir William MacGregor'.[2]

No such claims were forthcoming for German administrators while GNG was under the control of NGC. Blum was not alone in his derogatory assessment on Imperial Judge and NGC Administrator George Schmiele, who was finally dismissed by NGC after more than 8 years' service in GNG. Schmiele in response arrogantly claimed: 'not a single person of the 600 employees he saw coming and going renewed his employment contract'.

While Schmiele's outburst was hyperbole, typical of a NGC officer who dosed his anger with daily consumption of spirits, NGC employment conditions were contentious. The inability to cope with frontier conditions caused employees to air their frustration in open letters to the government. Many staff were unable to complete their contracts for reason of insanity (*Tropenkoller*)—'gone troppo' as they called the condition across the border in BNG—malaria or dysentery, all outcomes of şometimes even brief stays in GNG. The high salary differential between senior and junior employees and the strict control—and regular rejection—of personal expenses, poor provisions and accommodation, were also reasons for breaking employment contracts. This high staff turnover came at a considerable economic cost to NGC.

Method of hiring personnel

The economist Karl Helfferich observed in 1905 that the German government, with little experience in colonial affairs, had to implement a system of colonial administration over the first 20 years of its existence.[3] During the first 14 years in GNG this responsibility fell to NGC. Here, the company had to employ suitably qualified personnel for both administration and infrastructure development in order to build a viable colonial enterprise. This was a huge challenge for Adolph von Hansemann and his fellow Directors since they had no experience in such work. The German bureaucracy, unlike the role models of England and The Netherlands had no history in colonial administration. Some members of the Foreign Office, naval officers, explorers and traders had tropical experience; only a handful had visited New Guinea. How then did Hansemann staff his management team to develop his protectorate and provide an administration as required by the government under the charter?

The first employees of the company came from a pool of people Hansemann knew from his association with DHPG or were engaged on the recommendation of heads of government departments or universities. It seems that NGC did not advertise its employment requirements in newspapers. Otto Finsch, Oscar Stübel, Carl Ludwig Sahl, Bartoholomäus von Werner and Georg von Schleinitz—all known to Hansemann—applied for the position of NGC Administrator in New Guinea. The enthusiasm shown by these eminent officers and explorers started a ripple effect from which other appointments evolved.[4] For instance, Finsch hired the experienced explorer Carl Hunstein and recommended the engagement of the Arctic explorer Captain Eduard Dallmann (SS *Samoa*) who in turn signed on first mate Hinrich Sechstroh and chief engineer, Lars Nielsen, in Bremen. Second mate, Peter Hansen, the second engineer, cook, seamen (4), stokers (3), and a boy—all Germans—signed on in Sydney.[5] The appointment of Jacob Weißer to the position of Administrator in the Bismarck Archipelago can also be linked to both Finsch and Dallmann, or to Imperial Commissioner von Oertzen. Weißer was purser on SMS *Hyäne* when the ship visited Mioko in 1884–85. The Polish-born Stanislaus Kubary would have been known to Finsch, Schleinitz and Hansemann because of his well-documented South Sea exploits with Godeffroys. Kubary, in turn, saw to it that his brother-in-law, David Yalliot, a carpenter by trade, was employed as overseer in Konstantinhafen.[6] Moritz von Hippel was 68 years old—not 80 years as claimed by NGC's Dr Otto Schellong—when he joined the company. Hippel, an engineer with many years' experience in Mexico, owed his position with NGC to his son-in-law, Administrator von Schleinitz.[7]

As a rule, explorers and scientists knew of each other through professional associations and personal connections. The explorer Fritz Grabowsky was a school friend of Dr Schellong; Dr Carl Schneider, Dr Carl Schrader, Graf Joachim von Pfeil were members—von Schleinitz the past chairman—of the Society for Geography, Berlin. They were also associate members of the Geographical Society, Hamburg, where Bismarck's adviser Heinrich von Kusserow was prominent. Dr Max Hollrung was a chemist with a keen interest in photography. He became the first person in GNG to record scientific discoveries on photographic plates. After working in north Australia for the German-Australian botanist Baron Ferdinand von Müller, 60-year-old Wilhelm Persieh joined NGC as a botanist in 1887.[8] The first scientific foray into GNG by the botanist Dr Carl Lauterbach was self-funded. The intrepid explorer was subsequently appointed leader of two NGC gold expeditions. The agriculturalist Ernst Tappenbeck chaired the committee for the development of GNG in the German Colonial Society before joining NGC. The medical doctor, economist and agriculturalist Dr Hermann Kersting, who joined the Lauterbach–Tappenbeck expedition, was a government scientist. He was well known in the Berlin scientific community for his work in the Congo Basin.

As an estate owner, Hansemann saw value in people who were connected to farming and forestry. At the beginning of 1885, he approached Minister for Agriculture and Forestry Baron Lucius von Ballhausen with a request for candidates for GNG,[9] and in June 1886 Hansemann wrote to Bismarck requesting assistance for the recruitment of non-commissioned army officers. Lieutenant (ret.), forester Richard Mentzel, Second Lieutenant (ret.) Rudolph von Oppen, Second Lieutenant (ret.), forester Otto Elle and landscape gardener Ernst Schollenbruch were some of the first NGC employees in the protectorate. Hansemann also approached War Minister General Schellendorff for recommendations of retired officers.[10] Notwithstanding government responsibility to provide military protection, Hansemann required suitable Prussian sergeants to train an indigenous police force; he also believed that their military training would ensure diligent reporting to Berlin on a regular basis. Thus, with the exception of Hans Arnold and Eduard Wissmann, NGC administrators in GNG until March 1899 were current or past officers in government departments or had served with the Prussian military. Imperial commissioners, judges and other legal personnel were appointed by, and responsible to, the chancellor. NGC was responsible for the cost of their employment, but had little involvement in the selection except that Hansemann had some influence over the appointments.

Under the company statute, the board of Directors had to authorise employment contracts exceeding 12 months or where the annual salary exceeded RM5,000.[11] Otherwise, the executive Directors were authorised to engage personnel without first seeking approval of Hansemann, E. Herzog or A. Lent. The extent to which the Administrator could employ personnel in the protectorate was stipulated in the management guidelines:

> The engagement of staff is generally conducted by the Board because, for the time being, the Administrator will not find suitable German personnel in the Protectorate nor will he have the opportunity to check the level of competency. The Board will take into consideration the numbers and positions recommended by the Administrator for employment. If suitable personnel are identified by the Administrator he is permitted to engage same, subject to funding within the

budget, and provided employment does not extend beyond one financial year, nor attracts an annual salary exceeding 3,000 Marks.[12]

While Hansemann oversaw the drafting of the statute and the Administrator's instruction manual, he readily ignored them when it suited him. As the majority shareholder, he engaged, dismissed and instructed NGC staff on a whim. His fellow Directors seemed unperturbed by his autocracy. Without reservation, Eckardstein-Prötzel and other board members retrospectively approved his commitments on behalf of NGC. Although authoritarian, Hansemann expected resourcefulness from his managers. He considered it quite appropriate for Captain Dallmann to sign on his friends Sechstroh and Nielsen, and in Sydney the Dane Peter Hansen and 13 seamen, and for Dr Finsch to hire Carl Hunstein and his Scottish carpenter mate in Cooktown. George von Schleinitz engaged the German architect Höppner as carpenter, the North American farmer A. White and the German farmer Hermann Rieck in either Sydney or Cooktown. Schleinitz's successor, Reihold Kraetke, hired Richard Parkinson from Queen Emma's Ralum plantation. Hansemann reasoned that it made sense to engage people from the neighbouring Dutch and British colonies rather than employ inexperienced bureaucrats from Germany. Administrator Wilhelm von Puttkamer, for instance, hired the tobacco farmers Lutz and Schoevers from Surabaya. In nearly all cases Hansemann approved the employment of overseas staff retrospectively.[13]

In 1890 NGC subsidiaries KWLPG and A-C engaged more than 20 European planters from the Dutch Possession of Sumatra for cacao and tobacco plantations on Astrolabe Bay. A former Prussian officer, Curt von Hagen, had established a tobacco plantation company in Deli, Sumatra in 1887. The venture failed but Hagen was hired by Hansemann in 1893 to manage A-C. He followed the two German-born planters, Woldemar von Hanneken and Carl Rohlack, four assistant planters (Maschmeyer, Brückner, Baumann and Camillo d'all Abacco) and the accountant Max Goebel. The Netherlands East Indies Acting Consul Eduard Wissmann, employed by the tobacco planter and trader Blützingslöwe & Co. in Surabaya from 1880 until 1889, moved to Finschhafen in July 1890 to take up employment with NGC as Acting Administrator.[14]

Employment motives

Economics and speedy promotion in the government system were generally the driving force behind German migration. Schellong, for example, had to pay off the debts he had incurred during his studies for a medical degree.[15] In contrast, the President of DKG, Count Hohenlohe-Langenburg, told the South Sea veteran, Eduard Hernsheim, in 1886 of his desire to be appointed the first Administrator of GNG. He believed that he should 'lead the German people to unexplored shores where he would set the foundations of a new Germany'. Hernsheim dismissed the verbose Hohenlohe-Langenburg as a rambling drunk.[16] Where German nobility and senior bureaucrats—often one and the same—claimed national interest as the reason for seeking employment in the colonies, it was often pretence; future career prospects were improved in the highly structured Prussian bureaucracy and the desire to earn money would have ranked foremost in making the decision to go overseas.[17]

Apart from Anthony Persieh (60), Moritz von Hippel (68), Georg von Schleinitz

(51), Richard Parkinson (45), Paul von Below (50), Reinhold Kraetke (42) and Johann Kubary (41), the colonial aspirants were young, generally barely over twenty years, inquisitive, often the family black sheep, and always short of money.[18] In Ludwig Kindt's mind, young men should serve time in the colonies. In his guidelines on 'Immigration of German farmers in Java' he wrote: 'disappointed parents wished all too often that they could send their wayward son to the tropics. I, for one, have always recommended New Guinea a panacea for such wayward youth'.[19] To some extent, Heinrich Schnee's father agreed with Kindt. To him, colonies were places for dropouts; not a launching platform for the career of a qualified lawyer like his son.[20] Notwithstanding well-meant fatherly advice, Schnee accepted the appointment of imperial judge at Herbertshöhe in December 1898.[21] Whether it was the rebellious nature of youth, the urge to venture far away from home and earn some money on the way or, as he claimed later, a carefully laid out career path, the decision worked for Schnee. For the young lawyers, George Schmiele and Albert Hahl, the appointment as Imperial Judges in GNG led to that of Administrator-cum-Governor. Schmiele climbed to the top position in GNG quickly. The *Reichskanzler* appointed him to the position of imperial judge for the Bismarck Archipelago on 15 November 1886. When Bismarck agreed to Hansemann's request to combine the offices of Administrator and Imperial Commissioner under Fritz Rose on 1 November 1889, Schmiele's position was transferred to the Colonial Department of the Foreign Office (AA-KA). This move allowed Rose to remain an imperial judge while also advancing to the position of imperial commissioner for the Bismarck Archipelago. Thus, within 3 years he bettered his annual salary of RM4,000 in Germany to RM15,000 plus expenses, free housing and servants in GNG.

On 1 September 1892 NGC confirmed Administrator Schmiele's annual salary of RM30,000. For Schmiele, the good times lasted until January 1895 when his contract expired. While in charge he wielded power and enjoyed prestige: both went to his head. Regarded as pompous and disliked by the natives and Europeans alike, he left GNG disillusioned and a physically sick man. Schmiele died of malaria in Batavia on 3 March 1895 en route to Germany.[22]

Assessor Hahl had a similar but lasting rise to the top in GNG. He quit a secure but lowly paid job with the Ministry of the Interior in Bavaria to accept a position with the AA-KA in Berlin. In January 1896 the government appointed him imperial judge at Herbertshöhe. By accepting this position, Hahl took charge of the protectorate's 'eastern jurisdictional and administrative district', and thus leapt three or four rungs up the career ladder. Indeed, an equivalent position in Germany may have been out of reach altogether. To advance to just the position of lower court judge in Germany would have taken at least 10 years. Possibly a greater attraction was the remuneration package—at least four times his likely salary in Bavaria. With the death of the Acting Administrator Curt von Hagen on 13 August 1897, Hahl performed the duties of Imperial Judge and Administrator for a month. At the age of 30, on 12 October 1899 he was appointed Vice-Governor of the Caroline Islands. After the retirement of Governor Rudolf von Bennigsen on 10 July 1901, Hahl was in charge of GNG and remained so until 4 May 1915. Earning an annual salary of RM36,000 plus expenses, free housing and servants, he was by far the highest paid officer in GNG.[23]

H. Schnee, Imperial Judge and Acting Administrator in GNG and Samoa from 1898 to 1903, was appointed imperial Governor for German East Africa in 1912. During his tenure in the AA-KA, Schnee advanced to the rank of High Privy Councillor (*Wirklicher Geheimrath*), which was senior to that of a Governor in German protectorates. While his base salary in Berlin was slightly higher than that of a Governor, the position did not carry the same level of pecuniary benefits, independence and prestige. It, therefore, comes as no surprise that Schnee accepted a slight demotion in rank for a more prestigious position in German East Africa.[24]

The opportunities in the colonies for law graduates who had not yet sat for their second state examination were considerably higher than at home, where many lawyers scrambled for the few positions. Where governments paid trainee lawyers at all, their salary was no higher than RM1,500, the remuneration of an articled clerk. Setting aside age and experience, the government seemed to have had little reservation in appointing a law 'Assessor' or even an articled clerk as an imperial judge in the protectorate. While Schmiele, Hahl, Schnee and Mellien were fully qualified lawyers, M. Krieger, F. Hasse and R. Jordan were appointed imperial judges in GNG even though they had not sat their second state examination.[25] The authority for such rapid promotion was entirely the privilege of the German chancellor who appointed the judges in the protectorates.

The doctor, Otto Schellong, was indebted to his landlady, grocer, tailor and everyone else who had lent him money before he finished university. The oldest of 10 children, Schellong grew up in a small town in East Prussia were his father was the parish pastor. 'At that time', he reminisced, 'the code of honour that existed between the creditor and the student demanded repayment of the debt once a permanent position was attained'. Medical registrars earned a paltry amount of money in 1885. The monthly salary of a junior doctor in the hospital of Königsberg was RM100 less RM70 for board. According to Schellong, the balance of RM30 was not enough to make ends meet, let alone pay off debts. He decided that 'a fat salary from NGC would pay off his commitments while giving him the opportunity to expand his somewhat limited horizon at the same time'. Schellong received an annual salary of RM6,000, NGC's highest level of remuneration after the Administrator whose annual salary was RM27,000 plus allowances according to Schellong.[26]

The position of Inspector-General would have earned Reinhold Kraetke RM8,000–10,000 annually. Hansemann offered an annual salary of RM33,000—the equivalent of a ministerial salary—for Kraetke to accept the Administrator's position in GNG. Rather than terminating his employment with the *Reichspost,* Kraetke applied for leave of absence. In his letter to the postmaster-general he advised of his interest in the development of the German colonies and his desire to gain some overseas experience. Widening his professional horizon earned Kraetke a fat salary during his 18 months stay with NGC. The experience in GNG also advanced the former inspector to the ministerial position of secretary of the post office in 1901.[27]

Low pay and harsh conditions were reasons for leaving the Prussian Army; unpaid debts were grounds for dismissal. German colonies gave insolvent officers the opportunity to discharge personal debt. Hans Blum was discharged from the Prussian Army for dishonouring personal debts. He may have regarded the position of assistant on a plantation in GNG below that of a lieutenant yet he signed on, most likely for financial reasons. The annual pay of a first lieutenant was RM1,080 plus rations. In GNG Hans Blum earned up to five times that amount. Similar examples are Lieutenants Paul von Below and Wilhelm von Puttkamer. The former joined the Dutch colonial army before setting up his own coffee plantation on Java. Below sought employment with NGC after 33 years in the Dutch East Indies. The reasons for the change were economic: at the end of the 19th century the good times for coffee crops had passed.[28]

Puttkamer was the son of Bismarck's minister for the interior, Robert von Puttkamer, who was also Otto von Bismarck's brother in law. While the Puttkamers belonged to the landed class, Wilhelm left the army seemingly indebted. His brother Jesko von Puttkamer became the long-serving Governor of German Kamerun and Togo, Wilhelm advanced no further than managing a failed tobacco enterprise in GNG.[29]

Curt von Hagen, an officer in the Prussian Army, retired from the services, after a riding accident, to venture to Sumatra in 1886 or 1887 and become a tobacco planter. Crop failure and the global tobacco crisis of 1891 bankrupted his company. In 1893 he became Astrolabe Compagnie's (A-C) General Manager and on 9 October 1896 Acting Administrator of NGC.

Stefan von Kotze, a grandnephew of Otto von Bismarck, was a rebel. A naval cadet, he was discharged in early 1887 without reasons given. He arrived in Finschhafen on 3 August 1887 to work as an assistant on Kerawara Station for RM4 per day plus food and quarters. Captain Dallmann signed him on as second officer on SS *Ysabel*, but he lasted only a few weeks. Dallmann sacked him because 'he gossiped too much' instead of working. Kotze then applied to the government in GNG for work but was rejected. Surprisingly, he stayed with NGC until the end of 1893 when he left on the *Ysabel* for Java. 'I survived the malaria hole Finschhafen', he wrote in his recollections, 'because I treated fever with copious amounts of alcohol, not swallowing quinine as prescribed by the company doctor.' Spirits was the remedy that 'I also applied to deal with the many regulations of NGC'.[30]

Whereas adventure was a driving force, money would have been the main enticement for most seeking employment with NGC. During the 1880s and early 1890s unemployment remained high in Germany and kept middle-class children at school for longer. The result was a group of educated paupers. Salaries for university graduates were no higher than those for tradesmen and barely higher than for clerks during the 1890s: the starting salary for an engineer was about RM1,500 p.a. while the average remuneration for clerical workers of all ages was RM2,400. This was in stark contrast to company managers whose salary range in Berlin was about RM6,600 plus annual performance bonuses of between RM1,500–14,000.[31]

Disastrous Ventures

Germans ventured to the Dutch East Indies in the late 1870s to participate in the buoyant tobacco market, with plantation managers paid between 3,000 and 5,000 Dutch Gulden (RM5,000–8,000) plus a 10% share in the profit. When the tobacco and coffee markets collapsed in 1891 and 1895 respectively, this expertise became available for GNG, with many personnel seeking employment with NGC or A-C.[32]

NGC staff with overseas experience and the occupational mix

Stewart Firth made a sweeping statement when he wrote: 'men with no experience of the Pacific suddenly found themselves living on the edge of the New Guinea jungle'.[33] Yet at least one-third of NGC employees recruited between 1885 and 1898 had worked, lived and explored in non-European parts of the globe. Some had specific knowledge of the South Sea. While this experience did not guarantee performance, NGC employees who were recruited in Australia, the Dutch East Indies or in Africa had a start on the colonial dreamers, German economic migrants or frustrated Berlin bureaucrats, who had barely travelled beyond the boundaries of their provinces. Of the 266 European staff, 93 are known to have had overseas experience. This is a surprisingly high figure for a company or country without colonial history.

Hansemann pushed for early and quick mobilisation of personnel; so much so that NGC's first doctor, Schellong, made a diary entry on 25 January 1888: 'again, no less than 11 staff have arrived from Germany; we are questioning with some despair, what all these people are supposed to do for now! They need to move on to other locations at present as we have no accommodation left'.[34] Schellong had a point; with only Finschhafen and Hatzfeldthafen and one out-station established, NGC employed 95 staff between 1885 and 1888 and a further 65 by March 1891. The first contingent of employees comprised 25 (26.3%) men who had previously worked overseas, eight of whom had local knowledge. Driven by the labour requirements of the cacao, tobacco and cotton plantations on Astrolabe Bay and in the Bismarck Archipelago the overseas experienced contingent rose to 68 (42.2%) out of a total of 161 by March 1891. From April 1891 to the end of 1898 NGC and its subsidiaries KWLPG and A-C employed an additional 102 staff. This group included 37 (36.3%) personnel with considerable overseas experience. But tropical experience alone did not automatically translate to performance. Of the 101 'expatriates', seven completed their employment contracts, 27 extended and the balance were murdered, died from disease or were unwilling to fulfil the agreement.[35] Captain Dallmann, who took recuperation leave in November 1893, was disappointed when NGC did not extend his contract for a fourth time.[36] Generally, resignations were due to unfulfilled expectations or sickness. Rather than finding an El Dorado people faced an overregulated administration and a malaria-infested environment. Adherence to copious company procedures and the filing of reports were for many akin to catching dysentery or coming down with malaria; and all were reasons for leaving GNG.[37]

Some regarded the tyranny of distance as a blessing. The 40-day turnaround of a telegram between Jaluit and Berlin was judge Eugen Brandeis' reason to 'do as I please, not as Berlin instructs me to do'[38]. Others saw little benefit in being provided with free housing and subsidised food. Accommodation was a do-it-yourself task until prefabricated quarters were erected. The cost of living was regarded as too high when measured against remuneration levels. Equally, the administration often had little alternative but to dismiss personnel for anarchic behaviour, including addiction to alcoholic liquor or plain incompetence. The majority left because of ill health.[39]

From 1885 to 1898 NGC employed on average 19 new staff annually. The most active employment period was from 1886 to 1888 when 29 additional staff were sent to GNG while 25 left for various reasons during the same period. The highest intake was in 1887 when 36 employees arrived. A peak staff intake was reached again in 1891 when 34—mainly Sumatran tobacco planters—were engaged to work on the Astrolabe and Jomba Plains. The mortality rate was also the highest during this period. A malaria and dysentery epidemic in Finschhafen was the chief factor in the loss of 30 European lives (15 NGC staff) during 1890–91. Other high levels of European recruitment occurred in 1886 (26) and 1898 (22). When NGC was assured of the *Reich* assuming administrative responsibility for GNG from 1 April 1899, legal officers and other senior NGC personnel were given the option to have their employment transferred to the government or their contract terminated. NGC was now concentrating on plantation work and trading. This required people with skill sets other than government administration.

The first arrivals in GNG were seamen, explorers, administrators and planters, with the last making up the by far largest group. Ten German foresters and landscape gardeners arrived in GNG in 1886 and 1887 to set up experimental gardens in the tropical environment. It was Hansemann's idea to produce a supply of seeds in these gardens so that settlers could start preparing their land soon after they arrived. When NGC was unable to attract the German-Australians it had targeted, the company moved from land developer to agriculturalist. This change in business direction brought 10 new planters to GNG in 1888 and more in 1891 when A-C commenced with large-scale tobacco plantations. While most of these employees came from Sumatra, Australia and German East Africa, the recent arrivals included five tobacco farmers from the Grand Duchy of Baden in southwest Germany. The 13 scientists engaged by NGC did not devote their time solely to exploration. H. Geisler, Grabowsky, Hunstein, Kubary, Pfeil and Tappenbeck were predominantly devoted to developing stations.

Carpenters, blacksmiths and divers made up the largest group of 22 tradesmen that were recruited between 1885 and 1888. Save for a butcher, all nine tradesmen employed between 1891 and 1898 were carpenters. Surprisingly, no skilled workers were engaged during the following six years. Similar to the trades, 11 of 20 engineers were employed during the first 4 years. In view of Hansemann's priority to sell agricultural land to settlers, this group included surveyors and civil engineers. When the company moved from land developer to agriculturalist only two surveyors were recruited, with mechanics now in demand for maintaining equipment and saw mills.

Salary structure

NGC adopted many of the business processes of Hansemann's Disconto Gesellschaft (D-C). NGC ranked salaried staff on three levels: (1) Directors, administrators and senior managers (*Gehobener und höherer Dienst),* (2) lawyers, accountants and engineers *(Mittlerer Dienst),* and (3) tradesmen and clerks *(Einfacher Dienst).*

It appears that the payroll journal of NGC and its subsidiaries did not survive World War II. Occasionally, the remuneration levels of senior staff are mentioned in annual reports. Budget proposals were submitted to NGC's board by management for the 1887/88 to 1894/95 financial years. Likewise, remuneration budgets for 1891/92 to 1893/94 are in A-C records.[40]

Did the employment and salary policies of NGC produce the quality of men Sir Walter Crocker regarded vital for a successful administration? Hansemann blamed management for much of what went wrong. Staff took ill because of alcohol abuse, settlers would not come to KWL because the infrastructure had not been established, food went off because of careless handling and staff broke employment contracts because they could not cope with the frontier conditions. But rather than change his *modus operandi* and adopt a slower pace, Hansemann remained unwavering. He told Bismarck that his employees were well aware that GNG was pioneering work and that this meant hardship.[41]

Wedged between the Prussian judicial system and a procedure-driven NGC head office in Berlin, the Finschhafen (later Friedrich Wilhelmshafen) administration was anything but self-regulating. With the centralised management structure imposed on the administration in GNG, NGC operated as a government bureaucracy. Employees were numbers not individuals; filing reports and filling in statistics was seen to be as important as establishing infrastructure or setting up plantations. In the eyes of Hansemann NGC staff were paid well and he expected his employees to attend to all requirements without questioning the rationale of his decisions. Ernst von Tappenbeck declared that Finschhafen was never more than a meeting place for an army of officers (*Heer von Beamten)* who had nothing better to do than produce paperwork for Berlin.[42] Otto Finsch claimed that station managers were obliged to keep 15 different journals during the first year of operation.[43] Eduard Hernsheim called the company's administration a farce and sought the foreign office intervention. In 1888, he recalled, the initial enthusiasm and energy of all of the employees gave way to such discontent that the suggested change of name from Finschhafen to *Schimpfhafen* (Whinge Harbour) seemed fully justified.[44]

But the principal, Hansemann, was certain NGC could only be managed by enacting ordinances and regulations, with instructions issued to the Administrator for maintaining visibility and accountability. It was this plethora of regulations—often impractical—that led to disillusionment and ridicule from NGC staff. Governor Schnee observed that Hansemann tried to run GNG from Berlin as if it was a feudal estate in Brandenburg.[45] Many NGC employees cited Hansemann's paper trail as the reason for resigning. The false expectations NGC's office manager in Berlin, Hans Arnold, instilled in eager applicants was probably as strong a contributor to low staff morale as was the unsuitability of the candidates for the remote tropical environment. Clearly, management was empowered to employ staff and make decisions within their ambit of financial responsibility. For Schleinitz to refer the free issue of tropical attire for Schellong's assistant to Berlin for decision is a meek excuse for not simply saying 'No'. Similarly, to brush off the German-Australian architect Höppner's request for the same daily allowance as paid to German expatriates by referring the matter to Berlin showed a lack of leadership. Within a rigid Prussian reporting system, Schleinitz was hiding behind Hansemann. A former naval officer he was reluctant to make decisions without first referring matters to his 'Commander in Chief' in Berlin.[46]

The difficulties NGC faced became clear very quickly. Low wages, poor housing, spoiled food, excessive paperwork, malaria and dysentery, a bachelor existence and boredom contributed to an unhappy setting among the Europeans. That Hansemann did not ever visit GNG is understandable because of both his advanced age and his responsibilities as executive chairman of his bank; but the failure of any of the other NGC Directors to visit GNG during 14 years of company rule was imprudent.

Tappenbeck complained that a young lawyer was paid up to RM30,000 to work in the NGC administration while experienced planters were paid a miserly RM15,000 [and that] such a low salary would not even attract second-raters, let alone 'experts who would command respect in Berlin.'[47] Setting aside Tappenbeck's exaggeration, the differential between salary levels 1 and 3 was cause for a high rate of attrition. Even though NGC staff earned more than they would have received in Germany, the living expenses in KWL were high and the conditions poor. All staff were obliged to use the company's mess and food could only be purchased from the company stores at cif prices. While every NGC employee had access to free medical treatment, junior employees did not enjoy generous allowances or have access to a pension fund, were not given leave of three to four months for every three years of service and were not sent on recuperation leave without losing benefits. In the opinion of the low salary earners, senior managers were selected for positions because of their connections in Berlin, not for their ability.[48]

However, the large salary gap between the ranks did not translate into contentment among the well-paid officers. One exception to this was Schellong. The surgeon, who served out his contract, believed that staff complaints were much ado about nothing. He was happy enough with his position: 'I have plenty of medicines to last me for two years [and] with my salary of RM6,000 I am the highest paid person [in GNG]. I am in a position to buy whatever I need compared to the lower paid staff'.[49] While Schellong considered the submission of a monthly medical report to Berlin an easy task, he agreed that the burdensome paperwork hopelessly overloaded the middle and lower ranks. Imperial Commissioner W. Knappe observed the inadequacy of the foodstuffs, which 'consisted of little more than salted meat and mouldy bread'. Captain Dallmann of the *Samoa* informed Hansemann's office in Berlin: 'most of the vats on the brig *Lübken* arrived half empty, and what was left was mouldy. Also, the sugar had turned into castor on arrival, the canned herrings no longer resemble fish and were cast overboard, and, due to shipping damage, many of the vinegar and syrup vats arrive empty'.[50] Schellong found that canned food cost twice as much as in Germany, and was either not available or substandard. Tappenbeck and missionary

Disastrous Ventures

Johann Flierl went as far as suggesting that the death of 14 NGC staff in Finschhafen in 1890–91 was caused by substandard Australian tinned meat, or, as Flierl observed, through high alcohol consumption. Whatever the cause—bad food, alcohol, sanitary conditions or other stress related factors—the European death rate at Finschhafen over 6 weeks in 1891 was a most significant set-back in the development of NGC.

Schellong's successors were more strident in their criticism. During the first 14 years NGC employed 16 doctors. Of these, seven (Danneil, Dempwolff, Fuhrmann, Frobenius, Hoffmann; Schellong and Wendland) served out the contracted period, with Danneil, Dempwolff, Hoffmann and Wendland serving a second term. Dr Weinland and Emmerling died after 20 months in GNG, in March 1891 and February 1893 respectively. Hagen (malaria) and Schlafke (tuberculosis) retired from NGC because of ill health, and Hermann and Diesing left due to disagreements with Schmiele.[51]

A well-documented quarrel between Dr Ernst Diesing and the Stephansort plantation manager Friedrich Wandres led to the resignation of two NGC officers. The doctor was concerned that Wandres was authorised to diagnose the state of health of labourers on his plantation. When Diesing learnt that Wandres caned coolies to encourage them to recover quickly he requested Acting Administrator Hugo Skopnik to intervene. Wandres in turn accused the doctor of wrongly diagnosing a female coolie. He complained that Diesing was quick to send coolies back to Singapore for recuperation and that his incompetence was costing the company dearly.[52]

Skopnik, who could not afford to lose either his plantation manager or doctor, advised Diesing that neither he nor Wandres were authorised to examine females without the knowledge and agreement of the Administrator.[53] In total disagreement with such ruling, the offended doctor lodged a complaint in the local court against Skopnik and Wandres. Citing mismanagement and mistreatment of workers Diesing also lodged his complaint against Friedrich Wilhelmshafen Administrator Joseph Loag and manager Oskar Haesner. For this 'audacity', Diesing was fined RM40 and, to even out matters, Wandres was fined RM10 for showing disrespect towards the medical profession. When the manager disregarded the charge and continued with the flogging of workers, Diesing resigned from the company, but not before taking his complaint to Judge P. Boether in Friedrich Wilhelmshafen and to NGC's Directors in Berlin.[54] To make matters worse for Skopnik, Wandres' assistant planter, Hans Blum, supported Diesing's accusation by citing 15 transgressions by the 'upstart' Wandres, who used his authority over workers in a 'most brutal and perverted manner', and who 'sexually abused female workers in a degrading manner'. Blum accused Skopnik, of tolerating this shameless conduct without showing the slightest concern of misappropriation, drunkenness and personal enrichment by cutting employee's entitlements.[55] Hansemann instructed his Administrator to contain the quarrel 'as it will only serve the opponents of NGC who have repeatedly accused company officers of the gross ill-treatment of coolies'. The agreement with the Batavian authority prohibited flogging and a new recruitment embargo could be invoked if the matter became widely known. Hansemann was also concerned that the complaints could undo the agreement to transfer administrative responsibility to the government.[56]

Apart from these concerns, Skopnik had to deal with an ongoing health crisis, the accusations of a young doctor and the demands of developing a profitable plantation industry. He, like everyone else in GNG, was aware that planters hit labourers from time to time. The workers were often lethargic and behaved like obstinate children. It was customary in Germany for army cadets to be caned for disobedience, just like as naughty children were.[57] For this reason Skopnik did not admonish Wandres. Rather, he joined his manager and sued for libel. He accused Blum of being 'a blatant liar who had not done an honest day's work since arriving in the protectorate'.[58] Judge Boether found in favour of the litigants. Wandres, in the judge's opinion, did no more than 'strike a recalcitrant, lazy and dirty Chinese with a twig a couple of times'.[59] He fined Blum RM80 for insolence towards a senior officer of NGC.

As farcical as this episode seemed, it highlighted the tension between NGC staff at all levels. The highly structured administrative and judicial process NGC had implemented was dysfunctional. The legal and procedural demands on the administration, NGC's commercial interests and the ethical conduct required of medical practitioner were at odds. A doctor could examine a recruit but he could not decide whether he was fit to work; this rested with the NGC station manager.[60] The uncontrolled outburst of two junior employees demonstrated inexperience and stress. It may have been as a result of their state of health, overuse of alcohol, a poor diet or monotonous social intercourse. No doubt it would also have been because of concern for the local and coolie populations. Clearly the lack of leadership, complex rules and minutely prescribed procedures were not conducive to successful colonisation. After handing over administrative responsibility to the government, NGC concentrated solely on its commercial ventures. Ethics aside, Hansemann now saw the value of Wandres in his ability to recruit coolies for the Stephansort plantation. Because of 'the

Table 6.1 **Annual salaries for Officers and staff of the NGC in 1888 (£1 = RM20).**

Position	Base Salary (£)	Housing	Travel (£ per diem) land	sea	Allowance (£/s/d)
Chief Administrator	1,500	free	16	8	50 / 0 / 0
Imperial Chancellor	750–1,000	free	12	6	15 / 0 / 0
Imperial Judges	500-750	free	8	4	15 / 0 / 0
Medical Officer	300-500	free	8	4	9 / 0 / 0
Station Manager	300-500	free	8	4	9 / 0 / 0
Engineer	250-300	free	4	3	9 / 0 / 0
Captain of a steamship	400-250	n.a.	n.a.	n.a.	n.a.
Master of a sailing vessel	180-250	n.a.	n.a.	n.a.	n.a.
Tradesman	110-150	free	n.a.	1	0 / 4 / 6
Seaman	15-36	n.a	4	n.a.	0 / 4 / 6
Clerk, Orderly	30-42	free	4	1	0 / 4 / 6

*Land and coastal travel in GNG. The allowance was paid during sick leave

**Travel within and outside GNG. Food and beverages are included in passenger fares.

***Until 1888 servants and furniture were supplied by NGC in lieu of an allowance.

Disastrous Ventures

Table 6.2 **BNG annual salaries/entitlements for officers and staff (£-Stg.) BNG 1890–1897.***

Position	Base Salary	Allowance	Housing
Lieutenant-Governor	1,500	200	free plus servant
Government Secretary	500	200	free plus servant
Private Secretary	300	Nil	free
Chief Judicial Officer	1,000	200	free plus servant
Resident Magistrate	500–300	50	free plus servant
Medical Officer	300	50	free
Master of the Merrie England	300	victuals/uniform	n.a.
Chief Engineer	252	victuals/uniform	n.a.
Seaman	84	victuals/uniform	n.a.
Commandant	250	20 plus uniform	free
Government Agent	250	20	free
Storekeeper	150	10	free

*AR-BNG, 1890, p. 15; 1897, pp. 40–1.

good relations the plantation manager entertained with both the Batavian and Straits governments, the accusations against him must have been groundless', he informed the AA-KA in February 1899.[61] When the government assumed administrative control of GNG on 1 April 1899 Wandres became police commissioner in Stephansort. Remuneration packages for employees of the British and German administrations in 1903 remained aligned. As can be seen in Tables 6.3 and 6.4 German officers benefited from the payment of a colonial allowance, while Australian officers, who made up the vast majority in BNG, benefited from working closer to home.

Despite the complaints, NGC was competitive in its remuneration policy. Java was the benchmark and experienced planters would not have transferred to GNG if the pay discrepancy was as large as Tappenbeck had suggested. As the comparison in Tables

Table 6.3 **Government salaries and allowances in GNG - 1910 quoted in £1-Stg (£1 = RM20)***

Position	Base Salary	Allowance	Salary increase after 3 years	Housing
Governor*	900–1200	600	n.a.	free plus servant
Imperial Judge	315–465	300	30	free plus servant
District Judges	210–360	270	25	free plus servant
Magistrates	155–360	235	25	free
Medical Officer	150–360	235	25	free
Station Manager	165–300	180	20	free
Engineers/Surveyor	135–240	165	20	free
Tradesmen and Teacher	90–165	165	20	free
Assistant Manager	90–165	165	20	free
Policeman, Clerk, etc.	70–105	120	15	free

*Schnee, (1920) vol. I, pp. 458–62; Imperial Treasury, 'Draft of Budget, 1915' (NAA, Canberra, AA G2 and F255, 1914 Budget Papers, p. 3). **includes £300 p.a. entertainment allowance.

6.1 and 6.2 show salaries for NGC staff and officers of the BNG administration were comparable. While medical officers received a higher salary in GNG, the judiciary, government secretaries and seamen were paid better BNG. Schellong observed: the low wages paid to NGC seamen led to many jumping ship in the Australian ports.[62]

The avid critics of NGC, and particularly of Hansemann, were not isolated. In 1889 *DKZ* condemned NGC for employing too many officers, which the paper believed was not warranted for the six Stations under its management However, considering NGC was responsible for government administration, infrastructure and plantation development until 31 March 1899, the 51 land-based personnel the company employed on average for this period was, if anything, low.[64] The ratio of NGC staff to workers was 1:34 (30 personnel in administration and justice, 12 medical and 45 technical and port staff, and an average workforce for the period of 5,188 labourers). By comparison BNG and Papua average numbers of bureaucrats from 1888 to 1914 was 1:27 (53 in administration, 34 in justice, 2 in medical and 16 technical, harbour and marine staff, and an average workforce for the period of 2,867 Papuans). All that can be said on this comparison is that BNG managed a much lower number of labourers with fewer medical and technical staff.

NGC did not fail in attracting capable staff. It payed appropriate salaries, provided medical care, endeavoured setting reasonable living standards. Where NGC failed was in the management of its staff. Hansemann came across as an aloof, process-driven banker. When the Administrator's office produced 10-fold sets of instructions on how to address officers and who could sit at whose table at dinner, it is no wonder that Schellong noted in his diary that valuable men would leave GNG as soon as they had saved enough money for the return fare: 'the rapport between senior management and the company's employees was not congenial' and Directors would be well advised 'to devote more time in keeping their capable staff', Dr Schellong observed.[65]

Table 6.4 **Salaries and entitlements for Officers and staff in Papua – 1910 (£-Stg.)**

Position	Base Salary (£)	Allowance	Housing
Lieutenant-Governor	1,250	200	free
Chief Judicial Officer	1,000	200	free
Deputy Chief Judicial Officer	800	225	free
Government Secretary	700	50	free
Private Secretary	225	Nil	free
Treasurer	450	50	free
Resident Magistrate	350–450	20	free
Government Surveyor	400–425	20	free
Chief Medical Officer	425	20	free
Commandant	300	uniform +20	free
2nd Clerk	175	6	n.a.

*AR-Papua, 1910, pp. 46–51 and 132–37

Notes

1   W.R. Crocker, *On Governing Colonies*, p. 119

2   H. Blum, *Neu Guinea und Der Bismarck-Archipel*, pp. 37-9 & 52; Jäckel, 'Die Neu Guinea Compagnie', pp. 50–1; C.W.A. Monckton, *New Guinea Recollections*, p. 140; H.N. Nelson, 'The Swinging Index', *JPH* 13, (1978) p. 130; G. Souter, *New Guinea: The Last Unknown*, p. 60; L. Lett, *The Papuan Achievement*, pp. 44–5, C. Price & E. Baker, 'Origins of Pacific Island labourers in Queensland, 1863–1904', *JPH* 11 (1976) p. 73

3   K. Helfferich, *Zur Reform der Kolonialen Verwaltungs-Organisation, Introduction.*

4   Hansemann to Bismarck, 18 Aug. 1885 (RKA 1001:2408, p. 38). See H.J. Hiery, 'Die deutsche Verwaltung Neuguineas 1884-1914' in *Die Deutsche Südsee 1884 -1914*, pp. 280–1. O. Finsch, 'Wie ich Kàiser Wilhelmsland erwarb', *Deutsche Monatsschrift für das gesamte Leben der Gegenwart* (1902) pp. 580–4 & 728–9

5   O. Finsch, *Samoafahrten*, p. 6

6   *NKWL* (1891) Heft i, p. 4

7   *NKWL* (1886) Heft ii, p. 61. O. Schellong, *Alte Dokumente aus der Südsee*, p. 85. Baumann, *Biographisches Handbuch*, p. 149

8   Schellong, p. 9 & 33; *Mittheilungen der Geographischen Gesellschaft in Hamburg von 1885–86*, vol. 1887, pp. 349, 351–2. Persieh had the protea *Hakea Persiahana* named after him.

9   (RKA 1001:2408, pp. 3–5, 17 & 30)

10   *NKWL* (1885) Heft i, pp. 6–7; Hansemann to Bismarck, 26 June 1886 (RKA 1001:2408, p. 59); Hansemann to Schellendorf (RKA 1001:2670)

11   ' Statute of the Neu Guinea Compagnie', 29 March 1886 (*NKWL* [1886] Heft ii, p. 41)

12   NGC, 'Instruction für den Landeshauptmann' §32, pp. 18-9

13   Employment contracts (RKA 1001: 2402, p. 6; 2408, pp. 67ff ; 2410, pp. 9 & 103); *NKWL* (1888) Heft iv, p 179; (1890) p. 4; Sack & Clark (1889–90) p. 48; H. Münch, *von Hansemann*, p. 358

14   Russel to Caprivi, 3 May 1890, Hansemann to Caprivi, 7 Oct. 1890 (RKA 1001:2409, pp. 54 & 77); *NKWL* (1892) Heft i, p. 32

15   Schellong, pp. 9–10

16   Hohenlohe-Langenburg: 'Das deutsche Volk unter Vortritt seiner Fürsten, wie einst die Heerscharen unter Hengist und Horsa nach neuen Gebieten zu führen, und dort ein neues Deutschland zu gründen' (E. Hernsheim, *Lebenserinnerungen*, p. 139)

17   C. Krause, *Die Aussichten des Kolonialdienstes*, p. 23

18   O. Dempwolff, 'Ärztliche Erfahrungen in Neu-Guinea', *Archiv für Schiffs- und Tropen-Hygiene*, 2 (1898) p. 136. Baumann, *Biographisches Handbuch Deutsch-Neu Guinea, passim.*

19   L. Kindt: 'Oft wünschen auch betrübte Eltern ein misratenes Pflänzchen in tropischen Boden zu verpflanzen. [Ich] habe daher die Besserungsbedürftigen stets auf Neu Guinea verwiesen' (L. Kindt, 'Auswanderung deutscher Landwirte nach Java', 1903 p. 10; *DKZ*, [1893] Nr. 1)

20   H. Schnee, *Als letzter Gouverneur in Deutsch-Ostafrika*, pp. 9–10. H. Gründer, *Geschichte der deutschen Kolonien*, p. 236

21   *DKBl* (1899) Nr. 4, p. 124

22   Jb (1890) p. 14; (1893/94) pp. 4–5; Sack & Clark (1893–94) p. 90. H.J. Hiery, 'Die deutsche Verwaltung Neuguineas in der Südsee, 1884–1914', pp. 282–8; P.G. Sack, *Phantom History*, pp. 182ff

23   Colonial Secretary B. Dernburg (1907–10) earned RM100,000 p.a.

24   Schnee, *Als letzter Gouverneur in Deutsch-Ostafrika*, pp. 102–3

25   *DKZ* (1890), 4 Jan., p. 16; Hansemann to AA-KA, 28 Nov. 1892, AA-KA to Hansemann, Dec.1892 (RKA 1001:2410, p. 12–8); H. Fenske, 'Bürokratie in Deutschland', p. 13. A. Lotz, *Geschichte des Deutschen Beamtentums*, p. 605. W. Apitzsch, 'Das Verwaltungspersonal der NGC', p. 70

26   Schellong, pp. 1–10 & 32

27   Kraetke to Stephan, 3 Nov. 1887 (RKA 1001:2409, p. 8, 2402–06, pp. 58ff). Lotz, pp. 604ff;

28 RT 10, Legislativ Periode. 1898/1900, Band 2, p. 1481. (RKA 1001:2410, p. 36ff); M. Messerschmidt, 'Die Preußische Armee' in G. Papke & W. Pretter, *Deutsche Militärgeschichte*, p. 32; L. Kindt, 'Auswanderung deutscher Landwirte nach Java', *KP&KW*, 4 (1903) p. 13; Blum, p. 97

29 Apitzsch, p. 66; Schnee, ed., *Deutsches Kolonial-Lexikon*, vol. iii, p. 117

30 RKA 1001:2409, p. 84; 'Marineverordnungsblatt', xviii, vol. 4, 1 March 1887, p. 24; P.M. Pawlik, *Von Sibirien nach Neu Guinea. Kapitän Dallmann und seine Reisen 1830-1896*, p. 124; S. von Kotze, *Aus Papuas Kulturmorgen*, p. 226

31 J. Kocka, 'Unternehmungsverwaltung und Angestelltenschaft' in W. Conze ed. *Schriftenreihe des Arbeitskreises für moderne Sozialgeschichte*, pp. 90, 92, 164–5, 263, 473–4, 493–4, 498 & 542

32 W. von Hanneken, *Sumatra*, pp. 63ff and 'Eine Kolonie in der Wirklichkeit: Ilusionsfreie Betrachtungen eines ehemaligen Stationsvorstehers im Schutzgebiet der NGC', *Die Nation* (1895) pp. 54ff

33 S.G. Firth, *New Guinea under the Germans*, p. 24

34 Schellong, p. 187

35 The standard contract period was 3 years. NGC Statute §28 later increased to 4 years (Jb [1893/94] p.5; Sack & Clark [1893-94] p. 90). Employment contracts with planters from the Dutch Indies were generally for 5 years (Jb A-C, Dec. 1892, p. 7, RKA 1001:2427, pp. 7 and 189). L. Kindt had a 10-year contract, dissolved after one year, *Hamburgischer Correspondent*, 25 Dec. 1895 (RKA 1001:2425, p. 62). Jb (1887 to 1899), *NKWL* (1892) Heft i, p. 26 & (1893) Heft i, p. 22

36 Dallmann in a letter addressed to Sister Auguste Herzer in FWH on 7 Mar. 1894 blamed Administrator Schmiele for his downfall, Museum Schloß Schönebeck. See Pawlik, pp. 175–6

37 Firth, *New Guinea under the Germans*, pp. 24 & 27; S. Firth, 'The New Guinea Company 1885–1899: A Case of Unprofitable Imperialism', *HS.ANZ*, XV (1972) p. 362; P.J. Hempenstall, *Pacific Islanders under German Rule*, p.165

38 D. Spennemann, 'An Officer, Yes; but a Gentleman? A Biographical Sketch of Eugen Brandeis', *Pacific Studies*, 21 (1998]); S. von Kotze, *Aus Papuas Kultormorgen*, p. 226

39 The known average annual European death rate, including children, from 1886 to 1899, was 6.17% (*NKWL* [1886 to 1898]); see M. Davies, *Public Health and Colonialism*, pp. 209–15

40 PV-NGC 4 Apr. 1887, 9 Mar. 1888, pp. 58 ff, 10 Apr. 1889, pp. 132 ff (RKA 1001:2402, pp. 17ff). 6 Apr. 1892, pp. 98 ff, 24 Apr. 1893, pp. 154 ff (RKA 1001:2403–4). A-C Budgets (RKA 1001:2427, pp. 166–75; 2428, pp. 35–43)

41 Hansemann to Bismarck, 2 Jan. 1886 (RKA 1001:2408, pp. 42–3)

42 Tappenbeck, p. 31

43 O. Finsch, 'Wie ich Kaiser Wilhelms-Land Erwarb', *Deutsche Monatsschrift*, (1902), p. 742

44 P.G. Sack & D. Clark, *Eduard Hernsheim South Sea Merchant*, p. 200 and *Die Neu Guinea Compagnie in Kaiser Wilhelmsland und im Bismarck-Archipel*, p. 17); see Schellong, p. 31

45 Schnee, *Als letzter Gouverneur in Deutsch-Ostafrika*, p. 26

46 Schellong, p. 31, n. 11 & p. 88 (RKA 1001:2408, pp. 67–9)

47 E. Tappenbeck, p. 35

48 NGC, 'Allgemeine Bestimmungen der Neu Guinea Compagnie, 1891', §§ 10 & 11; Schellong, p. 201, n. 65; Blum (p. 52); Kotze, p. 22.

49 Schellong, p. 32 and 'Die Neu-Guinea Malaria einst und jetzt', *Archiv für Schiffs- und Tropenhygiene* (1901) p. 303.

50 Dallmann to NGC, 11 Jan. 1886 (Dallmann notes, Schloß Schönebeck). See Pawlik pp. 109–10

51 *NKWL* (1886) Heft iv, pp. 128–33; (RKA 1001:2977, pp. 11–31). Davies, pp. 31–2; 72–5 & 174–5. Schellong, *Alte Dokumente*, p. 41; Tappenbeck, p. 31.J. Flier, 'Die Bedeutung der Alkoholfrage für unsere Kolonien', *Kolonialpolitik und Kolonialwirtschaft*, X (1908) p. 546. (Frobenius was employed by the *Rheinische Mission* and worked as locum for NGC in Stephansort)

52 Wandres to Diesing, 9 Feb. 1898, Wandres to Skopnik, 5 May 1898 (RKA 1001:2414, pp. 6 & 89ff)

53 Skopnik to Diesing, 26 May 1898 (RKA 1001:2414, p. 57ff)

54 Diesing to Board of Directors, 25 Aug. 1898 (RKA 1001:2414, p. 38)

55 (RKA 1001:2414, p. 78ff)

56   Hansemann to Skopnik, 16 Oct. 1898; Blum to Hohenlohe, 9 Feb. 1899 (RKA 1001:2414, pp. 49ff)

57   Hempenstall, p.166, Firth, pp. 109–10 & 120, H.J. Hiery, pp. 3–6

58   Wandres, 16 Dec. 1898 (RKA 1001:2414, pp. 104–6)

59   Skopnik to Hansemann, 3 Aug. 1898 (RKA 1001:2414, p. 51)

60   NGC, 'Verordnung betreffend die gesundheitliche Controlle der im Schutzgebiet der Neu Guinea Compagnie als Arbeiter angeworbenen Eingeborenen, 18 Oct. 1890' (RKA 1001:2301, pp. 79–82)

61   Hansemann to AA-RKA 27 Feb. 1899 (RKA 1001:2414, p. 145)

62   Schellong (p. 100)

63   *DKZ,* (1889) Nr. 2, p. 13

64   J.W. Spidle, 'The German Colonial Civil Service' (Stanford, 1972)

65   Schellong, p. 138

IN SEARCH OF WORKERS

7

NGC's decision to become an agriculturalist rather than a pure land developer resulted in a need for experienced plantation staff. German-Australians were no longer encouraged to migrate to GNG. Approximately 1,100 Germans lived in the Dutch East Indies in the early 1890s, and Hansemann now targeted the German and Dutch coffee and tobacco planters in Java and Sumatra.[1]

Initially the company expected New Guineans to meet its labour needs, with artisans from Java to fill the gap in carpenters and other trades. However, with a few exceptions, Papuans were unwilling to work outside their village districts and were not interested in engaging in any long-term indentures. In any event, there were not many of them, and by 1889, the NGC workforce was overwhelmingly Melanesian, engaged from the Bismarck Archipelago and the Solomon Islands, with only a few Javanese and Peranakans employed then for special tasks. The smallest group of workers came from a few Papuan tribes in KWL. Here, only the Jabim (Yabem) people on the Huon Peninsula met the expectations of the Germans.[2]

A group of NGC Jabim workers ca. 1899 (F. Hutter, *Das überseeische Deutschland,* p. 555)

Disastrous Ventures

Coolies from The Netherlands East Indies and the Straits Settlements

The move into tobacco farming in 1891 necessitated a radical change in NGC's labour policy. Tobacco cultivation required skills that were not available in GNG. According to Dutch statistics, 469,534 Chinese lived in the Dutch East Indies in 1890. Starting in 1864, crimping agents in Singapore recruited thousands of Chinese coolies for the Dutch tobacco planters. After 1888 and until 1931, some 305,000 Chinese landed in Belawan-Deli, the major port in northeast Sumatra. The majority came from Swatow and Hong Kong where the Association of Deli Planters had recruiting offices.[3]

The well-known expertise of the Sumatran coolies was in particular demand for the careful harvesting, curing, grading and packaging of the tobacco leaves. The Dutch East Indies was therefore the obvious choice for NGC to attract such workers. To obtain these skills, Hansemann requested assistance from the AA-KA to gain approval from Batavia and the Straits Settlements for the importation of coolies on a large scale. A collapse of the price for Sumatran tobacco wrapper provided NGC with the opportunity to engage experienced coolies, *tandils* (overseers) and plantation managers from the Dutch colony.[4]

Before the Dutch agreed to the German request, NGC needed to meet the requirements of Dutch colonial law; the NGC 'Ordinance regarding the Maintenance of Discipline among the Coloured Workforce' of 22 October 1888 did not satisfy the requirements of the Batavian administration. The Dutch insisted that the rates of pay valid in Java and Sumatra were also applicable to coolies on indenture in GNG.[5] Conditions such as category of work, contract duration, rates of pay, hours of work, messing, accommodation, transportation and repatriation had to be declared on Dutch contract forms. Each labour contract required validation by a Dutch government official before embarkation. Compliance with employment conditions, contracted to a third party or working directly for NGC, remained the responsibility of the administration in GNG.[6] Because local workers received five strokes for the smallest misdemeanour, a further condition of employment was the renunciation of corporal punishment. In compliance with Dutch law, the Batavian administration sought assurances from NGC not to cane workers from its colony and to lodge a 10% advance payment on wages prior to the departure to GNG of any coolie. With the implementation of this requirement by NGC on 19 December 1889, the Dutch Colonial Secretary Pieter E. Keuchenius recommended to Governor C. P. Hordijk of the Dutch East Indies to permit the recruitment of coolies for GNG.[7]

Apart from a handful of Chinese and Javanese NGC hired in Cooktown and Surabaya, and the coolies (79 Chinese, 1 *tandil* and 5 Kalimantan Malays) the former Sumatran planter Lutz had indentured in Singapore; the first 25 Javanese artisans arrived on 2-year indentures in Finschhafen in April and May 1890. Under the Batavia—NGC agreement some 100 Javanese arrived between July and September 1890 to work on the tobacco fields in Hatzfeldthafen.[8]

The importation of coolies was costly, both in monetary cost and in human life. Of the first 'cargo' of Chinese workers, the *tandil* and three coolies died before they embarked in Singapore, 5 died on the steamer *Ysabel* Captain Otto Schneider was at the helm of the steamer, and 13 perished after landing in KWL. In addition, 15 Melanesian and Javanese workers died from cholera shortly after their arrival on the plantation. Few coolies worked properly at all because of their opium addiction, which also heightened their susceptibility to infectious diseases. Johan Schoevers quickly repatriated the few who survived the cholera epidemic. According to this former Sumatra planter, the coolies had never worked on a tobacco plantation before and were therefore of no use to him at Hatzfeldthafen. Rose advised *Reichskanzler* Caprivi on 21 December 1890: 31 out of 57 Chinese were addicted to opium.[9]

The revelation of opium addiction did not come as a surprise to NGC. Since the early days of the Vereenigde Oost-Indische Compagnie (VOC) the importation of opium and the cultivation of *Papaver somniferum* (opium poppy) by licensed Peranakans had been a major source of income for the Batavian administration. When Hansemann advised Bismarck of the company's intention to commence large-scale tobacco cultivation in KWL, he drew attention to the indispensability of Chinese coolies and to the related opium problems. 'To attract more Chinese to GNG', he told the AA-KA, 'a continuing ban on the importation of opium may not be maintainable if a black market is to be avoided and if some level of labour output is to be achieved'. Two years later, the government issued NGC with a restricted licence for the importation and distribution of opium in KWL.[10]

The intake of Javanese and Chinese coolies increased moderately in 1891. On 27 October, Wilhelm Puttkamer transferred 250 Chinese from Sumatra and Java to Singapore for onward transportation by the NDL steamer *Nierstein* to Stephansort. NGC chartered the Scottish steamer *Devawongse* to deliver 436 Singapore coolies and 12 Totoks from Sumatra to Stephansort on in December. A similar number of planters and coolies arrived on the second voyage of the *Devawongse* during February 1892. A new agreement with NDL saw the Scottish vessel replaced by the SS *Schwalbe* and SS *Lübeck*. With the increased shipping capacity, 1,085 Chinese and 757 Javanese arrived in Stephansort from Batavia, Tanjungbalai and Singapore between June 1891 and March 1892. NGC's tobacco subsidiary, Astrolabe Compagnie (A-C), was now awash with coolie labour and NGC informed its shareholders with a measure of confidence, 'work has been energetically started on the plantations with the intention of harvesting a crop from all fields in 1892'. The optimistic forecast by NGC was short lived. A malaria and dysentery outbreak in 1891 had a devastating effect on both the European and the Asian workforce. A European-introduced influenza epidemic affecting the Melanesian workers was equally devastating.[11]

Notwithstanding efforts to bring the mortality and morbidity under control, the toll escalated. A new outbreak of smallpox occurred in GNG in June 1892. Introduced by a Javanese stoker on the *Lübeck*, the infectious disease first attacked the Melanesian workers at Stephansort and then spread to Erima village, Konstantinhafen, Gorima, now Maraga, and Jomba plantations. This epidemic on these A-C plantations killed 351 workers within a few weeks. Mortality along the coast of KWL was worst, with the local population of regions like Kelana Island all but wiped out.[12]

Influenza became endemic during the wet season; beri-beri never abated in the

Chinese population, spreading ultimately to the Melanesian workforce. Malaria and dysentery affected most workers, with an equally devastating effect on the white population. Other ailments of concern were elephantiasis, tinea, framboesia, intestinal parasites and the European-introduced smallpox, rubella, venereal diseases, and tuberculosis. The Rev. Isaac Rooney was particularly concerned about the 'disease-ridden natives returning to the Bismarck Archipelago from Queensland. 'The return of many men from Queensland, Fiji and Samoa' he noted to Rev. George Brown on July 5 1887, 'has not been an unmixed blessing … Contagious and epidemical diseases have been introduced by them and have carried off large numbers both on New Britain and New Ireland.'[13]

After the catastrophic losses of European life at Finschhafen in early 1891, Hansemann became particularly concerned at the loss of three experienced managers at Erima and the station manager at Maraga a few months later. Influenza and dysentery severely affected the workforce from December 1891 to March 1892. During this period, 1,085 Chinese and 757 Javanese had arrived in KWL. On 30 June 1892, the company accounted for only 950 coolies. The high loss of life was a severe setback for A-C; it was also a slap in the face for Hansemann, who had told his shareholders 12 months earlier that the wellbeing of the staff and the workers was the most important issue for A-C if the tobacco grower was to become successful.

NGC and A-C were often remiss in recording the number of arrivals, departures, sickness and mortalities of its coolie workforce. The available data for Jomba indicates that 313 Chinese arrived in the second half of 1891. Of these, 110 were capable of performing some duty 8 weeks later. By Christmas 83 had died.[14] The decision to defer planting on two out of four stations until the 1893 season highlighted the impact of mortality and morbidity of labour on A-C's plantations. In April 1892 the company reported a 2,396 strong workforce on its four Astrolabe Bay plantations; only 1,570 workers registered with A-C's labour supplier NGC the following year.[15] With the death rate reaching 35% the Astrolabe Bay tobacco fields became NGC's charnel house. W. von Hanneken graphically illustrated this when reporting in 1895:

> [T]he epidemic was so severe that 'the sick lay with the pigs underneath their huts as they were too weak to climb the few steps to their bunks, with the corpses left for a considerable time with sick coolies before they were carried off to makeshift graveyards.[16]

Taking into consideration the number of recruits repatriated because of ill-health and the number of Chinese who fled into the jungle where they lived by looting and pillaging,[17] the death rate of 60% reported by the German Navy in 1903 may not have been far off the mark. This catastrophic mortality rate occurred despite the commissioning of a new European hospital on Beliao Island and a new hospital on Kutter Island for the Asian, Melanesian and Papuan workers. The number of physicians, nurses and orderlies was also increased. Dr R. Hagge transferred to A-C from NGC in early 1892 and Dr P. Emmerling arrived in Stephansort on 22 June 1891.[18] Dr B. Hagen worked in Sumatra for 13 years—including as government surgeon—before joining NGC on 12 November 1893. His knowledge of Chinese and Javanese customs qualified him to address dietary and sanitary requirements in the workforce. In addition, Dr W. Frobenius, who worked at the nearby Rhenish Mission, acted as locum in Stephansort. In order to prevent communicable diseases NGC inoculated all workers for smallpox before embarkation. Sister Auguste Hertzer three nurses an four orderlies staffed the native hospital on Kutter Island.[19] And NDL employed a health official in Singapore for its GNG service.

While the Berlin officials were gravely concerned, the new Administrator and former Imperial Judge in the Bismarck Archipelago, George Schmiele, did not seem overly troubled with the situation. He claimed that the Dutch suffered a much greater loss of life in their coolie workforce than was the case in GNG. In stating that 'to maintain a constant number of labourers over the period of one year, five times as many coolies had to be employed [by the Dutch] for the same period', Schmiele signalled his indifference to the human suffering. While the company admitted to the poor sanitary facilities and an insufficient supply of medication at Jomba and Stephansort, Schmiele put the casualty rate down to the poor quality of coolies the company received from the Dutch and the British colonies.[20]

Notwithstanding Schmiele's view, the high mortality rate in KWL prompted the Batavian administration to enforce an embargo on the recruitment of coolies for GNG. Articles by embittered former NGC/KWLPG employees Dr E. Herrmann, L. Kindt and R. Rohde ensured that no coolies would leave Java for the Protectorate from October 1892. The Dutch wanted to ensure the embargo was effective by requesting the co-operation of the Straits Settlements. The British Colonial Office was willing to oblige because the Dutch request met the demand by the Australian colonial governments to prevent Chinese migration to BNG via GNG.[21]

When tensions between England and France escalated over Siam in 1893 the British government sought support from Germany for its actions in Southeast Asia. This political atmosphere favoured NGC, resulting in a lift on the embargo on Chinese to GNG by the Straits government. Following the explicit undertaking by NGC that any vessel repatriating coolies from GNG would not enter BNG or Australia waters, the Straits government agreed to the immediate embarkation of 466 coolies for GNG. In all Singapore signed an agreement with NGC for 800 coolies within three years.[22]

The German consul in Batavia, Dr H. Gabriël, was also successful with an application for 180 coolies to leave for Stephansort on March 1893. When Gabriël applied for the recruitment of a further 200 Javanese in late 1893, the Dutch administration wanted to find out about the living and working conditions of their subjects in GNG before agreeing to this request. In the interim, on 24 April 1894, resident administrator, J. C. Kroesen of Surabaya reinstated the earlier embargo.

The Dutch official, H. B. Schmalhausen, visited Friedrich Wilhelmshafen in June 1894 to gain first-hand impressions of the conditions under which Javanese and Sumatran coolies worked.[23] The outcome was a 'clean bill of health'. Schmalhausen did not detect any mistreatment of coolies and concluded that the reports by Herrmann and Kindt were overstatements. 'No doubt coolies receive a clip behind the ears from time to time', he reported to his superior. 'However, even I, who cannot recall having beaten a Javanese since 1879, was tempted to hand out a few slaps in their face'.[24]

Government native hospital at Stephansort, ca 1910, (Goethe University Frankfurt a. M. No 014-4045-6)

A visit to Stephansort in October 1894 by Prince Hariman of Tidore and the Dutch East Indies health commissioner, Dr van der Horst, also produced strong approval.

NGC reported in 1893/94 that Dr van der Horst expressed satisfaction with the arrangements made by A-C for its workers in GNG. 'The hospitals in Friedrich Wilhelmshafen and Stephansort have surprised because of the high standard, [with] the conditions on Astrolabe Bay being declared exemplary, especially as regards coolie accommodation and medical amenities'. With only a 9-hour-working-day and a diet prepared to suit the physical and cultural needs of the coolies, Dr Horst found that the hitherto experienced high mortality rate was entirely due to the unhealthy and feeble state of the Javanese at their point of departure. In their meeting with A-C's Acting General Manager Carl Weydig, the visitors expressed surprise at the 'unexpected scale of development' found on Astrolabe Bay. 'Experience has shown that the climate of KWL suits strong Javanese better than the Melanesian labourers', according to the Dutch physician.[25]

With the help of the *Niederländische Kuhpockeninstitut of Batavia* the 1893 smallpox epidemic became manageable. NGC and A-C inoculated every employee, all workers—men, women and children—and villagers with the smallpox serum they had received from the Batavian health administration. In addition to quarantining, the Dutch authorities now screened every worker before travelling to the port of embarkation and again before embarking for GNG.

Following the Dutch commissioner's visit to Friedrich Wilhelmshafen, A-C's senior surgeon, Dr B. Hagen, left for Deli to study the prevailing health conditions on the Dutch tobacco plantations. Rather than finding exemplary conditions, Hagen concluded that the malaria-infected coolies in GNG arrived weakened from previous attacks of fever in Sumatra. The German physician observed that working conditions in GNG were generally better than in Deli. All Dr Hagen could recommend from his visit to Sumatra was to improve health screening before embarking for GNG.[26]

The 1895 tobacco season suffered from lack of rain in June–October and, according to NGC, because of the inferior quality of the coolies. Because of the persistently high mortality rate, NGC urged A-C in 1895 to repatriate all Chinese and Javanese who were unfit for regular work. It also advised of the temporary cessation of coolie importation. When NGC reported 494 fatalities in May 1896, the exasperated Directors pointed the finger at the feeble state of the Chinese coolies.[27]

A-C General Manager Curt von Hagen had already closed Jomba and Maraga on the understanding that the recruitment of coolies from the Dutch East Indies would not resume in the near future. The decision remained firm when the Straits government agreed unexpectedly to permit coolies to leave for GNG on a 3-year trial period. The change of mind in Singapore found resonance in Batavia. From December 1894 to October 1895, Dutch officials signed 897 coolie indentures, while the agreement with Britain delivered 503 Chinese during the same period for GNG. Yet sickness, death and early repatriations left A-C with only 308 Chinese and 406 Javanese in May 1896. Even though A-C reported some 100 Chinese and 50 Javanese staying permanently with the company,[28] the pervasive health issues led to the discontinuation of recruitment from the Netherlands East Indies and the Straits Settlements in 1896. After 5 years of quasi-independent operation, NGC closed the books on A-C on 1 November 1896 to take over the operational control of the plantations.[29]

Schmiele's view that KWL could only become economically viable with the mass migration of a people who were 'culturally further advanced than the uncivilised autochthones of KWL' was no longer accepted. A self-proclaimed expert on 'native' labour Schmiele claimed that the Javanese, Sumatrans and Ceylonese workers were more resistant to tropical diseases and, when engaged on piecework, cheaper than the Melanesians and Papuans. NGC replaced coolies with Melanesian and the highly regarded Jabim workers when it assumed managerial control of A-C in 1897.[30] It was a necessary economic decision. The Dutch tobacco planters had a large reserve of coolie labour. Unfit workers with recurring ailments were recorded (by tattoo) as unemployable. The Germans did not benefit from this procedure. The Directors of A-C advised in 1895: 'all endeavours to recruit capable people had been unsuccessful because of the particular restrictions under which recruited labourers are processed in Singapore'.[31] Directors blamed the venal conduct of the Chinese crimping agents as they kept coolies in spaces as cramped as eight square feet per man for 30 to 40 day voyages before delivering them to collection agents in Singapore.[32] The company also blamed sham medical screening and the switching of recruits during embarkations with worn-out, morally corrupt coolies for the malaise. These weak coolies, who were particularly susceptible to cholera and malaria, were the main reason for not meeting forecast profit in the opinion of the A-C.[33]

Hansemann also valued the entrepreneurship of the Chinese. He sought agreement from the British to allow Chinese from the Straits Settlement to settle in GNG if they so wished.[34] But because of the position taken by the Australian colonies on Chinese immigration, the British government, unlike the Dutch, did not oblige.[35]

Disastrous Ventures

A self-imposed ban by NGC reduced the number of Chinese coolies from a high of 1,085 in 1892/93 to a temporary low of 156 in 1898/99. Yet NGC was unable to operate its tobacco plantations entirely without them. Forty-six Chinese coolies and *tandils*, 84 Javanese workers and *mandurs*, and 40 Maeassars from the South Celebes arrived in 1898. Moreover, with the opening during the same year of a NGC agency in Hong Kong, 266 Chinese recruits arrived from the mainland for the first time.[36] Because of difficulties with the authorities in Swatow (Shantou) NGC managed to recruit only 372 Chinese in 1899/1900. Efforts to recruit coolies in Singapore for renewed tobacco planting at Jomba failed and the number of Chinese fell to 178 the following year, rising again to 306 in April 1901 with the arrival in April 1901 of 270 Swatow Chinese. With the termination by NGC of all tobacco cultivation in late 1901 collie recruitment had all but ended.[37] While the Chinese population in GNG had risen to 1,377 men, women and children by 1913, only 43 Chinese and 35 Javanese indentures were signed by NGC during the preceding years. E. E. Forsayth GmbH lodged an application in 1913 to contract 1,000 coolies from Java which Batavia rejected. When Berlin lodged a complaint with The Hague, the Dutch government reacted by ending the coolie transport to GNG altogether. It instructed Batavia not to engage in any new labour negotiations with GNG.[38]

The cost of coolie labour

Apart from the human dimension, NGC was acutely aware of the financial cost it incurred for medication, hospitalisation and early repatriation of feeble coolies. Its subsidiary, A-C, informed shareholders in December 1893 that the 'improvement of health is not only important, rather it is central to the survival and ongoing development of our enterprise'.[39]

Chinese from the Straits Settlements and later from Hong Kong and Swatow received generally less than the Javanese did; however, NGC paid both groups up to six times the benefits received by Melanesians and higher still compared to that paid to Papuan workers. Grabowsky paid the first group of Javanese carpenters and cooks hired by him in 1885 RM76–102/month and coolies RM20.50/month. Coolies earned considerably higher wages when performing specified tasks on a 'start and finish' basis. Preparing tobacco fields, planting, weeding, harvesting and curing formed part of such activities. An industrious coolie could earn up to four times the daily wage, often in much shorter working hours and it was, therefore, much sought-after work. Apart from wages NGC had to pay for recruitment fees, sea transport, food, medical, and housing costs. Independent recruiters received RM80–120/person— NGC agents in Singapore, Swatow and the Dutch East Indies received RM50–60/ person delivered to GNG.[40] The working hours of coolies varied. Until acclimatised new recruits worked for 2 hours in the morning and 2 hours in the afternoon. The working week was Monday to Saturday from 06.00 to 11.00 hours with a 2-hour lunch break and then until 18.00 hours; Sunday was a rest day. Approximately RM40 (10%) of the annual wage of the indentured worker had to be paid in advance at the point of engagement.[41] Dutch or British and German officials witnessed the indenture and ensured payments in Dutch Gulden or Straits dollars respectively. All money, including accrued interest, owed to the workers at the completion of their contract was paid in the presence of a NGC official (after 1898 a German government official). In the event an indentured worker went missing or died, the company paid all money accrued to either the next of kin or an official of the country from where the person was hired.[42] The advance of payouts after completion of contracts was not without problems either. Cayley-Webster, sailing on the SS *Lübeck* from Batavia to Friedrich Wilhelmshafen in September 1893 observed:

> Immediately after the vessel had left port, the Chinese contractor who had come from New Guinea to engage the coolies, proceeded to open a gambling saloon ... The thirty dollars which each coolie had received as an advance of wages was speedily transferred to his pocket.[43]

The charter of a *Lübeck*-class steamer was RM20,000–25,000/month. For the passage of a coolie not to exceed RM100, NGC calculated 500 coolies (1.5 m^3 space per coolie) on each of the six annual return voyages to Southeast Asia. When the company returned coolies because of their incapacity, utilisation space on the vessels increased albeit at a cost to NGC. Deceased coolies were cost savings of a sort: their burial was no more than a hole in the ground in GNG.[44]

NGC attained a minor benefit by retaining two-thirds of the wages paid to the Malays and Chinese in an interest-bearing account with D-G in Berlin, and until the introduction of German money in 1887, NGC derived a significant benefit by paying Papuans and Melanesians in truck (axes, hoop iron, smoking pipes and tobacco).[45]

The eating, living and working habits of the Javanese differed from the Peranakans and the Sumatran Chinese and the coolies recruited in Singapore, Hong Kong or Swatow. The company provided wooden-framed houses with plaited bamboo walls, atap roofs and earth-tamped floors for family units. Single Javanese or Chinese lived in large Malay houses.

NGC provided 30 catties (15 kg) of rice and 1 cattie (500 g) of salt, supplemented with tuber, taro corn and yams per month. The NGC 'Labour Ordinances of 15 and 16 August 1888' prescribed the recruitment, transportation, accommodation, medical care and victuals of coolies in minute detail. For example, bunks had to be 1.8 m long, 0.75 m wide and 1 m above ground. Headroom was not to be less than 1.25 m. Each labourer received a sisal mat, a blanket, pannikin, soup bowl and soap (25 g). The daily food ration during the voyage was 500 g rice, 1.5 kg yam or root crops and 4 litre of drinking water. They also collected 750 g of salted meat or dried fish, a clay pipe and 60 g of tobacco weekly.

Monthly wages (RM) of indentured and casual labour in KWL in 1889

Position	Wages	Provision	Sundries	Medical	Travel	Total p.a.
Chinese tandil	30–40.00	8.00	0.50	0.50	20.00	708–828
Chinese coolie	15–60.00	8.00	0.50	0.50	20.00	528–1,068
Journeyman	30–40.00	8.00	0.50	0.50	20.00	708–828
Javanese	27.00	8.00	0.50	0.50	20.00	671
Javanese woman	21.00	8.00	0.50	0.50	20.00	600
Melanesian*	6–10.00	6.00	0.50	0.50	10.00	276–324
Papuan*	3–8.00	6.00	0.50	0.50	5.00	180–240

*in this context Melanesians are from the Bismarck Archipelago and Solomon Isl. - Papuans are recruited in KWL

Disastrous Ventures

The same rations were applicable in the labour depôts of Finschhafen, Friedrich Wilhelmshafen and Herbertshöhe and, although not regulated by the ordinance, on the plantation. For variation, coolies could request bread, corn, fresh coconut and corn flour in lieu of rice, with tea, sugar and biscuits issued on special occasions. Each compound had a plot of land that was available for workers and families to grow their own vegetables and fruits. A-C informed its and NGC's shareholders in 1893, that 'in general, the coolies looked after themselves. While rice, the staple of their diet, is provided by the company, as is dried fish and conserves of vegetables', the supply of fresh fruit and vegetables is the responsibility of the workers. Some 100 enterprising Chinese and 50 Javanese established co-operatives or *kadehs* on company-provided land to produce for their own requirements and to sell to the workers 'at prices which are agreed and supervised by the station manager'.[46] A-C discharged its responsibility for providing a balanced diet by stating that Chinese and Malays could purchase a hearty meal at 15 cents per serve'. It was a service the gambling-prone, opium-smoking coolie would not have availed himself of readily, and once on the sick list he did not have the means to pay for extra food.

In 1901 Acting Governor Hahl mandated medicine cabinets on recruiting vessels and on stations. Thermometers, scissors, band-aids, cotton wool, bandages and slings were standard items. Other supplies, including iodine, opium, quinine sulphate, hydrogen peroxide, Epsom salt, hydrochloric acid, petroleum jelly, lime and cognac had to be available in quantities commensurate with the number of labourers.[47]

NGC made much of its care for its workforce. Paul Preuß wrote in *Der Tropenplanzer* that 'the much improved physical condition after only a few months was proof of the quality and quantity of food the local people received on the plantations. It is considerably better than what is customary in their home villages', the long-serving NGC Director boasted.[48] But many NGC managers and overseers did not adhere to the mandated requirements as vigorously as Preuß would have it. Whereas the atrocious health conditions prevalent on the tobacco plantations during the 1890s were largely a result of feeble recruits, an unbalanced diet and opium addiction, the local management often reduced the quantity and quality of food because of stringent budgetary requirements.

When the government physician Dr Wendland demanded a change to the diet of workers in 1908 because 'each company provided rations that it considered appropriate, even if this meant poor quality salt meat or rotten dried fish',[49] NGC protested that higher quality and larger food rations would increase its operational costs substantially. It was joined in its objection by E. E. Forsayth & Co. which argued that the new regulation would increase its cost per worker of RM96 to RM124/year or RM37,500 annually for its 1,340 workers. The Bismarck-Archipel-Gesellschaft estimated the cost increases at RM6 for each of its 400 employees. Wendland and Born rejected these complaints since a lack in nutritional values in the diet led to the spread of dysentery and pneumonia and therefore much higher operating costs.[50]

With the promulgation of the *Labour Ordinance, 1909*, the GNG administration sought to balance the demands of the planters with the minimum requirements set by the surgeons. From now on food rations for workers became a function of body weight. The minimum ration for a worker was now 625 g rice or 3 kg root crops plus a weekly allowance of 750 g of meat or fish. Workers with a body weight exceeding 60 kg received additional provisions.[51] Although Dr Born argued that the rations for labourers performing moderately heavy work required 760 g rice and 150 g of meat daily, the problem was not an increase in calorific requirements but one of nutritional values. Until the Polish-born researcher Casimir Funk made the discovery of thiamine (vitamin B1) in 1911 NGC remained unaware of the link between polished rice and malnutrition. The true understanding of the nexus between beri-beri and folic acid deficiency took another 20 years. Until then empirical evidence was largely restricted to hospital cases where doctors changed the diets of beri-beri sufferers to predominantly legumes in 1903, while Dr Hoffmann changed the diet from polished to cured rice. Dr Runge changed the diet to more yams, taro, fish, coconut and some rice in 1909, and noticed an immediate improvement in his beri-beri patients.[52] Funk's discovery found its way into the draft report on the 'Labour Ordinance of 1914'. The 1913 GNG government submission by Dr Wick recommended a 50% reduction in the daily intake of rice, while increasing the daily intake of root crops and fresh fruits to 1 kg and 125 grams respectively. In addition, Wick regarded the weekly intake of tea, biscuits, some sugar, lard and 500 g of meat as essential.[53] This time Preuß protested the loudest. By claiming the proposed legislation would cost it annually RM218 per worker (RM872,000 p.a. based on 4,000 employees), NGC advised the government that 'if implemented it would favour labourers over plantation owners'.[54] In reply to administrator Geisler's statement at the 5 March 1914 council meeting in Rabaul, to the effect that amended labour ordinance will double the cost of employing a worker, Governor Hahl pointed out that the annual health budget for GNG was nearly 25 per cent of total annual government outlays. 'If we are not improving drastically the wellbeing of our workers, we have failed in our endeavor to settle GNG', Hahl exclaimed.[55] World War I intervened and the legislation was never enacted.

Melanesian and Papuan labour

On 8 June 1885, the German government enacted an imperial decree, prohibiting the recruitment of Papuan and Melanesians for work outside GNG.[56] NGC was the beneficiary of this decree. Under its charter, it had the sole right and obligation to recruit indigenous labour in GNG. While Hernsheim lobbied Bismarck to prevent Queenslanders from recruiting in the Melanesian archipelago, the enactment of the decree disadvantaged all companies operating in GNG other than NGC, with companies and individuals now obliged to hire indigenous labour through NGC. Excluded were the requirements of DHPG. Under the supervision of NGC, the company continued recruiting Melanesian labour for its plantations in Polynesia.

When coolies proved too expensive and the tobacco industry faltered, the importance of Melanesian labour came to the fore. From August 1888 to 30 June 1892, New Ireland and the Solomons provided 3,930 workers to the labour depôts of NGC. Of these, 1,905 went to KWL: some went to Forsayth, Hernsheim and Mouton, with the balance going to DHPG plantations on Samoa.[57]

NGC opened its labour depôt in Finschhafen in March 1890. One month later, a second depôt was set up in Herbertshöhe on the Gazelle Peninsula. The Friedrich Wilhelmshafen administration attached the specially built recruiting brig *Senta* to Herbertshöhe in April 1890 to hasten the labour supply for the new plantation on the Gazelle Peninsula. However, past methods used by Queensland recruiters and the abuses committed on the indigenous workers by settlers made recruiting difficult. The coastal Tolai of the Gazelle Peninsula would not work for the Europeans under any circumstances. Moreover, many men from the coastal regions of New Ireland and the Duke of York suffered from the consumption of rum, and, coupled with the knowledge they had gained in the use of firearms while working on the sugar plantations, made them dangerous warriors and unsuitable for recruitment.[58]

Administrator Kraetke believed that the veteran planter Richard Parkinson was the only person who could deal with this uncontrollable, yet indispensable, human resource. When Parkinson joined NGC in June 1889, he called the native hostilities 'a permanent state of war'.[59] Yet he successfully recruited 764 Tolai, New Irelanders and Bukamen in the first few months of his engagement. The following year, Parkinson recruited 1,044 men in New Hannover, 130 in the Duke of York Group and 99 in Buka to satisfy both the Herbertshöhe plantation and Finschhafen depôt requirements. When Parkinson commenced planting at Herbertshöhe Captain Böhmermann of the *Senta* took over the recruiting. During 1891 he engaged 1,064 Melanesians, 760 of whom went to Stephansort to work for A-C, with the balance distributed to other plantation companies.[60] With the *Senta* in dry dock for much of 1892, Captain Dallmann, again in charge of the *Ysabel*, worked the Huon Gulf and the Solomon Islands, the Le Maire Islands and the north coast of KWL, back to Finschhafen and into the Huon Gulf and on several smaller islands north of Dallmannhafen.

The haul was poor. The first expedition tallied four men on short-term indentures. On the second voyage along the coast, Dallmann succeeded in engaging 132 men from the Bertrand (Tarawai) and other nearby islands, and from around Berlinhafen (Aitape). The number would have been larger, according to Dallmann, if five illegal sailing ships had not visited the area during the preceding months. Moreover, the barter conditions of the Queenslanders made recruiting particularly difficult on Bougainville where the Chiefs demanded guns and ammunition in exchange for strong young men; beads, hoop iron and other trinkets offered by the Germans would no longer suffice. The local people across the Buka Strait were more responsive. Here Dallmann signed on 144 Bukamen and he convinced Commissioner Rose to issue an amended labour recruitment ordinance. The 12 July 1892 regulation was to remind illegal recruiters that the Bougainville, Buka and adjacent islands were part of the Protectorate of NGC. Penalties of up to 3 months' jail or fines of up to RM3,000 were applicable also for this part of the German possessions.

The return of the *Senta* to GNG saw also the return of Ludwig Kärnbach for his second term with NGC. Kärnbach joined Captain Böhmermann to work the northeast coast of New Ireland and Buka Island. On their first voyage (August–December 1892), they managed to engage 731 men, but only 312 men from January to September

1893. In fact, trips to New Ireland, the outlying Gerrit Denys Islands, New Hanover, the Sandwich, French and Solomon Islands by the *Senta* resulted in more indentured workers returning to their villages rather than the engagement of new labourers.

Kärnbach left NGC in July 1893 to set up his own plantation company on Sainson (Seleo) near Berlinhafen. While NGC vessels were laid up or engaged on other work, he recruited for the company with his cutter the *Dora* for much of 1894 and 1895.

The hard-nosed recruiting practices of Kärnbach and his two European hands, Willy Rohde and the Englishman Diack, brought some relief to the labour-starved Astrolabe Compagnie. Of the 633 Papuans they recruited in 1893 and 1894, A-C received 526 recruits. In April 1895, the Stephansort and Erima tobacco plantations employed 646 labourers. During the course of the following year the company engaged 268 new recruits, while shedding 363 men who had completed their indentures, were sick, had died or absconded. The tally in May 1896 of 551 A-C labourers included 187 Jabim people who, according to the company, were most efficient workers. The major employer of Melanesian labour, the DHPG, signed 826 indentures in 1895. Contractors delivered the recruits to the company's depôt on Mioko Island for transport to Samoa.[61]

Only a year later the recruitment came to a virtual standstill. The *Ysabel* struck a reef on the north coast of the Gazelle and, after undergoing repairs in Sydney, Burns Philp bought the vessel in October 1896. Kärnbach died in February 1897 on a voyage to Stephansort. Father Franz Vormann of the 'Heilig-Geist-Mission' on Tamara (Tumleo) Island near Seleo continued with some recruiting until the purchase of Seleo by NGC toward the end of that year.[62]

The new Seleo manager, Paul Lücker, arrived on the island in June 1898 with three Chinese *tandils* and two Javanese *mandurs*, two Jabims and six Melanesians. His immediate concern was the construction of a new, larger station on Seleo. Recruiting for NGC continued for a brief period with the cutter *Dora*, now named the *Seleo*, but only yielding 14 men from the sparsely populated Lemieng area.[63]

Although largely unsuccessful in recruiting workers, Paul Lücker was doing well in procuring large tracts of land on islands around Berlinhafen. According to Albert Hahl, the NGC manager acquired 165,000 ha.[64] Lücker discovered the valuable *Calophyllum* tree for medicinal oil extraction, set up six trading stations and planted some 7,000 coconut palms on Seleo, Tarawai and Rabuin. Chinese traders supplied him with copra, trepang and pearl shell, which he exported on behalf of NGC to Singapore. Paul Behse took over from Lücker who resigned from NGC in 1899.[65]

The Governor of the Straits Settlements, W. E. Maxwell, summed up the sorts of labour problems NGC encountered in a paper delivered to the London Royal Colonial Institute in 1892. 'There is first the difficulty of managing Chinese labour', he told his audience, 'The Chinese were unruly and difficult to control, and did not make an acceptable worker who would subordinate himself to the will of a foreign employer'. Maxwell also mentioned that British scorn was balanced by an admiration for the Chinese instinct for capitalism and profit.[66] The British experience mirrored NGC's. Hansemann recognised the economic benefits of mass migration, but NGC's policies did not make use of the industriousness and artisanal skills of the Chinese to their advantage. When the shift from tobacco to coconut plantations in 1896 the number of Melanesians employed by NGC in the archipelago rose from 556 (October 1897) to 706 (July 1898). Chinese coolies employed by NGC in KWL declined from 518 in 1895 to 168 in 1897.[67] Asian labour increased again slightly from 1898 to 1900, however, by then the locals made up 75% of NGC's workforce. By 1906 the company employed 3,370 Melanesians and Papuans, only 95 Chinese, and 39 Javanese.

Labour shortages and inferior labour resources were the root causes of A-C's failure according to NGC. The agreement to provide the Chinese with opium was a curse, not a cure. Most of the 2,000 coolies recruited for the tobacco industry on Astrolabe Bay in the first 2 years died either during transportation or shortly after their arrival in GNG. The main causes of death were cholera, malaria and thiamine deficiency. That coolies worked harder when provided with a measure of opium was a short-lived gain. No matter how well they worked while under the influence of the drug, the resultant higher death rate was no compensation for the higher work output derived from the prescription. Opium importation to GNG tripled from 1890 to 1894. For NGC it became a moral as well as a financial dilemma.[68]

The German traders were generally opposed to Chinese immigration. Independent Chinese traders bought copra from the local people at prices they were unwilling or unable to match. In 1911 the *Amtsblatt* wrote that GNG had more than enough Chinese and their immigration should be stopped.[69] The Australian colonial governments prohibited Asian migration to Papua because it was concerned that the Chinese could migrate from Papua to Australia. Towards the end of German colonial rule Governor Albert Hahl became an advocate for Chinese migration. He, like Hansemann before him, encouraged the Chinese presence for economic reasons. Hahl believed that the entrepreneurship of the Chinese would make GNG self-supporting. He almost succeeded in persuading Berlin to give the Chinese equal status as the Europeans, a privilege the Japanese in GNG had from the outset.

Notes

1   Reichsamt für Statistik, 'Die Deutschen Schutzgebiete', *Statistisches Jahrbuch*, 1894, pp. 195-9.

2   Deutsche Kolonialgesellschaft, *Koloniales Jahrbuch*, vol. ii, 1889, p. 278. *NKWL* (1886) Heft ii, pp. 6, 83 and 133; (1887) Heft ii, p. 80 & Heft iii, p. 80.

3   Centraal Kanttor voor Statisiek, 'Jaaroverzicht van den Nederlandsche–Indie'. See H. Blum, *Neu Guinea und der Bismarck-Archipel*, p. 167; V. Purcell, *The Chinese in Southeast Asia*, p. 386.

4   Hansemann to Bismarck, 18 Mar. 1889 (RKA 1001:2299, pp. 137–40). *NKWL* (1891) Heft i, p. 21. See R. Hindorf, 'Einige Vorschläge für die Praktische Kolonisation im Schutzgebiet der *NGC*' (*DKZ* [1890] pp. 9ff.). K. Pelzer, *Die Arbeiterwanderungen in Südostasien.* pp. 90–6; Purcell, p. 434).

5   Jb (1891/92) p. 12; Sack & Clark (1890–91) p. 66

6   'Labour Ordinance for the East Coast of Sumatra no. 138/139' 15 July 1889 (*NKWL* 1893, p. 37). Dutch Ambassador to Bismarck 25 May and 29 June 1889, NGC to AA-KA, 1 June 1889, AA-KA to NGC 3 July 1889 (RKA 1001:2299, pp 184, 187–88, 199 & 203; 2300, p. 99).

7   P. Biskup, 'Foreign Coloured Labour in German New Guinea: a study of economic development', *Pacific History*, 5, p. 91; S. von Kotze, *Aus Papuas Kulturmorgen*, pp. 15–6. W. van den Doel, 'Kulis für

Deutschland' in H.J. Hiery, ed., *Die Deutsche Südsee*, pp. 777–8

8   NGC to AA-KA, 23 Dec.1890 (RKA 1001:2301, p. 16); *NKWL* (1890) Heft ii, p. 85, NGC Recruitment Ordinance, 15 Aug. 1888' (DKG, vol. 1, p. 535). Sack & Clark (1889–90) pp. 48–51.

9   Herzog to AA-KA, 23 Dec. 1890 (RKA 1001:2301, pp. 16 & 109; *NKWL* 1890, Heft i, p. 85; (1891) Heft i, p. 13. See S. Firth, 'German Recruitment of Labourers in the Western Pacific', p. 97.

10   'Opium Handel Deutsch Neu Guinea 1890–1914'(RKA 1001:2535/6), Hansemann to Bismarck, 18 March 1889. J. Rush, *Opium to Java: 1860–1910*; Purcell, p. 431.

11   *NKWL* (1891) Heft i, pp. 20–1 and (1892) Heft i, pp. 31–2 & 40–1; Jb A-C, Dec. 1892, (RKA 1001:2427, p. 6); Jb (1891/92) p. 12–3, Sack & Clark (1890–91) pp. 66–7.

12   Jb A-C (1 Oct.1892 to 30 Sep. 1893) p. 10; Jb A-C (1893/94) p. 6, (1894/95) p. 3 (RKA 1001: 2428–29). Jb (1892/93) p. 14, Sack & Clark (1892–93) p. 81; *NKWL* (1894) p. 23.

13   D.G. Pilhofer, *Die Geschichte der Neuendettelsauer Mission in Neuguinea*, p. 116–8; B. Hagen, *Unter den Papuas*, pp. 34–7. Firth, *New Guinea under the Germans*, pp. 51, n.10 & 125.

14   Rose to AA, 30 Jun. 1892 (RKA 1001:6512. pp. 45–52); Rose to Caprivi, 24 Dec. 1891 (RKA 1001:2980, p. 196). *NKWL* (1892) Heft i, p. 32; (1893), pp. 33–1; Jb (1890/91) p. 12.

15   A-C, (1892/93) budget, RKA 1001:2427, pp. 167–8. NGC and A-C employees in *NKWL* 1890– 95 (RKA 1001:2427, pp. 167–8); Jb A-C (Dec. 1892) pp. 4–6; (Dec. 1893) pp. 6–7.

16   W. von Hanneken, 'Eine Kolonie in der Wirklichkeit', *Die Nation* (1895) p. 134. Hiery, ed., *Die Deutsche Südsee 1884–1914*, p. 288; Firth, 'German Recruitment and Employment of Labour in the Western Pacific before the First War', p. 105, n. 3.

17   W. Wendland, *Im Wunderland der Papuas: Ein deutscher Kolonialarzt erlebt die Südsee*, p. 25.

18   *Oberkommando der Marine*, 8 Feb. 1893 (RKA 1001:2982, p. 95; *NKWL* (1893) pp. 62–3). Emmeling died of 'fever and nephritis' on 20 Feb. 1893; Hagge left A-C in 1893 (M. Davies, *Public Health and Colonialism*, p. 203).

19   *NKWL* (1893) p. 34; Jb (1891/92) p. 13; Sack & Clark (1890-91) p. 67.

20   *NKWL* (1892) Heft, i, pp. 32 & 45–7; *DKBl*, (1892) pp. 470–1. A-C AGM Dec. 1892 (RKA 1001:2427)

21   Jb (1891/92) p. 12.

22   Hatzfeldt to Caprivi, 18 Oct. 1893 (RKA 1001:2304, pp. 69–73). German Consul in Singapore to Caprivi, 14 Aug. 1893 (RKA 1001:2303, p. 182).

23   Jb A-C, Dec. 1893; RKA 1001:2427, p. 6; *NKWL* 1893, p. 31.

24   Doel, 'Kulis für Deutschland', p. 781.

25   Wendland, *Im Wunderland der Papuas*, pp. 24–7; Jb (1893/94) p. 14; Sack & Clark (1893–94) p. 97.Jb (1894/95) p. 13; Sack & Clark (1894–95) p. 115.

26   *NKWL* (1894) pp. 23–4 & 27

27   NGC to AA-KA, 29 May 1896 (RKA 1001:2985, p. 109). *NKWL*, (1896), pp. 23–4; Jb (1895/96) p. 6; Sack & Clark (1895–96) pp. 120–1.

28   *NKWL* (1995) pp. 32–3; Jb A-C, (1894/95) p. 6. NGC to AA-KA, 20 Aug. 1896 (RKA 1001:2305).

29   *NKWL* (1896) p. 4; (1897), p. 12; Jb (1896/97) p. 1–2; Sack & Clark (1896–97) p. 127.

30   *NKWL* (1893) p. 48; G. Schmiele, 'Charakteristik des Schutzgebietes der Neu-Guinea-Compagnie' (*DKBl* (1892) pp. 469–73). *NKWL* (1895) p. 36. Krieger, *Neu Guinea* (pp. 260–1).

31   Jb A-C (1894/95) p. 4.

32   Purcell, p.286.

33   Jb A-C (1894/95) p. 4 (RKA 1001:2429; see H. Cayley-Webster, *Through New Guinea and the Cannibal Countries*, 19; D.R. Snodgrass, *Inequality of Economic Development in Malaysia*, p. 36.

34   NGC to AA-KA, 6 Aug. 1896 (RKA 1001:2305, pp. 116–17).

35   RKA 1001:2305, p. 146.

36   *NKWL* (1898) pp. 24–5; Jb (1898/99) p. 23 and (1899/1900) p. 24; Sack & Clark (1898– 99) p. 164

37   Jb 1899/00, pp. 23– 4, and 1901/02, pp. 5, 9, 15 & 38–9; Sack & Clark (1899–1900) p. 208 and (1901–02) p. 233.

38   *AB*, (1914) Nr. 9

39   Jb A-C (1892/93) p. 7.

40   Jb (1887) p. 19; Sack & Clark (1886–87) p. 19. P. Preuß, *Die Kokuspalme und ihre Kultur*, p. 557; *Koloniales Jahrbuch*, vol. ii, (1889) pp. 278–9; vol. vi, 1893, p. 272.The government collected a licence fee of RM30 from 1 Apr. 1899 for a worker recruited overseas.

41   Jb A-C (1893), pp.13–17.

42   'Verordnung der NGC betreffend die Reichsmarksrechnung vom 19 Jan. 1887', 'NGC und AC Geschäftsreglement für die Vereinigte Verwaltung, 1896', §§6 & 18 (RKA 1001:2422, p.17); *NKWL* (1886) Heft i, pp. 1–3, (1888) Heft iii, p. 125; DKG, vol. 1, p. 511;

43   H. Cayley-Webster, *Through New Guinea and the Cannibal Countries*, pp. 19–20.

44   P. Preuß, pp. 557–8; F.M. Sieben, 'Über die Aussichten von tropischen Kulturen in Ost-Afrika und Neu Guinea', *Koloniales Jahrbuch*,6, (1893) pp. 18–19; Tappenbeck, *Deutsch Neuguinea*, p. 175; Blum, p. 164; *NKWL* (1888) Heft iii, p. 125 p. 126 (RKA 1001:2311, pp. 44–5).

45   *NKWL* (1888) Heft iv, p. 125 & 1891, Heft i, pp.34, 54 & 61; *Koloniales Jahrbuch*, vol. Ii, (1889) p. 278; T. Helmreich, *Das Geldwesen in den deutschen Schutzgebieten, Teil I: Neu-Guinea*, pp. 23–8.

46   DKG, vol. 1, p. 535. 'Verordnung betreffend die Arbeiter-Depots im Schutzgebiet der NGC', §§3, 6 &13; DKG, vol. 1, p. 549; *NKWL* (1888), Heft iii, pp. 127 & 140–1; Jb (1887) p. 19; *(*1893) pp. 37–8; (1895) p. 33; Sack & Clark (1886–87) p. 19. Preuß, p. 558.

47   Krieger: 60% of Chinese in GNG were addicted to opium (*Neu Guinea*, pp. 128, 237 & 261).

48   Preuß, p. 558.

49   Wendland to Hahl, 3 Dec. 1908 (RKA 1001:2312, p. 30 ff and 5769, p. 178).

50   Forsayth to Hahl, 16 Feb. 1909 (RKA 1001:2311, pp. 43ff); Bismarck-Archipel-Gesellschaft (RKA 1001:2311, pp. 44–5).Born to Hahl, 25 Oct. 1909 (RKA 1001:2311, p. 202).s

51   'Verordnung des Gouverneurs von Deutsch-Neuguinea betreffend die Ausführung und Anwerbung von Eingeborenen', 4 March 1909, enacted on 1 Jan. 1910 (DKG, vol. 13, pp. 147–57).

52   *Medizinal-Berichte über die deutschen Schutzgebiete*, (RKA, MB 1903/04, p. 235). R. Runge, 'Beriberifälle in Käwieng' (*AB*, [1909] Nr. 1, pp. 138–40). M. Davies, *Public Health*, pp. 119–27.

53   Wick to Hahl, 1913 (RKA 1001:5773, pp 29–39 and 52–64).

54   Herzog and Preuß to AA-KA, 29 July 1914 (RKA 1001:2314, pp. 8ff).

55   *AB*, (1914), Nr. 7, p. 104

56   'Erlaß des Reichskanzlers' in *NKWL* (1885), Heft i, p. 5. The 21 Aug. 1886 amendment prohibited the recruitment in the northern part of New Ireland (*NKWL* [1886] Heft ii, p. 59).

57   *NKWL* (1894) pp. 24–5; Jb (1891/92) p. 12; Sack & Clark (1890–91) pp. 65–6.

58   Sack & Clark [1889–90] p. 47. Firth, *New Guinea under the Germans*, pp. 47–65.

59   R. Parkinson, *Dreißig Jahre in der Südsee*, pp. 77–140;

60   *NKWL* (1890), Heft ii, p. 85; (1891) p. 16; (1892) p. 30; (1893) p. 28; Sack & Clark (1889–90) p. 51.

61   *NKWL* (1895) p. 36. Firth, *New Guinea under the Germans*, p. 40. P. Steffen, 'Die Katholischen Missionen in Deutsch-Neuguinea' in Hiery, ed., *Die Deutsche Südsee 1884–1914*, p. 361.

62   *NKWL* (1897) pp. 22–3; Jb (1896/97) p. 9; Sack & Clark (1896–97) p. 130

63   Jb (1897/98) p. 6; Sack & Clark (1897–98) p. 143.

64   Hahl to AA-KA, 22 Nov. 1898 (RKA 1001:2278).

65   Jb (1898/99) p. 21; Sack & Clark (1898–99) pp. 166–7.

66   W.E. Maxwell, 'The Malay Peninsula', *Royal Colonial Institute*, (1892) vol. 23, pp. 1–46

67   *NKWL* (1897) p. 25 & (1898), p. 23.

68   NGC to AA-KA, 18 June 1895, (RKA 1001:29040, p. 16).

69   'Chinesenplage', *OAL* (1906) p. 1016

OPENING THE COUNTRY: SCIENTIFIC AND COMMERCIAL EXPEDITIONS AND ILL-FATED ADVENTURES

8

The Schrader and Schleinitz expeditions

The first German scientific expedition arrived in Finschhafen on 19 April 1886. The leader of the party was the astronomer Dr Carl Schrader, explorer of South Georgia, Antarctica. He was supported by the botanist and agriculturist Dr Max Hollrung and the geologist Dr Carl Schneider. Hansemann had commissioned the scientists to explore the German possession on mainland New Guinea 'in a manner, which was to benefit the territorial expansion of the Compagnie'. While Hansemann advised the government that this expedition was not set up 'specifically for [economic] explorations, which must be left for a later date', he told his staff that they must become 'acquainted with the languages, customs and cultures of the natives' if NGC was to become a successful economic enterprise. During the course of the first 2 years, the scientists were to proceed as far as possible inland towards the British border and return to the coast by a different route.[1]

Schrader's party was equipped with instruments to enable all manner of scientific investigations. Apart from scientific research, the explorers' brief was to examine tree and plant species on their suitability for house, furniture, and shipbuilding materials. Tree sap was to be analysed for gutta-percha, copal and camphor, and the biochemical properties of tannic acid and organic pigments such as indigo measured. The value of staple and fatty substances in coco, sago and other palm genera were to be assessed. Mapping out his new Protectorate from Berlin, Hansemann wanted to know whether the tropical condition of GNG was suitable for European livestock and poultry. He also hoped that native animal species would be discovered for domestication to secure supply of fresh milk, butter, meat and pork was regarded by him as being of equal importance as finding suitable draught animals. In addition to economic discoveries of valuable minerals, he instructed his scientists to look on this expedition for hard coal for the company's ships and the fleet of the *Reichsmarine*.[2] As a rule, specimens were to be classified, numbered, tagged and catalogued. The explorers had to photograph the locations, map and document the elevations and general environments of the discoveries. Hansemann insisted that all journal entries were to be executed in duplicate, with a copy left in safekeeping at the camp during daily excursions. Schrader, Hollrung and Schneider were to prepare detailed reports on their observations, and discoveries of economic value.[3]

The explorers quickly learnt that the British/Dutch border in the southwest corner of GNG could not be reached under prevailing conditions. The topography required a considerably greater number of coolies than the 10 Chinese carriers they had hired in Cooktown. Used to the arid climate of the Australian goldfields rather than the humid, malaria infested, conditions of New Guinea, the Chinese were replaced by people of the Jabim tribe after barely coping with a 15 km excursion in a tropical rainforest. However, the number of carriers required for the investigations envisaged by Hansemann could not be marshalled in the sparsely populated area around Finschhafen either, and the few men who signed up were not prepared to journey beyond their village influence, also about 15 km. Schrader decided therefore to abandon the exploration of the interior and to investigate the coastal mainland region and some islands in the archipelago to assist in establishing NGC stations.[4]

From June 1886 to November 1887 the explorers investigated some 660 of the 800 kilometer north coast of mainland German New Guinea (*Kaiser-Wilhelms-Land*). Coastal expeditions started from Finschhafen with the 900 meter climb of the Sattelberg. Schrader and Hollrung explored the foothills of the Torricelli Range, northwest of the Sepik River *(Kaiserin Augusta-Fluß)*, travelled the Ramu River (*Ottilie Fluß*) for some 100 km, and the Sepik for more than 500 km. The the Purdy Islands were investigated for guano deposits, the Duke of York Group and the Gazelle Peninsula were paid a cursory visit. With discoveries of rivers, creeks, mountains and islands plotted on the scientists' expanding map, Hollrung recorded the many coastal inlets as 'ideally suited for harbours'. But much of the coastal strip was a mere 25 km wide, and where dense mangrove swamps did not compete with potential plantation land precipitous rock formations met the sea in a foaming interplay. From the British border in the south to immediately north of Hatzfeldthafen, almost 80% of the topography was mountainous. 'It is not easy to make geological sense from this chaos of ridges', Hollrung noted. 'The mountains appear in narrow formation, with the Finisterre Range—called mána-bórro (very high mountains) by the local people—standing out from this cluster'. The deep escarpments of this range defines the Rai Coast of southeast New Guinea before the range ends abruptly in the north, while merging with the Rawlinson Range in the south.[5]

On a second expedition in April 1886, led by Captain Dallmann on the *Samoa*, Dr Schellong, Mentzel and Hunstein advanced 41 nautical miles on the Sepik to gather geographical and hydrographical information. A follow-up group left Finschhafen on 24 July under Administrator von Schleinitz. The party included the Commissioner for the Marshall Islands, Wilhelm Knappe, Dr Schrader, Dr Hollrung and Carl Hunstein. The *Ottilie* had just arrived in GNG, provided the best in cabin accommodation. Accompanied by a steam launch for shallow waters, Captain Rasch to take the vessel 300 nautical miles upstream where the river still flows 300 to 400 meter wide.

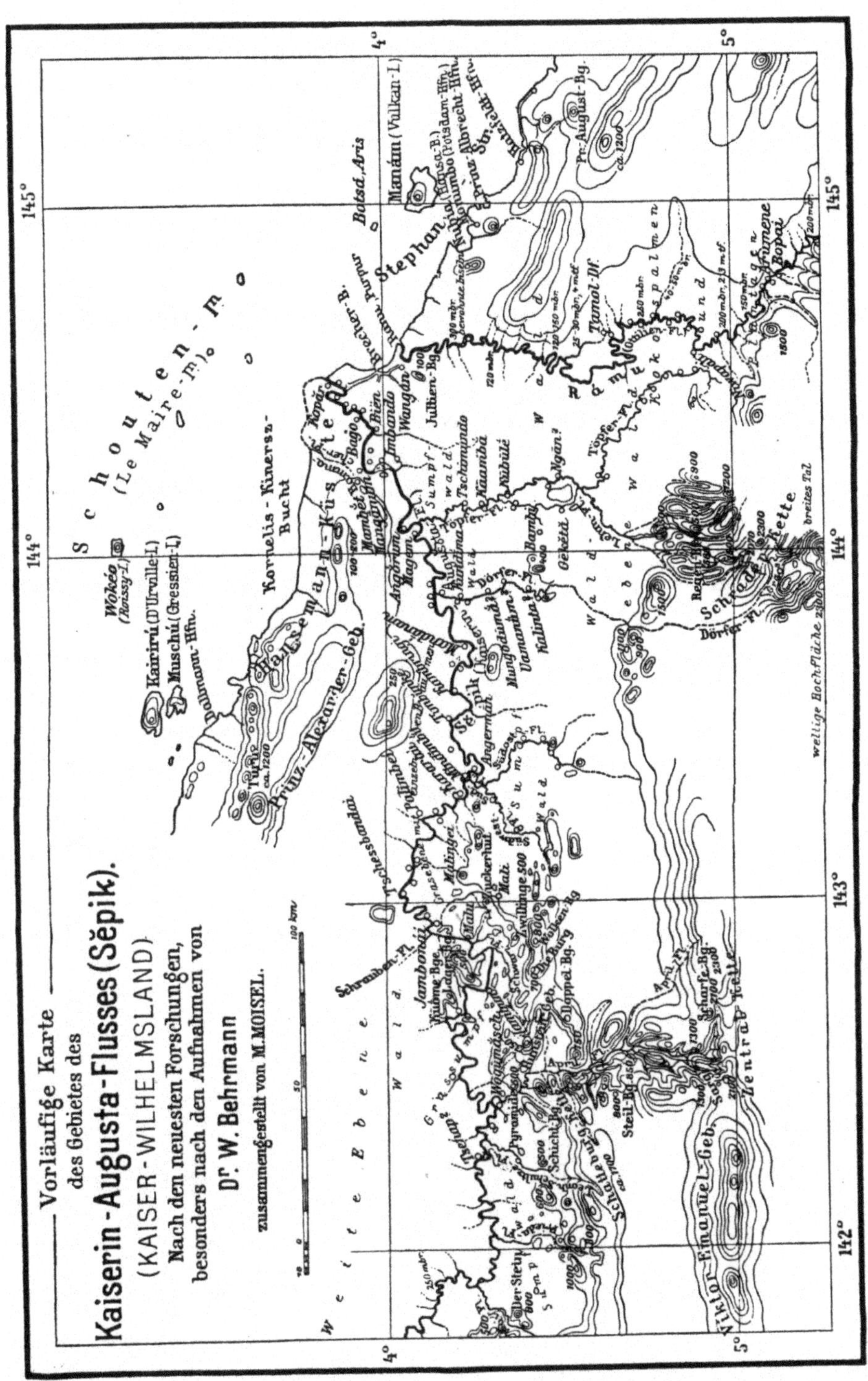

Map 6: **The Kaiserin Augusta (Sepik) River Expeditions** (Deutsches Kolonial Lexikon, B. II, p. 145)

Disastrous Ventures

Intent on discovering the source of the Sepik, Schleinitz navigated the launch from this point through shallow waters to about 100 km from the British border.[6] After 60 hours of steaming on what had turned into a foaming rapid the party returned to the *Ottilie* to continue exploration further downstream. The adventure ended when the ship's boiler was running low on coal. Rather than taking soundings and collecting specimens all hands were now required to cut wood. And, by sailing close to the river bank the *Ottilie.* was claimed several times by Sepik mud. A ragged group of explorers returned to Finschhafen three weeks later, on 13 August.

Notwithstanding the mishaps Schleinitz claimed that the Upper Sepik had enormous economic potential: 'as soon as suitable labour is available', read his report to Berlin, 'I intend to set up a Station at a point where the river leaves the mountain onto an expansive plain'. He planned to launch expeditions from there, chart the river and assess the agricultural potential of the flats. A feat completed by A. Stollé, W. Behrmann and R. Turnwald during the 1912-13 Sepik exploration mission.

Schrader referred in his report to the 'numerous, unusually large villages comprising 100 houses or more'. To deal with the regular floods and currents, houses were built on stronger piers than seen elsewhere in GNG. Within the vicinity of the villages palms grew 'as far as the eye could see'. Apart from the economic potential of the nut, Schrader surmised that 'the many hundreds of thousands of square kilometers overgrown with sugar cane would be terrain suitable for cattle breeding'. Schrader found the local people, who he believed had never seen a white man before, shy if not hostile. Where contact was made, the tribes offered spears decorated with human vertebrae, pottery, tobacco and other trinkets in exchange for cloth, bottles, pearls and, in the upper Sepik, shells. 'We also managed to barter for some human skulls', Schrader commented with apparent satisfaction.

Hollrung recorded the vegetation of swamp cypress, coir and wild sugarcane. He observed substantial forests in the mountainous area of the Upper Sepik, 'which will prove ideal for building material' and discovered two species of 'Garcinia Morella which produces the highest quality gamboge or gum resin'. As regards agriculture, he advised Schleinitz that the river flats on the Upper Sepik were ideally suited for plantations, 'whereas the lower region may prove to be too flood prone and would require further assessment before proceeding'.

A third Sepik expedition departed from Finschhafen on 24 June 1887. This time, Schrader, Hollrung, Schneider and Hunstein were supported by seaman Faßholz, 12 Malays and four Melanesians. The party reached the foothills of the Hunstein Range, some 240 km upstream, by mid-August. Setting up camp north of the village Malu, the party was able to procure food locally; other supplies, the mail and instructions from Schleinitz arrived once a month by steamship.[7]

Schrader reported that relations with the villagers were friendly to begin with but became hostile with the occurrence of their ever-increasing thieving. Because of this and the demanding terrain the expedition only worked within a radius of 8 km from the camp. Apart from conducting research in their respective fields, the scientists evaluated locations for future tobacco plantations, which ranked high on

Hansemann's agenda. In all, investigations in this remote area had lasted for about 5 weeks when Schleinitz ordered the group to move 13 km downstream and continue the work they had abandoned in 1886.

Hollrung dealt with the topography and vegetation whereas Schrader and Schneider concentrated on the hydrological and meteorological data. Hollrung recommended setting up a small, mobile lumber mill as soon as practicable in order to exploit the immense timber resource along the river and further inland. He believed the felling and processing of timber along the *Augusta-Fluß* to be straight forward and the transportation of the logs on the river not overly difficult. In light of the rich soil and moderate climate the expedition assessed the river plains as generally suitable for setting up plantations. Their only concern was occasional substantial flooding of the river as indicated by the marks on the trees.

Schrader left for the Purdy Islands on 7 November 1887 to prove-up phosphate minerals. Notwithstanding a high concentration in nitrogen, phosphoric acid and potash they determined the discoveries made by the surveyor August Rocholl and Administrator Schleinitz some 12 months earlier were not commercial as it only appeared in thin layers.

As one of their last tasks before returning to Germany, the explorers took probes from all four islands in the group for assaying in Germany. The probes proved to contain high concentration of carbonate-apatite and, according to Hollrung, were the most valuable phosphate discovered to date.[8]

Hansemann offered Hollrung an attractive annual salary of RM6,000 plus a performance bonus to stay on as plantation manager, which Hollrung turned down. He found the scarcity of suitable labour a huge impediment to successful farming and mining in GNG. The atomistic Papuan society, with its many different languages and cultures, meant that the local workers would not move outside the security of their village environment, if indeed they could be hired at all. Hollrung also believed that Chinese coolies could not be successfully employed in GNG. 'They will not work for the white man', he surmised. Rather, they will 'with a high degree of certainty control commerce and trade, slowly and surely, just like they have done in Java, Borneo, in the Philippines and in California'. Hollrung left for Germany a month before Schrader departed in November and Schneider in December 1887.[9]

If, as Blum suggests, the expeditions did not fulfil expectations, the reasons may be found in the unrealistic objectives set by Hansemann, not the achievements per se.[10] Schrader's decision to remain in the coastal region to first get a feel for the terrain was sound judgement. Strenuous mountain climbing in a hostile environment would have been highly risky. It may have satisfied the 'need to know' of the geographers; however, it would not have addressed the economic opportunities of GNG which, for some time to come, were restricted to the coastal region.

For the benefit of the wider scientific community, Hollrung's collection of flora specimens became the subject of careful scientific study by the *Königliche Botanische Museum* in Berlin. NGC regarded his catalogue as a valuable indicator for future commercial exploitation of the New Guinea flora. The Hollrung glossary on languages and dialects of the tribes around Hatzfeldthafen was not as extensive as the words, songs and rhymes collated by Schellong on the Jabim people. Both contributed to better communication, with Schellong's study of particular importance as the Jabims proving to be the most resilient, hard-working people in all of GNG.[11]

Schneider accompanied Schleinitz on other surveys along the north coast and into the Bismarck Archipelago. Assisted by planter Charles Barthélémy, who had moved from Fiji to GNG, and the surveyor and cartographer, Max Dreger, who drew many of the early maps on GNG, they were the first Europeans to travel the *Ottilie-Fluß* for the short distance of 13 km in mid November 1886. His participation in the Huon Gulf expeditions in October and in December led Schneider into hot water. The cryptic telegram by Schleinitz to Hansemann in October: 'surveyed Huon Gulf, many harbours, found gold', raised false expectations in Berlin. Professor Märker of the *Landwirtschaftliche Zentralverein* in Halle, Saxony, determined it to be metamorphic rock phosphor containing iron sulphide FeS_2 (pyrite). The 'nugget' found by Schneider on the Markham River was therefore fool's gold, not the coveted yellow metal. Generally, samples collected were examined by the *Preußische Geologische Landesanstalt* in Berlin where they were left for safe-keeping.[12]

Schneider's and Schrader's geographical and hydrographical reports led to the drawing of charts that laid the foundation for a more defined geography of GNG. For instance, the seismological instruments set up by Schrader allowed a detailed analysis of the Ritter Island volcano incident.[13] The weather stations at Finschhafen, Konstantinhafen and Hatzfeldthafen provided information for future agricultural management, as did the numerous readings taken along the seaboard, on the Ramu and Sepik Rivers. Schrader recorded temperatures on the coast at +19° to +35° Celsius and calculated an annual mean temperature of +26° C. At 1000 m altitude the temperature was +14° C. The weather pattern differed on the west coast of Finschhafen compared to Hatzfeldthafen. From December to April precipitation in Finschhafen was less than 20% of the annual total, while from Astrolabe Bay to Hatzfeldthafen it exceeded 60%. From June to September the pattern reversed. The highest average rainfall was recorded in the foothills of the Finisterre Range.[14]

Hansemann kept many specimens for his private collection and presented artefacts to the *Königliche Museum für Völkerkunde* and to the *Königliches Zoologisches Museum* in Berlin, to other German institutions and to private collectors. Hollrung summed up the explorers' view in the 1888 edition of the company's publication: 'With greater certainty than Admiral Moresby could predict from the deck of his ship the north coast of New Guinea can become another Java', with the prevailing southeast and northwest sea breeze making the climate of KWL particularly European friendly.[15] Such assessment may have been a reflection on the good health the three explorers enjoyed during their 20 months in GNG. It was a view not shared by anyone living in Finschhafen. Here, they found miasmatic mangroves as the cause of rampant malaria infections. If Hollrung's view influenced Hansemann to set up tobacco plantations on Astrolabe Plain three years later, it was costly advice indeed. The breeze was evidently not strong enough to contain the malaria-carrying mosquitoes that caused death and despair.

Schleinitz made substantial corrections to the British Admiralty charts of the north coast of New Guinea and the Bismarck Archipelago. A retired Vice-Admiral of the *Reichsmarine* and an expert in hydrography, he worked on board the *Samoa, Ottilie* and *Ysabel* to chart the Huon Gulf, the coastline from Cape Cretin to the Legoarant Islands and the islands west of Dampier Strait.[16] Schleinitz combined the 'dead-reckoning' method of course–speed–time with trigonometric readings taken from mountain ranges, rivers and other topographical features to draw his charts. Regardless of the difficulties in keeping the vessels at a constant speed and working with unreliable ship's compasses, Schleinitz claimed that his charts were accurate and that discrepancies in the British Admiralty charts were now corrected. His claim to accuracy was based on a reliance on the exact position of the land beacons defined by Schrader and his repetition of soundings until the data was repeated consistently. Schleinitz varied this slow and tedious work with the survey of a number of reefs on the otherwise steep coast of the mainland. Contradicting Finsch's observation, Schleinitz did not regard navigation along the coast of KWL as hazardous: 'Now that the coast is more or less accurately charted', he reported, 'it would be valid to claim that virtually nowhere will one find such an easy and safe sea lane to navigate as the one along this coast'. With moderate prevailing winds and steady currents running parallel to the coast, with a minimal tidal difference and therefore insignificant tidal currents, Schleinitz claimed that it was 'safe to sail within one cable—often no more than two boat lengths—from the shore'.[17]

The Hellwig-Zöller-Warburg expeditions

The botanist Dr Franz Hellwig arrived in Finschhafen for NGC on 7 May 1888 to continue with scientific explorations in KWL. His most notable achievement was his contribution to the Finisterre Range expedition from 3 to 21 October 1888. The undertaking was initiated by the correspondent of the *Kölnische Zeitung*, Hugo Zöller, who had previously explored some parts of the Amazon in South America, the Ganges River in India, the mountain ranges of south Cameroon and the coast of Togo. This venture was jointly funded by the newspaper's proprietors and NGC. The two explorers made it to a ridge in the Finisterre Range to view the expansive Bismarck Range. From this vantage point they named the four highest peaks – *Wilhelmberg* (4,300 m), *Herbertberg* (4,000 m), *Ottoberg* (3,500 m) and *Marienberg* (3,000 m). While Zöller expanded his studies to include the Bismarck Archipelago, Bougainville and Buka islands, Hellwig and the botanist Dr Otto Warburg of the Humboldt University of Berlin, who had arrived in Finschhafen on 6 April 1889, carried out ethnological and botanical studies on the Sattelberg and around Fortification Point. Further, he explored the surroundings of Konstantinhafen, Bilil-Bili and Siar Island and paid a brief visit to regions in the Bismarck Archipelago.[18] Apart from scientific investigations Hellwig worked for NGC by recruiting labour and by making economic assessments on potential plantation land. Hellwig died in Finschhafen from dysentery in June 1889. Warburg returned to Berlin in late 1889 and, apart from his own botanical collections, took Hellwig's specimens with him for cataloguing. He published a paper on his 'role in the understanding of the Papuan flora', and Hellwig's, *Die Bergpflanzen aus Kaiser-Wilhelms-Land,* and *Plantae Hellwigianae,* in cooperation with the renowned taxonomist and phytogeographer, Prof. Adolf Engler.[19]

Zöller returned to Germany in 1889 and wrote a book on GNG. Far from restricting his comments to geographical and other scientific discoveries he suggested improvements NGC should make to achieve economic success. In particular, he pointed to the successes of gold prospecting in BNG, and proposed for measures to be taken to assure similar results. Zöller insisted that payable gold would be discovered in GNG if the methods across the border were followed. Australian prospectors should be encouraged and rewarded to enter German territory: such men had 100 times more chance of locating gold than geologists or mining officials, Zöller suggested.

Hansemann did not take up Zöller's suggestion. During the first 4 years of scientific expeditions NGC amassed an impressive collection of ethnographic and botanical specimens. This generated knowledge in the fields of zoology, geography and meteorology. It was also a costly start to colonisation for NGC as it consumed by far the largest proportion of the 1885–1890 (RM3,437,086) budgets.[20]

The first Ramu expedition

From April 1890 to January 1891 the East Prussian estate owner and botanist Dr Carl Lauterbach collected specimens and artefacts on the central coast of KWL at his own expense while on an excursion around the world. During this period the agriculturalist Ernst Tappenbeck also spent time in GNG. A notable achievement of Tappenbeck was the first ascent by a European of Mount Hansemann which he undertook with Gustav Bergmann of the Rhenish Mission in June 1892. Bergmann's

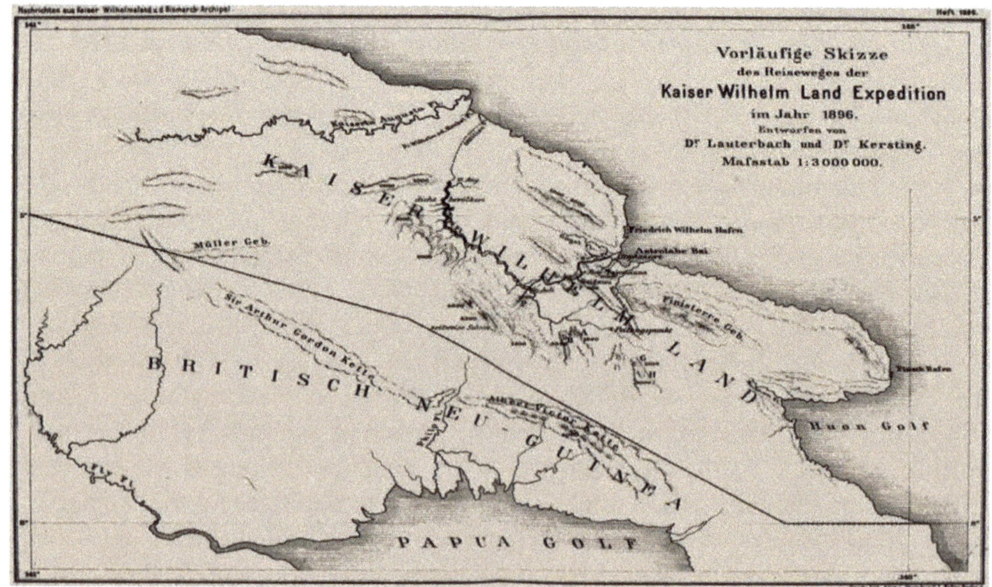

Map 7: **The Lauterbach–Tappenbeck–Kersting 1896 Bismarck Range Expedition** (*NKWL*, 1896)

knowledge of the Siar language made contacts with the tribes easier which assisted in completing the expedition quickly and successfully.[21]

Lauterbach and Tappenbeck returned to GNG in April 1896. Sponsored by the Colonial Department of the Foreign Office (KA-AA), the German Colonial Society of Kassel and the Geographical Society of Berlin, they joined the medical doctor Hermann Kersting of the KA-AA to explore the Bismarck Range. NGC provided staff and porters to the expedition for four months. The party included Albert Hoffmann of the Rhenish Mission near Stephansort and his 24 Bogadjim men, plus 4 pack horses and 40 goats for fresh meat. The leaders investigated the Gogol, Elisabeth and Narua Rivers on the Gogol and Astrolabe Plains, climbed to the 1,100 m summit of Mount Tayomann in the Oertzen Range and travelled by canoe the Yagéi (Ramu) River downstream for some 250 km. From a 1000 m vantage point Lauterbach and Kersting followed the flow of the river towards the Huon Gulf for some 100 km. They concluded that the headwaters of the Yagéi and the Markham Rivers sprang from the same mountain range. The explorers believed that the river was identical with the *Ottilie Fluß,* so named by Schleinitz in 1887. All told, they covered a distance of approximately 1700 km on foot and by boat during which they drew relief maps and established elevations.[22] The explorers determined positions by theodolite and astronomical observations and recorded natural occurrences such as earthquakes, cloud cover, precipitation, wind direction and wind strength. Lauterbach documented the taxonomy of some 150 birds and the sighting of crocodiles. Cassowaries were roaming in abundance on the Ramu Plains. Except for dogs and wild pigs the explorers sighted no mammals. Inadequate transport restricted the collection and shipment of live animals with only two cassowaries and two dogs shipped to the Berlin Zoo.

Lauterbach, like Zöller, believed the western tributaries of the Ramu contained gold, but this, he argued, would require thorough exploration. The party concurred that the vast area of fertile land stretching from the Sepik to the Ramu River Valley would be suitable for cultivation. Of particular interest to them was the alpine region of the Bismarck Range because of its European-friendly climate. They believed that plantations, to be established on the wide expanse of the lower lying valley, could be managed from this vantage point. Lauterbach concluded: 'the foothills of the Bismarck Range open up fresh, undreamt-of prospects for the utilisation of KWL'.[23]

The ill-fated Ehlers adventure

Otto Ehlers, a newspaper correspondent and professional traveller arrived in 1895 to trek across East New Guinea. Despite being warned by Acting Administrator Hugo Rüdiger not to attempt the precipitous crossing, Ehlers set out confidently on the journey from the Huon Gulf to the Gulf of Papua. Accompanied by Wilhelm Piering, Police Officer at Friedrich Wilhelmshafen, the two Germans were supported by 43 carriers and one servant. Ehlers calculated that his expedition would average 6 km a day, therefore reaching the south coast of BNG in 30 days. Other than rations for 5 weeks and some trade-goods, eight rifles and two shot guns, the explorers carried no more than the clothes on their backs. Geographical instruments were left behind as was photographic and other scientific equipment, regarded as unnecessary baggage.

Disastrous Ventures

The party started inland from the mouth of the Francisca River on 14 August 1895. Nothing was heard or seen of them until 20 members of the party were picked up by the Mobiabi tribe on the Lakekamu River in BNG on 21 October, 67 days after they had begun the journey overland. Ehlers and Piering were not among them. Rain had set in before they reached the only inland village on their track, with the first carrier dead within the first 10 days. After 5 weeks of unrelenting rain and cold fog, cutting their way through dense rain-forest, up and down steep mountains and across precipitous ravines, wading through leech-infested creeks, Ehlers and his men had run out of food. Reduced to eating grass and leaves and distressed by dysentery and other ailments, fewer than 35 men reached a tributary of the Lakekamu around 30 September. They scrambled along the river for 9 days before the stream could be negotiated by raft. After another 6 days of navigating rapids and narrow waterways full of snags 20 men reached the village Motumotu. When one raft capsized with two Buka policemen, Ranga and Upia (Opiha) shot Ehlers, Piering and several carriers dead to make room for them and their mates on the remaining raft. When apprehanded by Mr Kowald, BNG government agent for the Mekeo district, the two renegades concocted the story that the Germans had drowned. Only after Port Moresby returned the few survivors to Friedrich Wilhelmshafen did the truth emerge.

Awaiting their trial for murder, Ranga and Upia escaped and shot dead Administrator Curt von Hagen when pursued. The two escapees were subsequently speared to death by the Gogol people, their heads severed and taken to Stephansort as evidence for the reward set by NGC.[24]

In search of precious metals: The second Ramu expedition

Lauterbach's assumption of the presence of gold-bearing quartz and the discovery in 1896 of alluvial gold by Australian fossickers on the Upper Mambare River of BNG persuaded Hansemann to reverse his decision on scientific exploration. The NGC chairman now saw the future of his venture on the other side of the globe in the discovery of gold. He wrote in the *Nachrichten* that Australian prospectors found gold in the riverbed of the Mambare and that 40 to 50 Europeans were working goldfields in the Sudest and Misima Islands, and in the Louisiade Group. Oddly, he informed his shareholders of the requirement for new funds to equip yet another scientific expedition to GNG in 1897. Rather than disclosing the purpose of the venture, Hansemann spoke of the need to confirm that the Ottilie and Ramu Rivers were one river system. And, before gold exploration could commence friendly relations with the local people needed to be established. For this to happen it was necessary in Hansemann's mind to establish in the central region of the Ramu Valley; indeed, first of all he required the mapping of the entire valley. Then, and after the search for gold during this exploration was completed, the explorers were to attempt an inland crossing from the Ramu to the Markham River and exit at Huon Gulf.[25]

Hansemann appointed Tappenbeck the leader of this expedition. The experienced explorer had a free hand to select his team, equipment and provisions. In this, Tappenbeck regarded the construction in Germany of a flat bottom paddle-wheel steamboat a priority if the investigations of the Upper Ramu and its tributaries.

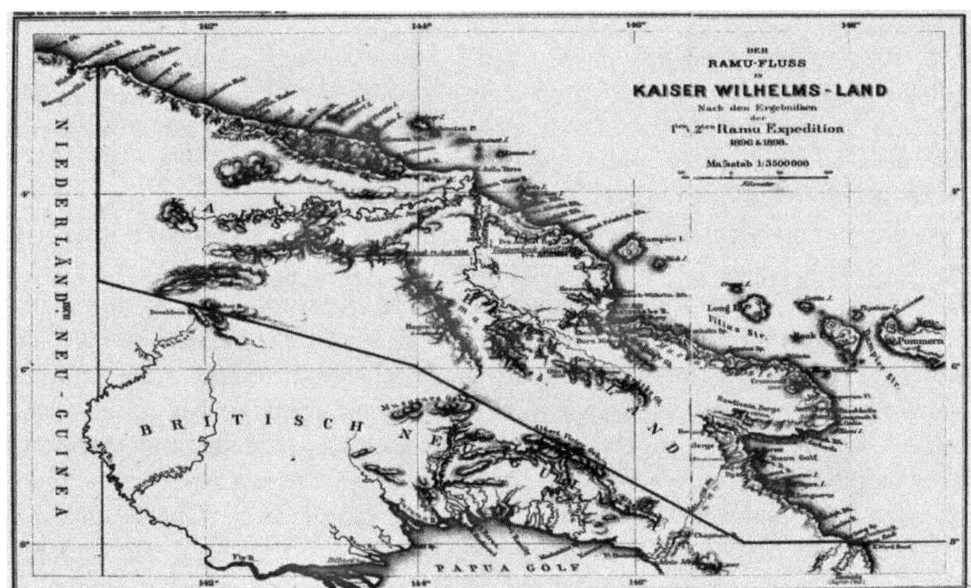

Map 8: **The 1896 Ramu expeditions** *(NKWL,* 1896)

Rather than relying on German geologists, Tappenbeck hired two gold prospectors from Australia; the architect-turned-gold fossicker Hans Klink and Robert Phillip from Sydney, who had worked the Palmer River goldfields, near Cooktown. Tappenbeck completed his European team with the engagement of Hans Blum, Peter Hansen and Hans Rodatz. Two Chinese cooks, six Javanese tradesmen and 36 Melanesian carriers provided support. The exploration barge was crewed by a Chinese machinist, a stoker and a coxswain from Singapore and 10 Melanesian deckhands. Tappenbeck procured geological instruments, assaying tools, guns and dynamite which, together with sections of the paddle steamer and pre-fabricated houses, were shipped to the Protectorate on NGC's *Johann Albrecht.* The loading in Singapore of rice, dried fish, building material, goats, pigs, fowls and ducks completed the provisioning of the expedition.[26] Following his arrival in Friedrich Wilhelmshafen Tappenbeck assembled the *Herzogin Elisabeth* and briefed his team on the task ahead.

Engine failure delayed his departure until 3 April 1898. Then the venture went no further than Cape Croisilles. The barge, with an 18.2 m overall length, a 3.9 m beam and a 1 m moulded depth, was not designed to handle the heavy swell in the Bismarck Sea. The paddle-steamer had to make for Adalberthafen, some 70 km northwest of FWH, while the *Johann Albrecht* sailed for the Ottilie River to unload the stores. The much larger steamer was able to cope with the roll of the sea; however, the livestock was much the worse for it. Captain Sanders was forced to return to the calm water of Adalberthafen and unload the few goats, pigs and fowls that had not perished.

With the arrival of calmer weather Sanders successfully crossed the sandbar at the mouth of the Ottilie on 13 August, with the paddle steamer still trapped by the rolling waves at Adalberthafen. After the *Johann Albrecht* journeyed some 300 km upstream—never much further than 140 km from the coast—Sanders confirmed

Disastrous Ventures

Lauterbach's finding: the Ramu and Ottilie were the same rivers. Here the rapids of the river made it necessary on 19 April for the explorers to land the stores and equipment on the riverbank and set up camp. The *Johann Albrecht* returned to assist the *Herzogin Elisabeth* to the river inlet so that the barge could proceed upstream under its own steam. It became a long, lonely stay for the team left behind. The *Johann Albrecht* was shipwrecked on 15 May 1898 on a Hermit Island reef.

While the *Herzogin Elisabeth* rode at anchor in Albrechtshafen (Bogia) near Ramumünde; Klink and Rodatz, a Javanese hunter, dissectors (2), carpenters (3), a Chinese cook and a boy, and 21 Papuans (including four women) set up NGC's first inland station on the foothills of what became known as the Hagen Range. Calm August weather provided the opportunity for Tappenbeck, Philipp, Ernst Schirmer and a fresh team of labourers to reach Ramu Station on the paddle steamer unassisted. During his involuntary stay on the coast, Tappenbeck established Ramumünde Station on the mouth of the river where he fabricated buildings for the Ramu Station. In the meantime Klink and Rodatz cleared some 5,000 m² of rainforest to set up makeshift houses and huts. Expecting that the wait would not have been long, the explorers traded mirrors and pearls with the local people for taro, yam, coconuts and sugar cane rather than setting up their own garden. They also built canoes to explore further afield or attempt a 300 km escape to the open sea if required.[27]

Building canoes was different from building houses, however. While the use of steel tools was an advantage, it took some time to master the selection of the right trees, to become skilled in hewing and to learn the fire treatment for water tightness. Despite the newly gained mobility, Klink and Rodatz found canoeing upstream too demanding and too dangerous. The headwaters of the Ramu were not investigated nor was there any attempt to go overland to the Markham River. During the four-month wait Rodatz collected insects, plants and artefacts. He recorded air temperatures, dew points and precipitations daily. He also took regular readings on the water level of the Ramu which, according to his report varied considerably with the amount of rain that had fallen. Klink examined rock faces and panned the riverbed for gold.[28]

Heavy rain in September and October made further prospecting impossible. It was also the end of Tappenbeck's employment with NGC. Even though the last 2 months of the expedition produced some gold on the Upper Ramu between latitudes 5° 33' and 5° 45' south, Klink was handed responsibility to bring the expedition to a close.

The third Ramu expedition

When scientific investigations transferred from NGC to the *Reich* on 7 October 1898 the government granted NGC exclusive prospecting rights in the Ramu Valley. Under the 1 April 1899 agreement NGC pays a royalty of 10% on the net income derived from mining. Spurred on by the successes of the gold miners in BNG, Hansemann re-engaged the experienced Carl Lauterbach and Hans Klink to lead a new Ramu expedition.[29] Before proceeding to Stephansort Klink travelled to Berlin for a meeting with Hansemann, and for the purchase of Fritsch & Benator gold-assaying equipment. On his return trip to GNG he stopped in Australia to engage the experienced gold prospector Herr Holst.

So that he would not be left stranded again, Klink decided to build a 15 km track from Stephansort to the foothills of the Bismarck Range. Holst, who was in charge of the construction, completed two-thirds of the trail in less than 8 months. At that point he contracted blackwater fever that required hospitalization in Friedrich Wilhelmshafen and eventually repatriation to Australia. The German engineer Peter Behrendt, who, like Klink and Holst, had been gold prospecting in Australia, completed the track in late 1900. Barring landslides and heavy rain it was now possible to reach the Ramu Station from Stephansort in 10 days.[30]

Lauterbach caught up with Klink, Rodatz and Philipp at Ramu Station on 4 October 1899. Fourteen days later the third Ramu expedition was underway. The party, including 51 carriers, commenced the journey upstream in 19 canoes. The investigations started with the re-examination of the eleventh tributary on the left side of the river. Lauterbach confirmed the presence of gold traces at this point and further upstream on the Ramu banks.

Some 100 km past the point of the 1896 expedition the Ramu became unnavigable. Unable to reach the headwater Lauterbach returned to Germany on 9 January 1900. Klink and Rodatz went to Australia on leave and Phillip left NGC for good. Schirmer and 12 men stayed on the Ramu Station, awaiting further instructions from Berlin.

The paddle-steamer *Herzogin Elisabeth* **on the Ramu River** (Goethe University, Frankfurt a. M. No. 014-4050-8). **Expedition leaders Dr C. Lauterbach (seated), standing left to right H. Klink, H. Rodatz, and Robert Phillip,** ca. 1899 (F. Hutter, eds. *Neu Guinea*, p. 541). **Start of the Third Ramu expedition,** ca 1898 (Goethe University, No. 014-4048-6). **Upper Ramu Station,** ca. 1900 (Goethe University, No. 014-4048-7)

Disastrous Ventures

Undaunted by the lack of success, Hansemann promoted further investigation by reporting to shareholders in March 1900 that valuable discoveries had already been made by Dr Lauterbach the previous year, viz:

1) During the wet season the Ramu is negotiable by barge from the coast to latitude 5°45' south or even further when the currents are moderate. 2) The Upper Ramu Station is reachable from Stephansort and Friedrich Wilhelmshafen via a land route. 3) The river flows in sections through picturesque, flat, arable, land. 4) Despite the presence of highland swamps, the climate in this part of KWL is conducive to a European way of life. 5) The Ramu Valley contains auriferous soil. An extensive ridge, containing alluvial gold, was discovered. Gold was also discovered in the tributaries. Evidence of gold traces heightens the probability of discoveries, with soil samples brought from the area presently undergoing examination in Germany.[31]

Hans Klink returned to New Guinea in May 1901 to set up a camp on the northeast side of the Ramu where a few specks of gold were found the previous year. Yet again the preparations suffered serious setbacks. In the course of ferrying equipment the *Herzogin Elisabeth* struck a snag which rendered the barge unserviceable. It took 6 months before the necessary equipment and buildings were laboured into place.[32]

In the meantime, from 10 to 24 January 1902, Klink diverted his interest in gold prospecting to accompany the botanist Rudolf Schlechter on an exploration of the Bismarck Range. Commissioned by the *Kolonialwirtschaftliches Komitee,* Schlechter found in what he was sent for: the white, milky latex of the rubber trees for which the German electrical cable industry had an increasing demand.[33]

Back on his original assignment in February 1902, Klink had to deal with a number of thorny situations. Behrendt proved unable to deal with the tropical conditions and had to be replaced with the experienced Wilhelm Dammköhler who had previously worked in the Dutch East Indies as a pearl fisher and as a gold prospector in Western Australia The bosun of the *Herzogin Elisabeth* could not handle the hard work on land, took ill and returned to Germany. A heavy storm, dumping 200 mm in two hours, washed away two canoes and most of the provisions. Shortly after these adversities, three labourers were killed by tribesmen.[34]

Klink prospected some 5,000 km^2 on the Ramu and its tributaries. He found gold traces in shallow sand and gravel beds and in pockets of rock outcrops. Many of the quartz samples turned out to be pyrite. In June 1902 Klink was relieved by the mining engineer Johannes Schlenzig. Together with Dammköhler, Ludwig Sommer and the prospectors Gundlich and Bradley, Schlenzig confirmed much of what Klink and Lauterbach had reported: the Bismarck Range contained gold, most likely buried under mud and gravel accumulated over millions of years in the riverbeds. The delineation of goldfields required time and money. But the NGC Board no longer had the stomach to request further funds from their shareholders. The Ramu concession was *in perpetuity and* the knowledge gained could be transferred to the *Huon Golf Syndikat.* In the Board's opinion NGC could again engage in speculative exploration when the company made a profit. For now, the Directors focussed NGC on the coconut plantations on the Gazelle Peninsula and on the Astrolabe Plain. The accumulated expenditure for the 1899 to 1902 Ramu expeditions was RM475,538. This sum was written off in the 1903/04.[35]

The Huon Golf Syndikat

After the *Reich* assumed responsibility for GNG on 1 April 1899 Berlin embarked on an agenda of speedy economic development. In the opinion of the *Reichskanzler* and more to the point, Kaiser Wilhelm II, NGC had been slow in establishing the economy of GNG. During an audience on 8 January 1901 the Kaiser let the new Governor of GNG, Albert Hahl, know that he was disappointed with the economic progress of the German colonies. 'Germany had embarked on developing its overseas economy at the eleventh hour, perhaps too late', he told Hahl: 'it was therefore imperative to make progress quickly and deliver results'. In reply to Hahl's concerns that GNG would develop slowly because of the vast area under his administration, the impenetrable terrain of the mainland and the low cultural and economic level of the indigenous people; the Kaiser pointed to the importance of discovering gold and silver to strengthen the *Reichs Mark*. 'The gold-bearing country near the border with BNG should be quickly explored and developed', he demanded of Hahl.[36]

Equipped with good advice but without the budget to realize the Kaiser's wishes, Hahl would have been pleased to find that Hansemann had facilitated a joint venture between Disconto Gesellschaft, Deutsche Bank, Norddeutsche Bank, Sal. Oppenheim jr & Co., Berliner Handels-Gesellschaft and NGC for the purpose of exploring the hinterland of the Huon Gulf south of Cape Arkon to the British border.[37] Thus the government awarded the *Huon Golf Syndikat* an exclusive concession on 17 June 1901 to explore for platinum, gold and silver, precious stones, lignite, anthracite, petroleum and other minerals of industrial value in this region.[38]

The 20-year mining agreement required the syndicate to form a colonial company within 5 years with an authorised capitalof at least RM10 million paid-up to no less than five million *Reichs Mark*. Under the agreement the government was required to waive tariffs on materials and equipment required for the construction of harbour and marine facilities, housing and mine infrastructure. It was also obliged to approve the lease of unoccupied land which was required for mining developments and to support the syndicate or companies in the purchase of land owned by the local people. In the event of the combined leaseholds exceeding 200 km^2 inland or 10 km of coastal strip, the GNG government, was entitled to a royalty of RM1/ha after 5 years. It also would reveive a 20% fee on profits when dividends exceeded 5%.[39]

The syndicate engaged H. Rodatz to lead the expedition who, with an available budget of RM500,000 assembled a team of experts. Former NGC employee Dauben became Rodatz's assistant. The Australian Robert Lindsay, a Sydney-based Norwegian (Ellington) and a Dane (Nissen) were hired as prospectors. The German geologist Herr Gode, who studied mining engineering in Australia, and the Australian geologist Mackenzie were engaged to provide scientific expertise. However, Mackenzie fell sick soon after arriving in GNG and returned home before the expedition began.

Rodatz acquired the schooner *Papua* in Friedrich Wilhelmshafen and hired Klaus Burmeister to skipper the 20t sailing vessel. Responsibility for the steam launch he bought in Sydney for this expedition was handed to the Scandinavian sailor Uhr. Finschhafen served as a depôt for recruiting Jabim people.[40]

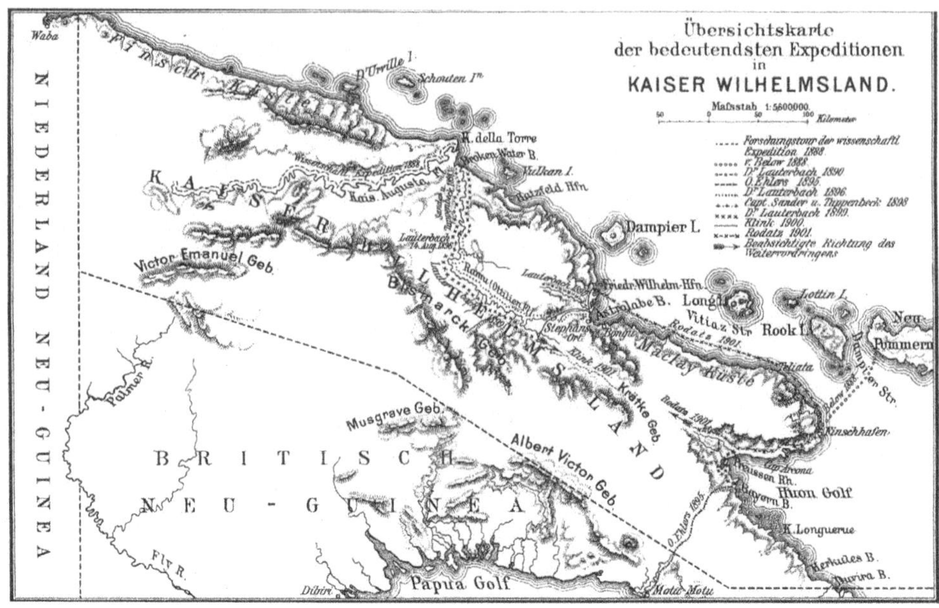

Map 9: **Expeditions in GNG to 1901** (F. Hutter, p. 523)

The preparatory work was completed in the Lugama district near the mouth of the Markham River and in October 1901 the explorers set off with about 160 carriers to explore the creeks and rivers fed from the Rawlinson Range into the Huon Gulf. They found that the rock formations in this region were of recent volcanic origin. With little prospect of discovering minerals and metals, they abandoned Laguma Station soon after in favour of Salamaua on Samoahafen. What happened during the next 2 years is not clear. NGC informed its shareholders in 1902 that Rodatz had made progress despite great difficulties along the Franziska River in a southwesterly direction to reach the British border. He planned a survey of the Markham and Adler Rivers but took ill in late 1902. In 1903 NGC reported that Johannes Schlenzig had assumed responsibility for the Huon Gulf expedition. In 1904 traces of gold and other minerals had been found in several areas, but that the significance of the discoveries could only be confirmed after the samples had been assayed: 'Herr Schlenzig is currently preparing a detailed report which will be circulated to the syndicate members as soon as it becomes available", NGC report. A year later, and without publishing the promised report, the company reported: 'the Huon Gulf expedition concluded at the end of November 1903, with the expedition terminated'.[41]

NGC's investment in the syndicate was RM187,500 which was shown as an expense in the 1903/04 accounts. Because the syndicate was not transformed into a colonial company, as stipulated in §5 of the agreement with the government, Colonial Secretary Bernhard Dernburg terminated the concession on 7 February 1908. He informed the Directors of Disconto Gesellschaft that he was only prepared to discuss an extension of the agreement if the syndicate put in place an appropriately funded company. Failing this the GNG government would, in accordance with §93 of the Mining Act of 27 February 1906, assume the exclusive mining rights in the area.[42]

Gold prospecting in German New Guinea

It appears Hansemann did not learn about the gold discovery on the Gira River in late 1897. BNG's Lt Governor W. MacGregor reported that prospectors yielded 8 to 10dwt of gold from fourteen dishes, but that it would be absurd to prospect as 'the Gira River encroaches on German territory [and] if Germany should prove unfriendly it would be useless'. MacGregor proposed 'to ask the German authorities to make the middle of the river the boundary, and leave navigation free to both colonies'.[43]

By 1908 Hahl would have been aware the Gira River was in Australian territory. He would also have been aware of the gold-bearing potential of the Huon Gulf district. And now that exploration of this region became his responsibility he sought Rodatz's view on his findings on the Huon Gulf Expedition. Rodatz, although careful not to divulge drawings and details of his report to NGC without first receiving permission from his former employer, admitted to Hahl: 'As leader of the expedition I had conducted a detailed survey of the land from Cape Arkona to the British border, with 'gold only discovered southeast of the Herculesfluß (Waria River)'. Rodatz said that he visited the BNG government Station Tamata on the Mambare–Tamata River several times and that he was shown a drawing by Australian resident magistrate, Archibald Walker, with locations where gold was being panned. Walker admitted to Rodatz that 'several of the gold-bearing districts, marked in a red circle, were situated on German territory'.[44]

All the gold discoveries on the map were in the Waria River and Mambare River districts. But the fields on the German side were only accessible by climbing the steep ridges of the many peaks leading to the headwater of the Waria. The river itself was only navigable for short distances and the path along the riverbank mostly cut off by rock faces, plunging almost vertically into a chain of rapids. Rodatz claimed that the geology of the area indicated the existence of gold 'which would only be found in pockets and therefore will only be profitable to a prospector. In his view, the likely occurrence of large gold veins could not be exploited by small operators:

> It requires the mobilisation of substantial mining equipment. [But] the opening up of the area can also not be undertaken by large expeditions, financed by corporations, because the investments will never return a profit. An expedition, which is instructed by Berlin how to proceed and which area to investigate, is too handicapped to operate successfully in this difficult terrain. The logistics for a large exploration team are difficult and slow and would encounter insurmountable obstacle with every step taken, while two miners with four carriers would find a way through the most difficult landscape. The self-denial of these tough men guarantees their successes.

Based on the British experience and his perception of the situation, Rodatz advised Hahl not to award an exploration concession to a company: 'the development of GNG would suffer and the company will lose its money'. Instead he suggested that Hahl open up GNG to prospectors and encourage companies 'to supply these fearless men with goods and services and providing them with the required labourers'.[45]

The El Dorado that Hansemann, Hahl and the Kaiser hoped for never materialised, though not for want of trying. In 1907 Hahl marched from Astrolabe Bay through the Minjen Valley to the Middle Ramu, crossing the Great Range beyond the watershed of the Ramu and onto the Markham River. One year later Hahl, together with Judge

Disastrous Ventures

Rudolf Karlowa, surveyor Karl Warnicke and Captain Möller of the SS *Seestern,* made the strenuous climb to the Waria Valley. Here, on the Pio, Waria and Jatuna Rivers, they surprised Australian miners panning for gold on GNG territory. At the village Ugo, the Governor met a village chief who was familiar was the whereabouts of the gold prospectors in the region. He told Hahl that magistrate Walker and the prospectors believed that they were still on British territory. Rather than chasing the prospectors off the river Hahl requested them to wash for gold at locations selected by him 'with the result that every dish showed gold specks'.[46]

The confirmation of gold prompted the German authorities to press for clarification of the exact colonial boundary in this gold-producing area. Both the Australian and German governments believed that delimiting the territories would benefit their colony's respective economic interests. For this reason few difficulties stood in the way for Hahl and Papua's Lieutenant-Governor Murray to establish an Anglo-German Boundary Commission in 1908. Captain Förster and the government geologist Artur Stollé were appointed to lead the German team; chief government Surveyor, Gustavus Sabine, together with Resident Magistrate for the Eastern Division, Owen Turner, led the Australian contingent. A licensed surveyor, an assistant, 20 native police and 20 Papuan carriers completed the Australian party. The Australian deputation, including Murray, landed at Warsong Point near the mouth of the Gira River on 27 December. A year later, on 7 January 1909, the German cruiser *Condor* arrived with Hahl, Förster and Stollé. After agreeing on the best method of carrying out the undertaking the joint expedition set off in the second week of January.

The boundary to be marked followed the 8th parallel of South latitude from the east coast to its intersection with the 147th meridian of East Longitude. After six months hard work the two teams had only set survey markers to longitude 147° 25' 48.28", a distance of approximately 30 miles from the east coast. Förster became too ill to continue and had to leave the expedition. Labour problems, sickness, pelting rain and the sheer impenetrability of the terrain forced the decision to determine the remainder of the Anglo–German boundary by triangulation.[47]

Before Stollé transferred in 1910 to join the expedition set up by the government to determine the German-Dutch New Guinea boundary,[48] he followed the Waria to its upper basin as far as the Unu River. There he discovered traces of gold in many of the creeks, which he estimated to contain 800,000,000 m^3 of low-grade wash.[49]

Gold traces were also confirmed by Wilhelm Dammköhler who, with Rudolf Oldörp, attempted to confirm the existence of gold deposits from the Ramu Valley. Starting the expedition from Astrolabe Bay in early 1909 the pair advanced to the Upper Ramu without hitting pay dirt. Dissatisfied with their findings they crossed the watersheds of the Ramu and Markham Rivers in July 1909 to enter the Herzog Range. On the Watut and most likely the Bulolo, a tributary of the Markham River, they discovered promising gold deposits.[50]

Short of provisions and fatigued, aided by only a handful of carriers, the two explorers were attacked by the Watut people. With Dammköhler falling to the warriors, an injured Oldörp managed to escape the assault and raft down the Markham River.

After an eventful, perilous journey he eventually found safety at the Neuendettelsauer Mission at Cape Arkon. To confirm his discovery Oldörp made a further attempt 10 months later. Together with Captain Bröker of the schooner *Lettie* he set off for the Watut on in April 1910. This time luck was not on his side; the schooner sank on 15 April, with only four carriers making it back to shore. Rudolf Oldörp took his knowledge of the gold's location to the bottom of the Huon Gulf.[51]

A group of German-Australian miners arrived in FWH on the SS *Prinz Sigismund* in 1909, among them August Aubry, Jacob Fox, J. H. Reinhardt, Cornelius Runk and George Sievers. This coterie of individuals had formed a company to explore for gold in GNG. Since Hahl had already granted the Frenchman Joubert and the Australians, Tooth and Ivory, prospecting rights, he also confirmed rights to this group.

The setup in September 1909 on Morobe Harbour served to support the joint border commission and government licensed explorers. Morobe Station was also set up to pacify the aggressive tribes in the highlands and to function as a base from where Australian gold prospectors on German territory could be kept in check. Despite rumours in Samarai that the Germans would not let Australian prospectors reach the Upper Waria from the mouth of the river, Hahl let it be kown in 1909 that Australian prospectors were free to use the Waria for transport where it passed through GNG territory.[52] He told the Australian veteran gold miners Frank and Jim Pryke: 'the impression is wrong that we want to hunt the Australian prospectors. We have good geologists, but we know that the Australian prospectors are the best in the world to open up new country. And we want this country opened up'. On another occasion, when William (Sharkeye) Park, Matt Crowe and Jim Preston were caught panning gold on the German side of the Waria the men were told by Hahl:

> You can enter the country as bird of paradise shooters as well as prospectors. Your boys can be shooting the birds while you are prospecting. Then if you find no gold, you will still make money by the sale of the bird's skins. If you find gold, you will make a fortune; never fear that we will be hard on you. You can peg out prospectors' claims just as you would in BNG (Papua). And the gold you will win will be yours, less a very small royalty such as you are charged in BNG (sic). We are thinking of adopting the Queensland or BNG Ordinances in the event of discovery of a goldfield. Whether or not, you men can rest assured that whatever you may find will be yours. [53]

Some Australians accepted Hahl's invitation but found it prudent to keep discoveries to themselves. In a letter to Townsville's *North Queensland Register* Frank Pryke wrote that Hahl permits the Australian miners into GNG because he knew they were 'the best class of people to open up new country'.[54] Hahl did not disagree. He believed that Germany had the better scientists and Australia the better practitioners.

In 1913 Rabaul granted mining concession to Emil Kempf from Alsace. After some wildly adventurous experiences on the Upper Waria Kempf located what looked like a dredging proposition.[55] At last it seemed that GNG would produce gold on a large scale. Eduard Haber, deputising for Hahl, cabled Berlin in 1914: 'the Upper Waria contains several billions of gold and much platinum, for the exploitation of which only equipment and access to the mine sites are missing'. Berlin dismissed Haber's telegram with *Katzengold* (fools gold),[56] correctly assuming that the major gold deposits were not on the Waria River.

Disastrous Ventures

Australian miners had worked the Waria since 1906 with modest success. In 1913 Jimmy Preston and Sharkeye Park made a request to Rabaul to prospect Koranga Creek and Watut River near Wau. Park remained on the Bulolo Ridge during most of World War I. He and Jack Nettleton confirmed strikes on the Koronga in 1922. But neither the prospectors of the time envisaged that the banks of the Upper Edie Creek and Bulolo River contained gold up to 2.5 metres deep for several kilometres. What became known as the Morobe goldfield produced over 80 tons of gold between 1923 and the outbreak of World War II. In 1937/38 this field yielded 403,652 oz. more than the entire gold production of Papua from 1888 to 1915.[57]

Miners' shacks at Eddie Creek, ca 1919 (M. von Hein colletion, Mitchell Library, fm3/846)

Notes

1   Hansemann to Bismarck, 2 Jan. 1886 (RKA 1001:2408, pp. 30–7 & 42–3)

2   *NKWL* (1886) Heft i, pp. 4-6; 'Instruction für den Landeshauptmann', §§ 14 & 19

3   'Instruction für die wissenschaftliche Forschungsexpedition', §§2, 8, 11, 12 & 18

4   *NKWL* (1886) Heft. iii, pp. 84 & 87–8, (1888), Heft iv, p. 228; Jb (1887) p. 5; Sack & Clark (1886–87) pp. 6–7; O. Schellong, *Alte Dokumente aus der Südsee*, p. 44

5   *NKWL* (1886) Heft iv, pp. 119–128, (1887) Heft ii, pp. 54–5, (1888) Heft iv, pp. 188–91

6   *Illustrated Australian News* (1886), 18 Sep. p. 155

7   *NKWL* (1887) Heft ii, pp. 32–7, Heft iv, p. 152. A. Hahl, 'Deutsch-Neuguinea und die ersten Jahre seiner Verwaltung' (*DKZ*, [1934] Nr. 46, p. 263). See Schellong, p. 57

8   *NKWL* (1887) Heft i, pp. 23ff; Heft ii, pp. 57; Heft iv, p. 153; (1888) Heft, i, p. 23, Heft iv, pp. 238ff

9   NGC, 18 Oct. 1887 (RKA 1001:2409, p. 30); *NKWL* (1888) Heft i, p.17; Heft iv, p. 236

10 H. Blum, *Neu Guinea und der Bismarck Archipel*, pp. 193–4

11 M. Hollrung, & K. Schumann, 'Die Flora von Kaiser Wilhelms Land', *Beiheft NKWL* (1889); M. Hollrung, 'Bericht über Wissenschaftliche Expeditionen in Kaiser Wilhelmsland' (*NKWL* [1887] Heft v, pp. 178ff; Heft iv, pp. 183ff; Jb [1889] p. 6; Sack & Clark [1889–89] p. 41). E. Sachau. 'First lexicon on New Guinean languages', (*NKWL* [1886] Heft iii, pp. 80–7). H. Zöller's 8,000-word-glossary on 24 languages spoken in the Bismarck Archipelago, KWL, Solomon and Admiralty Islands (*NKWL* [1890] Heft ii, pp. 97–8). Schellong, pp. 129ff. O. Dempwolff, 'Beiträge zur Kenntnis der Sprache von Neu Guinea', *Seminar für Orientalische Sprachen* (1905) pp. 182–254; Dempwolff, 'Beiträge zur Kenntnis der Sprache von Bilibili',

Seminar (1909) pp. 221–61; Dempwolff; 'Musikalischetonhöhen, Ein Problem für Papuasprachen', *Zeitschrift für Kolonialsprachen* (1912) pp. 327–30

12   Fortification Point to *Kaiserin Augusta-Fluß*; Purdy Islands, Mioko, Matupi in the Bismarck Archipelago, (*NKWL* [1887] Heft i, pp. 5–26, Heft ii, pp. 32ff; Heft v, pp. 164–78). North and south coast of New Britain, 17 Sep.–17 Oct. and 10–19 Dec. 1887, (*NKWL* [1888] Heft i, pp. 34-41). Schneider, 'Geologische Berichte über die Bucht von Finschhafen', *NKWL* (1887) Heft iii, pp. 84–7, 'Forschungstouren im Umkreis der Station Konstantinhafen', *NKWL* (1887) Heft iv, pp. 144–8; 'Nordküste von Neu-Guinea' (*DKBl* [1890], Nr. 1 pp. 70–1 & 131)

13   *NKWL* (1887) Heft i; pp. 27–8; *NKWL* (1888) Heft ii, pp. 76–9, (1889) Heft ii, pp. 81 & 83. Jb (1888) pp. 4–5; Sack & Clark (1887–88) p. 25. The phreatic eruption of Ritter Island, known as *Vulcan Insel*, led to the collapse on 13 March 1888 of 640 vertical metres (roughly 5 km^3) of the volcano. The subsequent tsunami of 8–15 m caused destruction on the north coast and the southwest promontory of New Britain. S.N. Ward & S. Day, 'Ritter, Island Volcano - Lateral Collapse and the Tsunami of 1888' (*Geographical Journal International* (issue 154 [2003]

14   *NKWL* (1887) Heft i, pp. 27–8; Heft iii, p. 84ff; Heft iv, pp. 33–4 & 153–5; Heft v, pp. 196–7; (1888) Heft ii, pp. 72–4; Heft iii, pp. 160–5. Climate data collected in GNG from 1886 to 1914 showed gaps over the course of a year; Chart 36. Data for 1886 to 1898 in A. von Danckelman, 'Die Fortschritte der Geographischen Forschung im Jahre 1891' (*Das Ausland*, 1891) to 1913 in H. Marquardsen & A.v. Danckelman, 'Berichte über das Meterologische Beobachtungswesen im Schutzgebiet Deutsch-Neu Guinea' (*DKBl*, Nrs. 3–27).

15   *NKWL* (1888) Heft iv, pp. 193 & 198.

16   *NKWL* (1889) Heft ii, pp. 48–87

17   G. v. Schleinitz, 'Beschreibung der Nordküste von Kaiser Wilhelms-Land von Kap Cretin bis zu den Legorant-Inseln' (*NKWL* [1889] Heft iii, pp. 137–54 and [1896] pp. 44–6, 54 & 82). Cartographical results of the Neu Pommern north and west coast, *NKWL* (1896) Heft i, pp. 44–6

18   *NKWL* (1888) Heft i, p. 144; (1889) Heft i, pp. 3–15; Heft ii, pp. 36–44 and (1890), Heft i, pp. 19–21. H. Zöller, 'Meine Untersuchungen in das Finisterre-Gebirge', *PGM* (1890) Nr 36, pp. 233-5; Zöller, 'Meine Expedition in das Innere von Deutsch-Neuguinea', *Geographische Gesellschaft München*, (1891) pp. 1-19. Zöller, 'Die Deutschen Salomon-Inseln Buka und Bougainville', *PGM*, (1891) Nr 37, pp. 8–11

19   A. Engler, *Botanische Jahrbücher für Systematik, Pflanzengeschichte und Pflanzengeographie* (Leipzig, 1891, 1892 & 1893). Hellwig's New Guinea diary in G. Thilenius, 'Eine Durchquerung des Gebietes zwischen dem Kaiserin-Augusta-Fluß und der Küste von Neuguinea', *Mitteilungen aus den Deutschen Schutzgebieten*, (1913) pp. 357–63. Jb (1889) pp. 6–7; Sack & Clark, (1888–89) pp. 38–9

20   Jb (1886/87) p. 25. H. Zöller, *Deutsch-Neu-Guinea und meine Ersteigung des Finisterre-Gebirges*, pp. 181–2. H. Jäckel, 'Die Neu Guinea Compagnie', p. 37

21   *NKWL* (1891) Heft i, pp. 31ff; (1892) p. 25; Jb (1894/95) p. 6; Sack & Clark (1894-95) p. 109.

22   C. v. Beck, 'Neu Guinea Compagnie', *Südseebote* (1918) p. 49.

23   'Ergebnisse der Kaiser Wilhelmsland Expedition', *NKWL* (1896) pp. 36–44; Jb (1895/96) pp. 9–10; Sack & Clark (1895–96) pp. 123–4.

24   *NKWL* (1895) p. 53; AR-BNG (1895/96) p. xxxiv; *SMH* (1896) 8 Apr., p. 3.H. Rüdiger, 'Bericht über den Verlauf der Ehlersschen Expedition', *DKBl* (1896), Nr. 7, pp. 448–53. See Hiery, 'Die Deutsche Verwaltung Neuguineas 1884–1914', pp. 292 & 315; Tappenbeck, *Deutsch Neuguinea*, pp.109-11

25   *NKWL* (1894) p. 53; (1897) pp. 52–3; Jb (1896/97) p. 12; Sack & Clark (1896–97) pp. 135–6

26   *NKWL* (1897) p. 55

27   *NKWL* (1898) pp. 39–41 & 55–9

28   Jb (1896/97) p. 12; Sack & Clark (1898–97) p. 136

29   NGC to shareholders, Jb (1897/98) pp. 9–10; (1901/02) p. 20; Sack & Clark (1897–98) p. 146

30   Jb (1899/1900) pp. 22–3; (1900/01) p. 27 (RKA 1001:3113, p. 19)

31   Jb (1898/99) pp. 19–20; Sack & Clark (1898–99) pp. 167–8

32   Jb (1900/01) p. 28

33   Jb (1901/02) p. 21; Sack & Clark (1901–02) p. 233. F. Schlechter, 'Die Guttapercha- und Kautschuk Expedition des Kolonial Wirschaftlichen Komitees nach Kaiser Wilhelmsland 1907–1909) KWK (1911) p. 171; *DKZ* (1907), Nr. 25, pp. 521ff; 'Kautschuk', *OAL* (1910) pp. 478–9

34   Jb (1901/02) p. 21; W.C. Dammköhler, 'Im Innern von Deutsch-Neuguinea', *KuH* 1907) Nr. 20

35   Jb (1901/02) pp. 22–4 & 36–7; Jb (1903/04) pp. 15–16; Sack & Clark (1902–03) p. 242

36   Hahl, *Gouverneursjahre*, p. 165–6; Sack & Clark, *Albert Hahl, Governor in New Guinea*, pp. 95–6

37   Syndicate letter of intent, to KA-AA, 9 Apr. 1900; Hansemann to KA-AA, 11 Apr. 1900 'Konzession zum Bergbau im Hinterland des Huongolfs' (RKA 1001:2347–8, pp. 1–4, 61–8

38   Beck, 'Neu Guinea Compagnie', p. 50

39   *RGBl.* 1900 (p. 813) §5, p. 5; §6, pp. 5–6; §7, p. 7; §§9–10, p. 9. Royalties on other minerals were 10% where dividend payments were 5% to 8%, increasing to 20% on payments above 8%.

40   Jb (1901/02) p. 28

41   Jb (1902/03) p. 26; The German Mines Department records were destroyed during WW II

42   Dernburg to D-G, 7 Feb. 1908 (RKA 1001:2349, p. 12)

43   'Sir William MacGregor, The New Guinea Goldfields', *BC* (1897) 20 Dec., p. 5

44   Hahl to Dernburg, 11 Oct. 1907 (RKA 1001:2349, pp. 3–5)

45   Rodatz to Hahl, 27 Aug. 1907 (RKA 1001:2349, pp. 4–5)

46   Hahl, *Gouverneursjahre*, pp. 205–6; Hahl, *Governor in New Guinea*, p. 125

47   'Delimitation of the Boundary between Papua & GNG', 1899–1910 (NAA Series A1–1914/4329; AR-Papua [1908/09] pp. 17 & 127; Sack & Clark [1909–10] p. 305); *Mercury,* (1908) 22 May, p. 5

48   Sack & Clark (1909–10) p. 305

49   H.H. Taylour & I. Morley, 'The Development of Gold Mining in Morobe', *The Australian Institute of Mining & Metallurgy*, 89 (1933) p. 5. See Hahl, *Gouverneursjahre*, p. 207; Hahl, *Governor*, p. 129

50   R. Oldörp & W. Dammköhler, 'Bericht über eine Reise in Neuguinea 1908–09' (*ABl* [1909] Nr. 19, pp. 135–6); Hahl, *Gouverneursjahre*, p. 210; Hahl, *Governor in New Guinea*, p. 130

51   Hahl, 'Der Aufbau der Station Morobe auf Kaiser Wilhelms-Land', (*DKZ*, [1935] Nr. 47, p. 237)

52   H.N. Nelson, *Black White & Gold*, p. 141

53   I.L. Idriess cited an interview with Hahl, *Gold-Dust and Ashes*, pp. 13 & 16; A.M. Healy, 'Ophir to Bulolo: The History of the Gold Search in NG', *HS,* XII (1965) pp. 112–13

54   Pryke to the editor of the *North Queensland Register* (NLA MS 1826, mfm PMB 913)

55   Idriess, p. 29; Hahl, *Gouverneursjahre*, p. 210; Hahl, *Governor in New Guinea*, pp. 125 & 130

56   Haber, 27 Aug. 1914; 'Der Krieg in New Guinea' (RKA 1001:2612)

57   Nelson, 'N.G. Goldfield Pioneers', pp. 258ff. E. Auerbach, 'Death of "Sharkeye" Park: Extraordinary Man who found a New Guinea Goldfield' , *Pacific Islands Monthly*, X, (1940) 15 Mar p. 22, 15 Jul p. 58

Other explorations in GNG: Hydrography by the auxiliary cruiser SMS *Möve* from 1895 to 1905, followed by the SMS *Planet* until Oct. 1914. Dr E. Stephan, later Augustin Krämer, led the German Naval-Expedition of 1907-09 to explore the Bismarck Archipelago. A. Stollé, engaged by the Colonial Society, joined C. Ledermann, J. Bürgers, A. Roesicke, W. Behrmann and R. Thurnwald to explore the Sepik region (March 1912 to Oct. 1913). W. Behrmann, *Im Stromgebiet Des Sepik. Eine Deutsche Forschungsreise in Neuguinea*, pp. 346–7; A. Stollé & W. Behrmann, 'Expedition zur Erforschung des Kaiserin-Augusta-Stromes', *DKZ* [1912] Nr. 29, pp. 743–4 & 793 and *DKZ* [1913] Nr. 30, pp. 6ff). R. Thurnwald used photography, cinematography and phonographic cylinders to record his findings on the Sepik and on Bougainville (1906–09), 'Forschung Dr. Thurnwalds im Gebiet zwischen Kaiserin-Augusta-Fluss und Küste', *DKZ* [1914] Nr. 31, p. 20. K. Sapper (vulcanologist) and G. Friederici (anthropologist) explored New Ireland for the *Landeskundliche Kommission für Erforschung der Schutzgebiete* (April–Sept. 1908). The Hamburgische Südsee-Expedition (1908-11) was the most comprehensive expedition ever undertaken in GNG. Led by F. Fülleborn of the *Institut für Schiffs- und Tropenkrankheiten*, Hamburg, the expedition included O. Reche (anthropologist), W. Müller (linguist), H. Vogel (painter), G. Ducker (natural scientist), Prof. Krämer and Elisabeth Krämer-Bannow, P. Hambruch & E. Sarfert (anthropologists). The discoveries of some 18,000 ethnographical and anthropological objects were published by G. Thilenius in 'Eine Durchquerung des Gebietes Zwischen dem Kaiserin-Augusta Fluß und der Küste von Neuguinea', *Mitteilungen aus den Deutschen Schutzgebieten* (1913) pp. 357-63. Dr L. Külz (appointed Chief Medical Officer for GNG in 1913) and Prof Dr A. Leber (ophthalmologist) were in charge of the *Medizinisch-Demographische Deutsch-Neuguinea Expedition des Reichs-Kolonialmat* (1913). Leber was charged with conducting a health survey of the whole of GNG, including population growth. He started his investigations on Bougainville and Buka and by undertaking a crossing of Manus Island (Centrale Durchquerung der Insel Manus, Mai 1914). Külz examined the population of villages south-west of Herbertshöhe (M. Davies, *Public Health and Colonialism* pp. 162--74)

SHIPPING SERVICES IN GERMAN NEW GUINEA

The chronic lack of sea transport hindered successful expeditions by the New Guinea Compagnie. Yet the prerequisite for the development of any overseas dependency was transportation. As early as September 1880 Hansemann had proposed the establishment of a government-subsidised steamer connection between Apia and Mioko. After many *Reichstag* debates and committee sittings the Mail Shipping Subsidy Bill was passed on 26 April 1885.[1] The subsequent agreement on 4 July 1885 between the Reich and Norddeutsche Lloyd (NDL) provided for a regular service from Hamburg and Bremen to Hong Kong with a connection to Japan and a second service from Hamburg and Bremen to Sydney via Singapore with a link to Apia. Until then no regular German steamship had called on any port in the southwest Pacific.[2]

The Union Steamship Company of New Zealand commenced a New Zealand government subsidised four-weekly service between Auckland, Tonga and Samoa in early 1885. The Pacific Mail Steamship Co. of New York, which delivered the Royal Mail to Sydney via San Francisco, also commenced a service in 1885 from San Francisco to Sydney, with calls on Honolulu, Fiji and Auckland.[3] While these shipping services benefited DHPG in Samoa, they did not assist NGC and other enterprises in German New Guinea.

In 1885 the only regular steamship connection between GNG and Europe was via Cooktown and Brisbane. The British-Indian Steam Navigation Co. of London maintained a monthly service from Batavia through the Torres Strait to Brisbane with a connection to London. Subject to the availability of cargo and passengers, ships would call at Cooktown, with NGC vessels connecting to GNG. In 1886 it took 66 days for cargo, 56 days for passengers and 42–49 days for mail to make the Hamburg–Finschhafen journey. NGC's operations depended entirely on this service when it began its settlement in GNG.[4]

Preceding the arrival of NGC personnel, Captain G. Inhülsen delivered the first consignment of building materials and provisions on his brig *J. H. Lübken* to Finschhafen on 18 October 1885. Hansemann bought the entire cargo from DHPG when the vessel was en route from Hamburg to Mioko in the Bismarck Archipelago.

NGC's monthly Cooktown–Finschhafen service rarely met the needs of the young colony; it most definitely did not meet the requirements of Hansemann's ambitious mobilisation schedule. With a top speed of 7.5 knots, the *Samoa* (165 BRT) could, at best, make Finschhafen to Cooktown in 4 days and 18 hours and return in 5 days and 5 hours. The *Samoa* ferried goods, passengers, the scientific explorers, the administrator and managers. The situation demanded at least one additional vessel.

Disastrous Ventures

A dearth of cargo and passenger space was made worse by the *Samoa's* poor seakeeping. Pitching and rolling in the slightest sea, the strain on the hull and boiler caused frequent breakdowns, with the crew barely able to hold the vessel together. In early June 1885 the *Samoa* pulled into Sydney to drop off Finsch for his return voyage to Germany. This provided the opportunity to carry out urgent work on the steamer in a Sydney dry-dock. It gave Captain Dallmann a well-earned rest; GNG, however, was without effective sea transport for the best part of 5 months.[5]

Hansemann needed a fleet of ships to develop and service his new Protectorate. In addition to the *Samoa* he ordered two steamships and purchased three old square-riggers even before NGC had received the Royal charter. A third steamer was ordered in November 1886. The three ships and three barques, fully fitted out, ran down the cash position of NGC by RM607,500 and RM107,000 respectively.

The steamer *Papua* and her sister ship the *Ottilie* (171 BRT) were laid down at F. Devrient & Co. in Danzig in December 1884 and March 1885 respectively. Six months later, the Directors of NGC proudly took delivery of their first steamship in Bremen. Devrient built the *Papua* to withstand the moody waters of the Indian and Pacific Oceans and the unpredictable tropical waters of the South Sea. The ship's steel scantlings and teak hull were to guard against the razor-sharp coral reefs, while copper cladding prevented excessive barnacle growth on the hull, thus ensuring a transit-speed of 9 knots. With 180 tons of coal on board Captain Pfeiffer and his crew of 13 set NGC's flagship the course for GNG on 21 June 1885. After an uneventful voyage the *Papua* linked up with the refurbished SS *Samoa* in Cooktown on 19 October. The experienced Dallmann piloted the two vessels through the treacherous Coral Sea to make Finschhafen safely by November 1885.[6]

After completion of sea trials the *Ottilie* left Danzig-Neufahrwasser for GNG on 2 April 1886. Barely a week at sea Captain W. Rasch had to call into Bremerhaven for emergency repairs because of damage sustained during a gale that swept up the

The SS *Papua* (170 BRT) ca. 1885 (*Illustrirte Zeitung*, Leipzig, 15 Aug. 1885)

Skagerrak. Weighing anchor again on 18 April 1886, the *Ottilie* made safe passage through the North Sea and the Mediterranean to arrive in Port Said on 6 May. After loading coal and taking fresh provisions in Colombo she set off east-southeast on 1 June. Making good time along the Sumatra and Java coasts, then through the Timor and Arafura Seas, a strong current and the coral reefs in the Torres Strait slowed down the *Ottilie* again. It was not until 20 June 1886 that the Administrator's secretary, H. Fischer, surveyor P. Schneider, and missionaries J. Flierl and T. Braun—who joined the party in Cooktown—disembarked in Finschhafen.[7]

Captain A. Dücker took prefabricated houses on the barque *Norma* (282 RT) to GNG in April 1886.[8] Built for Konitzky & Thiermann in 1864 by Johann Lang in Bremen, the primary function of this 40.7m long and 9.4m wide three-masted square rigger was to serve as temporary housing for the Administrator and his family and other NGC officers during the early building phase of Finschhafen. After the Station was sufficiently established, the square-rigger was converted to a 'hulk' for coal and other stores. When Finschhafen was abandoned in 1891, the *Norma* delivered dismantled houses and equipment to Stephansort. However, before unloading started the barque broke her mooring and foundered. This was probably the best outcome for NGC as the vessel was fully insured.[9]

A second barque, the *Florence Danvers* (492 RT) was procured in May 1886.[10] Under the command of Captain Hutter the vessel left Hamburg on 17 July 1886 with houses and a new NGC employee, the retired Prussian Army officer C. Ludwig. According to her logbook, the barque arrived at Sydney on 12 November to load coal, timber and provisions for GNG. The square-rigger proved cumbersome in shifting winds and strong currents. Shortly after her arrival in GNG she was taken off local work to haul coal from Australia to Finschhafen. In 1891 the vessel was laid up in Friedrich Wilhelmshafen to serve as coal hulk. In December 1892 she was beached and stripped for spare parts.[11]

The Hulk *Norma*, the SS *Ysabel* and the Barque *Esmeralda* at Finschhafen, ca. 1889 (*NKWL*, 1889)

Disastrous Ventures

The three-masted wooden barque *Esmeralda* (788 RT), purchased in December 1886 for approximately RM47,000, was the largest of NGC's vessels. The square-rigger left Cuxhaven for Finschhafen on 20 December 1886 with four Swedish houses, machinery, equipment and 600 t of coal. Captain Dücker, who had returned to Germany after delivering the *Norma,* sailed the *Esmeralda* directly to Finschhafen where he arrived on 10 May 1887.[12] Thereafter Dücker returned to the *Norma,* and Harbour Master R. Weller took command of the *Esmeralda.*

Like her sister ships the *Norma* and *Florence Danvers,* the windjammer shuttled the 2,500 nautical miles between Finschhafen and Sydney shipping building materials, coal and provisions. Shareholders were informed in 1890 that the *Esmeralda* had loaded approximately 1,000 t of phosphate on Mole Island in the Purdy Group and 40 logs of *Calophyllum Inophyllum* and two logs of *Malawa* at Finschhafen.[13] Shortly after leaving for Hamburg on 19 September 1890, Captain Weller and two deckhands died of fever while the rest of the crew were gravely ill.[14] The few remaining able hands took the *Esmeralda* to Brisbane for an emergency stop-over. Then under the command of her First Mate Wagner and a new Australian crew, the *Esmeralda* continued on to Hamburg where the phosphate was sold at RM40 per tonne. The keen interest for the timber extracted premium prices. Following the low return on the phosphate NGC entered into negotiation with Rabone, Feez & Co of Sydney for the mining of the Mole Island deposit. But the commercial discussions came to an abrupt end when a cyclone destroyed the island's mooring and mining facilities.

The square–riggers proved expensive to operate. In contrast to the steamers, where Chinese and Javanese stokers, cooks and stewards made up the crew, Europeans manned the sailing ships. The complement of a German barque typically comprised a captain, first and second mate and 18 sailors, and it was therefore not surprising that the *Esmeralda* was sold on her return to Hamburg.[15]

The German Navigators were not familiar with the narrow shipping lanes of the Coral Sea and remained unimpressed by the substandard harbour facilities at Cooktown.[16] Yet the skippers rarely chose the time-consuming alternative sea-lanes, rather, they travelled the largely uncharted waters of the Coral Sea at their and NGC's peril, and it was here where the company lost ships with predictable regularity.

On the evening of 9 December 1885, her first voyage from Finschhafen to North Queensland, the *Papua* was shipwrecked.[17] The incident occurred when Captain Pfeiffer struck the Osprey Reef, 60 miles east of Cooktown, on high tide. Efforts to refloat the ship were unsuccessful and the hull broke up the following morning. While the crew of 15 and two passengers made it safely to Cooktown they had little more than the clothes on their backs. The entire cargo of copra and other merchandise was lost; luckily the mail for Germany was secured, water-soaked, but legible.[18]

Although fully insured, the loss was a blow to NGC's development timetable. The company's first major ship acquisition lay on a reef off Cooktown after 34 days in New Guinean waters. The dismissal of Captain Pfeiffer, who was severely reprimanded by the Hamburg Maritime Court for reckless conduct did not help NGC; the company was again down to only one steamer.[19]

Until the *Ottilie* arrived in Finschhafen, NGC chartered the SS *Truganini* (130 BRT) from the Queensland Steam Shipping Co. at an approximate cost of RM50,000.[20] However, the *Ottilie* did not fare any better than the *Papua*. Apart from the early problems encountered in the Skagerrak, the copper-clad timber hull was damaged in the Coral Sea during her outward voyage. The repair required a docking in Brisbane during May and June 1887. A catastrophic event occurred on a return voyage from Surabaya to Astrolabe Bay. On 14 March 1891 an utterly drunk Captain Budde ran the *Ottilie* onto the aptly named Latent Reef in the Purdy Islands. The crew and the three passengers were able to take to the life rafts and reach nearby Mole and Mouse Islands before the steamer broke up, spilling her cargo of rice and cattle. Fortuitously, Captain Schneider of the *Ysabel* was able to pick up the survivors a month later when passing the island on her way to Surabaya. While the crew and passengers of the *Ottilie* remained in GNG, her captain, like Pfeiffer, faced the Maritime Court in Hamburg for gross incompetence. Again, the decision by the Court to revoke Budde's license was no compensation for the loss of NGC's second steamer.[21]

The *Ysabel*, built by Blohm & Voss (B&V) in Hamburg in 1886 for RM212,500, became NGC's most expensive, but also longest serving steamship. After the *Papua* disaster Hansemann placed the order with B&V on his own account.[22] To be better prepared for the unforgiving reefs of the Coral Sea, he agreed to Blohm's proposal to have the hull constructed entirely in steel. At the time, the German shipyards were slow in adopting the much lighter English designs because of concerns for corrosion and cracking prevalent in the early steel hulls. For B&V the *Ysabel* was their first ship that was not built in the wooden, copper-clad and iron traditions. Dallmann, who had handed command of the *Samoa* in Cooktown to H. Sechstroh on 1 July 1886, conducted acceptance trials of the *Ysabel* on the Elbe River in October 1886. He advised NGC's manager, Hans Arnold: B&V performed acceptably, 'as well as or better than any other German shipyard'. But Dallmann also listed a number of concerns.

The SS *Ysabel* (524 BRT) on the River Elbe, ca. 1886 (courtesy B & V, Hamburg)

Blohm's carpenter used some softwood on the hardwood decking, crew cabins were small, the coal bunkers too small, and the ship engine was undersized. 'It hurts a bit when any old collier leaves the *Ysabel* in her wake', Dallmann told Arnold.[23]

NGC decided to sell the *Samoa* to Burns, Philp (BP) for DM86,000 and book a profit of RM16,484 when an unscheduled docking in February 1890 was estimated to cost RM30,000.[24]

The increasing demand for plantation labour made it necessary to purchase a small sailing boat suitable for recruiting. Preceding the sale of the *Samoa*, the schooner *Senta* (60 BRT) was ordered in Sydney in May 1888 from Rabone, Feez & Co. at a cost of £2,632.[25] The vessel arrived in GNG 12 months later to commence labour recruiting in the Solomon Islands and the Bismarck Archipelago.[26]

After the loss of six ships in 5 years, the company added the steam-launch *Freiwald* to its fleet of two. The launch was purchased second-hand in Singapore towards the end of 1891 to provide transport for the Administrator and to service the tobacco plantations Maraga, Erima, Stephansort and Konstantinhafen. Passengers were charged RM15 for a return fare from Friedrich Wilhelmshafen to any of these Stations and RM4 for travelling between the Stations. The *Freiwald* was also available for charter at RM100 per day. Although it is unlikely that this little enterprise returned a profit, the *Freiwald* provided indispensable service to Astrolabe Compagnie (A-C) and NGC until she was shipwrecked at Erimahafen on 31 May 1895.[27]

Down again to only two ships, NGC took the *Ysabel* off the Stephansort–Surabaya–Singapore leg to work in the Bismarck Archipelago and on the seaboard of KWL, with Captain Voogdt of the *Senta* exploring the north-east coast of New Britain for timber, while also recruiting for the Herbertshöhe labour depôt. Hansemann was now forced to rethink his transportation strategy for GNG. If his new plan to develop a plantation industry on Astrolabe Bay was to be given any chance of success he had the choice of ordering new ships, only to see them wrecked on a New Guinea reef, or opt for the expensive but more reliable alternative of charter vessels.

The SS *Ysabel* at Stephansort, ca. 1890 (courtesy P-M Pawlik, Hauschild Verlag, 1996)

Until the government relieved NGC of the onerous task of providing marine services in GNG, the company kept losing ships. The exception was the *Ysabel*. While this steamer was not wrecked like all the other NGC ships, after 11 years in service the vessel became expensive to maintain and at an annual cost of RM 100,000 inefficient to operate at her top speed of 8 kt. The decision to sell the *Ysabel* to Burns, Philp (BP) in October 1896 realised a profit of £5,000 or 47% of the original purchase price. To NGC it was a good deal; to Wilhelm Joest it was surprising that NGC persisted with the vessel for such a long time. Embarking in Sydney for New Caledonia on 25 July 1897, the German explorer described the *Ysabel* as pitching and rolling in even calm waters, 'which one could only tolerate after a few dozen bottles of Pilsner'. Her skipper, Carl Ettling, regarded the *Ysabel* a reliable workhorse. He joined BP to remain with the steamer until she was stranded in the Marshall Islands on 7 June 1907.[28]

The purpose-built replacement vessel, *Johann Albrecht*, a 10 kt state-of-the-art recruiting vessel ordered from Bremer Vulkan in 1897, struck a reef near Mérit in the French Islands shortly after arriving in GNG on 25 November 1897.[29] Whereas this time the damage was minor and the vessel refloated after jettisoning the cargo, the *Johann Albrecht* ran hard aground on Hermit Islands 6 months later.[30] The incident occurred on 13 May 1898 after Captain Sanders rushed to the aid of the R&H brig *Welcome*, which had bottomed on the northwest side of the islands. Both the *Johann Albrecht* and the *Welcome* were beyond salvage, and after less than 6 months in GNG the latest NGC vessel was a total write-off. If the risky salvage attempt of the two vessels by the *Stettin* had also ended in the stranding of the NDL steamer, it would have left the schooner *Senta* at Herbertshöhe, the cutter *Seleo* at Apia and the chartered schooner the *Captain Cook* to provide sea transport along the 800km coast of KWL and an archipelago comprising several hundred islands.[31]

The urgent mobilisation in 1898 of the cutter *Baltic* for the loading and unloading of seagoing vessels and for services to the nearby out Stations on the Gazelle Peninsula, and in February 1899 the ketch *Alexandra* from Sydney provided little

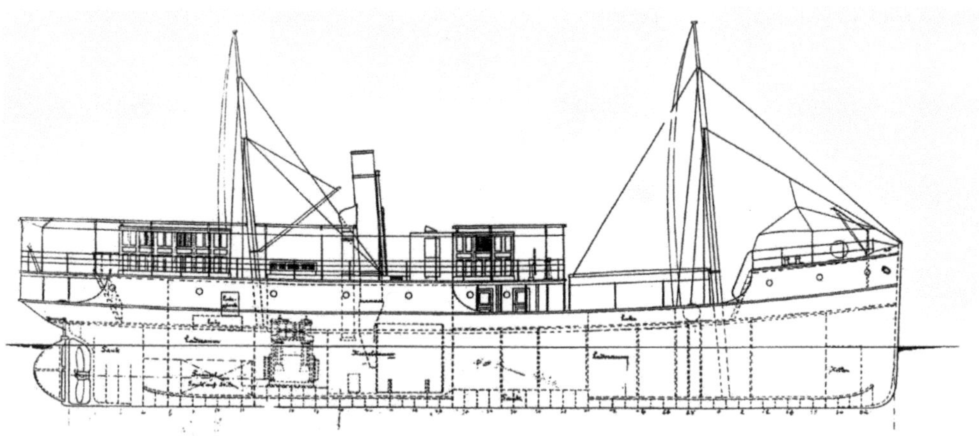

Outline drawing of the SS *Johann Albrecht* (287 BRT) ca. 1897 (StaB)

relief to the transportation bottleneck.[32] Both sailing vessels were fair-weather boats, with the poor sea-keeping capability of the *Alexandra* marginally improved after a bilge keel and larger sails were fitted. In 1901 NGC decided to cut its losses and sell the ketch. But yet again, before the decision could be put into effect the *Alexandra* sank near the island of Teripar on 13 July 1902.[33]

Soon after the loss of the *Johann Albrecht,* NGC placed an order for a motorsailer. Built to high standards in only 12 months by Schömer, Jensen & Co. of Tönning in Schleswig Holstein, the new NGC flagship did not fare any better than her predecessor. On her way to GNG, Captain Buchal found it difficult to keep the *Herzog Johann Albrecht* on course in the heavy seas over the 7 month voyage. The motorsailer unloaded her cargo of machinery and sawmill at Herbertshöhe and Warangoi Station on 15 November 1899. The strong currents and shifting winds in the archipelago proved an even bigger problem to the *Herzog Johann Albrecht*. In 1901 the decision was made to take the vessel to Hong Kong for a refit. While in transit, two typhoons damaged the vessel to such an extent that towing assistance to Hong Kong was required. Repairs and modifications took almost 9 months and it was not until November 1902 that the NGC flagship recommenced work.

Notwithstanding the modifications, the ship remained difficult to keep on course and the *Herzog Johann Albrecht* was reassigned to Herbertshöhe on 25 October 1902 to work as a labour recruitment vessel in the archipelago. A cryptic message in the 1903/04 annual report read like a relief: 'the *Herzog Johann Albrecht* was lost after stranding on the north coast of New Hanover; vessel and cargo were fully insured'. The vessel never operated to specification and insurance recovery was the cheapest way out.[34] The schooner *Otti* (70 BRT), procured by the company in 1899, took over recruitment work out of Berlinhafen. With the labour resources diminishing in the region, the schooner transferred to Friedrich Wilhelmshafen and then to Rabaul from where she worked as a recruiter until outbreak of the World War I.[35]

Fifteen years of maritime experience in GNG was conceptualized in the steamer

MS Herzog Johann Albrecht (189 BRT) ca. 1902 (Courtesy Hauschild Verlag, [H. Karting, *Deutsche Schoner,* Bd ii])

Siar. Built by Bremer Vulkan in 1901/02, the design of the vessel was based on that of the SS *Johann Albrecht,* except for a strengthened hull and better accommodation. In the absence of a regular shipping service to Singapore, the *Siar* made this run until 1909 to deliver produce for transhipment to Europe and return with passengers and goods for NGC.[36] On 1 April 1909 NDL took over this service and the *Siar* was again deployed mainly as a labour recruiter. By 1914 NGC worked its two remaining steamers—the *Siar* and the *Madang*—to ferry passengers and goods to and from the Stations, and deliver copra to Simpsonhafen or Friedrich Wilhelmshafen for on-shipment by NDL, or to provide shipping for exploration activities. Labour recruitment was then conducted with motor schooners which were purpose built in GNG.[37]

Other noteworthy ship acquisitions by NGC were the paddle-steamer *Herzogin Elisabeth* (60 BRT) and the small steamer *Meto.* The *Herzogin Elisabeth* was built for the second and third Ramu expedition by Bremer Vulkan in 1897. The five sections that make up the 18.2m long by 3.9m wide flat-bottom barge were constructed in less than 8 weeks. The sections were shipped as deck cargo to Singapore and from there by the SS *Stettin* to Friedrich Wilhelmshafen for assembly. The boiler, engine and other appurtenances were delivered by the *Johann Albrecht* on her maiden voyage from Germany. The deckhouse and accommodation module were built in GNG. The teak superstructure was designed to accommodate four Europeans, 60 labourers

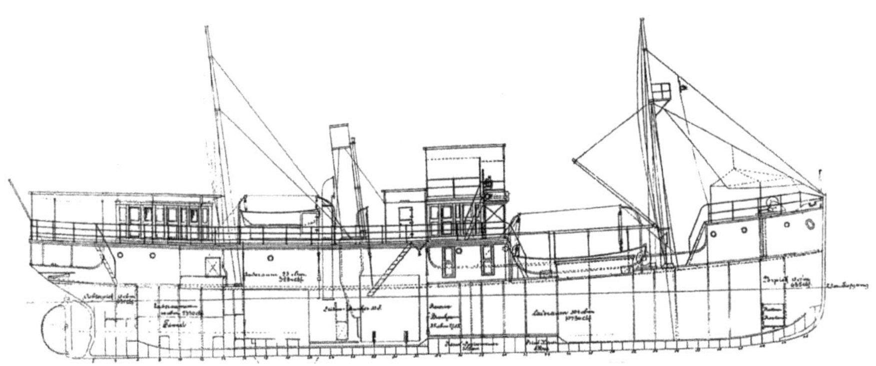

Outline drawing of SS *Siar* (BRT 324). **The *Siar* in the Bismarck Archipelago,** ca. 1910 (StaB)

and victuals for a 200-day voyage. The *Herzogin Elisabeth* maintained the line of communication between the explorers and gold prospectors on the Upper Ramu and Ramumünde at the mouth of the River for just over 3 years. The barge sank on the Ramu River in November 1901 after colliding with a submerged log.[38]

NGC purchased the *Meto* from Peter Hansen's with the acquisition of the Witu Islands in 1902 to work chiefly as a copra trader and recruiter. However, the rebellious islanders of Garowe ransacked Peterhafen in November 1903, killing Hansen's marine engineer, Doell, five Chinese carpenters and eighteen Malay workers. The assailants, their families and helpers made a run for New Britain. Amply provisioned, riffles and ammunition, the *Meto*'s location was only discovered when Captain Möller of the *Seestern* identified a funnel sticking out of the mud on the riverbed on the Willaumez Peninsular of the archipelago[39]

After the 'Mail Steamer Subsidy Bill' was passed in the *Reichstag* in 1885, NDL began a 4-weekly Bremerhaven—Singapore service.[40] In the absence of any government-assisted service to GNG, Hansemann decided to charter a steamer for the regular delivery of mail, passengers, goods, coal and Chinese coolies. Brought into immediate effect following the loss of the *Ottilie* the service commenced with the charter of the steamer *Nierstein* (948 BRT) from the Deutsche Dampfschiffahrts Gesellschaft 'Hansa', Bremen. From October 1891 to March 1892, the *Nierstein* left Singapore—via Surabaya when required—for Hatzfeldthafen, Stephansort, Friedrich Wilhelmshafen and the Bismarck Archipelago every two months.[41]

In 1891 NGC entered into an exclusive agreement with NDL. An interconnecting service started with the departure from Singapore of SS *Schwalbe* (932 BRT) on 15 April 1892. 'This arrangement,' Hansemann told his shareholders, 'has established the fastest and shortest service to the Protectorate possible at the present time'. By embarking in the Adriatic Port of Brindisi, he said, 'it only takes 37 steaming-days to reach the Protectorate of the NGC'. This, according to NGC's 1892 annual report, 'compares with a travelling time of 62 days via Surabaya or 57 days via Cooktown'.

Because the coal depôts had to be replenished to meet in-house supplies and those of the navy, NGC provided also a bunkering service for NDL in GNG. For these activities NGC chartered the brigs *Buste* and *Vagabund* among other vessels. [42]

Efforts by Hansemann to establish a profitable shipping business in GNG never succeeded and the interconnecting service with Europe increasingly affected the company's financial resources. The annual charter of SS *Schwalbe* came to RM276,000 to which was added the annual running cost of RM165,000 for the three NGC vessels. By 31 March 1891 NGC had incurred RM1,871,852 for charters, with income from freight, mail and passengers only marginally off-setting the outlay. 'Even if the increased business activities of the Astrolabe Compagnie bring to bear a boost in receipts from freight,' Hansemann cautioned his shareholders, 'the shipping cost is the enterprise's Achilles heel'.[43] Yet on 5 December 1891 and again on 5 February 1892 NGC chartered the steamer *Devawongse* (1643 BRT) from the Scottish and Oriental Steam Ship Co to meet the labour requirements of A-C's newly established tobacco plantations on Astrolabe Bay. The vessel transported Chinese and Javanese coolies, rice and building materials from Singapore and Surabaya to Stephansort, and even though the RM95,000 charter cost for the two journeys was back charged to A-C, the negative cash flow of NGC escalated alarmingly.

The requests by the *Reichsmarine* for NGC to build docking and ship-repair facilities in GNG remained therefore unanswered. Hansemann was not prepared to subsidise the occasional appearances of a German light cruiser in New Guinea waters. At the same time as repairs to the steam-launch *Freiwald* could be carried out in a small repair shop at Friedrich Wilhelmshafen, the decision not to invest in a larger local yard is open to question. Not a year would pass without the requirement of major repairs on at least one of NGC's small fleet. Dry docking in Sydney, Brisbane or Singapore was made particularly expensive by the transfer costs of special crewing, fuel and victualling.[44] Of particular cost impact were the short-term charters from Singapore, Batavia or Australia for the out of service NGC vessels.

NGC's transport pains eased when NDL redirected its Sydney–Samoa service to Singapore–GNG. The *Lübeck* (1815 BRT) started this new service in GNG on 21 April 1893. A typical consignment of coal, cattle, salted meat, flour and other goods was unloaded at Friedrich Wilhelmshafen before the steamer continued her voyage to the home-port of Singapore.[45] The demand for inward-bound shipping space soon exceeded the capacity of the *Lübeck*. Despite a dearth of outbound cargo—NGC took up shipping space mainly to repatriate coolies to Singapore and Batavia, with independent growers and traders exporting some merchandise—NDL replaced the *Lübeck* with the larger SS *Stettin* (2230 BRT) before the end of the year.

With the RM200,000 annual government subsidies in place sea transportation was now cheaper and, importantly, the eight-weekly government services allowed better planning of the operations in GNG. But while the charter of the SS *Schwalbe* was discontinued, shipping expenses continued to drain the company's funds.[46]

From 1898 the profitability of NDL's Singapore–Batavia–Herbertshöhe service was threatened by the entry of Australia's Burns Philp & Co. (BP). Over a 2-year period BP shipped 2,175 t of cargo in 13 voyages on their flag-ship the SS *Moresby* (1763 GRT) from Sydney to their newly established depôt at Herbertshöhe. Australian-bound cargo of 1,549 t was mainly copra from the Ralum plantation of E. E. Forsayth. Initially not pleased with the entry of a competitor, NDL soon recognised that the BP service provided a better connection for its passengers and cargo from Herbertshöhe to Australia. Also, rather than entering into fierce competition with the subsidised NDL, the pragmatic James Burns entered into a pooling arrangement with his German competitor. The agreement between BP and NDL split the profits on the cargo shipped between Sydney and New Britain. After allowing 20–25% for cost, NDL received two-thirds and BP one-third of the revenue, while net receipts from coal shipments were divided equally between the two companies.

Although Burns entered into an agency agreement with E.E. Forsayth soon after the arrangement with NDL, the pooling arrangement between BP and NDL worked well for a while for both companies. The start by NDL of a new Sydney–Hong Kong–Shanghai service via GNG and the Island Territory in 1900 had little effect on the arrangement as the service ended when the SS *München* (4,800 BRT) struck a reef in Yap Harbour on only her third voyage on 3 February 1901.[47] When the agreement expired in August 1903 BP decided to compete with NDL and run vessels to New Britain bi-monthly. NDL countered by setting a highly attractive copra freight rate of RM55/t for the Rabaul—Hamburg and Bremen run in 1905. The shift on the rate removed the company's major competitor from doing business in GNG.[48]

The turn of the century saw the introduction of a subsidised mail steamer service from Sydney to Jaluit, Yap and Palau. It came as a result of a 6 August 1900 agreement between the German government and the Jaluit Gesellschaft (J-G). For an annual subsidy of RM120,000 the Berlin contracted J-G to deliver mail every three months from German Pacific islands to Yap for shipment by NDL to Sydney.[49]

The service commenced on 1 January 1901 with the J-G steamer *Oceana* (684 BRT) which was refitted for this task in 1899 by the Scottish shipyard of S. McKnight & Co.[50] When NDL terminated the Sydney—Hong Kong run, J-G extended its service to the British owned Gilbert Islands and included on-demand calls to Rabaul. In a repetition of the problems that had beset NGC and NDL, the *Oceana* ran aground on a Jaluit reef on 23 December 1903. Too expensive to repair and subsequently sold for scrap metal in Singapore, J-G ordered a new steamer, the SS *Germania* (1,096 BRT), from the Germania-Werft in Kiel. With a 1000 h.p. steam engine providing a cruising speed of 11.25 kt., J-G's most luxurious steamer, boasting 20 first class and 12 second class berths, recommenced the 12-weekly service from Sydney to Rabaul, the Marshall and Micronesian Islands and Hong Kong in December 1904.[51]

NGC viewed the new connection to Australia as hardly ideal. The *Germania* called on Rabaul subject to availability of cargo, and, due to the added leg to Sydney, the frequency of NDL's Singapore service decreased to 12 compared to the 8 weeks provided by the *Stettin*. Her replacement in 1903 with the new *Feldherren* Class, the *Prinz Waldemar* and the *Prinz Sigismund, brought* the service back to 8 weeks.

When passenger demand called for the introduction of a shipping service from Australia to the Far East, NDL made a further change to the schedule. The Singapore—Sydney run was replaced in 1904 with a Sydney—Hong Kong service with connections to Kobe and Yokohama. The increasing volume of exports from GNG to Australia and Asia—by now exceeding exports to Europe—ensured that the NDL would continue to call on Simpsonhafen (Rabaul) and later Friedrich Wilhelmshafen but bypassing all other ports in GNG.

The change from Singapore and Batavia to Hong Kong troubled NGC. Burns, Philp had already withdrawn its regular service to GNG because of the highly subsidised competition from NDL. With no regular shipping service to Friedrich Wilhelmshafen, the development of KWL would slow down even further. Only the company steamer the *Siar* added to the NGC fleet in 1902, was available to make the journey to Southeast Asia. Serving the mainland coast was now left to a few owner-traders with their small boats.[52]

In 1903 NDL's Directors decided to invest in a 240 m deep-water pier with a 47 m long, 12.5 m wide and 4.5 m high shed complete with freshwater tanks and other amenities at Simpsonhafen.[53] The works, including onshore facilities comprising houses, office buildings, roads and a 12 km narrow gauge railway were completed on 12 October 1905. NDL could now safely berth its largest ships and the cruisers of the *Reichsmarine* on both sides of the pier.[54]

Coinciding with the completion of the harbour installations, NDL started an inter-island service on 1 October 1905. The SS *Sumatra* (584 BRT) sailed to a time schedule from Simpsonhafen to Buka and Kieta in the Solomons, Namatanai on the central coast of New Ireland, Kaewieng, New Hanover, Admiralty and Hermit Islands, turning south to Aitape on the northern coast of KWL, to Friedrich Wilhelmshafen, then to Peterhafen on the French Islands and back to Simpsonhafen. Assisted by the steamers *Langeoog* and *Roland* (90 BRT), later, by the steamer *Meklong* (175 DWT) some 5,000 t of internal freight was handled by this service annually until 1914.[55]

In 1909 annual assistance to NDL was increased to RM700,000. Payment was dependent on re-establishing the service to Singapore via The Netherlands East Indies. NDL commenced the new service with the SS *Manila* on 4 April 1909 from Singapore. After calling on Batavia, Semarang and Surabaya, then Macassar, Ambiona and Banda Aceh, Berlinhafen, Potsdamhafen, Friedrich Wilhelmshafen, Stephansort and Finschhafen, the steamer arrived in Simpsonhafen some 4 weeks later. The ports of call and the schedule were adjusted to meet the customers 'requirements.[56]

NGC could finally be satisfied with the shipping arrangement. From 1909 until the outbreak of World War I, a fleet of five NDL steamers called on Friedrich Wilhelmshafen and Rabaul, Aitape, Potsdamhafen, Finschhafen, Morobe and Peterhafen. Trade was now shipped economically to and from the major ports in Australia, Asia, North America and Europe. Apart from the two trunkline services, NDL worked several tugs in Simpsonhafen and was given responsibility for the government steamers.[57] In conjunction with the vessels of E .E. Forsayth, Hernsheim & Co., O. Mouton & Co, McDonald and the Christian missions, and the occasional visit by cruisers of the navy, there was now sufficient sea transportation for passengers and cargo alike.[58]

The *Sumatra* was laid up shortly before the outbreak of World War I. Despite a government subsidy of RM70,000 from 1909 onward, the annual loss by NDL's island service averaged RM81,000. The losses for the Rabaul/Simpsonhafen–Singapore run amounted to RM100,000 for the first 3 years. NDL posted a maiden profit of RM20,000 for this service in 1913. With an annual subsidy of RM500,000 the Australia–Hong Kong service averaged RM16,000 annual profits.[59]

With Hansemann's death in 1903 major ship acquisitions by NGC also came to an end. Only when NDL advised the company of its intentions to increase freight rates and passenger fares in 1909 did NGC place an order for a steamer, the wooden-hulled *Madang* (194 BRT). [60] Built in Hong Kong the ship took over from the *Siar* on the north coast of KWL on 8 August 1910, with the latter transferred to Herbertshöhe.

The long service of the *Senta* came to an end when the brig was dismasted near the French Islands in February 1911. The motor schooner *Witu* was then ordered from the same Hong Kong yard. When she wrecked on a reef 12 months later, a vessel of the same name and size was ordered from either the Chinese shipbuilder Ah Tam in

Matupi or the Japanese ship builder who had established yards in Simpsonhafen by 1911. NGC had come to the conclusion that wooden hulls were cheaper to build and maintain, and that they could now be built efficiently in GNG. Before the NGC enterprise came to a halt in 1914, three motor schooners were built in the archipelago for Kaewieng, Aitape and Herbertshöhe Station. The pinnace *Maski* was built to provide a passenger service between Herbertshöhe and Rabaul. The *Madang*, *Siar* and *Witu II* were redeployed to ferry cargo to and from the plantations in KWL and the archipelago. Briefly before GNG was shut down, the long-serving ketch *Frida* sank while riding anchor off Aitape and the cutter *Tamberan* was scuttled.[61]

For NGC the shipping costs relative to overall expenditures were significant in the first three years. The 31 March 1887 balance sheet showed RM595,279 in the fixed asset account for ships. This compared to 'Total Assets' of RM883,391. Twenty years later, the March 1914 accounts disclosed the total value of ships at RM139,512 against total assets of RM12,818,859. NGC treated ship assets conservatively. Apart from annual depreciation of 10–15%, RM70,000 was expensed between 1887 and 1891. A RM60,000 provision was booked to a special reserve account in the March 1903, which had grown to RM200,000 by March 1912.

NGC ships and cargo were insured, but losses translated into opportunity costs and increased insurance premiums. Hansemann's plan to commence the development of his colony with three vessels may have worked if the ships had stayed afloat and were better suited for the prevailing sea conditions. The significant ship losses by NDL, Hernsheim, DHPG, Forsayth and other planters imposed an additional burden on Hansemann to develop his colony in the short time-frame he had set himself.[62]

The NDL SS *Prinz Waldemar* at FWH, ca. 1910. The *Germania* at Howaldtswerke Kiel, ca. 1904 (courtesy, HDW Kiel). The Jaluit Gesellschaft steamship was confiscated in Sydney by Australia in 1914 and renamed the *Mawatta* (mf. John Oxley Library). The government steamer *Seestern* was lost on a voyage from Brisbane to Samarai around 3 June 1909 (B. Frommund, *Deutsch-Neuguinea*, 1926). The government yacht *Komet*, launched at Bremer Vulcan on 4 June 1911, was captured on the north coast of New Britain by Cmdr. J Jackson of HMAS *Nusa* on 11 Oct. 1914 (Australian War Memorial, H03242). The NDL SS *Lübeck*, ca. 1894 (NKWL, 1894). The NDL SS *Sumatra* at Howaldtswerke Kiel, ca. 1889 (courtesy HWD, Kiel). The NDL SS *Stettin* at Friedrich-Wilhelmshafen, ca. 1900 (Hesse-Wartegg, *Samoa, Bismarckarchipel und Neuguinea*, p. 48)

Disastrous Ventures

Notes

1   H. Münch, *Adolph von Hansemann,* p. 226; Hagen, *Bismarcks Kolonialpolitik,* pp. 73 & 108

2   P. Neubauer, 'Die Wirtschaftliche Bedeutung Der Deutschen Kolonien,' *Marine Rundschau,* 12

3   Gallus, 'Schiffsverbindungen mit unseren Kolonien', *Jahrbuch Deutschen Kolonien* (1908) pp.149f

4   *DKZ* (1888) p. 21 and (1889) p. 75. Jb (1887) p. 8; Sack & D. Clark (1886–87) pp. 7–8. W. Treue, *Die Jaluit-Gesellschaft auf den Marshall-Inseln 1887–1914,* p. 92

5   *NKWL* (1885) Heft i, pp. 2, 6 & 22; (1886) Heft i, p. 2; Heft iv, p. 102; Jb (1887) pp. 3 & 7; Sack & D. Clark (1886–87) pp. 4 & 8

6   The *Papua* -36m long, 6.2m beam, 3.4m draught - luxurious cabins, a steam-powered tender, two whaleboats, two cannons. The 300-hp engine consumed 155kg/hr of coal at 9 knots.With a bunker capacity of 180 t the *Papua* travelled up to 10,000 miles. *Illustrirte Zeitung* 15 Aug., 1885 (p. 157)

7   *NKWL* (1886) Heft i, p. 3; Heft iii, pp. 60, 79 and iv, p. 114; Jb (1887) p. 7.

8   R. Thiel, *Die Geschichte des Bremer Vulkan 1805–1997,* p. 155

9   *NKWL* (1991) Heft i, pp. 7 & 28.

10 *NKWL* (1886) Heft ii, p. 61; Sack & Clark (1886–87) p. 8, Jb (1887) pp. 7, 23 & 27.

11 *NKWL* (1887) Heft i, p. 4, Heft iv, p. 129; (1890) Heft i, p. 46; (1892) Heft i, p. 22; (1893), Heft i, p. 61 Sack & Clark (1888–89) p. 41, (1889–90) p. 55; Jb (1889) p. 10; (1890/91) p. 32

12 *NKWL* (1887) Heft i, p. 4, Heft iv, p. 129; Sack & Clark (1886–87) p. 8; Jb (1887) pp. 7 & 23)

13 *NKWL* (1890) Heft i, p. 46; Heft ii, p. 76; (1891) Heft i; p. 14; Sack & Clark 1887–88) p. 30, (1889–90) p. 49. Jb (1888) p. 11, (1889) p. 5

14 *NKWL* (1891) Heft i, p. 17. *Weser-Zeitung* (1891) 30. Jan. p. 4

15 Jb (1889/90) p. 12, (1890/91) pp. 9, 32 & 65, (1891/92) pp. 36–7; Sack & Clark (1889–90) p. 55; see P.M. Pawlik, Vol. 1, *Von der Weser in die Welt,* pp. 466–7

16 Gallus, p. 158; H. Blum, *Neu Guinea und der Bismarck-Archipel,* p. 56; Dallmann to R. Mentzel (Finschhafen) 7 Sep., 1885 in P.M. Pawlik, *Von Sibirien nach Neu Guinea,* p. 104

17 *NKWL* (1886) Heft ii, p. 61; Sack & Clark (1886–87) p. 8; Jb (1887) p. 8

18 *NKWL* (1886) Heft i, p. 2. O. Schellong, *Alte Documente aus der Südsee,* pp. 14–15

19 P.M. Pawlik, *Von Sibirien nach Neu Guinea,* p. 192, n.50. Schellong, p. 16

20 *NKWL* (1886) Heft i, p. 3.The *Papua* and cargo were insured. Salvage costs came to RM38,513; the charter for the *Truganini* amounted to RM49,819

21 *NKWL* (1887) Heft iii, p. 80; Heft iv, p. 129; (1891) Heft i, pp. 5 & 26–7. Insurance recovery on the *Ottilie* was RM53,761 (Jb [1890/91] p. 31). Budde file, Maritime Jurisdiction (*Seeamt*) Hamburg 1 Sep. 1891; compare Pawlik, p. 192

22 *NKWL* (1886) Heft ii, p. 61, Heft iv, p. 113. Jb (1887 pp. 7 & 23. H.J. Witthöft, *Tradition und Fortschritt 125 Jahre Blohm + Voss,* p. 23

23 Dallmann to Arnold, 20 Jan., 1887 (Museum Schloß Schönebeck); see Pawlik, pp. 123–4.

24 *NKWL* (1890) Heft i, p. 46; Sack & Clark (1888–89) p. 40; (1889–90) p. 55

25 Jb (1889) p. 8; (1890) p. 40; Sack & Clark (1888–89) p. 40; the currency stated ($) is incorrect.

26 Jb (1890) p. 12; Sack & Clark (1889–90) p. 55; *NKWL* (1890), Heft i, p. 46, Heft ii, p. 95

27 *NKWL* (1892) Heft i, p. 42, (1893) Heft i, p. 60; Jb (1892/93) p. 16; Sack & Clark (1892–93) p. 83

28 Jb 1895/96, p. 9, Sack & Clark 1895–96, p. 123; *NKWL* 1896, p. 28. A. Baessler, *Neue Südsee-Bilder,* pp. 365-6. Buckley & Klugman, *The History of B.P,* p. 71; Ettling, *Unter Pflanzern,* pp. 11-2

29 The *Johann Albrecht* (36 m long, 6.5 m beam, and 2.7 m draught) had a crew of 8 Europeans, and 15 Papuan/Melanesian; it accommodated 150 coolies on the upper deck. A 260 h.p. steam engine provided a cruising speed of 10 kt, 8.8 kt fully laden (*NKWL* [1897] pp. 41–3)

30 Jb (1896/97) p. 13; Sack & Clark (1896–97) p. 137.

31 *NKWL* (1898) pp. 39–40. Jb (1897/98)] p. 6; Sack & Clark (1897–98) p. 143

32 Jb (1898/99) pp. 13 & 23–4, and (1902/03) p. 10; Sack & Clark (1898–99) pp. 156 & 163–4

33   Jb (1899/00) p. 9; Jb (1901/02) p. 15; Jb (1902/03) pp. 10 & 14.

34   *SMH* (1903) 3 Nov., p. 8.

35   *NKWL* (1898) pp. 41–2; Jb (1897/98) p. 9; (1898/99) p. 25; (1900/01) p. 17; (1901/02) pp. 15; (1903/04) p. 11; Sack & Clark (1897–98) p. 145; (1898–99) p. 165; (1899–1900) p. 191; (1902/03) p. 10

36   Jb (1906/07) p. 23; Sack & Clark (1906–07) p. 266

37   Jb (1908/09) p. 5; (1909/10) p. 7; (1913/14) p. 7; Sack & Clark (1908–09) p. 293.

38   Jb (1896/97) p. 12; (1897/98) p. 4; (1899/00) p. 16; (1900/01) p. 28; (1901/02) p. 21; Sack & Clark (1896–97) p. 136; (1897–98) p. 140; (1899–00) p. 207; (RKA 1001:2419, pp. 33–6)

39   W.C. Crowes, 'Peter the Island King' (1922), Jb (1903/04) p. 2; Sack & Clark (1903–04) p. 244,

40   The government payed NDL RM4,000,000 *annually* for shipping services Bremerhaven to Shanghai, and Bremerhaven to Sydney (Hagen, pp. 97–114)

41   *NKWL* (1892) Heft i, p. 27.

42   The 15 April departure date contradicts the 11 June 1892 date in *NKWL* (1893) Heft i, p. 59; Jb (1891/92) pp. 14–15. *NKWL* (1890) Heft ii, p. 95; Jb (1892/93) p. 16; Sack & Clark (1892–93) p. 83;

43   Shipping expenditures to March 1891—excluding receipts from insurance recovery—were RM1,711,422 against income of RM277,174 (Jb [1891/92] pp. 14–15, 34–42; [1892/93] p. 56–8).

44   *NKWL* (1892) Heft i, pp. 40–2.

45   *NKWL* (1893) Heft i, pp. 60–1; Jb (1892/93) p. 16; Sack & Clark (1892–93) p. 83.

46   *Denkschrift*, 17 March 1914, RT 13 Leg., 1 Ses. 1914, Band 304, Nr. 1473, pp. 61ff.

47   The *München* commenced the Sydney–Hong Kong service on 28 July 1900. *Drucksache des Reichstages* 'Denkschrift zu den Gesetzentwürfen betr. Postdampferschiffs-Verbindungen mit überseeischen Ländern' (RT 13 Leg., 1 Session 1914, Band 304, Nr. 1473, p. 39).s

48   K. Buckley & K. Klugman, *The History of Burns Philp*, pp. 83–4 & 152–3.

49   W. Treue, *Die Jaluit Gesellschaft auf den Marshall Inseln*, pp. 87–8.

50   The SS *Harold* was built in 1891 by S. McKnight & Co. and registered in 1900 by J-G as SS *Oceana* (*Lloyds Register of British and Foreign Shipping*, 1895–1901; Jb-J-G (1900) p. 1.

51   Jb-J-G (1903) p. 1, AGM, 23 Apr. 1904. A. Hahl, *Gouverneursjahre*, p. 146.Treue, p. 91. 'Probefahrt des Dampfers *Germania* der Jaluit Gesellschaft' in *DKBl.* (1903) Nr. 15, p. 594

52   Jb (1902/03) p. 7, (1903/04) p. 11; Sack & Clark (1902–03) p. 242, (1903–04) p. 250.

53   E. Hernsheim, 'Der Pierbau des NDL in Simpsonhafen' (*DKZ* [1904] Nr. 21, pp. 467–8.

54   Jb (1906/07) pp. 9–10.

55   Sack & Clark (1912–13) p. 369; S.S. Mackenzie, *The Australians at Rabaul*, pp. 200–1.

56   *Denkschrift*, RT 13 Leg., 1 (1914 sitting), Vol. 304, Nr. 1473, p. 41 (P. Neubaur, ed., *Jahrbuch des Norddeutschen Lloyd*, p. 275).

57   A. Hahl, *Gouverneursjahre in Neu Guinea*, p. 67; P.G. Sack & D. Clark, eds., *Hahl Governor*, p. 94.

58   *NKWL* (1895) Heft i, p. 46; Sack & Clark (1899–00) p. 191 & 194. Jb (1892/93) p. 18; (1894/95) pp. 9, 13; Sack & Clark (1892–93) p. 84; (1894–95) pp. 114–15; (1898–99) p. 172; (1909–10) pp. 304–5

59   Sack & Clark (1912–13) p. 369. Mackenzie, p. 201; À. Kludas, 'Deutsche Passagierschiffs-Verbindungen in der Südsee 1886–1914', in H.J. Hiery (ed.) *Die Deutsche Südsee*, p. 171.

60   Jb (1909/10) p. 7, (1910/11) p. 7.

61   Jb (1909/10) p. 7; (1911/12) p. 8; (1912/13) p. 13; (1913/14) pp. 7–8; Sack & Clark (1905–06) p. 263; (1912–13) p. 370. David Y. H. Wu, *The Chinese in Papua New Guinea, 1880–1980*, p. 52.

62   The R&H *Welcome* struck a Hermit Island reef in 1898, the *Else* stranded in the Admiralty Islands in 1899, the *Arima* disappeared in 1901, the *Mascotte* caught fire in the König Albert Strait in July 1901. The E.E. Forsayth *Eudora* stranded in Jan. 1892 on the Gerrit Denys Is., the *Nukumanu* grounded in the Duke of York n 1899. The DHPG schooner *Suga* ran aground off New Hanover in Aug. 1901. The *Muruna* was lost at sea 1903/4. After completing a refit in Sydney, partner-owner of O. Mouton & Co., Axel Monad, captained the schooner on her last voyage to the Protectorate. O. Mouton replaced the vessel with the *Monantha*. Captain J. Strasburg wrecked the schooner near Buka in 1905. The *Minna* stranded on the north coast of New Britain in Dec 1900. Refloated a year later Mouton sold the schooner in March 1902 to Otto Schneider, former captain of NGC's *Ysabel*. O. Mouton ordered the building of the *Takubar* in 1914 . Chartered to NGC. Shipwrecked in 1917 (P. Biskup, *JHP* 1974)

THE START OF PLANTATION ENTERPRISES AND THE COLOSSAL LOSS OF HUMAN LIFE

10

Adolph von Hansemann founded his protectorate in 1884 with the ambition of establishing a settler colony. This first period lasted until 1889. When the expected settlers did not arrive, NGC started its second stage of economic development of GNG. The company now planted coffee, tobacco and cotton—more or less successfully, but unprofitably—at three locations in KWL and on the Gazelle Peninsula. The difficulty of managing three stations nearly one thousand kilometres apart in KWL and a new enterprise in the Bismarck Archipelago was part of the reason for concentrating a large-scale plantation industry on Astrolabe Bay in 1892. This started NGC's third and most costly phase in GNG. The focus on tobacco and cotton increased the cash flow; it also increased the financial losses. A combination of high labour costs, a dearth of coolies, epidemics, pests, unfavourable weather patterns and weak tobacco prices ended this experiment in 1902. After 12 years of unsuccessful toiling with tobacco and cotton agriculture, NGC settled on large-scale coconut plantations with copra becoming the mainstay of its business enterprise.

Administrator Georg von Schleinitz met Richard Parkinson on the E. E. Forsayth & Co plantation, at Ralum, on the Gazelle Peninsula of New Britain in 1887. In the course of the meeting, Schleinitz spoke of NGC's acquisition of substantial tracts of unoccupied land. Acting on Hansemann's instruction, he informed Parkinson of his intention to purchase fertile pasture from the local people with the aim of selling it to European settlers. Parkinson doubted that such plan was feasible in GNG. It required too much start-up capital and considerable experience in tropical farming. Instead Parkinson encouraged Schleinitz to grow NGC into a plantation enterprise based on the E. E. Forsayth model, set up by him for the American-Samoan Emma Coe, and which he now managed for her.

The first attempt by NGC to establish two large coffee plantations on New Britain in early 1888 lay on the seabed of the Bismarck Sea, washed out to sea by a tsunami.[1] Schleinitz's station manager, Carl Hunstein and the former Java coffee planter, Paul Below, 4 Javanese and 12 Melanesians from Mioko were pegging an area on the west coast of the island when a 15-m high wave took their lives on 13 March 1888. Also lost was newly imported agricultural equipment, building material and a boat.[2]

Ascending Mt Kombiu or Mother Volcano (632m), July 1900, standing left to right Dr H. Schnee, M. Thiel, Governor R. von Bennigsen, Dr R. Koch (A. Pflüger, *Smaragdinsel der Südsee*, p. 229); **ascending Mt Wunakokor - Varzin-Berg, 603m, approx.16 km southwest of Herbertshöhe** (R. Parkinson on the left, G. Schmiele third from right, J. von Pfeil on the right; **Punitive expedition in response to the 1893 Tolai attempt to sack Herbertshöhe** - Imperial Judge G. Schmiele right of centre wearing a pith helmet (courtesy K. Baumann)

The tsunami caused a more setbacks for NGC than Hansemann first realised. Rather than taking Parkinson's advice and starting with plantations on the fertile soils of the Bismarck Archipelago, he transferred NGC land in Kaiser Wilhelms-Land (KWL) to subsidiary companies for cash crop plantations. Experimental tobacco fields had proven successful in Finschhafen-Butaueng, Konstantinhafen and Hatzfeldthafen. He judged the soil quality, weather pattern, low indigenous resistance to large-scale plantations and the availability of local labour rendered better opportunities than other locations, including the Gazelle Peninsula. This assessment by Hansemann - from his desk in Berlin - proved to be a costly mistake.

The establishment of a large-scale plantation industry began in June 1890 with the formation of two new subsidiary companies. The business of the Kaiser Wilhelm's-Land-Plantagen-Gesellschaft (KWLPG) concentrated on coffee and cacao, while the Neu-Guinea Tabak-Gesellschaft (NGTG) focused on growing and marketing tobacco. The foundation meeting of KWLPG took place in Hamburg in the offices of the Deutsche Ost-Afrika-Linie (DOAL) on 13 November 1890. The principal of DOAL, A. Woermann, became the chairman of KWLPG; other members of the Board of Directors included A. Hansemann, A. Lent and C. Beck. The Board approved the company's statute, the 'General Conditions of the Articles of Association'. Berlin sanctioned the formation of the company on 26 June 1890,[3] and appointed C. Bohlen General Manager. The principal activities of KWLPG were the growing of coffee and cacao on land acquired from NGC in KWL.

KWLPG issued 1,000 partly paid shares with a nominal value of RM500 each to individuals and registered companies, totalling 35 equity holders on the share register. Shares paid up to 10% were eligible to vote at shareholder meetings when called by the Board. At the discretion of the Directors, shareholders were required to inject additional capital of up to 100% of the issued capital, with each call not exceeding 30% of the share face value. Under the statute, KWLPG had the right to redeem, sell or cancel shares with unpaid calls, and recover legal costs and interest from the equity holders.[4]

At the 1890 annual NGC meeting Hansemann informed shareholders of the formation in Hamburg of a colonial company for the purpose of cultivating cacao and coffee in KWL. Shareholders learnt of the successful trials with coffee and cacao by NGC and of the transfer of 3,000 ha prime agricultural NGC land for 12.5% equity (RM20/ha) in the new venture.[5]

In addition to the equity held by NGC, Hansemann underwrote personally 24% (RM120,000) of the issued capital, with his bank, Disconto Gesellschaft (D-G), taking up 3.4%. Other substantial shareholders in KWLPG were NGC Directors Russell and Lent (6% each), Eckardstein-Prötzel (4%) and A. Woermann (2%). The large share holding by related parties should have provided minority KWLPG equity holders a measure of security. This was not the case. The cacao and coffee venture failed. It was a fiasco that rendered all shares in KWLPG worthless. The government requirement for NGC to be the guarantor of KWLPG left NGC to clean up the mess.[6]

Cacao plantations

The first attempt by NGC to operate a major plantation enterprise ended within six months of its legal formation. Hansemann had hired the Trinidad-based German cacao expert, Ludwig Kindt, because of his impressive credentials. A cacao grower for many years, Kindt convinced Hansemann that Ceylon rather than Caribbean cacao was the best in the world. He suggested starting the enterprise in GNG with a variety he would procure in Colombo, *en route* to the protectorate. Kindt expected these seeds to germinate in his Wardian Case (terrarium) so that he could commence planting immediately on his arrival in GNG in September 1890. To ensure a prompt start, Berlin instructed the administration in Finschhafen to provide Melanesian and Papuan labourers while Kindt stopped over in Surabaya to recruit 18 Javanese workers.[7] Hansemann and Imperial Commissioner for GNG, Friedrich Rose, agreed on the selection of the fertile soils of the Astrolabe and Gogol Plains and issued instructions to start preparing land near the village of Gorima. According to the *NKWL*, 'all efforts were made to ensure a successful launch of the venture by filling in the mosquito infested swamps and by planting shade-providing Erythrina trees'.[8]

The extensive preparatory work did not produce the desired results. NGC had no proficiency in tropical plantation work. Inexperienced executives in Berlin selected, interviewed and appointed nearly all senior employees for its protectorate during the first few years. The employment of a plantation manager who regarded the ending of slave labour as the end of tropical agriculture sent the wrong signal to the NGC staff and settlers in GNG; it pervaded the corporate culture of NGC, which was not in the interest of the company and did not reflect Hansemann's belief. Kindt was clearly the wrong choice. So as not to miss the first planting season, his priority was the clearing and tilling of the land rather than completing the work on labour accommodation and sanitary installations. With most of the seeds procured in Ceylon not germinating and unseasonal rainfall wiping much of the remainder, Kindt blamed the failure of the first crop on 'the niggers'. The Bilbil people of Astrolabe Bay were accomplished potters and garden farmers, displaying an economic culture entirely different from that of the Europeans. And rather than recognising inexperience in agriculture and providing guidance and training while seeking the respect and cooperation of his workers, he routinely relied on flogging. Kindt regarded his workers as obstinate and disobedient, treating hunger and sickness by providing ever-smaller food rations.[9]

On 2 December 1890, 10 Melanesian workers out of group of 15 New Irelanders—who had arrived in Gorima 7 days earlier—found their way to Finschhafen. They had fled Gorima Station because the 'master belong glass' (the bespectacled Kindt) punished them 'by tying their hands behind their backs, forcing them to the ground and, with his boot in their neck, flogged them'. The ringleader who organised another 40 workers to escape to Finschhafen 14 days later had received the same harsh treatment. Kindt denied the accusations. In particular, he rejected any involvement in the death of a worker. 'All I did', he told Commissioner Rose, was to give them 'a clip behind the ear or a few smacks to their backs'. Kindt seemed more concerned with his own predicament than becoming familiar with local requirements and the regulations of the NGC. The grief for the loss of his child to malaria and his eagerness to get the plantation started would leave him with neither time nor inclination to study the tedious NGC labour regulation or to consider how the men would respond to more considerate treatment. Kindt regarded the regulation of punishing a culprit to a maximum of 10 lashes a week as pathetic. He belonged to a generation of planters that was more in keeping with the Dutch *Cultuurstelsel* in the East Indies of the 1830s. As a 'real planter', he believed in the God-given right to make use of 'natives' without needing to show empathy or kindness or to pay them much for their toil. Kindt's Caribbean workers were accustomed to corporal punishment. 'Should the Papuans, Javanese or Chinese be treated any differently,' he would have asked.[10]

Commissioner Rose disagreed. He was now in charge of NGC's protectorate and determined to assert his authority. Answerable to Bismarck, it mattered little to him that he received his salary from NGC. Hansemann entered into an agreement with the *Reich* on 23 May 1889 under which NGC officers were relieved from performing the administration of justice, the collection of taxes and duty. Berlin accepted this responsibility on the condition that NGC remained accountable for the cost. In order to lessen this burden, Hansemann approved the appointment of Rose on 1 February 1890 in the dual position of Imperial Commissioner and NGC Administrator.[11]

Circumstances led to the merging of the positions of Imperial Commissioner for the Bismarck Archipelago and NGC's Administrator when Schleinitz's replacement, Kraetke, left the protectorate at short notice. His hurried replacement with NGC's office manager in Berlin, Hans Arnold, was short lived. He died from malaria on 31 January 1890, less than 3 months into the job. [12] Imperial Commissioner Rose took charge of affairs in GNG by agreement between the colonial desk in the *Auswärtige Amt* (AA-KA) and NGC. While briefly relinquishing the responsibility for NGC to Arnold's replacement, Eduard Wißmann, on 17 July 1890, Rose was again responsible for the protectorate of the New Guinea Company when Wißmann died—also of malaria—on 28 February 1891.

Hansemann expected Rose to be a compliant manager. However, the 34-year-old lawyer who arrived in Finschhafen on 30 October 1889 was anything but subservient. Rose set to work on improving the general health conditions of Europeans and workers alike and on upholding the law. He was determined to curtail the callous treatment of labourers by the European planters. His far-reaching authority enabled him to amend the Labour Act, now requiring every indentured labourer to register with the administration in Finschhafen before commencing work anywhere in the protectorate. In view of rampant venereal infections in Finschhafen, Rose mandated medical check-ups and ongoing medical supervision of the Europeans and the workers. Moreover, Rose removed Kindt from the position of plantation manager.[13]

For NGC the appointment of the Imperial Commissioner was troublesome and expensive as the following vignette demonstrates. In January 1890 Rose informed the AA-KA of his misgivings about Kindt while also advising KWLPG and NGC of his reservations about the manager's conduct: 'The example set by the Company's General Manager', he informed Woermann, 'will pervade the management of the NGC'. Rose predicted labour abuse would lead to more workers absconding and that arduous employment conditions would make it increasingly difficult to attract new workers. For that reason he imposed a financial bond on Kindt for every worker under his care, which he would forfeit in case of proven mistreatment. Predictably, Kindt ignored Rose's instructions, leading to his dismissal on 30 April 1891, which in Rose's view was 'in the best interest of NGC and the *Reich*'. The Gorima plantation had not progressed. The workers and European staff alike were sick, had died, had abrogated their employment contract or were generally dissatisfied.[14]

Hansemann was in two minds regarding the dismissal of Kindt. He had complained previously that Rose's moralising was damaging the company's interests and that the responsibility of the imperial government was to further NGC's interests. In January 1891 he demanded that the AA-KA instruct its Imperial Commissioner 'to avoid, as far as possible, all measures that were likely to impede on the NGC's businesses'.[15] In this instance, however, he agreed to the dismissal of Kindt as it provided a useful explanation as to why KWLPG did not prosper. 'The success of a plantation', according to the *Nachrichten über Kaiser Wilhelms-Land und den Bismarck-Archipel (NKWL)*, 'depends entirely on the competency of the plantation manager'.[16] Kindt stood accused of having procured poor quality cacao seeds; but his dismissal was primarily based on his uncivilised behaviour towards the Javanese, Melanesian and Papuan workers. Kindt responded with indignation. *En route* to Germany he wrote to Chancellor Count Leo von Caprivi who had replaced Bismarck:

> I have been around the world and have seen many new and established colonies. The hopeless conditions, as they exist in New Guinea in every respect, I have not experienced anywhere else ... In New Guinea, my colleagues and I have never enjoyed two consecutive days without a fever and all this because of the poorest of standards in food. The Administration cares for the workers as badly as it cares for the Europeans and complaints are discouraged. I blame the Directors of NGC in Berlin for making promises on accommodation and food, which they knew, could never be fulfilled, and because of it my child had to die. I write this letter so that decent German families are spared a like fate to that my family and I endured in KWL.[17]

Kindt also took his grievance to the Higher District Court in Hamburg. The statement of claim sought compensation of RM70,000 for breach of contract. The Directors of KWLPG and Commissioner Rose, who testified at the trial, did not dispute Kindt's 10-year employment contract and his annual salary of RM12,000 plus expenses. They submitted to the court the company was entitled to give 6 months' notice of termination of employment if: (a) KWLPG was insolvent, (b) went into voluntary liquidation, (c) plantations did not develop to expectation, (d) the plantation manager demonstrated incompetence or negligence in the performance of his duties. The court found in favour of the now defunct KWLPG and dismissed the claim and again Kindt's appeal against the primary judgement.[18]

Far from solving the problem of labour relations by dismissing Kindt, Rose now had to deal with the murder of the missionaries W. Scheidt and F. Bösch, and Hatzfeldthafen planter B. von Moisy on 26 May 1891 together with a number of NGC workers. He also had to respond to the slaying of two Javanese overseers and six labourers on the Astrolabe Bay Gorima plantation in June and July.[19] The Gorima and Bogadjim traditional landowners felt particularly aggrieved at the intrusion of other Papuan and Melanesian tribes on their territory and the Europeans' theft of their land. Rose tried to hunt down the killers with little success. When evidence of stolen goods from the Gorima plantation surfaced in nearby Myou village, he ordered the burning of the houses with the villagers' livestock and food supplies.[20]

The Hatzfeldthafen and Gorima actions created a confrontational mood that spread through the protectorate and lasted for many years. Rose had to deal with these major disruptions while establishing plantations in KWL, the Gazelle Peninsula and the northeast coast of New Ireland. He sought for police and armed forces to deal with the hostilities. Hansemann rejected Rose's request. Under the imperial charter the government was obligated to provide order and security in GNG.[21]

Berlin had its hands full in Africa and refused to engage militarily in Hansemann's protectorate except for the occasional visit by a light cruiser from its East Asian squadron in Tsingtao. When Rose's contract expired on 31 August 1892 NGC reverted to the *status quo* of appointing the administrator while the government continued to appoint the Judiciary for GNG. NGC blamed NGC's poor finances a result of Rose's tenure. However, much worse was to come with the formation of Astrolabe Compagnie, Hansemann's next great experiment in his colony New Guinea.

Tobacco: the unprofitable start to a plantation industry

The plantation industry of the Dutch East Indies was Hansemann's paradigm. He believed that what thrived on Java and Sumatra would also grow well in GNG. Cacao seemed a good idea to him. But, its cultivation was slow to generate profits because seeds took 4 years to grow into fruit-bearing trees. An abundance of wild sugar cane had little appeal to NGC's board. The cultivation and harvesting of plantation cane was labour intensive, and for it to compete with European beet required major investment in industrial plant. Hansemann, therefore, gave preference to cultivating tobacco. Although requiring higher labour input, tobacco is harvested within 4 months of planting and, subject to favourable environmental and market conditions, yielded higher returns than slow-growing crops like coffee, cacao or coconuts.

In 1863 the Dutch trader Jacobus Nienhuys started to plant tobacco in the small Sultanate of Deli in northeast Sumatra. By 1872 his company, the Deli Maatschappij, exported 1,000,000 Gulden worth of tobacco, increasing to 2,500,000 Gulden the following year. By 1889 Deli produced 182,399 bales of tobacco worth more than 40,000,000 Gulden. It allowed the company to pay sustained annual dividends of around 75% on the issued capital.[22] Such impressive results drove Hansemann to aim for similar success in GNG.

Even as land acquisitions remained an important factor in colonising the protectorate, cultivating tobacco became central to NGC's commercialisation program. A fervent cigar smoker, Hansemann understood the value of a good quality leaf: from the outset he instructed his scientific explorers, station managers and Administrator to identify suitable land for cultivating tobacco. Station manager Fritz Grabowsky reported the first positive signs with the discovery of substantial quantities of 'wild' tobacco that grew on the rich loam of the Kunai Plains west of Hatzfeldthafen. 'The tobacco grown around Hatzfeldthafen', the former explorer noted in his February 1886 report to Hansemann, 'has a first-class aroma; the leaves are slim and elastic and with appropriate cultivation the tobacco grown in this region would promise to supply a valuable product for the European market'.[23]

By 1891 the moderate plan Hansemann had in mind for the Neu-Guinea Tabak-Gesellschaft had developed into a new grand vision for his protectorate. NGC withdrew from operating commercial plantations by selling its interests in KWL to a new company in which it held the controlling interest. Astrolabe Compagnie (A-C) was founded on 27 October 1891 to cultivate and manufacture tobacco on Astrolabe Bay.[24] After 5 year's backbreaking work and human suffering A-C was insolvent with its assets and liabilities taken over by NGC. After another 5 years Hansemann's dream to grow the world's best tobacco on Sumatran scale in GNG ended in disaster, in both financial and human terms.

NGC appointed Jacob Weisser in August 1886 area Adminstrator of the Central Station at Mioko in the Bismarck Archipelago. A former purser with the *Reichsmarine*, the 'old salt' with South Sea experience was instructed to visit Deli for 3 months to acquire knowledge in tobacco cultivation and fermentation and thereafter investigate the viability of growing commercial tobacco in GNG.[25] In the absence of land sales to settlers 'income producing enterprises under our management, in particular the cultivation of tobacco, are uppermost on my mind', Hansemann wrote to Weisser on 7 May 1887. 'With the knowledge you have gained in Sumatra we believe you are best suited to carry out the task of managing the intended tobacco enterprises.'[26] By the time Weisser had returned from Sumatra and settled on Mioko, NGC's botanist Max Hollrung had discovered wild tobacco grown by tribes in the Sepik River region. The samples he procured from the natives were sent to Germany for assessment. But even before the results were known, Hansemann had decided on large-scale tobacco farming in his Protectorate. Weisser had succumed to Malaria fever within a year of his arrival in Mioko, and Hansemann considered that tobacco could be grown anywhere in KWL, with land identification therefore no longer a prerequisite. What was needed foremost, he told his shareholders in the 1887 Annual Report, were experienced managers and planters, and that the engagement of personnel experienced in managing tobacco plantations are already under way.[27]

There was no shortage of respondents. The agricultural scientist, Dr Richard Hindorf, who had worked in Ceylon, Java, Sumatra and Australia, applied for a position in tropical cultivation with NGC in June 1887. In December 1887 Philipp Leiby left his tobacco farm in the German State of Baden to work for NGC for five years before returning to his home in St Ilgen. Others like Adolf Hermes (1888) and Franz Koch (1889) went from German East-Africa and Cameroon to GNG.[28]

While NGC hired tobacco experts from East Africa and the Dutch East Indies, Grabowsky continued his solitary path. He set up an experimental garden on Tschirimotsch (Mahde) Island to germinate local tobacco seeds. A request by head office in Berlin to send soil samples to Germany for analysis was only followed reluctantly. The evidence was already at hand: tobacco thrived at Hatzfeldthafen. Without waiting for the results from Berlin, he returned to Surabaya to recruit 50–60 'Malays', four Chinese and bullocks in order to prepare fields for the coming season.

Grabowsky and his 95 workers planted a 10 ha plot with the first commercial quantity of tobacco on the Hatzfeldthafen hills in June 1887. The move away from the safety of the island was premature, though. Under attack by the Dugumor, Tombenam or Tschiriar tribes, it was difficult to keep the workers on the job. A call in July for a warship to avenge the murder of a plantation worker went unanswered. The *Reichsmarine* showed little interest in chasing tribesmen in the hostile terrain of New Guinea. Grabowsky had to wait for the arrival on 27 August of the company steamers *Ottilie* and *Samoa* with complements of armed sailors from the Finschhafen district to put an end to the hostilities. It was a temporary calm. The warriors resumed aggression as soon as the ships left. Unable to harvest the first plantation tobacco of GNG, a frustrated Grabowsky resigned from the company in November 1887.[29]

Ernst Schollenbruch transferred from Butaueng—where he was in charge of experimental plantations—to Hatzfeldthafen to continue Grabowsky's work. He cut, looped and dried the first NGC leaves from Deli seeds in May 1888. By June quality cured leaves were graded, batched and sent to Germany for evaluation. In September Schollenbruch cleared rainforest on the river flats of the Daigun for the second

1888 tobacco harvest. In this he consolidated all farming activities—tobacco, yams, sorghum and grazing—within the vicinity of Hatzfeldthafen Station. It provided for better protection and rationalised his scarce labour resource.

The quantity and the quality of the second 1888 harvest were not as high as Schollenbruch had hoped. Yet, according to an 'expert report', the quality of the first cigars made from Hatzfeldthafen tobacco was above expectations: 'The elasticity of the leaves was exceptionally high, of firm structure, sticky and therefore most suitable for cigar-wrappers'. Hansemann and his colleagues would have praised cigars from their protectorate regardless. The first fully cured tobacco was sold in Bremen in 1889. Although badly graded, the sale exceeded the NGC break-even price of RM1.05/lb. While Hansemann should have been pleased with the mean price of RM1.51/lb (excluding duty) for the lot on offer, he was unhappy that inferior local tobacco seeds had been mixed with Sumatran seeds. Hansemann's strongest critic, Eduard Hernsheim, agreed. 'NGC tobacco appears to have none of the characteristics of the highly priced Deli leaf. It is worth no more than RM0.25/lb on the European market', he declared.[30]

Not to be distracted by sniping remarks of a South Sea rival, the first two commercial tobacco harvests in GNG did whet the appetite of the NGC board. Henceforth, tobacco planting was authorised on a large scale. For this to succeed, NGC required more planters with experience in tropical agriculture. The German tobacco industry employed few, if any, personnel with tropical experience and in 1888 the German and Dutch planters in Sumatra and Java had secure positions. So Hansemann decided that NGC would train its managers. Franz Koch, who had farming experience in German East Africa, retired Lieutenant-Commander Ernst Rodig and Commercial manager Ernst Wegner headed for the Dutch East Indies in September 1888 to learn about planting, picking, curing and grading tobacco. But the signs were ominous for Hansemann's ambition to create a second Deli in his protectorate. A viral fever infected many passengers and crew on the Hamburg Kinsin-Line steamer which was to take the party to Singapore. Rodig died and Wegner was hospitalised in Singapore for weeks before being sent back to Germany. Only Koch, who disembarked in Penang, recovered sufficiently to visit Sumatra; he arrived in GNG in 1890.[31]

Inexperience led to black root rot, a result of not properly draining the tobacco fields, and mildew, cat-worms and other infestations. Hansemann dealt with the situation by turning his attention to the European planters who had established themselves in Deli. In 1890 he informed shareholders: 'for success to be assured events thus far have shown that the management of tobacco plantations in New Guinea can only be entrusted to qualified growers who are familiar with Sumatran tobacco cultivation'.[32]

When Schollenbruch returned to Germany in March 1889, Wilhelm von Puttkamer, assistant manager at Hatzfeldthafen since 1886, was given responsibility for the plantation until the experienced Sumatran planter, Johan Schoevers, joined NGC in 1890. At that time Puttkamer was sent to the Dutch East Indies to attract Sumatran farmers to join NGC and to sign up Chinese coolies there. Hansemann recognised the necessity for these labour resources for the successful planting, curing and grading of tobacco.

Schoevers prepared the 20 ha immediately east from Hatzfeldthafen, where first-class tobacco loam was available on a wide expanse. He expected much improved results from the move inland as the impact of the onshore wind, which he knew inhibited growth and the aroma of the tobacco, was mitigated. With 163 local people and 15 Javanese Schoevers harvested approximately 7,800 kg of tobacco from some 200,000 plants in 1890. Heavy rain hampered the second planting in 1890. The 120 bales from this crop arrived in Bremen on 9 September 1891 and were auctioned with 115 and 75 bales respectively from the new Stephansort and Erima plantations achieving the best price. In late 1890 Schoevers was temporarily joined by the Sumatran planter Lutz who, in conjunction with Puttkamer, indentured 79 coolies, one Chinese overseer (*tandil*) and five Banjurese in Singapore at the end of October 1890 for the 1891 Hatzfeldthafen planting season. In January 1891 Schoevers had sufficient workers to plant 343,000 seedlings of tobacco. High wind and heavy rain delayed cutting until April. After an inferior harvest, with the leaves not cured and sorted in time for shipment Hansemann ordered Hatzfeldthafen to be closed. It was a disappointed Johan Schoevers who returned to Sumatra with his family.[33]

The precursor to large-scale tobacco and cotton agriculture

Richard Hindorf, who had returned to Germany after close to three years in the protectorate, delivered an enthusiastic account on the prospects of NGC. His speech to the Cologne Colonial Society in 1890 was taken up by the Queensland newspapers a few months later:

> The German New Guinea Company now concentrates its energy on plantation work, and very important results, particularly in the cultivation of a very superior cigar tobacco leaf and excellent cotton have been obtained. The shipments to Germany in both respects have proved that the cultivation of a superior tobacco leaf and of cotton is eminently profitable undertakings. The plantations at Hatzfeldthafen, Konstantinhafen, Stephansort, and Butaueng are in full swing, and several companies are now being formed in Germany for the extension of this profitable plantation work. As the administrative machinery of the territory is now completely organised, all questions of title to land, administration of justice, police protection, etc., are fully provided for. The chief result of the changes above referred to are, however, the ample provision of obtaining an unlimited supply of tropical labour.[34]

The situation depicted did not remotely reflect reality: Hindorf should have recognized that NGC's financial pain had barely started and that 'eminently profitable undertakings' were to be out of reach for many more years.

The former German East African farmer Adolf Hermes founded Stephansort on Astrolabe Bay in August 1888. He was given the go-ahead by the administration in Berlin to clear some 500 ha for tobacco cultivation and to set up appropriate infrastructure and facilities.[35] Within 11 months he had 19 ha of dense rainforest cleared, and constructed a leaf drying and curing shed, accommodation for four Chinese overseers and their families, and living quarters for Jabim people. A jetty, causeway paths, Hermes' house, a prison and a further tobacco barn were completed by end of the year so as not to miss the early season in the following year. In January

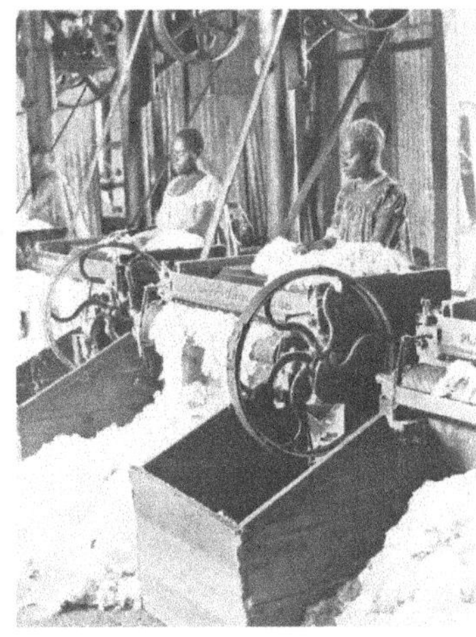

Workers at Herbertshöhe delivering the cotton harvest to the NGC gin house. Melanesian women operating the gins to separate cotton seeds from the fibre, ca. 1895 (F. Hutter, pp. 515 and 517)

1889 Hermes planted 14 ha with tobacco and, like his colleague in Konstantinhafen, 5 ha with maize, yam, taro, bananas and sweet potatoes for his workers and himself. The start Hermes hoped for did not eventuate. Pests similar to those in Hatzfeldthafen affected the first planting and an unseasonal dry spell in July–August affected the second. The workers' inexperience showed up in the slowness of picking and preparing the tobacco; and despite the use of *tandils*, sorting and packaging was inconsistent. The first Stephansort tobacco, 151 bales of approximately 56 kg each, left New Guinea in November 1889 and were sold off-market in Bremen in February 1890 at undisclosed prices.[36] The problems of the 1889 seasons were overcome in 1890. Of a total of 45 ha farmed, 14 ha were planted with cotton (yielding 10 tonnes); cereal and vegetables were planted on 15 ha (producing 30 t maize); and the 16 ha of tobacco yielded 158 bales of 79 kg each of 'the finest tobacco yet produced in GNG'. The Bremer tobacco experts praised the richness of the essential oils in the tobacco, and the width and texture of the leaves. Free from heavy veins, the tobacco leaves had fine elasticity, were lustrous and smooth, and was ideally suited for binders and wrappers. The average price attained at auction in Bremen for the 1890 crop was RM3.26/lb, with 'prime cut' leaves fetching RM5.20/lb. 'The high-quality tobacco, regarded by the merchants as superior to Deli's and close to the exceptional products of Mexico and Havana, would fetch even higher prices if the finely structured leaves were produced in a lighter, more even tan'.[37]

On the back of the tobacco produced by Hermes in Stephansort, Franz Koch started his assignment in March 1890 with the establishment of the nearby Erima Station. Within 3 months of his arrival he had built from local timber a Malay house with a community kitchen—typically built on 2 m stilts, 6 m wide and 13.5 m long—an accommodation block for 100 Chinese coolies, one for 200 Melanesians, and a boat shed. Koch's residence, completed in early November 1890, stood, in Papuan tradition, also on stilts. The 50 m jetty was near completion, with the 50 m connecting causeway finished in August ahead of the marine work.[38]

Disastrous Ventures

After the closure of Hatzfeldthafen the veteran Dutch tobacco planter Lutz went to work on Erima. By following Deli practise he started with 5.5 km of trenching so that the fields would be properly drained. Lutz oversaw the completion of the accommodation blocks, and for the roofs of the fermentation and drying sheds to be covered with local nipa-palm-fronds. This was significantly quicker and cheaper than importing atap from Southeast Asia. In May 1891 Lutz planted the first 100,000 seedlings. He did not see these harvested: after 18 months in GNG a severe fever hospitalised him in Finschhafen where he died in July 1891. Hermes, presumably with the assistance of Koch, oversaw the first picking of Erima tobacco and 75 bundles readied for shipping to Bremen. Erima had superior loam, but it was also one of the deadliest places. Like Lutz, Koch and Hermes did not live to see how the Erima tobacco was received in Germany. Koch, already cheating death once, succumbed to malaria fever on 26 December 1891, eight days after Hermes died of influenza.[39]

The first Erima tobacco was despatched in May 1892 by Erima's fourth manager in 12 months, Woldemar von Hanneken. When the consignment was auctioned in Bremen in September, together with the Stephansort and Hatzfeldthafen harvests, the results exceeded the expectations. The Erima tobacco was remarked on by the Bremer auctioneers as being of a finer quality than the Stephansort leaf. It led Hansemann to tell his shareholders that 'the tobacco was once more beautifully grown, had exceptional burning properties—evenly and snow-white—was of exceptional quality and sufficiently flavoured for today's taste'. The *NKWL* reflected the chairman's view by telling its readers that 'the tobacco was extraordinarily beautiful, which proves that growing conditions in Erima were even better than those present in Stephansort'. But Hansemann disapproved the use of high-quality Erima wrappers and binders with inferior fillers from other tobacco regions. It did not meet with the approval of many smokers, he believed, and decided to market NGC's own brand of cigars, rolled exclusively from Astrolabe Bay tobacco. By offering these cigars to the shareholders, employees and a circle of acquaintances, the cigars sold quickly and the NGC returned a modest profit on this product.[40]

The mean price of RM3.26/lb cif European ports attained for Stephansort tobacco in 1890 was RM1.25/lb above the upset price set by the head office Berlin. A year later the Erima harvest auctioned in Bremen averaged only RM2.10/lb cif. The result compared favourably with the mean price of RM2.17/lb for Sumatra tobacco sold in Amsterdam. However, some 26,000,000 lb of Deli tobacco fetched *f*33,128,000 in Amsterdam in 1888 alone. NGC sold 106,705 lb of tobacco in the first 4 years for RM242,666. Low volume and labour cost far exceeded the value of NGC's sales,

Import of NGC tobacco (lb) through the port of Bremen

Year	Hatzfeldthafen	Stephansort	Erima	Total
1888	1,600	0	0	1,600
1889	3,704	16,952	0	20,656
1890	12,878	24,994	0	37,872
1891	18,499	16,744	11,334	46,577
Total	36,681	58,690	11,334	106,705

with Stephansort the notable exception in 1891/92.[41]

Notwithstanding the high quality tobacco grown in Hatzfeldthafen and on Astrolabe Bay, Hindorf's account of the situation in 1890 was off the mark. The tobacco harvests in GNG were small and production costs high; most cotton harvests had failed. Tobacco gown in Sumatra in 1890 was built on more than 30 years of ruthless coolie exploitation. It was established by experienced European planters on fertile volcanic soil. To emulate this success NGC projected sales of 400,000 lb in 1897. But this planned increase was not nearly enough to make the enterprise profitable. In a depressed tobacco market production costs had to be lowered also.[42]

Hansemann recognised this. Already in 1889/90 he advised shareholders that the management of tobacco plantations in New Guinea could only be entrusted to experienced planters. To lower costs, all plantations in KWL needed to be consolidated in a region where unlimited highly fertile land was available and harbour facilities could be constructed quickly at a reasonable cost. Such an area existed in Astrolabe Bay near Stephansort and Erima. Hansemann engaged the Sumatra tobacco planter Bluntschli in February 1890 to assess the suitability of growing tobacco on the Jomba and Astrolabe Plains on a scale similar to that undertaken at Deli.[43]

The Astrolabe Compagnie

Hansemann's modest plans for NGTG shifted to a more ambitious scheme. NGC informed its shareholders on 9 December 1892 that tobacco land at Hatzfeldthafen was poor compared to the soil on Astrolabe Bay. Hatzfeldthafen will be abandoned, with tobacco plantations consolidated on the Jomba and Astrolabe Plains under a new enterprise, the Astrolabe Compagnie (A-C). Prospective investors in NGTG and KWLPG shareholders were encouraged to subscribe for shares in the new company.[44]

The closure of Hatzfeldthafen was against Puttkamer's advice. He informed von Hansemann in 1890 that first-class tobacco land was available there. In the opinion of Hans Blum and Ernst von Tappenbeck the closure of the Hatzfeldthafen was a waste of a valuable resources.[45] However, the problem for NGC was the lack of financial and management resources and the collapse of the international tobacco market, not the quality and quantity of suitable tobacco land at Hatzfeldthafen. The company's tobacco activities needed to be consolidated geographically and output increased substantially to become commercially viable. Hansemann speculated that the 1890 McKinley Tariff would set in train a world-wide crisis for non-USA premium leaf tobacco growers. This, he hoped, would benefit NGC/A-C.[46] Over 1,000 Germans worked in the hundred million Guilder Sumatran tobacco industry, and the collapse of the tobacco price should make Deli planters and coolies available for GNG.[47] The market dictated that these planters could be engaged at competitive wages to bring about better productivity and superior tobacco leaf quality in his protectorate.[48]

On 25 March 1891 the draft statute of A-C and a company prospectus was sent to the Foreign Office for review and to potential shareholders. It informed, *inter alia,*

Nominal capital of RM2,400,000 (4,800 shares with a face value of RM500). NGC to sell 14,000 ha prime agricultural land and harbour installations in return for 12.5% equity.

Soil probes taken during 1887 in nine locations, from FWH to Stephansort and six hours distance inland were assayed. A report by Professor Märker identifies six probes rich in humus, nitrogen, saltpetre, limestone and phosphates. The analysis compares favourably with soil analysed by the Moor Laboratories for the tobacco growing region of Deli in northeast Sumatra. With the exception of three probes nutrients exceed those of Deli by between 3% and 35%. The Astrolabe soil is particularly rich in lime which averages 2.5% compared to 0.3% in Deli.

NGC will be responsible for the supply of native labour suitable for the clearing of jungle, road work and other simple tasks. The NGC operates a purpose-built recruitment vessel. NGC will also be responsible for the recruitment of Javanese and other labour from the Dutch East Indies.

Six Europeans and 500 coolies are required to supervise and cultivate 400 tobacco fields.

Long-term projection is four to five plantations of 400 fields each. One plantation of 200 fields is planned for the 1891/92 season. Until the activities of Stephansort and Erima are transferred further inland, the surplus of recruited Chinese collies and *tandils* will be absorbed by NGC.

Generally, a tobacco field will only be productive for one, maximum two seasons. Experience in East Sumatra has shown that tobacco fields need to lie fallow for eight to nine years before planted with tobacco again. The 14,000 ha purchased from NGC will therefore not be sufficient for the planned number of stations and additional land will have to be acquired by A-C in the future.

NGC will establish a more frequent shipping service between the Protectorate and Surabaya.

The trials with tobacco conducted in Hatzfeldthafen and Stephansort from 1887 to 1889 provide important lessons. The colour and length of the tobacco leaf produced to date has impressed the experts. It is expected that a wrapper leaf quality can be grown on the Astrolabe/Jomba Plains that will match or exceed the quality of the leaves from the Deli once the inland plantation, Erima, is established. The engagement of experts from Sumatra and the recruitment of coolies from China are essential to achieve this objective.

East coast Sumatra (Deli) produced 4 t of tobacco in 1864 which was sold at f0.48/lb; in 1888 the region produced 12,840 t, selling at a mean price of f1.29/lb cif Amsterdam. The production cost for Sumatra tobacco is estimated at RM1.60/lb cif Amsterdam with a selling price of RM2.10 to RM2.80/lb achievable. This would generate profits of 30% to 75%.[49]

The prospectus kept silent on a number of salient points. For instance, the health problems in New Guinea and hostility towards the planters by many tribes did not rate a mention, nor did the unpredictable weather pattern. In any event, despite the optimistic contents of the prospectus it did not generate much interest and 80% of the shares were placed with related parties.

Wilhelm von Puttkamer was optimistic in buying 100 A-C shares. The confidence he conveyed to Hansemann on the prospects of New Guinea tobacco must have impressed the Chairman because he appointed him A-C's General Manager when he visited NGC's office in Berlin in early 1891. Curt von Hagen, who replaced Puttkamer at the beginning of 1893, was not as upbeat. Much the wiser from the failure of his own tobacco plantation on Sumatra he only subscribed to one share.

The *Bundesrath* approved of A-C commencing business on 22 December 1891. The overall administrative and legal responsibilities for the protectorate remained with Imperial Commissioner and NGC Administrator Friedrich Rose until Georg Schmiele was appointed Administrator of GNG on 2 September 1892. Puttkamer, who recommended his work in GNG by joining Koch on Maraga Station on 15 July 1891, took up the appointment as A-C's Administrator on 1 June 1892. The legal transfer to A-C of Erima Station took place on 1 January 1892 and that of Stephansort on 1 March 1892. Under the shareholder agreement NGC transferred to

A-C 14,500 ha of prime tobacco planting land on the Astrolabe and Jomba Plains in early 1892. Included in the conveyance were the new Maraga and Jomba Stations, with the latter planned 6 km northeast of Friedrich Wilhelmshafen on Jomba Creek.[50]

Tobacco plantations on Astrolabe Bay

The availability of Sumatra's tobacco planters changed A-C's mind.[51] Rather than limiting planting in the first year to Stephansort and Erima Stations, A-C now decided to plant tobacco also at Maraga and Jomba. The charter of the SS *Devawongse* in December 1891 provided additional capacity to transport coolies, rice and materials from Singapore and Sumatra to GNG. In two voyages 1,085 Chinese and 757 Javanese coolies, *tandils* and *mandurs,* experienced in the growing and manufacturing of tobacco, arrived in KWL in January and March 1892.[52]

A hasty start-up led to immediate problems. Coolies had been poorly selected and the living conditions were inadequate to deal with the large influx of workers. Addicted to opium, the coolies' health deteriorated quickly. A labour force at first thought to be too large was soon so small that barely 120 tobacco fields were planted at

Dr. Robert Koch and entourage on the Stephansort to Erimahafen 'Zebu Express', ca. 1899 (Deutsches Historisches Museum No. ZD025062, Hesse-Wartegg, p. 61)

Disastrous Ventures

Curt von Hagen, tobacco grading, cigar twisters, tobacco seedbeds, ca. 1895 (Archive Mission Eine Welt, J.H. Hiery, plate 18; F Hutter, pp. 513 & 559).

Stephansort and Jomba, and planting at Erima and Maraga was postponed until 1893 because many coolies had died shortly after their arrival and several Melanesians had succumbed to the influenza epidemic which had been partly responsible for the shut-down of Finschhafen a few months earlier. The rushed hiring of workers, their demise and subsequent diminishing farm returns accelerated negative cash flow. By December 1892 A-C had incurred debts of RM312,764. With shareholder funds of RM1,200,000 spent, it mandated a call up of the remaining 50% of unissued shares.[53]

Stephansort

Until NGC moved its headquarters from Finschhafen to Friedrich Wilhelmshafen in late 1892, Stephansort was the administrative centre for NGC and A-C.[54] Even before Berlin approved the new centre, staff residences and a hospital for Europeans were completed. Between October 1891 and April 1892 four accommodation quarters for Chinese, two Malay longhouses for 80 Javanese, one house for 20 Klingalese (Javanese Tamils), a kitchen and an isolation hospital for dysentery-infected workers were constructed. By the time Puttkamer assumed responsibility for the Stephansort plantation in June 1892, 100 ha were cleared, with 60 fields prepared, including the digging of the all-important drainage trenches, for tobacco. Fallow fields were planted with maize and sweet potatoes to provide the staple for workers. The out-planting of seedlings had started on 1 April. In July Puttkamer reported an estimated 60,000 lb harvest of better quality than had been grown previously.[55]

Maraga Station

The planter Rohlack arrived from Sumatra on the *Devawongse* with 150 Chinese and Javanese in March 1892 to assume responsibility for Maraga. The work on this plantation, started by Franz Koch, had been continued after his death by Puttkamer when he returned from Germany in the first half of 1891. Workers' quarters, complete with a *kadeh*, the manager's residence and the houses for European staff were complete. However, hardly any rainforest had been cleared for planting. The Finschhafen influenza epidemic had reached Stephansort by December 1891. The contagion was rampant among the local people, while the outbreak of dysentery started with the arrival of Chinese and Malay coolies. Combined with the ubiquitous malaria fever hardly any field-work was performed from the end 1891 to March 1892. With little possibility of planting tobacco at Maraga in 1892, Rohlack made the remaining Chinese coolies available to other Stations and carried on preparing 60 to 80 tobacco fields for the 1893 season using the Javanese and Melanesian workers. But he died of malaria on 22 July 1892, after less than 5 months in GNG. As a result, little work was done at Maraga in 1892.

Erima Station

A similar situation beset Erima Station. No work of substance was done until March 1892 because of the virulent influenza pandemic. With the early planting season missed and only a few coolies left, Hanneken built sanitary facilities and a 48-bed native hospital. The drainage of the plantation land was improved by separating the field from the rainforest by a deep trench. A corridor was constructed through the plantation with lateral paths providing better access to the fields. Because the tobacco had to be transported to Stephansort by bullock or horseback, Hanneken cut a 5 km riding path through the rainforest to connect Erima and Stephansort.

Jomba Station

The Jomba plantation was started by Georg Pfaff and his assistants Ernst Küchenthal, Rudolf Wolff and Herr Bolle. First assessed by Puttkamer and his surveyor E. Kleist in July 1891, approximately 3,500 ha of the Jomba Plains—immediately to the west of the Schering Peninsula—had been chosen for the fourth tobacco plantation. The undulating country was interrupted with timber standing on 40 cm of humus and then a deep layer of loam. The responsibility for Jomba was given to Pfaff. Highly recommended by A-C's adviser Herr Herring for whom he worked for several years on Sumatra, Pfaff arrived in Friedrich Wilhelmshafen in early September 1891 on the NDL steamer *Schwalbe.* He brought with him with two *mandurs* from Singapore, 54 Javanese coolies and artisans, 48 Chinese and 10 Sikhs from Java, 9 *tandils,* 263 Chinese coolies and 10 Chinese timber workers from Sumatra. The company's objective to have 150 fields ready for planting in February 1892 was unachievable. Heavy rain slowed tree-felling and prevented scrub from being burnt. Despite influenza, beri-beri, dysentery and malaria, the workers were cutting atap and digging trenches. Pfaff's residence, houses for his assistants, worker accommodation, two drying sheds, a boat shed and several shelters were completed. A hospital for coolies and a *kadeh* were finished by the end of the year. Before planting could begin, Pfaff germinated tobacco in 120 seedbeds. After a late planting, he reported proudly in July that his tobacco stood nearly as well as the 6-week older Stephansort crop.[56]

The 1892 Jomba harvest brought in 261 bales and for Stephansort 422 bales. Weighing in at 108,630 lb, the Stephansort lot was sold in Bremen in 1893 at a much lower price than the RM3.26/lb attained for the 1890 crop. Pfaff's judgement on the quality of his tobacco did not translate into earnings. No acceptable bid was received for the Jomba tobacco at auction in Bremen: the consignment remained unsold at the end of 1893. After the poor reception of New Guinea tobacco in Germany Puttkamer predicting a much-improved result for 1893.[57] He forecast a harvest of 265,000 lb from 410 to 420 fields in his plan to Berlin for 1893. Leading by example, Puttkamer planned 150 to 160 fields for Stephansort alone, the Station for which he was directly responsible, but only 60 fields for Maraga where a replacement for Rohlack was required. Hanneken and Pfaff projected 100 fields for Erima and Jomba respectively.

The forecast was again optimistic. The company had failed to control mortality and morbidity amongst the workforce and European staff. Apart from malaria and beri-beri, affecting the Chinese in particular, many workers fell to the smallpox outbreak in June 1892. The vaccination program, which included all inbound passengers and coolies, slowed the rate of new infections. But the sick were slow in rejoining the workforce, and the deceased could not be replaced in time for Puttkamer to meet his planting objectives. Stephansort and Erima suffered the largest reduction, with only 99 and 54 fields respectively planted with tobacco in 1893, while Maraga had 40 fields. The lower contagion in Jomba enabled Pfaff to meet his forecast.

Puttkamer was spared from influenza, smallpox and malaria; he was not spared by an impatient chairman. Hansemann, who was eager to see a return on his considerable investment, told shareholders in December 1892 that A-C was seeking to employ a person with considerable experience in tropical tobacco agriculture. In December 1893 he informed the shareholders that Puttkamer had handed over the administration of A-C to Curt von Hagen. A few months later a short note from the Berlin office read 'Herr W. v. Puttkamer has returned to Germany… The Company is currently negotiating the severance conditions for his [5-year] contract'.[58] Despite Hansemann's dead hand of control, Puttkamer's legacy in GNG was impressive. With 23 staff and a workforce of approximately 1,600 more-or-less able bodies, he built 146 structures of various kinds 'to high standards' from local timber and atap. These included 'native' hospitals at Erima, Maraga and Jomba, Europeans' residences, General Manager offices and amenities, houses for station managers and assistant managers. Worker Quarters for 140 Melanese, two blocks for 40 men and one for 60 men, two *tandil* cottages, one communal kitchen; two Malay houses for around 75 men each, four Malay houses for 60 men – including two kitchens for 80 men, one Malay house for 15 men, one *mandur* cottage, two with kitchen for 70 men, and six cottages with a kitchen for 50 men, three cottages with a kitchen for 40 men and four *kongsies* for 40 men. Tobacco sheds: 12 drying and three fermentation barns. One horse stable with eight boxes, one cow and bullock shed for approximately 100 head. Other buildings included two Chinese and one Malay *kadeh,* three rail-cart sheds and six warehouses. Two atap storage and a boat shed. A 7.5 km road connecting Stephansort with Maraga via Erima and Erimahafen and a 600 mm light-rail track was completed, with rails and carts due to arrive from Germany in late 1893.[59]

In 1893 Puttkamer harvested 47% more tobacco than the previous season. A consignment of 44,160 lb sold in Amsterdam at a mean price of 1.50/lb Dutch guilder (*f*). A-C felt relieved when comparing this sale with a Deli batch auctioned at the same time at *f*1.23/lb. A second batch, consisting of Erima (17,352 lb), Stephansort (7,324 lb), Jomba (37,100 lb) and Maraga (8,824 lb) tobacco was shipped to Bremen in the last quarter of 1893. While the Stephansort tobacco was high quality, the dark colour of the Erima, Maraga and Jomba leafs, and a depressed market, achieved poorer results than those attained in Amsterdam.[60]

The Curt von Hagen administration

C. von Hagen, ca. 1895

Curt von Hagen was not impressed with the situation he found on Astrolabe Bay when he arrived there in June 1893. The layout of the fields were unsatisfactory and he found the paperwork to be a shambles. Hanneken suffered from malaria fever and mostly bedridden, Pfaff, who transferred from Jomba to Stephansort after Puttkamer's departure, left the company on short notice. Hagen's main concern was, however, the high morbidity and mortality rates in the workforce. Hagen reported that 'the parlous state of the workers will affect the very existence of the company if not brought under control'.

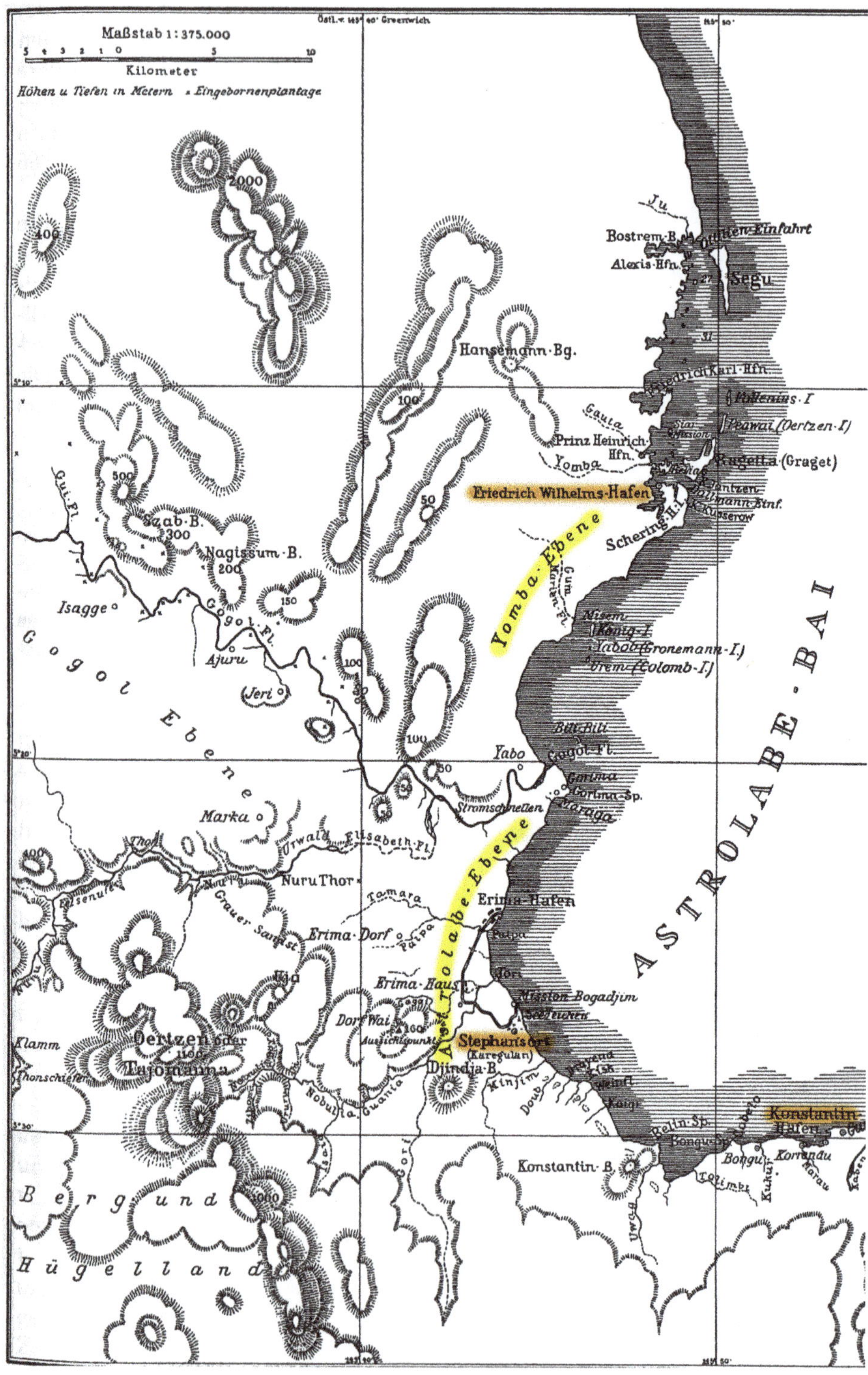

Map 10: **Tobacco land on the Astrolabe and Jomba Plains** (Krieger, 1899)

To mitigate malaria carrying mosquito infestation he started with the immediate clearing of the land around the living quarters, filling in swamps and compacting pathways with gravel. However, when von Hagen's recruit, the experienced surgeon, Dr Bernhard Hagen, arrived in Stephansort from Sumatra on 12 November 1893 he found the improved sanitary conditions had not reduced the death rate. The Javanese were better able to deal with the conditions, the Melanesians and the Chinese were not. Diagnosing nutritional deficiency, Hagen changed the diet by increasing intake of tuber roots and other vegetables. He demanded that new arrivals be put on light duties until the coolies had acclimatised. Dr Hagen promoted the construction of a central hospital on the high banks of the Gori River between Erima and Stephansort.[61]

Given the low number of coolies available and their poor state of health, C. von Hagen decided on limiting the planting of tobacco in 1894 to 200 fields in Stephansort and 100 fields in Erima. On account of the weak 1893 sales, the Jomba soil was considered inferior to the Stephansort soil, and Hagen closed the Station. Maraga, where the fields lay fallow in 1894, was also closed, as were the atap factories in Maraga and Friedrich Wilhelmshafen. The cost of the closures was considerable. For the dismantling and re-erection of buildings and barns, A-C booked losses of RM482,837 for Jomba and RM230,449 for Maraga in its 1892/93 and 1893/94 accounts. In capital improvements, the light rail system was no longer required for Maraga. However, it proved most efficient for transporting tobacco, atap and other goods between Stephansort and Erima (3.5 km) and then northeast to Erimahafen (4 km). The success of the narrow-gauge railway was such that Hagen proposed to extend the system on the Erima and Stephansort plantations to a total of 16 km. Part-approval was received from Berlin and tracks for an initial 5 km were ordered in 1894 for the following year. Also completed at Erimahafen during 1894 were a jetty for seagoing vessels, large storage sheds and a building for the new atap factory.[62]

For A-C tobacco to become better known in East Asia and to generate local revenue, Hagen set in train the requirement to 'roll cigars made of genuine New Guinea tobacco in Stephansort' for local consumption and export. The implements for manufacturing cigars were sent from Berlin and the German consul-general in Manila assisted in 1894 to hire women with expertise in cigar making. While the Filipinas' stay in Stephansort was brief—they did not cope well with the environment, they imparted the skills of rolling a fine cigar to several Javanese women before returning to Manila. Cigars made in GNG were, apparently, so popular in KWL and the Bismarck Archipelago that demand outstripped supply. Whether the scheme was an indulgence or a commercial success is not known. The cost of sales is unreported and no further reference is found on the sale of cigars to East Asia.[63]

The 1894 harvest did not generate even halfway acceptable sales results. Hansemann requested that Hagen see him in Berlin and explain the unsatisfactory situation. Leaving GNG on 7 June 1894 Hagen stayed over in the Dutch East Indies and Singapore for about one month to compare his experience in KWL with old tobacco hands from his Sumatra days. Little is known of his discussions with Hansemann except that Hagen strongly endorsed his deputy Carl Weydig who was in charge of A-C until he returned to Stephansort on 25 April 1895. Weydig, who started as a plantation assistant on Erima in October 1891 took the top job with the optimistic report that the Stephansort and Erima harvests would deliver 153,000–190,000 lb from 270 fields of the best-quality tobacco yet produced in GNG. The Stephansort tobacco had been grown from New Guinea sources and a mixture of New Guinean and Sumatran seeds produced a less favourable result for Erima. While it was a small batch of 8,000 lb from Erima that arrived in Amsterdam in April 1895, it fetched the best price of the entire 1894 crop. The second batch of 24,000 lb (10,080 lb from Erima and 13,920 lb from Stephansort) arrived in Amsterdam 10 weeks later. In a dead market, it was held back to be auctioned with the remaining consignment which was due to arrive in September. While the company advised that it intended to retain 'a not insignificant' amount of the 1894 harvest for the manufacture of cigars, it seems inconceivable that it was as much as 32,000 lb as the remaining two batches were 69,120 lb and approximately 20,000 lb rather than 121,120 lb advised earlier.

Whatever the difference, the tobacco did not attract an acceptable offer. The first lot was sold privately at below production cost. The second lot sent to Bremen was sold for an undisclosed price. A-C informed its shareholders that the poor sales were attributable to circumstances that require investigation: 'we intend to inform the esteemed shareholder of the necessary measures we need to undertake during an EGM', Hansemann commented on 30 September 1895.[64]

Shareholders at the EGM on 28 November 1895 were presented with a new calamity. Although considerable sums of money had been spent to complete the central hospital, the morbidity and mortality remained unacceptably high. While only one European had died during 1894 (the assistant planter Richter), the Melanesian workers again fell to influenza in great numbers during the rainy season of October to December. Smallpox, rampant earlier in the year, was reasonably contained, but fear of infection slowed down the hiring of new recruits from the archipelago and the Huon Gulf area. The plight of the Chinese remained unchanged; weakened by opium consumption and diet deficiencies, their illnesses continued to be dysentery, beri-beri or malaria fever—often all three ailments at the same time. According to Dr Hagen 45% of all diseases were infectious, with 67% leading to death. The most resilient workers were the Javanese who rarely took ill; if they did, they recovered quickly.[65]

A dearth of able workers was not the reason for poor crops. A-C advised in early 1895 that the tobacco in Stephansort and Erima stood exceptionally well and that a harvest of 340,000 lb, later revised to 200,000 lb, was expected. A severe drought from June to September put an end to this forecast. Stephansort and Erima received hardly any rain during the important months July and August. Of the 240 fields Weydig prepared in 1895 for 2,032,400 plants one-third fell to the drought. The tobacco cut from the remaining 1,361,790 stalks was damaged by flea beetle, June larvae and cutworm that was introduced to Stephansort by Manila cigar makers the previous year. What started off as a promising crop, ended up with only 112,000 lb shipped to Bremen. A-C had to inform its shareholders in the annual accounts that adverse climate in 1895 combined with low prices and the loss-making atap factory

in Friedrich Wilhelmshafen realised a loss of RM591,837.

In December 1895 Hagen prepared 400 fields to atone for the harvest failure. By February 4,240,000 seedlings had germinated in 2,120 beds. But again by the time planting out was completed in May 1896 drought had returned. Yet under the circumstances the harvest of 106,666 lb was higher than expected. Also higher was the prices fetched at the auctions in Bremen. The tobacco offered was delicate, of an even, light-brown colour. The leaves had good burning qualities but not of wrapper or binder-leaf quality. 606 bales were auctioned in Bremen in March, May, July and September of 1897 with satisfactory results.[66]

Merging A-C and NGC

The poor financial position of A-C forced the takeover of its plantations by NGC on 1 October 1895. Hagen was not blamed for the misfortunes of the company and was promoted to manage the combined enterprises while the employment of Administrator Rüdiger was terminated while on sick leave in Java in August 1896.

Map 11: **Layout of tobacco fields at Stephansort Station** (*NKWL*, 1892)

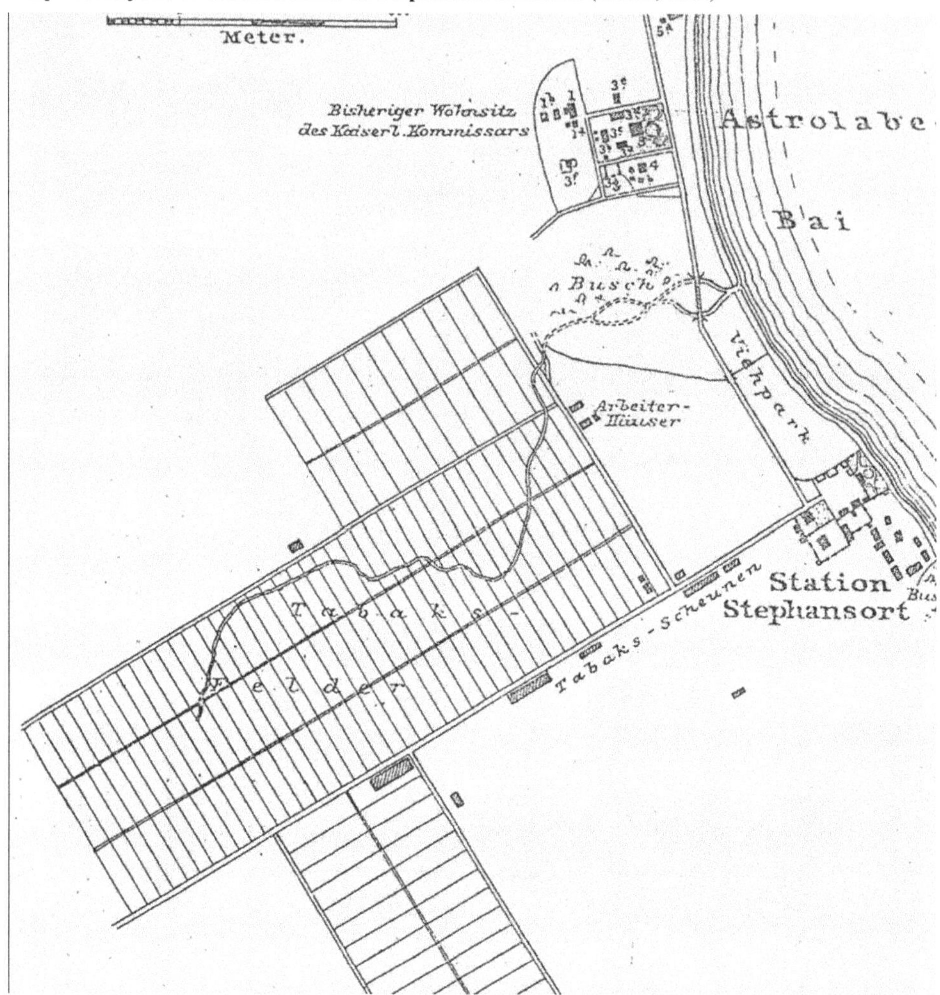

1) Prison, 1a) police residence, 1b) Chinese and Javanese prison, 2) Manager's residence, 2a) annex, 2b) bathhouse, 2c) fowl pen, 2d) kitchen, e) servants' quarters, 2f) pig pen, 2g) vegetable garden, 3) staff quarter, 3a) bathhouse, 3b) visitors' accommodation, 4) kitchen

Prior to the takeover being completed on 1 November 1896, Hagen's employment changed once again. On 9 October 1896 he was appointed *Generaldirektor* (Managing Director) responsible for all NGC and A-C operations in GNG. Saddled with new company regulations, 67 paragraphs in all, Hagen was commissioned by NGC's board to merge and restructure the management of the two organisations. As the legal representative of the two companies in GNG, Hagen was to remain in Stephansort, with the plantation managers s of Herbertshöhe, Friedrich Wilhelmshafen and Stephansort reporting to him. The restructure was to be completed by 1 April 1897, when the new regulations came into force. Hagen then transferred the Central Station from Friedrich Wilhelmshafen back to Stephansort. Since the closure of the Jomba plantation in 1894, Friedrich Wilhelmshafen served principally as the administrative centre of GNG. Now that government and company operations were again conducted by one person, Hagen considered it inefficient and expensive to maintain two centres. With the exception of three staff, one doctor, and approximately 100 locals for harbour services and police work, all personnel were either released or transferred to Stephansort. Activities maintained in Friedrich Wilhelmshafen were the labour depôt, sawmill and maintenance workshops, and the bunkering facilities for the mail steamers and the navy. The small hospital for Europeans moved from Beliao Island to the former residence of Administrator Schmiele on the Schering Peninsula. Buildings were demolished and moved to nearby Yap Peninsula with livestock.[67]

After suffering two consecutive droughts, Hagen wanted to avoid the dry months of June and July by starting the 1896 tobacco planting season in February and completing a maximum of 150 fields by May. 'This', he claimed, 'would ensure with much greater certainty that 100,000 to 150,000 lb can be grown and harvested with fewer workers and staff'. Rather than planting two seasons of tobacco on different fields, Hagen also decided to replant the same fields twice before turning the land over to different crops. Savings were to be achieved by replacing Chinese and Javanese coolies with Melanesian workers who were to be supervised by Sumatran *tandils* and Javanese *mandurs*. Coupled with the availability of labour for much of the year the fallow tobacco fields were exploited with the planting of coffee, cacao, nutmeg, ramie, gutta-percha and caoutchouc. In December Hagen planted 80,000 *coffea arabica* seedlings on 60 ha and, to increase cash flow, renewed planting of 150 ha Sea Island cotton took place in January 1897. As a long-term investment the planting of coconut palms was intensified, with 27,300 trees planted by 1896.[68]

Hansemann failed to realise that the quantity and desirability of the Dutch East Indies tobacco had taken many years to attain and that an untold number of Chinese coolies had paid for it with their lives. Negative reports continued to reach Berlin. Rather than an expected 100,000 lb in fermented tobacco, only 79,300 lb were shipped to Bremen in 1898. The optimism displayed with the growing of coffee at Stephansort was also much more guarded now. Many trees did not develop, though the experiment was continued for a time. These latest setbacks earned Hagen his dismissal less than a year into his new appointment. Accused by Hansemann of worker mistreatment—an issue raised with Weydig but never with Hagen before— and 'irreconcilable differences of opinion on the economic management of the enterprise', Hagen was due to leave NGC on 30 September 1897. Termination of another sort, however, occurred: He was shot dead near Jomba on 13 August 1897 while participating in a punitive expedition to capture two escaped former Buka policemen. The pair was held responsible for the murder of the explorer Ehlers.[69]

Until Judge Hugo Skonpik (Stephansort) was confirmed as the new Administrator on 11 September 1897 Albert Hahl, the 28-year-old Imperial Judge in Herbertshöhe, was acting in this position. The duties of the General Manager were entrusted in Oscar Baumüller, who previously worked under Richard Parkinson at Herbertshöhe.[70]

Friedrich Wilhelmshafen would again become the main port in KWL. An extension to 60 metres of the collapsed pier was carried out, the houses for staff, local workers, Malays and Chinese coolies, were refurbished. Coconut palms were planted along the foreshore and on the island of Beliao. Baumüller, who had transferred from Stephansort, restarted the tobacco plantation Jomba on account of the 'high quality' tobacco grown there previously. The construction of a narrow-gauge railway connecting the plantation with FWH was- in his view - both necessary and financially justifiable. He also reversed Hagen's policy of replacing Chinese coolies with Melanesian workers. But a shortage of both, coolies and Melanesians, put his plan for tobacco at Jomba on hold until 1901. In the meantime Baumüller planted the corridor between Friedrich Wilhelmshafen and Jomba with coconut palms. It was a task continued by Joseph Loag who became the new manager for Friedrich Wilhelmshafen after Baumüller's death from blackwater fever on 5 May 1898.[71]

Loag, the author of NGC's 1902 business plan, became Friedrich Wilhelmshafen's most successful manager. With a staff of six Europeans and 450 workers he completed the relocation of NGC's administrative centre from Stephansort in 1900. The port facilities were extended to take the largest mail steamers of NDL and the ships of the German Navy. Loag oversaw the widening and deepening of the Gauta River which was now navigable for steam barges to Jomba. A large warehouse was built and a retail outlet for merchandise established. By 1900 Friedrich Wilhelmshafen was again the largest and most important trading station in KWL. The main plantation and station and nearby islands were populated with 15,500 coconut palms and 5,000 Kapok trees. Cacao (4,714) and gutta-percha trees (2,293) were added to the existing 2,624 palms that had been planted on Jomba during the early 1890s.

When the 1899 and 1900 tobacco sales fetched a meagre RM45,878 the NGC tobacco chapter came to an end. Erima, elevated by Hagen in 1893 to the premier tobacco-growing area at the expense of Jomba and Maraga, no longer grew tobacco; this also applied to the centre of GNG tobacco, Stephansort. Only Jomba remained productive. Loag was not about to waste the efforts expended by Baumüller on re-establishing the plantation. Fermentation sheds, the manager's residence and workers' accommodation were in good state of repair, 140 fields were prepared. Loag planned for additional coolies from Hong Kong to add to the few Chinese transferred from Stephansort. This would enable him to increase the number of fields to 300. But the overseas arrivals did not eventuate and Jomba's much-heralded rebirth all but ended with the planting of only 90 fields, yielding approximately 58,000 lb of tobacco.

Directors praised the 'beautiful tobacco' that NGC grew on the Jomba Plains for some time after the decision had been made that the company would discontinue with tobacco in GNG. Only planting for domestic trading and personal use was continued on a small scale. After Hansemann retired from executive duties in March 1900 shareholders were informed that the trend in cigar smoking had moved to light-grey wrapper leaf of exquisitely fine texture. This, the board advised, required each tobacco leaf to be picked carefully, dried, fermented and graded by specialised coolies. Even in the unlikely event that tobacco prices would increase substantially in the future, according to the new management of NGC, there was no likelihood that a reliable source of coolies could be secured. The 1901 Jomba harvest drew the curtain on tobacco for NGC. A batch of 45,000 lb went to the bottom of Yap harbour when the *München* struck a reef in on 3 February 1901. The final consignment of 134,000 lb left Friedrich Wilhelmshafen on 25 January 1902: this included 50,000 lb from the previous year. It was again sold at well below production cost, and the board advised shareholders it felt relieved to have closed its tobacco episode.[72]

Hansemann's decision to engage in a plantation industry in 1889 to the exclusion of trading in copra put all NGC's financial eggs in one basket. Cotton was expected to generate cash flow and early profits; cacao, coffee and coconut palms were long-term prospects. It was tobacco, however, that Hansemann determined would make the company: 14 years later it had all but broken the company. Tobacco had destroyed RM2,400,000 of A-C shareholder equity, and with it most of NGC's managerial and labour resources. The more prevalent malaria on the coast and the spread of influenza and smallpox from Finschhafen to Stephansort killed more Europeans, Chinese, Javanese, Melanesians and local people during the height of tobacco activities from 1892 to 1896 than during the remaining 18 years of German administration in GNG.[73]

It cost NGC dearly, both morally and financially. The company blamed the feeble condition in which coolies arrived on Astrolabe Bay for the downfall of its tobacco venture. It produced figures to prove that Chinese coolies were weaker than their Javanese counterparts. According to the 1900 Stephansort numbers 3,737 sick days were taken by 78 Chinese during that year compared to only 1,124 sick days taken by 69 Javanese for the same period. The company first believed that the high death rate in the Chinese was a result of opium addiction and dysentery. When Robert Koch visited Stephansort in 1899 he drew attention to the prevalence of *anchylostoma duodenale* (hookworm) in the Chinese, resulting in anaemia due to iron deficiency. 'Extreme weakness', called beri-beri by the Sinhalese, was caused by an unbalanced diet of polished rice. NGC's doctors understood that beri-beri was an illness, not an excuse for not wanting to work. However, in the 1890s they had no cure. The planters did not share the doctors' opinion: they regarded the Chinese as inherently lazy.

After 1897 the majority of the workforce was Melanesians. A more selective employment policy, a balanced diet and better sanitary and hospital facilities improved health generally after 1900. The fundamental ingredient for successful tobacco agriculture was present by then. The soil of the Astrolabe and Jomba Plains was as good as that found in Deli. Early recognition that the Jabim and Melanesian people could be taught to become capable tobacco workers would have increased labour availability and lowered operational costs substantially. A better working relationship between Hansemann and, for instance, Puttkamer, Pfaff, Hanneken and Hagen would have exerted less pressure on staff in an already stressful situation.

Tobacco could have been grown commercially in KWL with a different mindset. A lower intake of coolies initially and a gradual start-up would have been sensible. A smaller workforce would have reduced the risk of infectious diseases and greater numbers of smaller plantations would have mitigated plant infestations. Growing tobacco in GNG required patient capital. An improved international tobacco market would have helped. The tobacco industry in GNG needed time to mature in the 1890s like the Dutch industry required in Sumatra in the 1850s. But time was not on the side of Adolph von Hansemann.

Notes

1   *DKZ* (1887) Nr. 4, p. 693; *NKWL* (1887) Heft ii, pp. 60–3 & 76–7, Heft iii, pp. 147–9, (1888) Heft ii, p. 71; see R. Parkinson, *Dreißig Jahre in der Südsee*, pp. 26–7

2   Jb (1888) p. 2; Sack & Clark, (1887–88) p. 22. E. Tappenbeck, *Deutsch Neu Guinea*, p. 18

3   'Die Kaiser Wilhelmsland-Plantagen-Gesellschaft' (RKA 1001:2425, pp. 5–7). Hansemann to Krauel, 26 Jun. 1890. Sack & Clark [1889–90] p. 50; Jb [1890] p. 7)

4   Share Register 1892 (RKA 1001:2425, pp. 45–52). KWLPG statute, §§9 & 12 (R1001:2425, p. 3)

5   Jb (1890) p. 7; Sack & Clark (1889–90) p. 50; *NKWL* (1890) Heft i, p. 18, Heft ii, pp. 76–7

6   Hansemann file note, 17 May 1890 (RKA 1001:2425, p. 3)

7   Jb (1894/95) p. 8; Sack & Clark (1894–95) p. 113

8   *NKWL* (1890) Heft i, p. 77

9   *NKWL* (1891) Heft i, p. 22; Rose memo 15 Dec. 1890 (RKA 1001:2425, pp. 37–40)

10 Rose to AA-KA, 27 Jan. 1891 (RKA 1001:2425, pp. 30–2). *NKWL* (1891) Heft i, p. 22; Adult males were punished with a wooden stick (25 strokes maximum), minors with the cane. The Dutch–German agreement of 11 Jul. 1900 permitted coolies from the Dutch East Indies to be caned . After 28 Oct. 1908 corporal punishment was restricted to the use of a rope (*Die Deutsche Kolonialgesetzgebung*, vol. vi, no. 157, 1909)

11 Hansemann to Bismarck, 22 Nov. 1888 (RKA 1001:2939, p. 5–10). *NKWL* (1889) Heft ii, pp. 31–2; (1891) pp. 3, 5 & 63–4, (1893) p. 15; Jb (1890/91) pp. 2–5; Sack & Clark (1890-91) pp. 56–8

12 *NKWL* (1889) Heft ii, p. 32; Jb (1890) p. 2; Sack & Clark (1889–90) p. 46. *TQ* (1890) 15 Feb., p. 336

13 *NKWL* (1890) Heft i, pp. 7 & 9. P. Sack, *Phantom History:* pp. 321–2

14 Rose to Caprivi, 21 Oct. 1890 (RKA 1001:2301, pp. 79–82); Rose to Woermann and to Kindt, 27 Jan. 1890 27 Jan. 1890; KWLPG to AA-KA, 30 April 1891; AA-KA to Woermann, 1 Apr. 1891 (RKA 1001:2425, pp 28–41); Rose to Caprivi, 27 Feb. 1891 (RKA 1001:2980); (RKA 1001:2409)

15 Hansemann to AA-KA, 4 Jan. 1891 (RKA 1001:2301, p. 57); AA-KA to Rose, 13 Jan. 1891 (RKA 1001:2939, pp. 86–7); NGC to AA-KA, 10 Feb. 1891 (RKA 1001:2409, pp. 125–9)

16 *NKWL* (1891) Heft i, p. 22

17 Kindt to Caprivi, 2 Sep. 1891 (RKA 1001:2410)

18 *Hamburgischer Correspondent*, 25 Dec. 1895 (R1001:2425, pp. 62–3). NGC to AA-KA, 5 Jan. 1895 (RKA1001:2939, p. 9). *NKWL* (1891) Heft i, p. 22

19 M. Krieger, ed., *Neu-Guinea*, pp. 125–6. *NAZ* (1891), 11 Nov.

20 Rose to AA-KA, 27 Jun. and 1 Sep. 1891 (RKA 1001:2980)

21 AA-KA to NGC, 9 Nov. 1891; NGC to AA-KA 22 Dec. 1891 (RKA 1001:2980)

22 F.M. Sieben, 'Über die Aussichten von Tropischen Kulturen in Ost-Afrika und Neu Guinea'

23 *NKWL* (1886) Heft ii, p. 63

24 *Bundesrath* approval, 22 Dec. 1891, *NKWL* (1891) pp. 18-21, (1892) p. 30–1

25 H. Münch, *Hansemann*, pp. 238–9

26 *NKWL* (1886) Heft iv, p. 113; (1887) Heft i, p. 4, iii, p. 130; Jb (1887) p. 22; Sack & Clark (1887) p. 21

27 E. Dallmann (Museum Schloß Schönebeck) P.M. Pawlik, *Von Sibirien nach Neu Guinea*, p. 133

28 *NKWL* (1888) Heft ii, p. 79; Heft iv, p. 179; (1889) Heft ii, p. 33, (1890) Heft i, p. 9

29 *NKWL* (1887) Heft ii, p. 32, Heft iv, pp. 181–2; Heft v, pp. 163 & 192–4. Jb (1887) p. 16; Sack & Clark (1886–87) p. 16. O. Schellong, *Alte Documente*, p. 114. P.G. Sack, *Phantom of History,* pp. 533ff.

30 *NKWL* (1888) Heft i, p. 19, Heft iii, p. 150, Heft iv, p. 179; (1889) Heft ii, p. 33; Jb A-C (1892) p. 7

31 Jb (1889) p. 6; Sack & Clark (1888–89) p. 38. See P.G. Sack, *Eduard Hernsheim*, p. 201

32 *NKWL* (1889) Heft ii, p. 35–6, (1890) Heft i, p. 14; Jb (1889) p. 3, (1890) p. 4; Sack & Clark (1888–89) p. 35, (1889–90) p. 48

33 *NKWL* (1890) Heft ii, pp. 73& 85, (1891) Heft i pp. 12–13 & 19, (1892) Heft i, pp. 21, 27–37, (1893) Heft ii, pp. 18–21; Jb (1890) pp. 5 & 8; Sack & Clark (1889–90) p. 48 (Bales ranged from 30 to 40 kg)

34   *TQ* 25 Oct. 1890, p. 834; *The Morning Bulletin*, Rockhampton (1890) 27 Oct. p. 4

35   *NKWL* (1889) Heft i, p. 24, Heft ii, p. 35; Jb (1888) p. 4, (1889) p. 4; Sack & Clark (1887–88) p. 24, (1888-89) p. 36

36   *NKWL* (1890) Heft i, p. 13, Heft ii, pp. 71–2; Jb (1889) pp. 3–5; Sack & Clark (1888–89) p. 48

37   *NKWL* (1891) Heft i, pp. 9–10; Jb (1890/91) p. 10; Sack & Clark (1890–91) p. 63

38   *NKWL* (1890) Heft ii, pp. 72–3

39   *NKWL* (1891) Heft i, p. 12; Jb (1889) p. 3-4; Jb (1891/92) p. 12; Sack & Clark (1890–91) p. 66

40   *NKWL* (1892) Heft i, pp. 28 & 36, Jb (1890/91) p. 10

41   *NKWL* (1890) Heft ii, pp. 77–81, (1892) p. 30; Sack & Clark, (1890–91) pp. 63–4. Jb (1890)] pp. 22-7, (1890/91) pp. 9 & 22-7, (1891/92) pp. 9, 13, 28-33). Sieben, p. 40

42   Jb A-C (1894/95) p. 4

43   *NKWL* (1891) Heft i, p. 20; (1892) p. 32

44   *NKWL* (1890) Heft ii, pp. 77–81, (1891), pp. 18-22. Jb (1890-91) pp. 1–2, 7-8, 10 & 42; Sack & Clark, (1890–91) pp. 56, 61–2 & 64

45   *NKWL* (1889) Heft ii, p.45; (1890) Heft i, pp. 21 & 26; (1891) Heft i, p, 14 & (1892) Heft i, p. 21; Jb (1890/91) p.5; Sack & Clark, (1890–91) p. 60. Blum, pp. 174–76; Tappenbeck, pp. 31–2

46   Deli wrapper leaf, selling at ƒ1.40/lb crashed to ƒ0.73 after the McKinley tariff Bill (Sieben, p. 40)

47   Blum, p. 175; R. Cohen, ed., *The Cambridge Survey of World Migration*, pp. 21–2

48   *NKWL* (1891) Heft i, p. 21, (1892) Heft i, p. 31

49   'Verzeichnis der Zeichner der Astrolabe Compagnie', Berlin 27 Oct. 1891' (Jb A-C [9 Dec. 1892] p. 1; (RKA 1001:2427, pp. 5-6 & 64-6).

50   *NKWL* (1991) pp. 8 & 19, (1892) p. 31; 48; Jb A-C (1892) p. 7 (RKA 1001:2427, p. 1)

51   *NKWL* (1991) Heft i, p. 21; (1892) p. 20)

52   *NKWL* (1892) Heft i, p. 31

53   AGM Dec.1892, pp. 4, 8-9, 18 & 33 (RKA 1001:2427)

54   *NKWL* (1893) pp. 18–21

55   Jb (1892/93) pp. 10–11; Jb A-C (1892) pp. 6-8; Sack & Clark (1891–92) p. 77 and (1892–93) p. 77.

56   *NKWL* (1891) pp. 20–1, (1892), Heft i, pp. 35–6, (1893) Heft i, p. 33

57   Jb (1892/93) p. 10; Jb A-C (1893) pp. 5–6

58   Jb A-C (1893) pp. 2– 6

59   *NKWL* (1893) p. 35; Jb A-C (1893) p. 3, (1893/94) pp. 9–10; McKillop, R.F. 'Tramways and Oxen: The New Guinea Kompagnie Tramways of Astrolabe Bay', in *Light Railways*, 81 (1983)

60   Jb A-C (1893) pp. 4 & 7–8, (1893/94), pp. 3–4 & 12; Jb (1893/94) p. 12

61   *NKWL* (1893) pp. 33–5 & 37–8; Jb A-C (1892/93) pp. 7, 9–10

62   Jb (1893/94) pp. 11–12; Sack & Clark (1893–94) pp. 95–6

63   *NKWL* (1893) pp. 35–6; Jb (1883/94) p. 13; Sack & Clark (1893–94) p. 96; Jb A-C (1892/93) p. 18, (1893/94) pp. 3, 11 & 17, (1894/95) p. 7

64   *NKWL* (1894) p. 30, (1895) pp. 12 & 31; A-C report (1893) p. 5; Jb A-C (1893/94) pp. 2–4 & 11, (1894/95) pp. 3–4; Jb NGC (1893/94) p. 13; Sack & Clark (1893–94) p. 96

65   *Die Nation*, 30 Nov. 1895; *NKWL* (1895) pp. 32–3; Jb A-C (1893/94) pp. 5–6

66   Jb A-C (1894/95) pp. 9 & 11–13; *NKWL* (1896) pp. 11, 58 & 67; (1897) pp. 17–18

67   *NKWL* (1895) p. 16; (1896) pp. 4–6, 9–10; Jb (1895/96) pp. 3–4; Sack & Clark (1895–96) p. 118 (RKA 1001:2422, 17ff)

68   *NKWL*, (1897), pp. 18–20; Jb A-C (1894/95) p. 10; Jb (1895/96) pp. 4–6, (1896/97) p. 6; Sack & Clark (1895–96) p. 118-21, (1896–97) pp. 130–1. Sieben, pp. 1 & 38

69   *BC* (1897) 25 Sep., p. 5

70   *NKWL*, (1897) pp. 13–18; Jb (1896/97) p. 4; Sack & Clark (1896–97) p. 129

71   *NKWL*, (1898), pp. 10–13; Jb (189/98) pp. 3–4 and 6; Sack & Clark (1897–98) 140–3

72   Jb (1899/00) pp. 15 & 18; (1900/01) pp. 26 & 39; (1901/02) p. 7

73   NGC to AA-KA, 29 May 1896 (RKA 1001:2985, p. 109); Hahl to AA-KA, 4 Sep. 1904, (RKA1001:2309)

Tapping of wild rubber (Ficus microcarpa and ficus pumila) on New Ireland, ca. 1902 (Bismarck-Archipel-Gesellschaft, 1909) **Herringbone-tapping, and on a felled India rubber tree,** ca. 1908 (Goethe University Frankfurt a.M. Nos. 025-0289-28F & 043-4006-13)

Typical atap thatched European house at Stephansort (F. Hutter, *Das überseeische Deutschland*, p. 553), **Stephansort tobacco plantation,** ca. 1895 (Hutter p. 557), HJ Hiery, plate 19, **tobacco shed under construction** (*NKWL*, 1894)

The Mapping of Manus Island (Admiralty Group) by S.M.S. *Möwe* **surveyor and assistant,** ca. 1903
(courtesy K. Baumann)

TRIALS AND TRAVAILS OF A PLANTATION INDUSTRY

When the opportunity arose to engage Richard Parkinson, NGC's Chairman Adolph von Hansemann thought of his Administrator's advice: NGC could be as successful as Ralum on the Gazelle Peninsula was for Queen Emma of Forsayth & Co. if it decided on establishing plantations on the Gazelle Peninsula in New Britain.[1]

With Administrator von Schleinitz' retirement from NGC in March 1888 and the short-lived appearance of his successor, Reinhold Kraetke, NGC's third Administrator in as many years, Hans Arnold, presided over the foundation of a new administration centre. Situated next to the coastal village Kokopo, halfway between Cape Ralum and Cape Gazelle, Arnold tasked Parkinson on 3 January 1890 to commence with its relocation. Named 'Herbertshöhe' after Bismarck's oldest son Herbert, the new township was to become the seat of the Imperial Chancellor and the Administrator of NGC for the Eastern District (Bismarck Archipelago & Solomon Islands).

Parkinson found the relocation of NGC's buildings from Kerawara in The Duke of York Group to Herbertshöhe, as difficult as Schleinitz experienced in establishing Finschhafen, Stephansort and Hatzfeldthafen. The coastal Tolai on the Gazelle Peninsula could be as aggressive as the tribes were in KWL. Engaged in early commercial transactions with European traders, the Tolai harvested coconuts for the foreigners who visited their shores in exchange for a few sticks of tobacco or glass beads well before German annexation. Soon, after they learnt to make copra, they traded their produce for Snider rifles and cartridges, explosives and steel axes. When the Europeans started to acquire their land and set up their plantations the Tolai robbed, mugged and murdered the foreign intruders. Mostly the Tolai were resisting coconut plantations since market gardening and coconut collection provided them with an agreeable way of life. They were reluctant to work for the Europeans for wages. This made the establishment of a new European settlement and plantations an arduous task. Further, the sudden death of Arnold after only a few weeks in the Administrator's job delivered Parkinson the worse possible start with NGC.[2]

Forsayth at Ralum and now NGC at Herbertshöhe were systematically expanding their land holdings to the west and east. When Parkinson endeavoured to recruit labour locally he could only convince 139 Tolai to work for him. He had to travel to New Ireland (Neu Mecklenburg) where he obtained 1044 men in one swoop.[3]

Rather than recruiting workers and preparing land for cotton and coconuts,

Disastrous Ventures

Parkinson became involved in fighting the Tolai who rebelled against the road construction linking Kokopo with Ralum. Following the northern coast on Blanche Bay, the road cut through Tolai fishing grounds and sacred places on the peninsula. The destruction of houses during the work led to the death by clubbing in April 1890 of a Forsayth overseer, the Filipino John Moses. Swift European reprisals aggravated an already difficult situation. In the previous month a coalition of Tolai from the Vunamami, Keravi, Bitarebarebe and Tingenavudu districts attacked Ralum, which ended in an indiscriminate response from NGC's and Queen Emma's planters. Under Imperial Judge George Schmiele's direction and Parkinson's leadership, five Europeans and more

The founding of Herbertshöhe, ca. 1888 (photo by E. Dallmann, Museum Schloß Schönebeck).

than 80 indentured workers drove the Tolai inland, with the outcome of 80 Tolai killed and some 60 villages destroyed.[4] A temporary stay in fighting enabled Parkinson to start farming at Herbertshöhe. It was not to last. Dissatisfied with life in general and having to deal with an interfering Berlin head office and with a pompous Imperial Judge, Parkinson walked away from his contract with NGC on 1 October 1891. A disconsolate man, all he wanted to do was to spend time with his wife and children on their small plantation Maulapao at Ralum. Fighting the Tolai since his arrival from Samoa, he now wanted to improve relations with the local people. He also wanted collect artefacts and study the archipelago's flora and fauna in more detail. Rather than filing reports to a chairman who had questionable knowledge of tropical agriculture, Parkinson wanted to write a book on his New Guinea experience.[5]

When Judge Schmiele—promoted by Bismarck to the position of Administrator (*Landeshauptmann*)—visited Herbertshöhe in November 1892, he found the labour depôt completed and 155 ha planted with cotton and some 8,500-palm seedlings planted. The gin and the cotton press buildings were operational and the quarters for the workers completed. The first two crops Parkinson had planted yielded 9,482 kg and 3,328 kg of scoured lint, which sold in Bremen for about RM1.28/kg. Parkinson had fenced grazing land for horses and cattle and gardens were yielding batata, yams and corn for the workers at Herbertshöhe and Friedrich Wilhelmshafen.

August Rocholl assumed provisional responsibilities for Herbertshöhe after Parkinson's sudden departure. A land surveyor by profession and an enthusiastic explorer, Rocholl discovered guano on the Purdy Islands in 1887 but proved ineffective in administration and plantation work. Earlier quarrels with Schmiele led to Rocholl's temporary retirement from NGC in 1889. Differences with Schmiele over etiquette resurfaced when Rocholl assumed responsibility for Herbertshöhe. This led to the severance of his employment for the second time in February 1893, and to the appointment of the retired Prussian Officer-cum-sugarcane planter Paul Kolbe to manage Herbertshöhe.[6]

Kolbe, who had worked in the Hawaiian sugar cane fields for 3 years, and who learnt from the Australian farmer James Smith how to plant cotton in Konstantinhafen, arrived in Herbertshöhe on 1 February 1893. Again, retaliatory missions rather than setting up plantations took much of Kolbe's time. For instance, on 6 and 18 July 1893 Tolai rampaged in Ralum, killing managers Robert Anderson and Georg Möller, and went on to destroy cotton fields around Herbertshöhe.[7] A few months later, local tribes made an audacious attempt to sack Herbertshöhe and the nearby Kinigunan Station of Octave Mouton.

An obviously frustrated Administrator decided on teaching the Tolai a lesson they would not forget. Calling up the light cruiser SMS *Sperber* in December 1893, sixty soldiers of His Majesty's Ship advanced several kilometers inland. Preventing the troublesome tribes from escaping, Schmiele, Parkinson and Queen Emma's men covered the northern flank, with Kolbe, including the Imperial Judge in Herbertshöhe, Eugen Brandeis and his secretary, Arno Senfft, and Octave Mouton set to drive the Tolai to the coast where they would be in the range of the German warship's heavy guns. It was Kolbe, however, who was bombarded: the eager 'soldiers' lost their way and were greeted by 'friendly fire' from the marines when appearing on the beach. Kolbe reached an outcome nonetheless. The deafening noise of exploding artillery frightened the warriors into submission.[8]

The many punitive expeditions gave Kolbe little time for his main job. Yet, according to NGC's periodical *Nachrichten* (NKWL), the 1893 cotton harvests yielded approximately 126,500 pounds (lbs), with the scoured product weighing in at 26,000 lbs, 114% more than the previous year's consignment to Liverpool. The company considered the mean price of sixteen pence per pound (d/lb) satisfactory, but hastened to add that the 19,085 lbs of scoured cotton from the 1894 harvest was of higher quality and was likely to sell in Liverpool at considerably higher prices.[9]

Despite NGC's advertising of its quality cotton from the Gazelle Peninsula, the exported quantities were too small to make Herbertshöhe profitable. As the exclusive provider of indigenous labour in GNG, this part of the business generated RM245,110 during 1890 to 1894, while farm and sundry income for the same period contributed a paltry RM46,877 to the bottom line of NGC's balance sheet.[10]

A few kilometres west of Herbertshöhe, Forsayth & Co produced cotton in much bigger quantities on Ralum, and suffering harvest failures on a much larger scale. Their financial pain was, however, short-lived, since Queen Emma decided in 1892 on ploughing up the cotton fields to concentrate on trade-copra as the major source of income for Forsayth. The Tolai gradually succumbed to European goods and this was their motivation to accept peace (for the time being) with Ralum. It provided the opportunity for Forsayth to enter into copra supply agreements with the locals and throughout the archipelago. The company became profitable by exporting 2,000 t of trade-copra in 1893. NGC on the other hand was unable to secure reliable sources of copra from the islanders and, while tentatively starting with plantation copra, could not expect any revenue from this resource for eight to nine years.

Schmiele continued to bully and nag. Grumbling over Kolbe's lack of leadership during punitive mission, matters came to a head when Schmiele vented his spleen on Kolbe by trying to foil his marriage to Queen Emma, 'an older woman of mixed blood' he barked at the NGC manager. When an enraged Kolbe horsewhipped the Imperial Judge across the face, his departure from NGC was assured.[11]

Kolbe's departure brought NGC's fourth manager to Herbertshöhe in as many years. The construction engineer from German East Africa, Wasa Mende, assumed interim responsibilities for the plantations until a permanent replacement arrived in May 1894. The appointment of the new manager, former A-C tobacco grower Woldemar von Hanneken, was short-lived too: he suffered from high fever soon after his arrival and was unable to fulfil his job,[12] forcing Mende to resume responsibility for the plantations. Given his engineering skill, he turned his attention to constructing a narrow-gauge railway from the wharf to the warehouse. While he built roads to the future plantation sites and dug wells, which, according to him, provided an inexhaustible supply of cool water for the growing township, Hansemann was searching for an experienced plantation manager.[13]

Dr Albert Hahl, ca. 1902

Albert Hahl: Imperial Chancellor at Herbertshöhe

NGC's dual role of governing the protectorate in accordance with the requirements of the Imperial Charter while progressing their trading and plantation businesses proved particularly onerous in the Bismarck Archipelago. Competing with established traders and planters and collecting taxes from them while also fighting the Tolai, was impossible. After protracted negotiations, Hansemann and the Colonial Department of the Foreign Office in Berlin (AA-KA) reached in principle agreement for the *Reich* to assume administrative responsibilities in the Eastern District from 8 April 1895. Police work, the collection of fines, fees, taxes and customs duty came under the responsibility of the newly appointed Imperial Judge, E. Mellien. NGC wanted to concentrate on making its plantation enterprises profitable, but, the arrangement with the government was short-lived yet again: the *Reichstag* did not accede to the agreement the Chancellor entered into with Hansemann. Mellien quit his post in Herbertshöhe seven months into a 3-year contract, and W. Mende continued to perform administrative and judicial duties until Albert Hahl relieved him in 1896.[14]

Albert Hahl was born on 10 September 1868 in Gern, the sixth of eight surviving siblings. With a population of about 2000, Gern was a typical rural village in Lower Bavaria, with the only noteworthy industry a small brewery run by Albert's father, Jacob Hahl, in conjunction with the family farm. Also typical for the time and the era was Albert's frugal upbringing. Notwithstanding the Protestant Hahls lived in Catholic Bavaria, their honesty, reliability and hard work made them respected members of their community. This upbringing saw Albert successfully complete high school in Freising (120km west of Gern) in 1887, followed with a law and economics degree at the University of Würzburg, to which, in 1893, he added a doctorate in law.

Hahl chose an economic history subject (*The History of Economic Ideas in England at the end of the Middle Ages)* for his dissertation. While this was unusual for a law graduate at the time, Hahl's attention to British economic history disclosed an Anglophilic interest in overseas economic development. Hahl became a fully qualified lawyer when he passed his third state examination in 1894, and, after working for a short time in the Bavarian civil service, he began a jurisdictional career in the newly created Colonial Department of the Foreign Office in Berlin.

A stocky man, with a Kaiser Wilhelm II moustache dominating a squarish face, the twenty-seven-year-young lawyer arrived in Herbertshöhe as imperial official of the Protectorate of the Neu Guinea Compagnie on 14 January 1896. While Hahl had desired posting to German East Africa, he gratefully accepted the foreign office's decision to give him greater responsibilities in Germany's less important colony.

Short on experience—having completed just a six-month induction at the Foreign Office—Hahl's first assignment in New Guinea was to assume responsibility for the 'Eastern Jurisdictional and Administrative District'. In directing government business for the region, Hahl was accountable to Acting Administrator Captain Hugo Rüdiger in Friedrich Wilhelmshafen (FWH). Hubert Geisler, NGC manager at Herbertshöhe, to Hansemann. In practice, Hahl and Geisler were their own masters. Instructions from FWH took as long as orders from Berlin, and during Hahl's 3-year tenure four Administrators—including Hahl for a brief period—were in charge of GNG.[15]

Hahl's next appointment—after a briefing in Berlin—was as the Deputy Governor of GNG with a seat in Ponape in the Caroline Islands. This appointment took effect one month after Germany purchased the Pacific Ocean territory from Spain in June 1899. On 10 July 1901 he returned to Herbertshöhe to stand in for Imperial Governor Rudolf von Bennigsen who had returned to Germany because of ill health. Less than twelve months into this provisional assignment, Hahl came also down with a life-threatening blackwater fever and returned home to recuperate.

His short-term replacement, Imperial Judge Wilhelm Knake, was not of the quality the Colonial Department in Berlin had in mind for GNG, so, on 20 November 1902, Chancellor Bernd von Bülow appointed Albert Hahl as Governor of German New Guinea. Before returning to the South Sea Hahl was received by Wilhelm II. During the audience, the Kaiser made it very clear that he expected his new Governor to discover gold in his Protectorate. Before returning Hahl also married Luise von Seckendorff–Aberdar whom he met while convalescing in Germany. The freshly wedded couple had several weeks on the SS *Stettin* and in Singapore to enjoy their honeymoon before arriving in Herbertshöhe at the beginning of March 1903.[16]

During Hahl's absence, NGC worked on plans to move some of their trading and export activities to Simpsonhafen (Simpson Harbour) at Blanche Bay, 20km by sea north-northwest from Herbertshöhe, where Hernsheim & Co and DHPG had establishments on Matupi Island in the 1870s. Hahl concurred, the protection of Blanche Bay offered a suitable location for a trading port and for the government's administration centre in the Bismarck Archipelago.

When Berlin showed little interest in finding a new port, let alone another new capital, Hahl took his idea to construct a port at Simpsonhafen to the General Manager of the Norddeutscher Lloyd (NDL). Barely 12 months into his new appointment, a confident Albert Hahl envisioned the establishment of the *Reich's* South Sea capital at Simpsonhafen should NDL agree to his idea.

Six years later, in October 1909, Hahl authorised the shift from Herbertshöhe to Simpsonhafen. In his 1905/06 annual report, he advised Berlin of the completion by NDL of a deep-water wharf for ocean-going vessels, sheds, stores and administration buildings (see chapter 9). Two years later, he reported Simpsonhafen was now the busiest and most efficient seaport in GNG and that the township housed several hundred NDL employees and personnel from NGC, DHPG, Hernsheim & Co, Forsayth and other companies.

Albert and Luise Hahl's compassion for the local people drove the construction of schools and a hospital for the European and local population at Namanula Ridge and elsewhere. Overlooking the port of Simpsonhafen, Namanula Ridge became the government district. Here the building of an impressive new post office and several other department offices, including the Governor's residence were completed when, in January 1910, the proud town became the capital of GNG. Because the Tolai people called the mangroves lined Blanche Bay foreshore 'ra baul', the Germans thought this to be a fitting name for their new capital and when Hahl received permission from Berlin, he re-named the place Rabaul.

Albert Hahl left GNG with his wife and two daughters, Berta and Carola, in April 1914. Whether he intended to apply for a senior position in the Colonial Department is not clear. World War I brought to an end Hahl's public service career. On 1 October 1918, he accepted the position of Executive Director with NGC in Berlin where he remained until his retirement in 1938.[17]

With his uncomplicated, down-to-earth personality, Hahl made friends easily. Richard Parkinson informed him about the ecology and geography of the Archipelago, Tolai culture and the influences they had on economic outcome for the European planters and traders. Parkinson's wife, Phoebe, who introduced the Hahls to her sister Emma, became an important intermediary in disputes with the local people. Luise Hahl soon became patron of the European women in the Archipelago. Deeply concerned with health and educational issues, she contributed as chair of the *Schulverein* (School Association) and the *Frauenbund der Deutschen Kolonialgesellschft* (Women's Association of the German Colonial Society) in Rabaul. As next-door neighbours on Vunatali Heights, above Herbertshöhe, Hahl and Geisler became close personally and professionally. Hahl often accompanied the NGC manager on foot or horseback to learn from Geisler's experience in constructing roads and bridges and plantation management. Geisler, in turn, recognised Hahl foremost as a person with considerable intellect and energy who got things done.[18]

Hahl was energetic. He explored the Gazelle Peninsula and travelled widely to learn about the lie of the land, local custom and economic exchange among the many tribes. He learnt that the Tolai were keen traders but also harboured an uncompromising hatred for the European intruders. Unmistakably, Hahl understood the Kaiser's message: 'The economic progress of the Protectorate and its contribution to the *Reich's* prestige will determine the future of GNG and therefore his future'.[19]

The Bismarck Archipelago prospered compared to KWL. By 1896 it accounted for 53 of the 58 NGC plantation and trading establishments, cultivating 858 ha of cotton and coconuts compared to 333 ha of unprofitable tobacco and some coconuts on mainland KWL. The population in the archipelago was also larger with 139 Europeans, including 64 Germans, 34 British and 13 Dutchmen. This compared to 121 Europeans in KWL, which included 44 Germans, 17 British and 7 Dutchmen. Twice as many indentured workers were engaged in the archipelago (1,813 Melanesians) than in KWL (495 Papuans, 168 Chinese and 254 Javanese). The archipelago also exported more; in 1897/98 nearly four times as much as KWL, while importing nearly twice as much.[20] This gave Hahl an important economic platform from which to start his governorship.

In his small office next to Geisler's, Hahl's workload varied but was not overly demanding. He was the Imperial Judge with consular powers to act for the *Reich*. His responsibilities for public administration involved the Seamen's Registration Office, which kept him occupied with the occasional arrival in Herbertshöhe of a steamer from overseas.[21] Hahl had taken the opportunity during his 2-month outbound voyage to study his new territory and identify the issues he believed needed addressing after his arrival in Herbertshöhe on 14 January 1896. Administrator Schmiele's reports on skirmishes with the Tolai and his recommendation in 1891—when he was still the Imperial Judge—to appoint trusted agents from the local community to act as intermediaries, made sense to Hahl, the local people required government safeguarding from extensive loss of their land.[22]

The economic exploitation of the Eastern District was limited to the northeast coast of the *Neu Pommern* (New Britain) peninsula, and NGC rule had made little progress in developing the archipelago. Some of Hahl's solutions were the same as Hansemann's: explore the country, build infrastructure, and provide GNG with a greater number of ships. However, in a departure from NGC policy, Hahl favoured irenic engagements with the local people. He recognised the need to empower the tribes with trade opportunities and to settle the issue of land ownership to attain economic growth. His solution for the latter was to set aside 'native reserves'.

Hahl gained respect by adopting a proactive policy of becoming acquainted with local customs. Within three months of his arrival he could converse with the Tolai people in the Kuanua language. Listening to their grievances, he became aware the Tolai had no understanding of the meaning of the sale of their land. Protecting village land was therefore one of Hahl's first initiatives that made a difference in GNG. On 22 July 1896, he suggested to Acting Administrator Rüdiger that Schmiele's idea of setting up 'native reserves' would lessen Tolai discontent. Hahl ensured that European planters did not intrude on sacred sites or take possession of land where the ownership was not clearly established. He was devoted to setting up reserves for the local people (*Schutzländereien für die Eingeborenen*) so that the people would work their land and become involved in the economy of their districts by growing produce. Hahl believed his scheme would advantage the settlers, in particular the biggest groups—NGC, Forsayth, DHPG and Mouton. Keeping the Tolai near the coast would retain a ready supply of day labour for the plantations and furnish an important labour resource for road building. While his 'native reserve' scheme would only take shape when he assumed the role of Acting Imperial Governor on 10 July 1901 Hansemann gave him some early support. In a May 1898 despatch to Acting Administrator Skopnik, Hansemann reminded him that land purchases by Europeans had to be in accordance with a valid NGC contract, including evidence that the sellers understood their actions. Hansemann also offered to have a clause in future contracts for the owner to retain usufructuary right to the sold land for an agreed period.[23] It was the latter point that Hahl fostered in particular. If the local people retained use of the land, he surmised, they could grow vegetables, fruits and coconuts for sale to the Europeans. This would provide them with a purchasing power, and over time, a local economy would emerge on European terms. Where the villagers did not work or populate the land, over time (50 years) it would revert to the European planters.

Hahl agreed with the planters and traders to put an end to bartering and only buy copra from the native people with *Reichsmark* or NGC currency. The arrangement lasted only a year though. The quality of the copra dropped significantly as soon as the forced payment was in Marks. Nevertheless, it was the start, of the Eastern District moving to a more regulated payment system.[24] Until 1888 Melanesians collected coconuts for Hernsheim, Forsayth, DHPG and other traders in exchange for a few pieces of hoop iron, glass beads or tobacco sticks. Generally, the currency for buying coconuts from the locals was equivalent to RM1/t. From 1890 the coastal Tolai increasingly bought nuts from the inlanders to sell to the Europeans at considerable profit.[25] Because the trading currency of the Tolai was *Tabu, Tapsoka* or *Diwarra* shell money rather than *Reichsmark*—the legal tender in GNG since 1 April 1887—or the *Neu Guinea Münze* circulated by NGC since 1 August 1894, they insisted on payment in the local currency. This was an expensive transaction for traders. To buy nuts they had to first procure shell money or, in the case of NGC, use shell money it received for goods it sold to the Tolai. (The value of one fathom *Tabu* [6 ft of 400 shells] ranged between RM2 and RM2.50).[26]

NGC's harmful idea idea of reproducing *Nassa* shells in Germany was discarded quickly: The locals had no problems in separating genuine *Tabu* from the imitation shell and the company could not find a manufacturer capable of replicating the North New Ireland *Tapsoka* and the Duke of York Group *Diwarra* economically. NGC also walked away from a scheme to dredge for *Nassa* shells in the Nakanai district of West New Britain because of the inflationary effect mass-produced shell money would have on the local community. Instead, on 21 May 1894 the *Reichskanzler* approved the issue of a local NGC currency.[27] The *Preußische Münzstätte Berlin* struck RM100,000 of NGC gold coins (RM20 and RM10), RM400,000 of silver coins (RM5, RM2, RM1, RM0.50), and RM5,000 of bronze coins (10 *Pfennig* [Pf.]) and copper coins (2 and 1 Pf).

When the *Reich* finally assumed responsibility for GNG on 1 April 1899, Governor Rudolf von Bennigsen withdrew the NGC currency in favour of the *Reichsmark*. By then many indigenous traders accepted coin money. Of course, they had no choice in the matter, because the Hahl-invoked Ordinance of 18 October 1900 prohibited trading in *Diwarra* on the Gazelle Peninsula and conveying *Diwarra* to other parts

of the Protectorate after 31 May 1901. The Ordinance of 1 April 1902 prohibited the dealing in any shell money by Europeans and 'natives'.[28]

Road building was another aspect of Hahl's policy that would bring the Tolai into a money economy. Apart from plantation corridors and the stretches of coastal road between Herbertshöhe and Ralum that caused so much trouble in 1890, only a bridleway from Bishop Couppé's Sacred Heart of Jesus Mission at Takabur (Utaulatawa district) to the coast was completed. Notwithstanding Hahl's tenuous relationship with the Tolai he managed to organise road building on a larger scale. While NGC was constructing a 30 km pack mule track from its sawmill site on the Warangoi River in the Massawa district to Herbertshöhe, and a road from its Gunanur plantation inland, Hahl used local people for road building elsewhere on the peninsula, in Fissaua on New Ireland and the smaller islands where European traders were present.[29] To finance these undertakings, NGC donated shovels, spades, axes, wheelbarrows and tobacco. Hahl marshalled prisoners sentenced to hard labour for this work, while landholders made their European staff and Asian workers available to oversee the work when the road cut through their area. Further, despite the testy relationship between the planters and Bishop Couppé, Hahl's good relations with Couppé and the Christian missions in general, enabled him to make use of missionaries for supervising the local workers.

Thus, when Hahl left GNG in 1898 he had set in train a road-building program stretching from Herbertshöhe to Simpsonhafen and inland to Mt Vunakoko. Built at a cost of a monthly fathom *Tabu* and a daily meal per worker, Hahl's roads connected Herbertshöhe with Ralum, Mt Varzin, Kabakaul and Tavui. Another road started at Herbertshöhe to follow the coastline of Blanche Bay to a point opposite Matupi and to Nodup. Hahl continued the program in the Bismarck Archipelago and KWL after he became Imperial Governor on 10 November 1902.[30]

When Hahl first arrived in GNG he lacked military support and an effective means of dealing with local customs. Therefore, he engaged village elders (*lualuas* or *luluais*) to facilitate the administration of justice to the local people, appointing three chiefs in August 1896 near Ralum and others in the Duke of York Group and the northern Gazelle Peninsula. The empowered chiefs became Hahl's magistrates in deciding disputes on quarrels about money, *Tabu*, pigs, or property. The *luluai* was not to judge family disputes, or quarrels about land and boundaries, or matters involving inter-village warfare. *Luluais* could impose fines on behalf of the government but could not impose or exercise corporal punishment and other local customs. Hahl also determined that every charged person could appeal the decisions of the *luluai* in his court in Herbertshöhe, where proceedings took place in the native language of the accused or appellant. Apart from police and administrative duties, *luluais* were responsible for maintaining roads and bridges in their villages. They also ensured people attended to their gardens and provided food for the villagers. When the *Reich* assumed responsibility for GNG, Imperial Governor Rudolf von Bennigsen expanded Hahl's *luluai* system by empowering the chiefs to decide minor legal disputes involving property up to a value of RM25. Until the government outlawed shell money in April 1902, the people paid their fines mostly in the local currency of *Tabu, Tapsoka* and *Diwarra.* [31]

While Hahl succeeded in bringing the coastal Tolai into a trading relationship with the Europeans, the killings of settlers and cannibalism continued in the hinterland and particularly on New Ireland.[32] Hahl answered with punitive expeditions. When attempts to raise a 24-strong indigenous police force by calling on the financial resources of NGC failed, he trained 75 volunteers from nearby villages. Sharing the 36 rifles that made up NGC's arsenal, the unpaid recruits never failed to turn up for the morning 6 o'clock drill, and in a short time, Hahl had a well-trained police force.[33]

Where pacification failed, Hahl resorted to inflicting punishment. He answered the frequent killings of Europeans by calling on the *Reichsmarine* in support of his punitive expeditions. He also believed NGC should deploy a steamer with 100-trained troops 'in the interest and the safety of recruiting vessels and trade'. Hansemann saw this the responsibility of the *Reich* and passed on Hahl's suggestion to the AA-KA, with little success. And the navy had little appetite for pursuits of tribesmen.[34]

Albert Hahl could effortlessly switch from a stern disciplinarian into an avuncular, understanding, person. 'The success of weapons always seems highly questionable to me', Hahl wrote in his report to the AA-KA in August 1896. After he sentenced a Tolai to death by shooting for killing the trader H. Hilson he became aware that the Tolai was driven to the murder because of ill-treatment at the hands of Hilson. Hahl granted a reprieve: 'Five months in the Herbertshöhe gaol is as severe as death itself' he told Geisler and commuted the Tolai's sentence to one-year hard labour.[35]

For the coastal Tolai to decide that they would work for and trade with the Europeans was not felt 'on the edge of the colony'.[36] Hahl's influence did not reach the Solomons, New Ireland, Duke of York nor New Hanover. Here cannibalism

GNG constabulary at Rabaul, ca. 1912 (Goethe University Frankfurt a. M. No. 043-4008-01)

remained central to the local culture; the European 'intruders' were killed and the tribes continued to fight each other.

The tolerance of Hahl towards the indigenous people also faced resistance from the European landholders and traders. They doubted his ability to establish an orderly administration among the tribal communities.

When Heinrich Schnee succeeded Hahl in December 1898, he found in favour of a 6,000 ha claim by the Tolai against NGC. Even though the local people became co-operative in their dealings with the Europeans Hansemann was furious that a German judge upheld a claim by an uncivilised tribe over valuable tracts of land.[37]

Whereas the coastal Tolai co-operated with the planters only to the extent of their wants, the appointment of Hahl to Governor of GNG in 1902 changed the situation. A poll tax, already levied in German East Africa, provided the framework for Hahl to draft similar legislation in GNG. From 1907, able-bodied men from selected areas in the Bismarck Archipelago paid an annual tax of RM5 each.[38] Hahl targeted the labour of northern New Ireland and New Hanover first, extending the scheme gradually to other areas in the archipelago and to KWL. By 1910 the head tax had increased to RM7 and in some districts to RM10.[39] Hahl's collection method was straightforward: *Luluais* eagerly gathered the tax from their people as they received a handsome premium (up to 10%) for every *Reichsmark* they returned to the government. ·

The tax was effectively a conscription ordinance. It raised revenue and encouraged the men work. It was a poll tax designed for villagers to become cash croppers and copra producers and, failing that, provide cheap labour to the plantations. Tax defaulters were 'collected' by the constabulary and forced to work off their debt on

Government building on Namanula Ridge, Rabaul, ca. 1911 (postcard)**; Governor Hahl and his wife Luise on a Sunday outing, ca. 1913** (Rabaul Museum)**; Lloydstrasse leading from Rabaul wharf to Namanula Ridge,** ca. 1914 (Goethe University Frankfurt a. M. No. 043–410–12)

government projects at RM1/week. The trading Tolai welcomed the tax as it relieved them from working on roads. Tribes who did not possess palm trees resented it.[40]

The New Guinea Company Plantation businesses

NGC and its tobacco plantation enterprise, Astrolabe Company (A-C), merged in November 1896. The merger also initiated the reorganization of the Eastern and Western Districts into three business units: Herbertshöhe, Friedrich Wilhelmshafen (FWH) and Stephansort. Initially, Seleo and Berlinhafen in the north, Finschhafen in the south, later the French or Witu Islands to the west of New Britain, came under the management in FWH. A General Manager for Friedrich Wilhelmshafen and for Stephansort was responsible for development and plantation profitability. The Administrator, resident in FWH, retained the political responsibility for GNG until April 1899. The Witu Islands became a separate district in 1903/04 with Peterhafen as its administrative centre.

Hubert Geisler determined the development of NGC's Eastern District from the day he started with NGC as an assistant plantation manager in 1891. He assumed responsibility for Herbertshöhe Station in 1895, managing the NGC plantations in the entire Bismarck Archipelago. His early achievements at Herbertshöhe were lauded when the German 'gentleman explorer' Wilhelm Joest visited GNG in 1897. Joest was above all impressed with the urban development of Herbertshöhe that he recounts in a quaint but telling prose.

> The buildings of NGC, with warehouses and cotton gins, outshone by the residence of the Imperial Judge and the Company Manager, the shops, several large sheds, accommodation for the European employees and the neighbourhood setting of spacious villas belonging to the relatives of Queen Emma', he wrote, 'find no comparison to the corrugated iron shacks which we saw in the Solomon Islands.[41]

The successes and wealth Joest describes were attained at considerable financial cost though. The 1897 growing seasons were particularly poor. Geisler had 431 ha under cotton and coconut palms, 12 ha were planted with coffee and the first monoculture of coconut palms was planted on a 5.5 ha experimental plot. But the Station generated little revenue. Rain destroyed the cotton planted in May. The November harvest was not much better, yielding only 24,300 lb. The return of only 56.5 lb of cotton to the acre was less than half that expected and with no income derived from labour hire due to a lack in shipping, Herbertshöhe incurred a loss of RM74,555 in 1896/97.[42] The only positive in 1897 was the first export of plantation copra. While the quantity of nuts converted to only 3.5 t in copra, its quality assured higher prices than generally obtained for trade-copra.[43] Geisler abandoned expansion of the coffee fields south of Herbertshöhe in favour of the more suitable county at Massawa Bay on the north coast. The rich soil of this area convinced the NGC man anger to acquire tracts of land for a future coffee and cacao enterprise. He authorised Ernst Kusserow, who had been with NGC since 1891, to set up on Massawa Island and commence a plantation.[44]

Geisler also introduced 35 cows from Java and a stud bull from Australia in 1897. He planned to make NGC independent from meat imports in the same manner he was going to replace Australian building material with a local timber.[45] A fully mechanised sawmill was ordered from Germany to work the seemingly unlimited timber resource of the Upper Warangoi River. While NGC had exported logs since the early 1890s, this sawmill, in conjunction with the FWH setup, met the local demand for dressed timber while also feeding into the Europe market where tropical timber was in great demand.[46] A latecomer in trade-copra, Geisler established NGC's first trading stations in 1897. The archipelago produced over 3,000 t of trade-copra annually, which E.E. Forsayth, R&H and, more recently, Octave Mouton bought locally at around RM4/t. Before Geisler could buy at this rate, he had to establish a trading network with a fleet of schooners. Until then he paid more than RM40/t for copra delivered to Herbertshöhe by independent traders.

The Philippine–American War of 1899 to 1902 proved a turning point for the South Sea copra producers. The drying up of exports from the Philippines drove copra prices up for the first time in more than a decade. Trade-copra now fetched RM200/t cif Singapore with higher prices attained for the plantation product.[47] While the market for Sea-Island cotton was firm, the failed crop of 1897 set in train rationalisation at Herbertshöhe. NGC followed E. E. Forsayth who had stopped planting cotton in 1899. The Australian cotton grower, James Smith, had abandoned his dream shared by Hansemann of emulating the cotton-growing eastern seaboard of North America as early as 1892. Engaged by NGC in 1891 to set up broad-acre cotton farming on the Astrolabe and Jomba Plains, the experienced Smith realised within the first two seasons that he could not grow cotton reliably in KWL.[48] Florida cotton did not germinate well in the moist onshore wind.[49] A switch to Sea Island cotton, which grew well on Ralum, yielded 4,627 kg (9,253 lb) of lint quality from 101 ha, but sold in Bremen at the lamentable price of RM0.30/kg. Further trials with 'Kidney' seeds also proved disappointing.[50]

NGC persevered with cotton on Astrolabe Bay until 1901, thus extending an unprofitable experiment. This weighed on Herbertshöhe. While Geisler followed the other planters on the Gazelle Peninsula and switched from cotton to coconut, he had to continue with the processing, baling and exporting of the fibre for his mainland colleagues until 1902 as Herbertshöhe operated the only gins in GNG.[51]

The drawn-out negotiations for the handover of administrative and fiscal responsibilities gave Geisler the opportunity to set up infrastructure at Herbertshöhe that would enable him to remain independent from government installations. With the transfer of NGC's marine installations to the government, Geisler constructed new NGC moorings and a 30 m jetty at the eastern end of Herbertshöhe harbour well before the hand-over on 31 March 1899. He completed a 1 km narrow-gauge rail track from the jetty to three new warehouses, built new dwellings for staff and extended the European hospital. Separate from the handover, Geisler installed a 17 km telephone network on the main Stations, built 14 drying sheds on Kenabot, Raniolo, Gunanur and Tobera, and improved sanitary facilities, native kitchens, several warehouses and equipment sheds. He developed the out-stations to plantation enterprises, including Wunawutung, Wangaramut, Towakundum, Ungan and those on Schröder and Kabotheron Islands. He also installed brick and limestone kilns at Massawa for the manufacture of building materials previously imported from Australia, and a ten horse-power sawmill, including tracks, steel frames and jinkers, a squaring saw, a cylindrical planer and a tongue and groove saw on the Warangoi River. Geisler completed a pack mule track from Herbertshöhe to Warangoi Station, a wharf at the mouth of the Warangoi River and he expanded the Raniolo plantation by constructing a funicular system across the ravine that divided the acreage.[52] All these installations remained with NGC after the Protectorate of the New Guinea Company became the Protectorate of German New Guinea in April 1899.

The haphazard NGC business model changed with the transfer of responsibility for the protectorate. No longer responsible for government business NGC was able to concentrate its financial and human resources on developing plantations. After Chancellor Hohenlohe appointed Rudolf von Bennigsen, the first Governor of GNG took up residence in Herbertshöhe on 24 July 1899. With the centre of GNG now in the Bismarck Archipelago and the Administrator no longer required, NGC moved its central administration from Stephansort to Friedrich Wilhelmshafen. Also effective from 1 April 1899 was a new NGC reporting structure. Predictably, Hansemann appointed Geisler Administrator for the Eastern District, exclusive of the Witu Islands. NGC's Western District was divided into two economic zones. Friedrich Wilhelmshafen manager Josef Loag, who was assistant manager for the Stephansort and Erima tobacco plantations from 1897, took over from Carl Heinrich Müller to become the NGC Administrator for Friedrich Wilhelmshafen, Peterhafen (Witu Islands), Purdy Islands and Finschhafen (Southern Region) in 1901. Tobacco planter Friedrich Wandres, who had joined NGC in 1896 from Sumatra, remained responsible for Stephansort and the plantation activities in the southern region of Astrolabe Bay. The three Administrators and Paul Behse, who returned to GNG on a new 3-year contract to replace Paul Lücker on Seleo (Northern Region), were directly accountable to Hansemann.[53]

Tobacco and cotton dominated the commodity exports of the Western District until 1899. The end of tobacco in Stephansort and Erima, and the haphazard re-start of Jomba left KWL with little to export in 1900 and 1901. While the plantation area in KWL was greater than the holdings at Herbertshöhe (1,441 ha *vs* 1,165 ha), in 1901 most of the mainland plantations were unproductive. FWH still employed 233 Chinese, 83 Javanese, 308 Melanesians and 34 Papuans. While this was a decline of some 125 workers over the previous year, it remained a high cost.

By 1901 Loag had planted some 37,000 palm-trees at FWH, Beliao and Kalobobo, and on Seleo. NGC expected a meaningful financial return from these trees in about six to eight years. Only 1,000 palms had started to reach maturity in 1901. To gain some earlier cash flow, Loag prepared—inexplicably—140 tobacco-fields and planted some 17,000 gutta-percha trees at Jomba in 1900/01.[54] It turned out to be the last commercial tobacco experiment for NGC.

The company's circumstances at Stephansort and Erima were no better. Wandres spent five months of 1898 in Singapore on coolie recruitment and left Stephansort for Germany—accused of labour mistreatment—the following year. Josef Loag, who then assumed temporary responsibility for Stephansort, reduced the number of Chinese and Javanese on the Station by nearly 40% in 1901. Some 120 workers (73 Chinese and 47 Javanese) attended to the 30,000 Liberia coffee shrubs planted in 1895 and rubber trees trial planted in 1897. Coffee had become a year-by-year proposition, 'bearing luxuriantly' when the soil moisture was moderate.[55]

The planting of *ficus elastica* and *castilloa markhamiana* was more promising. Botanist Schlechter oversaw the first tapping of the trees in 1901, with the latex sent to the 'Gummikamm-Compagnie' and 'Kautschuk-Firma Weber-Schärt', both in Hamburg, for market analysis. While the result of RM4.60 to RM6/kg for either class was not as high as hoped,[56] newly appointed Administrator for the Stephansort region, Karl B. Müller, planted more caoutchouc on the now fallow tobacco fields. By November 1901 some 42,869 *castilloa,* 1,050 *hevea brasiliensis* and 3,296 *elastica* were growing on the Stephansort plantations, with an additional 137,000 seedlings germinating. An increasing number of Melanesian workers (270) attended mainly to the 34,218 palms planted at Stephansort and 5,733 palms at Konstantinhafen. Then fires, lit by the locals to clear land for their own use, destroyed many of the young coconut palms. To counteract this Karl Müller planted 18,000 sisal stalks on the border of the plantations and between palms. Apart from its rope-making use, the fire-retarding properties of agave proved to be beneficial to the plantation.[57]

The only export revenue generated in KWL during 1900/01 was from 176 t of trade-copra, yielding a net income of RM24,989. Fifty-eight head of cattle at Friedrich Wilhelmshafen and 178 head at Stephansort filled 20,014 milk bottles and produced 175.5 kg butter for domestic sales.[58] NGC booked RM13,143 to the 1900/01 accounts from the sales of meat, stores and dairy product. Similarly, the building timber cut at the Erimahafen and FWH sawmills was for domestic use.

The palm inventory in the Eastern District stood at 120,000 trees on 1,165 ha in 1901. Geisler's 781 Melanesian workers had planted 18,200 coconut trees and planted 2000 coffee seedlings on 187 ha during the year. The first 14.5 t of kapok was harvested in 1901, and the 87.5 ha planted with coffee produced 455 kg, selling at RM1.60/kg locally. Between April 1901 and March 1902 Herbertshöhe picked 1,169 kg coffee. Geisler hoped to repeat the satisfactory ratio of 0.25 kg/tree from the first planting in 1902 of cacao. The November 1901 livestock tally stood at 15 horses, 148 cattle and 27 goats. Herbertshöhe sold all the milk it produced, the setting up of centrifugal cream separators in 1902 sped up the butter-making process. Like Friedrich Wilhelmshafen and Stephansort, the Herbertshöhe plantation workers grew their own food. In 1900/01 they harvested 1.2 t of beans, 8 t of corn, 13.4 t of yam, 146 t of cassava (manioc) and 7.7 t of taro on land made available to them by NGC.

The first comprehensive NGC business plan

While NGC ploughed up its tobacco and cotton fields in KWL, it extended its economic dominance in the Bismarck Archipelago. In 1901/02 goods worth RM1,190,701 were exported through Herbertshöhe compared to a paltry RM292,106 from KWL and the Witu Islands. Even at the height of tobacco and cotton production in 1894/95 exports from the archipelago (RM597,350) were greater than that from KWL (RM433,163).

To address this imbalance Hansemann instructed Administrators J. Loag and O. Häsner to submit a 10-year plantation strategy for board approval by 1902.[59]

Loag planned on an increase in coconut plantations from 3,528 ha to 8,000 ha by 1912. Trade copra and general merchandise were to make up the cash flow losses suffered from the discontinuation of tobacco and cotton. Coffee had not developed satisfactorily at Stephansort and the planting of cacao had not progressed much since the Kindt debacle. Loag recommended therefore to extend the coffee trials Geisler had started in the early 1890s on the Gazelle Peninsula. The discovery in 1902 of natural gutta-percha in KWL warranted systematic exploitation according to the botanist Rudolf Schlechter.[60]

Loag heeded this advice in his plantation plan. He was particularly keen to build on the experience Karl B. Müller had with India or natural rubber in Stephansort and, with a booming international market for caoutchouc, elsewhere in GNG. Seeds procured by Schlechter in Kalimantan, Singapore, in addition to locally produced seeds, were to provide him with a flying start. Initially, Loag intended to plant India rubber with coffee, coconut palms and ceiba or kapok trees (*ceiba pentandra*) on the old tobacco fields of Jomba and Erima.[61] He confirmed kapok as a suitable shade tree for the gutta-percha seedlings, and intended to export the fibre from its pods for mattresses, low-cost blankets and other industrial applications.

For a yearly sum to the GNG government of RM100 and a 5% royalty on sales exceeding RM5,000 annually, Loag negotiated an exclusive 10-year concession to exploit the India rubber resources from the Franziska River to the English border and 50 km inland.[62] Around Finschhafen, reopened as a support base for the Huon Gulf expedition in 1901, Loag identified the Station's coconut and coffee plantations at Butaueng for redevelopment. Further, his business plan foresaw the local Jabim people increasingly working with the company to expand this area into a large coconut plantation, with Finschhafen to become an important trading station for NGC again. (Because of isolation from Friedrich Wilhelmshafen and the Astrolabe Bay plantations NGC sold the Finschhafen plantation to Johann Flier's Neuendettelsauer Mission in 1907 for RM32,714).[63]

Another major area targeted by Loag was the Witu Islands. The Danish seafarer Peter Hansen, who previously worked for Captain Dallmann and Otto Finsch, had set up a little kingdom on Garove (Ile Des Lacs) Island where he established Peterhafen. The rich volcanic soil of the eight major islands in the group had an abundance of coconut palms. Hansen knew how to make a living without too much hard work. He taught the islanders how to make copra, which he obtained from them at an equivalent price of RM15/t and selling to Queen Emma of Forsayth for about RM180/t.[64]

Despite a smallpox epidemic wiping out a large number of islanders in 1896–97,[65] NGC set its sights on obtaining privileged concession from the foreign office for the Witus. And 1898, much to the chagrin of Queen Emma, Hansen revived his relations with NGC. In 1900/01 he delivered 176 t trade-copra to NGC rather than Forsayth, with about 100 tons left behind in Peterhafen because of a lack in shipping capacity. The intake, more than the copra gathered by NGC on the mainland of KWL (134.5 t) during the year, would have been higher still if it had not been for attacks by the islanders on the trading stations in 1899 and 1900.[66]

Queen Emma claimed to have bought the Witus from the islanders in 1881 for £50; an assertion disputed by NGC. Neither it nor the *Reich* recognised E.E. Forsayth's ownership of the island group and in 1902 NGC took possession of the Witus, except Unea Island, which the German government retained.[67]

When islanders sacked Peterhafen yet again in 1903, killing engineer Döll of the SS *Meto,* NGC overseer Max Reinhardt, five Chinese coolies and 18 Melanesians, and destroying Hansen's villa and barns, Hansen left the island to become NGC manager in Bogadjim and shortly after also for Walis Island near Aitape.[68]

Trouble with the Witu islanders aside, the board was particularly pleased with its purchase of Iles des Lacs (now Garove Island) and informed NGC shareholders in 1903: 'the ownership of the 4,600 ha island, with its abundance in coconut palms, will turn into one of the company's most valuable possessions'.[69]

With that in mind, NGC turned its attention to the acquisition of Unea Island (500 ha). The company estimated that exclusive trading here would generate 350 t of copra annually, increasing substantially after a coconut-planting programme had come to fruition. Further, NGC outlined plans to set up gutta-percha and cacao plantations on several of the islands. In order to secure agreement from Berlin, NGC proposed a 30-year lease for land on all eight islands for native reserves (*Schutzländereien*) which Governor Hahl was keen to establish.

On 24 May 1904, the GNG administration set aside 908.5 ha on Garowe and 237 ha on Mundua Island for 12 reserves and acreage for a number of smaller protected areas on the sparsely populated remaining six islands.[70] Concurrently Berlin agreed to sell NGC Unea and grant it a 30-year trade concession for all the other islands in the group. Under the agreement, effective on 1 Jan. 1905, NGC leased land on Garowe, Mundua, Naraga, Undagu, Ngoru, Wambu and Chileng free of charge for 30 years.[71] It bought the entire annual coconut harvests from the islanders and sold them European good and tobacco. NGC also signed a 30-year exclusive concession for pearl and pearl shell harvesting. For these rights NGC paid the Rabaul government an annual fee of RM500 until 31 December 1914. Thereafter the licence was set at RM2,000 for each year until 1 January 1934. For fishing rights, NGC paid RM250 annually and RM100/t for export-trepang. NGC also agreed to grant government officers a 40% discounted fare on its ships to and from the Witus.[72]

The new business direction

NGC's board in Berlin approved Loag's plan in November 1902. One year later the company had 2,324 ha under cultivation in the Archipelago and 2,388 ha in the Witu Group and KWL. Ten years later the plantation area for export crops in the Bismarck Archipelago had increased to 3,810 ha, in KWL to 3,077 ha and in the Witus to 1,401 ha. By then the only crops exported by NGC were copra and gutta-percha, a little cacao and low-cost, low margin, sisal agave.[73]

After many failures, the decision to plant mainly palms proved to be correct; the population explosion in Germany in the late 19th century and the introduction of vegetable oils (margarine) to the North American consumer at the turn of the century drove demand for palm oil. Prices for quality plantation copra rose from RM335/t in 1903 to RM655/t in 1913. Continuing strong demand for palm oil encouraged NGC to accelerate the 10-year planting programme of 650,000 palms. The company achieved its target as early as 1906, with 144,400 additional trees planted by late 1913.[74] Although most of the palms would not reach maturity until 1918, at average production of 1/t of copra from 100 mature (13-year-old) trees, NGC could look forward to a healthy return on this investment if prices remained firm.[75]

In contrast, the decision to plant rubber trees did not pay dividends. Oversupply in caoutchouc led to the collapse of the world rubber market in 1913. The original NGC plan foresaw significant acreage to be planted with rubber, however, the weak market post 1912 left the company with a mere 252,000 trees on 890 ha at Stephansort and Peterhafen. Even though the company thinned out uneconomical varieties and weak trees progressively, the financial return from the rubber plantations in 1913 was marginal at best. The only other significant crops identified in the Loag plan were cacao and coffee. Interplanted with coconuts and caoutchouc, some 50,000 *criollo* and *forastero* trees on the Witus and the Gazelle Peninsula produced 83.5 t of cacao in 1913. Coffee production reached its peak in 1908 when NGC sold 16 t in Hamburg. However, the growing rubber trees choked the Arabica shrubs and by 1910, export-quality coffee from the Witu Islands was no longer produced.[76]

The appointment of the experienced Dr Paul Preuß to the position of joint Managing Director of NGC on 13 June 1903 was decisive. The considerable knowledge in tropical agriculture Preuß had acquired in Africa he now applied in GNG. During his first inspection of NGC's plantations from September 1903 to April 1904, Preuß observed a dearth of experienced planters, labour and transportation. He ordered an immediate halt to plantation expansion, while bringing to an immediate end planting of kapok because of the high freight cost for this lowly priced fibre. Preuß made a considered decision to increase the planting of rubber because caoutchouc was in steep demand and he believed the trend would continue.[77] On his return to Berlin, Preuß submitted a plan for a successful industry in GNG to the board:

1) Plantation activities are to be concentrated on coconuts, caoutchouc and cacao.

2) Plantations shall be on a stand-alone basis. The speed of development depends on labour availability.

3) The existing coffee plantations are to be kept with no further expansion

4) Kapok fibre shall no longer be exported.

5) No new plantations are to be started outside the established Stations.

6) Planting of corn, rice, yam and tobacco for domestic consumption is to increase.

7) New intermediate crops such as lemon grass and Sichuan pepper are to be introduced.

8) Plantation development and trade in the Witu Islands is to be intensified.

Until NGC produced caoutchouc latex and plantation copra in meaningful quantities, revenue from trade-copra, trepang and European merchandise was to fill the gap left by the discontinuation of tobacco. While sales of food, tobacco, alcoholic

Disastrous Ventures

NGC income and expenditure breakdown 1903 - 1912

Location	1903	1906	1908	1909	1912
Herbertshöhe/Rabaul					
Plantation Income	90,948	253,071	257,691	309,368	983,498
Trade & Shipping Income	117,966	160,934	198,638	197,518	294,168
Expenditure	335,536	632,395	635,904	614,363	1,296,723
Cash flow	-126,622	-218,390	-179,575	-107,477	-19,057
Friedrich Wilhelmshafen					
Plantation Income	87,185	31,963	257,691	78,931	206,457
Trade & Shipping Income	29,900	57,685	63,059	82,671	170,203
Expenditure	272,359	288,880	289,398	363,650	309,865
Cash flow	-155,274	-199,232	-181,029	-202,048	66,795
Seleo/Potsdamhafen					
Plantation Income	5,009	10,155	19,729	26,162	29,552
Trade & Shipping Income	22,233	36,473	24,518	37,953	46,717
Expenditure	37,750	51,977	62,001	61,679	157,474
Cash flow	-10,508	-5,349	-17,754	2,436	-81,205
Peterhafen					
Plantation Income	0	114,627	105,590	105,021	236,136
Trade & Shipping Income	35,492	105,471	140,580	160,813	19,347
Expenditure		122,090	172,292	163,307	313,002
Cash flow		98,008	73,878	102,527	-57,519
Stephansort					
Plantation Income	7,457	24,544	57,507	88,847	125,234
Trade & Shipping Income	31,353	30,511	7,568	11,536	19,783
Expenditure	129,249	242,379	241,549	276,463	239,495
Cash flow	-90,439	-187,324	-176,473	-176,080	-94,478
Σ Plantation Income	190,599	434,360	698,208	608,329	1,580,877
Σ Trade & Shipping Income	236,944	391,074	434,363	490,491	550,218
Σ Expenditure	774,894	1,337,721	1,401,144	1,479,462	2,316,559
Cash Flow	-382,843	-512,287	-480,953	-380,642	-185,464

beverages, household goods and building materials from the Herbertshöhe, FWH and Stephansort warehouses exceeded RM1,000,000 by 1902/03, growth accelerated further with an increasing European population. Preuß insisted for European goods to be sold to all settlers in GNG and increasingly to the local people.[78]

NGC discontinued providing shareholders with detailed information on its major stations (planting, turn-over, employment, health) after 1903. The annual losses incurred on tobacco and cotton, the unproductive investments in Stations, shipping and exploration had become recurring embarrassments.[79] As of 1904 the company only reported mandatory activities and consolidated financial data. According to trial balances 12 months after the implementation of the new 10-year business plan, the outlays by the Western District (RM439,358) were 30% higher than those incurred by the Herbertshöhe administration. Peterhafen traded profitable, but the acquisition costs for the Witu Group—if incurred—were not shown in the balance sheet. Conclusively, the Eastern District performed better than all other commercial activities of NGC. The income and expenditure statement suggest that Herberstshöhe traded profitably from 1903 onward save for capital expenditure.

Livestock farming became another business stream. NGC provided increasing amounts of fresh milk, meat and poultry for its employees, and bred draught bullocks for agricultural work. Hansemann advised shareholders in 1887 of NGC's decision to import horses, cattle, pigs, sheep, goats and poultry from Australia and Java. While sheep suffered in the humidity, horses, cattle and pigs thrived on the coastal pastures.[80] By 1893 NGC spent RM53,000 on meat imports. In 1894 Ernst Tappenbeck issued a prospectus to raise RM150,000 for a cattle-breeding venture in KWL. He estimated the annual importation of meat was closer to RM100,000 when ship supplies and demands of other GNG consumers were added. Tappenbeck's Kabenau-Viehzucht-Gesellschaft entered into a 5-year agreement with NGC to lease 2000 ha at RM2,000 p.a. on the Kabenau River near Konstantinhafen. He was unable, however, to place the 750 shares on issue with investors and the scheme collapsed.[81]

Trialling shorthorn cattle and other breeds from Australia proved unsuccessful. The herds had low resistance to tropical diseases. When redwater fever affected cattle in the Gazelle Peninsula in 1897 NGC switched to the Javanese and Mandura 'hump-cattle'. While more resistant to ticks and other parasites, an outbreak of tuberculosis led to a large reduction in the Herbertshöhe herd in 1901.[82] Javanese and Manduran bullocks proved too small to perform sustained fieldwork and the cows produced little milk compared to European dairy cattle. The introduction of Zebus (Brahman) and white Zebus from Siam and Bengal respectively better met the requirements of the NGC managers: they were strong, acclimatised and resistant to ticks.[83] But breeding stock imported from Singapore in 1903 carried a malignant form of foot-and-mouth disease to the Stephansort and FWH herds with catastrophic consequences. Within a few weeks 133 head had died. A further problem occurred in Herbertshöhe in 1905 when rinderpest struck down 68 head in February and March.[84] A shortage in bullocks caused impasses in plantation upkeep: 'the requirement for draught bullocks is particularly high', NGC wrote in 1907/08, 'to pull the mechanical grass cutters, specially designed to slash the hardy Alang-Alang (Kunai) thatching grass, which is rampant in the coconut plantations'.[85]

Despite pests and diseases, the NGC herds increased from 308 in 1905 to 1258 head in 1914, but much lower than was planned. Growth in the European population and in the labour force translated into higher consumption. For this reason, NGC made increasing use of water buffalos and set aside an island in the Witus for pig breeding.[86]

Disastrous Ventures

Herbertshöhe, ca .1900 (*Illustrirte Zeitung* Nr 2994, 15 Nov. 1900); **The Road from Herbertshöhe to Kabakaul through NGC plantation,** ca. 1914 (Mackenzie, p. 67). **The Road from Rabaul Wharf to Government House on Namanula Ridge**, ca. 1914 (Mackenzie, p. 320), *to face* p. 232 **Rabaul Harbour with NGC warehouse and buildings in the distance**, ca. 1914 (NLA -obj-152972364), **House of the Administrator on the Schering Peninsula**, ca. 1903 (Goethe University Frankfurt a. M. No. 043-4025-2) **Friedrich-Wilhelmshafen**, ca. 1914 (courtesy H.J. Hiery, plate 31)

Disastrous Ventures

Sorting coffee at Matanatar Plantation, Gazelle Peninsula (Ralum) ca. 1914 (Mackenzie, p. 232). **Girre Girre plantation on the Gazelle Peninsula,** ca. 1914 (Goethe Univ. Frankfurt a. M. No. 024-z-52). **Husking coconuts for copra, Gazelle Peninsula** (SS Mackenzie, p. 276). **Water buffaloes carting coconuts** (Catalogue of Sale, p. 11). **Husk-fired copra kiln** (Bismarck-Archipel-Gesellschaft, 1909 shareholder report)

Governor Hahl negotiating with the people of New Ireland (Neumecklenburg) ca. 1900 (Hesse-Wartegg, p. 122). **Target shooting at the NGC Astrolabe Club (1) Karl Müller, (2) Josef Loag, (3) Franz Boluminski** (F. Hutter eds., p. 561; **Dr Robert Koch at Herbertshöhe on 16 April 1900, and Administrator Karl B. Müller at his Stephansort residence,** ca. 1905 (Hesse-Wartegg, p. 66). **25-year anniversary of the Matupi flag-raising ceremony,** ca. 1910. **Albert Halhl** with the local people (Goethe University Frankfurt a. M. No 043-4012-13).

Disastrous Ventures

An inconsistent legacy of Neu Guinea Compagnie

Hansemann attempted to copy Jacobus Nienhuys to become a tobacco baron rather than adopt the business templates of successful South Sea trading and plantation companies. He failed to recognise the time and the hardship it took for the Sumatran tobacco plantations to reach profitability; most importantly, Hansemann ignored, or had no knowledge, of the thousands of coolie lives it cost to produce the sought after Deli tobacco wrapper leaf. Under similar circumstances, the Dutch were equally successful in growing sugarcane on Java. New Guinea was rich in wild sugarcane from which NGC could propagate plantation cane. Here Hansemann seemed to recognise that sugar prices fluctuated as strongly as tobacco on the international market in which Queensland, Fiji and Java were major players. However, the high labour input and the very high cost in capital equipment would have been the determining factors for Hansemann not to involve NGC in this industry. Southeast Asia and the Indian subcontinent grew fine cotton successfully for centuries; by the 19th century the east coast of North America was the major supplier of this fibre to the world market. Hansemann was keen to repeat the American success, albeit on a smaller scale. Unreliable weather patterns, pests and diseases closed down this option. Caesar Godeffroy, the Hernsheim brothers and Queen Emma amassed a fortune from copra. It took NGC until 1909 to trade profitably on the back of the coconut plantations Geisler, Loag and Müller established in 1902.

Increased production and high copra and caoutchouc prices ensured the company became profitable without the government's annual instalments of RM400,000. Hansemann's successors in NGC, Beck and Preuß, were capable managers. Would they have made similar mistakes? The answer is probably yes. Preuß, a qualified botanist with special interest in gutta-percha, planted predominantly *castilloa* and later a *kickxia* genus. It proved to be a mistake because of the trees' low production rate compared with *havea*. The collapse of the caoutchouc market in 1912/13 was not foreseeable in 1903. Hansemann speculated that the tobacco market was nearing the bottom when deciding on tobacco farming. He and Preuß misread the future market.

By the outbreak of World War I NGC employed 81 European staff, 4,236 Melanesians and Papuans, 43 Chinese and 35 Javanese on 47 plantation and trading stations. General advancements in medicine, better hospitals and medication, better sanitary facilities and a better nutritional regime had improved European health in GNG. Notwithstanding these improvements, mortality in the indigenous workforce remained unacceptably high in 1914.[87] Yet NGC managers accomplished much. Of the General Managers, Loag had been with the company for over seven years, K.B. Müller, who took over responsibility for the Bismarck Archipel Gesellschaft in 1912, was a 12-year veteran of NGC. C. H. Müller left GNG for DOA around 1910. During his 13-year employment with NGC he was in charge of Stephansort, Friedrich Wilhelmshafen, Peterhafen and Herbertshöhe. Hubert Geisler - shortly before the administration centre moved from Herbertshöhe to Simpsonhafen (Rabaul) in 1909 - transferred to Stephansort to assume responsibility for the NGC business on Astrolabe Bay. In 1913 Geisler returned to his old job at Herbertshöhe where he ran

NGC's plantation businesses until the 'Australian Naval and Military Expeditionary Force' captured Rabaul on 13 September 1914.[88] These NGC managers were largely responsible for establishing roads, cuttings, viaducts and tunnels through mountainous terrain. They constructed river crossings, a 43 metre suspension bridge across the Jori River, and completed harbour installations, including wharfs at Herbertshöhe and Friedrich Wilhelmshafen for NDL steamships. A narrow gauge railway of some 40 kilometres in KWL and around Herbertshöhe included two funicular systems. The three managers oversaw the erection of over one thousand offices, dwellings, sheds and warehouses, of which Geisler accounted for some 688 buildings.

By 31 March 1914 NGC grew 794,400 palms on 7,143 ha, producing 2,647 t of copra. NGC plantation copra gained a reputation for its high content of vegetable oil whereas the lower valued trade-copra remained a valuable ingredient for soap and detergents. With one ton of copra equating to approximately 6,000 nuts, NGC workers harvested, husked, cut, dried and packaged the meat of 15,882,000 nuts in 1913/14. With only 29% of the plantation palms having reached maturity at that time, the company was gearing up to process 50,000,000 nuts annually by 1919.[89] These were encouraging prospects for NGC.[90]

NGC did not find itself in the same favourable position with gutta-percha. The most productive tree proved to be *havea*, which, often yielded twice the quantity of latex produced by other genera. The irregular shape of the *ficus elastica* trunk was time consuming to tap. Only 14,547 kg of latex was tapped in 1913/14, a reduction of 5,128 kg over the previous year. While prices had dropped from a high of RM8.50 in 1911/12 to RM4.70 in 1913, the prolific latex flow of the *havea* tree rendered plantation rubber still profitable at that price. The company valued a hectare with 10-year *havea* at RM8,000 compared to a hectare of 15-year *elastica* at RM3,000.[91] Because of the oversupply in rubber, NGC decided in 1914 to replace *elastica* and *castilloa* with palm trees and only maintain a small plantation of *havea*.[92]

The NGC cocoa harvest reached its highest point with 135,263 kg in early 1914. Although producing better quality cocoa, *criollo* was less resistant to fungus diseases and had been replaced with 140,000 *forastero* plants. By 1916 NGC expected to harvest some 250 tons of cocoa earning it approximately RM320,000 annually. While this sum was less than half the amount German planters generated in Samoa, it was, all the same, the second highest plantation income after copra for NGC. During the first quarter of 1914/15 NGC shipped 1218 t copra, 63 t cocoa, 53 t caoutchouc and 28 t of pearl shell. Not a tonne of these consignments reached the port of their destination due to the outbreak of the war. By September 1914 NGC's Berlin office had lost contact with the company's employees in GNG.[93]

From 1885 to 1913 NGC realised 1.38% p.a. on assets invested. Return on equity averaged 1.18% p.a. With the benefit of the annual instalments paid by Berlin for activities undertaken prior to 1899 NGC became marginally profitable. During the last 3 years of its operational life in GNG, the company benefited from the maturing of its coconut plantations, expanded trading and a strong copra market. The first dividend of 5% (RM358,425) was paid in the 1912/13 financial year.

Disastrous Ventures

The businesses of J-G in the Marshall Islands and DHPG in Samoa were commercially successful almost from the beginning. Both companies benefited from a ruthless Eduard Hernsheim and an inventive Theodor Weber. While J-G was primarily a successful trader and guano investor, DHPG and its predecessor Godeffroy built a highly profitable coconut and cacao plantation industry in Samoa.[94] Like NGC, the companies were searching for labour, suffered uprisings by the local people and had to deal with pests and natural disasters. What Hansemann and his managers ignored were the trading successes of DHPG and J-G. Before these companies commenced with the development of plantations they derived cash-flow from trading with the local communities. Importantly, the two companies did not risk their funds on the growing of cotton and tobacco. They made copra their financial staple.

NGC deemed expenditure on government administration a distractions that competed for funds required elsewhere. Only Arnold (NGC's Berlin office manager) and Wißmann (Surabaya coffee trader) had a private-sector background. All other administrators were either retired army/navy officers or had taken leave-of-absence from a government position in Germany. With the exception of Curt von Hagen they were administrators rather than plantation managers. They possessed little - if any - business sense. Contrary to Bismarck's view, Hansemann believed—at least initially—qualifications to manage a colony were best found with bureaucrats or military personnel. And that he could manage a tropical enterprise from his desk in Berlin.

Transhipment and warehousing of copra at Rabaul Harbour, ca. 1915 (NLA.obj-152984815-7)

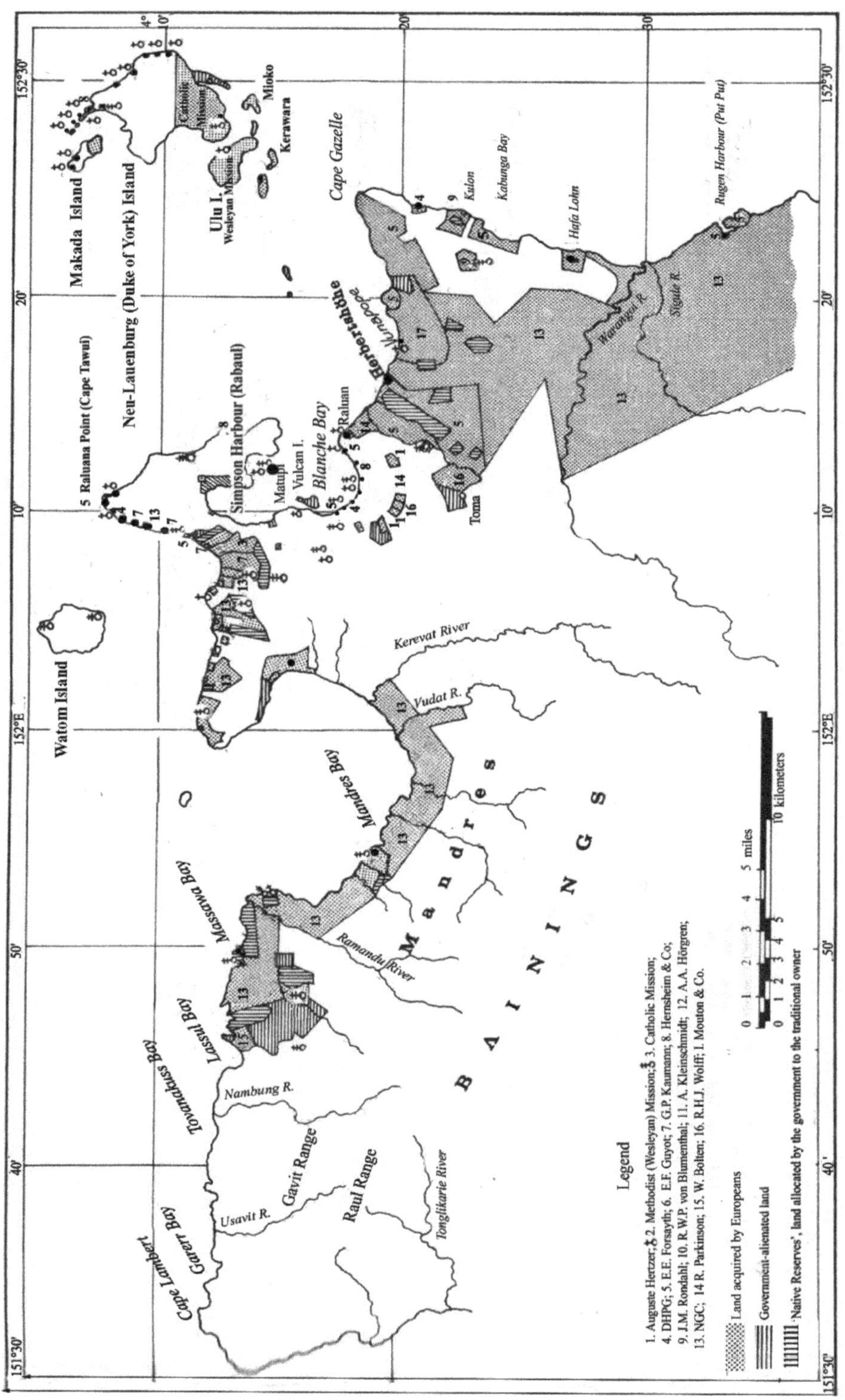

Map 12: **Plantations on the Gazelle Peninsula,** ca. 1910 (HJ Ohff, [adapted])

Disastrous Ventures

The successes of the Deli tobacco planters blinded Hansemann. He rushed into a tobacco venture without understanding the labour requirements, local weather cycles and soil conditions. He misread the long-term effect of President McKinley's tariff on the international tobacco market. Past his 70th birthday in 1896, Adolph von Hansemann was impatiently chasing success in GNG with tobacco. The long-term investments in coconut palms did not align with his life expectancy.

Notes

1   *NKWL* (1887) Heft i, pp. 60–1; Jb (1888) p. 3, (1889) p. 5; Sack & Clark (1887–88) p. 33, (1888–89) p. 37; R.W. Robson, *Queen Emma,* pp. 167–9. R. Parkinson, *Dreißig Jahre in der Südsee,* p. 34

2   *NKWL* (1890) Heft i, p. 9, Heft ii, pp. 63 & 74–5; Jb (1890) pp. 2–3; Sack & Clark (1889–90) p. 46. See P.J. Hempenstall, *Pacific Islanders under German Rule,* p. 127; S.G. Firth, *New Guinea under the Germans,* pp. 45–7. K. Neumann, *Not the Way it Really Was,* chapters 1 & 13

3   R. Parkinson, *Im Bismarckarchipel,* p. 77. *NKWL* (1890) Heft ii, p. 75, (1891) p. 16; J. Forsayth to Schmiele, 29 Mar. 1890; (NAA G255–CS95)

4   Schmiele to AA-KA, 8 April 1890 (RKA 1001:2979, p. 69); Firth, pp. 58–61

5   R. Parkinson, *Dreißig Jahre in der Südsee,* p. 27

6   *NKWL* (1892) p. 28, (1893) p. 23; Jb. (1891/92) pp. 7, 24, 35, (1892/93) p. 7; Sack & Clark (1892–93) p. 74

7   *NKWL* (1894) pp. 17–19; Jb (1892/93) p. 8; Sack & Clark (1892–93) p. 75

8   *NKWL* (1893) pp. 67–8; (1894) pp. 17–19; NGC to AA-KA, 11 Jan. 1894 (RKA 1001:2983). Eugen Brandeis, appointed Administrator for the Marshall Islands on 22 Feb. 1900, retired from public office on 18 Jan. 1906 due to brutality towards the islanders (D. Spennemann, 'An Officer, Yes; but a Gentleman? A Biographical Sketch of Eugen Brandeis', *PSM,* 21 (1998). Colourful exposés on how the Tolai fought under the medicine man Talarai (Tavalai), who 'invented' a bullet proof paint in B. Jinks, P. Biskup & H. Nelson, eds., *Readings in New Guinea History* pp. 112–15

9   *NKWL* (1893) p. 24; (1894) p. 16. The sales do not reconcile with the annual accounts for 1893/94

10 Jb (1889/90) pp. 28–9; (1890/91) pp. 28–9; (1891/92) pp. 34–5, (1892/93) pp. 54–5, (1893/94) p. 28)

11 *NKWL* (1893), p. 26; Jb (1893/94) p. 29; Jb (1893/94) pp. 4–5; Sack & Clark (1893–94) p. 90. 'Beamte des Schutzgebietes 1885–1901' (RKA 1001:2411)

12 W. von Hanneken, 'Eine Kolonie in der Wirklichkeit:', *Die Nation,* (1895) Nr. 9, pp. 133–6 & 155

13 Jb (1893/94) p. 10; Sack & Clark (1893–94) p. 94

14 Jb (1893/94) p. 8; (1894/95) p. 6; Sack & Clark (1893–94) pp. 89–90; (1894–95) p. 108

15 Hahl's leadership was seriously tested when he had to deal with the murder of Administrator von Hagen in August 1897, putting him temporarily in charge of GNG, and an outbreak of smallpox that had spread from KWL to the Gazelle Peninsular. *Morning Bulletin,* Rockhampton (1897) 27 Sep. p. 5

16 Jb (1895/96) pp. 6 & 8; Sack & Clark (1895–96) pp. 119 & 122.H. Rüdiger (acting, 17 Feb. 1895–18 Aug. 96), C. von Hagen (9 Oct. 1896 to 14 Aug. 97). A. Hahl (acting, 15 Aug. 1897 to 11 Sep. 97) H. Skopnik (acting, 11 Sep. 1897 to 31 May 99). H. Blum, *Neu Guinea und der Bismarck Archipel,* pp. 53–5. P. G. Sack , *Albert Hahl,* Editor's Íntroduction', S.G. Firth, *New Guinea under the Germans,* pp. 62–5, P. Biskup, Hahl at Herbertshöhe, 1896–8. H.J. Hiery (ed.) *Die Deutsche Südsee,* 'Die Deutsche Verwaltung Neuguineas', pp. 280ff

17 P. Sack preface to W. Wagner's edition of *Albert Hahl: Gouverneursjahre in Neuguinea.*

18 A.Hahl, *Gouverneursjahre in Neuguinea,* p. 75; B. Pullen-Burry, *In a German Colony or Four Weeks in New Britain,* p. 127

19 Sack & Clark, *Albert Hahl,* pp. 95–6, 142 & 145

20 Charts 22 & 23

21 Hahl, *Gouverneursjahre,* p. 48; Sack & Clark, *Albert Hahl,* p. 11

22 Hempenstall, *Pacific Islanders under German Rule*, pp. 131–2. Hiery, 'Die Deutsche Verwaltung Neuguineas' (p. 301) suggests that Schmiele's predecessor, Judge A. Geissler, first involved the local people in government affairs.

23 Hansemann to Skopnik, 4 May 1898 (RKA 1001:2276, pp. 14ff)

24 Hahl, *Gouverneursjahre*, pp. 92–3

25 O. Finsch, 'Über Naturprodukte der Westlichen Südsee', *DKZ* (1887) p. 525; see R.F. Salisbury, *From Stone to Steel: Economic Consequences of a Technology Change in New Guinea*, p. 337

26 *DKBl* (1894) p. 420; Jb (1893/94) pp. 2–3; *NKWL* (1894) pp.4–6; Sack & Clark (1893–94) pp. 86–8, Helmreich, *Das Geldwesen in den Deutschen Schutzgebieten*, pp. 28ff; Parkinson, pp. 62–5

27 Helmreich, p. 51

28 Jb (1900/01) p. 83; Sack & Clark (1900–01) p. 220.

29 Jb (1897/98) pp. 8–9 and (1898/99) p. 14; Sack & Clark (1897–98) p. 145 and (1898–99) p. 155.

30 *NKWL* (1897) pp. 49–50; Jb (1898/99), pp. 166–7; (1900/01) pp. 77–9; Sack & Clark (1898–99) pp. 177–8; (1899–1900) p. 205.

31 P.G. Sack, *Land Between Laws*, p. 112, Hahl, *Gouverneursjahre*, pp. 41–4; C.D. Rowley, *Australians in German New Guinea*, pp. 214ff.

32 'Bericht betreffend die Unruhen am Varzin in 1902' (RKA1001:2989)

33 Hahl, *Gouverneursjahre*, p. 56; Sack & Clark, *Albert Hahl*, p. 16

34 Hahl to NGC, 24 June 1898; NGC to AA-KA, 14 Oct. 1898 (RKA 1001:2987, pp. 7–9)

35 Hahl to AA-KA 25 Aug. 1896 (RKA 1001:2985; Station Court Herbertshöhe: Trial against Totaia for the murder of the trader H. Hilson, employee of the firm E.E. Forsayth. NAA G 255- 170-no. 1038174

36 S.G. Firth, *Albert Hahl, Governor of German New Guinea*, p. 32

37 Sack, *Land Between Two Laws*, p. 152; H. Schnee, *Als Letzter Gouverneur in Deutsch-Ostafrika*, pp. 26–34; S.G. Firth, *New Guinea*, pp. 5, 25 & 70

38 Sack & Clark (1901–02) p. 229; (1908–09) p. 293

39 Sack & Clark (1909–10) p. 308; (1910–11) p. 320; (1911–12) p. 337–8.

40 'Steuerwesen in Neuguinea' (RKA 1001:2763); *AB*, 1 May 1910; Sack & Clark (1907–08) p. 278, (1908–09) p. 289. Hempenstall, *Pacific Islanders*, pp. 142–3, & 187; R.F. Salisbury, *Vunamami*; Firth, *New Guinea*, p. 106; K. Neumann, Not the Way It Was: Constructing the Tolai Past.

41 A. Baessler, *Neue Südsee-Bilder*, p. 359

42 Jb (1896/97) p. 30; *DKBl*, (1898), pp. 405–6

43 *NKWL* (1897) p. 24, (1898), p. 21

44 Jb (1897/98) pp. 6 and 7; Sack & Clark (1897–98) p. 144

45 *NKWL* (1897) p. 24

46 *NKWL* (1896) pp. 16–18, (1897) pp. 24–5; Jb (1893/94) p. 9, (1896/97) p. 10, (1897/98) pp. 6 & 9; Sack & Clark (1893–94) p. 92 (1896–97) p. 134, (1897–98) pp. 142 & 145

47 *NKWL* (1898) p. 22

48 *NKWL* (1889) Heft ii, p. 33, (1891) Heft i, pp. 11–12 & 14, (1892) pp. 26–8, (1893) p. 22; Jb (1893/94) p. 9; Sack & Clark (1893–94) p. 93

49 *NKWL* (1891) Heft i, p. 11, (1892), Heft i, p. 26.

50 *NKWL* (1894) Heft i, pp. 16 & 20, (1894), Heft i, pp. 16 & 20; Jb (1890) p. 5, (1891/92) pp. 7 & 10, (1892/93) pp. 6 & 11, (1893/94) p. 15; Sack & Clark (1889–90) p. 49; (1890–91) pp. 61–4

51 Jb (1899/1900) pp. 7 & 19; Sack & Clark, (1899–1900) p. 208

52 *NKWL* 1896, p. 18; (1897), p. 25; (1898), p. 21; Jb (1897/98) pp. 7–9, (1898/99) p. 9; Sack & Clark (1897–98) pp. 144–5; (1898–99) pp. 152–3; Geisler to Hansemann (RKA 100:2419, pp. 23–6)

53 Jb (1896/97) pp. 4–5; (1897/98) pp. 4–5, (1898/99) pp. 7–8; Sack & Clark (1896–97) pp. 132–3, (1897–98) pp. 140–1; (1898–99) pp. 151 & 163

54 Jb (1900/01) p. 15

55 Jb (1896/97) p. 6; (1897/98) p. 5; (1898/99) p. 20; (1899/00) p. 19

56   Jb (1900/01) pp. 20–1

57   Jb (1899/1900) p. 18; (1900/01) pp. 20–2

58   Jb (1900/01) pp. 16, 22 & 37

59   Jb (1901/02) pp. 1 & 4

60   *NKWL* (1888) Heft iii, p. 149; (1896) p. 11; (1897) p. 20; (1897) p. 18; Jb (1897/98) p. 5, (1899/1900) pp. 7 & 19; (1901/02) pp. 4 & 8. Sack & Clark (1901–02) p. 223

61   Jb (1900/01) p. 15; (1902/03) p. 13; DKZ (1907) Nr. 24, pp. 520–1

62   Hahl to AA-KA, 11 Jun. 1904, NGC to AA-KA, 8 Jul. and 22 Aug. 1904; 'Erteilung einer Konzession an die Neu Guinea Compagnie im Gebiet vom Huon Golf' (RKA 1001:2423)

63   Jb (1900/01) p. 16; (1907/08) pp. 3, 6 & 10

64   Robson, p. 202

65   M. Davies, *Public Health and Colonialism*, pp. 109–11

66   Jb (1898/99) p. 25; (1900/01) p. 16; Sack & Clark (1900–01) p. 211

67 . Hahl to AA-KA, 15 Apr. 1904; 'Untersuchungen der NGC auf den Französischen Inseln' (RKA 1001:2424); Jb (1900/01) p. 84)

68   W.C. Groves, 'Peter the Island King' (NLA–ANU, mfm PMB MS 612)

69   Jb (1902/03) p. 15

70   Land mass of the group is about 9,000 ha (Garowe 4,500 ha and Mundua 1,000 ha)

71   RKA 1001:2424, pp. 16–19

72   Hahl charged NGC RM2,444 retrospectively for Unea in 1908 (488.787ha x RM5). NGC recovered the amount on 26 Jun. 1908. Correspondence NGC – Hahl – AA-KA (RKA1001:2424, pp. 4–119).

73   Jb (1912/13) pp. 5–6

74   Jb (1905/06) p. 2, (1912/13). p. 7, (1913/14) p. 4. The tally includes 53,346 'wild palms' planted randomly on harbour foreshores, along waterways, roads and lanes

75   Preuß, 'Wirtschafliche Werte in den Südseekolonien' (1916) p. 543.

76   Jb (1905/06) p. 3; (1907/08) p. 5, (1908/09) p. 3 and (1909/10) p. 5; (1912/13) pp. 8–9

77   (*NKWL* (1897) p. 19); Jb (1903/04) pp. 8–9. Kapok fetched RM 0.25–0.63 cif Amsterdam in 1897.

78   Jb (1903/04) p. 6; (1902/03) pp. 23–4; Charts 23 & 24

79   Chart 38

80   Jb (1887) p. 17

81   Prospectus of the Kabenau Viehzucht-Gesellschaft (RKA 1001:2430)

82   Jb (1897/98) p. 8; (1901/02) p. 4. Sack & Clark (1899-1900) pp. 188–9

83   Beck, 'Neu Guinea Compagnie', *Südseebote* (1918) pp. 68–9

84   Jb (1903/04) p. 10; (1904/05) p. 8

85   Jb (197/08) p. 5, Jb (1908/09) p. 4

86   Wambu Island, Jb (1913/14) p. 6

87   Chart 10

88   H. Geisler established his own plantation in GNG during the war. The Australian Government Expropriation Board expelled Geisler in 1921

89   *Wirtschaftliche und Finanzielle Rundschau* (1914) p. 377

90   Copra prices remained high until 1919 to then decline to a level of unprofitability by 1929.

91   Preuß, 'Wirtschafliche Werte in den Südseekolonien', p. 55

92   *DKBl* (1914) p. 286

93   NGC to KA-AA, 7 Sep. 1915, Jb (1913/14) pp. 3–15

94   Until 1905 Western Samoa exported four times more copra and ten times more cocoa than GNG (O. Mayer, *Die Entwicklung Der Handelsbeziehungen Deutschlands Zu Seinen Kolonien*, pp. 102ff; Preuß, 'Wirtschafliche Werte in den Südseekolonien', pp. 546 & 550

Cacao (*Theobroma cacao*) DKL vol. ii *to face* p.162

Coffee (*Coffea arabica*) DKL vol. ii *to face* p.136

Sea-Island cotton (*Gossypium barbadense*) DKL vol. i *to face* p.152

Sisal-Agave (*Agave sisalana*) DKL vol. iii *to face* p.368

Map 13: **The German Possessions in the Central and South Pacific – marked in red**
(*Bibliographisches Institut*, J. Meyer, 1910)

DER
DEUTSCHEN SÜDSEE - KOLONIEN.
Mafistab 1:28 000 000
Kilometer
Deutsch   Britisch   Französisch   Niederländ.
Portugiesisch   Besitz d. Ver. Staaten v. Nord-Am.
Grenzen der Bezirke.
Gouverneurssitze sind Rabaul (Simpsonh.) u. Apia. Die Namen der
deutschen Bezirksämter sind unterstrichen, die Namen der
Regierungsstationen sind unterstrichelt.
Deutsche Dampferlinien   Englische Dampferlinien
Französ.   Amerikan.
Japan.   16 Fahrtdauer in Tagen.
Kabel   Schiffbare Flüsse.
P Postanstalt   T Telegraphenanstalt   Z Zollamt
Evangelische   Katholische Missionsstationen
Die Missionsstationen auf Kaiser-Wilhelms-Land, dem
Bismarck-Archipel u. auf den Samoa-Inseln, sowie
die Postanstalten auf letzteren sind auf den betr.
Spezialkarten zu finden.
Wake
Taongi (Bogas)-In.
M a r s h a l l - In.
Bikini-In.
Bikar-In.
Eniwetok-In.   Rongelab-In.   Utirik
Ailinginae-In.   Rongerik-In.   Taka   Jabwot
Wotho   Likiebi   Ailuk-In.
Ujelang-In.   Ujae-In.   Kwajelin   Wotje-In.   Mejit
Lae-In.   Kr.(kab)In.   Chatham-In.
Iab-In.   Maloelab-In.
Namo-In.   Culvert-In.
Ailinglaplap-In.   Aur-In.
Maturo-In.
Arno-In.
(Jaluit-Ges.)   Jaluit-In.   Mile
Pingelap-In.   Jaluit-In.   Jabor   Keats-B.
Namorik-In.   Narik-In.
Kusaie (Ualan)-I.   Ebon-In.   Kili
M I K R O N E S I E N
S T I L L E R   O Z E A N
Butaritari   Makin (Pitt)-In.
N. Makin-In.
Apaiang   Maraki
Marana   Tarawa
Gilbert   Kuria   Aranuka   Apamama
In.   Nonouti   Kingsmill-In.
Nauru   Tapu_   Nukunau
Pacific Phosphate Co.   Tuputuea   Peru   Onoatoa
Ni-Peru-In.   Arorai
Tamana
Nauru 6-Jaluit 10   Howland-I.
Jaluit-Ges.   Baker-I.   Äquator
Winslow-B.
Nukumanu (Tasman-In.)   Canton (Mary)-I.
Liueniua   Mac Kean-I.   Birnie-I.   Enderbury
Ongtong, Java, Lord Howe In.   Gardner-I.   Phönix-In.   Phönix-I.
Hull   Sydney-I.
Nanomea
Naxomana   Nutao
Ellice-Ins.   Vattupu
Nui   Nukufetau
Funafuti
Nikalailai
S A L O M O N - In.   (S Ü D)
Sikajana (Stewart)   Motuiti
Isabel
Malaita   Atafu   Tokelau-
Maramasiki   Tuomako   (Union)-In.
Nukunono   Fakaafu
Guadalcanal   Matema (Swalloi)-Riff-In.   Nurakita   Robbie-B.   Gente Hermosa
Nitru   Sa Cruz (Kgn.Charlotte)-In.   (Swains)
Bauro   Tapua/Uapua   Anuda   Tuscarora
(S.Cristoval)   Voikoro   Fataka   Combe-B.   Wetterwitch   Field-B.   Samoa-In.
Muarn (Rennell-I.)   Ticopia   Rotuma   Teagaila-In.   Savaii   Apia
Torres-In.   Rowa-Lava   Horne-In.   Upolu   Tutuila
Banks-In.   Fatuna   Alofa   Pago Pago   Namua
Merena   Ganac (Meta)   Balmoral   Thikimbia   Muidor   Tataki   Rose-In.
(Espiritu Santo)   Maivo   Riff   Fidschi-In.   (G.Raxa-I.)   Niutobutabu
Araga   Vanua-Levu
Mallikolo   Ambrym   Yasawa   Koriu   Exploring-In.   Fonua Lai
Neue-Hebriden   Gr.   Koro   Lau (Oat)   Toku
Marabau (unter brit. u. franz.   Viti-Levu   Lakemba   Vavau-Gr.   Niue
D'Entrecasteaux   Verwaltung)   Gr.
Efaté (Sandw.)   Eromanga   Vatu Leilo   Late-I.
Tanna   Erronan (Futuna)   Kandavu   Makoa   Haapai-Gr.   Tonga-In.
Aneityum   Vatoa   Tofua   Kotu-Gr.   Niu
Bolep-I.   Astrolabe   Matuku   Nukualofa   Ata Tolu-In.
Wegoa   Riff   One-i-lau   Mika-Gr.   Buffon-R.
Neu-   Loyalty-(Loyauté)   Tirana-In.   Tongatabu   Eu   Harans-R.
Kaledonien   In.   Oniway Riff   Ata (Pylstaart)
Noumea   Mire   Pelorus-R.
Kreis d. Steinbocks   Matthew   Walpole   Nord-In.
Süd-In.
Minerra-Riff

Flag of British New Guinea (1886–1906)

Flag of the Territory (Papua) New Guinea

Flag of the Lieutenant-Governor

Flag of the Lieutenant-Governors from 1906 to 1946

Emblem of Papua New Guinea

BRITISH AND AUSTRALIAN COLONIAL INTENTIONS AND PRACTICES IN SOUTH-EAST NEW GUINEA

Part III

Stone club making and drilling of a skullcap (Papua, annual report 1914, p. 209)

Attack of Natives, Traitor's Bay (*CAP J. Moresby, Discoveries & Surveys in New Guinea*, p. 277)

BRITISH NEW GUINEA: A POLITICAL CONSTRUCT DOOMED TO FAILURE

Theodore Bevan, intrepid trader and explorer, viewed the British Protectorate in southeast New Guinea as one of the richest dependencies of the British Crown that was a failure in every sense of the word. Bevan was not alone in his opinion. Particularly during the first 4 years in the development of the Protectorate, a constant barrage of critical comments appeared in Australian newspapers. The Sydney *Daily Telegraph* reported on 10 March 1888 'British New Guinea is the rankest commercial failure south of the line'. A week later, the paper stated:

> The German New Guinea Company has spent already £250,000 in starting the colonization of New Guinea and adjacent islands. They have erected a great many Stations along the coast, started a local government, and surveyed all the harbours; besides, they have been having trials in agriculture, and now, after this experience, have started large plantations in New Guinea. This scheme, we believe will be the success of the country, owing to the cheapness and abundance of native labour. Already they have five hundred natives from the adjacent islands and two hundred Malays. They are employed in growing cotton, coffee, and tobacco. The company has forbidden home emigration, and has the country open now, wishing the emigration to come from Australia.[1]

Bevan's view in 1888 that the colony was 'an effete and meretricious system' had changed little 10 years later. In a paper delivered to the Royal Geographical Society of Australasia in Melbourne, he warned of the failure and disaster prospectors and settlers would face in BNG. The Protectorate 'had no adequate Government machinery, no postal system, hospital, or hotel [and] no lines of rails or telegraphs' 14 years after its proclamation. 'New Guinea wanted a Cecil Rhodes', he told the Society members, 'with [land] concessions made on similar lines to that of British South Africa in Rhodesia'. *The Sydney Morning Herald* shared this view along with many Australian newspapers by contrasting the German approach to the colonisation of New Guinea to that of 'British slackness. Already there are lands under cultivation, mills erected, a perfect system of police and administrative control, and a fine service of steamers connecting German New Guinea with the East Indies and the world's markets. Against all this', the *Herald* bemoaned in 1907, 'the British New Guinea is hardly out of swaddling dollies'.[2]

Of course, there were participants on both sides of East New Guinea with contrary views, exaggerating the perceived successes and failures in BNG or GNG. For instance, the NGC employee, Hans Blum, saw only the positive side of MacGregor in BNG. Deriding his own company's performance in GNG, he wrote in 1900:

Disastrous Ventures

> The clear and unwavering farsightedness of the British New Guinea Administration, whose architect set the framework with a steady hand and creative mind before he sketched out the vision, where the outline and colours are determined by daily progress, is contrasted on the eastern side by a canvas which, to put it mildly, would not even please a dilettante.[3]

Other disgruntled NGC employees shared Blum's view on GNG. But it was not a commonly held belief by the explorers, traders and gold prospectors whose unenthusiastic judgement on the BNG administration and the Colonial Office in London were coloured by their commercial interest in BNG.

The inconspicuous start of BNG

The approaches adopted by Adolph von Hansemann and Lord Derby's government department in colonising East New Guinea could not have been more different. The German was impetuous, wanting to commercialise his northeast Protectorate within a few years, while Britain's Colonial Office took its time by declaring BNG merely an interim arrangement on 6 November 1884. Nearly 4 years were to pass before a final settlement was made and the annexation of BNG was effected. Much to the chagrin of the explorers, traders, collectors and gold prospectors, they were at first prevented from entering BNG because, according to Deputy Commissioner Romilly, no regulations had been framed for the admission of Europeans to the Protectorate. Romilly issued a proclamation, confirmed by Commodore Erskine, which specifically referred to the protection of the New Guineans and banned settlement of any kind. To make his point, in Port Moresby he ordered Bevan and Ned Snow (a gold prospector) on 25 November 1884 not to disembark from the Chinese junk *Wong Hing* on which they had travelled from Cooktown.[4]

While Romilly eventually allowed Bevan—the whereabouts of Snow was unknown—to stay at or near Port Moresby for up to 6 weeks, he deported two Europeans, Guise and Currie, immediately after it was brought to his attention that their 'seduction of native woman threatened to lead to trouble on the coast'. The situation did not change much with the arrival in Port Moresby of Special Commissioner General Sir Peter Scratchley in August 1885. A veteran of the Crimean War, who also served in India before advising the colonial governments of Australia on their defence requirements, Scratchley took charge of BNG under the Western Pacific Orders in Council of 1877, 1879 and 1880 'until Her Majesty shall be pleased to make further provisions for administering law in the Protectorate'. As a deputy commissioner for the Western Pacific Scratchley's powers were limited. He was unable to implement 'regulations having the force of law, or impose or collect any taxes or licence fees upon exports or imports, or otherwise to exercise any legislative or judicial functions in the Protectorate'.[5] Scratchley was to do no more than make himself acquainted with the country, its harbours and general features, and enter into friendly relations with the 'natives'. He reported directly to Secretary of State, Lord Derby, who accredited him with the discretional powers within the limits assigned to a deputy commissioner of the Western Pacific. Scratchley was to uphold the regulations for BNG issued by the high commissioner in Fiji on 5 April 1884 that prohibited the supply of arms, ammunition, explosives, or liquor to the indigenous people.

Scratchley's restricted legal powers concerned him. He was not convinced that he could ban Bevan and Snow from BNG, nor did he agree with Romilly's dismissal of commentary in Melbourne on white settlement in BNG as 'very delusive'. Scratchley thought that discouraging firms, British or foreign, who wished to conduct business in BNG, would be 'impolitic' as it would forego valuable sources of income. He requested Derby to confer on him the necessary judicial powers over foreigners. Until then, he told Romilly, he would not encourage prospective settlers.[6]

Consistent with the British government's position on colonial acquisitions, the Colonial Office would not accede to Scratchley's request until the Australian colonies underwrote the funding of the administration in BNG. This required protracted negotiations which Scratchley was barely able to start: he fell ill soon after arriving in Port Moresby and died there on 2 December 1885. Romilly was once more in charge of the Protectorate until John Douglas, Queensland's government resident on Thursday Island, arrived in July 1886. However, neither he nor Douglas was able to hasten the Australian colonial governments to act. Thus, the Protectorate was left without aims other than the protection of its indigenous population.

After Britain declared southeast New Guinea a British Protectorate, the Australian colonies showed little interest in its future. While unhappy that their demand to annex all of East New Guinea remained unanswered, they accepted that Queensland's concern of a foreign power encroaching on its border had been dealt with. The Australians took particular umbrage at Commodore Erskine's speech that told the Hanuabada (Motuo) tribes of Port Moresby: 'from this time forth you are placed under the protection of Her Majesty's Government: that evil-disposed men will not be able to occupy your country, to seize your lands, or take you away from your own homes'.[7] With this anti-European stance by the British government and with cheap South Sea labour no longer available to the Queensland sugar planters, the interests of the Brisbane, Melbourne and Sydney traders in New Guinea as a source of opportunities also fell away.

Finance was one of the main obstacles to BNG progressing from a protectorate to a possession. Derby was concerned that the Australian colonies had not agreed to permanent funding and instructed Scratchley to ascertain 'whether the Colonies will provide in subsequent years a sum adequate to the due maintenance of the Protectorate'.[8] Derby insisted that BNG was an initiative by the Australian colonies and was not to be a source of expense to England.

While the main Australian colonies—Victoria, New South Wales and Queensland—were prepared to recognise some responsibility, this was not the case for the other colonial agitators. In 1885 all Australian, New Zealand and Fiji governments contributed equally to an agreed fund of £15,000.[9] South Australia and Fiji did not make a further contribution the following year, a position New Zealand and Tasmania adopted in 1887. West Australia continued to pay a token annual amount of £161 16s 9d. The three eastern colonies shared the balance of the costs incurred by BNG.[10]

From an Australian perspective, this financial arrangement remained provisional as long as the Colonial Office refrained from contributing (except for the Home

Office's expenses and travelling costs for its officers) while exercising executive power in the Protectorate. Queensland's Premier Samuel Griffith reminded the Colonial Office in 1886 that Britain was not living up to the agreement reached at the Intercolonial Convention held in Sydney at the end of 1883. Britain's offer of a steamship, inclusive of the annual running cost, had still not been committed, and London rejected Douglas' submission to underwrite a £75,000 loan. The Colonial Office believed BNG would not generate a profit for any time soon [11]

It took the gathering of the Australian governments at the first Colonial Conference from April to May 1887 in London to reach agreement. In line with the earlier proposal, Victoria, New South Wales and Queensland agreed to contribute £15,000 annually for 10 years. Britain agreed to supply the steamship *Merrie England* (260 BRT) at a cost not exceeding £18,500 and its maintenance for 3 years at £3,500 per annum.[12]

London also agreed to Griffith's demand for budgetary and expenditure control over the colony's contributions. With back-to-back guarantees from the other two colonies, his government passed the *British New Guinea (Queensland) Act, 1887* under which Queensland accepted the obligation of providing the agreed sum and making up the shortfall in the running costs for the steamship. With the funding of the Protectorate assured until 1898, the British government agreed with the three Australian colonies to commence drafting a constitution in preparation for the annexation of the territory. Letters Patent for 'Erecting Certain British Territory in New Guinea and the Adjacent Islands into a Separate Possession' of 8 June 1888, and BNG's first Administrator, Dr William MacGregor's 'Commission and Instructions of 4 September 1888', proclaimed Queen Victoria's sovereignty over the new British possession.[13]

HMS *Merrie England* on the Brisbane River, ca. 1898 (*The Queenslander*, 1 April 1898)

After four years of dithering, the Queensland government was practically in charge of this British colony. The procedure of joint control was unwieldy; although in practice Queensland approved the BNG budgets, had the right to veto the employment and dismissal of the public servants, exercised supervision over its administration and received the despatches from BNG's Administrator before distributing transcriptions to the Colonial Office and the relevant Australian governments. While Britain retained reserve powers, she was patently not interested in the development of her youngest colony. Only the influence of the Aborigines' Protection Society, Christian missions and humanitarian factions in the former Gladstone government saw to it that the Australian colonies could not exercise singular control over BNG. Alienation of land, the local people's employment by Europeans and the supply of alcoholic beverages, guns, ammunition and explosives to natives were Gladstone's concerns, not the development of a territory, which the British government always regarded as an Australian responsibility. Therefore, Whitehall insisted on the protective rights of the indigenous people being firmly written into law.

The early years were indeed lost years in the eyes of the few Europeans who chanced their luck in the territory. Andrew Goldie, who had lived there since the 1870s, was responsible for the first gold rush to New Guinea in 1878.[14] The territory's only storekeeper, he was a man of few words: 'the Protectorate', he told Bevan when the two met for the first time in Port Moresby, 'had so far been a blow to the country, as the missionaries wished to prevent settlement'. Bevan shared Goldie's sentiments. Yet he returned to explore BNG on four occasions. On 12 August 1885 he was granted a permit 'to explore and trade in BNG' only because Scratchley 'had not the power to keep traders out of New Guinea'.[15]

Bevan took full advantage of the opportunity by exploring the western part of the British territory and set up profitable trading stations in late 1887. While Queensland government surveyor, Hemmy, assisted Bevan with the mapping of the Aird and the Queen Jubilee rivers, Bevan claimed the credit when the two explorers returned to Australia on their small launch the *Mable*. 'Upon my return to Sydney in January 1888, I received the full share of those amenities which fall to the lot of successful explorers', he noted proudly. 'Among them was the acclamation of the President of the Royal Geographical Society of Australasia, Sir Edward Strickland', who told Society members: 'the work of the dashing and successful explorer—Mr. Bevan— is of high importance [as it] has largely contributed to the unfolding of the hidden secrets of New Guinea to an extent which never has been equalled'.[16]

However, other than praise and the mouth of the Aird River named after him, Bevan left empty-handed. Following five voyages to southeast New Guinea, one sponsored by Robert Philp of Burns, Philp, Bevan sought land concessions totalling some 254,000 ac in recognition of his work. The young explorer-cum-businessman aspired to become the first plantation owner of BNG. He had demonstrated entrepreneurship in 1885 by employing more than 1,000 local people along 100 miles of the Papuan Gulf coastline to catch, boil and cure trepang. It proved a profitable business for all concerned and could have hastened economic development if applied more widely.

But Douglas rejected Bevan's request. Believing that a land purchase of that scale was speculative, which would not add to the development of BNG, Douglas also asserted that he had 'no authority to make any such grants'.[17]

The land policy of Britain in New Guinea also frustrated Burns, Philp. Although Douglas granted the company a £50 monthly shipping subsidy for providing a mail steamer service from Thursday Island to Port Moresby, James Burns was disappointed at the delays in deciding British policy on New Guinea. For want of profitable trade in copra, trepang, sandalwood and other goods BP terminated the contract 18 months into a three-year agreement. Burns told Douglas in Sydney in 1887:

> The outlay, which will be necessary to establish anything like a decent trade with New Guinea, is very great and the only chance we would have of recompensing ourselves would be that we acquired properties, which in time will increase in value and so wipe off the losses made in opening up the case.[18]

The termination ended BP's first foray into New Guinea. For the time being the company saw greater opportunity in handling agency work for NGC in Cooktown than in setting up a branch in Port Moresby. But the agreement between the Germans and the Australian firm did not live up to expectations either: NGC decided in 1889 to ship cargo through Brisbane, Batavia and Singapore, and onward to GNG using its own or charter vessels.

Another company interested in doing business in BNG was DHPG. With established trading and plantation interests in Apia and Mioko, the Hamburg firm was keen to set up a trading base in Port Moresby. Scratchley was interested in the German proposition. Under proper supervision and restriction, he informed the Colonial Office; the German company would develop the resources of southeast New Guinea, which would ultimately benefit the islanders.[19] But Derby had already rejected a request by an English syndicate wishing to establish an agricultural and trading company in BNG in 1886 and he rebuffed Scratchley's DHPG proposal.

Dr William MacGregor, first Administrator, explorer and reluctant developer

Dr W. MacGregor, ca. 1898

William MacGregor was 41 years old when appointed the first Administrator of BNG in 1888.[20] By then he was an experienced colonial administrator who had worked in Fiji under High Commissioner for the Western Pacific, Sir Arthur Gordon, since 1874. MacGregor was concerned that the Foreign Office would ignore the desired promotion because of his age and middle-class Scottish upbringing. With the opportunity of high office in the new British colony, he argued the importance of his experience as medical officer, colonial secretary and acting Governor to Fiji. To Gordon, his paragon and mentor he said in 1886:

> The lessons I have learnt from you are I feel lessons that fit me better for administration of the particular kind required in New Guinea, than for anything else. There I could put into practice many of the principles, which I believe, are founded on a high sense of justice. In New Guinea, I might do more good or better prevent the doing of evil than a man that has had few opportunities of studying the government of native races than I have had the good luck to meet with.[21]

He also wrote to Queensland's Premier, Sir Samuel Griffith, whose friendship he made when delivering a speech on behalf of the Colonial Office at the annual meeting of the Federal Council in Hobart in 1885:

> I have thought that I might be able to carry out your policy there as well as perhaps anyone else, because I believe your views on the matter are those I consider right. If Douglas does not wish to have the permanent appointment, I shall be glad to go and assist you there.[22]

As Queensland was managing the funding of BNG, Griffith's support for MacGregor's appointment carried considerable weight. Ultimately, however, his appointment was less a reflection of the Scotsman's demonstrated ability, than the result of a passionate speech MacGregor delivered on the rights of the Papuans at that Hobart meeting. Pointing the finger implicitly at the Australian delegates he warned:

> Nothing more exasperates a coloured race [than] being dispossessed of their hereditary lands. Were that system once introduced, the consequence would be a long train of murders, reprisals and revenge, and finally the war of extermination. That system, I feel, will never with the consent of the colonies be introduced into the protectorate [, and] I am very much inclined to think that no recruiting should be allowed in New Guinea of men intended to proceed beyond that colony to work on sugar plantations.[23]

Campaigning against the use of South Sea labour on Queensland sugar plantations, Griffith unseated Sir Thomas McIlwraith in the 1883 election. Thus it is not surprising therefore that MacGregor's deep sympathy for the Papuan people impressed Griffith. Of similar age and similar social upbringings, both university-educated, sharing an interest in the humanities, particularly Latin and Italian literature, Griffith and MacGregor formed a lifelong friendship built on a mutual concern to protect indigenous people from the destructive effects of Europeans.

MacGregor had effective autonomy to run the colony. Only when Queensland's new Governor, Sir Henry Norman, arrived in Brisbane in May 1889 were his actions scrutinised more closely. His friend Samuel Griffith was no longer in office and the reinstated McIlwraith showed no interest in BNG. Even though Queensland was required to consult Victoria and New South Wales on New Guinean matters, the southern colonies appeared content to receive little more than annual reports. The Administrator was required to report to Queensland's Governor who was to keep the Queensland government and the Colonial Office informed. MacGregor claimed a lack of staff, the priority in exploration and the infrequent shipping connections between Port Moresby and Brisbane as grounds for laxity in keeping the Governor up to date. Moreover, because Governor Norman, the Queensland government and the Colonial Office often took longer than 6 months to respond to despatches, MacGregor freely utilised this independence in conjunction with his self-assurance and stubbornness.[24]

MacGregor the Explorer

MacGregor's training as a medical doctor and a scientist provided him with the qualifications to discover as much as possible about New Guinea's flora and fauna, the country's geography and its people. He also wanted to learn much about his territory in order to extend influence and authority in the process of pacification.[25] While this is an accurate description of his brief, MacGregor preferred to collect, discover and set himself challenges not hitherto achieved by others; rather than subjugate the local tribes and establish economic opportunities. Rossel Island, he noted, was botanically the richest place he had seen. He discovered a pure white orchid; found taro, yams, bananas, papaya and sugar cane across BNG, and amassed artefacts and species in flora and fauna. Baron Ferdinand von Müller of the Botanical Garden in Melbourne and C. W. de Vies of the Queensland Museum assessed and catalogued many of these plants, while museums in Australia and England displayed the artefacts he collected.

Rossel Island, on the easternmost point of the Louisiade Archipelago, was also one of the deadliest places in New Guinea, where 'a shipload of Chinamen was wrecked, and to a man—upwards of 200—killed, cooked, and eaten'. Treated in the same way as cattle, these men were 'kept in pens, and so many each week drafted out to the place of sacrifice', according to *The Brisbane Courier*.[26]

MacGregor's first north–south crossing of BNG during August and September 1896 were demanding. The ascent of Mt Knutsford (3,380 m) and then Mt Victoria (4,036 m) in June 1889, only 6 months after his arrival in the territory, was risky and the tribesmen in the region were surprised he survived. MacGregor planned the Fly River expedition and the 1896 north–south crossing meticulously; however, with a measure of justification many in the European community of Port Moresby certified the Administrator as either mad or at least irresponsible.

The 39-day expedition on the Fly River from 26 December 1889 covered about 1,200 miles (1931 km). Apart from MacGregor, the river journey on an 11 m long shallow draught steam launch with two whaleboats in tow included W. Cameron, a district Resident Magistrate (R.M.), engineer Douglas, fireman Kowland and midshipman Belford from the *Merrie England,* three Papuans and nine 'coloured men' in his party. L. D'Albertis and L. Hargrave had previously explored the river close to 840 km in 1876, and H. C Everill travelled the river for 430 km before branching off at Everill Junction to follow the Strickland River in 1885. MacGregor's party went further than both did. They travelled 130 km past D'Albertis Junction (where the Ok-Tedi meets the Fly) or more than 900 km from the mouth of the Fly. With the current proving too strong there they continued by whaleboat to where the Fly and Palmer Rivers meet. Named by MacGregor after Queensland Premier Palmer, the river was easy to navigate for some 90 km upstream. Thereafter it proved a weary ascent with boats dragged by rope more often than propelled by oars. At about 1,000 km from the mouth of the Fly, MacGregor, Cameron, two Papuans and five Fijians—the others had stayed with the steam launch—set up 'The 600-mile Camp' on the banks of the Palmer. MacGregor and four carriers continued along the Palmer for 4 days towards Mt Donaldson—named after the then Treasurer of Queensland—ascending to a point where they could see the peak of Mt Blücher on the German side, some 10 km away. They were running out of food by then and prepared for the return journey on 24 January. MacGregor believed that a thorough exploration of the mountains would take at least three months longer, and besides that, he did not feel justified in entering on such an exploration without the concurrence of the GNG government.[27]

In his report, MacGregor observed that 240 km from the mouth of the river the sounding was 12.6 m, the current 3.25 miles/hour (5.23 km/hour) and the riverbed was 180 m wide. The river flow in this area was 180,000,000,000 gallons (820 GL) in 24 hours, 'enough to supply twice the present population of the globe with 60 gallons (273 litres) a day a head', MacGregor claimed.[28]

The expedition was a great personal achievement. However, it delivered few tangible benefits. 'From an administrative point of view', MacGregor claimed, 'the information acquired is important'. From the mouth of the Fly to the Tagota village, 180 km upstream, tribes grew tobacco and vegetables.[29] With patience, this land can be brought under some control, according to MacGregor. While the party did not notice any villages from Tagota to Everill Junction, a large settled community was present at the point where the Fly meets the Strickland. 'Above that, however, they are all nomadic in their habits', with only one tribe between the D'Albertis and the Palmer junctions. This was not new information, of course. It merely confirmed what D'Albertis and Everill had found years earlier.

Cedar and other valuable woods were present below Everill Junction. 'To cut and transport timber from the higher districts of the river seems to be out of the question, because of distance' according to MacGregor. '[In any event] it was unlikely that any European would care to settle there, so long as superior inducements are offered by Australia', he reported. Like D'Albertis, MacGregor found gold. The small granules deposited in the riverbed of the Fly above D'Albertis Junction and the Palmer confirms that 'we have clearly shown there is gold there. But here too, we have no reason or ground for believing that it can be procured in payable quantity', MacGregor commented disparagingly.[30]

MacGregor's 69-day dash across New Guinea started at the mouth of the Mambare on 6 August 1896. Tamata Station, on Tamata Creek, some 5 km from its junction with the Mambare River, was the point from where the land expedition started on 11 August. MacGregor and Albert English, the government agent for the Rigo District, with 20 carriers, followed the gold prospector track to a point where the Chirima River fed into the Mambare and onwards to Simpson's 'store' on Mt Otovia. After a few days' rest at the gold-miner's shack of William Shearing (alias William Simpson), the party continued the journey with the experienced Simpson through unexplored territory to the top of Mt Scratchley (3,810 m). With that mountain-climbing ordeal behind him, MacGregor made a 22 km diversion to the southeast to ascend Mt Victoria once more. In the meantime his men had cut a track to the Gosisis and Tobiri villages at the foot of Mt Knutsford and Mt Musgrave. From there the going became easier with the journey tracking along the bank of the Vanapa River. On 13 October 1896 the party reached the mouth of the Vanapa where the *Merrie England* awaited their arrival to take them to Port Moresby.[31]

These expeditions—journeys of inspection as MacGregor called them—fulfilled the adventurer's desire to explore and conquer hitherto unknown land. They were indeed achievements that tested a man's physical and mental stamina because for the greater part MacGregor tracked through seemingly impenetrable rain forest and skirted precipitous mountainous terrain as inhospitable as any other place in the world.

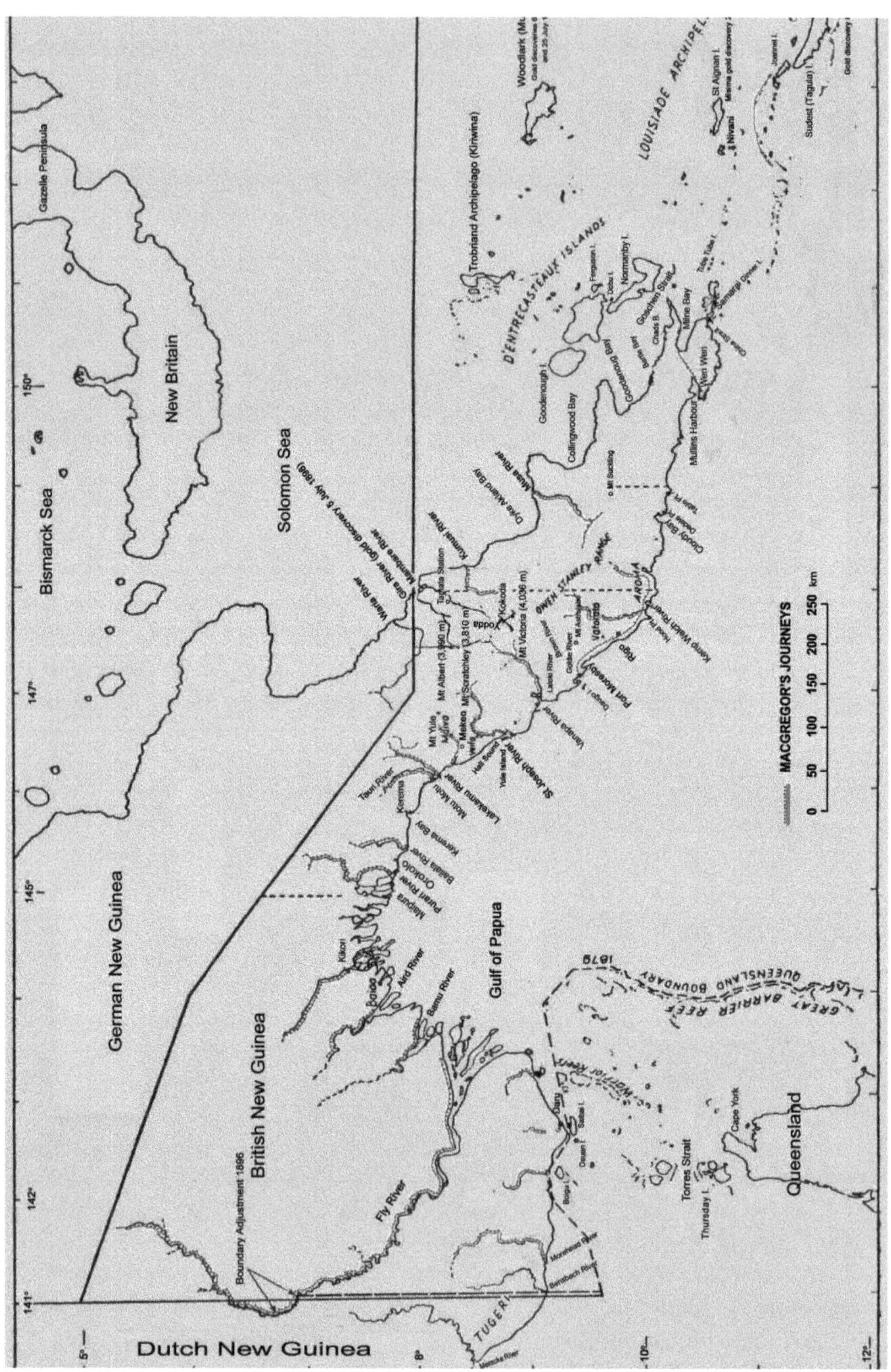

Map 14: **MacGregor's expeditions and gold discoveries** from 1888 - 1898 (Joyce, 1971 (HJ Ohff)

MacGregor viewed the expeditions as part of a pacification process: 'the people of Papua needed to meet the man who had arrived to protect them'. Scientifically, the expeditions added to the knowledge of the regions' geography and petrography. For instance, from the summit of Mt Scratchley, it became clear that the Owen Stanley Range was not a continuous ridge of mountains as shown on the charts, 'but a wide mass of ranges furrowed with deep gorges and bristling with peaks and pinnacle-like rock', containing hundreds of inaccessible crags and precipices.[32] The geological formation of this vast mountain mass was of schist and quartz where an abundance of 'the most beautiful rhododendrons were present' up to an elevation of 3,500 m, and where cypress and araucaria, one metre or more in diameter, standing 15 m tall. At higher altitude MacGregor discovered a white, sometimes pink, daisy of very 'delicate perfume of remarkable fragrance', and a 'black and yellow Bird of Paradise never seen by white men before'. The Gosisis and Tobiri men of the Owen Stanley Range, MacGregor described as the most impressive human specimens he had ever seen. They were of strong physique and bronze complexion compared to the small black people he expected in the interior.[33]

MacGregor's mapping of the northern rivers in March 1894 was the first survey by a European. He navigated the Mambare on the steam launch of the *Merrie England* upstream as far as possible and repeated the feat on the nearby Kumusi River. He explored the river systems tributaries, the Gira to the north and the Opi River to the south. Although enthralled by the northern area, which MacGregor declared 'without exception the most attractive I have seen in New Guinea', his work concentrated on tribes and population density for pacification purposes. In 1894 MacGregor regarded the provinces on the Upper Mambare as suitable plantation land. Further, in his economic assessment of the region, he pointed out the discovery of (precious) stones and large boulders of quartz, containing iron pyrite and occasionally traces of gold.[34] MacGregor returned to explore the Musa River. Where the river branched off to the north, he encountered six prospectors who revealed the discovery of gold. This, MacGregor reported on his return to Port Moresby, made the Upper Musa a fine field for the prospectors.[35]

In mid-1895 miners rushed to the Upper Mambare to wash gold on mainland New Guinea for the first time. Far from being pleased with the development, MacGregor regarded the gold miners a nuisance. In his mind they did not contribute to the economy of BNG, rather they interfered with his program of pacification.

When MacGregor returned to the region on his north–south crossing in 1896, he became involved in a major skirmish with the local people. The killing of the prospector George Clark of the Cairns Prospecting Association met a ferocious response that delivered 'thorough and complete' defeat of the recalcitrant natives.[36] It was a messy affair. Several warriors lost their lives at the hands of his native constabulary, and MacGregor saw the need to establish a government station at the Mambare–Tamata Junction to protect the miners from further attacks. Installing his secretary John Green as government agent and Assistant Magistrate (A.R.M.) for the Mambare turned out to be costly. Binandere warriors of the Orokaiva tribe attacked Tamata on 14 January 1897. Green, his servant and cook, four men of his constabulary, and three prisoners who were commandeered to build the station, were massacred by the Binandere.[37] Two weeks earlier the Orokaiva people killed two miners on the Mambare. On their way to repatriating six workers at the expiry of their indenture, John Olsen, David Davies, George Steele, Charles Fry and Alfred Haylor rafted canoes to the mouth of the Mambare River. They made it no further than Peu village, approximately 20 km from Tamata Junction. While they were setting up camp on the river bank villagers ambushed the party, clubbing Fry and his boy to death. Haylor and his boy died the following day when driven by the warriors into the river. In all during January 1897 the Binandere killed three Europeans and about 22 'natives' carriers, including prisoners and police. Luckily, the other three men (Olson, Davies and Steele), also reported missing, were found alive by the crew of the German hydrographic vessel the *Möve* in the 'Verrätherbucht' on the German side, near the mouth of the Mambare River.[38]

Despite MacGregor's ambivalent view on prospectors, the pioneering miner William Simpson rendered significant help to his expedition. By providing shelter, information on topography, and sending the explorers towards Mt Scratchley along a track he had cut, he made MacGregor's crossing much easier. Back in Port Moresby, he reported on the occasion when the indefatigable Simpson followed him to the top of Mt Scratchley and made the arduous journey back to Simpson's store, the location of his camp, the same day. Simpson appeared bemused that the Administrator, by now Lieutenant Governor, was interested in climbing mountains rather than finding gold: in the words of MacGregor, 'he did not think there was much likelihood of finding gold on the top of the mountain'. Rather, gold was more likely present in the riverbeds and foothills. 'Regarding the large area as the heart of BNG', MacGregor reported to the Queensland government, 'the country around Mt Albert Edward and the foot of the Wharton Chain deserves to be prospected [as it] undoubtedly contains not a little gold'. He finished his report on the first crossing of BNG:

> There can be no doubt that gold will now continue to be brought from the interior for many long years to come. The difficulties of getting there and back are great, but not insurmountable. For agricultural purposes the interior is useless, unless it were for growing a few vegetables for the miners.[39]

Simpson confirmed MacGregor's prediction with the gold and osmiridium specimens he took to Brisbane for analysis Thus he started the first gold rush on mainland BNG.

Administration

MacGregor's focus on exploration left little time and resources for general administration. He established a basic administrative structure but it was more reactive than proactive. He first established a bureaucracy of 12 officers, enacted seven ordinances and then almost immediately commenced his extensive and strenuous exploration of the territory. He divided the colony into Western and Eastern Division, with Mabudauan and Samarai as the respective administrative centres. In November 1889 the Central Division was created with Port Moresby proclaimed the capital of BNG. The Rigo and Mekeo districts, which already had government agents in place, became part of this division. With the influx of prospectors and miners, the Louisiades split from the Eastern Division in 1892 to become the South-Eastern Division. The Mabudauan administration moved to Daru in the Gulf of Papua to become the administrative centre for the Western Division in 1893.

The increasing number of prospectors in the Upper Mambare mandated the appointed of an agent in 1896, with the Port Moresby administration proclaiming this northern district the Northern and North-Eastern Divisions in 1898.

On legislative matters, MacGregor was obliged to seek advice from an Executive Council and obtain approval from a Legislative Council in accordance with the Letters Patent of 8 June 1888.[40] While the British and Queensland governments appointed the officers on the respective councils, MacGregor saw to the appointment of some trusted men. Of these, Francis Winter became the Administrator's principal support. Arriving in the colony within days of MacGregor, Winter assumed the position of chief judicial officer and Deputy Administrator. MacGregor also attracted A.M. Campbell from Fiji in 1896 for the position of Magistrate in the Eastern Division, which Campbell held until his promotion to government secretary in 1908. Anthony Musgrave—nephew of Queensland Governor, Sir Anthony Musgrave—had held this position since arriving in Port Moresby in 1885 despite his negative portrayal of the New Guineans. 'Most of the bad characteristics of a savage', he wrote to the Brisbane publisher Ferguson in 1890, 'are found in the Papuan. They are cowardly, selfish, thievish, untruthful, treacherous, grasping, bloodthirsty, and morbidly superstitious'. While MacGregor had doubts as to the Musgrave's suitability for public office in BNG, the Queenslander convinced the Administrator to keep him employed. Later, MacGregor even appointed Musgrave his private secretary when he became Queensland Governor in 1909.[41]

Another officer whom MacGregor took over from Douglas was Samarai R.M., Bingham Hely. The former government auditor was 'lazy and flatulent', MacGregor noted in his diary on 11 Jan. 1891. Hely remained a mainstay in his administration, though, first as R.M. in the Eastern Division then, in 1892, in the Western Division, a position he held until 1900 when he retired for health reasons.[42]

MacGregor lamented the budgetary constraints, preventing expansion of the civil service. He wanted to appoint officers to the Gulf of Papua, the Mairu, the northeast coast and on Kiriwina districts. While 'this would involve additional annual expenditures of nearly £2,000, the whole coastline for the Possession of 6798 km (3,664 miles)—3206 km on the mainland, 3592 km on the islands, would soon be completely under control', MacGregor proffered.[43]

During his 10-year tenure in BNG, a maximum of 64 permanent officers worked for the Port Moresby administration at any given time. Few of the staff had MacGregor's discipline and vigour—none fitted the description of 'iron Governor' attributed to MacGregor by J. T. Arundel. In recognising particular, MacGregor promoted 38 officers to the position of resident magistrate. Winter, Musgrave and Hely, the longest serving and most trusted officers, sat on the local Executive and Legislative Councils with Burns, Philp Port Moresby manager W. H. Gors (1892) and surgeon J. A. Blayney (1895).[44] As was the case in GNG, many officers resigned, left BNG for health reasons or died. MacGregor's persistent request for more staff, including medical professionals, remained unanswered. The administration of BNG was not a business enterprise compared to NGC in GNG, and the requests for additional personnel were not justified in the eyes of the Queensland government, which held the purse strings.

NGC employed fewer bureaucrats and legal officers. It regarded government administration, for which it was responsible until 1899, as an impost. Noticeably NGC outspent BNG in medical expenditures.

Health and quarantine regulations

The first local law dealing with health issues in BNG, The *Prison Ordinance, 1889*, stipulated food, clothing, bedding and rations, hours of work and personal cleanliness conditions. MacGregor invoked the Queensland *Health and Quarantine Act, 1886* against human diseases on several occasions. He increased quarantine measures for measles in 1893 because of an epidemic in Australia, and against smallpox in 1895, which was rampant in GNG. For the former he strengthened surveillance in Port Moresby and Samarai and gazetted his Resident Magistrates as health officers. On smallpox, he sent for vaccine to inoculate the constabulary, prisoners and local people employed by the government. A further precaution against introducing disease was the prohibition on ships entering BNG ports if they had transported Chinese coolies to or from GNG. The importation of domestic pigs into the possession exclusively from Australia and New Zealand safeguarded against rabies, trichinosis and bladder worms. The same law applied to horses, cattle, goats, and domesticated animals.[45]

In January 1895 MacGregor welcomed the part-time surgeon Dr J. A. Blayney to Port Moresby. When the Scotsman Blayney arrived from England, he found that he was also the appointed Magistrate for the Central Division and that no funds were available for building an urgently needed hospital in Port Moresby. The temporary 'hospital' was established in the local gaol and the warder's cottage of Port Moresby, supplemented by two hospital tents; and if it had not been for the efforts of the resident European community not even the most basic facilities would have been in place.[46]

The discovery of gold on the McLaughlin River, a tributary of the Mambare, in 1896 and on the nearby Gira River in 1897, demanded the presence of a resident doctor on Tamata Station to attend to the many sick and dying miners. At the time, Blayney was in Port Moresby on magistrate duties, while also dealing with a health crisis closer to Port Moresby. Some 400 ill-equipped miners had arrived in the first part of 1897. Inadequately prepared, lacking food rations, clothing and footwear, the miners tried to reach the Mambare via the Vanapa River or the steep Kapa Kapa trail, from the south coast to Kapa Kapa village at 3,130 m altitude. On either route, they had to cross the extremely rugged Owen Stanley Range, a task they found too difficult, forcing them to return to Port Moresby.[47] 'Deplorably weak they readily succumbed to fever and dysentery', according to Blayney, 10 patients died soon after they had arrived at his hospital. Of the 35 people he treated in the makeshift facilities, 10 suffered from malaria, three from diarrhoea, four had broken limbs, gunshot wounds or burns, with the rest suffering from nervous breakdowns and other ailments. The statistics on mortality (27.27%) refer only to the cases treated in this hospital: 'not having good accommodation here, and as our hospital arrangements were only temporary, as many cases as possible were forwarded to Cooktown', Blayney reported. Not included in this statistic are five Europeans who disappeared in the Owen Stanley Range and a prospector who died en route to Cooktown.

The rush to the Mambare resulted in mass casualties: at the hands of hostile tribes and because of the unforgiving terrain and climate: 'Let the madmen go', MacGregor exclaimed scathingly. 'At least the men from north Queensland, who are accustomed to similar climate, could perform some useful work by defining the location and value of the fields'. As regards medical care, he suggested for these 'lunatics' to take a bottle of sulphate and quinine pellets, Dover's powder pellets, anti-febrine tablets, anti-bilious pills, a revolver and a shotgun.[48]

Pills or not, the conditions on the goldfields remained chaotic with reports of scores of deaths continuing. Most of those who reached Tamata suffered from fever as sanitary facilities did not exist nor did they adhere to basic hygiene standards. In his account of the situation, Blayney blamed the miners for their predicament:

> Much of the sickness is brought on by the reckless mode of living unprovided with even the most ordinary medicine. They expect to be able to do the same amount of manual labour that they did in Australia. They are obliged to live on tinned meat, and often run short of stores. They drink heavily of alcoholic drinks. They use water which is polluted. The only wonder is that there has not been an epidemic of typhoid. [49]

Up to 150 European miners assisted by 600 Papuans worked the Gira (1898) and Yodda (1900) goldfields without the most basic sanitary facilities. The situation on Woodlark Island was worse still. Some 400 European miners and 1600 Papuans worked the Murua claims in 1896-97 in atrociously unhygienic conditions. Yet MacGregor did not take action or provide appropriate medical support. While, for instance, supplying 50 prisoners and the overseer and head gaoler, John Meredith, to a gold mining company for road clearing in the Sudest, he abrogated responsibility for the well-being of these men. Poor food and the lack of basic housing and medical supplies saw Meredith and a score of prisoners dead within 12 months. This was despite MacGregor's claim that the prisoners were 'in good physical condition, clean skinned, as contented as men in such circumstances could be'. The miners looked after themselves and their men. In this, they tried to improve their lot by funding a hospital at Tamata in December 1898. It closed 4 months later for lack of money and staff. In MacGregor's defence, he exceeded his annual 'Medical and Sanitary' budget of £100 by £54 in 1895-96. However, when he succeeded in having the health budget increased to £200, he surprisingly underspent the appropriation by £90.[50]

MacGregor adopted the Health Act immediately after taking office, but on the surface showed scant regard for the miners' and workers' health problems, particularly in the goldfields. The Administrator would have known annual mortality rates to be above 20%. Yet, he reported in 1889 'with the exception of that malady [Louisiade goldfields] there was little illness among them—in fact, were it not for fever, BNG would be a healthy country'. MacGregor concurred with Musgrave who had advised

Douglas earlier that no 'startling loss of life [was] discoverable' along the coast of BNG. He found the quarantine regulations at the two designated ports of entry—Port Moresby and Samarai—to be sufficient.[51]

While MacGregor never filed casualty numbers for BNG with his annual reports, the entomologist Margaret Spencer, who worked in Papua between 1953 and 1979, estimated the mortality rate among the Europeans and indigenous miners and workers at around 10% to 30% at the end of MacGregor's tenure in 1898.[52] Despite this, Spencer viewed MacGregor's achievement of establishing a public health system in BNG as impressive. The basic framework of legislation in quarantine, village hygiene, health of prisoners and labourers, and public hospitals were his main achievements in her view. Spencer cleared MacGregor from any responsibility for the disastrous mortality and morbidity rates on the goldfields. With 'such an obvious defect the answer must be not in MacGregor's failure', Spencer argued, 'but in the failure of his superiors to provide sufficient finance for such extra staff and assistance in employing them. His resources were already stretched to the limit'.[53] Whether more wardens would have made a difference to the mortality rate as Spencer suggested is doubtful. Information on sanitary requirements, checks on whether the prospectors and miners were suitably equipped and provisioned would have been as important as MacGregor's protest about the shortage of medical staff, medication and facilities.

Native Courts, the native armed constabulary and the village constable

When southeast New Guinea became a British Protectorate, the laws, acts and statutes of Queensland became the laws and ordinances of BNG. With the enactment of the *Native Affairs Ordinance, 1889*, MacGregor introduced a Native Administration Board. Comprising a minimum of two Legislative Council members and, besides the Administrator, two persons nominated by him, the ordinance considered matters bearing on or affecting the welfare of the 'natives'. A Magistrate sitting on civil and criminal cases would hear all proceedings in English, translated by the Secretary of Native Affairs into Motu, the most commonly understood Papuan language.[54]

In 1890 a duly constituted armed constabulary was established. Without police or a military force at his disposal, MacGregor required the men to perform the duties and functions of Queensland police officers. Authorised by the legislative council, a European officer started his command with 12 Solomon Islanders and two Fijian non-commissioned officers (NCOs). While the ordinance provided that the force was to consist entirely from unmarried Papuans who were of 'sound bodily constitution and between 17 and 40 years of age', the force of 50 NCOs still included 10 from the Solomon and New Hebrides Islands in 1892. It took time and training to attract suitable men to the discipline of a police force, and, initially Papuans responded the drafting for a period of up to 3 years with little enthusiasm. But regular provisions, a wage and a uniform eventually attracted 'the strongest men in the country' to the constabulary. The force expanded to about 25 men in each division by 1898.[55]

Scratchley recognised the atomistic nature of Papuan society lacked hierarchical authority through which a central administration could operate. He proposed in 1885 for the government to identify a man in every village as its agent. MacGregor took up Scratchley's suggestion. He realised that a constabulary, no matter how large their number, could not carry out police work on all points: 'it would take the whole of the funds at present provided for the expenses of the administration', he informed Governor Norman. To lessen his predicament MacGregor established a 'cheap auxiliary force' in 1890, consisting of a village policeman.[56]

On 31 December 1892 MacGregor gazetted the village constable system under 'Native Regulations'. Under the Act the Administrator appointed uniformed village constables at a rate of pay generally not exceeding £1 per year. Practicalities dictated for the R.M. to appoint a village elder to the position of village constable. MacGregor authorised the magistrates to give a ruling on village matters not covered under the native regulations. Where stealing, injuries to persons, property damage, non-burial of the dead, perjury, destruction of coconut trees or adultery was committed, the village constable could make arrests on behalf of the magistrate.[57]

At the end of MacGregor's term in BNG the police force numbered 110 Papuan men, growing to 287 under Lieutenant-Governor Hubert Murray by 1914. By then Papuans accepted police work more readily, although 'the right stamp of young, strong, and intelligent natives' remained difficult to recruit according to Murray.[58] While their main duties were the execution of orders from the courts and the protection of government officers, under Murray the constables also performed civilian tasks. In this regard, Murray viewed the pay of 10s per month in the first year, 15s in the second and £1 in the third year as too low when mail deliveries to the inland stations and plantations, wharf and bridge construction, and exploration assistance were included to their tasks. However, budget constraints prevented him from offering inducements to his police force other than words of encouragement.[59]

Unlike Albert Hahl who took MacGregor's idea of village constable a step further by introducing the *luluai* system in the Bismarck Archipelago, MacGregor did not appoint Papuan elders to adjudicate on misdemeanors committed by their indigenous brothers. Yet, the lessening of the tribal chiefs' authority was a keystone in MacGregor's policy. When retiring from BNG in 1898, MacGregor regarded the formation of the 200-strong native constabulary the finest and best institution he had established during his 10-year tenure in New Guinea.[60]

Labour laws

Increasing 'pacification' led to greater relaxation of constraints on the employment of Papuan labour. *The Natives Removal Prohibition Ordinance, 1888*, required that 'no deportation of natives be allowed, either from one part of the Possession to another, or to any place beyond the Possession, except under such conditions as may be established by order of Ourselves in Our Privy Council'. Four years later the BNG administration repealed the law in favour of the more 'development-friendly' labour ordinance. Passed by the Legislative Council on 23 May and receiving imperial assent three months later, the law was framed to free labour for the economic development of BNG. MacGregor regarded it as 'perhaps the most important legislative measure he had dealt with during 1892' because of the importance that the requirement of 'native protection' as set out in the Letters Patent of 1888 remained extant.[61]

Disastrous Ventures

Now MacGregor promoted the pressing need to mobilise local labour. 'The more the natives of one district are brought into contact with the natives of other districts', he tried to convince Queensland's Governor Norman, 'the better will they understand the protecting and pacifying power of law and Government'.[62] The salient passages of the ordinance addressed the need to provide workers to prospective planters and to assist miners. It stipulated:

Persons having bona fide residences in the Possession can only employ natives:

Natives can be engaged anywhere in the Possession provided that they are engaged before a Magistrate.

Before a Magistrate can sanction an engagement he must satisfy himself that the native is willing to enter into the contract and that he will be fairly treated and duly paid and returned to his home on the expiration of the engagement.

The period of engagement cannot exceed twelve months.

On the complaint of the employer or the employee a Magistrate may, at his discretion, cancel or vary the contract.

Residents can receive permits to let them take natives under engagement to them, entered into before a magistrate, to Cooktown or Thursday Island, on their own vessel, as boatmen, seamen or as personal attendants.

Payment of natives engaged before a magistrate must be made in the presence of the latter.

Natives can be employed within 45 km of their village for up to one month without the intervention of a Magistrate.

The Ordinance has been framed to permit the greatest freedom of contract between the employer and the native that is compatible with reasonable protection to the latter.[63]

The ordinance was applicable to workers employed by private persons or companies as distinct from the government. It was silent on pay rates, but obligated the employer to supply 'the native with food, water, medicine and shelter' until the worker is returned to his usual place of residence. The ordinance protected the employer from fulfilling his obligation if the worker deserted or left his place of employment before completing the indenture.

Under a regulation passed by the Legislative Council on 14 May 1892, government-employed labourers were entitled to a weekly portion of 10.5 lb rice, 2 lb biscuit, 4 lb meat, 2 lb sugar, 2 oz tea, 2 sticks tobacco and 0.5 lb soap. This was similar to the rations issued by NGC in GNG. When yams or other vegetables were available locally grown produce substituted rice and biscuit. This regulation was not applicable to company employees or private persons as prospectors and miners found it difficult to adhere to such conditions for logistical reasons.

To facilitate and encourage work contracts and to protect the employer from labourers abrogating their contract, MacGregor agreed to amend *The Native Labour Ordinance, 1892* in the following year. The 1893 ordinance gave government and private employers the necessary framework to employ indigenous people on contract work. Subject to the approval by an Inspector or Magistrate, private employers could now hire workers for the clearing of land, plantation work, road building or other specified scope of work on a lump sum or piecework basis. A written contract between the employer and the labourer was only required if the work took place more than

40 km from the employee's home village, the duration of the work extended over 12 months or total remuneration exceeded £5. The ordinance provided for a penalty of one-month's imprisonment and loss of wages for non-fulfilment of the employment contract. These provisions enabled the government, not the private employer, to penalise workers who failed to take up service after they had entered into a written agreement or if they deserted during the life of the agreement.[64]

Trying to develop BNG with the Papuans for the Papuans, MacGregor introduced two regulations in 1894 that he hoped would instil a greater sense of civic responsibility. In the first instance, he planned to have local people become engaged in the building and maintenance of roads. A Magistrate could direct village men to build roads or clear land for gardens. Non-compliance with an order to do the work was liable to imprisonment for a period not exceeding 7 days. Secondly, MacGregor mandated the planting of coconuts. In pacified districts the 'Magistrate for Native Matters' fixed the minimum number of coconuts that were to be planted each year by villagers. However, not even the threat of imprisonment rendered the scheme workable, and in 1898, MacGregor conceded that 'natives are not likely alone to ever add much to the exports of the colony'.[65]

Towards the end of his tenure MacGregor further reduced the restrictions on employing labour. With the implementation of the 1897 and 1898 labour laws he stated the south coast settled. Europeans could now employ Papuans without a written contract unless the work place was 100 km or more from their village. Another incentive to settlers was the clause providing for fourteen days imprisonment or loss of wages if workers were not carrying out the assigned tasks in a reasonable manner. Further, any person assisting a worker to run away was liable to punishment, with any deserter caught returned to the employer by the court.[66]

Economic development under MacGregor—land and labour

In 1889 MacGregor shifted the emphasis from the indigenous population to the European planter whom he now tried to attract to BNG. In 1888 he started from the premise that 'any plan for the systematic settlement of an agricultural population of Europeans in the country was inadmissible'. He believed that 'it was highly improbable that people of European descent could ever perform continuous manual labour in the field in New Guinea'.[67] He also argued that the Papuans occupied the best agricultural land and that so far 'no district has been found in the Possession in which any systematic plan for the settlement of Europeans could be carried out'. So MacGregor now started to pave the way for '*bona fide* settlers' to come to BNG to set up tobacco, tea, coffee, vanilla, banana, fibres or coconut plantations, 'as they would find good local labour, and soil and climate suited to any branch they took up'. MacGregor had brought Queensland's *Real Property Act* into force in 1889. The act provided the authority to grant settlers freehold title to land acquired by the Crown and register the ownership of real property in BNG.[68]

Twelve months later Port Moresby implemented a major departure from the 1888 land law to attract European settlers. 'There is no doubt', MacGregor now claimed, 'areas of good land of a few hundred acres each are procurable at very many places in the Possession, suitable almost for any form of tropical cultivation'.[69] Part one of the *Crown Lands Ordinance, 1890* regulated the settlement of land claims dating from before the declaration of sovereignty on 6 November 1888. Part two directed the process of land acquisition and the recording of the transactions. Explicitly, the Crown only took 'waste and vacant' land not required by the Papuans. Where the local people could establish ownership at a later stage, the law provided for it to return the land to them. Subject to this caveat, the Administrator was authorised to sell the land in fee simple to missions, for building allotments or agricultural purposes. Part four of the ordinance set out the payments and conditions for Crown land. While missions could acquire land in trust, the Crown sold town allotments by private bargain or by public auction subject to an improvement order. Where no obligations for carrying out improvements existed, Port Moresby offered agricultural land at 10 shillings per acre—5s/ac for coconut plantation land and 2s/ac for grazing lands. Settlers and companies acquiring plots for trading or fishing purposes paid £5 per acre. The Port Moresby administration also offered freehold land of up to 50 acres on 5-year deferred payment terms at a price of not less than £1 per acre.

Part five of the ordinance stipulated the lease of agricultural land for up to 25 years at one shilling per acre. For leased land with an enforceable improvement condition, a rent-free period of 3 years was applicable; thereafter the minimum rent was 6d/ac with an option to purchase the land during the leasehold. Interested parties leased coconut plantation land rent-free for the first five years provided the lessee planted 25% of the land with coconuts during this period. Irrespective of further planting, a charge of not less than 6d/ac was applicable for the following 5 years, and 1s/ac for the remainder of a 60-year lease.[70]

The 1891 ordinance invited white settlement to the exclusion of large enterprises. MacGregor sought to sell only small parcels of Crown land to European purchasers; he remained steadfastly opposed to inviting big business into BNG. Moreover, the executive council's long-winded dealings on claims predating the 1884 annexation delayed the registration of new land purchases. The Administrator-in-council accepted one small claim in February 1891, and took until 1898 before recognising 2,645 ac as bona fide transactions by Europeans prior to annexation.[71] Port Moresby rejected outright an application for 10,890 ac and 5 other claims because the council considered them 'so extensive that each of them would have covered the lands of several native tribes'. Torn between development and the protection of the indigenous population, MacGregor was keen not to have his fledging control over Papuans damaged by powerful companies who could easily become an *imperium in imperio*.[72]

Few, if any, settlers followed MacGregor's invitation to make the costly journey to BNG. The Australian land boom of the 1880s had come to a crushing halt. It gave way in 1891 to economic depression, creating high unemployment and ruining many businesses; it also amplified the popularity of the 'White Australia Policy'. While Chinese, or for that matter any Asian immigration, was not an option for MacGregor on racial grounds alone, the 1890s depression also prevented the entrepreneurial European settler making the move to an unexplored country where the government could repossess land if the local people could establish retrospective ownership. In 1891 MacGregor stated that he had received land applications for several thousand acres which he could not entertain because the granting of such applications would interfere with the native tribes. While maintaining 'the agricultural settler who is prepared to turn the land to use is the only land purchaser for whom there is any opening,' his 1891 annual report cautioned 'unfortunately that class of man is difficult to obtain, although every possible facility would be offered to him'.[73]

MacGregor had become so alarmed at the lack of settlers coming to BNG that he had a *Handbook for Intending Settlers in British New Guinea* published by the Queensland government. 'What is wanted,' MacGregor wrote in 1892, is 'the practical European settler, with a good head, strong arms, some capital, and sufficient expertise in tropical agriculture'. It was to no avail.[74] The planters did not come, leaving the administration to establish government coconut plantations. The government acquired Tauko (Fisherman Island) near Port Moresby as early as 1889 to establish an 80-acre government coconut plantation.[75] Subsequent land acquisitions at Tauko, 50 acres near Rigo Station in the Kapa Kapa district, the 46 acre Nivani Station on Samarai Island, 8 acres on Geisila Island near Samarai and 10 acres on Wagatutma Bay opposite Samarai, all became Port Moresby initiatives for coconut plantations. MacGregor started botanical gardens on some of the Stations to experiment with local and exotic plants: He procured coffee seeds from the Royal Botanic Gardens in Kew and other economic plants from the tropical garden in Rockhampton, Queensland. By 1891 some 15,000 coconuts had been planted. 'If successful', MacGregor reported, 'these plantations cannot but be an important item of revenue in half-a-score of years [leading to] the changes that will be found necessary to the full development of the coconut industry in BNG'.[76]

Initially MacGregor attached little importance to generating revenue. Rather, BNG's first Administrator frugally balanced annual outlays with the £15,000 annual funding, while complaining that he could not administer BNG on a shoestring budget. Once he had moved from establishing the authority of the government over wide areas of BNG, he became frustrated with the system of not attracting settlers. 'The establishment of some degree of supremacy on the part of the Government', he wrote in 1897, 'was preliminary essential to acquiring any extensive and exact knowledge of the physical nature and capability of the country'. When only a handful of settlers turned up he lamented, 'the most discouraging element in the administration of the Possession is the fact that no European planting on a scale of any importance has been started'. By June 1898 the Port Moresby had purchased or taken possession of land totalling 332,452 acres, private purchasers acquired only 6,572 acres. This included 2,645 acres attained by Europeans prior to 1888.[77]

After the miners, the teachers of the Christian missions were the largest group of white settlers. The missions had acquired 1,236 acres in 139 parcels for religious and agricultural applications to become self-sufficient in food production. The evangelists were also not averse to entering the commercial world of trading in copra and trepang for a profit. MacGregor encouraged this. He envisaged that the widely dispersed missions would supply the local people with seeds and encourage them to plant gardens of economic size.[78] The missions were indeed successful in horticultural education; but most of their agricultural land was less than 10 acres and was not of significant commercial scale. While some expansion of plantations, such as Arabica coffee on the Ravao mission and a coconut plantation on Yule Island took place,[79] it was sporadic and had no bearing on the overall development of BNG. Compared with the industrious undertakings of the Catholic and Lutheran missions in GNG, economically, the missions in BNG performed poorly.[80]

Private persons had taken up 27 blocks (109 ac) for residential and business use and 4 blocks for trading stations by 1898. Only three parcels of land were acquired for pastoral (1,366 ac) 11 for agricultural (2,986 ac) and 6 for plantations (874 ac) use. Rather than persuading Bevan to return to BNG and put to good use his experience, MacGregor favoured his principal surveyor, John Cameron, with 2,145 acres in the Kabadi district. Situated in the estuary of the Laloki, Vanapa and Brown Rivers, it was one of the most fertile lands in BNG. A year later Cameron acquired land at Cloudy Bay situated southeast of Port Moresby. Departing from 'the strict rules of the civil service', MacGregor saw no conflict of interest in favouring Cameron. The government surveyor was not on the 'civil list of officers' and, therefore, was not a public servant. Cameron never developed the land in any event. He died in 1898, his holdings taken up some 10 years later by an investor. A conflict of interest became obvious when in February 1894 the government agent for Rigo, A. C. English—who joined MacGregor in 1896 for the north-south crossing—took up five 10-ac parcels near the government nursery, 65 km southeast of Port Moresby. He planted *ficus rigo* next to existing native rubber, bringing the inventory to 12,000 trees in 1901. It became a valuable business for English with returns of £855 in 1900-01 growing to over £1,000 in the following years. About the time MacGregor left BNG in September 1898, he granted the collector of customs, David Ballantine, 100 ac of land in the Sorgi district, some 50 km inland from Port Moresby. The precursor to this transaction was Ballantine's expedition 'to induce the Hagari tribe to submit to the Government'. This month-long mission into the Sorgi hinterland was hardly successful, and neither was the coffee plantation Ballantine grew on the granted land. An outbreak of 'hemeleia vastatrix' or coffee rust followed the drought of 1902.[81]

When Andrew Goldie wanted to sell up, James Burns (BP) acquired the assets to open the trader's first branch in New Guinea in 1891. Walter Gors moved from the company's Thursday Island branch to manage Goldie's old store in Port Moresby. Within a short time Gors developed BP's BNG arm into a thriving business, buying and selling anything for a profit. With the opening of a second branch, also in 1891, BP became the supplier and shipper for the traders, miners and the government. Like NGC in GNG, the company issued its own bank notes (£1 and £5) which it accepted in any of its stores and branches, including Australia. In January 1893 MacGregor awarded BP a four year contract for an 8 weekly mail service from Cooktown to Port Moresby. The payment of £150 for each voyage enabled the company to expand a service to Yule Island, Samarai and the Louisiade goldfields. BP commenced with the construction of a jetty and warehouse at Port Moresby in 1891. The work, completed in 1895, included a 200-metre long tramline and rail carts.[82] Separate from BP, Gors acquired a grant from the government over 440 ac at Dedele on Cloudy Bay where he and his partner, Thomas Andersen, started a coconut plantation.

With the expansion of BP MacGregor commenced a large landfill project in Samarai in 1893. Faced with the alternative of moving the expanding town to another island or reclaim 9.5ac of swamp, MacGregor opted for the latter. A loan from the Queensland government for a light-rail-system and the employment of prison labour started the project. By June 1894 over 42,000 cubic yards of rock material had been placed. But because of the costly blasting required to procure the material, Port Moresby held over the remaining work of 13,000 cubic yards until 1897.[83] Also in 1893, MacGregor opened up the Gulf area by declaring Daru a BNG entry port. The transfer of cargo across the shallow water around Daru Island required the construction of a 174 m stone causeway and a 143 m pier at Daru port. Prison and local labour started this backbreaking work in 1897. The British New Guinea Trading Company completed the work 20 years later in 1917, with the construction of a tramway from the wharf to its warehouses and government stores.[84]

While the government was busy with the Samarai and Daru projects, BP built a slipway and its own wharf and store on Dinner (Samarai) Island. However, despite the mail steamer subsidy and land grants, the company would not book a profit at its Samarai branch until 1896-97. This stood in stark contrast with Port Moresby, where the sale of merchandise and the sandalwood operations contributed to BP's profits of £7,085 in the first financial year of operations BNG.

In 1896 Burns applied for 240 ac at Warirata on the Taluri Tableland at the northern end of the Astrolabe Range. The selected area on the Laloki River, 600 m above sea level, became particularly useful as a weekend sanatorium for staff and clients. Walter Gors wanted to demonstrate the suitability of the high country for coffee and cacao, which BP approved, provided Gors devote his energy and loyalty entirely to the firm and did not become involved in further private developments. [85]

The development of a BNG economy was so badly needed that MacGregor weighed up not returning to Port Moresby after taking leave in 1894. He lamented the glut of traders and collectors and the absence of producers when delivering a paper on BNG's economy to the Manchester Geographical Society. 'What is wanted in the Possession' he told his British audience,' is the man who will raise new products, or extend the range of those already existing. To facilitate this', he argued, 'the labour law has been made as little onerous as possible'.[86] The policy of attracting the small settler had failed and Papuans were neither able nor willing to contribute to the BNG's economy. MacGregor now looked for men of metropolitan influence and money to provide the turnaround he sought for his Protectorate.

Promoted on 13 March 1895 to the position of Lieutenant Governor, MacGregor started his second term in BNG with renewed vigour. Casting aside his fear that 'high finance' could undermine the authority of his office, he now felt comfortable holding discussions with 'the head of a great firm established in Sydney', the Colonial Sugar

Refining Company. His idea was to attract a sugar cane plantation industry to BNG based on the Fijian model.[87]

When these discussions proved fruitless, MacGregor was relieved to find Henry Alexander Wickham, of Para Rubber fame, take up land in BNG in 1895.[88] Wickham's sugar and coffee plantations in Queensland proved not viable and, now 50 years old, he ventured to BNG to investigate the native rubber trees for latex contents and quality. However, rather than investing in rubber he decided on large-scale coconut planting on Panasea Island near Samarai.[89] By 1906 Wickham's plantations generated 100 tons of copra annually from some 10,000 trees. Demonstrating his entrepreneurial skills, Wickham employed the local people to dive for trepang, shells and pearls. Taking a leaf out of William Saville-Kent's book, who began collecting live pearl oysters from Torres Strait in the late 1890s for pearl cultivation, Wickham brought a pearler to Panasea to investigate the culturing of pearl oysters there. Apart from his plantation, fishing and pearling interests Wickham advised the British New Guinea Development Company of London on the investment opportunities in BNG in Para rubber and coconut palms during the 1909–11 caoutchouc boom. Wickham sold his Conflict Islands Company in 1911 but retained his interest in BNG.

MacGregor's hopes also rested with John Lowles. This British parliamentarian who approached Queensland's Premier, Nelson, on behalf of Sir Somers Vine and Sir Charles Kennedy during Nelson's visit to London in 1896 to seek their views on the establishment of a large-scale rubber plantation in BNG. Nelson, enthusiastic about more rapid economic development in BNG, referred the matter to MacGregor.

After approving discussions with the Lieutenant-Governor an agreement acceptable to Vine, Kennedy and MacGregor was drafted. The newly formed British New Guinea Syndicate was to receive a land grant of 250,000 ac at 2s/ac payable over 8 years, conditional on specific improvements. MacGregor agreed to enact an ordinance that would make it easier to engage Papuan labour and permit the recruitment of indentured workers from India and the Pacific Islands. While the indenture of Chinese coolies remained banned in the 1898 Ordinance MacGregor submitted to the Queensland and British governments for approval, it gave the syndicate wide-ranging privileges.[90] Lord Lamington agreed, and forwarded it to the Colonial Office for assent. MacGregor and the Queensland Governor expected unqualified approvals from the Queensland, New South Wales and Victorian because the scheme lessened the demand on the Australian colonies for funding. However, while the Britain only asked for clarification before it would agree, the Premiers voiced their opposition to the scheme for not being consulted beforehand. *The Age* reminding its readers:

> Ever since British control had been established over part of New Guinea Australian enterprises in this direction had been severely discouraged if not absolutely blocked. [Now] we learn that the syndicate negotiator has met with amazing success in his dealings with the Administrator….The agreement completed between the representative of the British syndicate and the Administrator cannot fail to astonish and excite resentment, especially in the Australian colonies, which pay handsomely for the retention and the government of Southern New Guinea as a British possession…. The general Administrator makes his annual report in return for the £15,000 a year; but beyond that he stands aloof from Australia as if he were a denizen of some frozen island off the Siberian coast.[91]

Bevan could have written the vitriolic piece. He reminded Premier Turner that he, the veteran explorer, was denied the privilege of acquiring land in BNG when he intended setting up a major plantation industry there.[92] The free trader, Premier Reid of New South Wales, joined his Victorian counterpart in opposing the scheme. Turner told his Parliament on 29 June 1898: 'if we had the opportunities of fully investigating and discussing it, we might have come to the conclusion that some modified scheme would be advantageous to New Guinea. [Now] I am determined to do all I can to prevent this proposal being carried out'.[93]

Premier Byrnes, who had replaced Nelson in April 1898, was just as contrary. He argued that the syndicate was a danger to the Queensland sugar cane growers and to Australian interests. Byrnes would have paid attention to Burns' past intentions of 'reserving' plantation land for BP's expansionary plans in BNG. He would have been equally concerned if BNG had been 'dominated by a powerful British corporation'. Strong public sentiments, inflamed by a hostile press, generated fear of the influence of British capital in BNG. That the agitation made little sense since British capital all but controlled Australian commerce was ignored by the editors of the newspapers. Apart from missing the opportunity of transferring some of the development costs, the failure to implement the agreement cost the contributing colonies £5,000 in damages that the British New Guinea Syndicate claimed.

After Byrnes requested Nelson and Lamington to visit BNG in late 1898 and investigate investment opportunities, the eminent politicians filed a pejorative report. None of the lands they inspected on their 10-week tour were in their view suitable for small investors. 'While the most fertile land was along the banks of the rivers and was, therefore, suitable for agriculture, pioneers must make up their minds to have a very rough time for some years after starting operations', the report read. Further, Nelson pointed out:

> Without wishing to draw unfavourable comparisons, I may state that no lands came under my observation suitable for settlement in small areas; nor can any of them…compare with the lands on the Herbert, the Johnston, the Daintree, and other rivers in the tropical Queensland. If [this] country is to be developed it can only be accomplished by companies or individuals having command of large amounts of capital. [But] nothing came under my observation that would lead me to believe that the inducements to settlers on the Territory are sufficiently strong to attract farmers or others from Queensland or the other Australian colonies, where in addition to a healthy climate they enjoy all the advantages of civilisation—schools, police, protection, railways, post and telegraph services. [All] of which are yet unknown in the Possession.[94]

Sir William MacGregor conceded: 'at the present moment agricultural development is practically at a standstill on political considerations', his last annual report from Port Moresby read. In the *Sydney Morning Herald* on 31 October he accepted:

> There is very little settlement by Europeans in BNG for the reason that it is not a possible place for ordinary comfortable habitation. Australian hopes that the possession will soon become self-supporting, but without agricultural development that hope will not be realised. The country is admirably adapted for the production of tropical commercial vegetation. [It] only awaits the organising capacity of the European to grow lush in the admirable surroundings.[95]

Before leaving in September 1898 for Lagos, MacGregor expressed the hope that the mining industry may provide the profits to run BNG. For this to happen, he argued, 'further encouragement to prospectors to examine new districts' was needed.[96] Yet during his long term in office, he did not enunciate the administrative support, the infrastructure and the policies required in order to attract the desired prospectors. The employment and land laws were no longer impediments to investments. What the miners needed was better access to the interior, better security from attacks by the tribes, the abolition of import duties and a basic health system.

Hans Blum and many of his colleagues in GNG envied the achievements of MacGregor while NGC impressed British and Australian capital with its progress in GNG. The truth was that both colonies struggled to find their feet economically. Spending and wasting enormous funds, the Germans had at least gained the experience on what did not work for them in GNG while at the same time establishing infrastructure for future agricultural development. The future for BNG was more uncertain. The three Australian colonies were unwilling to fund BNG after their 10-year commitment expired in 1898. Notwithstanding this they strongly objected to British or foreign capital obtaining a foothold in BNG. Worse still, the colonies were incapable of agreeing to a large capital investment by BP. It was petty jealousy where New South Wales and Victoria were not prepared to provide Queensland with an economic advantage in BNG. As for Britain, she was not interested in New Guinea unless development could supply the revenue necessary to support its administration.

MacGregor deluded his supporters when claiming he had always been in support of European development. *The Brisbane Courier,* an enthusiastic supporter of MacGregor's achievements, lauds the Lieutenant-Governor's accomplishments as an explorer and pacifier, who 'implanted in the native mind some of the elementary ideas of civilisation, [teaching] the tribes to fear, respect, and trust the British Government'. However, the paper continued, 'Sir William MacGregor has not been anxious to precipitate settlement or the development of the natural resources. [Thus] it may be in his successor's time that we hear much more about New Guinea'. That is when the 'long hidden wealth of the island may yield itself to the daring search and intelligent methods of the British settler'.[97]

Notes

1   T. F. Bevan, 'The Gold Rush to British New Guinea', *The Royal Geographical Society of Australasia,* 1896–97, XV, pp. 18–23. T.F. Bevan, *Toil, Travel and Discovery in British New Guinea,* pp. 272 & 283ff. See also *Brisbane Courier (=BC),* (1888) 10 Mar., p. 4.

2   *Sydney Morning Herald (SMH);* 'German New Guinea', (1907) 14 Mar. p. 6.

3   '*Dem klaren einheitlichen Verwaltungsbild des Britisch-Neu-Guinea-Government, dem sein Schöpfer mit sicherer Hand und künstlerischen Blicks erst den treffenden Grundton gab, bevor er an die Zeichnung der Linie ging, deren Formen und Farben in stetem Fortschritt täglich bestimmter sich prägten, hängt an der östlichen Wand ein Gemälde gegenüber, das, um nicht härtere Worte zu gebrauchen, nicht einmal einem Dilettanten Ehre machen würde'* (H. Blum, *Neu Guinea,* p. 41).

4   Bevan, *Toil, Travel and Discovery,* pp. 4–6, 9, 11& 13

5   Instruction §3, R. Herbert to Scratchley (BPP, C–4273, p. 29). Legal opinion sought by Scratchley from Premier Griffith, 15 May 1885, enclosed in despatch to Derby, 28 May 1885; 'Sir Peter Scratchley: Correspondence and Notes' (NLA MS 1914–17, no. 761444); Great Britain: Special Commissioner for British New Guinea (Reports 1886–88, p. 5); J.D. Legge, *Australian Colonial Policy,* p. 33.

6 Herbert to Scratchley (BPP, C–4273, pp. 29 & 30). *The British Australasian (=BA)* (1884) 18 Oct.; *BC* (1885) 10 Jan., p. 6. Scratchley to Romilly, 14 April 1885; Scratchley to Derby, 8 May 1885. G.S. Fort, 'British New Guinea, notes by Sir Peter Scratchley'; see Legge, pp. 32–3, 37 & 92.

7 *SMH* (1884) 15 Nov., p. 9

8 Instructions §5, Herbert to Scratchley (BPP, C–4273, p. 29).

9 Premier Service to Colonial Office, *The Mercury* Hobart *(=MH)* (1885), 16 Feb., pp. 2–3.

10 AR-BNG (1888-89) p. 24.

11 Douglas to Derby, 26 April 1886; *BC,* (1886), 28 July, p. 6 and 8 Nov., p. 5.

12 The SS *Merrie England,* built in 1883, arrived at Port Moresby on 12 May 1889. The book value amounted to £15,121, leaving an unexpended balance of £3,879 (AR-BNG (1888-89) p. 20. The maintenance grant increased to £5,000 p.a. (AR-BNG [1889-90] pp. 20–1; [1890-91] p. xxiv; [1891-92] p. xxx). In 1893-94 (AR-BNG, p. xxv) the grant reduced to £4,000, in 1894-95 (AR-BNG p. xxiii) to £3,500, in 1895-96 (AR-BNG p. xxxii) and in 1896-97 (AR-BNG p. xxiv) to £3,000. The grant ran out in Sep. 1897. The annual expenditure of approximately £7,000 was now borne fully by the guaranteeing colonies (AR-BNG [1897-98] p. xxxvi and [1898-99] p. xxvii).

13 *British Government Gazette Extraordinary,* 4 Sep. 1888.

14 C.Wilkerson, 'Report on Auriferous and other Specimens from NG', AR-BNG (1888-89) p. 56

15 Bevan, pp. 133,135, 152; 185–86 & 260.

16 AR-BNG (1891-92) pp. 60–1; *TQ* (1887) 31 Dec., p. 1052; *SMH,* 'Exploration in New Guinea', *(1887)*

17 *SDT,* (1887) 9 July; *BC* (1887) 25 July, pp. 6–7. *SMH* (1888) 19 April, p. 12, Douglas to Bevan, 17 Mar. 1888, AR-BNG (1888) p. 9); Bevan, pp. 147–9.

18 AR-BNG (1888-89) p. 54.

19 Legge, p. 37.

20 W. MacGregor (1846–1919) studied medicine at the Universities of Aberdeen and Edinburgh. After internship at the Aberdeen Royal Lunatic Asylum in 1872 he joined the colonial service as assistant medical officer in the Seychelles and then as surgeon in Mauritius. After 10 years in BNG, MacGregor accepted postings in Lagos (1899), Newfoundland (1904) and Queensland (1909). MacGregor became the first chancellor of the University of Queensland in March 1910. During World War I MacGregor worked in the Colonial Office on Pacific issues (R.B. Joyce *Sir William MacGregor*).

21 MacGregor to Gordon, 5 June 1886, vol. 5 Stanmore Papers (NLA, Mfm 1628–37).

22 MacGregor to Griffith, 28 May 1886 (Griffith Papers, Mitchell Library, CY 2379 MLMSS 363-5x).

23 Quoted in R.B. Joyce, 'William MacGregor: The Role of the Individual', p. 35.

24 R.B. Joyce, *Sir William MacGregor,* pp. 109–19; Legge, pp. 54–7. 'First Annual Report of the Administrator', *BC,* (1890)19 April, pp. 5–6.

25 Joyce, p. 126

26 'Tribal Fights and Cannibal Feasts at Rossel Island', *BC* (1894) 26 Mar., p. 6.

27 Imperial measurements in the original text are metricised in this book.

28 MacGregor 'The Explorer', *The Queenslander (=TQ)* (1892) 30 Apr., pp. 842–3; 10 Sep., p. 506. AR-BNG (1889-90) pp. 49-64; (1890-91) pp. 93–100; (1891-92) pp. 102–09; (1893-94) pp. 89ff; (1895-96) pp. 91–2; (1896-97) pp. 81–93; (1897-98) pp. 130, 147–50. *SMH,* (1896), 8 Apr., p. 3.

29 *TQ* (1891) 3 Jan., p. 12.

30 AR-BNG (1889-90) pp. 49; 58–63.

31 AR-BNG (1896-97) pp. xii, xiii and 4–14; see J.H.P Murray, *Papua or British New Guinea,* pp. 291–6.

32 AR-BNG (1891-92) p. 57; 'Expedition to the Owen Stanley Range', *SA Register* (1889) 15 July, p. 5.

33 AR-BNG (1896-97) pp. xiii, 8ff. *SMH,* (1896) 29 Oct., p. 5; *BC* (1896) 31 Oct. p. 4.

34 AR-BNG (1893-94) pp. xvii & 30–7.

35 AR-BNG (1895-96) p. 25.

36 H. Nelson, *Black, White & Gold,* p. 97, *The West Australian (=WA)* (1885), 9 Sep. p. 4.

37 Joyce, *Sir William MacGregor,* p. 208; L. Lett, *Papuan Gold,* pp. 46–60; C.A.W. Monckton, *Some Experience of a New Guinea Resident Magistrate,* p. 193; AR-BNG (1896-97) p. xxvi & pp. 27–8.

38 'The Mambare Massacre', *BC* (1897) 11 Mar., p. 5; *NKWL* (1897) p. 57. Nelson, pp. 110–11.

39   AR-BNG (1896-97) pp. 10–11 &14

40   Letters Patent, clauses viii and ix.

41   AR-Papua, (1907-08) p. 45, Joyce, p. 152.

42   Joyce, p. 152. AR-BNG, (1891-92) p. xxiv; AR-Papua (1900-01) p. xli

43   AR-BNG (1891-92) p. xxiv

44   AR-BNG, (1894-95) p. xix. (Minutes of the Legislative Council 1888–1909, CO 436-2).

45   AR-BNG (1889-90) p. 5, (1894-95) pp. xxvi; M. Spencer, *Public Health in Papua New Guinea1870–1939*,
      p. 53 & 58. 'Smallpox in GNG', *SMH* (1895), 19 Feb., p. 5; *WA* (1896), 17 Jun., p. 5

46   AR-BNG (1896-97) p. 73

47   Nelson, pp. 114–15 (The Kapa Kapa trial runs 50 km to the southeast of the Kokoda track)

48   AR-BNG (1896-97) pp. 52, 74 & 114. Spencer, p. 62

49   AR-BNG (1898-99) p. 92

50   AR-BNG (1895-96) p. 98; (1896-97) pp. xxvi, 94; (1897-98) p. 125; *Western Mail* (1896) Jun. 17, p. 5.

51   AR-BNG (1888-89) pp. 7 & 25–6; (1890-91) p. xiv, (1891-92) pp. xxiv & 31–3. Chart 10

52   These are estimates. Mortality statistics for BNG appeared for the first time in 1902-03

53   Spencer, p. 63

54   Ordinance No. VI of 1889, AR-BNG (1889-90) p. 5). AR-BNG (1889-90) pp. 5–6. AR-BNG (1892-93) p.
      vii). See Joyce, pp. 182–95

55   AR-BNG (1897-98) p. xxv; (1898-99) p. 6

56   Legge, p. 64

57   AR-BNG (1892-93) pp. vi–vii; (1897-98) p. xxvi. See chapter 11, luluai system in GNG.

58   AR-Papua (1913-14) pp. 104–5.

59   ibid. J.H.P. Murray, *The Scientific Aspect of the Pacification of Papua*, pp. 1–18

60   J.H.P. Murray, *Papua or British New Guinea*, p. 27

61   AR-BNG (1891-92) p. vii

62   AR-BNG (1891-92), p. viii; 'Progress of the Natives and Native Labour', *BC* (1891) 17 Oct., p. 5

63   AR-BNG (1891-92) p. viii

64   AR-BNG (1893-94) p. v

65   AR-BNG (1897-98) p. xliii; Regulation No. I & 2 of 1894 (AR-BNG [1893-84] p. vii)

66   Ordinances Nos. II and VIII of 1897 and Ordinance No. II of 1898 (AR-BNG [1897-98] p. vi).

67   AR-BNG (1890-91) p. xxii.

68   AR-BNG (1889-90) p. 20; Ordinance No VIII 23 Nov. 1889 (AR-BNG [1889-90] pp. 6 and 20)

69   AR-BNG (1890-91) p. xxii

70   Ordinance No VII 15 Nov. 1890 (AR-BNG [1890-91] pp. v & vi)

71   AR-BNG (1897-98) p. xli

72   AR-BNG (1890-91) p. xxii; see Joyce, p. 210; Legge, p. 91

73   AR-BNG (1890-91) p. xxii. *Morning Bulletin* (Rockhampton, 1891) 29 Dec., p. 4; 'The Administrator's
      Yearly Report', *BC,* (1891) 30 Dec., p. 6; 'McGregor on New Guinea', *WA* (1892) 27 Jan., p. 6

74   *Handbook of Information for Intending Settlers in BNG. WA* (1893) 3 Jan., p. 4

75   AR-BNG (1889-90) p. 15

76   AR-BNG (1890-91) p. xviii; (1893-94) p. xxiii; (1895-96) p. xxix; (1896-97) p. xvi; (1906-07) p. 91.

77   AR-BNG (1895-96) pp. xxxiii, 127–8. Government land survey in AR-BNG (1896-97) pp. 71–2

78   AR-BNG (1893-94) p. 43

79   D.C Lewis, *The Plantation Dream*, p. 29

80   P. Steffen, 'Die katholischen Missionen in Deutsch-Neuguinea' and R. Pech, 'Deutsche evangelische
      Missionen in Deutsch-Neuguinea 1886–1921' in H.J. Hiery, ed., *Die Deutsche Südsee*, pp. 343–414.

81   AR-BNG (1897-98) pp. xli & 127-8. (1898-99) pp. xv–xvi, (1902-03) p. 17. 'Report of the Royal Commission
      of Enquiry into the Present Conditions of the Territory of Papua' (1906) pp. xvi–xviii.

82   Buckley & Klugman, pp. 56–7

83   AR-BNG (1893-94) pp. xxiii and 70–1; Station Journals, Patrol Reports from Out-Stations of British New Guinea (1890–1906) NAA Series A1 and G91–CA1419

84   AR-BNG (1995-96) pp. Xi & 67; (1897-98) pp. xxiv–v; Station Journals, (1890–1906) NAA Series A1 & G91–CA1419; see R.F McKillop, & M.R Pearson, *End of the Line: A History of Railways in Papua New Guinea.*

85   Buckley & Klugman, pp.88–9 & 95

86   *Manchester Geographical Society*, x, p. 284

87   MacGregor to Lamington, 4 Oct. 1898 (CO 422/12)

88   H.A. Wickham (1846–1928) collected some 70,000 *Hevea brasiliensis* seeds during 1876 in the Manaus region of the Amazon for the Kew Botanic Gardens. Dissemination of the seeds to Sri Lanka, India and Malaya and the Dutch East Indies helped create the rubber plantations of South East Asia and India. The superior quality of the cultivated seeds led to the collapse of the Amazon rubber boom that carried large sections of the Brazilian economy until 1912. In the early 1890s Wickham's went to North Queensland to plant coffee and sugar cane. The ventures were unsuccessful. H.A. Wickham, *On the Plantation, Cultivation and Curing of Para Indian Rubber.*

89   'Report of the Royal Commission into British New Guinea, 1907', p. xvi

90   AR-BNG (1897-98) pp. vi & 56

91   *The Age* (1898) 10 May and *BC* (1898) 17 May, p. 6

92   Bevan in the *Melbourne Age (=A)* (1898), 21 May; see Joyce, p. 407, fn.16

93   VPD, LC, vol. 88, p. 36

94   AR-BNG (1897-98) pp. 56–68 & 131–2; see Joyce, pp. 125, VPD, LC, vol. 88, p. 36; Legge, p. 96

95   *SMH* (1898) 31 Oct., p. 5; AR-BNG (1897-98) p. xliii

96   AR-BNG (1897-98), p. xliv

97   *BC* (1897) 21 Dec. p. 4. Joyce, p. 213

Expedition preparing for an excursion in the Owen Stanley Range, Port Moresby, ca. 1885 (University of Wollongong Archives, collection D160480)

The first Legislative Council of The Territory of Papua, ca. 1906, Head—Administrator, Capt. F. R. Barton, Left—Chief Judicial Officer, J. H. P. Murray, Resident Magistrate North-Eastern Division and Mambare District, C. A. W. Monckton, miner F. Weekley, Right —Treasurer, D. Ballantine, Resident Magistrate Eastern Division, A. J. Campbell, W. Whitten of Whitten Bros., prospector W. Little (J. A. K. Mackay, *Across Papua*, p. 182)

THE FIRST GRANDCHILD OF THE BRITISH EMPIRE

13

The BNG administration under MacGregor opposed economic settlement of any kind until 1890. It then tried to attract the small tropical planter and, that policy having failed, large firms. Despite generous offers of land and labour conditions, these attempts failed because the Australian colonies quarrelled among themselves and with the Colonial Office in London about the potential investors. More importantly, Australia suffered an unprecedented and prolonged financial depression throughout most of the 1890s. Triggered by the collapse of a speculative boom in Melbourne suburban land and house prices, the economy plummeted 17% across all the Australian colonies, with prices falling in real terms by 22% from 1890 to 1894. The banking crisis lasted until 1900. Forty Melbourne and Sydney building societies and mortgage banks failed between July 1891 and March 1892. Of the 64 Australian banks and finance companies that traded in 1891, 54 had ceased operating by 1893, the majority of them permanently. From April to May 1893 over half of the banks, holding 61.5% of total bank assets in Australia, suspended payments to depositors. The situation, partly related to a global economic downturn, deepened with the worst drought on record continuing until 1903. With 70% of Queensland in drought by 1902, total sheep numbers in eastern Australia fell from 106,000,000 to 54,000,000 and cattle stocks fell by more than 40% during this period. Plainly, the Australian people were not in a financial position to invest in property in Australia, let alone in an unknown, totally undeveloped country like New Guinea.[2]

The dawn of the Australian nation on 1 January 1901 instilled new optimism. The federal government in Melbourne busily bedded down the constitution and its new institutions; as to BNG, it hoped the Colonial Office would continue to take care of the possession for the time being. Whitehall, however, was in no mood to retain responsibility for BNG. Joseph Chamberlain, who was in charge of colonial policy, reminded the Australian colonies at the height of negotiations for a federated Australia that Britain annexed southeast New Guinea because of pressing Australian demand. In light of the British New Guinea Syndicate failure, Chamberlain told the Australian government in 1901 that British investment was plainly not welcome in BNG. 'Each year', he told Australia's first Prime Minister Edmund Barton, 'it is difficult to induce the House of Commons to vote money for the administration of a Colony' for the ultimate benefit of Australian capital and enterprise.[3]

Queensland, New South Wales and Victoria adopted a similar position. The annual payment of £5,000 pledged for 10 years by each of the colonies in 1888 terminated on 10 September 1898.[4] Over the years successive Premiers had been unable to agree on how to extract value from BNG, and they were now keen to shift the fiscal burden for BNG to the impending national government. Washing their hands of responsibilities, the Premiers believed that the administration could run BNG by drawing on the accumulated revenue fund established by MacGregor and the receipts from customs excise and gold mining permits. But with expenditures showing that savings plus proceeds from customs duty, licences and fines would last barely 18 months, the pressure was now on the Australian government to take control of BNG.[5]

In 1901 the new federal government drafted a bill for a 'White Australia Policy'. This led to the introduction in the Australian Parliament of an Immigration Restriction Bill in August. The Act effectively ended non-European immigration by providing for entrance examinations in a European language. With the 1890s depression influencing the thinking of many Australians, white working-class people objected to the competition of cheap 'black labour'. Barton pledged to ban all non-European migration to Australia and to repatriate all Pacific Islanders. Most members of both Houses of Parliament and the public supported Barton's election slogan. However, large landholders, particularly the Queensland cane growers opposed the idea. Melanesian workers, generally on three-year indentures at 10s a month pay and keep were a cheap resource not easily replaced with local workers. The industrious Chinese, who came to Australia during the 1850 gold rushes, did not intend to return to their ancestral homes. Apart from domestic politics, the Salisbury government opposed the Bill because Foreign Secretary Lord Lansdowne sought an alliance with Japan and Joseph Chamberlain—roasted in world opinion because of his enthusiastic support of the South African War—tried to avoid identification with the racism exercised in Australia.[6]

Against much criticism from many of Barton's parliamentary colleagues and his opponents—all pushing for complete prohibition of non-European migration—Parliament passed a watered down bill on 3 December 1901. Rather than race, permanent entry to Australia was now determined by passing a dictation test requiring a person seeking to immigrate to write a passage of 50 words in a European language chosen at the examiner's discretion.

The Immigration Restriction Act, 1901, contrasted with Barton's position on the South Pacific. During the election campaign he spoke of Australia's need for a national policy on the Pacific Islands. After the election the Prime Minister was keen to appease the Queensland sugar industry and to see the commercial interests of companies such as Burns, Philp & Co (BP) in the Pacific region protected. He also sought to restrict access to harbours in southeast New Guinea by possible future hostile powers (Russia, Japan, Germany, Holland or France). Whether for political, humanitarian, commercial or defence reasons, Barton believed strongly that Australia had an obligation to take over from Britain as the colonial power in BNG. In August 1901 he moved that Australia should accept BNG as 'Territory of the Commonwealth and that £20,000 a year is voted for 5 years as an interim measure to meet the cost of administration'.[7] Britain, Victoria and New South Wales were keen to hand over the territory and its costs. Queensland's past and present Premiers, Philp and Griffith, objected to a grab for power in BNG by the new federal government. Queensland had assumed responsibility for BNG on behalf of Britain and the Australian colonies in the past and saw no reason to relinquish this authority save for funding, which the Melbourne was welcome to provide.[8] The Queenslanders were not alone in criticising the Barton administration on BNG. Other detractors baulked at the cost of administering and developing BNG. The Member for New England (NSW), William Sewers, feared that assistance to agriculture in BNG, in particular for sugar, would be to the detriment of Australian farmers and that open territorial borders would overturn precisely what the Immigration Restriction Act tried to control. Senator Staniforth Smith from Western Australia lamented that Australia contemplated accepting responsibility for a territory when the country had hardly started developing its own resources.[9] Moreover, to complicate matters for Barton, the *Bulletin*—at the time a fanatically racist journal—did its best to ensure 'the bastard child was not brought into the Australian family of states'. Reflecting the views of many Australians, it caricatured Barton on 23 November 1901 whitewashing Papuans: 'in a few days', the magazine wrote, 'BNG will become part of Australia. If Australians persist in their cry for a White Australia there's a big job in front of Barton'.

Concerned that the bill for BNG could be defeated, Barton delayed a vote until November 1901 when it passed through both Houses. The resolution accepted BNG as a territory of Australia with a federal grant of £20,000 annually for 5 years. While the funding of the Port Moresby administration became effective retrospectively from 1 July 1901, it took four months before the *Commonwealth Gazette* proclaimed:

> The Senate and House of Representatives of the Commonwealth of Australia having passed resolutions authorising the acceptance of British New Guinea as a Territory of the Commonwealth, the United Kingdom placed British New Guinea under the authority of the Commonwealth of Australia on 18 March 1902.[10]

The federal government drafted the legislation for the territory's constitution with the caveat of limiting Australia's responsibility to five years. During this period the Governor of Queensland Governor would replace the Governor General of Australia.

Like Barton, Alfred Deakin saw no alternative to accepting responsibility for BNG when he became Prime Minister in 1903. Britain had annexed BNG at the request of the Australian colonies and Deakin argued that it was essential for Australia to assume control in the interest of 'the native people'. Appealing for compassion, he urged the members of the House to protect the Papuans and their land from 'irresponsible men who are a law unto themselves' and who, in the absence of sovereign control, would inevitably be drawn there.[11]

Parliament did not debate the bill again until Deakin tabled it in 1905. Passed by both Houses during the same year it became law on 1 September 1906. While BNG became the Territory of Papua on that day, the new Australian colony continued to lurch along without direction. Only after the Senate received the Report of a Royal Commission on 20 February 1907, which addressed the present conditions, the method of government and the best means of its improvement, did Melbourne pay attention to its responsibility for Papua.

G. R. Le Hunte, ca. 1880

The Le Hunte administration

The interregnum from 1899 to 1907 was a period of conflict and frustration within the Port Moresby administration. After the departure of Scotsman William MacGregor, the Welshman George Ruthven Le Hunte was installed as Lieutenant-Governor of BNG in 1898. Australia was preoccupied with becoming a federation, and the sporadic presence in Port Moresby by BNG's second administrator did not change the course of Australia's first and only colony until Prime Minister Deakin appointed J.H.P. Murray as the permanent replacement for Le Hunte in November 1908.

George Ruthven Le Hunte was born on 20 August 1852 in the small Wales fishing village of Porthgain in Pembrokeshire County. His father, George Le Hunte, and his mother Mary (daughter of E. Pennefather, Lord Justice of Ireland), lived on the Le Hunte estate at Artramont in Ireland until the family moved to Porthgain in 1877 where George Le Hunte started quarrying slate in 1837.

George junior was educated at Eton and then Trinity College, Cambridge. He graduated in Arts in 1873. Seven years later in 1881, after he had joined the British Foreign Office, he sat for a Master's degree in arts/law to join the bar of the Inner Temple, London. G. R. Le Hunte became the private secretary to Sir Arthur Gordon (Western Pacific High Commissioner in Fiji) in 1875. While in Suva he occupied several offices, including that of Judicial Commissioner in 1883. Before transferring to the West Indies in 1887 he became engaged to marry Caroline R. Clowes of Eardisland in Herefordshire.

Le Hunte served as President of Dominica from 1887 to 1894, and as colonial secretary on Barbados from 1894 to 1897. After a brief appointment as Colonial Secretary on Mauritius (1897) followed by a year's leave in England, Le Hunte succeeded William MacGregor in BNG in November 1898. When Baron Hallam Tennyson vacated his dual responsibilities of Governor of South Australia and acting Governor-General, to become Australia's second Governor-General in 1903, the Crown appointed Le Hunte Governor of South Australia.[12]

Le Hunte left BNG for South Australia on 9 June 1903, remarking in his final report to the Department of External Affairs: BNG in reasonable shape, 'a steady going machine on good common sense lines'.[13] On the positive side, he saw the first hospital and medical facilities of BNG established in Samarai. However, during the 4 years of Le Hunte's term, more Papuan lives were lost at the hands of his Magistrates and the miners and more Papuans were incarcerated than during the MacGregor decade. No significant sustainable development took place during Le Hunte's tenure. With New South Wales and Victoria preventing BP establishing the Hall Sound Co. in 1899, and therefore large-scale agricultural development, Le Hunte was ineffective in driving economic growth, blaming the lack of government funding and political support during the transition to the Australian federation. It is open to question whether Le Hunte was ever fully committed to BNG. Moving from the vibrancy of the Caribbean, the splendour of Government House in Roseau on Dominica, and the iconic parliament building in Bridgetown on Barbados, to the basic accommodation in Port Moresby was by no means a promotion. In contrast to BNG, agriculture in the West Indies employed a large number of experienced farmhands and Le Hunte could rely on educated staff and a suitably funded administration.

After becoming Governor of South Australia in 1903, the people recognised Le Hunte for his hard work and for his deep personal interest in the education and welfare of underprivileged children and the indigenous people of South Australia. His ambivalence toward BNG, however, delayed further the development of the Protectorate. On his departure from New Guinea, Chief Judicial Officer C.S. Robinson acted as the administrator for a year. Captain F. R. Barton, who replaced Robinson in mid-1904 resigned from his posting on 8 April 1908 due to the adverse findings of the 1907 Royal Commission into his administration. Unwanted by Britain and in the absence of meaningful interest by Australia, the future of BNG remained in doubt.

Notwithstanding that, Le Hunte spent nearly half of his tenure outside BNG, his fellow officers lauded his commitment to the pacification cause. A. Musgrave paid tribute to Le Hunte's devotion 'to the task of bringing the coastal natives largely under government influence, and concurrently, of adding to the knowledge of navigable waters of the Possession'. This foresight, according to Musgrave, 'was a striking example of Le Hunte's working and methods', while C.A.W. Monckton praised Le Hunte for committing to open up the north coast.[14]

Le Hunte recognised a gritty determination in Charles Monckton. This son of a New Zealand doctor panned for gold on Woodlark Island, dived for pearls and traded in the Louisiade Archipelago before returning to New Zealand in 1897 to study navigation. He left for Port Moresby on his small schooner later that year to accept an offer from MacGregor as relief officer in the Meko District. When Le Hunte created the North-Eastern Division with its seat at Cape Nelson in 1899, he chose the 25-year-old Monckton for the position of Resident Magistrate (R.M.) Shortly before Le Hunte left for South Australia, he facilitated the appointment of Monckton to both the Legislative and Executive Councils in Port Moresby.[15]

However, despite the praise from Musgrave and Monckton, Le Hunte did not measure up to his predecessor's commitment to BNG. He did not lead from the front as MacGregor had done. Rather, he favoured the comfort of the *Merrie England* and preferred to leave exploration to the prospecting miners and the pacification of the Papuans to his R.Ms. With the exception of two punitive expeditions, avenging the killing and eating of the missionaries James Chalmers, Oliver Tomkins and nine of their students on Goaribari Island, the Lieutenant Governor limited his duties to visiting coastal tribes and government stations. His inspections included the gold-producing islands of Louisiades, Sudest, Woodlark and Tamata Station on the Mambare River.

Disastrous Ventures

Increasing expenditures for want of money

Le Hunte would have been aware that he was taking over an administration that lacked infrastructure, particularly hospitals and roads, basic sanitary installations and an educated workforce. He would also have been conscious of opposition from the Australian contributing colonies and from Britain to providing further funding for BNG. Before taking office, he approached the Premiers of Queensland, New South Wales and Victoria for funding until BNG became self-supporting. More specifically, he requested that the appropriation of £15,000 be ongoing for another 5 years, the upkeep of the *Merrie England* to be paid for from accumulated funds and the balance to be drawn from annual revenue. After 5 years of such support, Le Hunte believed BNG would stand on its own feet.

As could be expected, the Premiers rejected his proposal. Victoria reflected the mood for financial disengagement in BNG nearly two years ago. Adopting the argument advanced by Chamberlain, Premier Turner had told MacGregor at the Premiers' Conference in January 1898:

> When I come to ask for further votes in connection with this [BNG], how am I going to explain to the House that I have been refusing expenditure on roads and bridges in our own colony, [with] an expenditure of £5,000 or £6,000 in New Guinea … not drawing one iota of benefit.[16]

Le Hunte had therefore no choice but to start his administration in BNG on the funds accumulated by MacGregor (£28,957) and the tax revenues for the first 12 months (£11,723). Initially, the sum available proved to be more than sufficient for Francis Winter, who was in charge of the administration for most of the 1898-99 fiscal year. Starting the new fiscal year with a balance of £20,904 in the accumulated fund account, Port Moresby collected £10,865 in import duties, £1,757 for mining permits, £403 from land sales and £810 for licences and fines.[17] The write-off of £3,697 in worthless or missing inventory did not affect the cash position. The appointments of an R.M. for the North-Eastern Division, additional mining wardens and two agents in the Eastern Division came at an additional cost of £971. Le Hunte increased annual spending on medical care fivefold to £620, and accelerated land surveys at a cost of £1,312. Total expenditure, including the running costs of the *Merrie England,* came to £28,301 for 1899-1900. This left a balance of £6,600. Following a special survey grant of £3,000 and a £3,000 loan from the Queensland government, and revenue forecast of £15,000, Le Hunte hoped to collect £27,600 in 1900-01.

While the new Australian federal government was bedding down its constitution, and the British government flatly refused to seek a vote in the House of Commons for further BNG appropriations, the financial position of BNG became increasingly precarious. Notwithstanding this impasse, the Port Moresby administration exercised little fiscal discipline. Increased spending on judicial administration, land surveys and health resulted in a budget blowout of £4,347 for 1900-01. Given the choice of walking away from BNG or balancing the shortfall, the Queensland government voted for further temporary financial relief in May 1901. Under the *Appropriation Ordinance, 1901*, the Le Hunte administration received £7,101 for general expenditures, and £1,750 for the maintenance of the *Merrie England.*[18]

Three months into the 1901-02 financial year, the Barton government had still not tabled an appropriation bill for New Guinea. Port Moresby was heading for a £20,000 unauthorised deficit by June 1902, and the colony was again in danger of defaulting. A last minute settlement in November 1901 saved the situation. The federal parliament in Melbourne belatedly recognised responsibility for BNG and voted £20,000 in annual grants for five years, retrospective to 1 July 1901. After the gazetting of the appropriation in March 1902, Le Hunte applied for a year's special leave. He did not return to his posting in Port Moresby.

The 1901-02 financial year ended with a £1,599 deficit. Queensland had insisted on the repayment of the £3,000 survey grant extended in 1901. In light of what could have been, the small deficit would hardly have spoilt the Lieutenant Governor's 12 month sojourn in England. His deputies, Judge Winter and A. Musgrave, delivered an even smaller deficit of £69 in 1902-03. They achieved this by reducing expenditure from £39,246 the preceding year to £37,577, while increasing revenue from £16,868 to £19,868, mainly because of increased land sales.[19]

Native policy through the gun

The excitement of gold discoveries on Sudest Island (1888) and on Misima Island (1889) was short-lived. The initial production of 3,850 oz. for the Louisiade goldfields had fallen to 560 oz. in 1896-97. By then most miners had moved to Woodlark Island, approximately 160 km north of Misima, or to the Upper Mambare River on the mainland, where gold was found in August 1895. Four years later 150 European miners panned the Yodda (Upper Mambare), Gira and Waria Rivers for gold. The reprisal by MacGregor on the Binandere people for the murder of the Cairns prospector Clark and the government agent Green established some control around Tamata Station. The death toll, however, among the miners and indentured labourers on the Upper Mambare continued to be 'quite horrifying' according to Monckton.[20]

Le Hunte maintained the principle of MacGregor's 'native policy' but his execution of the policy was harsher, resulting in greater loss of life. Responding to the miners' demand for better security, he consolidated the existing stations in the South-Eastern Division and created the North-Eastern Division. The problems in the Louisiades and on Woodlark were the miners, not the islanders. Alexander Campbell, R.M. for the South-Eastern Division, reported from Nivani Station in 1897, 'serious crime is almost unknown [and] the tribes of Misima, once so savage and troublesome as almost to make one despair of them, are now so completely pacified that only petty breaches of Native Regulations have to be dealt with'.[21] The influx of some 400 Europeans and 1,600 Papuan labourers to the islands made Woodlark the centre of the gold industry in BNG in 1897, and the centre of crime. The experienced diggers from Sudest Island were not the problem. Rather, it was the inexperienced and native fortune seekers and vagabonds who arrived from Australia with little money, stores and equipment, who created the problems. Campbell vented his frustration about them when he noted in his report, 'a dozen very bad characters, some of whom had served long prison sentences in the Australian colonies', were amongst the miners on Woodlark. Illustrating the problems he had to deal with, Campbell told the episode of two miners who had stolen 11 oz. of gold, a revolver and a watch from a deceased miner and found nothing wrong with their action. 'He was dead', was their simple explanation.[22]

While the local people in the southeast became the 'most law-abiding in the Possession', the situation was starkly different on the Upper Mambare, Upper Kumusi and Gira rivers. The killing of John Green in January 1897 saw the government secretary M. Shanahan installed as Resident Magistrate (R.M.) at Tamata Station. Shanahan and his surveyor, H. H. Stuart-Russell, managed to keep the area around the station relative safe. However, the influx of miners and indigenous workers in 1898 saw the death rate reach appalling levels further inland. Where the European miners avoided the spears and axes of the Orokaiva tribesmen, malaria and dysentery were frequently the cause of death. Shanahan, who had cut a 50 km track from Tamata Creek to the Gira River in 1897, and a further 90 km to within a few of the foot of Mt Albert Edward, the source of the Gira, was amongst them. He died from bilious fever on 5 August 1898.

In 1897 Robert Elliott and Alex Clunas prospected southwest of Tamata Station along the Kumusi River, and a few months later, with the inclusion of Sam MacClelland, followed the Mambare beyond MacLaughlins Creek into the Yodda Valley. They had to deal with the Orokaiva people whose territory stretched from the western side of the Owen Stanley Range to the GNG boundary in the north, the Hydrographer's Range in the southeast and along the coast of the Solomon Sea, from Oro Bay to the GNG border. The Yodda Valley people were one of the seven Orokaiva tribal groups, and were the most fearless warriors. Harassing, robbing and killing anyone who entered their territory they made life very difficult for the three prospectors and their men.

The Elliott group was particularly concerned that the carriers and native labourers had given much trouble by running away largely because of the belligerent local tribesmen. The problem worsened when more and more prospectors panned for gold on the Gira River and in the Yodda Valley. By the turn of the Century some 900 indentured workers, most of them from the Fly River region, worked for European miners in the Upper Mambare region. Then, cannibalism was also on the rise and, according to Shanahan's successor, William Armit, 'the local savages found many victims amongst the runaway carriers'. Judge Winter uttered surprise that so many indigenous workers went to the Mambare in the first instance. 'The whole country is clothed in dense forest, and the fall of rain is heavy ... the mortality amongst the native carriers in the district has been so heavy that it is unreasonable to expect that natives will engage as carriers for the Mambare', his 1898-99 Annual Report stated.[23] The miners called on Le Hunte for better protection by way of additional government stations. The Northern Division was, however, a huge region and to pacify and bring the Orokaiva people under government control required experienced staff and money which were resources the Port Moresby administration did not have.

Captain Archibald Butterworth, commander of the police in BNG, temporarily took charge of Tamata after Shanahan's death. He had already deputised for Green in

August 1896, when the latter accompanied MacGregor beyond the headwaters of the Mambare to Mt Scratchley and Mt Victoria. This time Butterworth was in the region to track down and arrest the two men responsible for the murder of his corporal, Sadu. Instead, he arrested the murderers of Fry and Haylor, the two miners who the Peu people slew a week before the massacre of the Green party. When illness forced Butterworth to leave the region on 1 September 1898, he installed Stuart-Russell as the officer-in-charge of Tamata.

Stuart-Russell's temporary assignment at Tamata lasted until 3 January 1899 when he returned to Port Moresby for a project to find easier access to the northern river goldfields. The Queensland surveyor's brief was to survey a possible road from Port Moresby, along the Brown River, to the Gap and to assess the possibility of a track towards the Mambare River or another suitable terminus on the northeast coast.

The arduous task commenced on 25 April 1899. Stuart-Russell's party consisted of J. MacDonald, head gaoler and overseer, 11 indigenous police, 16 prisoners as carriers, and warders. It also included Robert Hunter, who supervised three 'boys' looking after horses and mules. Returning 3 months later, Stuart-Russell spoke of his achievements and of the Yodda Valley people. The boisterous conduct of the locals was such as he had not seen in any other tribes before. Armed to the teeth, he reported:

> The fighting chief snatched a rifle from Warder "Paddy," and pointing it at MacDonald's tent clumsily [trying] to discharge it … Not being familiar with the effect of a bullet from a M. H. or Snider rifle, they imagined their shields sufficient protection, and come on with great confidence. The rifle practice, however, of Mr MacDonald, the two police, and Warders Aroa and "Norman," was too good, and, they came on again and again with the usual bravery of all natives belonging to that district, they were repulsed every time with loss, and eventually drew off, not a man in my party having been injured.

Apart from carrying out the survey, Stuart-Russell observed that 'colours of gold are obtainable almost anywhere in the valleys and tributaries of the Noaro and Lura Rivers'. On other commercial possibilities in the Owen Stanley region, he wrote:

> The trip has been a revelation to me as regards the potentialities of the New Guinea uplands. The soil is so luxuriantly fertile, and the climate delightful. The country on the southern side of the range strikes me as being richer than that on the northern side [where] sugar can thrive better, and is free from disease. The rubber trees, also, as far as I can judge, are of superior quality to those across the range. Oranges, pomegranates, etc., grow wild, and could readily be turned to account by an experienced gardener. The ordinary produce of the native gardens is taro, yams, taitu, pumpkins, maize, sugar cane, bananas, papaws, betel nut, tobacco, etc. In the Yodda Valley the coconut grows.

However, the valley can only be exploited, Stuart-Russell conceded, after the land from the Yodda Valley to the Opi River was made safe as the tribes were 'numerous, warlike, and treacherous', requiring careful patrolling before it will be safe for parties to pass through.

Le Hunte promoted Stuart-Russell to chief government surveyor of BNG for his remarkable work, but at an estimated cost of £10,000 he decided not to proceed with the road from Port Moresby to the northern goldfields. Le Hunte also dismissed the idea of providing support for agricultural industries in the highlands.

Yet on 31 July 1900 Le Hunte declared the Yodda Valley as a 'most valuable gold-bearing country' in BNG. By then intrepid miners had taken out the main gold-bearing leases on the northern rivers. On the Mambare, they extended from MacLaughlins Creek for about 55 km through the Yodda Valley. To the west of the Mambare, there were gold reefs on the headwaters of the Tamata Creek, the Gira and Aikora Rivers. It was a vast area, where European intrusion changed the social disposition of the Binandere and Orokaiva people as far as Mt Albert Edward. No longer were the local tribes solely concerned with raiding each other's villages. Their main target became the European miners. The miners' carriers, who often came from other parts of Papua, added another dimension to the disruption of tribal life in the Owen Stanley Range. The prospectors demanded they travel too far and their loads were too heavy. Rather than fulfilling their indentures, many carriers dumped their loads and absconded. Initially, the Binandere men went after the deserting carriers and returned them for tomahawks. After they realised the value of the men to the miners they extracted much greater booty before setting the boys free.[24]

When the bellicose William Armit arrived at Tamata the hostilities between the Europeans and the Binandere men escalated to a war-like level. W. E. Armit, born in Liège, Belgium, in 1848 arrived in Australia in 1870. He first worked as a stockman then as a sub-inspector in the Queensland Native Police. During this time he wrote newspaper articles under the pseudonym, 'A Queensland Police Officer', which, according to the *Bulletin,* included 'some first class alligator and nigger lies'. In 1883 the Melbourne *Argus* appointed him special correspondent to explore the north coast of southeast New Guinea. It gave Armit the opportunity to become MacGregor's private secretary in the same year. From deputy agent in charge of the Mekeo and Rigo districts in 1894, he advanced to sub-collector of customs at Samarai in November 1895.[25] Le Hunte engaged Armit in 1899, initially as assistant, then R.M. Northern Division. The former Belgian soldier regarded the tribes from Tamata Station to the foothills of Mt Albert Edward as treacherous people who lied abominably: 'it is almost impossible to eradicate the germ of suspicion from the mind of a savage' Armit reported. They are 'accustomed to employ every species of treachery and chicanery in their dealings with one another [and] they credit us with identical vices to which they cling with such pertinacity. [They are] cannibals from a sheer love of human flesh'. This makes it 'preposterous and intolerable to even dream of permitting a horde of savages to browbeat and intimidate'. Armit regarded it incumbent on himself 'to uphold the prestige of the Government, and secure the safety of the miners'. With this attitude, he set out on an expedition in early 1900 that became remarkable for its discoveries and terrible for its bloody encounters.

Armit left Tamata on 26 January to cut a track to the 'new diggings' on the Yodda Valley, which he believed would 'very soon become the premier goldfields in the Possession'. With eight constables, four village constables, 20 prisoners, 40 carriers and 3 personal attendants, he walked, climbed and waded through seemingly impenetrable, wet, country. Worn out and ill, he returned to Tamata on 1 April after trekking the Northern Division for some 620 km. His report to Le Hunte revealed lamentable encounters with the Kumusi and Yodda Valley tribes. The report also contained remarkable achievements in his nine-week journey—the building of a pack track to the Yodda Valley and the definition of the goldfields. He also sreported

> The following are the casualties in the several fights in which my police and myself were engaged: At Papangi, 16th February; 13 men killed; saw no wounded. 19th February, at Babagi; 17 killed. 22nd February, at Sisureta; 1 killed. 24th February, at Twidi; 6 killed. 26th February, at Koko; 4 killed. 16th March, at Berobesila, 13 killed. In no case did I see wounded man, as the scrub affords them ample opportunities to escape. The lamentable death of two women at Babagi, who carried spare spears for their husbands, were probably taken for men. [I followed] Sir MacGregor's instructions to me on more than one , "Never to allow a native to poise a spear preparatory to launching it, but always to fire before the spear could be thrown." I have invariably acted upon these instructions.

Clearly, Papuans did not scare Armit. Eight days out from Tamata, in the deserted village of Garawakita, two truculent warriors confronted him:

> Just as I was on the point of leaving two villainous-looking individuals, with blackened faces and wearing war plumes, marched defiantly into the village. To seize these gentlemen, tear off their plumes, and wash some of the black pigment from their faces was the work of about one minute. Then I clapped two heavy swags on their backs and sent them ahead'. They did not like it at all [when] they had to carry to camp, where I let them go.

Three weeks later, on 16 February, when he crossed the Pidza River in the direction of Papangi (Papaki) village some 250 warriors decorated in 'bullet-proof paint' and armed to the teeth, stood in the way of Armit's party:

> I ordered them to put away their arms, but they laughed at me, and one big man, taking two or three rapid strides forward, deliberately poised his spear at me. He was instantly shot dead. A fight commenced, but only lasted some few minutes …These are the stone-throwers who tried by many stratagems to secure [the prospectors] Crow, Walker, and party, and being very powerful and aggressive tribe, it became imperative to teach them a salutary lesson. [26]

Thirteen Papangi people died from gunshots, with an unknown number of wounded disappearing in the undergrowth. And as on nearly all expeditions in BNG then, there were several more encounters with tribal warriors. But in Armit's words, a 'well-directed volley [of gun shots] checked them'. While Le Hunte expressed concern at the large number of 'natives hurt', he hoped that the large loss of life was deterring them from mounting further attacks.

Armit, whose euphemism for killing was 'hurting', remained silent on the number of wounded and dead his own party had suffered on 'pacification and civilising' patrols other than to mention '30 deaths among the carriers, three of these being drowning' in 1899-1900. He was also unapologetic for the deaths he had inflicted on the warriors: 'In my opinion and I am competent to offer one—the natives of the Kumusi and Yodda Valley are among the most dangerous, as they are the most truculent, in the Possession, and it will take two years to pacify them'.

Armit and the prospector Matt Crowe—who came to his aide to repel the Papangi warriors—completed the track from Tamata Station through steep territory, swamps and dense rain forest to the Yodda Valley. They confirmed the source of the Yodda, discovered by MacGregor, but not marked on the official maps. Crucially, they examined the geology in the prospective gold-bearing areas. Summarising his detailed work he noted:

Disastrous Ventures

> I calculate that I have cut and marked over 100 miles of road, formed some dozen good camps, clearing away all timber, bridged 28 creeks, and pacified the native tribes, at least temporarily, for a distance of 100 miles from Tamata, and all this at a cost to the road vote of less than £40.[27]

Armit estimated the distance from Tamata to the Yodda goldfields at 130 miles or just over 200 km. Except for the Pidza River crossing between Korobama and Papangi, where he suggested a funicular system, most of the track was completed. The approach via the Kumusi River to the boat landing built by Clunas and Clark at Gobi village in 1897, and then overland to the fields, was approximately 300 km from the mouth of the river. Although preferred by many prospectors because it shortened the overland journey to 170 km, Armit considered the rapids and currents of the Kumusi too dangerous and the overland track in parts too swampy. He preferred to construct the Pidza crossing or cut a pack mule track from Gona on Holincote Bay, across the slope of Mt Lamington to Korobama. This, he estimated, would make the journey to the Yodda Valley a mere 135 km.

Corroborating Stuart-Russell's assessment 12 months earlier, Armit was impressed with the large area of good agricultural land he found at Papangi. In the Yodda Valley, he panned five sections of wash during his 10-day stay, with not a dish blank. Armit offered a similar opinion on the Kumusi and Pidza Valley, which he considered 'worthy of intelligent research', as the expected results would swell the gold returns of the Possession.

When Le Hunte voiced his concern as to the expedition cost, Armit replied with disgust, 'I endured unbelievable hardship, feeding myself and my party chiefly on native food for six months', and I need time to recuperate not to be told of my 'extravagant living'. He left for Australia on 19 August 1900 only to return to Tamata three months later without much physical improvement. Armit died, like his predecessor Shanahan, from bilious fever on 3 January 1901.

Le Hunte's new appointments—Archibald Walker and the Hon. Richard de Moleyns—arrived at Tamata on 28 February 1901. Walker was the errant son of Australian Senator J. T. Walker, a Director of BP and retired president of the Bank of New South Wales. Archibald Walker went to BNG in search of gold but ended up working as Chief Clerk in the Secretary's office. Forever in need of experienced men, Le Hunte believed the short stint in Port Moresby would be sufficient for Walker to qualify for the position of Assistant Resident Magistrate (A.R.M). Of similar ilk, de Moleyns, son of an Irish peer, arrived in BNG with an impressive family name but no money. Le Hunte rejected his application for 100,000 acres at Mullens Harbour on the grounds of de Moleyns' precarious financial position. Instead, he offered the Irish nobleman a spot as Assistant Officer at Bogi and then A.R.M. at Papangi (Papaki) Station. Both men did not last long. Like his two predecessors, Walker died of bilious fever, while de Moleyns escaped to Australia 1902 before malaria took him as well.[28]

This was not the end of the sorry saga of Tamata Station, which, according to Monckton, had been a death trap. F. W. Leetch, who followed Walker, transferred to Samarai because of his health: he died before October 1902. Robert Hislop, who replaced the German, Wilhelm Rohn as head gaoler at Tamata in 1900, transferred to Bogi to take de Moleyns' who moved to Papangi. Le Hunte appointed Robert Hislop and Halkett Parker A.R.M. in the Northern Division in place of Walker and Leetch. Hislop, whom Monckton called a 'weak, feeble individual, in no way capable of managing a district any more than a sixteen-year-old Quaker nursery governess would be of acting as sergeant-major to the Tyrone or Royal Irish', left the BNG administration on 1 September 1903. Monckton took on additional responsibilities with the Mambare region while remaining in charge of the North-Eastern Division. John Higginson, who arrived in BNG in 1903, supported Monckton's sacking of Parker and Hislop, and their replacement, G. Thomas. This left A. Elliott in charge of Bogi, A. Walsh in charge of Papangi and Higginson deputising at Tamata.[29]

The instability at senior management level in the Northern Division may have contributed to the ongoing bloody encounters with the Orokaiva people. Shortly before Walker came to Tamata, the mild-mannered, largely illiterate Elliott had to deal with the killing of the prospectors Tom Campion and John King and their three carriers. Under standing orders only to arrest perpetrators, Elliott and 12 police proceeded to the Upper Kumusi, the scene of the massacre. Sam MacClelland, who had escaped the attack, accompanied him. Any arrest of the perpetrators—if indeed intended—was unsuccessful. Instead, on the first day of the encounter, Elliott, MacClelland and their men shot four spearmen. During the next two days they slew 36 more warriors. 'Seventeen, their legs broken, were left to fend for themselves' and, according to Elliott, 'many more wounded got away'.[30]

The Europeans and their indentured carriers and workers encountered some 5,000 hostile Orokaiva people between Bogi Station and the head of the Kumusi River, and several times that number from the Kokoda Gap, the start of the Yodda Valley, and at Mt Albert Edward. The Papuan warriors resented the European intruders. They enjoyed warfare, European goods, (mainly trinkets), alcoholic beverages and tobacco. Whereas the miners saw them as primitive savages who savoured the white man's flesh, they also found them to be very skilful warriors. They quickly learned the white man's technology: the panning for gold, dynamite for fishing and guns in warfare. Most Australian miners saw themselves as the master with the God-given right to 'boot his own nigger', or in the extreme, use them for shooting practice.[31] There were, of course, also 'gentlemen miners' like Sam Faulkner and Frank Rochfort. They attained good results from their 'boys' by feeding them well and not working them like machines. Monckton despised such Europeans.

There was also Rayner Bellamy. The not yet fully qualified doctor from Cambridge University was highly regarded by all. Monckton agreed on the value of this medical officer because Bellamy 'brought to his work sympathy with natives, and acquired a knowledge of the peculiarities that is as rare as it is valuable, [whose] share in the pacification of the hitherto somewhat unruly tribes … has been no small one'.[32]

To attribute blame to the Le Hunte administration for appointing inexperienced, unrestrained or feeble officers would ignore the fact that Armit, Stuart-Russell, Elliott, Walker and others were required to protect the prospectors and miners while also establishing infrastructure under difficult circumstances. These officers were mainly young men trying to stop the prospectors from shooting, looting, destroying villages and gardens while in search of food. The government officers' excessive responses to attacks by tribal warriors identify a lack of training, but are also symptomatic of the time. Their inability to keep track of rampaging prospectors together with several hundred of their indentured labourers made the task of the district officers particularly difficult. Raiding, spearing, murdering and cannibalism by the tribesmen added to the chaotic environment that Walker and several of the Magistrates that followed him at Tamata tried to bring under some meaningful control.[33]

The appointment of Monckton to the Northern Division did not stop the carnage. 'Attacks on the miners, murder of their native employees, and pillage of their camps, followed by futile attempts at retaliatory raids by exasperated miners', were regular occurrences in the Yodda Valley according to the Magistrates.[34] Monckton blamed criminal activities largely on the inefficiency of the village constables. 'Coupled in many instances with actual criminality' led to the dismissal of three constables and the hanging of one man for murder, according to the A.R.M.'s report. The native magistrate court was not working properly either, and 'much weeding' was to be done according to Monckton. To start with, he kept the prison warden at Tamata busy with the incarceration of 60 Papuans in 1903-04 plus an unspecified number at Bogi Station. Seven Papuans and three miners were committed for murder, one for shooting with intent. Attempted murder (2), rape (5), manslaughter (1), wounding (5), assault (2), stealing (1) and harbouring prisoners (1) made up the other indictable offences during the year. While summary arrests (123) concerned the indentured labourers, with desertions (37), stealing (35) and disobedience (37) ranking highly, Monckton appeared powerless to make recalcitrant miners behave.

> Unfortunately, among the white community, there is a section by whom a native is regarded as a "nigger," who has no right of redress against a European for any injury sustained, even though it is a case of life itself. Lamentable though such bias is, it is there, and with that section, however atrocious a European's crime may be, he is certain of sympathy and assistance in evading the law.

Against the backdrop of this refractory behaviour, Monckton dealt with the looting of camps and attacks on miners 'by natives armed with stolen firearms'. In defence of the local people, Monckton claimed that 'by far the greatest numbers of these offences were committed by indentured labourers from faraway districts, and who had deserted their employers.[35]

In order to provide better protection for, and control over, the miners, Monckton decided to close Bogi and Papangi and establish Kokoda Station in 1904. The location was set up near Mt. Victoria, approximately 130 km from the south coast. It initially comprised barracks for the armed constables, a prison, officers' quarters, a Magistrate's office and storerooms. As the farthest inland station of BNG, Monckton suggested that it would prove the most healthy of sites, because mosquitoes were few and the malignant anopheles entirely absent.[36]

Concurrent with establishing this posting, Monckton started with the construction of a road from the coast to the Yodda Valley. He mapped out an easier route than the solution proposed by Armit 4 years earlier. With the road now starting at Buna

Bay rather than Gona in the north, Monckton engaged the 'rawest of wild savages—local tribes who, until very recently, refused to submit to, or even parley with, the Government'—for the project. By June 1904 Monckton had driven the greater part (95 km) of the road through dense rain forest and along rugged cliffs, with the bridges along this section also completed. However, the remaining 35 km to the Yodda Valley encroached largely on fiercely protected tribal land. To expedite the work Monckton convinced Bellamy to take up special duties by overseeing the completion of the project, and to then leave for England to complete his medical training'.

Bellamy's medical skills and his cool conduct helped to calm the tribes at Kokoda. Thus, he oversaw the completion of the tracks from Buna Bay to the Yodda and on to the Kokoda Gap in 1905. While Port Moresby bemoaned the cost of £1,000 and the ongoing repairs after flooding and landslides, Monckton put his case:

> Against this expenditure must be set the fact that the bulk of gold won in the Possession at present comes from this Division. No direct income is derived there from, but indirectly the 100 odd miners there contribute a considerable portion of the Possession's revenue.[37]

With the opening of a government station at Buna Bay, the Samarai firms Whitten Bros, and Clunas & Clark, relocated their stores from Bogi, on the Kumusi River, to Buna in 1905. The new stone jetty at Buna allowed cargo and people arrive from Port Moresby or Samarai directly at the port of entry to the Yodda goldfield, leading to safer transportation at substantially lower costs.[38]

Also completed in 1905 was Armit's suspension bridge across the Kumusi River and the move of the notoriously unhealthy Tamata Station 7.5 km upstream from Loma. Connected to the Gira goldfield via an upgraded 40-km track and 7.5 km of new road, it remained the second most important government station in the Owen Stanley Range after Kokoda.

Roads, improved facilities, better policing and a small step towards rapprochement all led to improved relationships with the local people by 1906. The Europeans on the Yodda and the Gira could now rely on locally grown fruits and vegetables. In addition, the replacement of some indentured labourers with resident people benefitted the miners and locals alike. No longer were miners required to pay Port Moresby recruiting fees or the travel costs to and from the point of hire, and the villagers participated to some degree in the local gold economy. Notwithstanding these improvements, the mortality rate amongst carriers (17.7% in 1906) remained unacceptably high, while during the same year 37% of the labour force left their employers stranded by not completing their indentures. The ratio of deserters was about the same on the Yodda fields where 83 out of 225 indentured labourers deserted.[39]

In his BNG assessment J. D. Legge observed that the gruesome 'affairs in the Northern Division must not be taken as typical of those in the Possession as a whole, for the system was as yet in its infancy there'.[40] Legge was clearly too charitable. After the demise of five R.Ms. in as many years and the true number of perished miners never known, it was not an issue of infancy; it was because of bad government policy. The Australian and British governments had successfully starved the Le Hunte administration revenue. To lessen the bloodshed in the Northern Division Le Hunte required experienced officers, and many of them. To keep them alive he needed to set up stations away from the mosquito-infested riverbanks, with infrastructure, stores and houses built to basic sanitary standards. With the large influx of itinerant people, basic health care was crucial. Le Hunte needed to build more roads for better access to the stations and the goldfields. He required better policing to keep the miners under control and contain the local people from attacking, harassing and stealing. Le Hunte was simply not in a position to provide this while allowing prospectors to roam the territory unchecked. While Le Hunte could have hoped a major gold find would hasten the Australian government's assumption of responsibility for BNG, his immediate access to funds was through taxes on foodstuff and other consumables. The prospectors and miners employed indigenous labour, purchased provisions and gear, drank and smoked. The goods, all imported from Australia, generated import duty. To quote Wyatt Earp, proprietor of the Golden Dust Saloon in Nome during the Alaskan gold rush, the government was 'mining the miners': the greater their number the larger the revenue from the high import tariffs.[41]

Improved medical care: Le Hunte's main legacy

With the lack of economic progress, it was no surprise that Port Moresby was still a backwater at the turn of the century. The capital had no roads, only pack mule tracks, few public buildings, and one ramshackle hotel. 'A well-appointed bath house' set up at a Tahitian mission teacher's house in Kalo village was 'a great step in civilisation and one of which Government House at Port Moresby cannot yet boast', Chief Medical Officer Dr Blayney observed.[42] Since 1899 he urged the construction of pit latrines in Port Moresby where Papuans urinated and defecated whenever and wherever.

In 1901, the Port Moresby European population of 59—nearly all men—worked almost exclusively for the government. While a site for a European hospital had been prepared in Port Moresby, and plans for water supplies and sanitary improvements drawn up, it was only in 1898, shortly before MacGregor left BNG, that the administration could consider these plans more seriously. The *Public Heath Ordinance, 1898* conferred on the executive wide powers for declaring infected districts and restrictions upon movement of people and ships. The administrator-in-council implemented regulations that he deemed necessary for preventing the spread of contagious diseases. He was empowered to quarantine people and livestock and mandate vaccinations. Even before arriving in BNG, Le Hunte secured a grant from the Queensland for the establishment of a medical department in Port Moresby. Under the Public Hospital Act, he started the long overdue construction of hospitals in BNG.[43] The largest town, Samarai, received preference over Port Moresby. Its fluctuating population of several hundred Europeans, combined with the high death rate on the goldfields, made this town in the Eastern Division the obvious place for BNG's first hospital.

Le Hunte appointed Cecil Vaughan as acting government medical officer in Samarai and A.R.M. for the Eastern Division in December 1899 even though the appointment raised eyebrows with the medical profession in Australia and England.

Unqualified as a surgeon, he came to BNG as a shareholder and manager of a Sydney-based company to exploit rubber in BNG not practice medicine. Le Hunte, however, was content with a medical officer of sorts, and with the experience Vaughan had gained in the Indian Medical Service, he appointed him to set up the first medical care facility in BNG in 1900.[44]

In addition to overseeing the hospital building work and running his rubber plantation, Vaughan's medical work stretched from the South-Eastern to the North-Eastern and as far as the Northern Division. He also organised a local committee to provide physical and financial assistance to expedite the work and extracted a commitment from Port Moresby to match dollar for dollar the amount collected (£136) and pledged (£200) by the mining and Samarai business community. And because Vaughan insisted for a 'native ward' to be included, the committee encouraged employers to arrange a voluntary deduction of 5% from their workers' wages.[45]

Vaughan completed the European hospital in 1901. He was unable to finish a native ward due to a lack of funds. The committee for the Port Moresby hospital finally received approval to proceed with its building a year later. Gazetted on 15 March 1902, construction took until August 1905—three years after Le Hunte had left BNG. The administration of Francis Barton provided £100 towards the building of the Native Hospital in Port Moresby, and £100 for completing the Samarai Native Hospital, both opening in 1905.[46] The setting up of a bush hospital at Tamata in 1898 was short-lived. Le Hunte also planned field hospitals on Woodlark Island and on the Mambare but found the expense too great.

Dr Blayney left BNG on 24 May 1901 after 6 years of service to study tropical medicine in England. Vaughan left for England on 1 February 1902, apparently to enrol at university to study for his medical exam. The two practitioners did not return to BNG, leaving only surgeon Dr Allen Craigen, who served as BNG's chief medical officer until 1904.[47]

One of Blayney's important legacies was the implementation of the *Health Act, 1900*. The sanitary board appointed under the regulation oversaw the disposal of excreta, rubbish and wastewater. Europeans and Papuans had public toilets in Port Moresby, a requirement still not mandated for Samarai at that time.

Vaughan's replacement, Dr Taylor Hancock, arrived in Samarai on 11 May 1903. He died 15 months later. The hospital there was still not receiving proper funding and, 'owing to the lamentable falling-off of public subscriptions,' the hospital closed on 31 March 1904. A derelict hospital residence used by Hancock would have contributed to his death from malaria on 4 August 1904.[48]

In 1904 Chief Medical Officer, Dr Colin Simson, reported the 'rapid spread of venereal diseases among the natives' in the Eastern and South-Eastern Divisions. This ongoing malaise made native hospitals an even higher priority. While the European hospital at Samarai remained closed, and Port Moresby's European population travelled to Cooktown or Brisbane for treatment until 1905, the Samarai Native Hospital treated 99 patients during its first 12 months of operations in 1904.[49] At the newly established Kulamadau Hospital on Woodlark Island the resident nurse treated 114 patients in the first year (1905-06) in less than ideal conditions. In a letter to a friend in Sydney, she wrote:

> We have not yet a doctor on the island, consequently a nurse's work is at times much out of her own sphere, and double anxiety and responsibility is incurred. The European ward of the Kulumadau is situated on the top of a very high hill, where it is healthier, and I can always get a cool breeze. The native hospital is situated about one mile away from the main hospital, where the natives have neither beds nor bedding; it is one large room with a fire in the middle, and they all gather around the fire, with a log of wood for a pillow and some rice mats for a covering, [and] where large swarms of mosquito and sandflies bring much malaria fever.[50]

In early 1905 the medical staff of BNG consisted of two surgeons, Dr. Craigen in Port Moresby and Dr Jones in Samarai. The handover from Craigen to Simson in March 1905 coincided with the completion of Port Moresby's European hospital. Private donations provided nearly all of the construction material and the equipment for the hospital. Port Moresby only committed to the expenditure for the building.[51] Then, following Australia finally taking responsibility for BNG in 1906, the number of surgeons increased to five. Apart from para-medical care provided by the Christian missions, the medical officers Simson and Beaumont (Port Moresby), Jones (Samarai), Bellamy (Woodlark) and W. Strong (A.R.M. in Mekeo) were tending to a European population of 687 and an indentured work force of 4,180 Papuans.[52]

Land and labour: the Hall Sound Company, an opportunity begging

The 1898 amended *Native Protection Ordinance* changed the BNG labour law in favour of the employer. Well before MacGregor left New Guinea, he realised that his plan to make the Papuans independent producers would fail. He became increasingly conscious of the need to develop agricultural industries if BNG was to become more than a British colony in name only. From the virtual prohibition of Papuan employment on plantations since 1888, MacGregor now foresaw lifting the 12-month term on employment contracts in the context that more Papuans had been pacified.

Le Hunte amended *The Native Labour Ordinance, 1900* soon after he arrived in Port Moresby. Under the new ordinance, he appointed labour District Magistrates with the authority to accept, cancel or vary labour contracts. After the completion of a 12-month indenture, European miners and settlers could now re-engage workers for a second term. It was conditional, however, that the men spend some time in their home village before commencing their second indenture. Apart from easing the employment conditions for labour the ordinance provided for the administration to raise funds by charging two shillings for every Papuan indentured to a company or person. To control unscrupulous recruiters, or rather, as a means of raising revenue, the administration issued recruiting licences with a £50 forfeitable bond.[53]

Subsequent to the labour reform and with the goal of making the BNG economy less reliant on gold mining, Le Hunte submitted a revision of the law on land acquisition to the Queensland government. MacGregor's scheme of making free grants to settlers had failed. Le Hunte opposed this in any case. He believed it would attract people without resources, who had little chance of becoming successful. Instead, Le Hunte intended to amend the land ordinance by removing the prohibition on the sale of government land, and to advertise sales in the *Government Gazette* and in leading newspapers in Australia and Britain. After a 6 month formal notification, Le Hunte recommended that the Administrator-in-Council deal with the applications. Provided the prospective purchaser visited the area of intended purchase with a government official before lodging a binding offer, Le Hunte suggested that the Administrator execute the land grants in full fee simple. The Lieutenant Governor, consistent with the wishes of the Executive Council, should then determine the price for the land and stipulate the conditions and timing of development.[54]

The Colonial Office concurred with Le Hunte while the Premiers of the contributing colonies demanded that any applications for land exceeding 50,000 acres require the prior approval by them. The Premiers reserved their right to consider any proposal for a minimum period of 3 months, and only after all three Premiers agreed to the sale could Le Hunte advertise the land.

The Land Ordinance, 1899 gave effect to the Premiers' amendment.[55] Port Moresby was now authorised to make freehold grants of up to 640 acres or one square mile without formal notification provided it was not included in any advertised area. In giving preference to companies and individuals who were physically present in BNG, Le Hunte was now empowered to make land grants of up to 6,400 acres.

It appears that Cecil Vaughan was the only person to take advantage of a larger grant. He acquired land in the Northern Division shortly after his arrival in 1899.[56] Prior to overseeing the building of the hospital in Samarai, Vaughan started clearing land for rubber planting. Arriving in Samarai on his motorsailer—built to his requirements in Sydney—he gained the only feasible access to his land on the mud plains of the Musa River by boat. The ketch-rigged motor launch, the *Musa,* drew a large crowd when Vaughan called on Brisbane in November 1898 on his way to Samarai. During the occasion of the Intercolonial Rowing Carnival, the owner of the *Musa,* according to *The Queenslander,* 'invited about twenty or thirty gentlemen for a trip on the Brisbane River to inspect this latest contraption in motorised propulsion'.[57]

Vaughan did not bring his rubber plantation to maturity, though. After escaping several attacks on his life by the tribes of the middle Musa, he returned his land to the government, and left Papua in early 1902.[58]

Port Moresby reallocated Vaughan's land and a few other plots to traders, miners and the Christian missions. John Clunn, the miner from Cooktown, discovered more profit in running a hotel at Samarai than in gold. The proceeds from selling spirits and beer gave him the opportunity to start Ramaga, a small plantation on the south side of Milne Bay in 1902. Another old hand, the miner Gus Nelsson, together with Wilhelm Shedden and Charles Arbouin, started a plantation on Blanchard Island near Samarai in 1903 while maintaining their previous occupations.[59] At about the same time the Swede Johann Olson had taken up land at Sebulagomwa on the southern part of Fergusson Island to plant coconut trees. He is also seen in the Witu Group around 1902. Two German brothers, Edward and George Auerbach, planted coconut trees on Muwo in the Trobriand in the late 1890s, but spent more time away from their plantation to continue prospecting, trading and recruiting labour. Ah Gow, a Chinese miner, arrived in the Sudest in the 1880s. He quickly turned to planting rice and coconuts on Nimoa rather than panning for gold. Also turning to agriculture in the

Disastrous Ventures

Sudest was Elizabeth Mahony. While her husband, John Mahony, was prospecting, his wife became a reliable grower of vegetables and rice for the miners and their men.

Le Hunte did not seem interested in the small number of agricultural developments though. Other than the Christian missions, most title-holders were undercapitalised and not in a position to stay the distance and become significant exporters of produce. In 1906 settlers occupied 1,434 acres of leasehold and 5,996 acres of freehold, but not a single plantation produced commercially. The caveat on the size of each allotment and the slow approval mechanism required by Melbourne for larger parcels prevented large companies from gaining foothold in BNG. This was no better illustrated than by the circumstances besetting the Hall Sound Company at the turn of the century.

In expectations that Le Hunte would lift the embargo on Asian immigration, Burns, Philp & Co., (BP) submitted a proposal to the Port Moresby administration for a land company—the Hall Sound Company—in BNG. James Burns suggested free migration of Asians to BNG would overcome the labour difficulty. On 5 September 1899 he wrote to his Chief Inspector, P.G.T. Black:

> Mr Le Hunte is anxious as far as possible, not to make too much noise about the importation of Japanese and other aliens, but he acknowledges it is absolutely necessary that some labour should be imported, and he would be likely to work quietly with us. [If] we can secure some large blocks of rich territory, there is no doubt in my mind that by introducing Japanese and Chinese we could lease the country to them, and they could grow fruits and other local products for the use of local diggers and probably for export to Australia as well.[60]

The grandiose scheme came to nothing. Le Hunte, like his predecessor, was in no position to permit coloured migration to BNG. He was also unsuccessful in obtaining the Premiers' agreement to sell to BP a large area of land for plantation development.

Burns, disappointed that his attempt to diversify BP into plantations had failed—'we were simply endeavouring to draw other capitalists in with ourselves in developing the country'—revived the idea 12 months later.[61] He instructed his Port Moresby manager, Walter Gors, to acquire 100,000 acres of land on Yule Island in Hall Sound. With Chinese and Japanese labour no longer a condition for successful development, Burns registered the Hall Sound Company in September 1900 with the purpose of establishing large-scale plantations in BNG. BP underwrote one-third of the capital of £30,000 in the belief that the influential Board of Directors, James Burns, J.T. Walker (Director Bank of New South Wales), Sir George Dibbs (previous Premier of NSW) Sir Malcolm McEacharn (principal McIlwraith, McEacharn & Co), James Forsayth and W. H. Gors could convince the Victorian and New South Wales Premiers to support the application.[62]

Not surprisingly, the Brisbane supported the Hall Sound concept with Le Hunte authorising the immediate grant to BP of 5,000 acres prime agricultural land on the St Joseph River. The other Premiers were not supportive, though. They required that the land application remain in abeyance pending federation. Premier Lyne (NSW) was strident in his opposition to the scheme, because he did 'not think that a lease of so large an area should be granted'. Lyne's comments also caused disquiet with the public who questioned the propriety of making a huge freehold land grant to a private company. It also frightened off investors. The public avoided the share offer when

BP floated the first tranche of 30,000 units at £1 each. While BP's Directors hoped the pending national government would be more sympathetic to the proposal, it took until 1903 before the federal parliament considered the application. Senator Staniforth Smith from West Australia toured East New Guinea (BNG, GNG and the Solomons) during that year. He was keen for the Hall Sound proposal to receive a fair hearing but to his dismay found barely 10 acres planted with chilli, with only a Samoan and two Papuans working for Hall Sound. 'I thought they were genuine investors', he stated scathingly on his return to Australia. 'The venture is a speculative fraud', and not worth supporting.[63]

The Brisbane Courier never pulled punches when it came to supporting Queensland's own Burns, Philp & Co. In 'Notes on New Guinea', it bemoaned the rejection of the land application by Hall Sound:

> One or more of the contributing colonies in Australia saw it in their wisdom to refuse the consent. Today the colony has no noteworthy industry. Pearl shelling and Bêche-de-mere fishing are carried out on a very small scale now. A good deal of desultory fossicking for alluvial gold is still going on, but whether the industry will ever play as important a part in the history of BNG as it has done in Australia is very doubtful. The country presents the appearance of a confused volcanic jumble, in which it would be hopeless to expect a 'strike' of gold to be traceable for any distance.... Papua must look to her agricultural land as her main course in revenue for its future.

The demise of the Hall Sound application brought down several other promising ventures, the paper continued, and it is time for 'the Commonwealth Government to appoint a commission of thoroughly practical expert men to go over there to inquire exhaustively into the whole governmental mechanism'.[64]

BP attacked the States and the Commonwealth for being 'completely out of harmony with the exigencies of the position in New Guinea' and wound up Hall Sound Company in 1903. Contrary to Smith's report, Gors had planted a variety of fruit trees on the on the St Joseph River land and had experimented with tobacco. While BP paid the government only £625 for the 5,000-acre parcel, the return on the small investment was equally meagre. The company reported in 1902 that the inferior quality of tobacco grown at Inawaia made the crop worthless. Other than the Warirata plantation, which grew Arabica coffee on a small scale, BP was finished with all agricultural ventures, at least for now. The collapse of the investment also spelled the end of Gors' employment with BP. His partner in the Dedele coconut plantation, Thomas Andersen, defrauded the business and committed suicide in late 1899. Gors sold out to BP's Samarai competitor Whitten Brothers before leaving New Guinea for good.[65]

Failure to permit the British New Guinea Syndicate and Hall Sound Company to commence large-scale plantation enterprises was not for want of Crown land. Notwithstanding the Administrator's limited power under Section V of the *Land Ordinances, 1888 & 1890*, Le Hunte started his tenure in BNG with an aggressive land acquisition program. Rejecting MacGregor's reluctance to acquire land for the Crown, he instructed his principal surveyor in 1899-1900 to acquire large tracts on the southwest coast of the Central Division. By June 1899 the administration had seized a mere 72,508 acres or 0.13% of the BNG land mass. A year later Le

Disastrous Ventures

Hunte had transferred 370,457 ac (1,500 km^2) of Papuan land to the government, bringing Crown land to 442,965 ac. Port Moresby requisitioned most of this land in the Central Division where Stuart-Russell declared,400 ac on the Laloki, Brown and Goldie River waste and vacant. Smaller tracts, totalling 22,857 ac, were 'purchased' from the coastal Motus and Koitapus, and the Koiari tribe of the Sogeri district in the hinterland of Port Moresby. This included an additional 2,100 acres for BP at Warirata even though the company showed no intention of expanding its 240-ac plantation there. During the same year the government procured 21,200 ac on the mouth of the Oriomo River in the Western Division. In the following year there were 24 surveys completed for the Christian missions, 35 grants for the purpose of cultivation, grazing and trading lands, 68 for gold mining leases and 9 leases for gold dredging, totalling 9,402 ac. To expedite this work, the Queensland offered to pay for five surveyors, their assistants and equipment at a cost up to £3,000.

The 98 land applications of 233,970 acres in 1900-01 included the BP submission. The request by de Moleyns for 100,000 acres on Mullens Harbour lapsed a year later because de Moleyns could not prove his financial bona fides. The administration also refused a 30,000-acre application for cutting sandalwood on Bioto Creek in the Hall Sound region. The total area granted in 1900-01 amounted to 8,580 acres. The tiny allocation of plantation land to prospective enterprises became even clearer in the following year. The Le Hunte administration granted only 1,115 acres from applications totalling 202,529 acres in 1901-02—most of it to the Christian missions. This was despite the 696,421 acres the Crown had amassed over the years.[66]

After the rejection of the Hall Sound application, the demand for agricultural land virtually stopped. To improve the situation Acting Administrator, Christopher Robinson, contemplated changes to the land law. He proposed that the Crown hold the title to all lands in European possession and for private persons, companies and missions to acquire land only under lease. Robinson expected very low returns on rental, with payments scaled to the capacity of an enterprise or person.[67]

Ignoring the demands of the planters and settlers Francis Barton ended the granting of freehold rights on 1 September 1906. The Port Moresby administration had alienated approximately 1,000,000 acres to the Crown, but after 24 years of European presence only 1,467 acres of land was developed for agricultural purposes. By 1906 the BNG administration had granted 465 land titles to the Christian missions, traders, Henry Wickham, the Whitten brothers, and to small-scale farmers.

Notes

1   Beatrice Grimshaw, *Papua the Marvellous: the Country of Chance*, p. 5

2   D.T. Merrett, 'Australian Banking Practice and the Crisis of 1893', *Australian Economic History Review*, 29, 1, (1990) pp. 60–85

3   CPP, 1902–2, vol. ii

4   AR-BNG (1898-99) p. 108

5   AR-BNG (1899-1900) p. xxvii

6   Bolton, pp. 243 & 246

7   CPD, vol. vi, 1901, p. 7092

8   Griffith to Barton, 6 July 1901 (NLA Mfm G27551 Series 1 MS 51/1/800)

9   Proceedings in the Senate, NLA Mfm G27551 Series 1 MS 51/1/800, p. 7477.

10   *Commonwealth Gazette* on 26 May 1902 (AR-BNG [1901-02] p. 7)

11   CPD, vol. vi, 1901, p. 7406

12   D. Langmore claims G.R. Le Hunte, son of George Le Hunte and his wife Mary, daughter of E. Pennefather, Lord Justice of Ireland, was born on 20 Aug. 1852 in Ireland on the family estate at Artramont, Wexford County (Australian Dictionary of Biography, vol. 10, pp. 66–7). *The Advertiser* (=*AA*) (1903) 9 May, p. 7 & (1925) 31 Jan., p. 13

13   Papers of Atlee Hunt (Correspondence, NLA MS 52); BC (1903) 19 June, p. 14

14   AR-BNG (1899-1900) p. x; (1902-03) p. 13

15   In 1906 Monckton became the first European to climb Mt Albert Edward (3,990m). He repeated MacGregor's expedition of 1896 by crossing into GNG north of the Waria River and then traversing BNG north to south Lutton, N., Australian Dictionary of Biography, vol. 10, pp. 549-50

16   Le Hunte to Premiers, 11 Sep. 1899, Despatches from the Lieutenant-Governor of BNG to the Governor of Queensland', 1896–1905 (NAA Series G73–CA1295); BNG 'Correspondence' (NLA MS 52)

17   AR-BNG (1898-99) pp. 108–9

18   AR-BNG (1900-01) p. vi

19   Chart 16 (annex)

20   C. Monckton, Last Days in New Guinea, p. 2. 'Natives on the Goldfields', *Brisbane Courier* (31 Jan. 1903, p. 14); *The Examiner & The Adelaide Register*, (21 Jan. 1903, pp. 5 & 6)

21   AR-BNG (1896-1897) p. xvi

22   NAA Series A1, G91–CO14 and G100–CA1419–CO14. *The West Australian* (1896) 17 June, p. 5 & 28 July 1897, p. 6, Western Mail (1896) 19 Jun., p. 31; *Kalgoorlie Western Argus* (1898) 5 May, p. 11. See H.N. Nelson, *Black, White & Gold*, p. 57

23   AR-BNG (1897-98) pp. xx, xxi & 93; (1898-99) pp. xvii, xviii & 92; (1899-1900) p. xxi; (1900-1901) p. xxx

24   AR-BNG (1899-1900) pp. xxi, 84 & 108–9. The 'Gap' referred to is the Kokoda Gap. AR-BNG (1898-99) p. 41–5

25   AR-BNG [1800–1901] p. xlii. H.J. Gibbney, Australian Dictionary of Biography, vol. 3, p. 48.

26   'Diary of a Trip to the Yodda Valley, Undertaken for the Purpose of Discovering a Practicable Road to the New Diggings, and of the Laying out of the Prospecting Claim at Blazed Tree Creek, by William .E. Armit. (AR-BNG (1899-1900) pp. 87–95

27   'Report of the New Road from Tamata to Yodda Valley, and on the Natives Inhabiting the Kumusi and Yodda Valleys' (AR-BNG (1899-1900) pp. 95–8

28   AR-BNG (1900-01) p. 51 and (1901-02) p. 21. On de Moleyns' ventures in BNG read B. Malinowski, *A Diary in the Strict Sense of the Term*, p. 39

29   BC (1902) 24 Dec., p.8; Monckton, pp. 40, 31 & 47. AR-BNG (1903-04) pp. 11–12, 35

30   AR-BNG (1900-01) pp. 48–9; Nelson, pp. 122–3

31   Nelson, pp. 124, 158 & 163; J.L. Indriess, *Gold-Dust and Ashes*, p. 12

32   AR-BNG (1904-05) p. 34.

33   AR-BNG [1900-01] pp. 48 & 55–6

34   AR-BNG (1903-04) pp. 39–40

35   AR-BNG (1903-04) p. 38; (1904-05) p. 37

36   AR-BNG (1904-05) pp. 13 & 34; (1903-04) pp. 11 & 39

37   AR-BNG (1904-05) pp. 13 & 34; AR-BNG (1905-06) p. 12

38   ibid, (1905-06) pp. 12 & 39

39   AR-BNG (1903-04) p. 36 (1905-06) pp. 12 & 39

40   Legge, p. 105

41   Chart 31

42   AR-BNG (1898-99) p.36; see M. Spencer, *Public Health in Papua New Guinea*, p. 71

43   AR-BNG (1898-99) p. vi; Spencer, pp. 62–3

44   C.R.B. Blackburn, 'Medicine in New Guinea: three and a half century of change', *Postgraduate Medical Journal*, Nr. 46 (Sydney, 1970, April)

45   AR-BNG (1899-1900) pp. 19, 32, 111 & 113. Spencer, p. 70

46   AR-BNG (1905-06) p. 76

47   AR-BNG (1900-01) p. vi; AR-BNG (1900-01) p. 37

48   AR-BNG (1902-03) p. 42, (1903-04) pp. 14 & 52. See Spencer, p. 74

49   AR-BNG (1903-04) pp. 53 & 66; (1904-05) pp. 17 & 64. D. Wetherell, *Reluctant Mission*, p. 225, referred to venereal disease as the 'white man's disease'

50   'Nursing in New Guinea', *TQ* (1906) 17 Feb. p. 6

51   AR-BNG (1904-05). pp. 17 & 64

52   AR-BNG (1905-06) pp. 76 & 84

53   AR-BNG (1899-1900) p. v

54   AR-BNG (1898-99) pp. 57–65

55   AR-BNG (1900-1901) p. v

56   AR-BNG (1899-1900) p. xxii ; V&P (Qld) 1899, p. 938; .Lewis, p. 36

57   'Novel Launch' *TQ* (1898) 26 Nov. pp. 1032–3

58   'Narrow Escape of Dr Vaughan' *Barrier Miner* (1899) 11 Sep. p. 2

59   Lewis, pp. 37–8.; Nelson, pp. 10, 42, 60 & 199

60   Burns to Black, 5 Sep. 1899, cited in Buckley & Klugman, p. 96

61   'Development of New Guinea', letter of James Burns to the editor *SMH* (1900) 6 Nov. p. 7

62   'The Hall Sound Company', *Morning Bulletin* (Rockhampton, 1900) 23 Nov., p. 4; 'Proposed Development', BC (1900) 19 Nov., p. 9.

63   BP minute of meeting, 11 Oct. 1900, ANU-NBAC, N 115/32; Staniforth Smith Papers (NLA MS 1709, item 1461); BC (1903) 5 May, p. 5. 'Development of New Guinea', *South Australian Register* (1900) 14 Nov., p. 4; *The West Australian* (1900) 16 Nov. p. 5

64   'Notes on New Guinea', BC (1902) 11 Aug. p. 2

65   BP, 'All About Burns, Philp & Company, Ltd.' (1903). 'New Guinea', W Gors, *Alexandra & Yea Standard* (1903) 13 Feb., supplement; BP, Report No 12, ANU- NBAC, N 115/32. AR-BNG (1898-99) p. xxvii, (1899-1900) p. 4; see Lewis, p. 25

66   AR-BNG (1889-90) pp. 23–4. (1899-1900) pp. xl & 110. (1900-01) pp. 104 & 106; (1901-02)

67   Minutes, Executive Council Meetings, Despatch no. 35, 12 Aug. 1903 (NAA Series G68–CA1417)

THE GOLD-BASED ECONOMY OF BNG AND PAPUA

At the helm of government in Port Moresby since 1907, Lieutenant-Governor Hubert Murray's reference to unlimited wealth suggested a thriving Papuan economy. The opposite was the case. No agricultural development of any note took place in BNG for its first 22 years. The anticipated discovery of minerals was patchy at best, and the colony's economy increasingly depended on government funding and import tariffs.

Lieutenant-Governor William MacGregor ended 1888-89, the first full year of BNG, with a surplus of £8,011. The trading account of the Protectorate deteriorated to a deficit of £11,140 in 1891-92, which was close to the typical balance for the following 5 years. MacGregor left BNG with a trade surplus of £2,888 in 1898, which increased to £16,236 under his successor, R. Le Hunte, in 1898-99. This was the highest surplus for the next 25 years. When Australia assumed responsibility for BNG in 1906/07, gold was the only meaningful industry. At that time, the export of gold amounted to £87,869 if the estimate is correct. With the exception of £915 worth of coffee beans there was no plantation industry producing exportable goods in 1906. Trade copra (£9,315) exceeded the combined exports of sandalwood (£2,522), trepang (£3,027) and pearl shell (£2,478) during that year.

By 1914 annual gold exports had fallen to £46,233. Revenue from copper ore, mined for the first time in BNG in 1906, rose briefly to £19,733 in 1914, declining thereafter to immaterial levels until mining of the vast Bougainville copper and gold deposit started in 1972. By the outbreak of World War I hopes of discovering a rich lode in Papua had all but vanished, and Australia's only colony turned its attention increasingly to the production of plantation copra to try to become economically self-sufficient.

Gold was in people's minds in Australia as the 19th Century ended. The rich deposits discovered in 1851 in the Ballarat and Bendigo region of Victoria set off the first large gold rush in Australia. The discovery of gold at Canoona near Rockhampton was the first of many discoveries that spurred development in Queensland and helped to protect that colony during the 1860s depression. Large nuggets found at Gympie in 1867 and at Charters Towers and the Etheridge River in 1872, and the rich placer deposits on the north bank of the Palmer River near Cooktown in 1873, underpinned the Queensland economy during this period. Gold production exceeded the value of all other commodities in Queensland well into the 1890s. One of the most profitable gold, silver and copper mines in the world commenced production at Mount Morgan (the mountain of gold) after its discovery in 1882. The Croydon discovery northwest of Charters Towers in 1885 was the last of the major gold finds in Queensland. With the gold mined out, prospectors trekked south to a new discovery in Tasmania at Mt Lyell in 1886 or to the East Kimberley of Western Australia. The last big rush in Australia followed the discoveries at Coolgardie (1892) and at Kalgoorlie (1893) in Western Australia. The last great gold rush in the world started with the discovery of rich placer deposits at Klondike on the Yukon River in northwest Canada in 1897. Many Australian prospectors went to Canada and Alaska, others stayed on to work the fields they knew best or ventured across the Coral Sea to southeast New Guinea and follow the naturalist John MacGillivray's suggestion in 1852:

> That gold exists in the western and northern portion of New Guinea has long been known; that it also exists on the south-eastern shores of that great island is equally true, as a specimen of pottery procured at Redscar Bay contained a few laminar grains of this precious metal. The clay in which the gold was imbedded was probably part of the great alluvial deposit on the banks of the rivers, the mouth of which we saw in that neighbourhood, doubtless originating in the high mountains behind, part of the Owen Stanley Range.[2]

The geologist and photographer, Richard Daintree, worked on the possibility in 1870 that the gold-bearing rock formation of the Peak Downs and parts of the Gilbert River in north Queensland should persist in the south-eastern extremity of New Guinea. 'If continuous it would give such rocks a large development in the interior, and so afford fair promise of goldfields when colonised', he surmised.[3]

Jimmy Caledonia, a Queensland miner, and Andrew Goldie thought they had confirmed Daintree's assumption with their discovery of gold dust at the junction of the Laloki and Goldie rivers northwest of Port Moresby. While many of the 100 or so miners who went there succumbed to malaria, hostile tribes, or aborted New Guinea's first gold rush in 1878 for the lack of discovering pay dirt, this unsuccessful quest for gold was the catalyst for the industry that formed BNG.[4]

The geology of British New Guinea

MacGregor despised the hordes of prospectors who roamed the country without considering the rights of the Papuans. But he also welcomed the knowledge and assistance that skilled miners like William Simpson and George Clark provided when exploring the country. Thus he arranged with Queensland's geologist, R. L. Jack, to send Andrew Gibb Maitland to BNG in 1891 to conduct exploratory inspections.

The Assistant Geological Surveyor of Queensland, 26-year-old Gibb Maitland left Port Moresby for Samarai on the *Merrie England* on 27 May. Over a period of four months, Gibb Maitland carried out geological examinations on the southeast coast and some adjacent islands (including Dinner Island on which Samarai was established). He investigated geological and geographical occurrences through Goschen Strait, as far as Bartle Bay, and in the D'Entrecasteaux Archipelago near Dawson Strait before returning to Samarai on 24 June. In the course of a hasty traverse of the Louisiade Archipelago in early July, he studied gold ore in the quartz reefs on Sudest and assessed alluvial gold found in the creeks on Misima (St. Aignan Island).

Back on the mainland, Gibb Maitland and M. H. Moreton (R.M. for the Eastern Division and secretary to MacGregor) climbed the largely inaccessible peak (3,676 m) of Mount Suckling to 2,553 metres while tracking from Awaiama on Chads Bay to Collingwood Bay. With the aid of the 40 carriers Moreton recruited from Tauputa village, the pair completed this strenuous expedition in just over 3 weeks. A month later, during the first 2 weeks of August, MacGregor relieved his secretary, Moreton, to accompany Gibb Maitland from Milne Bay to Mullins Harbour.

Following a brief return to Port Moresby on 13 August, Gibb Maitland travelled via the Laloki River to the Astrolabe Range and on to the St Joseph River. Here he was unable to do serious work though: 'the unsettled disposition of the natives, coupled with wet weather and attacks of fever prevented much geological work being done', he wrote in his diary.[5]

The excursion to the Morehead River on the Dutch border completed Gibb Maitland's 5 month geographical overview of BNG. He returned to Brisbane in October 1891 to write up his findings.

Drawing on literature, specimens and evidence picked up from prospectors, Gibb Maitland completed his 'Geological Observations in British New Guinea' in 1892. He advised the Queensland government:

> The list of minerals of economic importance hitherto met with in BNG is extremely small. Considering, however, the enormous area of country yet quite unknown, and the comparatively small number of persons who have hitherto made the search for minerals the object of their visit to New Guinea, and the fact that the natives of the country do not make use of the more important minerals, this scarcity need excite no surprise.[6]

In his 'Economic Geology', Gibb Maitland concerned himself mainly with the examination of the Caledonian Reef on Sudest and the prospecting activities on Misima. He confirmed gold specks in several bags of wash collected by MacGregor's party on the Vanapa River. He also reported an uneconomic quantity of gold in connection with cinnabar (mercury sulphide) on Normanby in the D'Entrecasteaux Islands and on St Joseph. Gibb Maitland believed the principal minerals in BNG to be gold, copper, iron, sulphur, graphite, lignite and mercury.

Sudest Island, the first discovery of payable gold in BNG

In 1886, George the Greek, a buccaneer from Cooktown, took a party of 23 men on his cutter to the Louisiade Archipelago in search for gold. With malaria fever and dysentery among their most vivid memories, they returned to Cooktown after seven months of fossicking in the dense scrub of Sudest Island. Their efforts to keep a campfire going during persisting rain and mist remained unrewarded. They returned home without a grain of gold.

Port Moresby granted Captain David Whyte permission to take nine prospectors from the Palmer field to the gold-bearing reef he had identified on Joannet Island (Sudest) in 1887. The party, financed by North Queensland businessmen, set sail from Cooktown on the *Juanita* in May 1888. Even though Whyte was unable to make out his previous discovery, the party returned to Cooktown three months later with 142 ounces (oz.) panned on the wash of the Runcie River on nearby Tagula Island.

Disastrous Ventures

Estimated returns from Louisiade (Sudest and Misima) Islands.

Year	European miners	Indentured Labour	Gold yield (oz.)	Value of gold (£)
1888-89	200	600	3,850	14,187
1889-90	400	1,200	3,470	12,140
1890-91	76	228	2,426	8,231
1891-92	65	195	1,235	4,322
1892-93	60	180	1,200	4,500
1893-94	38	114	1,128	3,906
1894-95	30	90	728	2,565
1895-96	20	84	600	2,100
1896-97	20	60	560	1,960
1897-98	28	84	600	2,100
1898-99	20	60	550	1,925
1899-00	16	48	450	1,575
1900-01	9	27	300	1,050
1901-02	13	39	400	1,400
1902-03	10	30	300	1,050
1903-04	8	24	300	1,050
1904-05	10	30	300	1,050
1905-06	14	42	400	1,400
1906-07	11	35	350	1,225
1907-08	11	35	350	1,225
1908-09	n.d.	n.d.	n.d.	n.d.
1909-10	7	30	200	700
1910-11	7	30	200	700
1911-12	9	90	600	2,100
1912-13	19	100	500	1,750
1913-14	19	100	421	1,200
1914-15	31	260	1,941	4,860
Total	Average 44	Average 147	23,359	80,271

Whyte's discovery caused much excitement in North Queensland; it set off the first gold rush to East New Guinea. Administrator MacGregor had gazetted the Runcie River goldfield in September 1888 and some 200 miners hastened to the Sudest. In early 1889, Walter Rose returned from the island with the news that about 300 men were working the rivers and creeks, and that on St Aignan, an island to the northwest of Sudest, 16 men got 9oz. between them in four days. 'For a man who is content with 2dwt. to 3dwt. per day the field will last a very long time', Rose reflected.

MacGregor, while unhappy about the uncontrolled arrival of the hundreds of fossickers, considered it prudent to send several hundred bags of gravel from the Louisiade to Logan, Jack & Clarke in Townsville. While the assays did not provide sufficient information to construct a picture on the geology of the islands, the Robert L. Jack report to MacGregor seem to confirm Daintree's proposition that rocks containing gold in Australia were also present in the Louisiade, viz:

The specimens reported on tell no connected tale such as would enable one to construct even a theory regarding the geology of the islands. They show, however, that palreozoic rocks such as are the matrices of gold and other metallic deposits in Australia and elsewhere are abundant,

Stamp-Battery at Mt Adelaide in Central Sudest, ca. 1898 (courtesy T. Neale)

and that basaltic lava are of common occurrence. The limestones may yield fossils which would be of great service in unravelling the structure of the islands. Four of the quartz samples give traces of gold by the iodine process, and this fact is of importance. Permit me to recommend that you should impress on prospectors the importance and simplicity of this test, which will detect the presence of gold in quartz or pyrites, even though present in such minute quantities as to be invisible in a dish ' prospect' with the most careful manipulation. The tincture of iodine of medicine is the only re-agent required, and the only apparatus necessary is a few test tubes, a spirit lamp, a glass funnel, white blotting paper and asbestos. Iodine is dissolved in alcohol till the solution is of a rich, but not too dark, port wine colour. The powdered mineral is then put in a china or glass dish, with its own bulk of the solution, and occasionally stirred for two hours. The solution is next decanted and filtered, and a bunch of asbestos fibres of the thickness of a penholder dipped into it. The asbestos (held with pincers) is then pushed into the flame of a spirit lamp. A purple tinge on the asbestos, after the spirit has been burnt off, is a certain indication of the presence of gold in the mineral.[7]

Hence, the main islands of the Louisiade Archipelago—Sudest, St Aignan, Rossel and Joannet—attracted the attention of even more prospectors. In February and March 1889, T. Downey and J. Blanchfield discovered gold on Gumonina Creek on the western side of St Aignan Island. It created a short-lived rush though. Of the 400 prospectors who followed them during that year, only 150 men worked the Misima field a year later. In June 1890 MacGregor reported disappointingly: 'I saw a great many dishes of stuff washed, none without "colours", but none yielding more than 2 to 4 grains (gr.), and the best below sometimes 8 feet (ft) or 10 ft of earth'.[8] A year later, the remaining 50 prospectors had dug the creek beds to the last recoverable grains of gold.

During the same year Messrs McLean and Samuelson started to work a promising vein in the southwest of Sudest they called the Caledonian Reef. Gibb Maitland reported this claim in June 1891. Samples he sent to Charters Towers for analysis gave 9 Pennyweights (dwt.) 17 gr. of gold and 1 ounce (oz.) of silver to the ton.[9] About 3 tons of ore shipped to Sydney yielded 4 oz. 18 dwt of gold and 1 oz. 21 gr. of silver per ton. While this was considerably better than the ore assayed by Gibb Maitland, the two miners were unable to repeat this early success, and after struggling on for another two years McLean & Samuelson abandoned the lease.[10]

For a brief period a new claim at the foot of Mt Adelaide in central Sudest, raised the hopes of the miners who kept an eye on the Louisiades. A few miles inland from Hinai Bay, outcrops of coloured quartz showed enough prospects of gold and silver for metropolitan money to back a new enterprise in 1896. MacGregor was keen for the venture to proceed. Quartz reefing did not interfere greatly with the fishing and hunting of the local people and he informed G. Hancock of the British New Guinea Goldfields Proprietary Co., Ltd. that his administration was ready to assist.

Hancock, aided by naturalist and prospector, Sam Day, recruited workers from nearby Rossel Island and from the faraway Fly River district; MacGregor supplied prison labour from Samarai for the construction of a boat landing on the mud flats of Hinai Bay and a 7.5 km track to the mine site.[11]

Nothing ever went to plan in New Guinea. During the first 12 months of the mine's establishment, the overseer and several mine workers died. Rotten food and poor living quarters affected the Europeans and the locals alike. While Hancock provided additional blankets to the workers and supplemented their daily staple of rice and sago with fish and vegetables, incessant rain made the working conditions treacherous and expensive. When the 10-head stamp battery was finally operational in September 1897, the *Sydney Morning Herald (SMH)* reported

> At Sudest, the British New Guinea Goldfields Propriety Company has had a trial crushing, which proved highly satisfactory.... Nearly all obstacles—and there were many—have now been overcome, and results may before long bear out the favourable opinions of the property entertained by Messrs Hancock and Day'.[12]

This optimism was not borne out by the facts though. Stockpiling of quartz commenced haphazardly, and the crushed ore did not yield the expected gold. Two years after the *SMH* article appeared, *The Brisbane Courier* reported on Le Hunte's assessment of the British New Guinea Goldfields Proprietary Company:

> The initial expenses of this company were heavy, probably much more so than its founders expected. In quite new country and under entirely novel conditions most people would be apt to underestimate the cost and labour required in landing heavy machinery, making roads over which to carry it through wooded hills of soft slippery clay, and hauling it over these roads. This work, has been done, and at present there is a quartz machine erected at the foot of the slope of the hill in which the reef is situated. The reef is reached by tunnels. A large quantity of quartz has been crushed. The return of gold is not known to the Government.[13]

In reality the return of gold was meagre. Apart from overspending on establishment Hancock underestimated the time and cost of driving into the hard rock of Mt. Adelaide. When he failed to raise new capital in 1900, the operations of British New Guinea Goldfields shut down.[14]

The Woodlark Mines, ca. 1906 (K. Mackay, *Across Papua*, p. 65)

Kulamadau Woodlark Island Gold Mining Company (S. Smith, *Handbook of the Territory of Papua, 1912)*

Prospecting on Joannet and Rossel Island in 1888, on Normanby in 1889 and 1895, and Fergusson Island in 1895 in the D'Entrecasteaux Archipelago proved unrewarding. Walter Gors of Burns, Philp (BP) warned in 1897, 'no payable gold is known of at present in the colony … and the few miners remaining on the field have not been able to earn their tucker'.[15] The prospectors on the Sudest had packed up their sluice boxes and the 16 Europeans still on the island traded for gold with the locals. Le Hunte took note of the poor state of New Guinea gold mining in his first annual account. On 30 June 1899 his deputy, Francis P. Winter reported:

> Matters are and have been dull in the Louisiade Gold Field. On Misima mining has practically ceased… Alluvial mining in Sudest Island has fallen very low. What there is, is chiefly carried on by natives. [But] that there is no more gold to be found would be a hasty conclusion to come to as what may exist in the bowels of its lofty, densely-wooded hills is unknown.[16]

Le Hunte declared the Milne Bay area—a short 50 km from Samarai—a commercial gold field on 6 December 1899, the rumoured 60 oz. to the ton proved unsubstantiated. Some 60 men sought their luck in the area for a short period. However, Milne Bay barely supported 20 miners at the best of times.[17]

Whatever the beliefs and hopes of the prospectors and the administration in Port Moresby, gold mining in New Guinea was a tough, dangerous and a mainly unprofitable business. A 'white man's grave', the diggers called BNG. Malaria, malnutrition and dysentery took many prospectors before they picked the first grain of gold from their dishes. Others died from brawling over claims or at the hands of ferocious tribes. Even during the most productive years from 1888 to 1893, miners in the Louisiades obtained yields less than £110 worth of gold per annum.[18]

Misima: hard rock ore and inadequate capital

The Misima field provided an illustration of the haphazard nature of the gold industry in BNG. In 1904, five European men and two European women resided on Sudest. Resident Magistrate Mathew Moreton's wife bred cattle on Nivani Station while the eight 'permanent' expatriates on Misima worked the terraces of the old claims, barely making rations. The miners' hopes lifted once more when J. W. Reed, A. Grant and J. R. Smith discovered several lodes towards the end of 1904. After pegging Quartz Mountain, Sisa Gold Mountain, The Galena and The Massive a metallurgist from the London-based firm of Bewick, Moreing & Co. assessed the discoveries on Misima. The results were encouraging, but ultimately disappointing: The Massive contained a big lode, except the gold was too fine requiring large capital investment to recover.[19]

Six years on renewed, in 1911, Mount Sisa Gold Mining Co., N.L. raised £5,000 on the Sydney equity market for a mining venture on Misima. The company acquired a 12-acre lease on the Engubinina Creek in the Mt Sisa district, Site clearing, the installation of a mill, stores, housing and native quarters was completed in 1912. Start-up problems and a lack of funds prevented the mine reaching economic production.

Estimated returns from the Murua (Woodlark Island) goldfields

Year	European miners	Indentured labour	Gold yield (oz.)	Value of gold (£)
1895-96	190	760	12,000	42,000
1896-97	400	1,600	20,000	70,000
1897-98	160	640	10,000	35,000
1898-99	62	248	5,000	17,500
1899-00	76	304	6,000	21,000
1900-01	150	600	7,500	26,250
1901-02	100	400	7,000	24,500
1902-03	115	374	8,500	29,750
1903-04	125	500	9,000	31,500
1904-05	100	400	9,689	33,911
1905-06	80	294	10,527	36,844
1906-07	69	227	5,296	18,536
1907-08	69	227	5,296	18,536
1908-09	70	252	6,339	19,721
1909-10	48	252	9,781	33,594
1910-11	89	343	8,632	32,276
1911-12	89	403	9,447	32,333
1912-13	93	420	12,147	41,515
1913-14	39	347	9,182	29,840
1914-15	58	450	7,171	24,449
Total	Average 109	Average 452	178,507	619,055

Twenty years later, The Mount Sisa Gold Fields (Papua) N.L. Co. drove a 3700 meter tunnel on the abandoned lease to reach a 'Peak Lode 14 ft wide by 100 ft leader, all highly payable', according to a report in the *Sydney Morning Herald*.[20]

The Misima Gold Mining Co. renamed St Aignan Mining Co. Ltd in 1914, preceded the Mt Sisa Co. Prospecting the same area and taking options on gold leases at Mt Sisa Umuna in 1910, Misima Gold Mining planned to start mining its Massive No. 1 claim in 1913. Two veins, assayed by government geologist, E. R. Stanley, contained sugar-like quartz in a 212 ft high wall. Prison labour built a 7.5 km-road from the harbour to the mine-site, and a road of similar length from the mine to a sodium cyanide plant. A saltwater sluicing pipeline and a 28-h.p. Hornsby Stockport gas engine, powering two Huntington Mills, saw the work completed by early 1915.[21]

Also in 1914, the New Guinea Option Syndicate N.L. entered into an agreement over its Massive Block (Umuna) and Massive No 1 South leases with the Broken Hill Proprietary Block 10 Co. Despite, or because the First World War BHP was seeking to invest some of its large cash reserves in gold opportunities outside Australia.[22]

After expending some £11,000 on ore delineation, BHP Block 10 Directors floated Block 10 Misima Gold Mines, N.L. on 8 September 1916 with the intention of amalgamating the lease on the line of lode at Misima. The consolidation of BHP Block 10 Co., Ltd.; St. Aignan Mining Co. Ltd.; R. Boyd and C. Coppard; Misima Gold Mines, N.L.; and St. Aignan Gold Options, N.L. provided a stockpile of approximately 100,000 tons of ore worth £1-19 a ton, and lodes which, in the opinion of the Directors, rendered the Misima mining enterprise viable. The venture never lived up to expectations though. With only modest returns on expenditures of some £300,000, Block 10 Misima Gold Mines' major shareholder, BHP Block 10 Co., Ltd., forced the closure of the mine in August 1922.[23]

Island: Papua's most prolific gold producing district to 1919

The trader Richard Ede, Cooktown miner Charlie Lobb and the Swede Soelberg were the first Europeans to wash gold from the Suloga and Okiduse Creeks. News of their discovery in the south of Woodlark in June 1895 did not take long to reach the Louisiades where the easy gold had been taken and the few miners left were eager to move on to more prolific grounds. When MacGregor inspected Woodlark (Murua) Island in November that year he found 20–30 European were 'doing fairly well'.[24] With good indications of gold at both locations, MacGregor proclaimed Murua as BNG's second goldfield on 6 November 1895. While miners were keen to keep a rich 500 oz. patch in the Okiduse Range secret, the news of a discovery at New Chum's Gully (later Karavakum or Bonivat) spread quickly.

On 19 June 1896, the Perth *Western Mail* wrote of two prospectors arriving in Cooktown by the *Titus* with 75 oz., and that after six months' prospecting on Woodlark the McPherson party arrived at Samarai with 1000 oz. of gold. These men reported 'a big future for gold mining in Papua Land, if it was not the forever present fever', the paper informed its readers. On 11 March 1897, *The Brisbane Courier* reported the arrival of the steamer *Burdekin* with 2,000 oz. of gold from Woodlark. Moreover, five days later, *The Adelaide Advertiser* reported the arrival in Cooktown of 32 passengers on the schooner *Ivanhoe* with about 300 oz. of gold on them. Besides this, the ship's manifest showed 800 oz. from Woodlark consigned to Messrs. Burns, Philp & Co.[25]

While a miner on the *Burdekin* wrote to the *Brisbane Courier* in March 1897, 'there is no inducement to go [to New Guinea] as, notwithstanding the new find, the field is practically worked out, [and] fever and dysentery is causing many deaths amongst the miners', the Woodlark discoveries started the third rush to BNG.[26]

When the *Merrie England* cast anchor in Suloga Bay in November 1895 MacGregor found about 190 miners on Woodlark who had shipped 1,373 oz. of gold valued at £4,375 in 1895-96. It was much less than McGregor's estimate. He believed that the gold taken from Woodlark during the 12 months to June 1896 amounted to some thousands of pound sterling in value and that many of the miners had done 'well, some of them very well'. He proclaimed Woodlark as BNG's second goldfield.[27]

With the last major Queensland gold discovery of the 1880s petering out, the Woodlark rush engendered renewed eagerness in the minds and bodies of the ever-hopeful gold fossickers. At the peak of activities, 400 miners dug and washed the gold-bearing riverbanks and beds of Woodlark. Some 1,600 Papuans were feeding the sluice boxes and performed most of the backbreaking work. The recovery of 20,000 oz. of gold in 1896-97 was a never to be repeated level of production on Woodlark during the pre-War years.

A. J. Campbell, R.M. South-Eastern Division, was responsible for law and order on the 100 square kilometer that made up this mineral-bearing country. With his headquarters on Nivani, 150 km to the south and Samarai, 335 km to the northeast of Woodlark, his mining warden found it difficult to control the fortune hunters who came without mining skills, money, equipment or stores. The leases would not support more than 170 miners in his opinion. 'I have before me several Northern papers', he wrote to MacGregor on 20 March 1897, 'but in none of them can I find a word of warning re the Woodlark Goldfields, although … there are plenty of, if not absolutely untrue, highly exaggerated, reports of the quantity of gold, the vessels, or miners, carry away with them from the island'.[28] The *Kalgoorlie Western Argus,* however, reported, 'the prospects of a speedy development of the gold mining industry in BNG are not promising. [W]hereas there would be metalliferrous wealth in New Guinea, the mistake made by the miners is that they come to New Guinea quite unprepared for the country, and in a very short time are totally without means'.[29]

With the help of negative publicity in Australia, death and sickness amongst the miners and their workers and a realization that gold was only found the hard way, the presence of European miners on Woodlark dwindled to 62 by April 1898. With this population, alluvial mining on the island again became profitable, and each miner and his team of four Papuans sluiced on average 80 oz. of gold during the year to June 1899. Annual earnings averaged a healthy £300, with similar results in 1899-1900 when 78 miners washed an estimated 6,000 oz. of gold on Woodlark.[30]

Changes to the Queensland Mining Act in 1899 had no bearing on the industry in BNG. While the declining number of gold leases in Queensland led to a reduction from ten to five shillings in the annual fees for a 'Miner's Right',[31] the original fees in BNG were retained.[32] Le Hunte believed new discoveries would attract the miners no matter the cost of a mining claim, and BNG needed the revenue, however low.

At that time, Australian mills were starting to replace the dishes of the alluvial miners. The testing of the Ivanhoe reefs at Kulamadau confirmed a new and seemingly profitable lode in 1899.[33] The prospect lay 3 km from Bonagai on the northern extreme of Kwaipan Bay. Initially worked by single alluvial miners, the confirmation of extensive reefs saw the formation in Sydney of the Woodlark Island Proprietary Gold Mining Company No Liability (N.L.)., Suloga Gold-Mining Co., N.L., in Adelaide the Woodlark-Ivanhoe Gold Mining Company, Ltd., and the Kulamadau Gold Mining Company, Ltd. of Charters Towers.

The Sydney investors who floated The Woodlark Island Proprietary Gold Mining Co. N.L. in 1899 (authorised capital £100,000) secured approximately 91 acres at Kulamadau for an outlay of £20,000 and 10,000 fully paid shares. After visiting the Woodlark Island mine site the company's manager, A.J. Webster, reported in glowing terms that 'the whole of the company's claims are gold-bearing … carrying ore estimated to yield at least 4 oz. to the ton'.[34] However, as nearly all ventures in Papua, Woodlark Island Proprietary had to overcome many hurdles before producing the first ounce of gold. When mine manager John Provis realised that the reef may not contain as much gold as first thought he cut the weekly wage of his expatriate miners from £5 to £4. It brought mine development to a halt. The men contended that owing to malaria fever they were unable to work more than half their time, and that £2.10 per week in Queensland was better than £5 at Woodlark. During the ensuing strike, and the threat by Provis to send south for hands, Woodlark Island Proprietary's General Manager in Sydney, R. N. Kirk, became concerned that the men could turn into a disorderly mob, where 'police and mining property might have fared badly'. He called on the administration in Samarai for an extra mining warden to maintain law and order, and for the engagement of W. B. Bramell, a treasury employee from Port Moresby, to help implement the (Queensland) mining regulations. Resident Magistrate Moreton invoked the return of the weekly wage. Then, by early 1901, the tramline from the mine to the harbour and the 20-head stamp battery completed, Le Hunte took the opportunity to open the first mechanised gold mine in BNG.[35]

The Woodlark Island Proprietary Gold Mining Co. N.L. operated until 1906 more or less successfully. What started as an open-cut soon developed into underground extraction. By early 1904 the miners cut rock 65 meters underground, yielding up to £3/t, but averaging only £1/t. Woodlark Island Proprietary announced a maiden profit of £2218 in 1904, and a maiden dividend of 2d per share at the company's sixth annual meeting a year later. In 1905 the mine crushed a record 10,895 tons of ore for 3,044 oz. gold and 248 oz. from the cyanide treatment of 640 tons tailings.[36]

Flooding kept the mine closed for the most part of 1906. At the annual general meeting on 3 February 1907, the Directors submitted that

> The past six months' operations compel them to ask the shareholders to agree to a scheme for the reconstruction of the company, as it is quite evident that the capital required to put the mine into a profit-earning condition cannot be raised from the present resources. Presuming the Directors' report is adopted, an extraordinary meeting will then be held, when the following reconstruction

motion will be submitted for approval: "That the Directors be authorised to sell and transfer the company's assets and liabilities to a new company, proposed to be formed under the name of 'Woodlark Island Mines, No Liability, having a capital of £12,500 in 50,000 shares of 5s each."

Shareholders passed the resolution at an extraordinary general meeting on 16 July 1907. Woodlark Island Mines, N.L. acquired the assets and liabilities of the Proprietary Company; the Board of Directors remained the same.

When the newly appointed manager W. J. Dawes arrived at the mine he found the main shaft in disrepair. His intention to sink a new shaft to at least 150 metres went no further than the previous level of 60 m. With the only revenue derived from the treatment of tailings, and with some 50 tons of rock crushed at the neighbouring company's mill, Woodlark Island Mines ceased to trade by selling its leases and assets to the Kulamadau (Woodlark Island) Gold Mining Co., Ltd.[37]

Adventurer and speculator, H. W. Clark, met with the Directors of the New Guinea Mining & Prospecting Syndicate N.L. in Adelaide in June 1900. 'The good reports respecting the Kulamadau goldfield were not exaggerated' he told the Directors hoping to engender their interest in the three claims he had secured next to the Woodlark Proprietary Company. 'From a small reef on the celebrated Kulamadau-Ivanhoe lode—said to be one of the richest in Australasia, £20,000 worth of gold had already been won, [and] this lode forms part of his leases', Clark told his prospective financiers. W. H. Gors of Burns, Philp who called on the Directors in Adelaide a month later agreed: 'Woodlark Island was one of the best things ever offered to the Australian public—second only to Mount Morgan. The formation was large and rich and the Adelaide people were fortunate to having secured their claim'.[38]

The Directors of the New Guinea Mining & Prospecting Syndicate N.L. (W. Finlayson, H. Giles and J. T. Ralph) advertised their prospectus on 13 June 1900 to float the Woodlark-Ivanhoe Gold Mining Co N.L. The issue of 25,000 shares of £1 each was fully paid, with an additional 25,000 shares offered for subscription at 2s 6d each and 2s 6d on allotment. The balance of unissued stock could be called by Directors, not exceeding 3d per share per month. With the registration of the company on 4 July 1900, H. C. Clark received £1,000 for the transfer to the company of his three mining leases totalling 34 acres.

Woodlark-Ivanhoe commenced full operations with the commissioning on 9 September 1901 of the second 15-head-battery, a Cornish fire-tube boiler, and a Huntington mill. The equipment was set in motion by H. C. Blunt of the London listed Australian Mining and Gold Recovery Company in the presence of Woodlark Island Proprietary manager, Mr MacFarlane, Oliver Jones of Kulamadau Gold Mining, and a large number of onlookers. MacFarlane proposed the toast of the Woodlark Island mining community. He expressed that 'the island had a great future [and that] the Ivanhoe would prove itself to be a great mine and a dividend paying one. Everything works smoothly. [And] and there will be no difficulty in keeping the plant running full time, as the lode is over 20 ft. wide and can be mined cheaply. The company has a splendid dam holding over 1,000,000 gallons of water, and a great saving is being effected by the use of local wood, which is proving a success in steaming with the Cornish boiler'.[39]

The future did not turn out as MacFarlane predicted though. When the alluvial leases were exhausted, mine manager Bob Boyd drove a 21 and a 30 metre declining tunnel into the hill. At the point of intersection he dug a 25 m shaft to reach a 4.2 m thick vein. It was an expensive undertaking that indebted Woodlark-Ivanhoe to an unsupported level. It required the placement of 60,000 new shares at 10s each. Paid up to 5s the issue was approved at an EGM on 16 September 1901. But, like so many other hopefuls, the venture failed. H. W Clark made some money by selling a piece of dirt that contained little gold and by working in a senior position for the firm. Burns, Philp benefited from shipping men and equipment to the site. The shareholders of ended up empty-handed. Woodlark-Ivanhoe abandoned the lease in 1904.[40]

When Charles Wood panned gold from the creeks at Suloga Harbour, Woodlark, Sydney speculators were eager to buy into his discovery. On Wood's initiative Suloga Gold-Mining Co. N.L. floated in Sydney in May 1900 with a capital of 48,000 shares of £1 each, of which 26,400 were fully paid and the balance paid up to 12s 6d. The company acquired Wood's 60-acre alluvial lease at Suloga and retained his services as the mine manager. The mobilisation of a pumps and sluice boxes was to generate immediate returns from the placer deposits. The reality was different. Most of the gold was water-borne, too fine for the sluice boxes to trap. In order to pay its debts the company made an unsuccessful call of 6d in August 1901. On 21 September 1901 the *Australian Town and Country Journal* reported that two large shareholders in the Suloga Gold Mine had acquired the property on tribute for twelve months. The returns from the property have been so unsatisfactory that the board decided to recall the manager and cease work'.[41]

The Kulamadau (Woodlark Island) Gold Mining Company Ltd. developed its 120-acre mine. The company raised £50,000 in 100,000 shares of 10s each on the Charters Towers Exchange on 16 June 1900. In 1903 Kulamadau (Woodlark Island) acquired the claims of the Woodlark-Ivanhoe Gold Mining Co. By 1904 the mine was a modern enterprise. A Sterling boiler delivered steam to head frames and to the de-watering pumps in the pit and tunnels. Air compressors and electric generators provided services to the shafts and tunnels. The 20-head battery delivered ore from the centrifugal rollers of a Huntington Mill to five Berdan Pan (grinding) mills to three Wilfrey vanners (tables). A cyanide plant for the treatment of tailings comprised a 50-ton leaching vat, a 15-ton mixer and a 40-ton sump vat. Designed for efficiency, the mine returned 3,588 oz. of gold from 4,388 t of ore in 1904-05, and 5,415 oz.. from 5,044 t in 1905-06. Directors declared a maiden dividend of six pence per share in 1904, followed by three pence for the 1904-05 financial year.[42]

With the depletion in 1906 of the short (60 ft) but rich vein, Kulamadau acquired the leases on the north and south of its mine from the Woodlark Island Co. and the nearby leases of the Murua Syndicate (formerly the Woodlark-Ivanhoe Gold Mining Co.). In 1908-09, the company crushed 5,846 t yielding 2,987 oz. from the Murua Syndicate acquisition. The cyanide treatment of 6,600 t tailing recovered 1,002 oz.[43] In 1911 Kulamadau crushed 11,850 t of ore and treated 3,700 t of tailings. By 1914, under the management of the company's Director and attorney, Harry Poole, the men had driven 604 ft of shafts that were timbered to a depth of 122 ft. Drifts and crosscuts extended over 1,298 ft, and numerous winzes (connecting shafts between 2 levels) totalled 34 vertical feet. Three Huntington mills crushed the 1913-14 production of 13,175 t, while 7,700 t of tailings underwent cyanide treatment. It yielded 3,028 oz. and 668.5 oz. respectively. At the mean price of £3-5 per oz., Kulamadau realised gross sales of £12,014 in that financial year. The 22 European miners generated £546 each in revenue for the company. With miners earning between £260 and £300, 'boss-boys' and specialist workers £18, and ordinary workers £6 per year,[44] the operational annual cost of the mine before interest and depreciation amounted to approximately £9,000. To attain a return on the investment and pay a 10% dividend, the company needed to sustain or better this return. It did not. While still realizing a half-year profit of £2,950 for the period ending 31 December 1916, Kulamadau went into voluntary liquidation in 1917-18. Papua Gold Mines Ltd. acquired the leases of Kulamadau (Woodlark Island) Gold Mining Co., Ltd. in 1934.[45]

There were more profitable, short-lived, mines on Woodlark. Soon after the 1900 rush, the McKenzie's Creek claim, approximately 10 km from the Kulamadau reefs, yielded several thousand ounces in a few months. It set a production record not broken in BNG. There was also the discovery of gold in Federation Reef near Busai in 1902. Located 8 km east-southeast from Kulamadau—known as the Busai Mining Centre—Coleman Creek showed high deposits of alluvial gold. At Reilly's Creek, 1 mile south of Busai, other extensive but short-lived alluvial fields were mined.

After declining returns, the syndicates working the Busai Mining Centre (Kikiti Vinai No. 15, Guiau No. 4, Mary Murua No. 19 and Murua No. 3) consolidated their holdings into one gold-mining lease (No. 84) and then, in 1908-09, into the Federation Busai Syndicate. Yielding 62 oz. from only 74 t of crushed ore during its first year, Federation Busai returned a satisfactory result in 1909-10 with 444 oz. of gold recovered from 289 t of ore. 'This property gives every promise of being most valuable', Murua's mining warden and A.R.M., Charles Norrie, observed in 1914. One miner and his 20 workers extracted 214 t from the mine in 1913-14. The crushed material yielded 208 oz. valued at £659. Cyanide treatment of 24 t concentrate extracted gold worth £383 and zinc worth £78. The mine continued at this level of operation until 1918 when the Busai Gold Mining Syndicate acquired the lease.[46]

Discovered in 1910 near McKenzie's Creek, a rich lode of 75% lead also contained 28 oz./t of silver. It did not contain gold though, and because the vein was only 1–5 inches thick, it was regarded non-commercial. The assessment of the Woodlark King, Illawarra and Little McKenzie No. 1 claims at Karavakum by the newly appointed government geologist E. R. Stanley proved a different proposition, however. 'Gold can be seen without the slightest difficulty in the stone [and] one cannot help thinking that this property will have a very bright future', read Stanley's diary entry in 1911.

Removal of overburden on the Little McKenzie No. 1 claim laid bare a rich vein. Trail crushing returned 40 oz. from 23 tons. The setting of a 12 ft diameter by 73 ft deep shaft, and the installation of a 25-head stamp-battery, accessed a lode yielding 228 oz. from 33 t; 162 oz. from 26 t, 287 oz. from 30 t, and 1,045 oz. from 612 tons.[47]

The good returns did not continue. The high concentration of gold was intermittent and was present largely in the initial lode. By 1914 the miners had extended the drift to 645 ft and had sunk the shaft to 125 ft. They only mined 38 t of ore during the year, yielding 17 oz. and 16 dwts. This result did not improve with the treatment of the ore by cyanide, with only £236 realised from processing 460 t.

Even though the gold in the Karavakum district was not uniformly present, Stanley regarded the region as potentially the most important gold-producing area on Woodlark. Like Little McKenzie the nearby Illawarra lease between the Muniai River and Thompson's Creek had a short but spectacularly productive life. Established in 1904, the mine crushed 48 t of ore in 1905-06 from a slender vein, returning 286 oz. of gold valued at £987. The following year it crushed the remaining 456 t yielding 256 oz. Thereafter the miners on the Illawarra leases worked predominantly on alluvial deposits.

The Woodlark King claim on Karavakum, produced an astonishing 599 oz. from only 65 t of ore in 1904-05, and 944 oz. from 188 t the following year. When theis mother lode was exhausted, the owners sold the lease to the J. M Leish syndicate. Owning half of the lease and working for tribute, Leish struck a rich lode in 1911. The initial crushing of 14 tons of rock yielded 350 oz. which is 25 oz. to the ton. With a more substantial mill, concentrator and cyanide plant installed in 1910, Woodlark King, Woodlark King South No. 148, the Woodlark King (No. 2 South) No. 155 and the Just-in-Time leases averaged 3 oz. of gold to the ton, with some results coming in at 162 oz. from 18 t and 466 oz. from 47 tons.[48]

New lodes were uncovered with the sluicing of the river and creek banks. In 1914 Norrie reported: 'This mine [Woodlark King] is still looked upon as a wonder, and great interest is exhibited by all in regard to its future'. This acclamation by a government officer is not surprising. The production by two miners and 22 'natives' of 1,596 oz. of gold from 372 t of ore realised approximately £5,350 in receipts during the year of the report. The Woodlark King mine had returned £50,000 since starting production in 1903.[49] However, as with all mines, this one was not without its problems. Groundwater recharge required large outlays for pumps and drainage systems. Leish and his syndicate tried unsuccessfully to float the company on the stock exchange in Australia in 1914. The de-watering pumps failed or could not cope with the large ingress of water in 1917. It resulted in the flooding of shafts, tunnels and drifts. A new prospectus issued in 1921 was also unsuccessful in raising capital, and the 'wonder mine' on Woodlark shut down.[50]

In 1912, seventeen years after the discovery of gold near Suloga Harbour, Stanley submitted his report on the geology of Woodlark Island. He found Murua massively more productive than the neighbouring Louisiade fields. Woodlark yielded by far the largest quantity of gold mined in Papua. In 1912-13 the miners on the island generated a record £41,515 in gold receipts. In 1914 Woodlark produced 46% of all the gold mined in Papua.[51]

Yet the majority of miners found it difficult to make a decent living. Their average annual income for 1895-96 and 1914-15 of £283 barely covered labour, equipment

Crossing the Yodda at Oila; log flume channelling water to the sluice boxes (Murray, *Papua of Today,* 1925)

and other operational expenses. The years 1905-06, 1909-10, 1912-13 and 1913-14, where the average annual income from mining ranged from £446 to £765, indicate general profitability. A handful of miners made a small fortune during this period. However, considering average earnings, the European miners on Papua's most prolific goldfields lived at a below subsistence level. Moreover, according to the *Cairns Post,* 'The Woodlark digger does not hang on to his money. Easy got, easy gone, is his motto. Consequently he has no money for developing his mine'.[52]

As to the indentured workers, they made some money, as did the local people who prospected the abandoned fields and who had learnt to win gold by amalgamating the crushed rock with mercury. Working the Woodlark fields was as hazardous for the Europeans as it was for the local population. The mortality rate of 10% in 1902-03 (37 of 374 workers) was mainly due to beri-beri (thiamine [B_1]) deficiency and dysentery. The hazardous undertaking of mercury separation increased their susceptibility to diseases. German measles, brought from Samarai on the Whitten Bros. steamer the *President* and the government ketch *Siai* between June and November 1902, became endemic among the workers and the local population; it also affected the European miners. An ore trolley crashing through a shaft-head in 1914, taking six workers to the bottom of the pit, exemplified the high accident rate among workers.[53]

Estimated returns from the Gira and Aikora goldfields

Year	European miners	Indentured labour	Gold yield (oz.)	Value of gold (£)
1897-98	23	115	1,222	4,582
1898-99	80	400	6,000	22,500
1899-00	90	450	7,000	26,250
1900-01	30	150	2,400	9,000
1901-02	50	250	5,500	20,625
1902-03	50	250	6,000	22,500
1903-04	55	275	6,000	22,500
1904-05	52	260	6,000	22,500
1905-06	55	330	6,000	22,500
1906-07	42	300	5,000	18,750
1907-08	37	473	5,000	18,125
1908-09	29	298	4,500	16,875
1909-10	3	40	2,000	10,500
1910-11	6	70	900	3,150
1911-12	2	37	200	700
1912-13	3	20	200	700
1913-14	2	27	516	2,000
1914-15	7	131	1,200	3,600
Total	Average 34	Average 215	65,638	247,357

The gold-bearing beaches and gullies of the Gira and Yodda Rivers

Michael Shanahan discovered the first major goldfield on mainland New Guinea on the Gira River in 1898. Some 80 miners worked the Gira and the creeks running into the Mambare, washing an estimated 6,000 oz. in under 12 months after Deputy Administrator, Judge Francis Winter, declared the Gira a commercial goldfield on 5 November 1898. Then, gold mining on the mainland was restricted to the alluvial fields of the main rivers in the north, the Tiveri and Arabi tributaries of the Lakekamu River in the Gulf Division, the small claims in the Keveri Valley of the East-Central Division and on Milne Bay in the Eastern Division. Here all mining was carried out by sluicing and panning, with dredging contemplated since 1900 but only trialed on the Lakekamu field after 1914. No noteworthy reef mining took place on the mainland during the period under review.

William Simpson and eight prospectors returned from the Upper Mambare in January 1896 with only a few ounces in their packs. It was a meagre reward for prospecting a hostile district for 5 months, a feat MacGregor described as 'by far the most arduous undertaking ever performed by any exploring party in the colony'.

Simpson was leading the Ivanhoe party that had joined up with Clark's Cairns Prospecting Association. He was encouraged by finding the geological make-up of the country to be mostly 'slate and quartz, with colour of gold in many creeks, with occasional traces of osmiridium and cinnabar' also present. The prospectors and their 22 Tauputa (D'Entrecasteaux Islands) carriers made camp on the Mambare approximately 25 km upstream from Tamata Junction. From there they tested the creeks for some 60 m, as far as the north-western and southern branches of the Mambare. Simpson and his men prospected along the western foothills of the Owen Stanley Range, investigated the Chirima, and tracked south into the Yodda Valley before returning to Samarai and Australia.[54]

'Nearly the whole of the area is auriferous', according to Simpson, 'but the gold is in very small quantities and not payable'. The 46 oz. he obtained in little over 3 weeks was from the gravel of the McLaughlin Creek at the foot of Mt Scratchley. It provided sufficient encouragement for Simpson, MacLaughlin and Clunas of the *Ivanhoe* party, and MacClelland who had prospected with Clark—together with four new miners—to return to the creek of the original discovery in March 1896. Carriers shifted 6-months of provisions and gear for 150 km up the Mambare over a two-week period. Three stores were set up near Tamata and along the track they cut to the MacLaughlin about 120 km away. Simpson reached the river in the third week of April, and by June he had panned nearly 200 oz. of gold from the gullies and the creek running into the MacLaughlin. By the middle of the year, four prospectors and 36 carriers, who picked up the news of 'a rich lode' on the Upper Mambare, joined them. The Perth *Inquirer* told its readers that Simson's party had 900 ounces of gold—worth between £3 18s and £4 per oz.— on them when they arrived back in Samarai. But Alex Clunas warned eager prospectors not to rush to the Mambare.

> Nothing had been discovered to warrant anybody going to New Guinea unless they were well equipped and prepared to go out prospecting. With reference to the Musa River, he said his party went upstream about sixty miles by steamer, and only got poor prospects, but these were better than the prospects obtained by the party the first time they tried the Mambare.[55]

And by year-end John Schmitt and David Davis, who arrived on the MacLaughlin in early October—along with one or two unidentified prospectors—were the only miners to remain in the region during the wet season.

Simpson had left BNG at the beginning of the rainy season. Arriving in Brisbane in early 1897, he talked about assisting MacGregor to cut a passage on the Lieutenant Governor's epic journey across BNG. After he and MacGregor had climbed Mt Scratchley, he carried on with armed constabulary and government carriers to prospect around the foothills of Mt Victoria, in the Moni, the Adaua and the Keveri Valley. He came across quartz and slate showing a few colours in the Moni Valley, but found no gold in the gullies of the Adaua. Simpson cautioned aspiring prospectors as to the unforgiving nature of New Guinea: 'The likelihood of succumbing to malaria, dysentery or a spear of an Orokaiva tribesman was much greater than finding payable gold in the highlands of BNG', he told his attentive listeners.

Before leaving BNG MacGregor referred to Simpson's gold discovery in his June 1898 report: 'There can be no doubt that gold will now continue to be brought from the interior for many long years to come. The difficulties of getting there and back are great, but not insurmountable', were his parting comments.[56]

The prospector who had experienced the thrill of payable gold in his dish required no encouragement. The Australian newspapers had raised hopes of the discovery of another mother lode for many years. In 1897 nearly one thousand prospectors sailed to BNG to work on Woodlark or prospect the Upper Mambare. There were men

Estimated returns from the MacLaughlin and the Yodda goldfields

Year	European miners	Indentured labour	Gold yield (oz.)	Value of gold (£)
1895-96	12	48	246	900
1896-97	3	15	300	1,125
1897-98	50	200	4,000	15,000
1898-99	70	280	6,000	22,500
1899-00	90	450	7,000	26,250
1900-01	150	600	10,000	37,500
1901-02	70	350	6,000	22,500
1902-03	70	350	6,000	22,500
1903-04	45	225	5,400	20,250
1904-05	48	180	5,000	18,750
1905-06	45	225	6,000	22,500
1906-07	61	305	5,000	18,750
1907-08	39	312	3,600	13,050
1908-09	24	312	3,700	13,875
1909-10	3	30	1,000	3,500
1910-11	4	40	675	2,362
1911-12	4	*70	300	*1,050
1912-13	5	*70	300	*1,050
1913-14	5	55	418	1,570
1914-15	9	96	1,750	6,562
Total	Average 40	Average 211	72,683	271,544

*Unreliable data

from Germany (W. R. Becker), Austria (L. Sirch), Sweden (Gus Nelsson), Scotland (J. Dourand) and Ireland (M. Mahoney and J. Hayes) among the new arrivals. The old hands, Alex Clunas and Robert Elliott, returned from Cooktown to the Upper Mambare on 20 April 1897. J. F. Close—also from Cooktown— together with 14 carriers and 6 tons of gear and stores accompanied them. Simpson returned to the Upper Mambare on 16 June 1897. Together with Moses MacClelland, he arrived from Samarai with 25 carriers and 6 t of provisions. Prepared for 6 months of mining and prospecting, he only lasted a few weeks, dying in September 1897 from exhaustion.[57]

Moses McaClelland and Gilbert Hudson continued to work their dishes at the foothills of Mt Scratchley without Simpson. They panned off 600 oz. from the gullies of the MacLaughlin and the nearby creeks. Sam MacClelland, Clunas and Elliott traced the Mambare east into the Yodda Valley. When M. Shanahan (A.R.M. Tamata) discovered a small nugget on the Gira they turned their attention to the new location. Sharing the wash with 20 miners, they obtained 1,200 oz. within a few days.[58]

Panning for gold in the narrow gullies and cold white water was exhausting work, and only a few men left the Gira fittingly rewarded. Eighty prospectors shared in an estimated £22,500 from some 6,000 oz. of gold recovered on this field in 1898-99. The average earnings of £281 in the first year of the discovery were, at first glance, satisfactory when compared to Woodlark. Was it worth the risk to life and limb?

The northern rivers emptying into the Mambare, the Gira, the MacLaughlin and

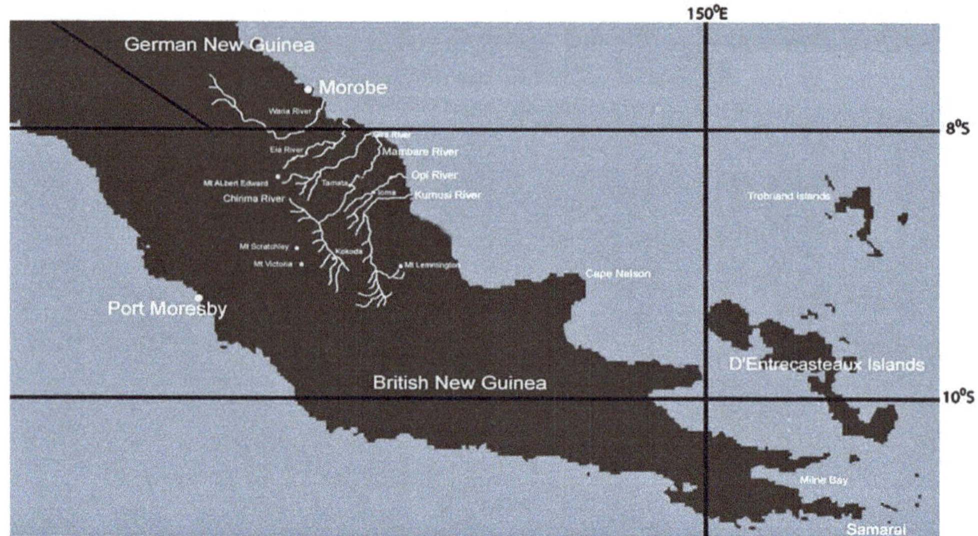

Map 15: **The Northern Rivers** (HJ Ohff)

the Aikora, did not measure up to the big discoveries in Australia. However, when the alluvial fields in the Louisiades were exhausted and the reefs on Woodlark returned a fraction of the gold of former years, these fields seemed a good proposition.

Two new fields were discovered towards the second half of 1899. Elliott prospected the headwaters of the Aikora, the south-western tributary of the Gira River. He found payable gold on a white water creek (Elliott's Creek) high on the slopes of Mt Albert Edward. Downstream, on the Aikora, Tom Champion made a second discovery that he called Champion's Beach. Because of the steepness of the terrain, where torrential rain cleaned out the crevasses and gullies daily, prospectors directed most of their attention towards the Yodda at the time. Yet Tom Champion and other miners averaged 100 oz. each of good quality gold under trying conditions. Two miners, it was rumoured, obtained 45 oz. for only 6 days' work.[59]

In 1898 Clunas, Clark, Nelson and Close cut a new track to the Yodda Valley from Tamata Station. Matt Crow, Sam MacClelland, William Day and Archibald Walker took the shortened route to the valley to prospect the area more thoroughly in mid 1899. When they returned six months later with the news that good gold existed in the much-easier-worked Yodda Valley, the prospectors on the Gira rushed to peg new claims in the Yodda Valley - hopefully this time on a placer deposit.[60]

The Yodda was dangerous territory. Day, writing to a friend in Cairns shortly before leaving with MacClelland for the Upper Mambare warned:

There is a great rush to the Mambare now, where there are 300 men, who are dying at the rate of three or four a week. I have great faith in the Mambare but it is no good without boys, and it is very hard to get them to go there, and no wonder, as from 50 to 75 per cent of the boys have died there and about 30 per cent of the whites. Sam and I are the only two men who have never lost a boy in New Guinea. I think nine out of every ten people who go to the Mambare consider it Hell upon earth … Keep all your friends from the Mambare if you ever want to see them again. I think New Guinea has a great future before it, but the natives are bad, the fever, etc., etc., is worst, and the Government the worse of the lot… Sam and I had to pay our boys 12 months wages to the Government in advance … I cleared two or three hundred pounds in five months, above all expenses. If New Guinea had a Cecil Rhodes she would be the best country on earth.[61]

In 1900-01 some 150 miners with some 600 Papuan panned in the Yodda Valley. Sam MacClelland was no longer among them. He died of fever in the second half of 1900. In the following two years the number of miners fell by more than half. When a drought in 1903 reduced the flow of the creeks to a trickle only 45 prospectors remained on the Yodda. Rather than sitting on their hands the prospectors completed a track from Champion's Beach to Elliott's Creek. The Port Moresby administration assisted with prison labour. The breaking of the drought in late 1903 and better communication with the coast ensured a consistent return of gold from the Aikora, the Gira and MacLaughlin's creeks and the Yodda Valley fields between 1904 and 1907. The miners panned on average 130 oz. Their annual taking of £500 was twice as much as the miners realised at the height of the rush in 1901.[62]

Harry Osborne went to the Aikora when he first came to BNG in 1899, then to the Yodda and back to the Aikora. He recalled 40 years later:

It was not until two years had passed and the richness of the Yodda was on the wane, that miners began to return to Elliott's. By this time the men had learned to utilise natives for mining work—especially those from the D'Entrecasteaux group. Several native villages up in the mountains had been induced to bring in sweet potatoes, which they traded away for knives and tomahawks, and so alleviate the food problems to some extent—and under these improved conditions rich terraces and beaches on Elliott's Creek were successfully worked.[63]

Gold mining in BNG was an expensive business. Shipping of men, equipment and foodstuff, combined with a 10% duty imposed on most items imported into Papua meant that the miners on the Upper Mambare required approximately £350 annually to recover their outlays. Until the completion of the Buna Bay to Kokoda Station track in 1905, the landing place for men and goods travelling to the Yodda was at Bogi Station. Established by the government in 1900, the location was 90 km from the mouth of the Kumusi, and from there it was 100 km to the first camps on the fields. Freight on the Kumusi River to Bogi was £5 per ton and from there to the Yodda Valley 1s per pound for ordinary articles and 5s per pound for dynamite, medicines and fragile goods. This was less than paying carriers to take the goods through the swamps, creeks and precipitous paths of the old 130-km route from Tamata. Still, depending on the 'obligatory' daily consumption of tobacco and rum, a miner required £3 to £4 a week to exist in the BNG goldfields. This cost did not include gear, ammunition and explosive, and the payment of wages and food for the indentured labourers. Each miner had on average five labourers, costing 10–20s per month and more for 'leading boys'. As each man required 50 lb of rice at £1-10, the cost of employing a Papuan on the Yodda amounted to 17 to 20s per week.[64]

While the cost of some provisions came down slightly when the miners managed to trade hardware and trinkets for food with villagers—a tomahawk was worth three bags of potatoes in 1901—it was the exception rather than the norm as the hostilities between the Europeans, their indentured workers and many of the Orokaiva tribes continued with customary ferocity.

Disastrous Ventures

The search for new goldfields to stem decline

The miners believed they would find 'real' gold under tons of gravel in the northern rivers. It was a view shared by geologists. And on 30 November 1900, Port Moresby awarded 52 km of dredging claims on the Mambare, 60 km on the Gira and 30 km on Tamata Creek. Gold syndicates took up 28 dredging claims on the Kumusi, Musa and Gira Rivers. W. Gors of BP proposed the formation of a company with a nominal capital of £240,000, of which £30,000 was to be set aside for the exploratory testing of the northern rivers. Dredging expert Wellman inspected some of the sites on behalf of the claim-owners. When faced with floods Wellman left what he considered a most hostile country. For the section of the Mambare he managed to inspect he recommended the mobilisation of a small dredge for experimental purposes.[65]

Three years later progress remained most unsatisfactory. Gors and the other claim-owners dumped the idea, and A.R.M. Monckton reported 'the project of dredging for gold in the Northern Rivers seems to have been entirely abandoned'. So as not to ring the alarm bells Monckton assured Port Moresby that the grounds for not proceeding with dredging was not because the lands were not auriferous. 'On the contrary', he assured Le Hunte, 'the beaches on the Aikora River were proved to be exceptionally rich in the precious metal'. The reason was the lack of funds. 'The plans of those who were supposed to be promoting the speculation were apparently not supported by any financial strength' the A.R.M. asserted.[66]

In search of a new mother lode, miners had crossed the Aikora in 1903 to prospect along the Waria River into GNG territory. It was not until late 1906 that Matt Crowe and Arthur (Buna) Darling claimed the discovery of payable gold in shallow depth on this river. As the German explorers had found out before them, the headwater of the Waria is in very inaccessible country, and it was only by chance that the two veteran prospectors ended up in this inhospitable part of East New Guinea. Starting from Finnegan's Creek on the Yodda with 35 carriers, they went in a northerly direction to the western foothills of Mt Albert Edward, crossed the Aikora and came to a larger river, which, after some help from villagers, they identified as the Waria. After working the river and its tributaries for some 50 km they returned to Tamata in mid-1906, four months after they had left the Yodda. Darling only admitted to collecting a few grains. The mining warden had no such qualms. He claimed that Crowe and Darling panned consistently two grains to the dish, and that the field was probably within the boundaries of the present Gira field, with the Waria as its most northern extremity of this 1700 square kilometer gold-bearing country.[67] Port Moresby's attitude towards the find was ambivalent. It agreed to send an expedition to the Waria. On 21 January 1907 the Rockhampton *Morning Bulletin* reported:

> There is no gold in paying quantities on the Waria River and that prospecting the country away from the stream can only be carried out at great expense and risk. The glowing accounts of a rich discovery have been proved untrue, and their falsity should act as a check on any future unauthenticated rumours being too readily believed.[68]

The sobering news did not prevent 10 prospectors, among them Fred Kruger and Pryke brothers, Frank and Jim, to make the long and difficult trek to the Waria. The brothers panned 300 oz. within a few months, enough to take a year's leave before returning to the district in 1908. However, Arthur Lyons, mining warden at Ioma, reported during the same year:

> Men, who hitherto had not tried the Waria, are now prospecting there, whilst others, to whom the Waria had not come up to expectations, have returned to resume work on these fields … Occasionally, a miner returning from there is reputed as having amassed a good "chamois", whilst others—experienced men too—declare the field a "duffer". One thing is certain, the gold generally which so far has there been won is of exceeding poor and fine quality.[69]

The Pryke brothers agreed; their claims yielded some 3,000 oz. worth £12,000 in 1907 and 1908 but little more than specks thereafter. The government employed over 200 prisoners to cut a track from Tamata to the upper Waria. It proved to be a wasted effort since the miners had all but abandoned the field by 1910.

In the same year the governments of Papua and GNG agreed to fund the Anglo-German Border Commission to survey the boundary between the colonies. Like the German explorers who had been defeated by malaria and the sheer impenetrability of the mountainous terrain, the parties abandoned the expedition after 6 months, in 1909, with only a few survey markers set.[70] The Australians were confident that they had done enough work to confirm a gold-bearing section on the Waria. It was a belief that proved to be of little benefit. The Waria and its creeks produced little gold.

The gold industry of BNG did not undergo much change under Papua's new Lieutenant-Governor, J.H.P. Murray and his right hand man, Commissioner for Lands and Director of Agriculture, Staniforth Smith. The small goldfield in Milne Bay attracted 72 miners when discovered in 1900. It was 75 km by boat from

Junction of Bulolo and Koranga Creek (NLA, No. A6510, 2306)**; gold washing on the Waria and the Lakekamu Rivers** (Goethe University Frankfurt a. M. Nos. 041-0240 - 31 & 041 – 0234 - 42)**; Sluicing on the Yodda** (Smith, 1903)

Samarai. The field only yielded 13,231 oz. between 1899-00 and 1906-07, with most of the gold (4,000 oz.) recovered during the first few months.[71] Even less productive were the alluvial fields on the eastern slopes of the Owen Stanley Range. Discovered by Frank Pryke and George Klotz in April and May 1901, the Keveri Valley goldfield was about 35 km inland from Cloudy Bay on the south coast. A cool and healthy spot, the find was on a portion of the watershed of the Musa River some 2,000 ft above sea level. Frank Pryke worked the field with his brother Dan in 1903 and 1904. The youngest Pryke, Jim, joined them in 1905. The field was worked out by 1907. It produced no more than 1,500 oz. per year, with the total output no greater than 3,670 oz..[72] The northern rivers had produced 4 tons of gold, 43.4% of the total production in the Territory. But 'the current decline cannot be taken as evidence that the mining industry is on the wane', Smith declared confidently:

> The surface has only been scratched, and only in a few places, and the mineral resources of the Territory are as yet a matter of conjecture, for there is no evidence upon which even an approximate estimate could be based.[73]

With the amendment of the 1899 mining regulation, Smith ensured in 1907 that all minerals, gems and precious stones on or under native lands were the property of the Crown. The Mining (1907) and Land (1906) ordinances provide for 'native land holders' to be awarded compensation for damage to land by mining operations'. If in the opinion of the mining warden the miners may cause extensive land denigration, a mining claim was not to be awarded unless the potentially injured party gave its explicit consent. The warden was obliged to estimate potential damages caused by the mining activity and determine the value of his assessment. The government would hold the money in escrow and refund the injured party after mining operations had

The government Mineral Laboratory at Port Moresby (Smith, *Handbook on the Territory of Papua*, 1909, p. 22)

ceased or the miner(s) had reinstated the land. Further, under the amended mining ordinance, Papuans retained the right to mine for gold on alluvial grounds while enjoying the privileges conferred by the Queensland Mining Act on the holders of miners' rights, but without the responsibilities the rights imposed on miners.[74]

Notwithstanding the expanded rights under the mining ordinance, the northern river fields declined to 35.8% of total Papuan gold production by 1915. The miners exploited the riverbanks, creeks, and gullies to depths that were humanly possible, but they were unable to test the deeper parts of the rivers. Commercial dredging—while encouraged by the administration—never went ahead. This left the miners with the proven but inefficient methods used in Australia since the beginning of alluvial mining in the 1850s—ground sluicing, 'wing damming' and 'blind stabbing'.[75]

With no new goldfield declared by Port Moresby since the small discovery in the Keveri Valley in 1904, Murray enacted the *Reward Ordinance, 1909* and the *Encouragement Ordinance, 1910*. Under the ordinances the administration was authorised to pay up to £1,000 to the discoverer of a new goldfield provided that

(a) For a period of 18 months within the three years immediately following the report of the discovery a population of not less than 200 miners of European descent has been employed upon the goldfield.

(b) The goldfield is distant more than 35 km in a straight line from the nearest place where payable gold had previously been obtained.

(c) This Ordinance shall not apply to parties that are subsidised by the Government.[76]

There was no worthwhile encouragement in these ordinances for the miners. The £150 contract awarded by Port Moresby for assessing the strata below the Yodda River gravel was a fruitless exercise: the contracted miners found no traces of gold. James Swanson—who had prospected and mined all over BNG since the turn of the century—explored the interior of the Central and Gulf Divisions with his son in 1907 and 1908. Apart from traces of gold in the Vailala and Tauri Rivers, they found nothing worthy to report.

In 1909, Buna Darling went 75 km up the Markham to prospect the Watut River, which, unbeknown to him, had taken the life of the German explorer Wilhelm Dammköhler only a few weeks earlier. Sick with fever, short of food and left for dead on the bank of the river by his Orokaiva carriers, Darling told the story of gold he had discovered when Les Joubert picked him up in his launch *Buna*. Apparently, he discovered gold in GNG somewhere between the headwaters of the Watut and the Tiveri Rivers. Darling never had the opportunity to prove his claim. Short of money and weakened from spear wounds, he died on his way to Australia in early 1912.[77] Thereafter not even experienced prospectors like Swanson, Darling, Preston, Crowe and the Pryke brothers came up with new discoveries. A properly equipped prospecting party would cost every bit of £1,000. It was well in excess of what the miners could raise amongst themselves.

In the first 20 years the ratio of indentured labour to European miners remained about constant at 5:1. Without new discoveries and with gold increasingly harder to mine, Europeans started to rely more on Papuans. After 1907 the local workers were given more and more responsibility. Generally, they were now sufficiently skilled to set up the water races, flumes and sluice boxes, and could reliably pick the gold from the prospector dishes. Where a Papuan oversaw the mining, the 'boss' prospected nearby. By 1914 the ratio had changed to approximately 10:1. This increased the average annual earnings from £200 to £400 for a European miner.

The Lakekamu River: a Papuan life for every 82 oz. of gold

By June 1909 Staniforth Smith admitted that gold was not to be found as easily as he had predicted when he first arrived in Papua: 'The Gira, Aikora, and Yodda Gold-fields on the mainland all tell the same tale: a gradually diminishing gold yield, and fewer miners'. He now advocated spending government money to change the situation as he set up the first fully funded prospecting party. Because the rivers flowing into the eastern part of the Gulf of Papua sprang close to the source of the Waria and the Aikora, Smith believed it was possible that the mountains releasing the gold into the northern rivers would do likewise on the southern slopes. The miners shared Smith's view: they were certain that auriferous country existed in the watersheds drained by these streams, and it was just a matter of finding it.

The Port Moresby government voted £800 for a prospecting party and sought a recommendation from miners in Papua as to the best person to lead the party. The choice was Matt Crowe. A very experienced prospector, both in Western Australia and Papua, Crowe picked his team and decided where to prospect in the Gulf country. Frank Pryke, also highly regarded by the miners, had worked the northern rivers and discovered the Keveri goldfield five years earlier. He and his brother Jim joined Crowe for the 6-month expedition in the eastern Gulf region. Two other experienced miners, James Swanson and his son, had already prospected the Vailala and Tauri Rivers in 1907 where they found traces of the precious metal. Chas Higginson, R.M. of the Gulf Division, believed success would have followed 'if these two men had been able to penetrate right into the heart of the mountains from which these streams rise'. Crowe and Pryke agreed on this assessment.

The *Merrie England* left Port Moresby on 6 June 1909 with 35 Papuan carriers and 3 months' provisions to take the party to the mouth of the Tauri River. Crowe and Frank Pryke had decided to explore this river as far as the main range first. They decided to have the steam launch *Ruby* land them about 100 km up the zigzagging river. The land expedition started on 19 June and progressed slowly to the tributaries and headwaters of the Tauri. The party found traces of gold, but nothing payable. After three gruelling months Crowe returned to the Lower Tauri for stores. He also informed Murray that he intended to prospect the nearby Lakekamu River.[78]

After six months of far-reaching exploration, the party returned to Port Moresby with three cocoa cans full of gold they had collected in the gullies and the creeks feeding the headwaters of the Lakekamu. Crowe informed Port Moresby that the prospect of his discovery is on a creek, yielding 2oz. of gold per day per miner, 110 km up the Lakekamu or Williams River and 20 km overland. Fourteen days later, on 24 December 1909, Murray gazetted the Lakekamu a goldfield. It comprised 1400 square kilometers from the northeast corner of the Gulf along the GNG border to the northwest corner of the Central Divisions. The Olipai River, which runs into the Lakekamu from the west, the East Tiveri with its tributary the Arabi, and the smaller West Tiveri, and many of the creeks feeding these rivers, carried the gold. Crowe and the Pryke brothers pegged their reward claims 1 mile above Ironstone Creek, approximately 14 km from where the Tiveri meets the Arabi.[79]

Murray left Port Moresby on 28 December for a 2-week inspection of what he hoped would become Papua's most productive goldfield that could establish Port Moresby to the same level of importance enjoyed by Kalgoorlie in Western Australia, or even Australia's young capital, Melbourne. Murray's private secretary, Charles Garrioch, police officer George Nicholls (A.R.M. Lakekamu goldfields) and Matt Crowe accompanied the Lieutenant-Governor and the Director for Mines. William Bowden (A.R.M. Central Division) left for Motu Motu—at the mouth of the Lakekamu—with 20 police, 5 tons of coal and supplies a few days earlier. Bobbing uncomfortably in the coastal swell, the *Ruby* made light work of the three fully laden whaleboats and a dinghy she was towing up the non-tidal Lakekamu River once the mud-bar at the mouth of the river had been negotiated. Passing Olipai junction after 3 days' travelling, Murray's little convoy anchored at an island sitting in the fork of the Tiveri and Arabi River. The island was about 170 km from the mouth of the Lakekamu, and was the same spot where Crowe and Pryke had previously established their base camp. Crossing to the mainland, the party walked for 15 km through dense mangrove-flats until they reached Rocky Creek with its gold-bearing sedimentary rock. After inspecting various locations where the prospecting party found gold, and after some rough climbing and much wading and swimming of creeks, Murray returned to Port Moresby on 11 January, satisfied with the importance of the new discovery.[80]

'Three cocoa tins of gold, and the 2 oz. a man per day are very exciting', reported the *Northern Territory Times* on 21 January, 'but' the paper cautioned, 'somehow, remarkably few "rushes" live up to the early reports of the field, and perhaps the latest may not be up to expectations. It is certain, however, that it will attract a large number of sturdy Australians'. The *Northern Territory Times* was correct on both counts.

Within a short few weeks after Murray's announcement several hundred Europeans of all nationalities rushed to the new discovery. The would-be miners tried to get there quickly, overland from Port Moresby, from Daru or by boat; they were in the

Estimated returns from the Lakekamu goldfields

Year	European miners	Indentured labour	Labour mortality	Gold yield (oz)	Gold value (£)
1909-10	61	643	*258	3,000	11,250
1910-11	38	428	57	8,000	30,000
1911-12	33	495	26	6,500	24,425
1912-13	14	141	8	5,000	18,750
1913-14	29	386	1	4,000	15,000
1914-15	22	224	11	3,000	11,250
1915-16	27	340	n.d	2,715	10,500
Total	Average 32	Average 379	361	32,215	121,175

*18 January to 30 June 1910

main inexperienced, arrived unprepared for the local conditions, and returned sick or perished for lack of funds. When J. F. Coghlan heard of the reported 'three ounces per man per day' discovery in New Guinea, 'he was immediately seized with an attack of the prevailing gold fever', writes the *Kalgoorlie Western Argus.*

> They took the ketch right up the river to the landing, ten miles from the alleged El Dorado, and reached the scene of the new rush on the 10th of January. At this time there were about 200 men on the field and an immense swarm of native labourers. When Mr Coghlan left about a month later, on the 7th February, there were only 50 miners left, mostly old New Guinea hands, and fully 500 boys. ...The conditions of mining, Mr Coghlan describes as simply terrible. A damp, sodden, humid country, dense scrub darkening everything, almost impossible for the new arrivals to make a fire; the eternal diet biscuit and tinned meat. The Queensland men had no idea of the conditions until they had experienced them. Mr Coghlan predicts that there is going to be a terrible epidemic of sickness. The sanitation is awful, and the regulations are fearfully inadequate. Cesspits have to be sunk 2 ft. deep in the moist ground for the native boys, and there are 500 of them at present in a small cramped space. The old miners who have been in the country for some time are gaunt spectres. It is a black outlook altogether.[81]

As Coghlan predicted, the new rush had dire consequences. By early 1909, the entire south coast was on health alert. The outbreak of whooping cough in March spread swiftly from the eastern islands to Samarai, then from Port Moresby to the Mekeo District and as far as the Gulf Division. To make matters worse a dysentery outbreak at Port Moresby, Sogeri and Galley Reach had spread to the Lakekamu fields with catastrophic consequences.

By the end of February 1910 Port Moresby reported that 120 miners had come from Australia. The desperation of the fortune hunters to find gold was so great according to Arthur Lyons, who had transferred from the Upper Mambare, that the ones who survived tore the creek beds out of all recognition. 'The landscape present more the appearance of having been through a seismic disturbance than having been altered by the hand of man' Lyons quipped.

But land degradation was of little concern to the Port Moresby government. When Murray and Rev Copland King rushed to the site on 30 March to inform themselves about the dysentery epidemic they were — in Murray's words — unprepared for what they found. The death rate among natives in the hospital was enormous—about 35%. Many prospectors had fled the field destitute and for fear of infections. Over 200 workers broke their indentures because their employer was dead, had left the field, or because they were too ill to work. 'The amount of sickness and the gravity of it among the natives have been appalling', Dr Julius Streeter observed when he arrived on replaced Dr Simson. Murray tried to stem the contagion by proclaiming:

> 1) The goldfield is closed to all recruiting. 2) No natives on the field are to leave, except for Port Moresby or Samarai; their arrival at either of these ports to be reported to the R.M. and Government Medical Officer. 3) Natives who have had dysentery are not to leave the field without permission of the Government Medical Officer.

Despite the gazetting of regulation to isolate villagers and by administering several thousand doses of medicine, the procurement of additional medical equipment, tents and bedding, the epidemic was at its worse in April 1910 when 80 deaths occurred. During the first six months of the rush 221 labourers and five Europeans had died from dysentery. The annual rate climbed to 76.8% by June, when 34 'boys' perished. It took until November 1910 for the contagious disease to be sufficiently contained, and for Murray to lift the recruiting ban.[82]

Without losing sight of the human tragedy Papua's latest goldfield yielded approximately 3,000 oz. of 'the best gold (£3 15s per oz.) discovered in the Territory during the first few months'. According to Lyons 'the yield would probably have been considerable larger had it not been for the action taken by Murray in stopping all recruiting of natives'. Some 80 miners and 920 labourers returned to the area briefly after the lifting of the embargo.

Crowe and the Prykes had stayed on during the difficult period to protect their claim on Ironstone Creek. In 1910-11 they came up with a lucky strike. Yielding 1,400 oz. over 12 months Crowe and the Pryke brothers had discovered a gold-bearing terrace in the fork of the Rocky and Ironstone Creeks. Their perseverance yielded 450 oz. at the head of Rocky Creek within a few days. And Fred Kruger collected 400 oz. in just over 6 months on the Cassowary Creek, 25 km northeast from Tiveri Landing and about 30 km southeast of Nepa Station.

The spirits of the Lakekamu miners rose sharply when E. R. Stanley found magnetite, ilmenite, zircon and 'grains of a rose-red, transparent mineral, possessing a well-defined crystal structure... not unlike Colas ruby'. I imagine, Stanley reported in early 1911, 'there is a splendid field of gems and gold in the vicinity of the Lakekamu, and I would have no hesitation in recommending an examination on this part of the district'.[83] It turned out to be an overly optimistic assumption.

Desperate measures

The goldfield required a lot of 'dead work' before miners could shovel the placer material into the sluice boxes. To deal with the overburden the miners employed more workers than on other fields in Papua, taking home less money. Dredging equipment sent to the Lakekamu fields in 1911 to test the river and creek-beds by wing damming was unsuccessful and abandoned after a few days. It was then clear that Lakekamu River carried little gold. While the 14 remaining miners yielded a healthy 5,000 oz. in 1912-13, the Lakekamu fields were exhausted and abandoned a few years later.[84]

The miners, forever hopeful that a large auriferous field would produce a mother lode, approached the government in 1911 to fund a further prospecting party. Port Moresby agreed to pay half the expenses incurred by prospecting parties. That is, for any money raised by the miners Port Moresby would contribute an equal sum. This arrangement resulted in two major prospecting expeditions in 1912.

By December 1911 the miners had raised £250 and voted on a new prospecting party. The government contributed an equal amount for Frank Pryke, Robert Elliott and Charles Priddle to prospect the Upper Vailala River in 1912. The Pryke brothers and Crowe had already investigated some of the area in 1910. Again, after 3 months during which an encounter with tribesmen on the GNG border nearly took Frank Pryke's life, the party returned empty handed. On their arrival in Port Moresby, Murray remarked, 'Mr Pryke is a man of iron nerve. An arrow went very nearly through his body, and would probably have killed anyone else: Mr Pryke, however, simply pulled it out and went on with his prospecting'.

A second prospecting party left Lakekamu on 10 May 1912 to examine the headwaters of the Tiveri River. Avard (Bob) Newcombe who, with Gordon Robertson and Arthur Hicks, prospected the creeks and watercourses running into the Tiveri and Olipai Rivers led this group. They obtained four and five grains to the dish below the watershed of the Tauri River and 10oz. where the river branched into two streams. It was not sufficient to warrant an application for a reward claim, or to offer sufficient inducement to return there and mine.

Murray was no longer confident Papua could produce another field like Woodlark or the Upper Mambare. He advised the Australian Federal Government in 1912:

> Gold mining has, on the whole, been less successful during the past year, for the Lakekamu field has been almost exhausted and the attempts of the prospectors to find a new field towards the Vailala have been unsuccessful. It must be admitted, though Lakekamu has produced 17,500 ounces of gold, has not proved a second Yodda, as it was once hoped would be the case.[85]

William (Sharkey) Park, Matt Crowe, James (Jimmy) Preston and Edward (Teddy) Auerbach agreed. In 1912 they travelled to German New Guinea via Morobe to prospect the Ramu and the Markham districts. They faced the same problems the Germans encountered: 'On the Markham', Auerbach recalled nearly 30 years later, 'we had all the fighting we wanted, two or three times a day. They used to like daylight and dawn to do their fighting. Those natives were game. If trained, they would make splendid soldiers'. As to gold, Auerbach retold the tale of Jimmy Preston's discovery on nearby Koranga Creek in *The Pacific Island Monthly*.

> Somewhere near the head of the Waria Jimmy Preston shot a bird of paradise. When he went to retrieve it, he found it on the outcrop of a reef. Preston sent the specimens to Sydney to be assayed through Klink, the German R.M. at Morobe. Klink opened the letter containing the assayer's report before he informed Jimmy, and others that the assay went for 4oz. to the ton. Preston also sent two assays from Samarai to Sydney. They both went for 4oz. to the ton. He intended to go back after the war, and peg out the reef.[86]

Whether this was the gold discovered by the party on the Koranga Creek near Wau, and which Sharkey Park worked secretly in 1922 until 1923 when a new Mining Act came into force is not clear.

Staniforth Smith undertook an expedition for black gold—anthracite coal—during Murray's absence in 1910-11 with disastrous consequences. The objective was to examine the headwaters of the Bamu and, if possible, reach the Strickland. However, the party did not succeed in travelling much beyond the Kikori River where Kenneth Mackay and Yodda Valley gold miner William Little had found coal two years earlier.[87] Rather than staying with the original plan, Smith decided to investigate whether these coal deposits extended westward towards the Omati, Turama and Bamu Rivers. If confirmed, Smith believed that the field could be cost effective.[88]

Staniforth Smith, Leslie Bell (Chief Inspector Native Affairs), Alfred Pratt (surveyor), Hubert Leonard Murray (Acting Private Secretary) and John Hennelly (R.M. Gulf Division) together with 25 armed constabulary and 50 carriers started an expedition on 20 November 1910 to examine the headwaters of the Turama and Bamu Rivers. After fourteen days of struggling across inaccessible mountainous country, the provisions for the police and the carriers ran too low to continue. Murray, Hennelly, 14 police and 33 carriers returned to Port Moresby on 7 December; Smith, Bell and Pratt continued on emergency rations. Smith reported after his return to Port Moresby four months later:

> I went up the Turama River to look for indications of coal there with Bell, Pratt, 11 police, and 17 carriers. We endeavoured to strike west. The country was exceedingly rough; we were forced north-west by high mountain ranges. We pushed on expecting to reach the level alluvial country drained by the Turama and Baum….Returned safely with party to Goaribari Island [on 18 March 1911]. Got to the vicinity of the upper waters of the Strickland River latitude 6deg. 20min., and resumed along the course of the western branch of the Kikori River. We travelled on foot 700 km and by river 280 km over totally unexplored country, completing the major exploration of the territory. Most important information was gained. We found a little loose coal in the creek near the Lower Kikori and a large field of excellent coal on the Upper Kikori. The western division, instead of being largely low-lying recent alluvial, consists in a great part of an elevated plateau. We travelled for 370 km over rough mountain country, the lowest valley being over 2,000ft. above the sea level. The country is composed of huge upraised masses of coral. The upper waters and watersheds of the great rivers emptying into the gulf are now fairly defined, completing our knowledge of the river systems of the territory. We have now data for estimating the population of the whole territory with some accuracy.[89]

Smith did not discover mineable 'black gold'. He found colours in some creek beds, but no placer deposits. Prime Minister Andrew Fisher congratulated Smith on his safe return. 'Messrs Smith, Bell, and Pratt, travelled through unknown country on foot for 700 km, and came down a new and unexplored river…These young intrepid Australians have explored unknown country in a determined, very practical and scientific way. It shows that they have not only grit and courage, but that they have that kind of determination which enables people to get out of difficulties,' Fisher proclaimed at a rally in Newcastle. For 11 carriers the rescue came too late, they had either drowned or succumbed to exhaustion. Lieutenant-Governor Murray reprimanded Smith; for he believed, 'the collapse of the expedition [was] mainly due to the deficient organization as regards carriers and supplies'. At an inquest in December 1911 he said 'The loss of a third of a party is something quite unprecedented in Papuan exploration, and the expedition cannot be looked upon otherwise than disastrous'. The expedition, Murray bemoaned, cost £5002.[90]

Sir Rupert Clarke, pastoralist, racehorse owner, politician, and land-speculator tried his hand at gold mining at Coolgardie and in banana, peanut, rubber and coconut plantations in Papua. In early 1914 he financed and led an expedition up the Fly River. Because of the isolation and the time and cost involved, no prospector had visited the Upper Fly since McGregor reported traces of gold on the banks of Papua's largest river 24 years previously. Frank Pryke, who went to Moree in New South Wales to recover from his arrow wound, and his brother Jim, accepted Clarke's invitation to participate in the expedition. Laden with stores they left Port Moresby on 10 May 1914 on Clarke's yachts the *Kismet* and *La Carabine,* and the launch *Ella.* The party included Clarke's Kanosia (Papua) plantation manager, Archibald MacAllpine and 30 Papuans. After establishing a camp at Cassowary Island, Pryke and his party explored the upper tributaries of the Fly, the Alice, Black and Tully creeks and gorges. Clarke went 1170 km up the Fly, further than any white man had journeyed before. He returned with much scientific information. The party did not return with any gold.[91]

Gold mining in Papua was hard work, unforgiving, for many it was fatal. The geological strata, which delivered the rich alluvial discoveries in north Queensland, did not continue into southeast New Guinea. The gold discovered in the Louisiade and Trobriand Archipelagos was formed differently. It was not as prolific or pure and did not occur in big nuggets as at Mt Morgan, Charters Towers or on the Palmer River in Queensland. Alluvial gold in Papua was mainly dust or granules.

Lakekamu was a tragedy. By June 1914 nearly £100,000 of gold had been mined for the loss of at least 361 Papuan and 11 European lives. The health problems on this field crystallised the human suffering the gold industry brought to Papua generally. Mortality on the Louisiade, Woodlark and Upper Mambare fields to 1903 is largely unknown. Many historians have adopted a peak rate of 33% in the Papuan workforce and the European prospectors for this period. It was probably higher. During the first 10 years of the Papuan gold industry, the mortality rate was never below 10%. The loss of lives was on a scale larger than that experienced in Finschhafen in 1891-92 and on a similar level of the fiasco suffered by the GNG tobacco growers from 1892 to 1895. The dysentery outbreaks in 1909-10 and again in 1911 resulted from an unrestrained gold industry, operating in an under-resourced, under-funded and practically nonexistent Papuan health system. The gold mining industry in BNG and Papua delivered few, if any, discernible gains, and none for the indigenous population.

Miners' claims in the Upper Mambare River region (Goethe University Frankfurt a. M. No. 067-0929-28)

Chapter 14: The Gold-based Economy of BNG and Papua

Miners at Woodlark Island, ca. 1900 (M. v. Hein collection, Mitschell Library, FM3/846)

Notes

1   J.H.P. Murray, *Papua or British New Guinea*, p. 316

2   MacGillivray, J. *Narrative of the Voyage of H.M.S. Rattlesnake*, vol. ii, p. 69

3   R. Daintree, 'General Report on the Northern Districts of Queensland', Brisbane (1870) p. 8

4   H.J. Gibbney, 'The New Guinea Gold Rush of 1878', *Journal of the Royal Australian Historical Society*, 58 (1972) pp. 284ff, 'Gold found in New Guinea', *ATCJ* (1878) 12 Jan. p. 12

5   *The West Australian* (=*WA*)(1951) 1 Feb., p. 24; 'Natural History Society', *BC* (1893) 22 Apr., p. 8; AR-BNG (1891-92), pp. xv-xvi, 53–5 & 88

6   A. Gibb Maitland, 'Geological Observations in British New Guinea in 1891', *QPP*, C.A 106–1892, pp. 695–728; AR-BNG (1891-92) attachment, p. 28

7   R.L. Jack and A.W. Clarke to MacGregor, 5 June 1889 (AR-BNG [1888-89] pp. 10 & 52). Also 'British New Guinea', *BC* (1889) 27 Feb., p. 7; (1890) 19 Apr., pp. 5-6; *The Queenslander*, 31 Aug. 1889, p. 418

8   AR-BNG (1889-90) p. 25; (1891-92) pp. 80 & 82

9   AR-BNG (1891-92) p. 81. (1 ounce [oz.] = 20 pennyweights [dwts] = 480 grains [gr.])

10   AR-BNG (1889-90) pp. 25-6; Pacific Islands Monthly, vol. 14 (1944); Nelson, pp. 22–3

11   'Important Gold Discovery at Sudest', and 'Papuan Fossickers', *BC* (1894) 26 Mar., p. 6. AR-BNG (1895-96) p. xvii; (1896-97) appendix DD (map on Mt Adelaide claim); (1896-97) p. 56

12   AR-BNG (1897-98) p. xix; *SMH* (1897) 2 Dec. p. 7. See H.N. Nelson, *Black, White & Gold*, p. 22

13   'The New Guinea Goldfields Report by the Lieutenant-Governor', *BC* (1900) 24 Feb., p. 10; *Cairns Post* (1940) Sep.,4, p. 8

14   AR-BNG (1899-00) p. 83

15   'A Rush for Gold, A Warning to Miners', *Adelaide Advertiser* (1997) 3 Mar. p. 5

16   AR-BNG (1898-1899) p. xxvi, (1900-01) p. xxxii; (1901-02) p. 19. *BC* (1900) 24 Feb., p. 10; (1899) 22 Jul., p. 6; *The South Australian Register* (1899) 7 Jul., p. 5. H.A. Borland, 'The Old British New Guinea Mining Days', *Cairns Post* (1940) 4 Sep. p. 8

17   AR-BNG (1899-1900) pp. xix, 17 & 83

18   *Cairns Post* (1940) 11 Sep., p. 3.

Disastrous Ventures

19 AB-BNG (1904-05) pp. 30–2 & (1905-06) pp. 13, 59 & 71; (1906-07) p. 84

20 'Gold in Papua', Mining Journal (1912) 23 May, AR-Papua (1912-13) p. 41. *SMH* (1930) 18 Feb.

21 'Mining in Papua', Australian Mining Standard (1911) 4 May

22 *SMH* (1914) 27 Nov., p. 9; *The Argus* (1914) 23 Nov., p. 13 and 28 Nov., p. 22; *The Adelaide Advertiser* (1914) 28 Nov., p. 13; AR-Papua (1913-14) p. 153; (1914-15) pp. 138 & 141–42

23 AR-Papua (1921-22) pp. 89–90; (1917-18) p. 49; BC (1923) 29 Mar, p. 4; *Barrier Miner* (1923) 4 Aug., p. 1; (1917) 17 Nov. p. 4

24 AR-BNG (1895-96) p. xviii

25 *Western Mail* (Perth, 1897) 19 June, p. 31; *The Advertiser* (1897) 16 Mar. p. 6

26 BC (1897) 11 Mar. p. 5

27 AR-BNG (1895-96), p. xxx; (1896-97) pp. xi & 56. C.A.W. Monckton, *Some Experience of a New Guinea Resident Magistrate*, p. 22. TQ (1896) 2 May, p. 821; *BC* (1896) 24 Apr., p. 5.*SMH*, (1896) 29 Oct. p. 5; The West Australian (1897) 28 Jul, p. 6

28 AR-BNG (1897-98) pp. 99–101; Nivani Correspondence, Station Journals and Patrol Reports, British New Guinea (1890–1906) NAA Series A1 and G91; see Nelson, pp.56–7

29 *Kalgoorlie Western Argus*, (1898) 5 May, p. 11

30 AR-BNG (1897-98) p. xix; (1898-99) pp. xxvi and 81–5

31 Queensland Mining Act, 1898

32 Mining Ordinance No. V, 1899, §4

33 AR-BNG (1899-1900) p. 83); *BC* (1900) 24 Feb. p. 10

34 AT (1899) 28 Oct., 15; *SMH* (1899) 11 Nov. p. 10 & 16 Dec., p. 18; *BC* (1900) 8 & 16 Jun. pp. 3f.

35 Nivani Station Journal, 1900-01, NAA Series A1, G91–CA1419–CO14 & 15 NAA Series A1, G91–CA1419–CO14 & 15; AR-BNG (1899-1900) pp. xx & 81–3; (1900-01) p. 78; (1902-03) p. 39. *Cairns Morning Post* (1900) 1 Sep., p. 2; (1901) 30 Apr. p. 3;

36 *SMH* (1904) 29 Jan., p. 5; *The Argus* (1905) 16 Feb., p. 8; *Australian Town and Country* (=*ATCJ*) (1904) 3 Feb. p. 53; (1906) 7 Feb. p. 54

37 *SMH* (1907) 19 Jul., p. 11 AR-Papua (1906-07) pp. 76, 81–2; (1907-08) p. 63

38 *South Australian Register* (1900) 8 Jun. p. 7; 11 July, p. 9. 13 June, p. 2, 'Prospectus Woodlark Island Gold Mining Company'.

39 AR-Papua (1900-01) p. 78; *BC* (1901) 6 Feb. p. 7; *The (Adelaide) Register* (1901) 15 Oct., pp. 7, 22. *The Adelaide Advertiser* (1901) 29 June, p. 9, *SMH* (1900) 10 Dec. p. 9, (1902) 19 May, p. 9, 7 Aug., p. 9

40 *Adelaide Register* (1901) 17 Sep., p. 7 & 24 Dec., p. 5; *Queenslander* (1903) 17 Oct., p. 33, *Launceston Examiner* (1904) 13 Feb; *BC* (1904) 10 June, p. 3, (1906) 19 Feb., p. 3; *SMH* (1907) 30 Jan., p. 11

41 *SMH* (1900) 8 May, p. 9; 31 Jul., p. 9; 8 Sep., p. 14; 6 Nov., p. 6; (1901) 7 Sep., p. 13; *BC* (1901) 6 Jun. p. 3; *Town and Country* (1901) p. 55

42 *BC* (1900) 16 Jun., p. 7; *ATCJ* (1904) 30 Mar., pp. 30–1, *SMH* (1905) 7 Dec., p. 7, *BC* (1906), 27 Nov. p. 5. AR-Papua (1904-05) pp. 55–8

43 AR-Papua (1906-07) pp. 76, 78 & 81–2; (1908-09) pp. 131-3. *Townsville Daily Bulletin* (1907) 24 Aug. p. 4. *SMH* (1909) 8 Apr. p. 11

44 Statement by Hon. Fred Weekley, MLC on the 'Miners and Leaseholders on Woodlark Island' (Report of the 1907 Royal Commission on the Territory of Papua, §§1360–99)

45 *SMH* (1912) 1 Jun., p. 12; (1913) 27 Nov., p. 11; (1914) 27 Oct., p.9; (1916) 6 Jan., p.9; 17 Aug. p. 4; (1934) 20 Jan., p. 17; BC (1917) 13 Mar., p. 4; AR-Papua (1916-17) p. 39, (1917-18) p. 45

46 AR-Papua (1913-14) p. 155; AR-Papua (1917-18) p. 48 and (1918-19) p. 82

47 AR-Papua (1904-05) pp. 55–6; (1906-07) pp. 76 & 82; (1911-12) pp. 193 & 201 (1911-12) p. 202.

48 AR-Papua (1911-12) p. 204; *Cairns Post* (1911) 6 Nov. p. 4

49 AR-Papua (1913-14) p. 155

50 AR-Papua (1917-18) p. 48; (1918-19) p. 82 $ (1919-20) p. 99

51 AR-Papua (1911-12) pp. 189–208, (1913-14) pp. 36 & 153. 'Gold in Papua', *Mining Journal* (1912) 23 Mar. The ratio remained above 43% after Block 10 reached full production in 1919 (AR-Papua (1919-20)

52 'Mining in Papua', *Cairns Post* (1911) 14 Aug., p. 2; 3 Oct., p. 8 and 6 Nov. p. 4

53 AR-BNG (1902-03) pp. 30–1; (1913-14) p. 155; see Nelson, p. 69.

54 AR-BNG (1895-96) p. 76; (1898-1899) pp. xxvi, xii & 22; SMH, (1896) 8 April, p. 3.

55 BC (1906) 3 Nov., p. 5; The Inquirer (1896) 6 Nov., p. 11; AR-BNG (1896-97) pp. xix & 36.

56 AR-BNG (1897-98) p.14.

57 AR-BNG (1896-97) p. 36; *BC* (1897) 13 Oct. p. 5; see Nelson, p. 112-18.

58 'Sir William MacGregor, 'The New Guinea Goldfields', BC (1897) 20 Dec., p. 5; (1898) 10 May, 4; ATCJ (1898) 1 Jan., p. 25; *SMH* (1898) 4 Apr., p. 5; *TQ* (1898) 30 July, p. 199.

59 AR-BNG (1898-99) p. xxvi; (1899-00) p. 85; D.H. Osborne, 'Gira and Yodda Goldfields' in *Pacific Islands Monthly*, xiii (1943) p. 30.

60 AR-BNG (1897-98) pp. xix, 53 & 150 (map).

61 *Morning Post* (Cairns, 1899) 28 Jun., p. 5.

62 *Northern Miner* (1900) 31 Oct., p. 5; *ATCJ* (1903) 21 Jan., p. 25; (1906) 3 Jan., p. 55; AR-Papua (1903-04) pp. 48-7.

63 Osborne, p. 30

64 AR-Papua (1900-01) pp. 19 and 48; (1903-04) pp. 35–6; (1906-07) p. 79

65 AR–Papua (1900-01) p. 49; (1907-08) p. 55, Lands, Surveys, Mines, p. 103; *BC* (1901) 15 Jun.   p. 14

66 AR-BNG (1902-03) p. 32.

67 'New Rush in New Guinea', *TQ* (1906) 24 Nov., p. 15; AR-BNG (1905-06) p. 71.

68 Morning Bulletin (Rockhampton, 1907) 12 Jan., p. 4; AR-BNG (1906-07) p. 85.

69 AR-Papua (1908-09) p. 134; D. Pryke, 'Correspondence and Papers' (NLA MS 1826, mfm PMB 913).

70 Delimitation of the Boundary between Papua and German New Guinea, 1899–1910 (NAA Series A1–1914-4329; AR-Papua [1908-09] p. 127).

71 AR-Papua (1906-07) p. 78.

72 H. N. Nelson, 'Frank Pryke: Prospector' in J. Griffin, ed., *Papua New Guinea Portraits*, pp. 75–100.

73 AR-Papua (1906-07) p. 19.

74 Mining Ordinance, 1907 assented to 2 May 1908 (AR-Papua (1907-08) p. 6.

75 *Northern Argus* (1900) 27 Sep., p. 5; *ATCJ* (1901) 16 Feb., p. 26; AR-Papua (1906-07) p. 76.

76 Goldfield Reward Ordinance, 1909 assented to 21 Oct. 1909; Gold Mining Encouragement Ordinance, 1909 assented to 12 April 1910.

77 E. Auerbach, 'N.G. Goldfield Pioneers', *Pacific Islands Monthly* (1940) 15 July, p. 59.

78 AR-Papua (1908-09) p. 129; *Morning Bulletin* (Rockhampton, 1909) 27 Feb., p. 6; *Northern Miner* (Charters Towers 1909, 5 Aug. p. 6; Cairns Post (1909) 6 Aug. p. 11

79 *Northern Territory Times and Gazette* (1910) 21 Jan., p. 10

80 AR-Papua (1909-10) pp 12-14. 'A Trip to the Lakekamu Goldfield.' *Cairns Post* (1910) 15 Apr., p. 2.

81 *Kalgoorlie Western Argus* (1912) 26 Jul., p. 4

82 AR-Papua (1909-10) pp 22–3, 32, 102–5, 117, 124–5 & 152; *SMH* (1910) 22 Apr., p. 6; see D. Lewis, *The Plantation Dream*, pp. 95

83 AR-Papua (1910-11) pp. 24–5

84 AR-Papua (1910-11) p. 25; (1918-19) p. 84. *Northern Miner* (1911) 1 Mar., p. 2; *Kalgoorlie Western Argus* (1912) 6 Apr., p. 6; (1915) 23 Apr., p. 4

85 AR-Papua (1911-12) pp. 6, 12, 35 & 38–9.; (1912-13) pp. 37–8 & 40

86 E. Auerbach, 'New Guinea Goldfield Pioneers'. *Pacific Islands Monthly*, (1940) 15 Jul.

87 AR-Papua (1908-09) pp. 14 & 128

88 *Financial News* (1911) 19 May, 'Exploration in Papua. Large coalfield found on the upper Kikori'.

89 AR-Papua (1910-11) pp. 6 & 165–71

90 Staniforth Smith Expeditions, Starvation and Cruelty Alleged', *Examiner* (1912) 1 Jan. p. 6

91 AR-Papua (1913-14) pp. 153; AA (1914) 19 Feb. p. 8; *Townsville Daily* (1914) 10 Jul. p. 6

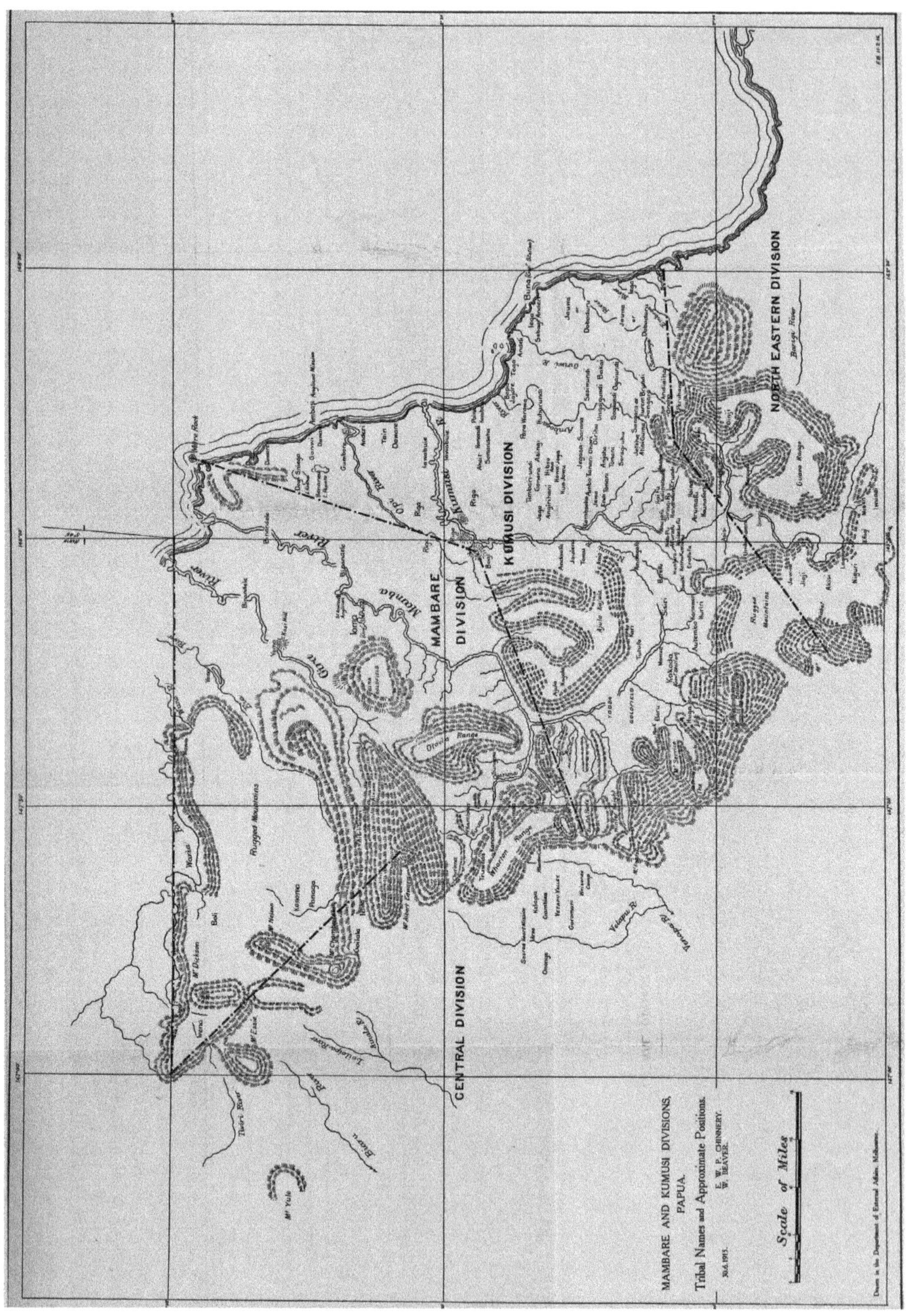

Map 16: **Mambare and Kumusi Divisions - Tribal names and approximate locations,** ca. 1914
(NLA ID 40203020)

BLUEPRINTS FOR TROPICAL PROSPERITY

The Department of Lands and Surveys, established by Lieutenant-Governor George Le Hunte in 1899/1900 under H. H. Stuart-Russell, reported on the land acquired by the Crown and what areas were available to settlers each year. In 1900, the number of surveyors was increased to six. This brought about the layout of streets and building sites in Port Moresby and Samarai, and the survey of the mountainous terrain for the planned road from Port Moresby to Kokoda, including the locations for bridge crossings, culverts and the gradients for water channels. The surveyors pegged mining leases, land for trading stations and some small agricultural plots, as well as numerous land grants to the Christian missions. However, following the debacle surrounding the British New Guinea Syndicate in 1898 and the Hall Sound Co. in 1902, the appetite for large-scale agricultural land ceased altogether until the Australian Federal Government assumed responsibility for BNG in 1906.

With the economic development of BNG going nowhere, Prime Minister George Reid requested Secretary of External Affairs Atlee Hunt in 1904 'to go to New Guinea, and report what was best to be done to promote the settlement, consistent with preserving the interest of the natives'.[1] The protectionist Alfred Deakin, who became Prime Minister for the second time on 5 July 1905, received Hunt's report. He was then as interested in finding a solution for BNG as Edmund Barton had been in 1903 and the free trader Reid in 1904. The Report urged the immediate passage of the Papuan Bill held over since 1902.

The self-proclaimed expert on tropical agriculture, Senator Staniforth Smith, sought Hunt's support in 1905 to obtain Deakin's agreement for him to tour BNG. Smith had been optimistic as to the colony's agricultural potential since he first visited there in 1903. He now wanted to inform the Commonwealth of his detailed findings. With one eye on the possible appointment as the first Lieutenant-Governor of the Territory of Papua, Smith outlined a plan in the Senate in late 1905 that identified agricultural prosperity leading to a self-supporting Papua, which would ultimately be a significant economic asset to Australia.

The government's procrastination in coming to terms with the reality that southeast New Guinea was now an Australian responsibility continued through 1906 when Deakin called a Royal Commission into the conditions in Papua. He also sought recommendations from the Commissioners on how to best develop Papua.

By the end of 1906 Deakin had before him three reports (Hunt, Smith and the Commissioners). Largely concurring in their recommendations the reports provided the Australian government with a blueprint for economic development in Papua.

Disastrous Ventures

New Guinea Affair: A complete muddle

Randolph Bedford, politician, miner, agriculturalist and renowned journalist filed a report from Port Moresby in October 1905 which made BNG the focus of attention before the colony became officially the responsibility of Australia in 1906.

'To guard against the Papuan Bill being passed in ignorance of the real conditions in existence in Papua', Bedford wrote, 'it is necessary to state with respect to the present disorganisation of the government that members of the Executive and Legislative Councils are at daggers drawn with one another'. Bedford found that public officers were given a preference over settlers and companies in the acquisition of crown land and that future settlement would be difficult if the undesirable situation continued.

> The only apologists—and their excuses are perfunctory—for the Government are the missionaries of the London Missionary Society (L.M.S.), who have an undue influence over this and past Administrations. [The] money voted formerly by the States and now by the Commonwealth, has helped only the native and the missionary, and of these latter the L.M.S. is a mere trader, working unpaid natives at boat-building and other timber work, in opposition to the white labour they undercut. [The] whole administration calls for a searching inquiry, with progress only visible in the eastern part of the colony, and that this is entirely due to the miners who provide nearly two-thirds of the revenue with the least assistance from the Government [If] the air is not cleared quickly [Bedford concluded his story] Australia's enforced attempt at Imperialism will continue to be comic opera chastened by Chadbandism, and played to a small audience.[2]

Prime Minister Deakin referred the Bedford allegations to the Secretaries of the Department of External Affairs and the Attorney-General's Department for examination. 'The Prime Minister', according to newspaper reports, 'very much regrets that such an unpleasant situation has arisen', more so as it is a matter absolutely devoid of importance.'[3] The Department Heads, however, considered the matter serious enough to recommend that the Prime Minister call a Royal Commission to 'Report on the Present Conditions and Method of the Government in The Territory of Papua'.

The Hunt Report on economic development

Atlee Hunt undertook his inspection of BNG from 13 July to 26 August 1905. He commenced his 43-day tour on the Burns, Philp (BP) steamer SS *Ysabel* destined for Port Moresby *via* Daru. Hunt discussed matters of concern with the leading officials of the administration in Port Moresby, Samarai and Cape Nelson. On Woodlark Island he met with some 50 members of the local Progress Association and noted their concerns. Visits to the headquarters of the four Christian missions were high on his agenda, as were inspections of the few existing plantations in order to form an idea of the agricultural possibilities in BNG. Due to time constraints, the labour, health and policing issues of the Yodda and Gira goldfields were only discussed with C.A.W. Monckton in Port Moresby.

Hunt started his mainland inspection on horseback at BP's Warirata coffee plantation on the Astrolabe Range and then went to the coffee plantation of the government's treasurer David Ballantine at Sogeri in the Laloki River Valley. The government steamer *Merrie England* took Hunt's party from there to the mining leases on Woodlark Island. Of the Christian missions, Hunt visited the headquarters of the Wesleyan Mission on Dobu Island in the D'Entrecasteaux Archipelago, the Anglican Mission in Wedau, Bartle Bay, the Society of the Sacred Heart Mission on Yule Island, and many of the London Missionary Society's establishments. Of the latter, the Milne Bay coconut plantation, Killerton, and the sawmill and boat-building establishment on Kwato Island—both managed by LMS missionary Charles Abel—stood out as potentially commercial developments in Hunt's view. He also visited the Samarai publican's John Clunn's Ramaga and government station at Rigo.

The son of a Queensland grazier and manufacturer, Hunt approached his task like a businessman. Starting from the premise that 'the management of a colony is, in many respects, merely the conduct of a commercial undertaking, [and] that an enterprise started on insufficient capital is doomed to failure', he quickly concluded that the BNG enterprise was massively underfunded. Before drafting his recommendations on the future of Papua, he discarded several unworkable propositions:

a) Having achieved ownership, to remain content with the fact that foreign nations may not use the territory as a base from which operations against Australia might be organized and conducted.

b) To hand over BNG to a chartered company

c) To limit Government interference to the preservation of peace among the natives.

d) To leave the natives alone as far as possible, interfering not at all with their mode of life, habits, and superstitions, the Government limiting its interposition to cases where it becomes necessary to secure protection for white settlers.

e) To promote the settlement of European families.

f) To encourage the development of the country under European auspices by the employment of imported capital to be expended under European direction, employing native labour, and at the same time extend the influence of the Government until the whole Possession is brought under control.

Hunt was unequivocal about one point: ownership involves responsibility to the inhabitants which cannot be evaded by any civilised nation. Whereas the handing over of responsibility for Papua to commercial interests would possibly relieve the government of much trouble and cost, Hunt distanced himself from this because a chartered company would not promote the welfare of their 'native subjects'. In any event, he believed that there were insufficient grounds for Australia to abnegate its duties in favour of a company whose main interest was to make money with a minimum outlay. At the same time Hunt was greatly concerned with the raising of revenue, as without it, Australia could not afford to run Papua. To meet 'all outlays with no revenue', he said, 'would be expensive' and should not be considered in the first instance because it would 'not be in the bluest interests of the natives themselves'. In regard to settlement by Australian families intending to take up land, Hunt believed that New Guinea could not be fairly promoted as a country for white men to settle in. He also addressed the dearth of capable men in Australia. The class of migrants Papua needed were 'the very kind of man of whom Australia stands in need herself and in Australia such a man can reasonably hope to find a home and raise a family'.

There was nothing in the prospects of Papua to warrant extravagant optimism according to Hunt. Developing the Territory, he cautioned, would require time, patience, energy and most of all money: 'in Australia millions have been and are being spent in opening up the country … it would be unreasonable to expect that Papua, a country where natural obstacles are far greater than in most parts of the Commonwealth [could be expected to prosper] by spending a very few thousand pounds each year'. Hunt calculated that 75% of the annual government expenditure in Papua was devoted to policing. The cost of bringing villages and tribes under government control and maintaining order and good government, left virtually nothing for building infrastructure and 'improving' the land.

Because the Australian government was unlikely to commit large sums of money to an enterprise which would not return a profit for many years, Hunt proposed the establishment of a sovereign loan fund of not less than £300,000 for the exclusive development of the commercial resources of Papua. The loan money was to be extended by the Australian government in a similar manner to the British government providing funding to the Australian colonies. Regarding Papua he suggested that the Commonwealth loan be advanced annually at £15,000 over a period of 20 years at an annual interest rate of 3–3.5%. The rate was to be increased by 1.5% when the total sum was drawn. Hunt did not address repayment other than by suggesting amendments to the contract reflecting changing circumstances in Papua. Hunt also envisaged that the Papuan administration would solicit venture capital for agricultural and mining enterprises, albeit solely at the risk of the investors. Separate from these financial arrangements he recommended a £5,000 annual increase for 10 years to the government subsidy of £20,000. He insisted that this sum should be spent exclusively on administrative matters and law and order. The duties of the Papuan government were first and foremost 'the subduing, the pacifying of the people, teaching them to respect the lives of others and better appreciate the value of their own'. In short, Hunt considered it mandatory for the annual subsidy to be spent on 'inculcating the doctrines of elementary civilization' into Papuans.

Java had provided the model of colonisation for Hansemann's New Guinea Protectorate in 1885. It was also Hunt's paradigm for Papua in 1905. He believed that the Dutch colony was remarkably like New Guinea, where millions had been spent on what seemed for many years a hopeless undertaking, but which 'now repays the Dutch government most handsomely for all its outlays'. Taking a leaf out of Hansemann's textbook on the development of GNG, Hunt pointed to the similar soil and climatic conditions that provided for excellent opportunities in the development of tropical agriculture. If applied professionally, it 'could also be the foundation for profitability in New Guinea … Crude methods of agriculture no longer sufficed in an increasingly competitive market in tropical products'. Therefore, he urged 'the adoption of the latest appliances and systems that experience and science suggested would be a fundamental requirement to be successful in the field in Papua'. Further, Hunt recommended that 'more experimental plantations and nurseries be established under the control of trained tropical agriculturists. Cotton, tobacco, vanilla, indigo, rubber, tea and cocoa should be grown'. However, 'most serious attention should be given to coffee of the Arabian and Liberian varieties which already grows well at an elevation of some 2,500 feet on the Astrolabe Range and at sea level in the valley of the Laloki River'. Special consideration was to be given to fibre plants in Hunt's business plan. While the 'Americans at present monopolize the supply of Manila hemp, the banana, to which this hemp is closely allied, flourishes widely in New Guinea' and would provide an opening for extensive cultivation.

Turning his attention to large-scale plantations, Hunt suggested that fibres, rubber and coconut, all growing wild in abundance, should be exploited in the controlled environment of plantations. Provided 'the planter can afford to tide over the necessary years of waiting', they were the three most desirable objects of cultivation, which would ultimately repay the outlays handsomely. Hunt was also keen on the cultivation of sugar of which several varieties were indigenous to Papua. No attempt had been made to grow it commercially in Papua because of the cost. While there was an abundance of suitable land to set up large sugar plantations, it required much more capital to set up a mechanised mill than had hitherto been contemplated by anyone in Papua. With the appropriate capital investment 'it may be that New Guinea will yet take rank with Java as a great sugar-producing country' were Hunt's encouraging remarks.

For a plantation and agriculture industry to emerge, the Report advocated repealing the cumbersome land laws and replacing them with a short and simple code. Hunt preferred a reversal of the existing policy and a law to enable the government to declare all Papuan land the property of the Crown. Failing that, he suggested that as much land as possible should be secured from the 'natives' in the areas chosen for agriculture. This land should then be made available to settlers and corporations on terms as attractive as possible. Indeed, 'I advocate', Hunt said, 'as a beginning, making [the terms] so easy that they practically amount to giving the land away [but] always under the strictest conditions as to improvements'. Survey maps of the localities chosen for agriculture should contain full disclosure on access, the conditions of the soil, the proximity to water, the proposed roads and the means of obtaining labour and other relevant information for prospective purchasers. To attract investors, the information should be advertised extensively in Australia, East Asia, Europe, Canada and California on attractive conditions, 'remembering always that the objective is not so much to sell the land as to induce permanent cultivation'.

While agriculture was to deliver the long-term prospects in Hunt's Papua model, gold mining was expected to increase in importance in the short term. Nothing drives miners more strongly than the discovery of a new payable goldfield. Hunt suggested, therefore, promoting the mining industry in Papua with the government establishing a prospecting vote either 'to be employed as a reward for new finds or to afford temporary assistance in prosecuting likely ventures'. An export tax on existing and future gold production was his answer to funding the prospectors.

The Report proposed several other revenue raising methods available to the government. On taxing the indigenous population, Hunt argued: 'Civilization has given the natives absolute security [and] it seems but fair that he should be asked to contribute something towards the expenses of maintaining the system that confers this inestimable benefit on him'. Other recommendations pointed to the introduction of a land tax as applied in India, a culture or land rent system applied by the Batavia administration since the 1830s, a poll tax as in Fiji, a hut tax as in Central Africa and Nigeria, or the village tax, which is apparently most suitable to the local conditions of life'. The introduction of a law requiring men to pay a fixed sum of money annually was regarded as the most desirable for Papuan conditions. The tax could be earned from the production of hemp, cotton and copra. However, since most of the planting and the preparing of crops would add to the workload of the Papuan women, without encouraging the men to work, Hunt proposed that each village furnish men for plantation work 'to be performed as a national duty, as military or naval service as in France and Germany, the government deducting, if thought desirable, a certain proportion from their wages as the tax for their village'. Whatever scheme was to be implemented, most important to Hunt was that a personal tax to be imposed on young, able, Papuan men. It was designed to make Papuans work because if their idleness could not be turned into productive activity, Hunt saw no future for Papua.

He also saw little future for the Territory unless the Australian government assumed full responsibility quickly: 'so far as expansion is concerned, the Territory is now at a standstill ...Investment had not been forthcoming in the past and there was no hope of this being reversed until the Papua Bill passed the Australian Parliament. People would not invest money in a country without having some idea of the character of the government and the applicable laws'.

The report restated the two 'duties' which he believed would be imposed on Australia when it assumed control of Papua: 'the one to our dark-skinned fellow subjects—to give them the advantages of civilization, divesting them so far as we are able from the evils that too often follow their train; the second, to ourselves—to make the fullest use of the goodly heritage it is our privilege to possess'.

Hunt delivered a forthright assessment with his 'British New Guinea Report' to Alfred Deakin on 25 October 1905. He excused possible charges of presumptuousness on the grounds that, as permanent head of the Department of External Affairs for the past 4 years, he had endeavoured to familiarise himself with the circumstances of BNG by reading all of the official reports and other available literature concerning the Territory, and neglecting no opportunity of meeting men with local experience.[4]

The Staniforth Smith model of economic development

Miles Staniforth Cater Smith (1869–1934) worked for the wool classers and merchants, Goldsborough Mort & Co., in Melbourne before moving to Kalgoorlie to work as a telegraph linesman on the Western Australian goldfields. In 1896 he opened an office for Reuter's Telegram Company in Kalgoorlie. Elected as a municipal councillor in 1898, he was Mayor of Kalgoorlie in 1900–01. Mayor Smith supported the working class by subsidising the freight of fresh produce from the coast to the town markets. In 1901 he nominated for the first Federal Senate election and received the most votes. In the Senate he sat in opposition to the Barton and Deakin governments. A staunch free trader and opponent of 'coloured' immigration, he supported the election of J. C. Watson to become the first Labour Party Prime Minister of Australia in April 1904.[5] The Labour government only lasted 112 days. Making use of his training with Goldsborough Mort, Smith took up the study of tropical agriculture and became the parliamentary authority on Papua. Smith enlisted in the Australian Imperial Force in January 1916. He was appointed Acting Administrator of the Northern Territory in September 1919 to settle the aftermath of the 'Darwin Rebellion'. Smith sided with the North Australian Workers' Union—against the local Chinese labourers—to resolve the dispute. His recommendation to accept the Baldwin Spencer solution to aboriginal problems by increasing reserved land and spending was rejected by the Federal Parliament. This led to his resignation from his post in 1921. Smith returned to Papua in 1921 as Commissioner for Crown Lands, Mines and Agriculture. He retired in 1930 and settled at Kulikup in southwest Western Australia.[6]

Copra, caoutchouc and other tropical commodities started to boom in the early part of the 20th century. Staniforth Smith, who considered in 1901 that Australia needed to concentrate her financial and labour capital on developing her own resources, discovered his fervour for BNG 2 years later. Visiting the Territory in 1903, he found 'a large and valuable estate', lying idle, which 'only requires money judiciously spent in cultivation to make it capable of yielding large revenue'. While vehemently opposed to BP's agricultural development proposal on Yule Island in Hall Sound, he saw opportunities for the Australian settler to become successful in BNG: 'The present revenue is sufficient to maintain the status quo', he reported to the Senate, but it also would ensure that 'New Guinea will remain undeveloped, and always be a financial burden [on the Commonwealth]'.[7] Smith's path to the creation of an economically thriving BNG was to attract settlers through the most liberal land and labour laws. Like Atlee Hunt, he suggested 'giving land away' in order to increase the population and develop the economy.

Smith would have been aware that MacGregor's policy to attract small landholders was unsuccessful. And even though the government now had at its disposal more and better quality land, he would have known that low-cost, high-quality land was but one factor in attracting settlers. Of even greater importance to settlers, in his opinion, was the availability of low-cost labour. Other issues of concern to them were the availability of seeds and seedlings, building materials, food and so forth, and all at affordable prices. The ability to export produce speedily and cost-effectively would also have ranked highly. This required coastal shipping for delivering goods to Port Moresby or Samarai. That all this was not available in BNG was precisely why Smith saw a pivotal role for himself in southeast New Guinea. He aspired to be Australia's first Lieutenant-Governor of Papua so that he could implement change and create a thriving tropical plantation industry.

Smith became an expert on all issues concerning East New Guinea. His visits included trips to GNG and the Solomon Islands, and by the time the *Papuan Act* was debated in the Senate in late 1905, there was no person more vociferous on the new constitution for the Territory of Papua than Smith. There were strong parallels between his and Hunt's vision of Papua's future and what Hansemann tried to achieve in GNG. The Dutch East Indies and the British achievements in the Straits Settlements and the Federated Malay States provided Smith with the template for BNG. To lend his model weight and to choose the best methods for developing Papua, Smith asked the government for permission to visit the British and Dutch East Asian colonies. Atlee Hunt agreed with Smith on the requirement of more rapid economic development in BNG. In conveying the Australian Prime Minister's desire to receive a report from the Senator on the British and Dutch colonies Hunt wrote:

> Mr Deakin wishes to say that he much appreciates the public spirit you display, and will be pleased to receive a report on the lines indicated by you. Your knowledge of the Territory of Papua will place you in a position enjoyed by very few others of making your report of such nature that it will have practical value in assisting the development of the Possession.[8]

Smith tabled his report in June 1906. His account of the Dutch East Indies mirrored Hansemann's and Hunt's convictions: Java, 'the Garden of the East', was at the same latitude and 'the same isotherm' as New Guinea, so any economic plant growing successfully there would also grow well in Papua. Smith strongly favoured coconut and rubber plantations, but also envisaged tobacco and coffee in Papua. He intended to overcome the absence of an experienced and productive labour force by adopting the Dutch method of educating people to work. His report ignored the recruitment of Chinese coolies: he pointed to an increasing apathy in the local people since Chinese coolies and Indian indentured workers had been recruited for work in Malaya. Smith saw a thriving Papua as dependent largely on the availability of very cheap farm and grazing land. He advocated that the Crown be the landlord to ensure that land speculators were kept out of Papua. But he also supported the idea of virtual freehold, provided the lessee developed the land in accordance with their agreement. The lease could then be a perpetual one, charged at a nominal annual rate for at least the first 30 years. He wanted the government to assist farmers with tropical agriculture research and to provide them with quality seeds and seedlings. He cited the support the Batavian government provided to their planters through the extensive experimental gardens of Buitenzog (Bogor) in the foothills of Mt Salak. Smith recommended the Port Moresby government set up similar experimental gardens on the coast and in the foothills. Such gardens could become part of an increasing number of government plantations which, Smith insisted, must be operated on a commercial basis. The senator believed that Australia had the advantage of being able to learn from other colonial administrators' mistakes: 'almost every difficulty regarding economic development has either been solved or has been the subject of prolonged investigation', Smith reported in the Senate. Preventing the mistakes of others required an agriculture department administered by a person with a thorough knowledge in tropical plantation work. With an eye on his own career, he suggested that such an expert need to be well connected to tropical enterprises overseas.[9]

Deakin offered Smith the position of Director of Agriculture, Mines and Public Works in Papua on 4 September 1906. The Senator accepted the offer. He believed he was only one step away from becoming Papua's first Lieutenant-Governor. He did not seek re-election when nominations closed for the federal elections in December 1906, and took up the new posting in Port Moresby on 16 May 1907.[10]

Deakin's equivocation

Prime Minister Deakin was reluctant to implement the recommendations of Atlee Hunt and Staniforth Smith. Their blunt conclusions were that the Papuans were to be endowed with the privilege of European civilization and for Australia to make full use of the economic opportunities offered. This was inconsistent with the compassionate passages in the Papua Bill. With the objective of Papuan welfare central to the Bill, Deakin was keen not to create divisions in the House of Representatives. He was aware of tensions that had long simmered between senior officers in BNG. The position of Lieutenant-Governor had not been settled since the departure of G.R. Le Hunte in 1903, when Captain Francis Barton was appointed Acting Administrator.

When Hunt requested clarification from the Lands Department in Port Moresby on the process for approving land transfers, John Richmond, who had replaced H.H. Stuart-Russell as Head of Public Works, Lands and Mines in December 1902, remonstrated. He blamed the slow process on Barton's interference in the paperwork, accusing him of destroying land certificates and general ineptitude.[11] On 16 June 1904, the Executive Council chaired by Barton suspended Richmond from duty until the matter was dealt with by a Commonwealth Public Service Enquiry Board in Melbourne. Hunt did not draw attention to the friction between Barton and his senior officer, and praised the Port Moresby administration for its excellent work: 'Now that the Australian government is entirely responsible for Papua, their keen spirit of enterprise and adventure' required appropriate remuneration. Hunt recommended that a pension system for government officers employed in the Territory should be adopted as soon as practicable.[12]

When the board found against the evidence tendered by Richmond and exonerated Barton, the aggrieved Richmond wrote to Hunt seeking a reconsideration of his case.

The handing down of the decision by the Public Service Board made Deakin aware of the discrepancy between Hunt's report on the quality of senior officers in Port Moresby and a senior officer's view of the administrator. Recognising Hunt's friendliness with Barton, he sought the confidential views of Chief Judicial Officer J.H.P. Murray in Port Moresby. 'What I wish from you,' Deakin wrote privately, 'is as complete a criticism of the circumstances in New Guinea as you can make off hand and without delay—I shall be glad to have the fullest and frankest judgement you can favour me with upon our officer's methods and aims'.[13] Murray, who had been given judicial responsibilities for BNG in September 1904, was clearly pleased to be asked by Deakin for his opinion. The Oxford-educated lawyer regarded himself intellectually superior to Barton and just about everyone else.[14] At age 43, with war experience in South Africa, and having been Crown prosecutor in New South Wales, he believed that he, not Barton, should have followed Robinson as the administrator.

Murray's 60-page handwritten reply to Deakin on 26 March 1906 reveals the character of the person who was to preside over the administration of Papua from 1907 until his death in office at Samarai on 27 February 1940. With BNG becoming the Australian colony of Papua in 1 September 1906, Murray played the anti-English, pro-Australian card to impress Deakin:

> Government officials here are divided into two parties, the "Colonial Office" party and the "Australian" party. The former strongly adhere to the old regime of MacGregor and Le Hunte, inwardly rejoicing if all white settlers—especially miners—could be removed from the country.

They would feel satisfied, Murray continued, if BNG never became anything more than a 'glorified curiosity shop and an extensive and very expensive ethnological museum'. This stands in stark contrast to the view of the Australian administration who is 'anxious for the development of the country, and are sincere in their dislike of a policy which … has retarded the progress of the Possession in the past … and under which large sums of Australian money have been expended with very little result'.[15]

Turning his attention to Barton, Murray attested to 'His Excellency's personal charm and the attractiveness of his manner: 'my personal relations with him have always been pleasant', he opened his observations on Barton, before back-stabbing his superior officer. Pointing to the necessity of developing Papua by white Australian settlement he noted that 'it is hardly an exaggeration to say that Captain Barton's administration is about as unsatisfactory as possible'. His sympathy with the 'natives', essential and admirable in itself, 'unfortunately misleads [him] into a policy … of "passive resistance" to white settlement'. Barton openly condemned gold mining Murray proffered: 'I have frequently heard [him] deplore the fact that gold had ever been found in the country'. The pugnacious Murray accused Barton of opposition or at least indifference to land conveyancing: 'the great hindrance to settlement in the past has been not so much that rents were too high, tenures too short, and survey fees excessive, as that it was impossible to get an application for land attended to within many months—sometimes years. [A]s a result', Murray argued, 'BNG had in land matters acquired a bad reputation which would take some time to overcome'. Summarising his opinion, Murray claimed that Barton 'is a man of weak character and indolent disposition who could therefore never be a satisfactory Administrator'.

After this malicious attack, Murray turned his attention to Treasurer David Ballantine. He accused this long-serving officer of lying 'drunk in his cottage for days together without going to his office' and with no reproof from the administrator. The strong-willed, pernicious Ballantine completely controlled the Administrator, with 'common talk through the Possession that [he] is the Governor, not Captain Barton'. Murray made no secret of his loathing for Ballantine: 'I have always disliked him, but shall endeavour not to do him an injustice'. He accused Ballantine of unscrupulously encouraging the anti-white proclivities of the administrator while leaving the accounts in an unsatisfactory condition. 'In my opinion one of the crying needs of BNG is the immediate appointment of a Treasury Inspector from Australia to make a thorough inspection of all the government accounts'. Prejudging the outcome of the audit, Murray proposed the appointment of an experienced treasurer.

Murray reserved particular resentment for the Magistrates. With the exception of R.M. Campbell of the Eastern Division, who he regarded an honourable man, he described them as 'on the whole, a shady lot'. Lacking legal training and making occasional errors in law, Murray hoped that under a strong and impartial administration they would run straight and do an excellent job. It must have come as some relief to Deakin that Murray had some kind words for officers in the Lands Department: 'so far as I am able to judge these officers have done their work conscientiously and I am unable to give the reason to His Excellency's objection to them'. The chief draftsman, Matthews, a friend of Murray, was recommended by him to replace Richmond if Barton did not lift the suspension from duty of the chief surveyor.[16]

By inviting Murray to provide him with 'complete criticism' of his superior and fellow officers Deakin got more than he had bargained for. Secretary Hunt thought highly of Barton and gave a generally satisfactory report on the officers in the administration. The Public Service Board also handed down a favourable report on Barton. Murray's harsh criticism of Barton and every person in the BNG administration who was 'English' pointed to him striving for the Lieutenant-Governor's position. There can be little doubt that he believed in the veracity of his account as BNG was rudderless and had not been dominated by an imposing man like MacGregor since 1898. Murray was also imposing. He was physically and intellectually strong. As a member of the governing council he influenced policy and administrative outcomes. But rather than contributing positively he resorted to complaining and conniving. In closing his letter to Deakin he recommended that an absolute stranger to be appointed Lieutenant-Governor. Murray's friends then and many historians today believe that he was sincere when he made the suggestion. It is possible his dislike for Barton was stronger than his own ambitions, and all that he wanted to see in BNG was a change of personnel for the better. However, Murray would also have known that his letter could become public knowledge, and it was useful to have demonstrated his integrity by openly not vying for the administrator's position.

In contrast to Murray, Staniforth Smith was frank as to his own ambitions in Papua. Rather than complaining about Murray's appointment, he wrote to Hunt: 'I am grateful for my appointment as a stepping stone to higher things [and] am doing my best to get the experience that Mr Deakin said was the one thing I lacked'.[17]

Before considering a Royal Commission Deakin contacted MacGregor, now Governor of Newfoundland, to ask him whether he was interested in resuming responsibility for Papua. Deakin believed the 38-year old Staniforth Smith would be a good appointment to the Lieutenant-Governor's position after some time spent as an understudy to MacGregor to gain experience for the job. MacGregor, who would not have found the fishing community of the most easterly part of North America overly challenging, was interested in moving back to a tropical climate. For him it only required agreement to a remuneration package that included a pension scheme. However, when Hunt informed Barton that adverse criticism had reached Deakin from Port Moresby, Barton wrote to Deakin on 4 July 1906 to request the appointment of a Royal Commission to enquire into his administration's performance. With requests from Richmond and Barton for an official enquiry and aware of MacGregor's availability to take charge of Papua subject to an acceptable remuneration package, Deakin was glad to be handed reasons for a Royal Commission, which Parliament established on 14 August. And, notwithstanding Murray's allegations, shortly before the Royal Commission took evidence in Port Moresby, Deakin appointed Barton the first Administrator of Papua on 1 September 1906.[18]

The Royal Commission's recommendation

> By reason of the fact that the persons and lands of the natives had to be guarded against "lawless and evil-disposed persons," that time in its original sense is past, and in the opinion of Your Commissioners the hour has struck for the commencement of a vigorous forward policy, so far as white settlement is concerned.[19]

On 13 September 1906 the Royal Commissioner Colonel J. A. K. Mackay (MLC, New South Wales), Chairman, W. E. Parry-Okeden (retired Queensland Police Commissioner) and Justice C. E. Herbert arrived in Port Moresby. The terms of reference went well beyond the 'present conditions [and] method of government' as the Commissioners were to recommended on all issues concerning the development of Papua.

Over 7 weeks the Commissioners travelled widely to take evidence from 71 witnesses on wide-ranging issues. Their inspections included the Christian missions and the government stations also visited by Hunt; Yule Island, (previously evaluated on its agricultural potential by W. Gors of Burns Philp (BP) and Senator Smith), the Whitten Bros coconut plantation on Cloudy Bay, and the gold-producing region of the Trobriands, Milne Bay and the Upper Mambare. The Commissioners did not go to the Gira and Aikora goldfields. Rather, they took evidence from a delegation of miners who came to the coast near the German border.

Magistrate Monckton led a party consisting of Kenneth Mackay, Charles Herbert, the Rigo Manager Georg Belford, a small escort of the Armed Native Constabulary and a number of carriers from Buna Bay on 15 October to march to Kanderita village which had been visited by Europeans only once before. The party reached Kokoda Station on 21 October and the mining centre of Yodda on the following day. At a height of 8,689 ft (2,600 m) the main range was ascended on 31 October and Monckton returned to Cape Nelson. He had been relieved by Police Commandant William Bruce at Kagi village who then led the party *via* Maneri, Iorobaia and Irutapuna to Port Moresby. The day before reaching the coast on 6 November the coffee plantations at Sogeri were inspected.

Murray, Barton and Robinson were not called to give evidence until the second week of November. Murray had sought permission from Deakin to submit the letter he wrote to him in March: 'I intend giving evidence to the same effect, and my letter will be useful in shewing that the opinion which I entertain of the Administration is not a mere transient impression or due to any momentary irritation'. Murray had no choice. He had thrown the first stone with his complaints to Deakin, and with the now public attack on Barton and the aspersions he had cast on many of the other officers in BNG, he would advance to the top in the administration of Papua or leave his posting in Port Moresby a scorned person.

On the immediate question—the 'Richmond case'—the Royal Commission exonerated Barton by agreeing with the Administrator that he was justified in suspending the surveyor. While not buying into the British versus Australian argument, the Commissioners recommended for the administration to be thoroughly reorganised.[20]

Giving credence to some of Murray's evidence, the report strongly recommended that Treasurer Ballantine 'be suspended by the appointment of a thoroughly competent man in his place'. Ralph Drummond's promotion to be Chief Government Survey was, in the opinion of the Commissioners, inadvisable. With neither sufficient experience nor administrative ability they recommended Drummond not be retained in his senior position. As regards the government Secretary's Department, it was found to be in much disorder:

In addition to the general administrative responsibility that rests [with] the Government Secretary as head of the Public Service, he should be held responsible for the work of all the officers grouped immediately under his Department [*viz.*] Magistracy, Police, Prisons, Native Affairs and Control, Census, Statistics, Supervision of Audit Work, Registrar-General, Registrar of Patents, Registrar of Joint Stock Companies, *Merrie England.*[21]

In its investigations the Commissioners considered complaints levelled against Commandant W. C. Bruce of the Armed Native Constabulary. The brash and garish Bruce was accused of using obscene language repeatedly in front of women and missionaries. Even though he pleaded diminished responsibility for his actions because of excessive drinking, the Commissioners concluded that Bruce was shielded by Barton: 'he should not have been retained in his position in the service after his serious offences'. They recommended that the commandant's position be abolished and the policing placed under the command of the R.M. of the Central Division.[22]

The Commissioners believed that Anthony Musgrave, who had nearly 22 years' service in BNG, should be assisted by a Chief Clerk and, because of the demands of the growing Public Service in Papua, retired in the foreseeable future. The Commissioners agreed with Murray that Alexander Campbell, R.M. of the Eastern Division, is the most competent officer in the administration and would succeed Musgrave. The report portrayed remuneration as generally inadequate:

The only possible way to induce capable young men to accept service in Papua is to offer them reasonable inducement:

a) Fair remuneration (no white clerk should be paid a less sum than £200, with junior positions in the Public Service to be performed by trained natives).;

b) Reasonable promotion;

c) Recognition of special merit and zeal;

d) Extended periodical furlough;

e) Some definite provision, such as an annuity on completion of service; (Australian Life Assurance Company of undoubted stability for the issue of a policy to each officer on appointment under which the Company will undertake to pay the assured officer on retirement, after he shall have served 15 years, an annual sum equal to the amount of quarter of his then salary, to be increased by one 60th of that salary for each additional year's service).

Promotions, retirement benefits and salaries of the experienced officers also required attention. C.A.W. Monckton was noted as a 'good officer [with] nearly ten years' service in Papua'. With the transfer of Campbell to be the government Secretary, Monckton was promoted to be R.M. of the Eastern Division, and his annual salary increased to £450. H. L. Griffin (R.M. Gulf Division) was transferred to the Northern Division with his annual salary increased to £350. The North-Eastern Division was recommended to be temporarily merged with the Northern Division, with Resident Magistrate, G. O. Manning, transferred to the Gulf Division.

Disastrous Ventures

Mathew Moreton (R.M. of the South-Eastern Division) was 60 years old. The Commissioners recommended his retirement after almost 18 years' service in BNG. The Commissioners viewed the private plantation interest of A. C. English as conflicting with the proper performance of his magisterial duties in the Rigo district. Proposing to overturn the policy favoured by Le Hunte, the report recommended that 'no public officer should be permitted to have private interests of the kind in the district or place in which he is stationed'. While not making a recommendation on Barton, the overall assessment of his administration found against him:

> A strong under-current of disaffection was found to be running through the Service, which, traced back along the channels opened up for enquiry through public records, and other evidence, disclosed its source mainly at the head of the administration… The two senior Executive officials in the Territory—the Government Secretary, Mr Musgrave; and the Treasurer, Mr Ballantine— form notable examples in this classification.[23]

The report did not offer an opinion on J.H.P. Murray other than to point out that 'the Chief Judicial Officer is not merely "Chief Magistrate" … but he is virtually a "Minister of Justice" and legislative draftsman ... It is therefore recommended that an officer familiar with Supreme Court procedure should be appointed'.[24]

The general thrust of the recommendations was the requirement of much stronger Australian support than had been hitherto provided. A better staffed, better paid and better run administration was to provide the framework for a 'vigorous forward policy'. The Commissioners concurred with the earlier reports by Hunt and Smith in emphasising the importance of encouraging white settlement to make Papua commercially viable.

The Commissioners recognised that European settlement 'was vitally interwoven with the native problem in all respects [and that] it cannot be too emphatically laid down that its successful future depends on the preservation of the native races, for the native is one of the best assets that Papua possesses'. However, the Papuans first needed to be awakened from their 'lotus-eater' dreams, and white settlement was, in the opinion of the Commissioners, one of the surest and most practical methods of arresting their present indolent, apathetic state. White settlement would create the laws, and the work and business environment that would achieve these aims. For the local people to understand European culture the teaching of English was to be made compulsory in mission schools which the 'native children' were compelled to attend. To pay for the benefit of being hurled into 'the iron period', the 'pacified' Papuans were required to contribute to the development of the country by working for either themselves or the Europeans. To force them to recognise the imposed 'obligations they owe to the government', the Commissioners suggested that a tax be imposed on the natives under government control. By considering several tax systems that could be adopted to create value in Papua; the Commissioners chose enforced labour as its preferred option. They considered cash payment acceptable in lieu of working for the government if the 'natives' preferred this. The Report did not recommend the level of taxation or the duration of work to be performed. Concerns that the administration would be hard pressed to use the large number of labourers available were dismissed. The activities generated by a 'vigorous Roads and Works policy, the creation of (four) government plantations and the government Recruiting scheme—with its necessary receiving and distribution depôt' would absorb the labour.

Another significant recommendation was for all free Papuan land to be declared Crown land. To achieve this would require amendments to the *Land Ordinance, 1906*, to give the government power to acquire land compulsorily. Under such legislation 'the natives in the settled districts' were required to mark off their land within, say, 6 months from the date of notification. Following that period, 'all land thereafter unmarked in any such district shall become Crown lands'. It was further suggested that action be taken promptly to purchase any land Papuans may be willing to sell.

Concerning land, the Commissioners pointed to an oversight in the *Mining Ordinance, 1899* which required immediate attention: 'all the privileges and powers attached to the ownership of miner's right, and the ownership of all mining tenements under the existing Mining Law, are absolutely confined to Crown lands [with] no ordinance regulating or permitting mining on private property'. With most prospecting taking place on land not owned by the Crown—a situation also applicable to the mining activities taking place on riverbeds—the commissioners expressed concern that many mine operations were conducted illegally in Papua. The acquisition of Crown land was, therefore, regarded as equally necessary for the miners as for agricultural settlement. In order to mine legitimately, the Commissioners recommended a law to declare all minerals to be the property of the Crown, and that 'such legislation should provide for regulations being made for the due protection of native rights and customs, and for compensation to the natives for damages sustained at the hands of those who mine upon their land'.[25]

Turning their attention to financial matters the Commissioners reported:

> In a sense the Commonwealth is on its trial as a governing power, and on the verdict which must soon be pronounced in this connexion will depend issues of the gravest import as regards her own future; for should she give practical assurance to the Imperial Government that she is capable of ruling Papua wisely and well, it is not unreasonable to suppose that other island possessions at present held by Great Britain may be handed over to her charge... The true destiny of the Commonwealth is to be the paramount power in the Southern Seas [this] must inevitably increase the respect in which Australia will be held by other nations, and will also cause her voice to be listened to with deeper attention in the councils of the Empire.

To achieve financial independence, the Commissioners believed that a subsidy of £20,000 and local revenue would not be sufficient to meet the extra cost of administration and development if most of their recommendations were to be adopted. Unable to forecast the revenue from agriculture, mining, timber and other pursuits, it was suggested that the Australian government advance the government of Papua sufficient interest free funds to cover the annual administrative and development costs: 'such advances [to] remain a credit to the Commonwealth and a debit against the revenue of the Territory, until such time as the latter may be in a position to extinguish the liability.' At the same time an audit by experts could identify existing and future commercial possibilities.

Further, the government was to make low-interest loans of between £25 and £500 available to settlers. Applications for the loans were to be authorised by a board of local government officers for land leases that had been in existence for at least 12 months and where a satisfactory proportion of the improvement conditions imposed by the *Land Ordinance, 1906* had been complied with. A similar funding arrangement was recommended for prospectors: 'where actual prospecting work has been carried out in suitable country, but where the prospectors find themselves unable to proceed from want of money', the Commissioners recommended the government make available cash advances. Such grants were to be made 'with the clear understanding that the money so provided be expended under the advice and supervision of the mining officials'.[26] In this context it was also recommended that a government geologist be appointed to explore the country in conjunction with a party of miners for minerals.[27]

In other areas of finance, commerce and trade, it was suggested that tariff preference be given by Australia to Papuan products, and that all government stores be purchased through the Queensland government Stores Department. A wireless telegraphy system could connect mainland Australia from Port Moresby *via* Thursday Island. A trans-Papuan telephone line should be erected from Port Moresby, *via* Sogeri and Kokoda, to Buna Bay.[28]

The reports by Smith, Hunt and the Royal Commission were bold, confident and consistent. The authors were untroubled by the meeting of two completely disparate cultures. They were not commissioned to address the 'native' injustices so frequently recounted in the Australian and British newspapers. Australia was burdened—in her view prematurely—with a responsibility to govern Papua. Success or failure in Papua was to be measured by economic success or failure, not by the degree of protection given to the indigenous population. The Reports identified the necessity for change at all levels. It was to be effected by changing the quality and number of personnel in the administration, by forcing plantation development and mining ventures, and by changing Papuan behaviour. The Papuan people were identified in this view as a resource, whose education would inculcate European practices, and whose training would provide the skills the Europeans needed to grow the economy.

The clarion call to settlers, investors and miners was the Report of the Royal Commission in 1907. The Commissioners believed that the outside world generally possessed only the vaguest knowledge of Papua. They recommended that the region's natural possibilities be placed before the public so that inaccuracies on climate and the aggressive nature of the indigenous people could be 'swept aside'.[29] The government followed the Commissioners' advice and encouraged Port Moresby to stimulate public interest in Papua by advertising in Australia the availability of land for settlement and the richness of the country.

For Deakin, compassion for the indigenous people remained a priority. When asked in August 1906, 'who should be supreme—blacks or whites—if their interest clashed in the course of the development of Papua,' the Prime Minister replied unwaveringly: 'Yes, in our opinion, Papua belongs first to the Papuans ... Their well-being is to be studied in most respects even before that of men of our own colour'.[30]

The tabling of the Royal Commission Report in February 1907 brought some immediate consequences. In view of the adverse judgment Administrator Barton could no longer hope to be confirmed Lieutenant-Governor. He went on leave early in April 1907 and retired 12 months later. Murray was in Melbourne at the time and he then met Deakin for the first time. Subsequently, the government asked Murray to act as the Administrator: this was confirmed on 9 April 1907. His temporary appointment brought about the immediate retirement of Treasurer Ballantine. After 18 years of book-keeping in BNG- thereafter Papua - Ballantine retired to his 100 ac coffee plantation at Sogeri where, aged 41, he died of alcoholism. Also retired from the Public Service immediately was Commandant Bruce. Murray did not abolish the Armed Native Constabulary but placed it under the command of the Central Division. Bruce remained in Papua to work as a planting contractor for private companies. Later he prospected for gold, cut timber on a concession he obtained along the Vanapa River, and cleared the land at Sogeri which he had obtained for planting. Bruce joined the former government printer, Edward Barker, and the Port Moresby merchant, Charles Baldwin, in starting Papua's first newspaper, the *Papuan Times,* in January 1911. The paper became a conduit for Bruce, who was its editor until 1917, to pursue a vendetta against Murray.[31] Secretary Anthony Musgrave retired after 20 years' service on 30 June 1908. MacGregor was appointed Queensland's Governor. As recommended in the report, A.M. Campbell succeeded Musgrave.

Three days after Murray was confirmed Acting Administrator, Monckton took 12 months' leave and subsequently retired from his posting in Papua. His proposed transfer to the Eastern Division attracted a 10% salary increase and better living conditions. It was not the Lieutenant-Governor's position, however, which Monckton believed he would have performed more effectively than Barton or the inexperienced Murray. Fifteen years later he explained his reasons for 'chucking in my hand':

> After the departure of Sir William MacGregor and Sir Francis Winter, no Administrator seemed strong enough to cope with the strangle-hold that the headquarters' Bureaucracy apparently were getting on everything, including commerce, mining, agriculture, and the pacification of the country. Sir George Le Hunte might possibly have squelched them, for he had both the knowledge and the training; but then he had been almost perpetually absent; he had been away from the Possession for no less than two of his four-year tenure.

Citing an example of the stranglehold, he continued:

> The Survey Department had in their employ six surveyors at salaries above those of the Resident Magistrates, and each with an Assistant drawing more pay than the Assistant R.M., and each with a large native establishment, and yet during twelve months they had only done work to the value of £125 in the aggregate, while at the same time an outside surveyor had … done work to the amount of £1,400, for which he was paid by the Government.[32]

Monckton had highlighted a contentious point which resonated with many officers. The remuneration for Magistrates had remained virtually unchanged since 1888. Living conditions for the R.M. in the remote Western and Northern Divisions had also hardly improved. The biggest annoyance to the Magistrates was that their pay was lower when compared to officers with less demanding tasks. Ignoring the fact that they were provided with a residence, house boys and gardeners, they drew the Commissioners' attention to their annual salaries. An A.R.M. received £225, an Acting R.M. £325 and a R.M. between £300 and £500. A draftsman in the Lands Department received £250 annually, a road overseer £300, the Chief Surveyor £375, and a field surveyor and a road engineer £400.[33]

Disastrous Ventures

It is therefore not surprising that G. O. Manning (R.M. North-Eastern Division) did not transfer to the Gulf Division on the same level of pay (£300). He resigned in 1907 but stayed on to clear land for the Laka River Rubber Co. at Marshal Lagoon. Other officers to leave the Public Service were A. C. English (A.R.M. Rigo), H. L. Griffin (R.M. Northern Division) and A. Jewell (Barton's private secretary). All stayed in Papua to pursue private interests. English had already exported small quantities of latex from his rubber plantation in Rigo, and intended to plant out his 50 ac estate with sisal. Jewell returned to Port Moresby after a year's leave in Australia to plant sisal at Tavai near Gaire, 50 km southeast of the capital. Griffin, who was not a member of the anti-Murray faction, transferred from the Gulf to the Northern Division. He had to resign in late 1908 when it was reported that he was shooting Bird of Paradise in contravention of the *Wild Birds Ordinance*. He subsequently developed 640 ac on the Vama Creek at Galley Reach with the intention of selling it to Melbourne investors.

The 1906 Royal Commissioners at Samarai, cw. W. E. Parry-Okeden, G. Belford, Col. J. A. K Mackay (Chairman), E. Harris (Secretary), Justice C. E. Herbert (J. K. Mackay, *Across Papua*, frontispiece)

In the Owen Stanley Range, cw, Justice E. Herbert, Resident Magistrate C. A. W. Monckton, Col K. Mackay (*Across Papua*, p. 124)

Notes

1   Hunt to Deakin, 25 Oct. 1905; 'British New Guinea Report' (CPP 1905, vol. ii, p. 4)

2   'New Guinea Affairs, A complete Muddle', *The Northern Miner* (1905) 9 Oct. p. 5

3   'Administration of New Guinea', *Kalgoorlie Western Argus* (1905) 17 Oct. p. 22

4   (CPP 1905, vol. ii, pp. 3–4, 6–7, 12, 14, 16, 20, 22, 24 & 28). See 'British New Guinea A Land Of Promise, The Atlee Hunt Report', *The Adelaide Advertiser* 1905, 1 Nov. p. 8

5   Australian Labor Party after 1912

6   S. Smith Papers, NLA MS 1709; H.J. Gibbney, *Australian Dictionary of Biography*, vol. 11, p. 657.

7   Smith Papers, NLA MS 1709, item 1461

8   Hunt to Smith, 3 Jan. 1906, Staniforth Smith Papers, NLA MS 1709, item 938. .

9   'Report on the Federated Malay States and Java' by Senator Staniforth Smith (CPP 1906, vol. 2).

10   Deakin to Smith, 4 Sep.; Smith to Deakin, 5 Sep. 1906, Staniforth Smith Papers, NLA MS 1709, 969.

11   Report of the Royal Commission (CPP 1907, pp. lxxxvii–lxxxxix & 151–4)

12   'British New Guinea Report', by Atlee Hunt (CPP 1905, vol ii, p. 26)

13   J.A. La Nauze, Alfred Deakin, vol. 2, p. 459; F. West, *Selected Letters of Hubert Murray*, p. 36, fn.

14   CPP 1907, Report of the Royal Commission, p. lxxxvii

15   West, p. 37, letter 32

16   Ibid, pp. 39–45

17   Smith to Hunt, 15 July 1907, Staniforth Smith Papers, NLA MS 1709; La Nauze, pp. 461–6 and 468–9.

18   Hunt to Barton 12 June 1906, Atlee Hunt Correspondence NLA MS 52.

19   Report of the Royal Commission (CPP 1907, pp. v & viii–ix)

20   Murray evidence 8, Nov. 1906 (CPP 1907, pp. 85ff). Barton p. 137, §§2038, 2048 & 2121. West, p. 47.

21   (CPP 1907, pp. xcix. cii &cxi–cxxiv)

22   ibid, pp. lxvii &cii.

23   ibid, pp. ci–cii &lxv–lxvii.

24   ibid, pp. civ–cv.

25   ibid, pp. xiii-xiv xlvi; road programme, see pp. xxxvi–xxxvii; Government Stations, pp. xxii–xxiv; Government labour-recruiting system, pp. xxix–xxx.

26   ibid, pp. l–li.

27   ibid, p. xxix.

28   ibid, pp. xlix, liv and lvii–lviii.

29   ibid, p. lxiv.

30   Question by H.B. Higgins in the House of Representatives (CPD, vol. xxxiii, p. 3345.

31   Lewis, pp. 123–4

32   Monckton, *Last Days in New Guinea*, p. 252–3

33   Salary list of officers (AR-Papua [1907/08] pp. 44–6)

Map 17: **The Territory of Papua,** ca. 1909 (Smith *Handbook* 2nd edition)

AMBITIONS, DREAMS AND DISAPPOINTMENTS: JHP MURRAY AND STANIFORTH SMITH

J.H. P. Murray
(NLA:24110142-v)

M.S. C. Smith
(slq.gov.au: 259263)

BNG did not progress economically during its first 20 years. A focus on marginal gold mining ventures and a failure to attract financially strong enterprises which could invest large sums of money in plantations are seen as the reasons for the stagnation. Australia had contributed £20,000 annually to the running of the colony since 1901. When the new nation assumed full responsibility for the Territory under the *Papuan Act, 1905* the Australian government was intent on reducing its financial liability as quickly as possible. The international boom in tropical agriculture, which started in 1901, underpinned the hope that economic growth and increased government revenue would deliver Papuan self-sufficiency. The recommendation in 1907 of the Royal Commission was that Papua should undergo rapid plantation development. An administration was to be installed that would establish a legal framework and create conditions that would attract settlers. Government-generated revenue was derived almost exclusively from import duties. It was the settler who was to create the economic environment that drove the consumption of Western goods in the European and Papuan communities in order for Papua to reduce its financial reliance on Australia.

There was no plantation industry in BNG. David Lewis' work on the Papuan plantation industry found that 'comparatively few white men made a living out of Papua'.[1] This was despite Papua's gold mining industry and a large international appetite for industrial rubber until 1911 and the strong price for copra to 1919.

In the same way NGC had profoundly influenced the development of GNG, the British New Guinea Development Company (BNGD), established in 1910, largely set the economic agenda for Papua. Both companies had strained relationships with their respective governments. NGC blamed Berlin for its inability to develop profitably when it was in charge of GNG. When the German government assumed responsibility for the Protectorate in 1899, the planters blamed Governor Hahl for the high cost of Papuan and Melanesian labour. BNGD went on the warpath over Lieutenant-Governor Murray's protective labour laws. Taking the side of the settlers and plantation developers, BNGD blamed Port Moresby for overselling the commercial opportunities in Papua while failing to enact appropriate labour laws.

In many ways the development of NGC and BNGD was surprisingly similar though in different time frames. Ten years after the German company had shut down its tobacco and cotton plantations, the British enterprise commenced with these same cash crops. It soon learnt the same lessons for which NGC had already paid dearly.

This chapter deals with the optimistic beginning of the Papuan plantation industry and its subsequent failure with the outbreak of World War I when all commodity prices other than copra collapsed. The future was obvious by 1914.

Discord between the planters and Lieutenant-Governor JHP Murray

> We must resign ourselves to a gradual development, and no longer cherish dreams of exploiting Papua and the Papuans in a single generation … This is hard upon company promoters and others but I cannot help thinking that is a good thing for the Papuan.

These were Lieutenant-Governor Murray's sobering words in 1912. Derided in 1907 by Exeter Hall and the Protestant missions in Papua as a champion of unbridled economic progress, 5 years later they saw the converted catholic Murray in a different light. The Christian missions believed he was now more attuned to Papuan society transforming itself to Western values, slowly and without exploitation by the European mining and settler communities.[2]

A contrary view was taken by the planters and the large plantation companies. As they failed to prosper they turned on the government which had promoted settlement and investment initially. By 1909 many of them accused Murray, appointed to the position in Port Moresby on an anti-English pro-Australian 'ticket', of the same indifference to their call for cheap labour and low taxes that had brought Administrator Francis Barton into disgrace. Their quarrels with a righteous Murray were over land, labour supply, labour cost, the prohibition on the importation of coolies and artisans from Asia, the high impost on imported goods and the tariffs on Australian and Papuan produce.

John Hubert Plunkett Murray was born in the northern Sydney suburb of Manly on 29 December 1861. His father, Sir Terrence Aubrey Murray, became one of the largest landholders and wealthiest man in Australia only to lose it all in 1865 because of persistent drought and financial overextension. Terrence Murray and his business partner, Thomas Walker, had obtained a grant of land in 1842 known as Yarrolumla. The Molonglo and Queanbeyan Rivers ran through this highly fertile 40,000-acre-estate, Winderradeen Station, today's site of the Australian Capital Territory. ('Yarrolumla House' built by Murray is the principal residence 'Yarralumla' of the Governor-General of Australia to this day).

T. A. Murray's first wife had died in 1857. Shortly thereafter he married Agnes Anne, née Edwards, the English-born teacher who had taken charge of his son and daughters since his wife's passing. By 1861 the Murray family had grown with the birth of John Hubert, and in 1866, with the birth of George Gilbert Aime.

Both brothers excelled academically but physically they were poles apart. Gilbert, extremely intelligent like his brother, was timid, his delicate health a perpetual source of anxiety. Hubert had inherited his Irish grandfather's nature and his mother's brain. During his adolescent years he was rebellious, short-tempered, and ill-disciplined. Most of these early traits remained with him throughout his life. At age sixteen, Hubert had grown into a 191 centimetre, 85 kilogram lad, who excelled in athletics and boxing, and was an exceptional horseman. But most of all he was academically gifted. Hubert was dux of his class at Sydney Grammar. Gaining the Fairfax prize in the Sydney University Junior Examination of 1876 and the University Medal at the senior public examination with first class honours in all subjects in 1878, he excelled at everything he put his mind to. He also indulged his liking for a pint of ale or two which frequently ended in a fight, with Hubert inevitably emerging as the unscathed victor, save for enhancing his reputation as a 'mad Irish brawler'.

After finishing at Sydney Grammar School, Hubert sailed for England in April 1878 to join his mother and brother Gilbert who had left Australia a year earlier.

Easily bored, his intemperate behaviour led to his expulsion from Brighton College where his mother had secured his admission for his final year before University. The curriculum was below Hubert's level of academic standard and he spent most of his time drinking. He broke the school record for shot-put and the hammer throw, while still coming first in all the tests. He was conscious of his Irish heritage and harboured a bitter dislike of the English. It was his English science master at Brighton whom he knocked off his feet with a left hook to the jaw after the teacher called him a 'Wild Irishman', leading to his dismissal from the school.

Murray was stranded. Expelled from Brighton College, his mother was unable to find a school that would accept her son, until the unrepentant Hubert ended up with Dr Schiltz near Cologne in Germany. Surprisingly he liked Dr Schiltz and took some pride his new teacher's nickname for him *'das Raubtier'* (wild animal). Under his German tutor Hubert Murray became proficient in German, French, Latin and Greek, and devoted much time to the understanding of German literature and poetry.

Finally admitted to Oxford he graduated in 1886 with first-class honours in Greats. He completed his formal education in England by reading for the Bar at Inner Temple in London and, without much enthusiasm, passing his final examination with flying colours, while also playing Rugby for the Harlequins and winning the English amateur heavyweight boxing title.

Returning to Sydney in late 1886, he was admitted to the Bar of New South Wales and appointed a crown prosecutor ten years later. In January 1900 Hubert Murray sailed to Cape Town as a special service officer in command of a troop ship. But Murray hated 'the whole business of war' and left the service after 10 months with the rank of lieutenant-colonel. Returning to what he regarded a tedious way of earning a living in the courts of NSW, the experience in South Africa led to him permanently abstaining from alcohol and an increased devotion to Catholicism.

Murray and his wife Sybil—whom he married in 1889—arrived in Port Moresby,

New Guinea, on 16 September 1904. Prime Minister Deakin had appointed J.H.P. Murray Chief Judicial Officer of BNG and acting administrator of the Territory of Papua in 1907, and then as Lieutenant-Governor in 1908.

Sybil Murray returned to her three children as quickly as she could book a suitable cabin on a steamer to Sydney. Port Moresby was not for her, not a place to bring up a young family. Consisting of about a dozen huts, and five ramshackle buildings covered in rusted iron, which the government called the administrative centre, it was the starkest possible contrast to her small but comfortable home in Sydney. Worse still, there were no roads other than rough tracks, no telephone, no electricity, no water supply except for galvanised iron tanks that were attached to the huts, and there was no hospital or any meaningful health care. While her husband remained Lieutenant-Governor of The Territory of Papua until he died at Samarai from lymphatic leukaemia on 7 Feb. 1940, she only visited him occasionally in Port Moresby until she passed away in 1929.[3]

Since the February 1907 *Report of the Royal Commission of Enquiry into the Condition of the Territory of Papua*, it had been common knowledge that Murray had caused Barton's downfall. The former commandant of the Native Armed Police, William Bruce, was particularly aggrieved by the 'fallacious accusations' Murray made against him during the Commission's hearings. A co-editor of the *Papuan Times* and the editor of the paper from January 1911, Bruce pursued a personal quarrel with Murray relentlessly. Calling him an ambitious liar, Bruce attacked the Lieutenant-Governor for his compassion for the 'natives' whose interest Murray placed above the law-abiding 'white pioneers'. According to Bruce there was no doubt in the settlers' minds that the 'brown person' was vastly inferior to the white man. In 1914 BNGD's General Manager, Lewis J. Cowley, acquired a financial interest in the newspaper. Couched in Bruce's preferred style of invective, the paper now presented the company's views on Murray's policies on labour supply, claimed to be responsible for BNGD's inability to develop rapidly and profitably in Papua.[4]

Murray seemed untroubled by the attack on his administration. He regarded himself as intellectually superior to any of his officers and all the settlers in Papua. Allegations of unfriendly behaviour towards business and a general lack of understanding of financial matters were offset by a universal acknowledgment of his sharp legal mind. He was an excellent drafter of ordinances and a highly literate person, whose supporters praised him for his humanity.

Accounting for the administration's achievements since BNG was placed under Australian control on 1 September 1906, Murray provided a scorecard on the economic performance of Papua in his 1909/10 annual report. The European population had increased by 27%, from 690 in 1907 to 879 in 1910 and government revenue by 60%, from £21,813 to £34,822. Whether Murray regarded the slower growth in government expenditure from £45,445 to £64,873 as positive or negative is not clear. He was unequivocal, however, in expressing deep satisfaction with the Papuan trade figures which had increased from £68,300 to £117,410 from 1901 to 1911. Ignoring that the actual increase was 72%, and most of it was based on gold earnings, he aggregated imports, customs receipts and other revenue to claim that 'total territorial revenue exclusive of the subsidy from the Commonwealth' had increased by 200%. When dealing in concrete numbers his assessment, while selective, was more to the point: 'the comparison of the progress made before and since the Commonwealth assumed control is to an Australian still more gratifying', he trumpeted his achievements. In the 4 years prior to Australia assuming full responsibility for the Territory revenue increased by £3,368. From the time Australia assumed full control, from 1906 to 1910/11, it grew by more than £24,158. Exports, £63,756 in 1906/07 had increased to £117,410 by 1910/11 and imports increased from £87,776 to £202,910.[5]

Murray also drew attention to the multitude of lease applications since the passing of Barton's Land Ordinance in September 1906. In the first few months after the ordinance was gazetted, the lease of land for agricultural, trading and residential purposes had risen from 7,544 ac to 70,512 ac from July 1906 to June 1907, and to 364,088 ac 5 years later. Similarly, the area of plantations had risen from 1,467 ac in 1907 to 15,881 ac in 1911. In his judicial capacity Murray had drafted the amendment to the 'employer friendly' *Native Labour Ordinance, 1906*. While this was carried out under Barton, it was under Murray's direction that the new law was assented to in April 1907. The ordinance provided for the engagement of labour on a casual basis for 3 months without an employment contract. The terms of indenture determined employment of up to 3 years (previously 1 year) except for miners and carriers whose period of engagement was not to exceed 18 months. Under the ordinance Murray was empowered to proclaim any portion of the Territory of Papua to be a settled labour district. This enabled employers to indenture labour up to 180 km from their village.[6]

The new labour law allowed the government to retain control over the movement of Papuans, thus preventing over-recruitment and the depopulation of particular districts. The wages and conditions stipulated under the ordinance set the cost of Papuan labourers marginally above Papuans in GNG. The obligations to pay minimum wages, specified standards of victuals, housing and care, were similar to the requirements mandated by the Germans. Of considerable concern to the miners were the high labour recruitment fees and the requirement to pay 3 months' wages in advance or lodge a security bond. This constituted a tax on capital which was particularly costly for the nascent Papuan plantation industry and it was a significant difference to other South Sea employers of plantation labour. But Murray was optimistic. With commodities booming and the number of plantations doubling from 76 in 1907 to 151 in 1910 he informed Melbourne

> The factors that I have enumerated combined with steadily increasing Customs revenue, justifies us in cherishing the belief that the time is not very remote when this Territory will be able to meet all its financial obligations without requiring any subsidies.[7]

And two years later, when the number of employed Papuans had increased to a record 10,270 workers on 192 plantations, Murray reported: 'in the face of these figures, and of those already given relating to land settlement, it can hardly be denied that the present administration has, so far, been successful as regards the development of the territory'.[8]

Disastrous Ventures

What Murray neglected to mention was the stagnant level of export sales. Five years after he had assumed responsibility for Papua, gold receipts were down and only a few tons of coffee had been exported. The planters laid the blame for under performing production squarely on the federal and local governments. The strict control on recruitment, enforced by Murray, was a problem. And of greater concern were the recurring dysentery outbreaks and the administration's lack of urgency on opening up and 'civilising' new districts for recruiting. Murray's Commissioner for Native Affairs and Control Department, established in 1910 to ensure that indentured labour was properly treated, aggravated the mistrust of the planters towards the administration. Inspectors, whose sole job it was to check whether labourers were 'supplied with good wholesome food, and properly housed and attended to when sick', harassed the plantation managers. The planters complained that Murray's 33 officers empowered under the Native Labour Ordinance had nothing better to do than annoy them. Murray remained unimpressed. He answered the settlers' protests with a laconic paragraph in his 1909/10 report:

> In spite of the difficulties, which are now rapidly disappearing, no complaints have been received from *bonâ fide* settlers, because they have recognised that, whatever their disabilities and hardships may have been, the Government has strained every nerve to remove the obstacles to settlement, and afford all reasonable facilities to those who are developing the latent resources of the Territory.[9]

Rupert Clarke, Papua's largest plantation developer at that time, disagreed. Apart from the restrictive local employment condition he demanded the importation of coolies. 'If rubber-growing in Papua is to be successful', he told the Melbourne *Age* in July 1909, 'the employment of Asiatic labor will have to be allowed. Melbourne businessman and chairman, F. G. Wilson of Domara River Plantation, Ltd, assigned the responsibility for not meeting the labour requirements of the Papuan plantations on the 'listlessness of the Federal Government'. When the Fisher government formally refused the admittance of Javanese skilled planters on Papuan plantations in June 1912, the headlines of the *Age* and *The Advertiser* screamed: 'Papuan Planters in Trouble'.

> The plantations are now approaching a condition of ripeness for tapping, an operation requiring skill and experience. For some time the planters have foreseen the necessity of obtaining skilled labor, and with the consent of the Papuan officials a scheme for the importation of a limited number of Javanese for three years, for whose return to Java the planters were to be responsible under heavy penalties, was brought before the Papuan Legislative Council.

The decision aggrieved the planters, who put the blame squarely on the Minister for External Affairs (J. Thomas) the *Advertiser* concluded its report.[10]

A land of opportunity

Francis Barton enacted that no estate in fee simple would be granted from 13 November 1906. Henceforth agricultural and pastoral land could only be leased. Under section 16 of the ordinance persons and companies could obtain 'leasehold of the best class of agricultural or pastoral land for any period up to 99 years, subject to improvement conditions'. The government charged no survey fees. During the first 10 years leasehold was 3d/ac for agricultural and 10s. per 1,000 acre for pastoral land. Thereafter Port Moresby determined the rent of agricultural land at 5% and on pastoral leases at 2.5% of the improved value, with reappraisals conducted every 20 years. Where the valuation rose 33% above the nominal rent for agricultural land and 25% for pastoral land, the lessee could renounce the lease and claim compensation for the improvements from the government.[11]

The planters and investors welcomed the new conditions. Staniforth Smith's appointment to the position of Director responsible for development across all issues concerning agriculture in May 1907 instilled confidence in Papua's commercial future. While on 30 June 1906 only 7,544 ac were held under lease, during the next 12 months 62,968 ac were taken up. Australia's interest in Papua since 1905 finally seemed to bear fruit.

'The land laws of Papua are liberal—probably the most liberal in any tropical country'—the Director for Agriculture Staniforth Smith wrote in the 1907 annual report. *Papua the Marvellous, the Country of Chance,* a booklet circulated in 1909 by Port Moresby in Australia and Britain, spelled out the generous leasing terms. Designed to attract the young and daring sons of wealthy estate owners, the pamphlet was written by Murray's confidant, the Anglo-Irish journalist Beatrice Grimshaw. Boldly confronting the misconception about Papua's climate and 'savages', Grimshaw wrote about the fertility of the soil and the high profits that could be made in this country of opportunities. She wrote about Murray's care for 'the Papuan Savage, the best treated black in the world, eager to work on plantations for the white man'.[12] The hyperbole in the book bothered Secretary A. Campbell. He complained to the Secretary of the Department of External Affairs about the misleading propaganda. Not so Murray; he saw the value of Grimshaw's booklet in attracting wealthy English investors to Papua: 'the sooner it appears the better', he told Atlee Hunt.[13]

Twenty years after NGC had started agricultural development in GNG, Australian and British investors started taking notice of the opportunities in agriculture in Papua. The boom years in copra and rubber attracted prospectors to turn their hands to plantations. Traders, managers, and government officers took up growing coffee, coconuts and rubber in Papua.

Papuan land was cheap. And even though the land had to be planted with government-approved crops, and a security deposit paid with every application— as a surety that the development guidelines were met—many officers leased land or purchased town allotments in Port Moresby and Samarai to build houses for themselves.

D. Ballantine, A. C. English, H. L. Griffin and A. Jewell stayed on in Papua to chance their luck in plantation development. John (Jack) Anderson, one of the first miners on the Sudest rush in 1888, hung up his prospector's pan in 1907 when he was 64 years old, to become a planter on Panamoti Island in the Calvados Chain. Other miners like Clunas and Clark (Giriwu River and Giropa Point, Buna Bay), G. Nelsson (Kwalapan Bay, Woodlark), E. Auerbach (Muwo, Trobriand Island), and D. H. Osborne (Kanadu and Abuleti, Rossel, Nimoa and Panapompom Islands) extended their plantation holdings after Australia assumed control.

Disastrous Ventures

The 6,400 ac Dr Cecil Vaughan had acquired on the Musa River in 1899 remained undeveloped and were returned to the government when he left BNG in 1902. His medical successor, Dr Robert Jones, maintained a one-sixth share in Henry Wickham's Conflict Island Planting Association for many years. Dr Colin Simson took up 500 ac at Hisiu on Redscar Bay in 1906, where his neighbour was Alearce Savery Anthony, a settler from Mauritius who had managed a property for Ballantine at Sogeri until 1905. The gold miner Fred Weekley managed Simson's property, while Simson became involved in other opportunities such as the Laloki Copper Mine in the Astrolabe Range. Dr Julius Streeter, Simson's replacement in 1910, partnered Robert Bunting to invest in a rubber plantation at Port Glasgow. Captain Archibald Hunter of the *Merrie England* was granted a 600 ac lease at Sogeri which he sold to BNGD in 1910 for equity in the company. Others like Head Gaoler John MacDonald and his subordinate Horace Hides each held a lease of 500 ac on the Lower Laloki, and Charles Garrioch (clerk of the Executive Council) started a partnership with bank clerk Henry Greene in 1902 to grow coffee on their Sagoro Tano plot at Sogeri. In 1907 Garrioch joined John Bensted (government stores clerk), Cyril Havilland and Albert Ardie (field assistants to the government surveyor) and applied for a £100 share each in the Papua Rubber Co. This venture, however, never got off the ground.[14]

Following some land speculation involving government surveyor Ralph Drummond, a December 1907 amendment to the *Land Ordinance, 1906* barred officers of the Lands Department from acquiring an interest in land other than for their place of residence or in land where their official duties were not compromised. It was a soft change, affecting two officers at the most. The section was repealed in 1914 when all government officers were again permitted to acquire land in Papua, subject to the transparency of their dealings.

Buccaneers, speculators, planters and the vegetable oil industry

The wake-up call for NGC in Friedrich Wilhelmshafen and Herbertshöhe came at the turn of the century. The Scotsmen, Dunlop and Thomson, had invented the pneumatic tyre which became a standard on the automobiles Henry Ford started to mass produce on his assembly line. The projection for caoutchouc consumption was on a steep upward curve. The other commodity increasingly in demand was vegetable oil. Petroleum had replaced whale oil in street lighting and tallow was no longer the favoured ingredient in finer soaps and cooking. Margarine, first produced in France around 1870, was commonly used in Europe in the late 19th century, and started to gain a foothold in the United States of America. The Lever Brothers were largely soap makers, and responsible for an increasing demand for oils in the English-speaking world. The Dutch specialised in making margarine and drove the demand for oils on continental Europe. When the price of copra more than doubled from £14/t in 1900 to £30/t in 1912, William Lever (later Viscount Leverhulme) wrote in his introduction to *Coconuts, the Consols of the East:* there is 'no field of Tropical Agriculture that is so promising at the present moment as coconut planting, and I do not think in the whole world there is the promise of so lucrative an investment of time and money as in this industry'.[15]

The Levers had recognised that copra would be in short supply as early as 1903. Initially their soap factory in Sydney relied on trade copra from the Fiji, Tonga and Gilbert Islands. In 1905 Joseph Meek, chairman of Lever Bros Australia Ltd and Managing Director of Lever's Pacific Plantations Ltd (LPPL), purchased 51,000 ac of freehold near Guadalcanal in the Solomon Islands for LPPL from Captain Olaf Svensson. By 1906 LPPL owned or leased in excess of 300,000 ac on which it grew coconuts. 'To leave the production of Coprah (sic) in the hands of natives, who stop producing as soon as they have supplied their own limited wants, will not give the world the Coprah it wants', William Lever observed in 1904. The family intended to make their companies independent of external supplies of vegetable oils. They planned to purchase copra and palm kernels at the lowest possible prices.[16]

Concerns about the uncommercial attitude of the Port Moresby administration and the lack of available plantation land and labour in BNG made Lever set up its South Sea copra plantations primarily in the Solomons rather than BNG. The company's first plantation purchase came in 1901 when it bought several widely-dispersed islands in the South Pacific from the phosphate trader and miner Pacific Islands Co. (PIC) for £25,000. In 1906 Lever acquired the PIC concession over 193,490 ac in the Solomon Islands. LPPL had already acquired the interests in three smaller islands (51,000 ac) from Svensson, and 29,000 ac from the Solomon Islanders. Dissatisfied with a 99-year lease, Lever renegotiated the terms of the occupancy of prime plantation land with the Colonial Office to 999 years at a peppercorn rent.

For Papua's plantation industry to become competitive with the Melanesian island plantation enterprises it had a lot of catching up to do. J. Kitchen & Sons Ltd of Melbourne was the first Australian company to take up this challenge in 1907.

Lever Bros. processed some 10,000 tons of copra in its Sydney Balmain factory to meet the requirements for its 'Sunlight' soap while also supplying Kitchen & Sons of Melbourne with coconut oil for their 'Velvet' soap. During a visit to the Balmain factory in 1906, J. H. Kitchen and John Ambrose found out that Lever was paying £17/t for trade copra and that in due course their plantations in the Solomons would produce copra for less than half this amount, and that they expected to be independent of the outside copra market very soon. These were sound reasons indeed for Kitchen to become involved in the industry.

Staniforth Smith worked on Kitchen & Sons to invest in Papua rather than the Solomon Islands. 'Coconuts', he wrote in his *Handbook*,

> are a very remunerative and most reliable industry, and one that should receive quite as much attention as rubber cultivation. The natural conditions are in every way suitable, and skilled labour and extensive plant is not required in the production of copra. Papua, being outside the hurricane belt, possesses a great avmatge in this respect over such places as Fiji, the New Hebrides, and Samoa. The trees begin to yield in five years, and are bearing heavily when eight or nine years old. A full grown tree should yield 60 nuts a year, and with 50 planted to the acre, that area should yield 3,000 nuts, or half a ton of copra, worth £10.

With the help of the London Missionary Society on Kwato Island he convinced Theo Kitchen that New Guinea was preferable to the Solomons because of lower labour cost, better climate, and that it was under Commonwealth Government control.[17]

Dedele on Cloudy Bay. First commercial plantation in BNG. Estd. in 1894 by Walter Gors and Thomas Anderson. Purchased by Whitten Bros of Samarai in 1900. Managed from 1907 to 1915 by Carl Ettling. CW: **husking coconuts, worker and staff housing, Dedele native hospital,** ca. 1914 (C. Ettling, *Unter Pflanzern und Goldgräbern im Kanibalenland Neu Guinea*, pp. 48-9)

Following a visit to Papua by Fred Kitchen the company committed to a long-term 5,000 ac lease of densely grown scrub on Gili-Gili Island in Milne Bay, approximately 50 km from Samarai. C. O. Turner (A.R.M. Eastern Division) and the Rev. C. W. Abel of the London Missionary Society recommended the island as most suitable for growing coconut trees. While Smith told Kitchen that the land was 'as good for coconuts as anything he had seen, with the possible exception of certain portions of Java, Kitchen remained sceptical because it consisted mainly of coral outcrops and sand. Pressed for time and relying heavily on the advice he had received from the Papuan government and from Rev. Abel, he engaged the Norwegian sailor Schröder as Kitchen's Papuan manager before returning to Australia.

Kitchen & Sons financed its new venture by incorporating the Commonwealth Copra Co. Pty. Ltd on 5 March 1908. The authorised capital was £150,000, initially issued to £50,000 in £1 shares. Kitchen & Son's subsidiary, Soap & Candle Co. of Sydney, acquired one-third, and the parent company's chairman (T. J. Davey) and Directors (J. A. Kitchen, F. W. Kitchen, J. H. Kitchen and G. P. Clarke) acquired the balance of the issued capital. The Commonwealth Copra Co. acquired Kitchen's plantation interest in Papua for £1,256, which was for costs incurred since acquiring the plantation land in 1907.

A newcomer, who started a plantation business on the advice of a missionary and bureaucrats, whose brief was to attract agricultural investment to Papua, was bound to learn an expensive lesson. Between 1907 and 1910 less than 10% (407 ac) had been cultivated. Schröder had difficulties in recruiting suitable labour, which did not improve after Kitchen complained to the Papuan and Australian governments on the shortage of suitable labour in Papua. Dissatisfied with his conditions of employment and general progress of the venture, Schröder resigned in October 1910, and an experienced Ceylon planter by the name of Wright became responsible for the venture. To 1914 Wright planted 3,228 ac, but had only produced a few bags of copra. It was found that the poor land on Gili-Gili would require £30/ac to bring coconuts into bearing compared to £20/ac Levers incurred on its plantations. Also, in the Solomons coconut palms started to bear fruit after 6 years, delivering an average 5 cwt (0.25 t) of copra; and Solomon Islanders were regarded as better workers, with 'the boys doing twice as much work as the boys from Gili-Gili'.

Smith's advice on copra (0.5 t/ac) must have applied to the Solomons, not Papua, Kitchen surmised. The copra plantations on Gili-Gili, Maiwara and Waigani produced 0.25 t/ac at best. In February 1915 Kitchen & Sons and Lever Bros. merged their Australian enterprises. It gave Levers a presence in Papua for the first time.[18]

By 1906 the Papuan plantation bug had infected Australian and English plantation interests. Promising quick and large returns on rubber, coconuts, coffee, and sisal investments, entrepreneurs sought to tap the Sydney, Melbourne, Adelaide and London capital markets. The Papua Trading and Planting Syndicate Ltd (PTPS), for instance, was the idea of Admiral Edward Davis, who had called on Papua in 1906 in one of his last tours of duty with the Royal Navy. Together with Alfred Copeland and William Ray he founded PTPS in May 1909 to plant rubber on the Imila and Kemp Welch rivers, some 120 km east of Port Moresby. The 12,600 ac leasehold PTPS acquired from the prospector Bert Hayes 'is in one of the most fertile of all the rich valleys of Papua, and perfectly adapted to the cultivation of rubber and all other tropical products', according to the Adelaide *Register*. 'Considering that plantation rubber fetches about 9/per pound and that at 2/per lb a mature plantation should pay dividends of 50%, … the investment should be a most profitable one', the paper informed its reader.[19] But rather than concentrating on planting rubber trees PTPS wasted its financial resources to suing BNGD for defamation, and the Directors defended alleged misrepresentation brought about in a London court by Sophie von Holstein-Rathlou of Copenhagen. In late 1913 Madame Rathlou sought to recover £5,750 she had invested in PTPS in 1909. The plaintiff in the first and the defendants in the second instance won in court, they were not successful with their venture in New Guinea. Papua Trading and Planting Syndicate Ltd folded in 1914.[20]

The Sydney printer, publisher and politician, William Brooks, garnered the interest of the ubiquitous Melbourne pastoralist and plantation owner, Rupert M Clarke, to float Sogeri Para Rubber Ltd (SPR) on the Sydney Exchange in 1910. The company was formed with capital of £50,000 in £1 shares to acquire the Papua Para Rubber

Co. Limited (PPR). Founded in 1907 chiefly by colonial government officers, and comprising 1,500 ac on the Sogeri Plateau, 55 km north-east of Port Moresby the land was returned to the government unimproved. Subsequently purchased by Henry Greene, the 99 year leasehold of PPR was known as the Kuitakinumu Estate. Greene received 20,000 fully paid SPR shares for the transfer of the improved leasehold, including houses, roads, and 125 acres planted with 12,000 Para rubber trees, 7 acres with sugar bananas and 5 acres with sisal hemp. More than one hundred thousand Para rubber and sisal hemp plants were in various states of maturity in the company's nursery. In contrast to many other plantation hopefuls, SPR manager Tom L. Sefton reported the successful planting of 500 ac with rubber, and the tapping of the older trees in early 1914. With the collapse of the international rubber market in 1911/12, Sefton moved SPR into additional tropical produce. He became one of Papua's most respected, successful and enduring plantation managers. When SPR merged with other plantation interests in the Sogeri region, Sefton retained his position to manage Kuitakinumu until the early 1950s.[21]

The Papuan Industries, Limited Company (PIL) was inaugurated in 1904 by Rev. F. W. Walker. When Walker severed his connection with the London Missionary Society the previous year, he also left behind Killerton Island, off Samarai, where he and the Rev. C. W. Abel had established a most recognised Papuan Christian mission.

Walker had come to the conclusion that Papuans would best be helped, spiritually and materially, if they were made to work productively. With support from Sir William Lever of Lever Bros., PIL was registered in London in December 1904, with half of the issued capital of £30,000 placed immediately with friends who, according to the Melbourne *Argus,* were deeply interested in missionary work in Papua. The object of the company, the paper told its readers, was the development of native industries in Papua and the islands of the Torres Straits. The company was controlled by a Board of Directors in England; F. W. Walker was managing Director designate of PIL in New Guinea and the Torres Strait.

Walker combining protestant ethos and business principles. He maintained that the first object of the company was for the permanent good of the natives. He, and his shareholders, expected that the company would also generate reasonable profits.

Walker established PIL's headquarters with a large store, dwellings and workshops on Badu Island, 46 km north of Thursday Island in the Torres Strait. He set up another establishment on the mainland near Daru in the Gulf of Papua. With only minor revenue derived from trading in pearl and tortoise shell and bêche-de-mer (trepang), the development of a coconut plantation at Dirimu on the Binaturi River and a rubber plantation at Madiri on the estuary of the Fly River consumed most of the raised funds. PIL's noble charter, proscribing the distribution to shareholders of annual dividend above 5% —with higher earnings reserved for the benefit of the workers— was far from being realised: Walker travelled to England and Australia on a regular basis to raise new funds for his cause. In an address he delivered on 28 October 1905 in the Victoria Hall, Adelaide, he expressed his delight with the sympathetic consideration the federal authorities and state politicians demonstrated towards the advancement of the people of New Guinea. He hoped the residents of Adelaide would take a similar interest in the natives and that Christian commercial men in Australia should take up shares in the concern, he told his audience.

When funds had all but dried up in 1913, Walker toured Australia once again to raise further funding. 'The principal object of my visit to Australia is to secure further capital', he told the people in Adelaide, The City of Churches.

> In the first place, we raised only half the authorized amount, which was £50,000. We started the work with that sum, but we stated that it would be necessary to get more, as it would be 10 years before the plantations could prove remunerative. I obtained £12,000 in England, including £1,000 from Sir William Lever.

How much money Walker raised in Adelaide and the other places he toured in Australia is not known. But when the Hon. H. Mahon (Acting Minister for External Affairs) announced on 14 October 1914 that the Federal Government would grant a first instalment of £1,000 to Papuan Industries Ltd, the future of PIL was secured. The company had to independently obtain £2,000 to receive the grant. Then, a government guarantee for up to £10,000 spread over a period of ten years, made the raising of additional capital much easier.[22]

On 22 May 1912, Papuan Plantations, Limited (PPL) held its seventh AGM. Applying for parcels of 5,500 ac and 1,500 ac on the Laloki River in 1905, Chairman Stephan S. Ralli informed shareholders that the company was now ready to commence with the first cutting of sisal. With 250 ac under sisal hemp at each of the plantations, and the latest type of machinery for the extraction of fibre in place, shareholders hoped that their patience would soon be rewarded with a maiden dividend. The sisal market was flat, though, and the plants needed to fully mature to harvest the quantity required for an export order. To meet liabilities and continue trading until the first full harvest in 1913, PPL needed to borrow £3,000 via the issue of a first mortgage debenture at an interest rate of 8% per annum. The shareholders authorised the Directors to borrow the required funds. They were rewarded by receiving the first dividend ever paid by a Papuan plantation company in 1914. The joy was short-lived. The War depressed sisal fibre further, and shipping of goods to and from Papua became difficult and expensive. PPL went into voluntary liquidation and sold its assets to the British New Guinea Development Company.[23]

Another ephemeral affair was the business promotion of another Adelaide syndicate. The Adelaide Papuan Rubber Syndicate, Limited, founded on 19 August 1910, had procured 3,000 acres at Galley Reach near the Veimauri River, 'in one of the best portions in Papua, adjoining Sir Rupert Clarke's plantation, situated within a few hours sail to Port Moresby', according to *The Adelaide Advertiser*. The idea of the company's Directors (S. A. Davenport, P. A. Wilson, and F. R. Ragiess) was to send a company representative (A. R. Burton) to London with instructions to place the property on the London market. Eight months later the company informed its shareholders: 'Mr Burton was unfortunate in arriving in London at a most inopportune time; just after the collapse of the boom in rubber, and while the state of affairs in Papua were in a somewhat chaotic state, he is still using his best endeavours, [however,] he has so far not met with any success'. The shareholders of the Adelaide Papuan Rubber Syndicate, Ltd passed a resolution on 15 November 1912 to place the company in voluntary liquidation. The Galley Reach property became part of the Clarke–Whiting Kanosia rubber plantation estate.[24]

Sir Rupert Clarke and Robert Whiting from Victoria had spent £220,000 on plantations in Papua by 1921. Although the two wealthy entrepreneurs lost a considerable sum of their investment during the collapse of the caoutchouc market, Clarke believed that rubber-growing in Papua could be successful with the employment of Asiatic workers.

In February 1907 Clarke and Whiting registered The Papua Rubber Plantations Propriety Limited (PRP) in Victoria, with the Melbourne accountant Arthur Bloomfield as the company secretary. By year-end Clarke had leased 5,000 ac on the western and northern sides of Galley Reach, 70 km west of Port Moresby, and Whiting 3,800 ac on the Veimauri River, which enters Galley Reach from the northwest. PRP developed Para rubber on Kanosia and coconuts on Rorona, both on Clarke's lease, with rubber planted on Veimauri under a separate arrangement. In 1909 Clarke and Whiting acquired a lease over 10,000 ac between Fairfax Harbour and Boera, immediately northwest of Port Moresby, to plant sisal hemp for the manufacture of ropes. Two proprietary limited companies—Fairfax Harbour Plantations and North Fairfax Harbour Plantations—were set up to develop this land.[25]

Bloomfield, who had become interested in Papua after meeting Alexander Campbell and Ralph Drummond in 1906, was the first to move into Galley Reach with a lease of 1,000 ac in early 1907. In 1908 he acquired in his wife's name an additional 1,280 ac nearby in order to sell the two properties to The Galley Reach Rubber Estate Ltd in which he retained a controlling interest. Clarke's and Whiting's manager at Galley Reach looked also after Bloomfield's company, which became 'a show case' according to Smith, with little of Bloomfield's money spent on it. During the same year Bloomfield promoted two other plantation ventures in Papua with the lease of 2,000 ac on the Kemp Welch River. After Smith told Atlee Hunt that Bloomfield was 'the most valuable man in the investment line' in Papua. Hunt invested personally £500 in the Kemp Welch River Rubber Estate Ltd. G. Syme of the Melbourne *Age* became Bloomfield's other 'victim', by becoming the major investor in his New Guinea Rubber Estate Ltd.

In 1909 Bloomfield wrote a pamphlet on Papua's agricultural opportunities. Speculators - like the prospectors before them - banked on striking it rich. In his book *The Plantation Dream* David Lewis gives an account of the well-funded and structured British New Guinea Development Company, and of the opportunists and buccaneers who were mostly flushed out by a collapsing rubber market.[26]

The British New Guinea Development Company

> One of the most important projects of Imperial development which have been brought before the British public since the Charter Company was introduced to them by Mr Cecil Rhodes is that of the British New Guinea Development Company. As every reader of the *British-Australasian* knows, British New Guinea (Picturesque Papua as it is familiarly called in Australia) is a country of vast natural resources which has received the attention of numerous adventurous sons of the Commonwealth in recent years.[27]

This upbeat opening paragraph in *The British-Australasian* coincided with the simultaneous launching in Britain and Australia of the British New Guinea Development Company, Limited, prospectus. The British newspapers still considered Papua a British domain, and the choice of company name for the new venture was obviously aimed at reassuring investors.

Opposition by the Victorian, New South Wales and Queensland to the British New Guinea Development Syndicate in 1898 on the grounds that it involved British interests and capital was long forgotten. Murray's concerns in 1906 that the development of BNG was held back by the colony's British administrators and officers no longer rated a mention. Development was the mantra of the Papuan administration. Smith seemed not greatly concerned with the nationality of the white settlers; he realised that any large plantation development could only succeed with the financial resources available from Britain, which would also bring with it experienced British managers.

Speculating on the land boom, a Queensland Papuan Syndicate was formed in late 1908 to acquire large tracts of plantation and agricultural land in Papua. The Brisbane stock and station agent, Claude Musson, set up the syndicate with the idea of selling the land to a company listed on the London Stock Exchange. The most notable member of Musson's syndicate was Queensland's Chief Justice Sir Pope Alexander Cooper who held nearly 16% (4,700) of the 30,000 shares. Other syndicate members were Queensland graziers J. H. McConnell and P. M. Bigge, and Brisbane merchants J. H. & T. H. Brown. Musson's share in the syndicate was 20%. The Papuan contacts and participants in the scheme were the public servants J. MacDonald and A. Hunter, and Port Moresby merchant A. M. Sinclair.

The Papuan Lands Ltd Co. was registered in London with the purpose of acquiring the Queensland Papuan Syndicate. While Musson was again the originator of this idea, his authority in the new venture transferred to the former South Australian premier and then South Australian agent-general in London, American-born John G. Jenkins, and Duncan Elliott Alves, who had already earned a considerable reputation as a pioneer of colonial undertakings. The two men assembled a list of eminent public figures, both in Australia and England, to impress the Papuan government with the seriousness of their intentions. Apart from Alves and Jenkins, the Hon. W. L. Baillieu of Melbourne (stockbroker and member of the Victorian Parliament), the Hon. Agar Wynne (Protectionist Member of the Federal House of the Representatives), Sir Alfred Cowley (ardent Queensland separatist, Chairman Bank of Queensland and Speaker of the Queensland Legislative Assembly), Charles A. Darling (chairman of Kuala Selangor Rubber) and W. H. Horn (Director of the Bank of Adelaide) sat on the Papuan Lands Company's advisory committee.[28] The intention of the Board of eminent Directors was to sell the assets of the Papuan Lands Company to The British New Guinea Development Company, Ltd (BNGD).

In preparation for a listing of BNGD on the London Stock Exchange in February 1910, Jenkins and Darling visited Australia and Papua to obtain 'official support and co-operation for the company, and information at first hand as to the conditions under which its work will be carried on'. H. A. Wickham of Para-rubber fame,

Disastrous Ventures

A.J. Boyd (Queensland Department of Agriculture), G. Burnett (Queensland Chief Forest Inspector), and A. S. Bloomfield (author of *Tropical Agriculture in Papua*) accompanied them to provide advice in their fields of expertise.

Darling and Jenkins submitted their 'Report' on the economic potential of Papua to the Papuan Lands Ltd board in late 1909. In his deliberation Darling expressed the experts' utmost confidence in the success of agricultural undertakings in Papua. His Report identified 112,000 ac of Queensland Papuan Syndicate land over which Papuan Lands Ltd. held options as excellent agricultural assets. Subject to the survey regulations under the *Papuan Land Ordinance, 1906,* the land was identified in the report as the foundation holdings of the new BNGD.

Except for Sogeri, the report read, the land was easily accessible by water, and was partly in Papua's dry belt (annual rainfall 750–1000 mm), suitable for sisal, tobacco, cotton, and in the wet belt (rainfall 2,550–3,825 mm p.a.) for the cultivation of rubber, sugar, cacao and coconuts. Darling claimed that Papua was outside the cyclone belt, and that its rich soil and reliable rainfall makes it exceptionally favourable for tropical agriculture. Moreover, as no export duties are levied the Company will possess an undoubted advantage over similar undertakings established in the Federal Malay States, the Straits Settlements and Java.

The Report pointed to the availability of cheap indentured labour as one of the most important factors in the success of the enterprise. 'Indentured Papuan labour', according to Darling, 'is considered by competent authorities as quite equal to that of the Kanaka of Polynesia or the Tamil of India and Ceylon', and that there were at present 'about 5,000 indentured Papuans working satisfactorily in the Territory … with wages ranging from 5s to 10s a month, with food and house accommodation'. Wickham highlighted the suitability of the land on Cloudy Bay for Para rubber. He added the observation that compared to Ceylon, where tree tapping begins in the seventh year, with Papuan rubber trees start producing after 5–6 years.

Ignorant of or disregarding the unprofitable cotton and tobacco plantations in GNG ten years earlier, the Report pointed to the immediate revenue that could be derived from these cash crops. Daniel Jones (Department of Agriculture, Brisbane) and Arthur Boyd relied on 40-years' experience in the Queensland cotton industry. They believed that Papua was well suited for cotton and recommended that it be planted on a large scale. Samples of cotton that had been grown on the land in the Laloki district—to be acquired by BNGD under the land deal with Musson—had been assessed by the Liverpool Cotton Association (Ltd) to be of 'most excellent qualities, and well worth further cultivation'. Jones estimated that the land he had inspected

Table 16.1 **BNGD land acquisition plan**

Location	Area (ac)	Location	Area (ac)
Brown River	40,000	Orangerie Bay	4,000
Cloudy Bay District	30,000	Milne Bay	5,000
Redscar Bay	11,000	Cape Rodney	2,700
Laloki River District	9,500	Sogeri District	600
Port Moresby District	8,700	Galley Reach	500

would yield 3,000 lb of cotton pods or £32/ac. After deducting for cultivation and harvesting, Darling adjusted Jones' prediction to £20/ac in the Report.

Musson took R. S. Nevill, a tobacco expert with the Queensland government, to Papua in early 1908. 'I am decidedly of the opinion that it would prove a most valuable crop', Nevill wrote to Musson. 'Here in Queensland we have been growing Cigar Tobacco for several years altogether with white labour; it has proved very profitable at the comparatively low price of 10½ d/lb average'. With the low labour cost in Papua and on the assumption that no more than one labourer was required to cultivate, harvest and cure tobacco for every 1½ ac, Nevill estimated the cost of tobacco production in Papua would not exceed 2 d/lb. This erroneous estimate was included in the prospectus. The production cost on the large-scale tobacco plantations in Sumatra averaged 1s 4d/lb and was publicised widely. The production cost on the NGC tobacco plantations in GNG was never below 2s 6d/lb.

Setting aside that the sugar industry in Queensland, Java and Fiji was highly competitive, Darling suggested that Queensland's considerable area under sugar depended largely on the Papuan varieties of cane . Oblivious to the fact that Queensland sugar growers may not have been in agreement with Darling on this, BNGD Directors provided a cost estimate for setting up sugar mills and related infrastructure. Investors were informed that the Company would undertake large-scale cane cultivation with the latest types of machinery'.[29]

Launch of the prospectus

The BNGD prospectus was launched simultaneously in England, the European Continent, Australia and New Zealand. Subscriptions opened on 21 February and closed 3 days later. The Earl of Ranfurly was presented in the prospectus as the Chairman of the Board of Directors. The other Board members were Sir Webster Brook Perceval (Director of Union Bank), W. A. Horn (Director Adelaide Bank), the Hon. F.C. Stanley (brother of Lord Derby), the Hon. John J. Jenkins, and D.E. Alves. Sir Alfred Cowley was to be appointed the 'Local Director' in Brisbane, C. Darling the General Manager for Papua and S. Thompson company secretary. Baillieu, Cowley and Wynne were appointed Associate Directors, with E. L. & C. Baillieu appointed the Australian brokers for the float.

With interests in plantations, banking, hydro-electricity generation, shipping and trading, BNGD was easily to become the largest enterprise in Papua. Mineral exploration and exploitation was vested in Papuan Minerals Exploration Ltd. BNGD would also provide capital and credit to white settlers in the manner of a chartered company like Cecil Rhode's British South African Co.[30]

Apart from the expert reports mentioned above, Darling contributed cash flow and profit projections based on a planting schedule in the prospectus (Table 16.2). In the sixth year he projected 10,000 ac planted with rubber and profits of £50,000 annually. The profit projections were based on initial outlays of £110,000 for clearing and planting, including the purchase of seeds (£5 7s. 6d/ac in the dry belt and £6 10s/ ac in the wet belt). The prospectus pointed to other income to be derived from the selling, leasing or cultivating of BNGD's vast landholdings and the harvesting of its timber resources. 'To those unacquainted with the extraordinary fertility of these lands', Darling declared, 'these estimates appear high; but it will be observed that in every instance my estimate is considerably below those of the experts employed to report upon the properties'. What Darling did not reveal or did not know was that the estimates of the 'experts' were unreasonably optimistic. It was also not clear from the information provided in the prospectus whether the cost estimate provided for the establishment of the necessary infrastructure.

The nominal capital of BNGD was £1,500,000 divided into 1,000,000 7% participating preference shares of £1 each and 500,000 ordinary shares of £1 each. The initial subscription was to comprise 500,000 participating preference shares offered at par and the issue of 248,000 ordinary shares in settlement to the vendors. Payment for the shares was 2s 6d/share on application; 2s 6d/share on allotment, and the balance in calls not exceeding 5s/share at intervals of not less than 3 months. After the distribution of 7% profit on the participating preference shares and 7% on the ordinary shares, available profits were to rank equally between the participating preference and the ordinary shares.

By way of consideration Papuan Lands Ltd was to receive £275,000, payable in 223,000 shares of £1 each and £52,000 in cash, with dividend payments on the ordinary shares ranking behind the participating preference shares. Under separate agreement BNGD was acquiring the leases from shareholders of Papuan Lands for a total consideration of £68,050, of which £1,800 was payable in cash and £66,250 in ordinary BNGD shares. BNGD had already procured 10,000 ac in Papua, and had incurred sizeable costs for the expeditions, the expert advice and negotiations.[31]

An unfulfilled plantation dream

> There was an element of romance about the registration in February 1910 of the BNGD, which was formed under the powerful auspices to exploit the resources of the practically unknown but enormously rich territory known as Papua.[32]

The romance the London *Daily Express* was writing about in 1911 reflected BNGD's first report of October 1910. *The Joint Stock Companies Journal* reported that the company was making good progress which showed that its Directors were 'bent on not allowing the grass to grow under their feet'.[33] *The Financial Times* and other dailies informed their readers that BNGD had employed local labour and subcontractors to clear 2,500 ac for Para rubber, 1,000 ac for coconuts and 250 ac for sisal hemp.

The company had developed plans to interplant cash crops such as maize, peanuts, rice and bananas and to cultivate another 750 ac of cotton, 500 ac of cigar leaf tobacco and 100 ac of tea. To make an early start on the harvesting of timber, a sawmilling plant had been erected, with the felling of timber well underway. Without checking the accuracy of the information, *The Financial Times* reported:

> The development of the territory is proceeding apace, and as a result the available plots for building in Port Moresby, the seat of the Government, are eagerly sought for. This was anticipated by the Directors, and a considerable number of plots have been acquired by the company on which houses, warehouses, shops and offices are being erected. The appreciation in value of the building sites has been very rapid, as the available space in Port Moresby is small.[34]

Table 16.2 **Planting and profit projections**

Year one Cloudy Bay (wet belt)	Area (ac)	Profit/ac (£)	Total (£)
Arrowroot	300	15	4,500
Bananas	300	30	9,000
Peanuts	100	8	800
Maize	500	8	4,000
Tobacco	500	20	10,000
Laloki District (dry belt)			
Maize	1,500	6	9,000
Tobacco (cigar leaf)	500	40	20,000
Rice (dry)	300	9	2,700
Year 2—Laloki			
Same as year 1 plus			60,000
Sugar cane	1,000	20	20,000
Cotton	750	20	15,000
Year 3—Laloki			
Doubling of year one planting plus			120,000
Sugar cane	1,000	20	20,000
Cotton	1,500	20	30,000
Sisal hemp	3,000	10	30,000
Total			200,000
Year 4 planting as per year 3			200,000
Year 5 planting as per year 4			200,000
Year 6 planting as per year 5 plus			200,000
Rubber	2,000	25	50,000
Total			250,000

A progress report on the Papuan Minerals Exploration Ltd, in which BNGD held rights to 20% of profit distributions, mentioned the options the company had secured over several high-grade copper and gold leases. In accordance with the option agreement the fields were delineated by Papuan Minerals to prove the extent and value of the lodes. 'Altogether', BNGD reported, 'the prospects of Papua as a payable mineral field are most hopeful'.[35]

A labour shortage was at the centre of the discussions Murray held with BNGD's Directors when he was in London in September 1910. He cautioned the board not to start on too many developments at once because of a general shortage of suitable plantation labour.[36] Conveying Murray's concerns, S. L. Thompson (the company secretary) advised Darling not to lay down any more plantations than originally planned unless sufficient labour was available.

Darling was only too aware of the problem. Captain Archibald Hunter, who started recruiting for him after exchanging his Sogeri leasehold for BNGD shares, sailed the company steamer *Wakefield* up and down the coast in search of labour without much success. Darling, the Rev. Charles Abel, Guy Manning (Laka River Rubber Estate), Raymond Dubois (Papua Plantation Ltd) and Wallace Westland (manager for Clarke and Whiting's rubber plantations in Galley Reach) together with eight other prominent plantation managers wrote to Staniforth Smith requesting an official inquiry into labour resources.

Disastrous Ventures

Smith, acting for Murray, mentioned the availability of labour in his 1909 *Handbook,* reminding Directors at the same time of the requirement of experienced overseers for successful industrial plantation development in Papua. Rather than discussing the issue with the plantation managers in Murray's absence, he forwarded their demands directly to Atlee Hunt who tabled them in Parliament. In a covering letter Smith explained the current shortage of labour on the dysentery epidemic in the Central and Gulf Divisions, and that only the managers in the Central Division out of 140 plantations in the Territory had complained. A month later Smith dispatched his 20-year forward estimate of labour requirements to the Federal Parliament in Melbourne. Based on 10% availability from a Papuan population of 400,000–500,000 he argued that the Territory could meet all the labour requirements.[37]

The labour problems, the debilitating dysentery and the stressful job of setting up a large plantation and trading enterprise led to Darling's resignation after only a few months into the job. Also short-lived was the appointment of D. E. Alves to BNGD's board. He was reluctant to meet calls on his shares and was replaced by Evelyn Metcalfe soon after the company became incorporated.[38]

The rate at which money was spent alarmed the board to such an extent that Metcalfe travelled to Papua in October/November 1910 to inspect BNGD's activities. Alfred Cowley arrived from Brisbane to join him in Port Moresby. They found that the business was not managed altogether satisfactorily, and attributed this to the poor state of health of Darling. A man of considerable energy and experience in plantation management, Metcalfe appointed Lewis Jesse Cowley as Darling's successor. According to his uncle, Alfred Cowley, Lewis was a planter of high repute and had considerable experience in Queensland extending over some 12 years.[39]

Notwithstanding L. J. Cowley's high reputation, profits failed to materialise and the share price of BNGD fell. The *Manchester Dispatch* lead a chorus of critics after the company issued an abbreviated annual report in June 1911.

> The first annual report of the BNGD is not a very informing document from the point of view of work done [it complained], but it is interesting in showing the very large amount of money paid away in underwriting commission, preliminary expenses, and brokerage. The issued capital—excluding vendors' figures—is £324,234 to obtain this the company appears to have paid £73,253 or 20%. Thus it starts heavily handicapped.[40]

More acerbic was the Sydney *Bulletin* when it wrote BNGD had 100,000 ac of plantation land for which it paid a 'shocking price considering the money ex-Premier and book agent Jenkins of S'Australia got'. The London *Stockbroker* called BNGD 'a perfectly hopeless affair [with] not the remotest chance of [it] ever paying a dividend'. The Australian broadsheet newspapers were more measured in their criticism. 'The company has made a fair start, [with] expenditures in Papua and Brisbane amounting to £27,883 to December 31, 1910, and trades showing a profit of £1200 for the same period', reported the *SMH*.[41]

A useful distraction—the discovery of oil

BNGD's Directors expressed their satisfaction about the 'zeal and energy' Lewis Cowley displayed. In the 1911 annual the company reported the planting of 2,814 ac of coconuts, 624 ac of rubber, 342 ac of sisal hemp, and 320 ac of tobacco and other staples. 'The experimental crop of Tobacco has been highly successful, and Cigars are being manufactured by the Company's staff in Papua', the report highlighted. Reminiscent of Hansemann's report to NGC's shareholders in 1891, Lord Ranfurly told shareholders: the cigars 'are sold as fast as they can be produced at 20s to 20s 6d per hundred, which price should provide a handsome profit on cost of production'.

Apart from tobacco, the Board forecast an early cash flow from a Para rubber (266 ac) and a coconut (96 ac) estate the company purchased for £1,500 plus 5,000 fully paid ordinary BNGD shares. 'The purchase price is a bargain', shareholders learnt, 'as it includes stores valued at £1,100'. The trial shipment of timber to Melbourne proved unsuccessful, though. Captain J. A. Rogers of the *Bentinck* was told not to bother unloading the second sawmill when he arrived in Port Moresby with the plant. The difficult terrain made the harvesting of timber close to impossible, Cowley told him, and BNGD decided to dispose of the newly acquired steamer including plant.[42]

In April 1912 *The Financial Times* took a lead from *Reuters* to report on a significant discovery of petroleum in Papua. 'The find', the paper informed its readers, 'is in Kiri, on the Vailala River; [where] a series of minute craters was discovered at intervals of a few yards for about a quarter of a mile. From these water and mud were issuing with every appearance of great pressure [and] the gas which exuded ignited easily and gave out a bluish flame.[43] London's *The Daily News* also reported on the discovery of petroleum in Papua; a fact 'not altogether a surprise', according to the petroleum expert J. D. Henry who wrote:

New Guinea has an important geological association with the Borneo fields, and there are oil indications at various points', Henry told the paper. 'In the case of the Australian markets [the discovery] is exceedingly important [because] the American exporting fields on the Pacific coast do not produce the more volatile oils [and] the oil fields in Europe are prevented by high transport charges for going into these far-away markets.[44]

The petroleum discovery BNGD shareholders read about in the London newspapers was made by Lewis Lett and G. Thomas. Lett, first engineer on the *Bentinck*, stayed on in Port Moresby when BNGD dissolved the charter for the steamer in early 1911. The colony promised opportunity for him and his mate Thomas and the pair found much suitable plantation land 150 km upstream of the Vailala River. In this vicinity, near the villages Opa and Akauda they also discovered mud springs in September 1911 that gave off a thick frothy scum with a decidedly petroliferous odour. These mud springs were 'in a state resembling ebullition by escaping inflammable gas' according to Lett.[45]

The discovery, first reported in the *Sydney Morning Herald* on 3 January 1912, spawned much excitement in Papua and Australia. The Federal Government announced that oil had been discovered at Akauda, Papua, on 22 February 1912, and the Commonwealth had proprietary rights over oil, gas and coal discoveries made in Australian territory. Melbourne foresaw a day when Papua would satisfy Australia's oil needs, and the Navy hoped for Australasia to become self-sufficient in oil production. BNGD jumped on the bandwagon by reporting the discovery of oil on the Gira River at its June 1912 annual meeting. 'Instructions have been telegraphed to the General Manager', the chairman advised, 'to proceed with the development of the field by means of hand wells in the localities of most promise'. Shareholders also learnt that a London petroleum engineer would carry out further testing.[46]

The expected discovery of oil provided a faint ray of hope. The company spent £1,477 on the expert from London and advised shareholders a year later:

> The Directors regret that the Government has so far declined to grant any leases for development of the oil field, although their intention to do so in June, 1912, when engineers were sent out by this Company, was quite clear. The decision of the Government is the more regrettable in that promising developments have taken place and the field is believed to extend over a large area.[47]

The Fisher Labor government was indeed of the opinion that a very large oilfield was present in the wider Vailala district and that initial delineation should be carried out by Mr E. Grebin, an American oil driller, in conjunction with Mr J. E. Carne, (assistant government geologist, NSW), to be followed by the experienced British geologist and oil expert Dr Arthur Wade. The results were both promising and disappointing. Hydrocarbon was present, but the geological structure was not a capped shale proposition, rather, the strata consisted of clayey rock with little permeability. After completing his geological assessment in 1914 Wade suggested an extensive drilling program be undertaken.[48]

Seventeen years later, Murray's intention to keep the petroleum exploration and production entirely in the Commonwealth's hands was overturned by the Federal Government when oil exploration was farmed out to the Anglo-Persian Oil Co. When this production-sharing agreement was discontinued for lack of success, Port Moresby decided to 'throw open to private enterprise all but a block of 1,000 square miles situated in a district where oil was first found'.[49]

BNGD was fortunate that it had not been given the opportunity to participate in oil exploration in Papua, for 17 years later no payable oil or gas had been discovered. The oil exploration expenditure of £1,498 was written off in 1923.

The prosperity Lett and Thomas had hoped to attain from their discovery never eventuated. In search for further gas and oil springs, Thomas succumbed to the tropical contagion– malaria and/or dysentery in 1912. Lett, after ridding himself of the oil bug, acquired the 2,500 acres coconut plantation on the Vailala from Robert E. Mawson – father of the Antarctic explorer Douglas Mawson – in about 1913.

BNGD's first informative annual report

In 1914 Lewis Cowley provided his first and only detailed report on BNGD's plantation. He resigned shortly after and was replaced by George Archibald Loudon, who had been the commercial manager of BNGD from November 1913.

Cowley's report included a map (18) and table (16.3) on the size and location of the plantations. It showed that on 31 January 1914 the area under cultivation was 7,231 ac, with nearly 6,000 ac planted and 1,248 ac prepared for planting by the end of the wet season. Cowley made a point of the three consecutive years of droughts: the condition was particularly prevalent during the second half of each year. Although the Port Moresby region, where many of the BNGD plantations were located, was in 'the so-called dry belt', Cowley explained that, 'the average for 17 years for the last six months, including 1910 was 11,162 inches of rain, while for the three years following and ending 1913, the average for the same period was only 4,825 inches'.[50] By way of explanation for not having generated any meaningful revenue, let alone profits, Cowley pointed to the difficulties all tropical plantation enterprises experienced in new countries. He noted the labour shortages and the persistence of malaria which affected everyone in Papua. A synopsis on farming outlined crop growing and plantation development in the report:

Para Rubber — 'because of the non-germination of the imported Para rubber seeds the company had decided to plant nearly all of its coastal land with coconuts. This still left an estate of some 800 ac of Para rubber at Itikinumu and Jawarare, where, at 1,500 ft above sea level, rainfall was more reliable. The tapping for 9 months of 700 Para trees produced satisfactory, albeit commercially insignificant, results. It was hoped that the depressed caoutchouc market would have recovered by the end of 1916, when about 18,000 trees would be ready for tapping. This tally was to increase to 54,000 trees in the following year. In contrast to the slower-growing Para class, the Ceara rubber planted on 176 ac at Katea and Baubauguina could be tapped when 3–4 years old'. Even without any rise in the current price in caoutchouc, Cowley suggested that it would pay to tap 15,000 of these trees in 1915, increasing to some 40,000 trees within in the following 2–3 years.

Coconuts — 58 ac with palms 4 years and older, had been purchased from the Aroa estate on Redscar Bay. Seed nuts from the 5 ac of mature palms at Aroa were mainly planted on the Eastern Division estates of Gadaisu at Orangerie Bay and Waigani at Milne Bay, and on Obu and on Redscar Bay. The more than 3,700 ac of coconuts that had been laid down in 1913 and 1914, included planting on the Otomata and Pailee estates at Cape Rodney, and at Vilirupu Harbour.

Sisal Hemp — some 360 ac of sisal was planted at Bomana on the Laloki River, a short distance from Port Moresby. The company reported that the first 70 ac could be harvested in 1914. However, because of the high milling, treatment and freight costs, and the low prices for the fibre in Australia, it was decided not to harvest until an economy of scale was attained. A sisal estate of at least 1,000 ac, yielding approximately 100 t of no. 1 fibre and about 5% of accompanying tow, was considered economical. Bomana grew 1,258 ac of sisal hemp in 1916, returning little or no profit.

Tobacco—the growing of a good tobacco leaf proved more difficult than the optimistic 1911 annual report conveyed. 'For two years', Cowley reported,

> we experimented on the growth of Tobacco, first of all with cigar leaf, and later with pipe. After great difficulty we managed to secure the services of a few skilled cigar makers, and manufactured what was pronounced by most of those who sampled them, a high grade article.[51]

William Bruce, who professed to know something about the smoking quality of these cigars, reported in February 1912: the 'Colorado Madura' type cigars were still too green, but over time the Papuan product should become as important a product as copra and rubber. The importance of tobacco that Bruce and BNGD identified lay more in the local consumption than in exporting it. Since the 1880s tobacco was a major trade item with the Papuans, comprising approximately 10% of the value of all imports annually until 1907 and, with growing terms of trade, still comprising 6.75% of annual imports in 1914. Trade or twist tobacco attracted import duty of 2s 3d/lb, rising to 8s/lb for cigars and cigarettes in 1914. In an expanding Papuan economy the Board expected local tobacco to be highly profitable.[52]

In 1913 the company started investing several thousand pounds sterling to prepare 200 ac of tobacco at Katea, approximately 40 km north of Port Moresby. Twenty large curing sheds were erected and equipment ordered from America and Europe. Cowley hoped to procure machinery and tobacco experts from Australia, but settled for the greater expertise residing in Holland and its Far East colony, with the Dutch tobacco 'twisters' Arie Otte and Willem Akkermann arriving in Port Moresby in late 1913. The first consignment of equipment for twist tobacco arrived at the end of 1914. The cigarette making machines ordered from America, together with an American tobacco expert, did not arrive in Papua until 1916.

Reminiscent of the NGC reports, BNGD informed its shareholders in 1916 that the commissioning of the 'up-to-date' tobacco factory, 'will show very satisfactory results'.[53] Twelve months later the Directors disclosed:

> The Preferential Tariff granted on tobacco manufactured in Papua has not given the results expected, as the Papuan Government has increased the Excise Duty on the [imported] ingredients of tobacco, and further, those ingredients are now costing 300 % more than in pre-war days.[54]

Subsequently the company withdrew from tobacco cultivation. The disclosed write off in tobacco equipment in 1917 (£3,029), in 1918 (£6,352) and in 1919 (£3,449) were a fraction of the total losses BNGD incurred on this failed venture.[55]

The financial returns on catch and cover crops, including cotton, were not much different, albeit not as expensive an investment as tobacco. After harvesting 160,376 lb of cotton ball in 1913, Cowley decided to interplant 917 ac with cotton in the 1914–15 seasons. The crop failed, with only 345.5 lb/ac of raw cotton harvested. BNGD made no further attempt to cultivate this crop.

BNGD was more successful in producing staples for domestic consumption. By interplanting the young coconut, rubber and sisal plantations with catch crops, the 1913 harvest was: Mauritius bean (112,784 lb), maize (164,528), sweet potatoes (169,344 lb), cow peas (1,176 lb), horse fodder (72,800 lb), 193 bunches of bananas and 636 pineapples. In 1919 the harvest of sweet potatoes had risen to 952,447 lb, far exceeding the in-house requirements of BNGD.[56]

Trading stations and general merchandising — the establishment of the coastal stations, set up as labour depôts, and for the barter of copra and sago, was unsuccessful. Little trade copra was procured, and the recruitment of labour was carried out by contractors. By 1914 the stations were leased to independent traders or closed.

While the merchandise section of BNGD was profitable from inception - the Port Moresby and Samarai stores returned gross profits of £6,000 in 1913/14 - the company was cash flow negative for the first 12 years. The 1914 balance sheet showed land and property investments of £283,402, capitalised plantation expenditures of £124,428, and buildings, ships, livestock, and inventory at £54,174. The debtors account stood at £6,704 with an additional £8,690 owed to creditors. Cash on-hand in Papua, London and in Australia amounted to £8,189. To remain afloat BNGD made calls on the outstanding preference shares, issued debentures and secured a loan from BP. G. A. Loudon assumed responsibility for BNGD in Papua on 1 January 1915. He remained with the company until 1926.[57]

BNGD sisal plantation and hemp decorticating plant - BOMANA Plantation (BNGD annual reports 1914 & 16); **Sisal hemp mill - Fairfax Harbour Plantation Company, and Ploughing by motor tractor BNGD's tobacco plantation KATEA - Laloki Valley** (S. Smith, *Handbook of the Territory of Papua*, 1912)

Disastrous Ventures

BNGD's funding requirements post 1914

The initial public offering was successful. The 500,000 participating preference issue fully subscribed at 5s, with an immediate call of 2s 6d also paid by the balance date of 31 December 1910. Papuan Lands, Limited subscribed for 96,114 of these shares, while only receiving 136,778 ordinary shares of £1 each and £36,043 for the land it transferred to BNGD, rather than the 223,000 ordinary shares and cash consideration of £52,000 outlined in the prospectus.[58]

In 1913 BNGD changed its balance date from 31 December to 31 January 1914. Lord Ranfurly and J. G. Jenkins resigned from the board in June 1913. W. A. Horn was elected chairman, with the other board members Perceval, Stanley and Metcalfe. Alfred Cowley retired from his Brisbane position in 1917.

Papuan Lands Ltd had failed to pay a 2s call made on 5 July 1912 forcing the BNGD board to call an extraordinary shareholder meeting on 17 December 1912. Apart from appointing the new Directors, shareholders of BNGD approved for Papuan Lands to pay one Shilling of the call immediately, with the balance of 1s by 1 August 1914. Further, Papuan Lands agreed to forfeit an entitlement of 70,000 ordinary shares subject to BNGD cancelling £50,000 in underwriting commission and £23,253 in. brokerage.[59]

Reminiscent of the frequent calls NGC Directors made on its shareholders, the Directors of BNGD made six calls between 1 January 1911 and 31 January 1917, when the original issue of 500,000 partly paid participating preference shares were fully paid. To finance what was a loss-making venture until then, the company issued 7% convertible debentures for £100,000 in 1919. By the balance date of 31 January 1921 the notes were fully paid and BNGD continued to draw heavily on its cash reserves. Expenditures on plantations and infrastructure had been capitalised in accordance with accounting practice. By January 1921 these non-performing assets had accrued to £608,556 in the 'Plantation Investment' account and a year later BNGD provided shareholders with the option of a capital restructure or liquidating the company. The shareholders voted for a restructure and changes to the board of Directors.

The application of the Australian *Navigation Act* to Papua in 1921 all but bankrupted the Papuan plantation industry. Under the Act all Papuan exports were required to be shipped to Australian ports on Australian-owned ships, crewed by European (Australian) seamen. The application of this Act to Papua, the classification of Papua as a foreign country under the *Import Tariff Act* and depressed commodity prices rendered BNGD unable to pay interest of £122,000 on the debentures. The fob price for copra had fallen to below £12/t. in 1920 and with excise of 25s/t applied from 20 Nov. 1920, copra became unprofitable to produce. An appeal to Murray for the removal of the levy on 22 March 1921 was rejected.[60]

At the June 1922 annual meeting Horn and Metcalfe resigned, Perceval (chairman) and Stanley were re-elected. O. J. Trinder (insurance and shipping broker), T. Boyd (planter from the Federated Malay States) and Sir William McCheyne Anderson from Sydney joined the board. Thompson remained the company secretary.

Shareholders supported a write down of the plantation assets by approximately

Category		Aroa	Baubauguina	Bomana	Gadaisu	Itikinumu	Jawarare	Katea	Obu	Otomata	Pailie	Waigani	Brown River	Nomo	Kapa Kapa	Total
Total expenditure (£)		1958	3722	1318	2698	3389	1410	6080	2746	2195	2940	4816	323	0	0	33595
Area of plantations (ac)		8101	6358	8578	4300	1522	180	4435	2098	2700	6166	5000	6613	6	21	56078
Tobacco under cultivation (ac)		726	797	433	862	637	160	331	1068	508	477	1106	100	6	20	7231
Area cleared for planting (ac)		340	–	72	230	25	10	165	48	40	116	102	100	–	–	1248
Tobacco	1914 crop	–	–	–	–	–	–	30	–	–	–	–	–	–	–	30
Sisal Hamp	2–3 Years	–	–	361	–	–	–	–	–	–	–	–	–	–	–	361
Ceara Rubber	Total	6	115	–	–	–	–	61	–	2	–	–	–	–	–	184
Ceara Rubber	1 Year	–	–	–	–	–	–	4	–	–	–	–	–	–	–	4
Ceara Rubber	2 Years	6	115	–	–	–	–	57	–	2	–	–	–	–	–	180
Para Rubber (ac)	Total	–	15	–	–	612	150	–	–	–	173	–	–	–	–	950
Para Rubber (ac)	< 1 Year	–	–	–	–	361	50	–	–	–	56	–	–	–	–	467
Para Rubber (ac)	2 Years	–	15	–	–	176	50	–	–	–	10	–	–	–	–	251
Para Rubber (ac)	3 Years	–	–	–	–	63	20	–	–	–	96	–	–	–	–	179
Para Rubber (ac)	4 Years	–	–	–	–	–	30	–	–	–	11	–	–	–	–	41
Para Rubber (ac)	8 Years	–	–	–	–	12	–	–	–	–	–	–	–	–	–	12
Coconuts (ac)	Total	380	667	–	632	–	–	75	1020	466	188	1004	–	6	20	4458
Coconuts (ac)	< 1 Year	215	404	–	241	–	–	53	270	240	128	432	–	–	–	1983
Coconuts (ac)	2 Years	45	147	–	391	–	–	22	500	129	–	572	–	–	–	1801
Coconuts (ac)	3 Years	115	115	–	–	–	–	–	250	67	37	–	–	6	20	611
Coconuts (ac)	4 Years	–	–	–	–	–	–	–	–	30	23	–	–	–	–	53
Coconuts (ac)	> 9 Years	5	–	–	–	–	–	–	–	–	–	–	–	–	–	5

Table 16.3 **BNGD Plantations and crops** (annual report 1914)

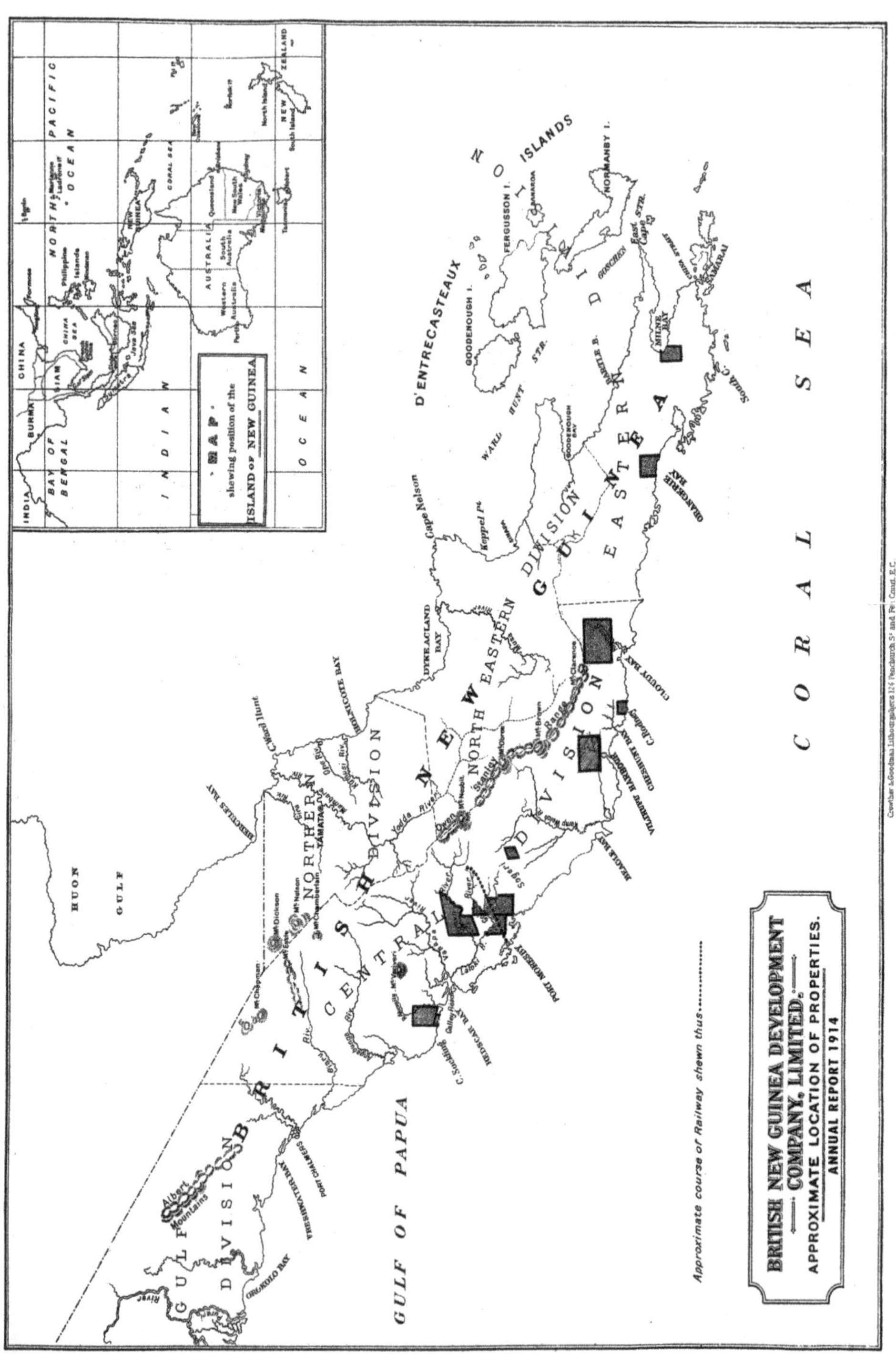

Map 18: **BNGD plantations** (AR-BNGD, 1914)

£200,000 and a first mortgage over the company's assets for a bank loan of £50,000. The conversion of three new 10s shares paid to 66.66% for each £1 BNGD share with the balance payable at call was also approved by the meeting. The share capital restructure required a change of the Papuan law (passed in May 1923) to provide the debenture holders of BNGD with security over the company's assets.

The restructure of BNGD and the lifting by the Australian government of the *Navigation Act* as it applied to Papua in 1925 enabled BNGD to pay its maiden dividend of 5% in 1926. However, a second capital restructure was necessary in 1935. The plantation assets of £478,531 were now written down to £191,412, a fraction of the original development costs. A rights issue in 1937 gave shareholders the opportunity to acquire two 2s shares for each 10s shares held. A tariff of 4d/lb on all rubber imported by Australia other than from the territories of the Commonwealth (Papua and the former GNG) in November 1930, and a 50% recovery in the rubber price in 1936 enabled the Directors to declare dividends of between 3% and 7.5%.[61]

The old Andrew Goldie wharf at Grenville West, Port Moresby, sold to Burns, Philp in 1891. The two-storied building was added by BP, ca. 1896 (BP archive (John Oxley Library, Brisbane).

Disastrous Ventures

Attempting to reconcile competing interest

MacGregor was bold and successful in exploring the territory. He travelled BNG more widely than could have ever been expected of a Lieutenant-Governor. He prepared maps, collected mineralogical samples, sent artefacts, flora and fauna specimens to museums in Britain and Australia. MacGregor appeased tribal communities and endeavoured to make them plant coconut palms to engender a local economy. When this failed, he made the labour and land laws more attractive for plantation investments. It was to no avail. At the end of his tenure BNG was still a backwater, with little infrastructure and without a basic health system. Gold had been discovered in the Sudest in 1888 and on Misima in 1889. Ten years later the alluvial fields in the Louisiades were exhausted and the miners had moved on to the Trobriand Archipelago where they discovered gold on Woodlark Island in 1895. BNG benefited little from these discoveries. The European prospectors and miners paid a pittance for mining licences and, notwithstanding their contribution to the coffers of BNG through a consumption tax (import duty), their presence exerted financial strain on the administration. This was particularly felt by the Le Hunte administration. While the goldfields brought death and misery to the miners, their carriers, the local tribes, it was also costly in economic terms. It was often left to the administration to sort out the estates of the deceased Europeans and pay the wages owed to the indentured workers. In case of morbidity, miners were generally repatriated to their villages at government expense. Where an employer had died or left the Territory without notifying the authorities, the workers where left stranded among hostile tribes.

The violent contacts between the Europeans, their workers and the local tribes required policing. The lawlessness in the goldfields of the Gira and the Yodda required courts of law, magistrates, prisons, wardens and gaolers. The Stations Tamata, Ioma, Bogi, Papangi and Kokoda, established solely to protect the European prospectors and miners, are examples of expenditures that weighed heavily on the government's purse strings.

The Australian, New Zealand and Fijian representatives at the 1883 Inter Colonial Conference in Sydney demanded the annexation of East New Guinea for reasons concerning the defence of Australia and the rapid extension of British trade in the region. The Erskine Proclamation of 1884 limited the Deputy Commissioner of the Western Pacific to securing the protection of the indigenous population of southeast New Guinea. When BNG became a protectorate of the British Empire in 1888 MacGregor continued with this objective. However, his aspiration to pacify, protect and educate the Papuans only succeeded to a degree and in a narrow manner. While the government settlements of Daru, Port Moresby, Rigo and Samarai enjoyed largely peaceful intercourse with the tribal communities, and the Trobriand and Louisiades islanders were relatively calm, European contact with the remote coastal and highland tribes remained bloody and often deadly. MacGregor, Le Hunte, Robinson and Barton left the education and acculturation of the Papuans to the Christian missions. There existed clearly greater emphasis by the administrators to support the missions with land grants than the requirement to promote agricultural development by European settlement energetically. MacGregor promoted the British New Guinea Syndicate only because his policy of encouraging the 'natives' to plant coconut palms and start a market garden economy failed. The syndicate scheme was politically naïve unless the premiers' support of the contributing colonies was secured. Similarly, Le Hunte stood accused of conspiring with the co-founder of BP's Robert Philp, then Premier of Queensland, to favour the Hall Sound Company. Unmindful of the shift in the political power in Australia, he did not invest the necessary time to convince the Barton government of the benefits the plan would bring to BNG.

Except for alluvial gold, trade copra, trepang, pearls, pearl shell, tortoise shell and artefacts made up the bulk of goods sent from BNG. While the governments in Brisbane, Sydney, Melbourne and London bear much responsibility for BNG's lack of economic growth, the Port Moresby administrations should have achieved some progress in tropical plantation and agricultural industry in BNG by being more proactive. When a 'mother lode' was not discovered after nearly 30 years of back-breaking alluvial mining, *The West Australian* voiced indifference by stating

> Papuan development was not expected, under any circumstances, to be sensationally rapid. It is not and never can be a white man's country in the accepted sense. Except for its strategic value the Commonwealth might well have had nothing to do with so troublesome a possession.[62]

The Papuan agricultural 'revolution' was at its most productive from 1907 to 1914. With virtually no plantations laid down by 1906, Smith, more so than Murray, facilitated the planting of 42,921 ac by 1914. Plantation numbers rising to 228 in 1914, most of it planted with coconuts (29,030 ac), caoutchouc (6,606 ac) and sisal hemp (3,110 ac). BNGD cultivated more acreage between 1910 and 1915 than in the company's history from then until 1950. Of the 14 plantations shown in table 16.3, Pailee (477 ac) was acquired from Laka River Rubber Plantation in which Bloomfield had an interest. Former gold miner Robert Hunter sold his large coconut estate Obu (1,068 ac) to BNGD in 1914. The company failed to develop its 40,000 ac lease on the Brown River and relinquished it in 1921.[63]

Generally, BNGD cultivated its plantations with subcontract labour thereby avoiding the worst of the labour problems in the Central Division. In many ways Smith was right: there was enough labour in Papua. For the planters the problems were, for the most part the low Papuan productivity and the protective rights provided under the Labour Ordinance.[64] The proposed 'native taxation' or work to be provided by 'natives' as promulgated by Atlee Hunt and the Royal Commission in 1907 was never enacted. Murray regarded the imposition of a tax to make natives work akin to forced labour. While the importation of labour from Southeast Asia. China and India would have greatly increased the planters' bargaining power with the Port Moresby government and the Papuans it was not sanctioned by the federal government nor was it supported by Murray.

Cash crops never became a paying proposition. BNGD put great store in the production of tobacco and cotton. They ignored NGC's unfortunate experience. The hardship of receiving not enough or too much rain, the cost of fertilising, pest and mould control, the building of drying and curing sheds, and warehouses, and the dearth of expert labour and overseers had already been experienced by the Germans on the other side of the divide. BNGD tobacco was grown solely for domestic consumption. This required investment in the importation of paper and aromatics for cigarette manufacturing and dry storage. Notwithstanding import duty protection on tobacco products entering Papua, BNGD spent approximately £150,000 on its tobacco venture before shutting it down in 1918/19.[65]

With cotton also not living up to expectations, BNGD's Directors were relieved when the prospect of oil in 1912 drew attention away from the underperforming plantations. Promoted as the new bedrock on which BNGD's prosperity was to grow, this optimism faded when the government prevented private enterprise from exploring for oil. And by the time BNGD became profitable on copra, and to a lesser extent, rubber in the late 1920s, Papuan oil prospects were all but forgotten.

Planter frustration grew with the Australian government's indifference towards the plight of a nascent Papuan industry. It boiled over into open conflict between BNGD and Murray during the war years. In April 1914 Murray wrote to his brother in Oxford: 'there is a gang of capitalists interested in Papua who want to get rid of me to have a free hand with the natives'. Justifying Papua's slow economic development, Murray considered it his duty to look after the weaker people. He conceded that 'the industrial races of Asia' would have made a difference to the economic development of Papua. He was worried, however, that Chinese success would cause other problems when he wrote in 1925: 'I shudder at the possibility of its practical application [Chinese immigration], for it is conceivable that a people might be discovered whose fitness for survival is superior to our own'. Returning to the mantra of Australian security, he contended that it was an obvious advantage to Australia 'to preserve a race like the present inhabitants of Papua, who can never be a menace to the Commonwealth'.[66]

When Robert Belfort and Johannes Hoyer wrote about the potential of Papuan agriculture in their coconut manual they drew on BNGD's statement:

> When Australia has realised what a valuable asset she possesses right at her very doors, Papua will have become the most prolific and richest exporter of tropical products outside Ceylon. Land is easily obtainable on the most liberal terms, and labour is plentiful and cheap.[67]

The prognosis remained unfulfilled. By 1914 Papua offered no discernible economic benefit to Australia. The Territory's soil lacked the nutrients for intensive agriculture, the dry belt was extensive; there was no efficiency to be gained with Papuan labour. With no new payable discoveries in precious metals, coal and oil, Australia had lost interest in Papua by 1914.

Murray survived the planters' discontent to remain in charge of Papua until his death in Samarai in 1940. Eastern Plantation Holdings, a subsidiary of the British Jessell Group, acquired BNGD in 1970. The Belgian plantation conglomerate S.A. SIPEF N.V. of Antwerp bought the BNGD plantation interests and other tangible assets in 1984.

page 391, **Elevala Island, Port Moresby from Mission House,** ca. 1885 (SLV No H24423)
Port Moresby, ca. 1909 (S. Smith, *Handbook of the Territory of Papua* [1912])
Port Moresby, ca. 1914 (National Archives Canberra, C5487 PH/0126)

Notes

1   D. C. Lewis, *The Plantation Dream*, p. 292

2   J.H.P. Murray, *Papua or British New Guinea*, pp. 350, 356. & 360

3   L. Lett, *Sir Hubert Murray of Papua*, pp. 11–69

4   *Papuan Times*, (1913) 7 May & (1914) 3 June; See Lewis, p. 120

5   Murray, p. 359; AR-Papua (1909/10) p. 25.

6   Land Ordinance, 1906 (AR-Papua [1906/07] pp. 19–21, [1909/10] p. 25, and [19010/11] p. 15.x). Smith, *Handbook* (1909) p. 119

7   AR-Papua (1909/10) p. 26

8   Murray, pp. 359–60

9   AR-Papua (1909/10) pp. 25 & 28

10   'Planter Complaint of Government Listlessness', *The Age* (1911) Sep. 1

11   AR-Papua (1906/07) p. 68; (1908/09) annex, p. 2

12   B. Grimshaw, *Papua the Marvellous, the Country of Chance*, pp. 3–59

13   Campbell and Murray to Hunt, 28 Sep. 1909 (Correspondence, NLA MS 52)

14   Lewis, pp. 98–102

15   H. H. Smith & F.A.G. Pape, *Coconuts: The Consols of the East*, p. v

16   Lever's Pacific Plantations Ltd, NLA mfm PMB 1139

17   Smith, *Handbook* (1909) pp.46–7; K. Buckley & K. Klugman, *The History of Burns Philp*, pp. 21ff

18   A. Riches, *History of J. Kitchen & Sons*, p. 20-5; AR-Papua (1906/07) p. 90; 'Rubber Plantations in Papua' (NAA, Series A606 – 1921/2/26)

19   'Rubber Growing In Papua', Adelaide, *The Register* (1910) 19 Feb. p. 12

20   *Barrier Miner* (1914) Jan. 24; London, *Financial Times* (1914) Feb. 13, 14, and 16

21   'New Rubber Company', *The Queenslander* (1910) 25 Jun., p. 38; 'The Prospectus', *SMH* (1910) 18 Jun., p. 9; *Townsville Daily Bulletin* (1913) 4 Jan. p. 12; *Cairns Post* (1936) 19 Aug. 13

22   ' Papuan Industries', *Melbourne Argus* (1904) 28 Dec., p. 3; 'Meeting of Business Men', *Register* (1905) 1 Nov., p. 9; 'BNG: A Land of Promise', *The Advertiser* (1905) 1 Nov. p. 8

23   *The Advertiser* (1912) 23 May, p. 7; *The Northern Miner* (1913) 22 Apr., p. 8; see Lewis, pp. 80–1

24   *Advertiser* (1910) 22 Aug., p. 7, (1912) 16 Nov., p. 12; *The Register* (1911) 1 May, p. 7

25   'Cultivation of Sisal Hemp', *The Register* (1908) 18 May, p. 5. 'Demand for Asiatic Labor', *Barrier Miner* (1909) 14 Jul. p. 4

26   A. S. Bloomfield, Tropical Agriculture in Papua; see Lewis, pp. 78–105

27   'New Guinea Development.', *The British-Australasian* (1910) 17 Feb. pp 16–17

28   *SMH* (1910) 9 Feb., p. 13 & 29 Mar., p. 11; see Lewis, p. 85

29   BNGD Prospectus, *SMH* (1910) 21 Feb. p. 13

30   *The Globe,* London (1910) 7 Oct. and *Daily Graphic,* London (1910) 17 Oct.

31   BNGD Prospectus

32   *Daily Express* (1911) 22 June.

33   *The Joint Stock Companies Journal* (1910) 19 Oct.

34   *The Financial Times* (1910) 18 Oct.

35   BNGD Prospectus, Glasgow *Evening Citizen* (1910)15 March, *The Westminster Gazette* (1910) 17 Mar.

36   Secretary to BNG Port Moresby, (1910) 8 Apr. (1915) 12 Mar., p. 101 (ANU, deposit 95/1/1)

37   *CPP* 1910, vol. iii, pp. 155–9, Despatch of Administrator of Papua relating to Native Labour

38   D. C. Lewis, 'Labour and Development in Papua, 1912–1922', p. 7 n.6

39   AR-BNGD (1910) p. 2; minutes of meeting, 1911

40   *Manchester Despatch* (1911) 21 June

41   *BC* (1911) 23 Jan., p. 3; *The Bulletin* (1911) 31 Aug.; *SMH* (1911) 8 Aug. p. 11

42   AR-BNGD (1910) p. 2; (1911) pp. 2–3; 'Gloomy View, *Register* (1911) 20 Feb. p. 6

43   'Important Petroleum Discovery in Papua', *The Financial Times* (1912) 4 April

44   'Petroleum in the Empire', *The Daily News* (1912) 5 April

45   'Petroleum in Papua', *Townsville Bulletin (1912)* 23 May, p. 3; 'Papua's Great Wealth',
       How oil was discovered', *Northern Star,* Lismore (1913) 13 Jun. p. 7

46   AR-Papua (1910/11) p. 23. 'Geological report on the 'Petroleum Oil Field, Vailala River'
       (AR-Papua [1911/12] pp. 33-4 & 174-80)

47   AR-BNGD (1912) p. 5; *SMH* (1913) 18 Aug. p. 11.

48   'Petroleum in Papua', *Townsville Bulletin* (1912) 23 May, p. 3. AR-BNGD (1914) p. 4; (1915) p. 21

49   *Murray, Papua of To-Da*y, p. 10

50   General Manager report, 28 Apr. 1914 (AR-BNGD [1914] p. 12)

51   AR-BNGD (1914) p. 14

52   Chart 31.

53   AR-BNGD (1914) p. 15; (1915) p. 21

54   AR-BNGD (1918) pp. 14–15

55   AR-BNGD (1917) pp. 4, 8, 15 & 16; (1918) pp.3, 4 & 14–15; (1919) pp. 2, 6 & 11

56   AR-BNGD (1914) p. 16; (1915) p. 17 and (1920) p. 9

57   AR-BNGD (1914) pp. 4 & 21

58   *SMH* (1910) 9 Feb., p. 13, 21 Feb., p. 13; *The Argus,* Melbourne (1910) 18 Feb. p. 7

59   AR-BNGD (1911 & 1912); *The British-Australasian,* 19 Dec. 1912; *Statistic,* 21 Dec. 1912

60   AR-Papua (1920/21) pp. 7-8 & 19, (1921/22) pp. 5–6. Murray, *Papua of To-Day,* pp. 142–3

61   AR-BNGD (1925–1940) *The Financial Times and Investor's Chronicle* (1911–39)

62   *The West Australian* (1911) 22 Feb. p. 6

63   Lewis, pp. 305–09

64   Champion to Murray, 10 Feb. 1919(NAA Series M2096–CA 1413 & A1–CA15)

65   AR-Papua (1915) p. 15; (1916) pp. 17 & 21; (1917) pp. 4 & 15; (1918) p. 3; Lewis, p. 230

66   F. West, *Selected Letter of Hubert Murray*, p. 80 & Murray, *Papua of To-Day,* pp. viii–ix.

67   R. Belfort & A. J. Hoyer, *All About Coconuts*, p. 45

Disastrous Ventures

Samarai, ca. 1905 (plates by Louis Budérus, collection John Oxley Library, Brisbane)

SIMILARITIES AND DIFFERENCES IN TWO NEIGHBOURING COLONIES

17

The two colonies in East New Guinea were remarkable for their similarities rather than their differences. A close study demonstrates that GNG's laws did not differ greatly from those in BNG and Papua, and that the conduct of individuals was, on balance, as good or as bad in both colonies. All of the salient differences between the two colonies had their base in commercial realities, not in the moral or the strategic intents of their founders. Commercial success, or the lack of it, was the key factor in the European development of East New Guinea.

Until the last quarter of the 19th century neither Germany nor Britain had expressed any real interest in colonising East New Guinea. However, following the last big wave of colonisation Chancellor Otto von Bismarck determined in 1884 that Germany should annex northeast New Guinea, but only if the cost of establishment was borne by private enterprise. This position had a remarkable parallel in Britain when Prime Minister William Gladstone agreed—also in 1884—to place southeast New Guinea under British protection with the proviso that the Australian colonies pay for the cost of administration.

GNG and BNG were established in response to German and British commercial ambitions in the Pacific. With prospects of large gold discoveries in East New Guinea, the two metropolitan countries expected that commercial interests would develop and fund the colonies, minimising the cost to government both financially and with respect to military deployments. While GNG's economic development differed from BNG's, both colonial administrations depended on a co-operative indigenous workforce and in both colonies the employment and productivity of local labour became a crucial issue. Both administrations regarded military intervention as an ineffective and undesirable way to pacify the indigenous people. Both tried to minimise expenditures and to stimulate exports. By 1914 the differences between the two colonies were largely due to the different commercial strategies and practices that had been developed.

German New Guinea

The commercial imperatives in GNG were clear from the start. Under the terms of the Imperial Charter of 17 May 1885 The Neu Guinea Compagnie (NGC) was granted the exclusive possession of 'ownerless land' and could acquire any land that the New Guineans were prepared to sell. Berlin permitted NGC to exploit the natural resources of the territory. The company was to exercise the sovereign authority vested in the Emperor, except in foreign relations and the administration of justice. In return the company was obliged to pay for the administration, explore the territory for its economic resources and potential, experiment with the economic exploitation of plants and create an economic environment for the benefit of all Europeans (and Japanese) living in The Protectorate of the New Guinea Company. The pacification of the New Guineans was to be left to the missions. NGC was obliged to protect the 'natives' without being instructed by the government what this actually entailed. Teaching the local people to work and to acquire European goods was seen as the main aim of their cultural advancement, this was to be achieved mostly while in employment with NGC.

NGC expected to defray the cost of governing by raising taxes and customs duties, fees and fines. Primarily established as a vehicle to raise funds and to colonise the country, Hansemann used NGC to requisition land for settlers. The company also aspired to become a miner of precious metals and coal. The revenue base was expected to grow as an increasing number of settlers arrived in response to NGC establishing infrastructure for agricultural development. But the settlers did not arrive. Malaria and dysentery decimated NGC's staff and workforce, and the inland region proved too difficult to explore and develop. As a result NGC switched from land promoter and explorer to plantation owner and operator

NGC experimented with cacao and coffee, invested in cotton, and embarked on large scale tobacco planting. After 10 years of failed crops the company switched exclusively to coconut and rubber. The cost of planting cotton and tobacco had reached unsustainable levels, both in human suffering and financial terms.

NGC had begun the cultivation of tobacco with optimism and determination, only to experience high labour mortality, labour shortages, a lack of expertise, a shortage of shipping capacity and harvest failures partly due to pests and inclement weather. NGC invested in cotton gins and tobacco curing barns only to find that at best every second harvest was moderately successful. High losses of European lives led to the abandonment of NGC's administration centre, Finschhafen, in 1892 and five years later the plantation establishments on the Astrolabe and Yomba Plains were also discarded. Keenly aware that shipping was central to establishing a colonial footprint in GNG, Hansemann was unwavering in ordering new vessels following the frequent losses of his ships on the reefs of the Bismarck Archipelago. Tobacco and cotton were never profitable for NGC. By 1902 the company had consumed all the cash injected by shareholders and lenders (RM10,000,000 [£500,000]) none of which was covered by operational cash-flow or the value of assets.

Negotiations by NGC in 1895 for the transfer of local sovereignty concluded with the signing of a settlement agreement in 1898. The Reich paid NGC RM4,000,000 (£200,000) in ten equal yearly instalments, and granted the company 50,000 ha and the exclusive exploration and mining rights in the Ramu Valley in recognition for colonising The Protectorate of the New Guinea Company until 1899. With the transfer of a few NGC buildings, inventory and harbour installations to the Reich, government administration began in German New Guinea (GNG) on 1 April 1899.

At that time NGC had RM8,212,100 (£410,605) of non-performing assets on its books. While this expenditure was largely the consequence of poor business decisions, it was akin to a subsidy payment for GNG. Seen in this way NGC's contribution towards the development of GNG until 1899 was considerably higher than the £223,822 in expenditure incurred by BNG in the decade from 1888–1898.[1]

In its first decade of operation NGC dissipated its shareholders' capital. The value that was eventually created by 1911/12 through the successful copra plantations on the KWL coast and in the Bismarck Archipelago required a government subsidy of RM4,000,000 and further substantial injections of shareholder funds for NGC to become profitable.

British New Guinea and Papua

Delegates at the 1883 Intercolonial Convention in Sydney urged the immediate incorporation of non-Dutch New Guinea into the British Empire on the grounds that the 'acquisition of territory south of the equator by any foreign power would be highly detrimental to the safety and well-being of Australia'.[2] The delegates left it open as to who posed a threat to Australia, and whether it was military or economic. If Germany, France, Holland, Spain, Japan, Russia or even the United States of America were identified as the countries that could threaten the safety of Australia, no consideration was given to those countries' military capabilities or political situations. Germany had only a small ocean-going navy in 1883 and France had offered Germany her Southeast Asian colonies in settlement for the 1870/71 war reparations. Holland was occupied with the ongoing development of her Southeast Asian colonial possessions while giving practically no attention to West New Guinea. Spain was an empire in decline; the United States was an ally of Great Britain, and was soon to be joined by Japan. This left Russia, which some Australians feared planned to invade Australia. Russo-phobia started with the Crimean War (1854–56) in which some colonial Australians fought. The Australian colonies started building coastal fortresses after Britain actively supported Turkey in her war with Russia in 1878. Fortification was intensified in Australian cities and townships when British and Russian colonial interests clashed in the north of Afghanistan in 1885, and when New South Wales Governor Henry Lock accused Russia of cutting an underwater telegraph cable connecting Australia with England via East Asia in 1888. There was, however, no significant political discussion or debate relating to the potential Russian occupation of East New Guinea as a staging post for invading Australia.

Adolph von Hansemann's interest in northeast New Guinea led him to inform Bismarck in 1880 that the territory could provide better access to an emerging market – Australia. If the Australians knew about Hansemann's memorandum they would have regarded it a threat to their agricultural industries, Queensland's sugar cane in particular. Clearly, the Australian colonies' first interest in New Guinea was to protect their own agricultural base at home. It was not in the interests of Queensland growers to see a new colony of cheap labour and land spring up on their doorstep. Attaining political control over the region could help prevent this.

Disastrous Ventures

There was also no incentive for a newly federated Australia in 1901 to actively engage in the creation of a strong economy in Papua. Subsidies for Papua declined as a percentage of government budgets after 1906, while from 1910 import duty receipts exceeded subsidies. This transfer increased the cost on business and held back the development of Australia's first and only colony.

Foreign labour was fundamental to the economies of the British and Dutch colonies in Southeast Asia, and in Fiji, Samoa and German Nauru. It could also have contributed to the development of Papua. However, the relatively small requirements by Australia for imported tropical goods were largely brought in from the low-cost producers of the South Sea Islands, including GNG and Southeast Asia, not BNG or Papua. The colony did not develop an economy of scale that would allow it to compete with north Queensland let alone in the international market place. By not producing significant quantities for a rising copra and rubber market by 1902, Papua missed a once-in-a-lifetime commercial opportunity.

Queensland Premier Thomas McIlwraith told the Royal Colonial Institute in 1894 that he had not insisted on the annexation of East New Guinea in 1883 because of the desire for 'more land or to get natives to work on the sugar plantations of Queensland'. Rather, he claimed that the desire to annex New Guinea 'arose simply for the purpose of preventing undesirable neighbours from coming near them'.[3] This statement by McIlwraith comes closest to explaining why the Australian colonies insisted on the annexation of southeast New Guinea. While the Australian and British governments were relieved at the outbreak of World War I that Papua was in Australian hands, this was not the result of McIlwraith's foresight in 1883: his thinking was not so much strategic as protectionist. When Melanesian labour was no longer available to Queensland's farmers, he aimed to protect his constituencies from low-cost producers on their doorstep in the already competitive sugar export market. This was best accomplished by annexing the southern part of New Guinea and restraining investments in agriculture there.

The European population of BNG in 1888/89 reached 735, nearly all prospectors. It declined to 97 in 1894 when the first gold rush had finished. It took until 1909/10 to again rise above that number (879 Europeans) and then to reach 1,219 people in 1913. The Papuan workforce in BNG climbed quickly to approximately 1,200 men in 1889/90, declining with the exhaustion of the first gold fields to 90 in 1894/95. When Australia assumed full responsibility for Papua (1906) employment stood at 4,180 workers, rising to 7,681 by June 1914, plus 3,702 casual and 2,391 prison labour.

While the European population in GNG was lower than that of its southern neighbour – rising from 122 people in 1886 to 1,130 in 1913 – the number of indentured Papuan and Melanesian workers in GNG was greater than at any time in BNG or in Papua, rising in 1886/87 from 351 to 17,529 workers in 1913.

A mix of a low population base, an uneducated workforce, and the absence of risk capital meant massive government funding was required for substantial development in BNG and Papua. Aggregate government revenue in the British/Australian colony from 1888–1914 amounted to £512,787, an average of £19,723 over 26 years.

Nearly 75% of the receipts were derived from import duty (£379,683), with land sales (£24,164), postal income (£21,904) and mining permits (£17,115) contributing only small amounts of revenue. No-one, including the Papuans, paid personal, business or land tax. By not implementing a poll tax, as suggested by the 1907 Royal Commission, Papua's tax system stood out from other colonies.

The total government subsidies by Britain and Australia for 1888–1914 amounted to £556,794, an average of £21,415 each year. Several Australian colonies and the Australian federal government from 1901 contributed £448,098 of this sum in annual subsidies and £36,634 in infrastructure grants and loans. The British government paid for the steamer *Merrie England* and contributed towards the vessel's operational costs of £72,062. Government subsidies for the 26-year period accounted for 48% of the total funds available to the Port Moresby administration. Shipping subsidies paid to Burns, Philp, survey work and other assistance provided by government officials, were not included in the annual government appropriations for BNG or Papua.

GNG Government activities

Bismarck recognised in Hansemann and Bleichröder two bankers who had the wealth and the determination to stay the distance before the Reich assumed administrative control of GNG. Without such industry leaders he would not have agreed to the colonisation of northeast New Guinea. To minimise expenditures NGC governed its Protectorate from 1885 to March 1899 with only eight full-time staff and a constabulary of 36 part-time local policemen. Company employees lent additional administrative assistance. Clearly, Hansemann's complaint that NGC spent too much time and money running GNG was not justified. Even though revenue raised by NGC

Government revenue, expenditure, subsidies and grants (£1=RM20)

Revenue (£)	1887–1899		1899–1914	
	GNG	BNG	GNG	BNG-Papua
Taxes	4,036	0	117,399	0
Customs duty	16,919	60,231	331,850	319,452
Miscellaneous	6,149	7,718	203,377	125,386
Total	**27,104**	**67,949**	**652,626**	**444,838**
Expenditure				
NGC payments	0	0	200,000	0
Administration	20,675	270,785	964,493	790,007
Capital	727,923	25,938	249,053	122,024
Total	**748,598**	**296,723**	**1,413,546**	**912,031**
Government and NGC subsidies	410,605	145,997	798,798	302,101
Extra Funding	0	7,537	38,143	29,097
Shipping subsidies	0	70,288	n.d	1,774
Total	**410,605**	**223,822**	**836,941**	**332,972**

from taxes, customs duty, fines and licence fees did not cover all administration cost for the 1889 to 1899 period. However, NGC and government outlays in GNG was a fraction of the money MacGregor expended over the same period on BNG.

Hansemann's request to have the NGC Protectorate administered with government officials from May 1889 so that management could devote its attention exclusively to commercial activities did not achieve the expected benefit for NGC. Rather, it added to the company's financial woes because the officers chosen by the government – for which NGC had to pay – were determined to establish government rather than NGC policies. When NGC reverted to govern the Protectorate with its own staff in September 1892, expenses declined but so did government services.

A considerably larger cost to NGC was the establishment and maintenance of government buildings, ports and other infrastructure. Until Berlin agreed to subsidise a shipping service between Sydney and Singapore via Samoa and GNG in 1893, maritime activities cost NGC at least RM250,000 (£12,500) annually. By comparison, the 25,000,000 Pesetas (£862,500) the Reich paid Spain in 1899 for her Caroline Islands was more than four-times the amount the government paid NGC for establishing GNG. However, in contrast to GNG, the Carolines together with Nauru and the Marshall Islands (The Island Territory) became self-sufficient based on strong guano and copra exports. Hence part of GNG required no subsidies after 30 June 1909. This benefited GNG when Albert Hahl rationalised the German Pacific possessions (excluding West Samoa) into a centralised administration in Rabaul.

Labour and racial issues

In both colonies severe outbreaks of influenza and dysentery, combined with the ever-present malaria, brought work on the plantations to a standstill for weeks on end. The introduction of Chinese coolies to NGC's tobacco plantations in 1891, and their susceptibility to beriberi due to an unbalanced rice diet, made an already catastrophic situation worse. Since the Dutch would not employ coolies infected with malaria on their Southeast Asian tobacco plantations, NGC was probably correct in claiming that it ended up with many of these unwanted coolies.

A switch to the recruitment of coolies from the Straits Settlements and China did not reduce the mortality among the Chinese either, and the Germans found it difficult to keep track of the thousands of workers dying on its plantations. Annual mortality rates in GNG of 15% among the Papuan and Melanesian workers and up to 60% among the coolies on the Astrolabe Bay tobacco fields during the 1890s may be a conservative estimate. Stewart Firth described the death rate in GNG as being on a scale never experienced in Queensland, Fiji or Samoa. Hank Nelson, however, estimated the annual mortality rate among the European prospectors and their indentured labourers in BNG during the late 1880s and through the 1890s at 30%, increasing to 40% at Lakekamu in 1909/10.[4]

Neither colonial administration knew the actual number of deceased other than to agree that it was unacceptably high. What was known was the effect that high rates of mortality and morbidity had on the profitability of the enterprises, and given the scale of death and sickness NGC experienced among its staff and workforce, the company's survival is surprising.

When Hahl accepted Japanese immigrants to GNG as culturally equal to Europeans, his administration could have gone the next step and also accept indentured Chinese and Javanese workers. Hahl did not follow this path partly for racial concerns and, given the possibility of mass Asian immigration, he was concerned as to his ability to retain effective social control over GNG. In this the German did not differ from the Australian government. Both Britain and Australia had banned Asian labour – particularly Chinese coolies – for fear of losing Managerial control in Papua, and because of a likely Chinese diaspora from Papua to mainland Australia.

Murray left the education of indigenous children to Christian missionaries. Hahl built government schools and set up trade schools to train Papuans in administration, woodwork, farming and other skills. Official health care was absent in BNG until the first surgeon arrived in 1895. The first hospital in Port Moresby was completed in 1905, not by the government, but through private initiatives and funding. Compared to their neighbour the Germans had spent sizeable funds on the GNG health system.

The 1908 land boom in Papua did not translate into the expected agricultural development, and the British New Guinea Development Company Ltd (BNGD) found it difficult to grow cash crops profitably. When government sponsored gold, coal and oil explorations remained unsuccessful, the wellbeing of the Papuan people again became Port Moresby's main focus. Murray opportunistically agreed with the British liberal – not the Australian – popular view that England had adopted the policy of holding her colonies in trust for the benefit of the indigenous people, not for the benefit of the European settlers as the plantation and mine owners demanded.

Germany stumbled into colonial conquest in 1884 without a strong legal framework in place for her new possessions; the labour ordinances proclaimed in GNG generally followed the British experience, based on similar Christian ethics.[5] However, neither Hansemann nor Hahl had plans of developing and maintaining a Protectorate primarily for the New Guineans. The German planters, like the Rabaul government, regarded the indigenous population as an important labour resource that was to be managed for productivity rather than for any humanitarian objective.

Lillian Overell observed this German assertiveness when she reported on the German policy regarding the natives, which 'was severe, and in the early day cruel floggings were common'. Stewart Firth agreed with this view, stating that although the Germans 'laid down more plantations, built more roads and bridges, provided better shipping, lived in more imposing official residences and at Rabaul constructed a capital with amenities far superior to those offered by Port Moresby'; he also pointed out that such development was not worth the price of mass mortality, floggings and summary executions that the indentured labourers in GNG paid.[6]

In the post-colonial history debate much is made of Hahl permitting the use of the cane. Murray regarded the practice as indefensible and preferred incarceration and prison labour to corporal punishment. But there is scant information on the treatment of prison labour in either colony. As for labour relations, like in any other colony they were largely the responsibility of individual Managers. Some Europeans were callous and cruel. But a sensible employer cared for his workers as much in GNG as he did in Papua. This was not solely a reflection of decency. It was common sense because equitable and humane treatment of labour and staff increased efficiency.

When Overell wrote about her visit to Samarai, 'the drinking hell of the Pacific' where an employer 'flogged a boy so brutally that he died two days afterwards', she believed that the law would have dealt with the (European) culprit appropriately. Flogging and other cruelties occurred in the German, British and Australian Protectorates of New Guinea as in colonies elsewhere notwithstanding that it was even then considered cruel and questionable behaviour.[7]

Long-term Governors of both colonies, Hahl and MacGregor were intrepid explorers, MacGregor in particular. Both had a genuine concern for the many diverse tribal peoples of East New Guinea, but they also invoked the laws of their governments sternly and used force to suppress resistance. They ordered the local people to plant coconut palms, and build and maintain roads, and both used prisoners as corvée labour. From the beginning, Hahl had no doubts that the aim of German colonisation was to open the country to European planters, miners and traders. 'I see the value of the archipelago', he wrote in 1896, 'above all in its resources – copra, ivory nut, trepang, turtle shell – which make it possible to exploit the region by way of trading before plantation undertaking are established'.[8] MacGregor held the British government's belief in protecting the indigenous population with his intentions to hold at bay unscrupulous European merchants, miners and planters. In his language, protection of the indigenous people was coextensive with pacification. Only when MacGregor considered the people 'pacified' and he was running out of funds did he turn his attention to commercial development of BNG.[9]

Better schools and hospitals did not necessarily make the Germans better colonisers; however, better public institutions deliver better economic outcomes. Murray, fluent in German and in occasional contact with Hahl, knew of the better government installations in GNG even before Australian troops occupied the German territory.

The comparative economies of GNG and BNG/Papua New Guinea

Greater commercial urgency determined a much larger GNG economy compared to BNG/Papua. For the period 1887 to 1913 total trade expressed in Pound Sterling was £5,350,802 in GNG, 68% larger than in BNG/Papua (£3,662,889). A similar ratio is evident in the import and export statistics (GNG imports £3,010,149–BNG/Papua £2,105,356; GNG exports £2,340,653–BNG/Papua £1,557,533).[10] A sharp difference between the GNG and Papuan export figures emerged with the maturing of the coconut plantations laid down – mainly by NGC – from 1900 onwards. In 1913 export of plantation copra from GNG amounted to £308,684, accounting for 76.7% of total exports for that year. This stood in stark contrast to £98,241 or 76% for the three highest commodities (gold £62,332, copper £18,997 and copra £16,912) exported from BNG/Papua in 1912/1913.

Arguably GNG should have delivered better economic results. The Bismarck Archipelago provided a distinct advantage over mainland East New Guinea. The climate was preferred by the European planters and administrators, and its volcanic soil was helpful for a productive plantation industry. While NGC replaced tobacco on Astrolabe Bay with palms and rubber after 1898, the hinterland of KWL remained largely unexplored by 1914 and the considerable labour resources – particularly in the Ramu and Sepik River Valleys – had not been exploited.

The Port Moresby administrations, from MacGregor to Murray, believed southeast New Guinea was a commercially viable proposition based on gold prospecting. Australia believed that Papuan gold would attract the similar numbers of people and economic benefits that were generated by the Victorian, Queensland and Western Australian rushes. While Wilhelm II had hoped that New Guinea gold would underpin the gold standard of the *Reichsmark*, the aspiration of the Australian government was not so ambitious. It hoped on sufficient gold to be extracted in Papua to make the colony financially independent.[11]

The discovery of high-grade copper ore (20–40%) in late 1906 on the Astrolabe Range, southeast of Port Moresby, raised expectations that it would be copper rather than gold that would generate the economic activity required to make Papua self-sufficient.[12] For this to materialise a railroad had to be constructed from Rona village to Port Moresby. However, neither the government nor the leaseholders were willing to make this investment, resulting in just 3,884 tons of copper ore taken to Port Moresby – all on pack mule – between 1907 and 1914.[13]

Only when no new gold was discovered and copper ore proved too expensive to export did Melbourne and Port Moresby take agriculture seriously. But the anticipated mainstay of the Papuan agricultural economy, BNGD, made the same mistakes as NGC some 18 years earlier. The company's staples of tobacco, cotton and sugar were either unprofitable or, in the case of sugar, not proceeded with. Imported Para rubber seeds had also proven unsuccessful, and the company's considerable coconut plantations were not productive during the boom years before the war.

Murray expressed a reluctance to compare the economic performance of Papua with that of GNG. 'Comparisons are proverbially odious and often misleading', he wrote in 1925. Yet it suited him to mention that Papua was catching up to GNG economically because by 1910 he believed Papua's agricultural development matched GNG's achievements in this area.[14] To make his point Murray took the liberty of comparing plantation land area without disclosing the full picture. The Port Moresby government had alienated – to a lesser extent purchased from the local people – 410,275 ha by June 1910. This compared to only 147,506 ha acquired by GNG by December 1909. However, planters in Papua had at that time only cultivated just over 4,000 ha with cash crops, coconut palms and rubber trees compared to a cultivated area of 23,810 ha in GNG. By June 1914 the planted area in Papua had increased to 17,379 ha, in GNG it had increased to 34,190 ha by December 1913. More troubling for the Port Moresby administration, by 1914 hardly any Papuan plantation contributed to export earnings. Apart from BNGD, agricultural investors and settlers had turned their backs on the Australian Protectorate, with one-third of the leases forfeited by 1914.

Disastrous Ventures

World War I ends a period

The outbreak of the Great War in August 1914 ended the German enterprises in GNG. By then NGC had set its investment strategy on a profitable growth path. It was better established and more profitable in 1914 than any other enterprise in East New Guinea. For Papua the economic pain continued. Its plantations did not come into full production until the early 1920s. Then the market in tropical produce had collapsed followed by the onset of the world economic crisis in 1928.

What had become obvious by 1914 was confirmed by Murray in 1925: gold mining in New Guinea was, on balance, a failure. Murray and Smith had staked Papua's economic future on extensive exploration and on dredging the northern rivers for alluvial deposits, and on increased revenue from the copper ore in the Astrolabe Range. However, between 1914 and 1921 only an estimated £232,845 worth of gold was taken out of Papua. The Misima mine, Murray hoped, 'was to prove the herald of a new era of gold-mining activity on a larger scale than ever known before'. But it was, he conceded years, later, 'the final flicker, before extinction'. Thus, the ephemeral successes of gold mining in Papua attracted a degree of attention that was disproportionate to the labour and pains invested.[15]

Looking at former GNG (a mandate was conferred by the League of Nations in 1921 upon Australia via Great Britain), Murray made out that East New Guinea under Australia's administration could be of great importance to Australia: 'It is probable that in time they may supply practically all the tropical requirements of the Commonwealth', he wrote in 1925.[16] Notwithstanding this bold forecast, unlike Papua, the development of the plantation industry in GNG accelerated during the war. By then the German coconut plantations were highly productive, and with the military administration preventing German nationals from repatriating profits, the available funds were reinvested in plantations and used to establish new ones in what was still thought of as GNG.

Colonel William Holmes, commander of the Australian Naval and Military Expeditionary Force, understood the German economic achievements. With similar numbers of Europeans in both colonies, the GNG economy employed two-and-a-half times as many indentured workers, producing nine times more copra and, despite Papua's gold production, one-third more in export earnings. Holmes advised his government that the German territories should be kept as valuable possessions. Prime Minister Hughes agreed. But neither Papua nor the Mandated Territory ever became the tropical food bowl. Australian interests were set on preventing an over-supply of tropical goods, and the trade unions were keen not to compete with low-cost Papuan, Melanesian or indeed Chinese labour from former GNG. Thus Murray declared

> I am one of those persons who put 'Australia' first and I should never seek any advantage to Papua which would be injurious to the Commonwealth. I quite understand and quite agree that the coloured labour of Papua should not be allowed to compete with the white labour of Australia, but where an industry obviously does not pay with white labour ... and where [there is] no Australian industry to protect ... I cannot see why Papuan coffee should not be admitted duty free ... The economic progress of the natives of Papua can be no disadvantage to Australia, for the tariff can always be used to prevent competition.[17]

Towards the end of German colonial rule Europeans, Japanese and the Chinese who remained there, enjoyed a comfortable life on the coast of KWL and more so in the Bismarck Archipelago. Lillian Overell described this lifestyle:

> Rabaul is a beautiful little town built on low-lying land with the steep ridge of hills for a background. The well-laid-out streets are lined with rows of trees … The wooden bungalows, standing on high piles, usually have only two or three rooms, but these are large and airy with many windows and doors. They are surrounded by wide verandas, opening here and there into spacious porches which are furnished as sitting-rooms … Behind the town the road winds up to Namanula where Government House, the hospital and various officials' residences stand on the saddle that overlooks Simpsonhafen on one side, and the open sea on the other. Near the wharf are the big stores of the New Guinea Company … Life in the Bismarck Archipelago under the German regime was a delightful thing. The planters had beautiful homes, cheap black labour, every encouragement from the Government, good roads, telephones, and a sanatorium in the hills … a regular shipping service, ice, fresh milk and meat.[18]

By then, both, Port Moresby and Samarai, and the plantation establishments also provided a measure of European comfort and liveability. However, the quality and quantity of streets and roads, sewer and water reticulation, electricity and telephone services were still basic and far behind those established in GNG.

Clearly, the foremost motivation for both the Australian Eastern Colonies and for Germany was to occupy East New Guinea for commercial objectives. Imperial ambitions and strategic posturing were not the motivations of the metropolitan governments in London and Berlin. 'Has it all been worthwhile,' asks Margrit Davies in her book on public health in German New Guinea.[19] Significant investments in medical research and health care, including the establishment of hospitals in all major centres of GNG provided health services for all, including the local people if and when they took up the opportunity. Germany and the international community enjoyed lasting benefits from the field-work Robert Koch conducted in GNG and in Africa. The Berlin Royal Prussian Institute for Infectious Diseases, established by Professor Koch, and the Hamburg Institute for Maritime and Tropical Diseases, established by Dr Bernhard Nocht in 1900, were recipients of lasting legacies.

Notwithstanding these achievements, and while many companies and settlers in GNG had chalked up commercial successes by the outbreak of World War I, they were attained with huge costs in lives and money to both the settlers and the local population. On 1 April 1899, according to Hermann Hiery, The Protectorate of the New Guinea Company was economically bankrupt, politically unsuccessful and morally incriminated. That NGC transferred colonial administration to the Reich on 1 April 1899 in a complete mess (*Scherbenhaufen*) is a proposition shared by Stewart Firth.[20] However, by June 1914 NGC had grown into a significant plantation company. From its New Guinea venture it generated income of RM 3,364 million and net profit of RM722,059. The revenue for 1913/14 equated the entire GNG government budget (RM3,834 million) for the same financial year.

Albert Hahl left GNG on extended leave in April 1914. Travelling with him to Germany were two Melanesians who had enrolled in the *Kolonialschule* (Colonial School) in Witzenhausen, northeast Hesse. Hahl believed the future administration of GNG should largely be conducted by New Guineans, and that these two young men would encourage others to make the long voyage to Germany and learn about German government administration and financial accounting. Hahl did not know that the looming War would change German polity totally, and that he would never return to New Guinea that reflected nearly 20 years of his work.

Albert Hahl left behind a German colony that was confident in its future. On indigenous and social issues Hahl was at one with Murray. William H. Cox of the Methodist Missionary Society of Australia in the Bismarck Archipelago wrote to the German Governor on his 13th of April 1914 departure day:

> Your Excellency's firm and invariable usage to resist all encroachments on the liberty of the subject, even though a coloured subject, and all attempts to unduly interfere with the rights of person and property of the natives has been a matter of genuine satisfaction to our Society. The united force of the European settlers has only too often been in an opposite direction, and we desire to congratulate Your Excellency on the consistency with which you have fought the cause of the native against the claims of those whose one admitted aim is to 'make money', as well as the measure of success which Your Excellency has achieved. [W]e cannot but recognise that the views of Your Excellency are liberal views, and beyond any doubt sincere and single in the intention to benefit the native people.[21]

The miners, planters and workers in Papua did not enjoy the same improvement in health-care that was prevalent in GNG. When Australia assumed full responsibility for the Territory of Papua in 1906 the federal government had few ideas on how to deliver medical services in her new colony. Australia still lacked the framework for its national health policy nine years after federation, and it was not until 1910 that Britain assisted Australia by providing the first specialist in tropical medicine for Papua.[22]

By 1914 Papua remained wedged between the interests of metropolitan capital, the white settlers' needs and a dithering administration in Port Moresby. MacGregor and Murray were ambivalent about striking a balance between the wants of the colonisers and the interests of the indigenous Papuan people. The tropical farmers of Queensland harboured little interest in seeing Papua develop a successful plantation industry. If gold production in Papua had matched that from the earlier discoveries in Australia, Papua would have received the political and financial attention required to develop the country economically. While this would hardly have benefited the larger Papuan population, the lack of material success also left the European settlers and companies empty-handed. It was a trend that continued until Australia combined former GNG and Papua into the Territory of Papua New Guinea post 1945.

Papua New Guinea was built on the faulty foundations laid down during the first 30 years of colonial development, and further weakened by two world wars and the great depression. The independent state of Papua New Guinea found very little in its colonial past on which it could build a traditional society but also a modern economy.

Notes

1   The quality of the capital investments made with the respective subsidies is set aside in this argument.

2   NSW V&P, vol. 9

3   W. MacGregor, 'British New Guinea', Proceedings of the Royal Colonial Institute, vol. xxvi, (1894–95)

4   S. G. Firth, *New Guinea under the Germans*, p. 35; H. N. Nelson, *Black, White & Gold*, pp. 69, 118 & 197, chart 10

5   P. G. Sack, *Phantom History: The Rule of Law and the Colonial State*, p. 52

6   Firth, 'German Recruitment and Employment of Labourers in the Western Pacific before the First World War', p. 314; Firth, *New Guinea under the Germans*, p. 174

7   L. Overell, *A Woman's Impression of German New Guinea.*

8   Hahl to AA-KA, 25 Aug. 1896 (RKA 1001:2985, p. 141)

9   W. MacGregor, *The British in New Guinea*

10   The trade figure does not account for the three steamships NGC acquired between 1884 and 1887. The Papuan accounts finished on 30 June 1914, while the GNG figure is taken up to 31 Dec. 1913 (Table 11 & 13 annex). Trade data for The Island Territory see charts 24, 25, 26, 27 &28

11   See Gold prospecting in GNG, chapter 8

12   S. Smith, 'Astrolabe Copper Field', report 17 July 1907, pp. 1–3 (AR-Papua [1906/07])

13   AR-Papua (1913/14) p. 158

14   J.H.P. Murray, *Papua of To-Day*, p. 141–47

15   ibid.

16   ibid., p. 294–5

17   ibid., p. 240

18   L. Overell, *A Woman's Impression of German New Guinea*, pp. 7–8 & 29.

19   M. Davies (*Public Health and Colonialism*, pp.175ff) borrowed the line from Dr R. Black's assessment of the achievements of western medicine in Papua and New Guinea, *PNGMed.J*, vol. 9, No. 3, 1966.

20   Hiery, *Die Deutsche Südsee*, p. 299; Firth, 'The New Guinea Company 1885–1899: A Case of Unprofitable Imperialism'.

21   (RKA 1001:2568), quoted in Hiery, p. 309

22   D. Denoon, K. Dugan, & A.J. Marshall, *Public Health in Papua New Guinea: Medical Possibility and Social Constraint, 1884–1984*

BIBLIOGRAPHY

A. Manuscript Sources and Government Publications:

Australian National University Archives, Canberra (ANU):
British New Guinea Development Co.: deposit 95/1/1: Gov. letters to the General Manager in Port Moresby, 8 Apr. 1910–12 Mar 1915; deposit 95/2/1: specimens of printed matters and circulars, 1910–48; deposit 95/3/1: newspaper cuttings, 1910–1940, mfm 37: a) prospectus, b) Memorandum of Articles of Association (1922) c) Directors' reports and annual accounts, 1914–18, newspaper cuttings from the *Financial Times* and *Investor's Chronicle* (1911–39).

Blohm & Voss Archive, Hamburg

Bundesarchiv Berlin-Lichterfelde (BAL):
Debatte im Reichstag Zwecks Übernahme der Deutsch Neu Guinea Compagnie', *German Reichstag, Deutsche Kolonialgesetzgebung. Sammlung der auf die Deutschen Schutzgebiete Bezüglichen Gesetze, Verordnungen, Erlasse und Internationale Vereinbarungen* (1901–05).

Kaiserliche Gouvernement von Deutsch-Neu Guinea', *Geltende Verordnungen für Deutsch-Neu-Guinea (Bismarck-Archipel, Deutsche Salomon-Inseln und Kaiser-Wilhelmsland)* (1903).

Reichsamt für Statistik, Die Deutschen Schutzgebiete, *Statistisches Jahrbuch* (1894) pp. 195-99 (1895) pp. 200-04 (1896) pp. 195-200 (1897) pp. 202-05 (, 1898) pp. 204-08 (1899) pp. 215-19 (1900) pp. 226-31 (1910) p. 396.

Statistisches Jahrbuch für das Deutsche Reich: Die Deutschen Schutzgebiete vol. xviii (1894–1915)

Reichs-Kolonialamt, Koloniale Abteilung:
Allgemeine Bestimmungen über die Stellung der Beamten im Schutzgebiet der NGC (1885–1901),
Allgemeine Bestimmungen für im Dienste der Neu Guinea Compagnie stehende Handwerker und ihren gleichgestellten Personen (1885–1901) RKA 1001:2410.

Allgemeine Statistik des Weltmarkts (1915) RKA 1001:7519.

Allgemeine Verhältnisse – Marshall Inseln (1885–1915) RKA 1001:3071–3175.

Arbeiteranwerbung Javanischer Arbeiter (1909 –1914) RKA 1001:2341–42.

Arbeiteranwerbung, Staatsvertrag mit China (1909–1914) RKA 1001:2338–40.

Arbeiterfragen (1884–1914) RKA 1001:2286–2313.

Arbeiterfürsorge in Deutsch Neu Guinea – Bericht von Dr. Wick (1903–13) RKA 1001:5773.

Astrolabe Compagnie (1891–97) RKA 1001:2427–29.

Astrolabe und NGC, Geschäftsreglement (1896–1897) RKA 1001:2422.

Beamte des Schutzgebietes (1885–1918) RKA 1001:2408–16.

Bergbau Deutsch Neuguinea (1890–1915) RKA 1001:2347–50.

Bismarck-Archipel-Gesellschaft (1907–1928) RKA 1001:2438.

Burns, Philp & Co. Ltd. (1908) RKA 1001:2442.

Denkschriften – Deutsch New Guinea, Karolinen, Marshall Inseln (1907–09) RKA 1001:6544–45.

Der Krieg in Neu Guinea (1914) RKA 1001:2612.

Deutsche Südsee-Phosphat A.G, Jahresberichte (1906–15) RKA 1001:2459–65.

Deutschlands Einfuhr an Landwirtschaftlichen Stoffen (1910–1927) RKA 1001:7520.

Deutsche Südsee-Phosphat-Gesellschaft (1906–1915) RKA 1001:2459–65.

Die deutschen Schutzgebiete in Afrika und der Südsee: Amtliche Jahresberichte (1898–1914)

E.E. Forsayth GmbH (1910–12) RKA 1001:2313.

Gewinnung von Gold in Neu Guinea (1906–1940) RKA 1001:2357–58

Geschäftsbericht der Neu Guinea Compagnie Direktion (1887–1914) RKA 1001:2419–20.

Gesundheitsverhältnisse in Neu Guinea (1896–1913) R1001:80539.

Gouvernmentsrat (1900–1914) RKA 1001:3103–4.

Grundsätze für die Niederlassungen von Missionaren (1886) RKA 1001:2409.

Handelsregister Deutsch Neu-Guinea (1899–1914) RKA 1001:5028.

Disastrous Ventures

Handelsregister Karoline' (1900–1912) RKA 1001:5029–5030.
Handel und Gewerbe in Deutsch Neu-Guinea (1906–1915) RKA 1001:2533.
NGC Instruktion für den Landeshauptmann (1885) RKA 1001:2408.
NGC Instruktion für die Wissenschaftliche Forschungsexpedition (1885) RKA 1001:2408.
Jaluit-Gesellschaft, Jahresberichte (1886–1921) RKA 1001:2502–05.
Jaluit Gesellschaft – Konzessionen (1899–1910) R1001:2454–8.
Jute und Kapok in Deutsch-Neuguinea (1905–1914) RKA 1001:82367.
Kaffee in Deutsch-Neuguinea (1885) RKA 1001:8072.
Kakao in Deutsch-Neuguinea (1902–1913) RKA 1001:8073.
Kautschuk und Guttapercha in Deutsch-Neu-Guinea (1902–1914) RKA 1001:8123–25.
Kaiserlich Statistisches Amt', *Statistisches Handbuch für das Deutsche Reich* (Berlin, 1907).
Kohlen und FlottenStationen (1901–1909) RKA 1001:2603.
Land und Grundstückerwerbungen Kronland in den Marschall Inseln (1887–1912) RKA 1001:2296–7
Land und Grundstückerwerbungen Kronland in den Karolinen (1899–1912) RKA 1001:2285/9.
Landwirtschaftliche Versuchswesen in Deutsch Neu-Guinea (1901–1916) RKA 1001:8675–6.
Marshall Inseln: Jahresberichte (1887–1911) RKA 1001:6524–26.
Meteorologische Beobachtungen in den Karolinen (1899–1908) RKA 1001:6147–48.
Meteorologische Beobachtungen in den Marshall Inseln (1914) R 1001:6152.
Meteorologische Beobachtungen in Neu-Guinea (1899–1918) RKA 1001:6147–48.
NGC Allgemeine Bestimmungen (1885–1901) RKA 1001:2403.
Deutsch-Neuguinea: Verhältnisse allgemein (1886–1915) RKA 1001:2976–96.
Pacific Island Compagnie, Phosphatausbeutung (1900–1920) RKA 1001:2507–11.
Petroleum Erforschung (1913) R1001:2352.
Plantagen-Gesellschaft (1890) RKA 1001:2425.
Plenarversammlungen der Direktion (1886–1920) RKA 1001:2402–07.
Prügelstrafe in Deutschen und anderen Kolonien (1900) RKA 1001:5381.
Reichstagsachen (1910–1913) RKA 1001:2716.
Rechnung über den Haushalt der Afrikanischen Schutzgebiete, das Schutzgebiets Neu-Guinea, der Verwaltung der Karolinen, Palau, Marianen und Samoa (1907–1914) RKA 1001:2716.
Rechtsverhältnisse im Schutzgebiet (1886–1903) RKA 1001:4780–4783
Sägewerk (1908) RKA 1001:2440.
Sechium Edule [Choko] in Deutsch-Neuguinea (1907–1908) RKA 1001:8238.
Schiffsregister Deutsch Neu-Guinea (1903–1920) RKA 1001:5387.
Sisalhanf und sonstige Agavenfasern in Deutsch-Neuguinea (1908–14). RKA 1001:8240
Statut und Organisation der NGC (1885–1914) RKA 1001:2395–2401.
Tabak in Deutsch-Neuguinea (1889–1903) RKA 1001:8075.
Trepang und Perlenfischerei in Deutsch-Neuguinea (1899–1915) RKA 1001:2562.
Verordnungen im Schutzgebiet Neu Guinea (1886–1914) RKA 1001:2959–62.
Zoll- und Steuerverordung (1886–1907) RKA 1001:2963 & 7419.

Deutsche Bank AG Archive, Frankfurt
Neu Guinea Compagnie (financial records)
Jaluit Gesellschaft (financial records)

Focke–Museum, Bremen
Dallmann Logbuch & photos

Goethe Universität Frankfurt am Main
Bildbestand der Deutschen Kolonialgesellschaft (plates, photographs, maps)

Hamburgisches Weltwirtschaftsarchiv, Hamburg
NGC, Hernsheim & Co. and Hamburgische Südsee AG – Submission to the Secretary of the Australian Royal Commission (Hamburg, 24 September 1919).

Howaldtswerke-Deutsche Werft (HDW) Archiv, Kiel

John Oxley Library, Brisbane
Cooktown Courier (18 Apr. 1874–1931 Dec. 1887 and 24 Jan. 1888–1924 Nov. 1896 (mfm 0150).

Museum Schloß Schönebeck, Bremen-Vegesack,
E. Dallmann journal and photo album (1878 – 1896)

National Archives of Australia, Canberra (NAA)
Papua New Guinea Record 1883–1942 mfc Series G2, 30, 100–17, 255, 254–5, 270 & 280 (CA 1419,
    1449, 1504, 1507–8, 1518 & Ca 7462 and goldfields CA 1904/1/65)
Department of External Affairs, Melbourne: Correspondence (1 Jan. 1903–14, Nov. 1916) NAA,
    Series A1–CA7.
German New Guinea: Correspondence (1 Jan. 1885–31.Dec.1914) NAA G255
Imperial Government of German New Guinea (1 April 1899–17 Sep. 1914) Series G255-CA 1449
J.H.P. Murray, Folders and Correspondence, reports, speeches relating to the general administration
    of Papua (1 Jan. 1915–31 Dec. 1938) NAA Series M2096–CA 1413
Papua: 'The Murray Administration', NAA Series A1–CA 1912/20688.
Minutes of the Executive Council Meetings of BNG (1888–1906) , Territory of Papua (1907–1942)
    NAA Series G68–CA 141718.)
Queensland Governors, Dispatches to the Administrator of BNG (1891–99) NAA, Series A1–2261.
The Woodlark Island Proprietary Gold Mining Company, NAA Series A1–CA 1905/8015

National Library Australia, Canberra (NLA)
Correspondence Respecting New Guinea, Public Record Office, London, NLA mfm PRO 2684–95
COA, Custodian of Expropriated Property, 'Sale of expropriated properties (first group) in the
    Territories of New Guinea and Papua', Libraries Australia ID 2062077 (Melbourne, 1925)
British New Guinea C.O. 422 Original Correspondence, Secretary of State, vols 1–15 (1884–00).
British New Guinea C.O. 436 Minutes of Executive & Legislative Councils, vols 1–4 (1888–06).
British New Guinea C.O. 453 Government Gazettes, vols 1–2 (1888–1906).
British New Guinea C.O. 200 Ordinances, vols 1–2 (1888–1906).
Atlee Hunt Papers, Correspondence, NLA MS 52.
British Administration – Late German New Guinea, 'Statistics Relating to Commerce, Native Tax,
    Population, Live-Stock and Agriculture, etc.' (1911–1915) NLA FERG/5822.
Australian national newspapers; *The Brisbane Courier (=BC); The Queenslander (=TQ); Sydney
    Morning Herald (=SMH), Sydney Daily Telegraph (=SDT), Melbourne Age (=A), Melbourne
    Argus (=MA), The Mercury Hobart (=MH),The (Adelaide) Advertiser (=AA), Launceston
    Examiner (=LE), Australian Town and Country Journal (=ATCJ), The British Australasian
    (=BA),The West Australian(=WA)*
German New Guinea, Annual Reports (1900–13) NLA MS361.
Finsch, O. *Neuguinea und seine Bewohner* (Bremen, 1865).
——, *Samoa-Fahrten: Reisen in Kaiser Wilhelms-Land und Englisch-Neu-Guinea in den Jahren 1884
    und 1885 an Bord des Deutschen Dampfers „Samoa"* (Leipzig, 1888).
——, *Systematische Übersicht der Ergebnisse seiner Reisen und Thätigkeiten 1859–91* (Berlin, 1899).
Fort, G.S, 'British New Guinea, from notes by the late Sir Peter Scratchley' (Melbourne, 1886).
Lever's Pacific Plantations Ltd, NLA mfm PMB 1139
Pryke, Daniel and Frank, Papers, diary, newspaper cuttings, notes, NLA MS 1826, mfm PMB 913.
    Papuan Times and Tropical Adviser (1911–17) NLA mfm NX 915.
R.B. Joyce papers: The administration of British New Guinea, 1888–1902, NLA, mfm G22814.
Report of the Royal Commission on the Affray at Goaribari Island (Sydney, 1904).
Report of the Royal Commission of Inquiry into the Present Conditions, Including the method of
Government of the Territory of Papua and the means of their Improvement (Melbourne, 1907).

Disastrous Ventures

Report of Royal Commission on Late German New Guinea (Melbourne, 1920).
Rev. J.D. Lang papers, NLA MS 3267
Staniforth Smith Papers, NLA MS 1709.
W.C. Groves, 'Peter the Island King', NLA mfm PMB MS 612
Smith, S., *Handbook of the Territory of Papua* (Port Moresby, 1907; 1909; 1912 & 1927).
Smith, R.M. (tr.) 'German Interests in the South Sea', Abstracts of the White Book presented to the *Reichstag* (Dec., 1884 & Feb., 1885).

Staatsarchiv Bremen (StaB)
Bremer Vulkan Archiv, Schiffsregister deposit 2–R.11. p.3.b.2.
Weser-Zeitung (1884–1914)

Staatsarchiv Hamburg (StaH)
Franz and Eduard Hernsheim, deposit. A700/001
Family Archive Tetens, mfm84/07, deposit 622–1/103
Skrîvan, A., Das Hamburgische Handelshaus Johann Cesar Godeffroy & Sohn, *Zeitschrift des Vereins für Hamburgische Geschichte* (*ZVHG*) Bd.81.1995, pp. 12955
Gossler, C. Der Kaufmann August Unshelm , *ZVHG*, Bd. 95.2009, pp. 2367
——, Zwischen Hamburg und Tahiti: Der Kaufmann Gustav Godeffroy und die Risiken des deutschen Südseehandels, *Hamburger Wirtschaftskronik*, Bd. 5.2005, pp. 3573
Die Jaluit Gesellschaft, deposit A906/0005

State Library of New South Wales (Mitchell Library) Sydney
Annual Reports on British New Guinea (BNG, 1888–1906):
MacGregor, W.M. (Port Moresby, 1888–98) deposit Q998.4/P.
Winter, F.P. (Port Moresby, 1898–99) deposit Q998.4/P.
Le Hunte, G.L. (Port Moresby, 1899–1903) deposit Q998.4/P.
Barton, F.R. (Port Moresby, 1904–06) deposit Q998.4/P.
Annual Reports on The Territory of Papua (Papua)
Murray, J.H.P. (Port Moresby, 1907–21).
BNG Government Gazette, vol. i (4 Sep 1888) Q342.984/T.
Griffith Papers, General Correspondence (1886–1916) CY 2379 MLMSS 363/5x).
Griffith Papers, Letters from MacGregor, CY 2381 MLMSS 363/6x).
Eduard Hernsheim papers, 18601917, MAN/FM4, 221820
Minutes of the Proceedings of the Intercolonial Conference (1881) DSM/Q354.9/N.
Territory of Papua Government Gazette, vol. i, NI (1906) vol. 8, N8 (1914) Q342.984/T.
The British New Guinea Development Company, Limited, Prospectus (1910) F91/56.
The British New Guinea Development Company, Limited (1910–20) Q 338.106 B.

State Library of Victoria, Melbourne,
Bloomfield, A.S., *Tropical Agriculture in Papua,* pp.1–24.
Victorian Parliament 'New Guinea Protectorate – Correspondence' (Melbourne, 1884) p. 23.
New Guinea – Correspondence (Melbourne, 1885) p. 15.

Sal. Oppenheim jr. & Cie., Cologne.
Die Kolonialen Unternehmungen in Samoa und Neu Guinea, , vol. 112–14 (1879–1914).

Zentralbibliothek für Wirtschaftswissenschaft, Hamburg/Kiel
Firmenarchiv Hernsheim, AG/P20

Bibliography

B. Books and Dissertations:

Ackermann, J. & Demison, J., eds., *Richard Parkinson: Dreißig Jahre in Der Südsee* (Sydney, 1999).

Ainsworth, C.J., *Report of Colonel Ainsworth on Administrative Arrangements and Matters Affecting the Interests of Natives in the Territory of New Guinea* (Melbourne, 1924).

Apitzsch, W. ,Das Wirtschafts- und Verwaltungspersonal der Neu-Guinea-Compagnie 1885–1899', *Fakultät Geisteswissenschaft* (Hamburg, 1988).

Aydelotte, W.O., *Bismarck and British Colonial Policy* (Philadelphia, 1937).

Bade, K.J., *Friedrich Fabri und der Imperialismus in der Bismarckzeit*(Freiburg, 1975)

Ballhaus, J. ,Wesen und Charakter der Kolonialen Landesgesellschaften Ende Des 19. Jahrhunderts', in *Jahrbuch Für Wirtschaftsgeschichte* (Berlin, 1972) pp. 95-115.

Bassett, M., *Letters from New Guinea 1921* (Melbourne, 1969).

Baum, E., *Deiheim und überm Meer - von der Deutschen Kolonialschule zum Deutschen Institut für Tropische und Subtropische Landwirtschaft* (Witzenhausen, 1997).

Baumann, K. Klein, D. & Apitzsch, W., *Biographisches Handbuch DNG* (Fassberg, 2002)

Baumann, K., *Lebenserinnerungen: Siedler und Reisende in Deutsch-Neuguinea* (Fassberg, 2008)

Behrmann, W., *Der Kaiserin-Augusta-Fluß; Expedition in 1912–1913* (Berlin, 1917).

——. *Im Stromgebiet des Sepik. Eine Deutsche Forschungsreise in Neuguinea* (Berlin, 1922).

Bein, A. & Goldschmidt, H., *Friedrich Hammacher, Lebensbild eines Parlamentariers und Wirtshaftführers 1824–1904* (Berlin, 1932).

Belfort, R. & Hoyer, A.J., *All About Coconuts* (London, 1914)

Bevan, T.F., *Toil, Travel and Discovery in British New Guinea* (London, 1890).

Biermer, M., *Fürst Bismarck als Volkswirt* (Greifswald, 1899).

Birke, A.M., *Deutschland und Großbritannien: Historische Beziehungen und Vergleiche* (München, 1999)

Bismarck, O. v. *Gedanken und Erinnerungen* (Stuttgart, 1898–1901).

——. ed., *Die Gesammelten Werke: Bis zur Ausrichtung des Deutschen Reiches* (Berlin, 1924).

——. ed., *Die Gesammelten Werke - Gespräche: Bis zur Entlassung* (Berlin, 1926)

——, ed., *Die Gesammelten Werke - Reden: 1878–1885* (Berlin, 1929).

——, ed., *Die Gesammelten Werke - Reden: 1885–1897* (Berlin, 1930).

Blum, H., *Neu Guinea und der Bismarckarchipel: Eine Wirtschaftliche Studie* (Berlin, 1900).

——, *Das Bevölkerungsproblem im Stillen Weltmeer* (Heidelberg, 1902).

Boehm, E.A., *Prosperity and Depression in Australia 1887–1897* (Oxford, 1971)

Böhme, H., *Deutschlands Weg zur Großmacht. Studien zum Verhältnis von Wirtschaft und Staat Während der Reichsgründungszeit 1848–1881* (Köln, 1966).

Bolton, G., *Spoils and Spoilers: Australians Make Their Environment 1788–1980* (Sydney, 1981).

——, *Edmund Barton: The One Man for the Job* (St. Leonards, 2000).

Bonn, M., *Nationale Kolonialpolitik* (München, 1910).

Booth, D.R., *Mountain, Gold and Cannibal* (Sydney, 1929).

British Foreign Office, *Former German Possessions in Oceania* (London, 1920).

Brooks, J., *The Mighty Leaf: Tobacco through the Centuries* (Boston, 1952).

Brown, R.G. 'The German Acquisition of the Caroline Islands, 1898', in J.A. Moses and P.M. Kennedy, eds., *Germany in the Pacific and Far East, 1870-1914* (Brisbane, 1977)

Brücke, O., *Die Entwicklung und Wirtschaftliche Bedeutung der Kopra- und Kokusölproduktion und Konsumation* (Nürnberg, 1930).

Buchholz, H., 'Die Naturräumliche Struktur der Ehemaligen Deutschen Südseekolonien', in J. Hiery ed., *Die Deutsche Südsee 1884–1914* (Paderborn, 2001).

Buchner, M., *Aurora Colonialis: Bruchstücke Eines Tagebuchs aus dem Ersten Beginn unserer Kolonialpolitik 1884/85* (München, 1914).

Bruce, C., *The Broad Stone of Empire* (London, 1910)

Buckley, K. & Klugman, K., *The History of Burns Philp* (Hong Kong, 1981).

——, *The Australian Presence in the Pacific: Burns Philp 1914–1946* (Sydney, 1983)

Disastrous Ventures

Bullerdiek, J. & Tilgner, D., ed., *Lloydmissionen, Robert Claessens' Fahrten um die Welt 1891–1955* (Bremen, 2012)

Burger, F., *Unter den Kannibalen der Südsee* (Dresden, 1923).

Burnell, F.S., *Australia v. Germany: The Story of the Taking of German New Guinea* (London, 1915).

Burns Philp, & Co., Ltd: *Their Shipping Agencies, Branches & Steamers* (Sydney, 1903)

——, *Branches around Australia and the Pacific* (John Oxley Library, Brisbane, 1913)

Burton, J.W., *Australian Mandate in New Guinea, Studies in Australian Affairs* (Melbourne, 1930).

——, *Missionary Survey of the Pacific Islands* (London, 1930).

Busch, J.H.M., *Tagebuchblätter* (Leipzig, 1899).

Bußmann, W., ed., *Staatssekretär Graf Herbert von Bismarck. Aus seiner Politischen Korrespondenz* (Göttingen 1964).

Canis, K., *Bismarcks Außenpolitik: 1870 Bis 1890* (Paderborn, 2004).

Carteret, P., *Reise um die Welt – Reisebeschreibungen* (Wien, 1785)

Cawston, G., *The Early Chartered Companies C. 1296–1858* (London, 1896)

Cayley-Webster, H., *Through New Guinea and the Cannibal Countries* (London, 1898).

Champion, I.F., *Across New Guinea from the Fly to the Sepik* (London, 1932)

Chalmers, J. *Pioneering in New Guinea* (London, 1887)

Chisholm, A.H., *Ferdinand von Mueller, Great Australians* (Melbourne, 1962)

Cohen, R., ed., *The Cambridge Survey of World Migration* (New York, 1995)

Commonwealth of Australia, *The New Guinea Handbook* (Canberra, 1937)

Cooper, H.S., *The Coral Lands of the Pacific* (London, 1888)

Creutzberg, P., ed., *Public Finance 1816–1939* (The Hague, 1976)

Crocker, W.R., *On Governing Colonies: Being an Outline of the Real Issues and Comparison of the British, French and Belgian Approach to the Theme* (London, 1947)

Crowe, S.E., *The Berlin African Conference 1884–1885* (London, 1942)

Daiber, A., *Eine Australien –und Südseefahrt* (Leipzig, 1902)

Davies, M., *Public Health and Colonialism: The Case of GNG 1884–1914* (Wiesbaden, 2002)

Dawson, W.H., *The German Empire, 1867–1914 and the Unity Movement* (London, 1919)

Decharme, P., *Compagnies Et Sociétés Coloniales Allemandes* (Paris, 1903)

Deckert, E., *Grundzüge der Handels- und Verkehrsgeographie* (Leipzig, 1902)

Deeken, R., *Die Auswanderungen nach den Deutschen Kolonien unter Berücksichtigung der Wirtschaftlichen und Klimatischen Verhältnisse* (Berlin, 1908)

Denoon, D., Dugan, K., & Marshall, A.J., *Public Health in Papua New Guinea: Medical Possibility and Social Constraint, 1884–1984* (Cambridge, 1989)

Denoon, D. & Snowden, C., eds., *A Time to Plant and a Time to Uproot: A History of Agriculture in Papua New Guinea* (Port Moresby, 1981)

Dernburg, B., *Koloniale Finanzprobleme* (Berlin, 1907)

——, *Koloniale Lehrjahre* (Stuttgart, 1907)

——, *Zielpunkte des Deutschen Kolonialwesens* (Berlin, 1907)

——, *Die Vorbedingungen für Erfolgreiche Koloniale und überseeische Betätigung* (Berlin, 1912)

Detzner, H., *Vier Jahre unter Kannibalen: Von 1914 bis zum Waffenstillstand unter Deutscher Flagge im Unerforschten Innern von Neu Guinea* (Berlin, 1921)

Deutsche Kolonialgesellschaft, *Koloniales Jahrbuch: Beiträge und Mitteilungen aus dem Gebiete der Kolonialwissenschaft und Praxis* (Berlin, 1888–1895)

——, *Deutscher Kolonialatlas mit Illustriertem Jahrbuch* (Berlin, 1901–1914)

Disconto Gesellschaft, *Denkschrift zum 50 Jährigen Jubiläum 1851–1901* (Berlin, 1901)

Docker, E.W., *The Blackbirders: A Brutal Story of the Kanaka Slave-Trade* (London, 1970)

Doel, W. v. d. ‚Kulis für Deutschland', in H.J. Hiery ed., *Die Deutsche Südsee 1884–1914,* (Paderborn, 2001).

Drabble, J., *Rubber in Malay 1876–1922: The Genesis of the Industry* (Oxford, 1973)

Dutton, G., *Queen Emma of the South Sea* (Melbourne, 1976)

Dugdale, E.T.S., ed., *Bismarck's Relations with England 1871–1890* (London, 1928)

Edwards, P.G., *Prime Minister and Diplomats: The making of Australian Foreign Policy 1901–1949*

(Melbourne, 1983).

Ellis, A.F., *Ocean Island and Nauru* (Sydney, 1935)

Elschner, C., *Korallogene Phosphatinseln Austral-Ozeaniens und ihre Produkte* (Lübeck, 1913)

Ettling, C., *Unter Pflanzern und Goldgräber im Kanibalenland Neuguinea* (Berlin, 1930)

Evans, R., Sauders, K. & Cronin, K., *Race Relations in Colonial Queensland: A History of Exclusion, Exploitation and Extermination* (Brisbane, 1988)

Fabri, F., *Bedarf Deutschland der Kolonien?* (Gotha, 1879)

Fabri, T., *Kolonien als Bedürfnis unser nationalen Entwicklung* (Heidelberg, 1884)

Fabricius, W., *Nauru 1888–1900* (Canberra, 1992).

Ferguson, J. &, A.M., *Coconut Planter's Manual or all about the Coconut Palm* (Colombo, 1885)

Finch-Hatton, H., *Advance Australia* (London, 1885)

Fieldhouse, D.K., *The Colonial Empire: A Comparative Survey from the Eighteenth Century,* (London, 1966)

——, *Economics and Empire, 1830–1914* (London, 1973).

Firth, S.G. 'German Recruitment and Employment of Labourers in the Western Pacific before the First World War', D. Phil. (Oxford, 1973).

——, ed., *Albert Hahl, Governor of German New Guinea* (Canberra, 1978).

——, *New Guinea under the Germans* (Melbourne, 1982).

——,'Captain Hernsheim: Pacific Venturer, Merchant Prince', in D. Scarr ed., *More Pacific Islands Portraits* (Canberra, 1978)

Fischer, D., *Unter Südsee-Insulaner das Leben des Forschers Miklouho-Maclay* (Leipzig, 1956).

——, *Germany's Aims in the First World War* (New York, 1967).

——, *Der Erste Weltkrieg und das Deutsche Geschichtsbild* (Düsseldorf, 1977).

Fitzner, R., *Deutsche Kolonial-Handbuch: Ergänzungsband* (Berlin, 1909).

Flierl, J., *Dreißig Jahre Missionsarbeiten in Wüsten und Wildnissen* (München, 1910).

Ferguson, *British New Guinea: An Abstract of Statistical Notes* (Almanac, Brisbane, 1891)

Frommund, B., *Deutsch-Neuguinea: Eine Perle der Südsee* (Hamburg, 1926)

Furnivall, J.S., *Netherlands India: A Study of Plural Economy* (Cambridge, 1939).

Furness, W.H., *The Island of Stone Money—Uap of the Carolines* (London, 1910)

Gall, L., Feldman, G.D., James, H., at al. *Die Deutsche Bank 1870–1995* (München, 1995)

Galloway, J.H., *The Sugar Cane Industry* (Cambridge, 1989).

Gallus, 'Schiffsverbindungen mit unseren Kolonien', *Jahrbuch Deutschen Kolonien,* (Essen, 1909)

Giordani, P. *The German Colonial Empire* (London, 1916)

Goldthorpe, C.G. *Plantation Agriculture in Papua New Guinea* (Port Moresby, 1985)

——, *Why Papua New Guinea needs Plantation* (Port Moresby, 1985)

Graichen, H., 'Goldfieber', in Hillrichs, H. and Graichen, H., eds., *von den Minen der Skythen zu den Schätzen Timbuktus* (München, 2002).

Gnielinskie, S. v. ,Struktur und Entwicklung Papuas und das von Australien Verwalteten, Ehemals Deutschen Gebietes der Insel Neu Guinea', Dissertation *Nat. Science* (Hamburg, 1957)

Godeffroy, G., *Schutzzoll und Freihandel unter Besonderer Berücksichtigung des Zollprogramms des Fürsten Bismarck* (Berlin, 1879).

Gordon, D.C., *The Australian Frontier in New Guinea 1870–1885* (New York, 1951).

Gräbner, F., ed., *Neu-Mecklenburg: Die Küste Ummuddu bis Kap St Gerorg* (Berlin, 1907).

Grapow, A. v., *Die Deutsche Flagge im Stillen Ozean* (Berlin, 1916).

Grattan, H.C., *The Southwest Pacific since 1900* (Ann Abor, 1963).

Greeve, W., *Seeschiffahrts - Subventionen der Gegenwart* (Hamburg, 1903).

Griffin, J., ed., *Papua New Guinea Portraits: The Expatriate Experience* (Canberra, 1978)

Griffin, J., Firth, S. & Nelson, H., *Papua New Guinea, a Political History* (Melbourne, 1979).

Grimshaw, Beatrice, *Papua the Marvellous: the Country of Chance* (Melbourne, 1909).

——, The New New Guinea (London, 1911).

——, *Guinea Gold* (London, 1912).

Groote, P. de, *Nouvelle-France, Colonie Libre de Port-Breton (Océanie)* (Paris, 1880).

Gründer, H., *Geschichte der Deutschen Kolonien* (Paderborn, 1984).

Disastrous Ventures

Hagen, B., *Unter den Papuas: Beobachtungen und Studien, Land und Leute, Thier- und Pflanzenwelt in Kaiser-Wilhelmsland* (Wiesbaden, 1899).

Hagen, M. v., *Bismarcks Kolonialpolitik* (Stuttgart, 1923).

Hahl, A., *Gouverneursjahre in Neu Guinea* (Berlin, 1937).

——, *Deutsch-Neuguinea* (Berlin, 1942).

Haller, H., *Die Phosphat-Gesellschaften der Südsee* (Leipzig, 1911).

Hannay, D., *The Great Chartered Companies* (London, 1926).

Hanneken, W. v., *Sumatra* (Berlin, 1902).

Healy, A.M., 'Colonial Law as Metropolitan Defence: The Curious Case of Australia in New Guinea', in H.J. Hiery & J. Mackenzie, eds., *European Impact and Pacific Influence: British and German Colonial Policy in the Pacific Islands and the Indigenous Response* (London, 1997).

Helfferich, K., *Zur Reform der Kolonialen Verwaltungs-Organisation* (Berlin, 1905).

Helmreich, T., *Das Geldwesen in den Deutschen Schutzgebieten: Neu-Guinea* (Fürth, 1912).

Hempenstall, P.J., *Pacific Islanders under German Rule: A Study in the Meaning of Colonial Resistance* (Canberra, 1978).

——, *Protest and Dissent in the Colonial Pacific* (Suva, 1984).

Henderson, W.O., *Studies in German Colonial History* (London, 1962).

Henley, T., *New Guinea and Australia's Pacific Islands Mandate* (Sydney, 1927).

Henning, H.J. ,Bismarcks Kolonialpolitik – Export Einer Krise?' in K.E. Born ed., *Gegenwartsprobleme der Wirtschaft und der Wirtschaftswissenschaft* (Tübingen, 1978).

Henshaw, D.J.B., *Black Consequences of Australia's White New Guinea Policies* (Burwood, 1989).

Herberger, S., 'Kannibalismus in Deutsch Neu-Guinea', in H.J. Hiery ed., *Die Deutsche Südsee 1884–1914* (Paderborn, 2001)

Herbert, C.E., ed., *Statute Law of the Territory of Papua from 1888 to 1916* (Port Moresby, 1918).

Hernsheim, E., *Tagebuch* (Hamburg, 1886).

——, *Lebenserinnerungen von Eduard Hernsheim* (Hamburg, 1910).

Hernsheim, F., *Südsee-Erinnerungen 1875–1880* (Berlin, 1883).

Hertz, R., *Das Hamburger Seehandelshaus J.C. Godeffroy & Sohn 1766–1879* (Hamburg, 1922).

Hesse-Wartegg, E. von, *Samoa, Bismarckarchipel und Neuguinea: Drei Deutsche Kolonien in der Südsee* (Leipzig, 1902)

Hiery, H.J., *Das Deutsche Reich in der Südsee (1900–1921). Eine Annäherung an die Erfahrungen Verschiedener Kulturen* (Freiburg, 1993).

——, *The Neglected War: The German South Pacific and the Influence of World War I*, (Honolulu, 1995)

——, 'Die Deutsche Verwaltung Neuguineas 1884–1914', in H.J. Hiery ed., *Die Deutsche Südsee 1884–1914* (Paderborn, 2001).

Hiery, H.J. & Mackenzie, J., *European Impact and Pacific Influence: British and German Colonial Policy in the Pacific Islands and the Indigenous Response* (London, 1997).

Hoffmann, G., *Wirtschaftsspionage in der Südsee: H.H. Meier & Joh. Ces. Godeffroy* (Bremisches Jahrbuch, 1997).

——, *Das Haus an der Elbchaussee. Die Geschichte einer Reederfamilie* (Hamburg, 1998).

Hoffmann, W.G. & Müller, J.H., *Das Deutsche Volkseinkommen 1851–1957* (Tübingen, 1959).

Howard, M. & Durntaloa, S., eds., *The Political Economy of the South Pacific to 1945* (Townsville, 1987).

Howe, K., *Where the Waves Fall: A South Sea Island History from First Settlement to Colonial Rule* (Sydney, 1984).

——, *Nature Culture and History. The Knowing of Oceania* (Honolulu, 2000).

Hübbe-Schleiden, W., *Deutsche Colonisation* (Hamburg, 1881).

Hudson, W.J., *Australia and Papua New Guinea* (Sydney, 1971).

Hughes, L.H., 'Observation on Malaria from Experience in New Guinea', in, *Medicine* (Sydney, 1921).

Huldermann, B., *Die Subventionen der Ausländischen Handelsflotten und ihre Bedeutung für die Entwicklung der Seefahrt* (Berlin, 1909).

Humphries, W.R., *Patrolling in Papua* (London, 1923).

Hutter, F., Dove, K. & Seidel, H., eds., *Das Überseeische Deutschland* (Stuttgart, 1911).

Hutter, F.K., *Das Überseeische Deutschland. Die deutschen Kolonien in Wort und Bild* (Leipzig 1890)

Idriess, I.L., *Gold-Dust and Ashes* (Sydney, 1939).

Inglis, G. *Papua: A Grandchild of the Empire* (London,1912)

Inglis, K.S., *John Moresby and Port Moresby: A Centenary View* (Port Moresby, 1974).

Irmer, G., *Völkerdämmerung im Stillen Ozean* (Leipzig, 1915).

Jäckel, H., *Die Landgesellschaften in den Deutschen Kolonien* (Jena, 1909).

Jackman, H.H., 'Nunquam Otiosus and the two Ottos: Malaria in GNG, in B. G. Burton-Bradley ed., *A History of Medicine in Papua New Guinea: Vignettes of an Earlier Period* (Kingsgrove, 1990).

Jinks, B., Biskup, P. & Nelson, H., eds., *Readings in New Guinea History* (Sydney, 1973).

Johannsen, K. & Kraft, H., *Germany's Colonial Problem* (London, 1937).

Jöhlinger, O., *Die Wirtschaftliche Bedeutung unserer Kolonien: Sechs Vorlesungen für Kaufleute*, (Berlin, 1910).

——, *Die Koloniale Handelspolitik der Weltmächte* (Berlin, 1914).

Joyce, R.B., *New Guinea* (Melbourne, 1960).

——, 'Australian Interests in New Guinea before 1906', in W.J. Hudson ed., *Papua New Guinea* (Sydney, 1971).

——, *Sir William MacGregor* (Melbourne, 1971).

Jukes, J.B., *Narrative of the Surveying Voyage of H.M.S. Fly, Commanded by Cpt. F.P. Blackwood R.N., in Torres Strait, New Guinea and Other Islands of the Eastern Archipelago during the Years 1842–1846* (London, 1847).

Jung, K.E., *Der Weltteil Australien* (Leipzig, 1883).

Kade, E., *Die Anfänge der Deutschen Kolonial-Zentralverwaltung* (Würzburg, 1939).

Kärnbach, L., *Die Bisherige Erforschung von Kaiser Wilhelms-Land und der Nutzen der Anlage einer Forschungs-Station* (Berlin, 1893).

Karting, H., *Deutsche Schoner,* (Bremen, 2003)

Kennedy, P.M., 'Germany and the Samoan Tridominium, 1889–98; A Study in Frustrated Imperialism', in J.A. Moses & P.M. Kennedy eds.*Germany in the Pacific and Far East, 1870–1914* (Brisbane, 1977)

——, *The Rise of the Anglo-German Antagonism 1860–1914* (London, 1980).

Killebrew, J.B. & Myrick, H., *Tobacco Leaf: Its Culture and Cure, Marketing and Manufacture*, (New York, 1909).

Klein, D., 'Neuguinea als Deutsches Utopia: August Engelhardt und sein Sonnenorden', in H.J. Hiery ed., *Die Deutsche Südsee1884–1914* (Paderborn, 2001).

Kludas, A., 'Deutsche Passagierschiffs-Verbindungen in der Südsee 1886–1914', in H.J. Hiery ed., *Die Deutsche Südsee* (Paderborn, 2001).

Knaplund, P., *Gladstone and Britain's Imperial Policy* (London, 1927).

——, ed., *Letters from the Berlin Embassy 1871–1874, 1880–1885* (Washington, 1944).

——, *Gladstone's Foreign Policy* (London, 1970).

Knapman, B., *Fiji's Economic History, 1874–1939, Pacific Research Monographs* (Canberra, 1987).

Knight, M.P., 'Britain, Germany and the Pacific, 1880–87', in J.A. Moses and P.M. Kennedy eds. *Germany in the Pacific and Far East, 1870–1914* (Brisbane, 1977) pp. 61-88.

Köbner & Gertsmeyer, *Die Deutsche Kolonialgesetzgebung,*(Berlin, 1906–1909).

König, H., *Heiß Flagge, Deutsche Kolonialgründung durch S.M.S. Elisabeth* (Leipzig, 1934).

Koschitzky, M. v., *Deutsche Colonialgeschichte* (Leipzig, 1887–1888).

Kotze, S. v., *Aus Papuas Kulturmorgen* (Berlin, 1905).

Kraft, H.H., *Chartergesellschaften als Mittel zur Erschließung Kolonialer Gebiete* (Hamburg, 1943).

Kratoska, P.H., ed., *Honourable Intentions: Talks on the British Empire in South-East Asia;* in *Proceedings of the Royal Colonial Institute 1874-1928* (Singapore, 1983).

Krause, C., *Die Aussichten des Kolonialdienstes: Grundsätze für die Verwendung von Beamten und Unterbeamten in den Deutschen Schutzgebieten* (Frankfurt a. M, 1908)

Krieger, M., ed., *Neu-Guinea* (Berlin, 1899).

Kucklentz, K., *Das Zollwesen der Deutschen Schutzgebiete in Afrika und der Südsee* (Berlin, 1914).

Kunze, G., *Im Dienst des Kreuzes auf ungebahnten Pfaden* (Barmen, 1901).

Kyllmann, A., *Aus dem Leben Adolph von Hansemanns* (Berlin, 1926).

La Nauze, J.A., *Alfred Deakin* (Melbourne, 1965).

Langhans, P., *Deutscher Kolonial-Atlas* (Gotha, 1897)

Lawson, J.A., *Wandering in the Interior of New Guinea* (London, 1875).

Legge, J.D., *Australian Colonial Policy: A Survey of Native Administration and European Development in Papua* (Sydney, 1956).

——, *Britain in Fiji* (London, 1958).

——, 'The Murray Period 1906–40', in W. Hudson ed., *Australia and Papua New Guinea* (Sydney, 1971).

Lett, L., *Knight Errant of Papua* (Edinburgh, 1935).

——, *The Official Handbook of Papua* (Port Moresby, 1938).

——, *The Papuan Achievement* (Melbourne, 1942).

——, *Papuan Gold* (Sydney, 1943).

——, *Sir Hubert Murray* (London, 1949).

Lewis, D.C., *The Plantation Dream: Developing British New Guinea and Papua* (Canberra, 1996).

Lotz, A., *Geschichte des Deutschen Beamtentums* (Berlin, 1909).

Lutton, N., 'C.A.W. Monckton', in J. Griffin ed., *Papua New Guinea Portraits* (Canberra, 1978)

Lyne, C.E., *New Guinea: an Account of the Establishment of the British Protectorate over the Southern Shores of New Guinea* (London, 1885).

Lyng, J., *Island Film: Reminiscence of German New Guinea* (Sydney, 1919).

——, *Our New Possessions of Late German New Guinea* (Melbourne, 1919).

MacGillivray, J. *Narrative of the Voyage of H.M.S. Rattlesnake*, vol. ii (London, 1852).

MacGregor, W., *Handbook of Information for Intending Settlers in British New Guinea* (Brisbane, 1892)

MacKay, J.A.K., *Across Papua, Being an Account of a Voyage Round, and a March Across The Territory of Papua with the Royal Commission* (London, 1909)

Mackellar C.D., *Scented Isles and Coral Gardens: Torres Straits, German New Guinea and the Dutch Indies* (London, 1912)

Mackenzie, S.S., *The Australians at Rabaul*, in *The Official History of Australia in the War of 1914–1918*, vol x (Sydney, 1938).

Mair, L.P., *Australia in New Guinea* (London, 1948).

Masterman, Sylvia, *The Origins of international Rivalry in Samoa, 1845–1884* (London, 1934)

Mayer, O., *Die Entwicklung der Handelsbeziehungen Deutschlands zu seinen Kolonien,* (München, 1913).

McKinney, R.Q., 'Micronesia under German Rule 1885–1914' (MA thesis, Leland Stanford University, 1947).

McKillop, R.F & Pearson, M.R., *End of the Line: A History of Railways in Papua New Guinea,* (Port Moresby, 1997)

Meyer, G., 'German Interests and Policy in the Netherlands East Indies and Malaya, 1870–1914', in J.A Moses and P.M. Kennedy eds., *Germany in the Pacific and the Far East, 1870–1914,* (Brisbane, 1977)

Meyer, H., ed., *Das Deutsche Kolonialreich, eine Länderkunde der Deutschen Schutzgebiete,* (Leipzig, 1910)

Monckton, C.A.W., *Some Experience of a New Guinea Resident Magistrate* (London, 1921)

——, *Last Days in New Guinea* (London, 1922)

——, *New Guinea Recollections* (London, 1934)

Moore, C., Griffin, J. & Griffin, A., *Colonial Intrusion - Papua New Guinea, 1884* (Port Moresby, 1984)

Moore, C., Leckie, J. & Munro, D. (eds), *Labour in the South Pacific* (Townsville, 1990).

——, 'Pacific Islanders in the Nineteenth Century Queensland', in C. Moore, J. Leckie & D. Munro eds., *Labour in the South Pacific* (James Cook University of Northern Queensland, Townsville).

Moresby, J.C., *Discovery and Surveys in New Guinea and the D'Entrecasteaux Islands* (London, 1876)

Morrell, A.J., *Narrative of a Voyage to the Ethiopic and South Atlantic Ocean* (New York, 1833)

Morrell, W.P., *Britain in the Pacific Islands* (Oxford, 1960).

Moses, I. 'The Extension of Colonial Rule in Kaiser Wilhelmsland', in J.A. Moses & P.M. Kennedy eds., *Germany in the Pacific and Far East, 1870– 1914* (Brisbane, 1977)

Moses, J.A., 'The Coolie Labour Question and German Colonial Policy in Samoa, 1900–14', in J.A. Moses & P.M. Kennedy eds., *Germany in the Pacific and Far East, 1870-1914* (Brisbane, 1973)

——, 'Imperial German Priorities in New Guinea 1885–1914', in S. Latukefu ed., *Papua New Guinea: A Century of Colonial Impact 1885–1984* (Port Moresby, 1989)

——, *Germany in the Pacific and Far East, 1870–1914* (Brisbane, 1977)

Moses, J.A. & Pugsley, C., eds., *The German Empire and Britain's Pacific Dominions 1871–1915* (Claremont, Calif., 2000)

Münch, H., *Adolph von Hansemann* (München, 1932)

Mulleit, A.J., *British Administration of German New Guinea - Statistics* (Melbourne 1916)

Murray, J.H.P., *Papua or British New Guinea* (London, 1912)

——, *Papua of Today, or an Australian Colony in the making* (London, 1925).

——, *Review of the Australian Administration in Papua from 1907–1920* (Port Moresby, 1926)

——, *The Scientific Aspect of the Pacification of Papua*, Address at the Australian and New Zealand Association for the Advancement of Science, Sydney Aug. 1932 (Port Moresby, 1932)

Nash, R.L., *Australian Joint Stock Companies Year Book* (Sydney, 1898).

Nelson, H.N., *Black, White & Gold: Goldmining in Papua New Guinea* (Canberra, 1976).

Neubaur, P., *Die Deutschen Reichspostdampferlinien nach Ostasien und Australien* (Berlin, 1906).

——, *Der Norddeutsche Lloyd. 50 Jahre Der Entwicklung* (Leipzig, 1907).

——, *Jahrbuch des Norddeutschen Lloyd* (Berlin, 1913/14).

Neuhauß, R., *Deutsch Neu-Guinea* (Berlin, 1911).

——, *Unsere Kolonie Deutsch-Neu-Guinea* (Weimar, 1914).

Neumann, A., *Kurs-Tabellen Der Berliner Fond–Börse* (Berlin, 1918).

Neumann, K., *Not The Way It Really Was: Constructing the Tolai Past* (Honolulu, 1992)

Nussbaum, M., *Vom „Kolonialenthusiasmus" zur Kolonialpolitik der Monopole: zur Deutschen Kolonialpolitik unter Bismarck, Caprivi, Hohenlohe* (Berlin, 1962).

Oechelhäuser, W., *Die Nachteile des Aktienwesens und die Reform der Aktiengesetzgebung,* (Berlin, 1878).

Ollivier, M., ed., *The Colonial and Imperial Conferences from 1887 to 1937* (London, 1954).

Osterroth, A. v., *Das Schuldwesen der Deutschen Gebiete* (Leipzig, 1911).

Overell, L., *A Woman's Impression of German New Guinea* (New York, 1923).

Overlack, P., 'The Imperial German Navy in the Pacific from 1900–1914 as an Instrument of Weltpolitik', PhD thesis (University of Queensland, 1996).

——, 'Australia and Germany: Challenge and Response before 1914', in D. Stevens ed. *Maritime Power in the 20th Century: The Australian Experience* (Sydney, 1998)

Parkinson, R., *Dreißig Jahre in der Südsee* (Stuttgart, 1926).

——, *Im Bismarck Archipel. Erlebnisse und Beobachtungen auf der Insel Neu Pommern* (Leipzig, 1887)

Parnaby, O.W., *Britain and the Labour Trade in the Southwest Pacific* (Durham, 1964).

Patzig, C.A., *Deutsche Kolonialunternehmungen und Postdampfersubventionen* (Hannover, 1884).

Pawlik, P.-M., *Von Sibirien nach Neu Guinea. Kapitän Dallmann und seine Reisen 1830–1896* (Bremen, 1996).

——, *Von der Weser in die Welt* Vol. III (Bremen, 2008)

Pelzer, K., *Die Arbeiterwanderungen in Südostasien. Eine Wirtschafts- und Bevölkerungsgeographische Untersuchung* (Hamburg, 1935).

Pfeil, J. v. & Ellguth, J.F., *Studien und Beobachtungen aus Der Südsee* (Braunschweig, 1899).

Pilhofer, D.G., *Die Geschichte Der Neuendettelsauer Mission in Neuguinea* (Neuendettelsau, 1961).

Pflüger, A., *Smaragdinseln der Südsee* (Bonn, 1901)

Poschinger, H. v., *Fürst Bismarck als Volkswirt* (Berlin, 1889–1891).

Powell, W., 'The Powell Trading Association, Limited', in *Powell Papers* (London, 1880).

——, *Wandering in a Wild Country or, Three Years amongst the Cannibals of New Britain*, (London, 1884).

Preuß, P., *Die Kokospalme und ihre Kultur* (Berlin, 1911).

Proudfoot, P., Maguire, R. & Freestone, R., eds., *Colonial City, Global City: Sydney's International Exhibition 1879* (Darlinghurst NSW, 2000).

Pullen-Burry, B., *In a German Colony or Four Weeks in New Britain* (London, 1909).

Purcell, V., *The Chinese in Southeast Asia* (London, 1965).

Reeves, L.C., *Australians in Action in New Guinea* (Sydney, 1915).

Rein, K., *Wie England die Deutschen Kolonien Bewertet* (Berlin, 1917).

Ribbe, C., *Zwei Jahre unter den Kanibalen der Salomon-Inseln* (Dresden, 1903).

——, *Unter dem südlichen Kreuz, Reisebilder aus Melanesia* (Dresden, 1924).

Riches, A., *History of Kitchen & Sons* (Melbourne, 1945).

Riebow, G., *Die Deutsche Kolonialgesetzgebung.* (Berlin, 1885–92).

Riehl, A.T.G., *Der „Tanz um den Äquator". Bismarcks Antienglische Kolonialpolitik und die Erwartung des Thronwechsels in Deutschland 1883-1885* (Berlin, 1993).

Riemer, G.A. *Tagebuchs-Auszug betreffend die Reise SMS Hertha nach Ost-Asien und den Südsee Inseln 1874-1877* (Berlin, 1878)

Robson, R.W., *Queen Emma: The Samoan-American Girl who founded an Empire in 19th cent. New Guinea* (Sydney, 1965).

Roe, M., 'History of South-East Papua to 1930', PhD thesis (ANU-Canberra, 1961).

Rohrbach, P., *Wie Machen Wir unsere Kolonien Rentable?* (Halle, 1907).

Romilly, H.H., *The Western Pacific and New Guinea: Notes on the Natives, Christian and Cannibal with Some Account of the old Labour Trade* (London, 1886).

Roskoschny, H., Die Deutschen in der Südsee: ein Beitrag zur Geschichte deutschen Handels und deutscher Kolonisation (Leipzig, 1886)

——, *Europas Kolonien: Die Deutschen in der Südsee* (Leipzig, 1889).

Rowley, C.D., *The Australians in German New Guinea, 1914–1921* (Melbourne, 1958).

——, 'The Occupation of German New Guinea 1914–21', in W.J. Hudson ed., *Australia and Papua New Guinea* (Sydney, 1971)

Rush, J., *Opium to Java: Revenue Farming and Chinese Enterprises in Colonial Indonesia 1860–1910* (New York, 1990).

Sack, P.G., 'Traditional Land Tenure and Early European Land Acquisition; the Clash between Primitive and Western Law in New Guinea', PhD thesis (ANU-Canberra, 1971).

——, *Land Between Two Laws: Early European Land Acquisition in New Guinea* (Canberra, 1973)

——, *Albert Hahl Governor in New Guinea* (Canberra, 1980).

——, *Phantom History: The Rule of Law and the Colonial State: The Case of German New Guinea* (Canberra, 2001).

Sack, P.G. & Clark, D., *German New Guinea: The Annual Reports* (Canberra, 1979)

——, *German New Guinea: The Draft Annual Report for 1913–1914* (Canberra, 1980).

Sack, P.G. & Sack, B., *The Land Law of German New Guinea* (Canberra, 1975).

——, eds., *Eduard Hernsheim: South Sea Merchant* (Boroko, 1983).

Sass, J., *Die Deutschen Weißbücher zur Auswärtigen Politik 1870–1914* (Berlin, 1928).

Scarr, D., *Fragments of Empire: a History of Western Pacific High Commission, 1877–1914*, (Canberra, 1967).

——, ed., *More Pacific Island Portraits* (Canberra, 1979).

Schanz, G., ed., *Kolonialschulden und Kolonialanleihen* (Berlin, 1914).

Scharpenberg, A., 'Die Bedeutung des Norddeutschen Lloyd für die Wirtschaftliche Erschließung der Deutschen Südseekolonien unter Besonderer Berücksichtigung der Deutschen Südseephosphat Aktiengesellschaft Bremen', PhD thesis (Münster, 1944).

Schellong, O., *Alte Dokumente aus der Südsee: Zur Geschichte der Gründung der Kolonie,*

(Königsberg, 1934).

Schindlbeck, M., 'Deutsche Wissenschaftliche Expeditionen und Forschungen in der Südsee bis 1914', in H.J. Hiery ed., *Die Deutsche Südsee 1884–1914* (Paderborn, 2001).

Schinzinger, F., *Die Kolonien und das Deutsche Reich. Die Wirtschaftliche Bedeutung der Deutschen Besitzungen in Übersee* (Stuttgart, 1984).

Schleinitz, G. v., ed., *Die Forschungsreise S.M.S. „Gazelle" In den Jahren 1874–1876* (Berlin, 1888).

Schmack, K., *J.C. Godeffroy & Sohn Kaufleute zu Hamburg. Leistung und Schicksal eines Welthandelshauses* (Hamburg, 1938).

Schmidt, R., *Deutschlands Kolonien: Ihre Gestaltung, Entwicklung und Hilfsquellen* (Berlin, 1895).

Schmidt, W. & Werner, H. eds. *Geschichte der deutschen Post in den Kolonien und im Ausland* (Leipzig 1942)

Schmoller, G. & Sering, M., eds., *Handels und Machtpolitik: Reden und Aufsätze* (Stuttgart, 1900).

Schnee, H., ed., *Deutsches Kolonial-Lexikon* (Leipzig, 1920).

Schneider, K., ed., *Jahrbuch über die Deutschen Kolonien* (Berlin, 1912).

Schramm, P.E., ed., *Kaufleute zu Hause und Übersee, Hamburgische Zeugnisse des 17, 18. & 1900* (Hamburg, 1949).

——, *Deutschland und Übersee* (Braunschweig, 1950).

Seidel, A., *Die Aussichten des Plantagenbaus in den Deutschen Schutzgebieten* (Wismar, 1905).

——, *Unsere Kolonien: Was sind sie Wert, wie können wir sie Erschießen?* (Leipzig, 1905).

Seiler, O.J., *Australien-Fahrt. Linienschiffahrt der Hapag-Lloyd im Wandel der Zeiten* (Herford, 1988).

Shineberg, D., *The People Trade: Pacific Island Labourers and New Caledonia, 1863–1930,* (Honolulu, 1999).

Silburn, P.A., *The Colonies and Imperial Defence* (London, 1909).

Smith, H.H. & Pape, F.A.G., *Coconuts: The Consols of the East* (London, 1913).

Smith, W.D., *The German Colonial Empire* (Chapel Hill, 1978).

Sontag, R.J., *Germany and England, 1848–1894* (New York, 1964).

Souter, G., *New Guinea: The Last Unknown* (Sydney, 1963).

Spellmeyer, H., *Deutsche Kolonialpolitik Im Reichstag* (Stuttgart, 1931).

Spencer, M., *Public Health in Papua New Guinea 1870–1939* (Brisbane, 1999).

Spidle, J.W., 'The German Colonial Civil Service: Organization, Selection and Training', PhD thesis (Stanford, 1972).

Steffen, P., 'Die Katholischen Missionen in Deutsch-Neuguinea', in H.J. Hiery ed., *Die Deutsche Südsee 1884–1914* (Paderborn, 2001).

Stern, E. R., *Gold and Iron: Bismarck, Bleichröder, and the Building of the German Empire,* (New York, 1977).

Stevenson, R.L., *A Footnote to History: Eight Years of Trouble in Samoa* (London, 1892)

Stolper, G., *Die Deutsche Wirtschaft seit 1870* (Tübingen, 1966).

Suchan-Galow, E., 'Die Deutsche Wirtschaftstätigkeit in der Südsee vor der ersten Besitzergreifung 1884', PhD thesis (Hamburg, 1940).

Swadling, P., *Plumes from Paradise* (Coorparoo, 1996).

Tampke, J., ed., *Ruthless Warfare: German Military Planning and Surveillance in the Australian – New Zealand Region before the Great War* (Canberra, 1998).

Tappenbeck, E., *Deutsch Neuguinea* (Berlin, 1901).

Taylor, A.J.P., *Germany's First Bid for Colonies 1884–1885* (London, 1938).

The British Foreign Office, *Former German Possessions in Oceania* (London 1920).

——, *Pacific Islands* (London 1920).

Thilenius, G., ed., *Ergebnisse der Südsee-Expedition 1908–1910* (Berlin, 1913).

Thompson, R.C., *Australian Imperialism in the Pacific: The Expansionist Era 1820–1920,* (Melbourne, 1980).

Thurnwald, R., Forschung auf den Salomon-Inseln und dem Bismarck-Archipel (Berlin, 1912)

Thiel, R., *Die Geschichte des Bremer Vulkan 1805–1997* (Bremen 2008)

Townsend, M.E., *Origins of Modern German Colonialism, 1871–1885* (New York, 1921).

——, *The Rise and Fall of Germany's Colonial Empire 1884–1918* (New York, 1930).

Treue, W., 'Der Erwerb und die Verwaltung der Marschall-Inseln. Ein Beitrag zur Geschichte der Jaluit-Gesellschaft', PhD thesis (Humboldt Universität, Berlin, 1940).

——, *Die Jaluit-Gesellschaft auf den Marshall-Inseln 1887–1914* (Berlin, 1976)

Trood, T., *Island Reminiscences* (Sydney, 1912).

Truppel, O.A. v., *Die Deutsche Südseekolonien: Zur Denkschrift der Südseefirmen an den Reichstag* (Weimar, 1917).

Veur, P.W. v. d., *Documents and Correspondence on New Guinea's Boundaries* (Canberra, 1966).

Vietor, J.K., *Geschichtliche und Kulturelle Entwicklung unserer Schutzgebiete* (Berlin, 1913).

Voigt, P., *Deutschland und der Weltmarkt* (Berlin, 1900).

Wächter, E., *Der Prestigegedanke in der Deutschen Politik von 1890 Bis 1914* (Aarau, 1941).

Wagner, W., ed., *Albert Hahl: Gouverneursjahre in Neuguinea* (Hamburg, 1997).

Walker, M., *Germany and the Emigration 1816–1885* (Cambridge Mass., 1964).

Warnicke, J., *System der Nationalen Schutzpolitik nach Außen* (Jena, 1896).

Washausen, H., *Hamburg und die Kolonialpolitik des Deutschen Reiches 1880—90* (Hamburg, 1968).

Weber, E. v., *Die Erweiterung des Deutschen Wirtschaftsgebietes* (Leipzig, 1878).

Weber, F., *Die Koloniale Finanzverwaltung* (Münster, 1909).

Wegner, G., *Deutschland im Stillen Ozean: Samoa, Karolinen, Marschall Inseln, Marianen, Kaiser Wilhelmsland, Bismarck Archipel und Salomon Inseln* (Leipzig, 1903).

Wehler, H.U., *Bismarck und der Imperialismus* (Frankfurt a. M., 1969).

Wendland, W., *Im Wunderland der Papuas: Ein Deutscher Kolonialarzt erlebt die Südsee*, (Berlin, 1939).

West, F.J., *Hubert Murray: The Australian Pro-Consul* (Melbourne, 1968).

——, ed., *Selected Letters of Hubert Murray* (Melbourne, 1970).

Westphal, W., *Geschichte der Deutschen Kolonien* (München, 1984).

Wickham, H.A., *On the Plantation, Cultivation, and Curing of Para Indian Rubber* (London, 1908)

Whitaker, J.L., Gash, N.G., Hookey, J.F. & Lacey, R.J., *Documents and Readings in New Guinea History* (Milton, 1975).

Wilda, J., *Reise auf der S.M.S. Möve* (Berlin, 1903).

Willard, M., *History of White Australian Policy to 1920* (Melbourne 1967).

Witthöft, H.J. *Tradition und Fortschritt, 125 Jahre Blohm + Voss* (Hamburg, 2002)

Wolfers, E.P., *Race Relations and Colonial Rule in Papua New Guinea* (Sydney, 1975)

Wolff, M.J., *Die Disconto-Gesellschaft* (Berlin, 1930).

Wu, D.Y.H., *The Chinese in Papua New Guinea, 1880–1980* (Hong Kong, 1982).

Ziebura, G., *Grundfragen der Deutschen Außenpolitik seit 1871* (Darmstadt, 1975).

Zimmermann, A., *Die Deutsche Kolonialgesetzgebung. Sammlung der auf die Deutschen Schutzgebiete Bezüglichen Gesetze und Internationale Vereinbarungen* (Berlin, 1893–1900).

——, *Die Handelspolitik des Deutschen Reiches vom Frankfurter Frieden bis zur Gegenwart*, (Berlin, 1901).

Zimmermann, A., ed., *Geschichte der Deutschen Kolonialpolitik* (Berlin, 1914).

Zöller, H., *Deutsch-Neuguinea und meine Ersteigung des Finisterre-Gebirges* (Stuttgart, 1891).

C. Journal and Newspaper Articles and Reports:

'Deutschlands Verpflichtungen in der Südsee', *Deutsche Kolonial Zeitung (=DKZ)* Supplement 1& 5–10 (1886) pp. 188–9.

'Die Entwicklung der Deutschen Interessen in der Südsee', *DKZ* (1886) pp. 367–74.

'Viehzuchtverhältnisse in Kaiser Wilhelmsland', *DKZ* (1894) pp. 109–10.

'Der Nachtragsetat Neu Guinea', *DKZ* (1896) pp. 185–6 and 205.

'Kulimißhandlungen in Deutsch-Neu-Guinea', *Vossische Zeitung (=VZ)* 19 Sep. 1896, Amsterdam.

'Gold in Neu-Guinea', *DKZ* (1898) pp. 339–40.

'Die Arbeiterfrage in unserer Kolonie', *Kölnische Volks-Zeitung (=KVZ)* July 1899.

'Die Chinesen für Kaiser Wilhelms-Land', *KVZ* (Feb. 1900).

'Ein Regierungsdampfer für Neu-Guinea', *DKZ* (1901) pp. 504–5.

'Ein Trauerspiel in der Südsee', *DKZ* (1901) pp. 225–6.

'Handelsstatistisches, Kohlenlager', *Der Ostasiatische Lloyd (=OAL)* 1901, pp. 205 & 763

'Wirtschaftliche Veränderungen in der Südsee?' *DKZ* (1901) p. 498.

'Die Arbeiterfrage', *OAL* (1902) p. 389.

'Über die Handelsunternehmungen in unseren Südsee-Kolonien', *Deutsche Asiatische Warte (=DAW)* 4 (1902)

'Die Zukunft des Bismarck-Archipels, Die Bedeutung der Südseeschutzgebiete, Kautschuk, Tabak,

'Etat der Südseekolonien', *OAL* (1903) pp. 96, 350, 436 & 890

'Steinkohle, Kakao, Zollerhöhung, Neu-Guinea Unerforscht, Kautschuk Kolonialbeiträge', *OAL* (1904) pp. 770, 743, 817, 869 & 920.

'Die Pflanzungen der Station Kavieng', *Deutsche Kolonialblatt (=DKBl)* 1905, pp. 52–3.

'Steinkohle', *OAL* (1905) p. 770.

'Auf der Suche nach Steinkohle', *Gott Will Es* (1906) pp. 55–63.

'Neu Guinea, Chinesenplage, Kohlenfunde, Kautschuk', *OAL* (1906) pp. 164–70, 832, 971, 1016 &1191

'Das Guttapercha und Kautschukunternehmen in Neu-Guinea', *DKZ,* 24 (1907) pp. 521–2 & 537–8.

'Wirtschaftliche Skizze, Einfuhr', *OAL* (1907) pp. 421 & 827.

'Deutsche Marine Expedition', *DKBl* 1–13 (1907–08).

'État, Beziehungen zu Australien, Goldfunde, Kautschuk, Phosphatlager, Kopragewinnung, Landordnung, Zölle &Grenzberichtigung', *OAL* (1908) pp. 926, , 826, 851. 876–7, 1158 & 1210.

'Neu-Guinea unter dem Druck des Neuen Zolltarifes', *DKZ* (1908) pp. 723–6.

'Queensländer Zuckermühlen nach Neu-Guinea', *OAL* (1908) p. 278

'Wegebau im Norden der Gazelle Halbinsel', *DKBl* (1908) pp. 743–4.

'Die Südseeexpedition der Hamburgischen Wissenschaftlichen Stiftung', *DKZ* (1909) pp. 549–50.

'Etat, Kautschuk, Umwandlung einer Englischen Firma, Wirtschaftliche Schmerzen, Zollermäßigung, zur Bevölkerungs- und Arbeiterfrage', *OAL* (1909) pp. 37, 89, 835, 921–2, 1024 &1322–5.

'Mineralvorkommen im Schutzgebiet', *Amtsblatt Rabaul (=ABl-R)* 1909, pp. 127–8.

'Die 25 Jährige Jubelfeier der Südsee-Kolonien', *Kolonie und Heimat (=KuH),* 11 (1909/10) p. 3.

'Die Südseeexpedition der Hamburgischen Wissenschaftlichen Stiftung', *DKZ* (1910) pp. 87–8.

'Eine Reise durch die Kolonien', vol. v, Südsee, *Kolonie und Heimat* (Berlin, 1911)

'Kautschuk', *OAL* (1910) pp. 478–9.

'Etat, Wirtschaftliches, Reformen, Chinesen', *OAL* (1911) pp. 14, 51–3, 88–90, 312 & 433–5

'Die Guttapercha- und Kautschuk -Expedition', *DKBl* (1911) pp. 459–60.

'Jahresbericht über die Weiterentwicklung von Kaiser-Wilhelmsland', *ABl-R* (1911) p. 242.

'Eine Reise durch die Deutsche Kolonien' vol. 5 Südsee, *Kolonialpolitischer Zeitschriften (=KPZ)* (1912).

'Heydt's Koloniales Handbuch', *Buch der deutschen Kolonial- und Überseeunternehmungen,* 6 (1912).

'Am Goldfluß von Kaiser Wilhelmsland', *DKZ* (1913) pp. 379–80.

'Etat, Wirtschaftliches', *OAL*(1913) p. 330 & 539.

'Deutschland in der Südsee', 'Wirtschaftliche Aussichten &Petroleum', *OAL* (1914)

'Eine Reise nach dem Südbezirk', *ABl-R* (1914) pp. 32–4.

'Forschungen Dr. Thurnwalds', *DKZ* (1914) p. 20.

'Death of "Sharkeye" Park: Extraordinary Man who found New Guinea Goldfield', *Pacific Islands Monthly (=PIM)* X, 15 March 1940, pp. 22–3.

Anton, G., 'Neues über unser Südseeschutzgebiet', *Jahrbücher für National-Ökonomie und Statistik* (1900) pp. 517–24.

Auerbach, E., 'Death of "Sharkeye" Park', 'N.G. Goldfield Pioniers, *PIM,* x, 15 March, pp. 21-3 and 15 July, pp.58-9.

Bächer, 'Eine Studienreise nach Neuguinea.' *DKBl* (1912) p. 542.

Badermann, G., 'von der Phosphatindustrie in den Südseeinseln', *DKZ* (1911) pp. 471–2.

Bahlke, G., 'Die Nationale Schiffahrt im Dienste unserer Kolonien', *KZ* (1911) p. 822.

Bast, W., 'Die Einfuhr des Deutschen Reiches aus den Tropen, 1897–1932', *Koloniale Rundschau - Beiheft (=KR)2* (1936).

Baumgartner, 'Geographisches aus Kaiser Wilhelms-Land und dem Bismarck-Archipel.' *Aus allen Weltteilen,* 26 (1894–95)

Beck, C. v., 'Expedition des Reichs-Kolonialamts und der Deutschen Kolonialgesellschaft zur Erforschung der Gebiete des Kaiserin-Augusta-Flusses', *DKZ* (1911) p. 652.

——, 'Die Arbeiterverhältnisse in Neuguinea', *essay* (1912) pp. 47-58.

——, 'Neu Guinea Compagnie, ein deutsches Kolonialunternehmen in der Südsee', *Südseebote (=SB)*1918 pp. 46ff.

Bee, M.C., 'The Origins of a German Far East Policy', *The Chinese Social and Political Science Review* (1937) pp. 65-97.

Bencke, A., 'Der Heutige Stand unserer Kenntnis Neu-Guinea', *Deutsche Rundschau für Geographie und Statistik (=DRGS)* 1910

Bennigsen, R., 'Bericht über Eine Expedition der Deutschen Polizeitruppe an Bord S.M.S. *Möve'*, *DKBl* (1899) pp. 697ff.

——, 'Bericht über eine Reise nach der Nordküste der Gazelle-Halbinsel', *DKBl* (1899) pp. 811–2.

——, 'Bericht über eine Expedition im Hinterlande von Friedrich-Wilhelmshafen und Stephansort' *DKBl* (1900) pp. 324ff.

Bensted, J.T., 'Sir Hubert Murray of Papua', *Australian School of Pacific Administration (=ASOP)* (1953) pp. 675–82.

Berg, M.L., 'Yapese politics, Yapese money and the *Sawel* tribute network before World War I.' *Journal of Pacific History (=JPH)* No. 27 Issue 2 (1992).

Bevan, T.F., 'The Gold Rush to British New Guinea', *Proceedings of the Royal Geographical Society of Australasia (Victoria) 1896–97*, vol. XV, pp. 16–23.

Biskup, P., 'Albert Hahl – Sketch of a German Colonial Official', *Australian Journal of Politics and History (=AJPH)* XIV (1968) pp. 342–57.

——, 'Hahl at Herbertshöhe, 1896–1898: The Genesis of German Native Administration in New Guinea', *Second Waitangi Seminar* (1968) pp. 77–99.

——, 'Foreign Coloured Labour in German New Guinea: A Study of Economic Development', *JPH* (1970) pp. 85–107.

——, 'The New Guinea Memoires of Jean Baptiste Octave Mouton', *JPH* (1974).

Blum, H., 'Curt von Hagen', *Tägliche Rundschau* (1897).

——, 'Die Bestrafung der Mörder des Landeshauptmann von Hagen', *Berliner Lokal-Anzeiger* (1897).

——, 'Das Wirtschaftsleben der Deutschen Südseeinsulaner', *Preußische Jahrbücher,* 2 (1899).

——, 'Neu-Guinea im Haushalte für die Schutzgebiete', *Deutsches Wochenblatt (=DW)*1899, pp. 186ff.

——, 'Noch einmal Neu Guinea', *Deutsches Wochenblatt* (1899) pp. 390–3.

——, 'Südseebilder', *Zukunft* 26 *(=Z)* 1899, pp. 383–6.

Bonn, M.J. ‚Nationale Kolonialpolitik' (München, 1910) p. 32.

——, 'Die Neugestaltung unserer Kolonialen Aufgaben', *essay* (1911) p. 48.

Bonn, O., 'Die Neugestaltungen unserer Kolonialen Aufgaben', *Bibliographisch Wirtschaftliches Magazin* (1911) p. 48.

Böther, P., 'Die Bedeutung einer Durchquerung Neu Guineas für die Wirtschaftliche Entwicklung Kaiser-Wilhelmslands', *KZ* (1903) pp. 240–3 & 2846

Bücher, 'Eine Studienreise nach Neuguinea', *DKBl* (1912) pp. 542–7.

Campbell, S., 'The Country between the Headwaters of the Fly and Sepik Rivers', *Geographical Rev.* 92 (1938) pp. 232ff.

Churchill, W., 'Germany's Lost Pacific Empire', *Geographical Review* (1920) pp. 84–90.

Corris, P., 'Pacific Island Labour Migration in Queensland', *JPH* (1970) pp. 43–64.

D'Albertis, L.M., 'New Guinea: its Fitness for Colonization', *Proceedings of the Royal Colonial Instutute* (1879).

Dammköhler, W.C., 'Im Innern von Deutsch-Neuguinea', *KuH,* 20 (1907–08) pp. 6–8.

——, 'Neues aus Dem Innern von Neu-Guinea', *KuH,* 5 (1909–10) p. 3.

Danckelman, A. v., 'die Fortschritte der Geographischen Forschung im Jahre 1891: Neu-Guinea und Bismarck-Archipel', *Das Ausland* (1891) p. 1027.

Davies, A.G., 'The Pacific Islands – Their Glamour and Their Tragedies', Historical Society of Queensland, 22 April 1943.

Deeken, R., 'Der Handel Neuguineas im Jahre 1911', *DKZ* (1912) pp. 631–2.

——, 'Die Wirtschaftlichen Verhältnisse in Kaiser-Wilhelmsland', *KuH,* 34 (1913) pp. 2 &41.

Dempwolff, O., 'Ärztliche Erfahrungen in Neu-Guinea', *Archiv für Schiffs-& Tropen-Hygiene, (=AfSuTH)* 2 (1898)

——, 'Die Erziehung der Papuas zur Arbeit', *Koloniales Jahrbuch,* 11 (1898).

——, 'Beiträge zur Kenntnis der Sprache von Neu Guinea', *Seminar für Orientalische Sprachen* (1905).

——, 'Beiträge zur Kenntnis der Sprache von Bilibili', *SfOS* (1909).

——, 'Ethnographische Schilderungen Eingeborenen-Sprachen', *ZfKS* 19 (1929)

Denoon, D., 'Book Review of Stewart Firth's 'New Guinea under the Germans'', *JPH* (1983) p. 68.

Dernburg, B. ,Koloniale Erziehung', *Münchner Neueste Nachrichten (=MNN)*1907.

Drew, G.J. 'Discovering Historic Burra', *Department of Mines and Energy, Adelaide*, 1988).

Drus, E., 'The Colonial Office and the Annexation of Fiji', *The Royal Historical Society (=RHS)* 4 (1950).

Ewers, W.H., 'Malaria in the early Years of German New Guinea', *Journal Papua and New Guinea Society,* 6.1 (1972)

Finsch, O. ,Über Naturprodukte der Westlichen Südsee', *DKZ* (1887) pp. 519–30, 543–51 & 593–6.

——, 'Deutsche Namensgebung in der Südsee', *Deutsche Erdkunde* (1902) pp. 42ff.

——,. ,Wie Ich Kaiser Wilhelms-Land Erwarb: Mein Anteil an dieser Kolonial-Gründung der NGC', *Deutsche Monatsschrift für das gesamte Leben der Gegenwart* (1902) pp. 406ff.

——, 'Südseearbeiten: Gewerbe -und Kunstfleiß, Tauschmittel und Geld der Eingeborenen auf Grundlage der Rohstoffe etc.', *Hamburgisches Kolonialinstitut,* 14 (1914).

Firth, S.G., 'German Firms in the Western Pacific Islands, 1857–1914', *JPH,* 8 (1973) pp. 10ff

——, 'The New Guinea Company 1885–1899: A Case of Unprofitable Imperialism', *Historical Studies, Australia & New Zealand (=HS.ANZ)* XV (1972) pp. 361ff.

——, 'German Labour Policy in Nauru and Angaur, 1906–1914', *JPH,* 13 (1978) pp. 36ff.

——, 'German New Guinea: The Archival Perspective', *JPH,* 20 (1985) pp. 95ff.

Fitzner, R., 'Die Bevölkerung der deutschen Südseekolonien', *Globus,* 84 (1903)

Fischer, H., 'Die Trommeln von Wuwulo', *Würtembergischer Verein für Handelsgeographie,* 25, (1907) p. 79.

Flierl, J., 'Die Bedeutung der Alkoholfrage für unseren Kolonien', *Kolonialpolitik und Kolonialwirtschaft,* X (1908).

Foster, R.J., 'Komine and Tanga: a Note on Writing the History of German New Guinea', *JPH,* 22 (1987) pp. 56ff.

Full, 'Berichte über eine Reise nach Morobe und um Neupommern.' *ABl-R* (1909) pp. 48ff.

Fülleborn, F., 'Hamburger Südsee-Expedition', *DKZ* (1908) p. 845.

Gammage, B., 'The Rabaul Strike, 1929', *JPH,* 10 (1975) pp. 3ff.

Germer, E., 'Miklucho Maklai und die Kolonial Annexion Neuguineas', *Museum für Völkerkunde.*

Gibbney, H.J., 'The Interregnum in the Government of Papua', *AJPH* (1966).

——, 'The New Guinea Gold Rush of 1878', *Journal of the Royal Australian Historical Society(=JRAHS)* 58,(1972) pp. 284ff

Grabowsky, F., 'Erinnerungen an Neu-Guinea', *Das Ausland* 63 (1889) pp. 121–3; (1890) pp. 91ff

——, 'Der Bezirk von Hatzfeldthafen und seine Bewohner', *Petermanns Geographische Mitteilung(=PGM)* 41 (1895) pp. 186–9.

——, 'Eine Wirtschaftliche Studie über Neu-Guinea und dem Bismarckarchipel.' *DKZ,* 51 (1899)

Hahl, A., 'Achtzehn Jahre in Deutsch-Neuguinea', *ZGEB* (1920) pp. 22f.

——, 'Berichte des Kaiserlichen Gouverneurs A. Hahl über eine Reise nach den Salomon-Inseln', *DKBl* (1904) pp. 61ff.

——, 'Das Mittlere Neumecklenburg', *Globus,* 9 (1907) pp. 310ff.

——, 'Der Bismarck - Archipel und die Salomons - Inseln', *DKZ,* 12 (1899) pp. 107ff.

——, 'Der Aufbau der Station Morobe auf Kaiser-Wilhelm-Land', *DKZ* (1935) p. 237.

——, 'Deutschland und die Inseln des Südlichen Ozeans', *Deutsche Presse-Korrespondenz* (1932)

——, 'Deutsch-Neuguinea und die Ersten Jahre Seiner Verwaltung', *DKZ* (1934) pp. 262–3.

——, 'Die Ansiedlung von Europäern in den Tropen', *Koloniale Rundschau (=KR)* 1920 pp. 168-76.

——, 'Die Australische Mandatsverwaltung in Neu Guinea', *essay* (1939) pp. 10–32.

——, 'Deutsche Kolonien in der Südsee', *essay* (Hamburg, 1938).

——, 'Geologie von Neuguinea', *Deutsche Geologische Gesellschaft, Berlin,* 66 (1914) pp. 250–4.

—— ,Guttapercha- und Kautschuk-Expedition in Neuguinea', *DKZ,* 25 (1908) p. 405.

——, 'Neu Guinea', *DKZ* (1904) p. 411.

——, 'Rechtsverhältnisses und Rechtsanschauungen der Eingeborenen', *Nachrichten über Kaiser Wilhelms-Land und dem Bismarck Archipel (=NKWL)* 1897, pp. 68–85.

——, 'Über die Entwickelung des Bismarck-Archipels in dem Jahre 1897/98', *DKBl* (1906) pp. 405-6.

——, *Jahrbuch über die deutschen Kolonien,* 5 (1912) pp. 161ff.

——, 'Über die Rechtsanschauungen der Eingeborenen eines Theiles der Blanchebucht und des Innern der Gazelle Halbinsel', *NKWL* (1897) pp. 68–85.

——, 'Wirtschaftliche und Technische Fragen in Neu-Guinea', *Kolonial-Wirtschaftliches-Komitee (=KWK)* 1910, pp. 6–17.

——, 'Wirtschaftliche Fragen in Neuguinea', *DKBl* (1911) pp. 55–6.

——, 'Zur Geographie des Schutzgebietes von Deutsch-Neu-Guinea', *DKZ* (1902).

Hahl, A. & Schlechter, R., 'Fortführung des Guttapercha- und Kautschuk-Unternehmens und Reisbau versuche in Neu-Guinea', *KWK,* 2 (1910) pp. 8–21.

Hanneken, W. v., 'Eine Kolonie in der Wirklichkeit: Ilusionsfreie Betrachtungen eines ehemaligen Stationsvorstehers im Schutzgebiet der NGC', *Die Nation* (1895) pp. 133–6, 54–5.

Hardach, G., 'Bausteine für ein Größeres Deutschland: die Annexion der Karolinen und Marianen 1898–1899', *Zeitschrift für Unternehmungsgeschichte,* 33 (1988) pp. 1–21.

Hayn, 'Vermessungsarbeiten S.M.S *Möve* an den Küsten von Kaiser Wilhelmsland, Neu-Pommern und Neu-Mecklenburg', *NKWL* (1896) p. 51.

Healy, A.M., 'Review of S. Firth's 'New Guinea under the Germans', *Pacific Studies (=PS)* 8 (1984)

——, 'Ophir to Bulolo: The History of the Gold Search in New Guinea', *HS,* XII (1965) pp. 105ff.

Henderson, L.O., 'Germany's Trade with Her Colonies, 1884–1914', *Economic History Review (=HER)* IX (1938) pp. 1–16.

Hernsheim, E. ,Der Bismarck-Archipel und seine Zukunft als Deutsche Colonie', *Hamburgischer Correspondent (=HC),* 1886.

——, *Die Neu-Guinea Compagnie in Kaiser Wilhelmsland und im Bismarck-Archipel* (1888)

——, 'Der Pierbau des Norddeutschen Lloyd in Simpsonhafen', *DKZ* (1904) p. 467ff.

Hernsheim, F., 'Die Marshall Inseln', *Geographische Gesellschaft* (1886) pp. 297–308.

Herrmann, E.D. and Weinland, C.D., 'Gesundheitsverhältnisse der Beamten und Arbeiter', *NKWL,* Heft i (1890) pp. 27ff.

Hesse-Wartegg, E. v., 'die Zukunft von Deutsch-Neu-Guinea', *Deutsche Rundschau für Geographie und Statistik (=DRGS)* 24 (1901/02) pp. 97–103.

Hezel, F. X., 'The Man who was reputed to be King: David Dean O'Keefe.' *JPH* No. 43 (2008)

——, *Strangers In Their Own Land: A Century of Colonial Rule in the Caroline and Marshall Islands* (Hawaii, 1995)

——, 'A Yankee Trader in Yap' in D. Scarr, ed., More Pacific Island Portraits (Canberra, 1978)

Hiery, H.J. ,der Melanesier und das „Böse", in W.A. Ritter and J.A. Schlumberger eds. *17th Bayreuther Historisches Kolloquium* (2001) pp. 137–47.

Hindorf, R., 'Einige Vorschläge für die Praktische Kolonisation im Schutzgebiet der Neu-Guinea-Kompagnie', *DKZ* (1890) pp. 9–23 & 102–5.

Hoffmann, A., 'Rechtsverhältnisse und Rechtsanschauungen der Eingeborenen', *NKWL* (1898) p. 72.

Hoffmann, G., 'Wirtschaftsspionage in der Südsee: H.H. Meier und Joh. Ces. Godeffroy', *Bremisches Jahrbuch,* 76 (1997).

Hogbin, H.I., 'Trading Expedition in Northern New Guinea', *Oceania*, 4 (1935) pp. 375-407.

——, 'Tillage and Economy: New Guinea ', *Oceania*, 2 & 3 (1938 & 1939) pp. 127–51 & 286–325.

Hollrung, M., 'Wissenschaftliche Expeditionen in Kaiser Wilhelmsland', *NKWL* (1887) pp. 178ff.

Hollrung, M. & Schumann, K., 'Die Flora von Kaiser Wilhelms Land', *NKWL Beiheft* (1889).

Hood, F.A., 'The Kanaka Mercantile Marine', *Walkabout*, 2 (1936) pp. 37–8.

Hüsker, Studer & Naumann, 'Die Naturwissenschaftlichen Ergebnisse der Expedition *S.M.S. Gazelle*', *ZGEB*, 11 (1876)

Jäckel, H., 'Die Neu Guinea Compagnie', *Kolonialpolitik, Kolonialrecht und Kolonialwirtschaft*, (1909) pp. 25ff

Jacobi, E., 'Die Bedeutung unserer Südsee-Kolonien für den Weltverkehr', *DKZ* (1901) pp. 462–3.

Jacobs, M., 'Bismarck and the Annexation of New Guinea', *HS.ANZ*, 5 (1952) pp. 15–26.

——, 'The Colonial Office and New Guinea 1874–1884', *HS.ANZ*, 5 (1952) pp. 106–18.

Jacobs, W.R., 'The Fatal Confrontation: Early Native-White Relations on the Frontiers of Australia, New Guinea and America, a Comparative Study', *PHR*, 40 (1971) pp. 283–309.

Jöhlinger, O., 'Das Heimische Kapital und die Kolonien', *Koloniale Rundschau* (=*KR*) 1912, pp. 662f

——, 'Weltpolitik und Kolonialpolitik', *KR* (1916) pp. 461–73.

Joyce, R.B., 'The British New Guinea Syndicate Affair', *The Royal Historical Society Queensland*, V (1953) pp. 771–93.

——, 'Sir William MacGregor: The Role of the Individual' *Waigani Seminar* (1968) pp. 33–43.

Jung, K.E., 'Die Arbeitsverhältnisse in der Südsee mit Bezug auf die Entwicklung unserer Dortigen Erwebungen', *Globus*, 48 (1885) pp. 282ff.

Kennedy, P.M., 'Bismarck's Imperialism: The Case of Samoa, 1880-1890', *HJ*, XV, 2 (1972)

——, 'German Colonial Expansion in the late Nineteenth Century: Has the "Manipulated Social Imperialism" Been Ante-Dated', *Past and Present*(=*PP*), 54 (1972).

Kersten, 'Bericht über eine Expedition nach Morobe.' *ABl-R* (1913) pp. 131–2.

Kienitz, E., 'Der Wert der Deutschen Schutzgebiete: Ein Schätzungsversuch', *TP* (1917) pp. 449–53.

Kindt, L., 'Das Schreckensgespenst der Chinesengefahr', *DKZ.* (1902).

——, 'Auswanderung deutscher Landwirte nach Java', *Kolonialpolitik und Kolonialwirtschaft*, 4 (1903).

Knaplund, P., Sir Arthur Gordon on the New Guinea Question, 1883', *HS.ANZ*, 7 (1956) pp. 328–35.

Kohl, K., 'die Verlegung des Gouvernements von Herbertshöhe nach Simpsonhafen', *ABl-R*, 1 (1909)

Kolonial-Wirtschaftliches Komitee, 'Wirtschaftsatlas der Deutschen Kolonien' (1900–1914)

König, B. v., 'Die Finanzen der Deutschen Schutzgebiete', *DKG* (1900/01) pp. 149ff.

Krämer, A., 'Die Chinesengefahr in den Deutschen Südseekolonien', *DKZ.* (1902) pp. 30–1.

Krauss. ,Expeditionsbericht aus Morobe', *ABl-R* (1912) pp. 7–9.

Krieger, M., 'Die Etats für die Südseeschutzgebiete', *DKZ* (1899) pp. 530–1.

——, 'Die Umwandlung der Neuguinea-Kompagnie in eine Kolonialgesellschaft', *DKZ* (1899) pp. 231f.

——, 'Über Das Arbeitsmaterial in Neuguinea', *DKZ*, 29 (1899) pp. 260–1.

——, 'Über Handel und Verkehr auf Neu-Guinea', *ZKPKW* (1899) p. 104.

——, 'Über die Handelsunternehmungen in unseren Südseekolonien', *DKZ*, 31 (1899) pp. 277–8.

——, 'Über die Gesundheitsverhältnisse in unseren Südseeschutzgebieten', *DKZ* (1900) pp. 316–7.

——, 'Kaiser Wilhelmsland und seine Nachbarkolonien', *DAW*, 4 (1902) p. 49.

——, 'Über Ansiedlung und Verwendung von Chinesen in Neu-Guinea', *DAW*, 4 (1902) p. 45.

——, 'Über Handel und Verkehr auf Neu-Guinea', *DAW*, 4 (1902) p. 30.

Kunze, G., 'Berichte', *Rheinische Missionsgesellschaft* (1891) pp. 46-54 & 339–41.

Lauterbach, C., 'Die Kaiser Wilhelmsland Expedition', *DKZ* (1896) p. 434.

——, 'Über den Abschluß der Kaiser Wilhelmsland Expedition', *DKBl* (1897) pp. 4–5.

——, 'Die Geographischen Ergebnisse der Kaiser Wilhelms-Land-Expedition', *ZGEB* (1898) pp. 141–7.

Legge, J.D., 'Australia and New Guinea to the Establishment of the British Protectorate, 1884', *HS.ANZ*, 4 (1950) pp. 34ff.

Leidecker, C., 'Einiges über die Entwicklung von Deutsch-Neu-Guinea', *Überall* (1909) p. 129.

Disastrous Ventures

Lewis, D.C., 'Labour and Development in Papua, 1912–1922: The case of the BNGD Company', MA (ANU, 1973) pp. 1-65.

Lewis, W.A., 'World Production, 1870–1960', *Manchester School of Economics M.Sch* (1952)

Lewis, W.A. & O'Leary, P.J., 'Secular Swings in Production and Trade, 1870–1913', *M.Sch* (1955).

Lorentz, H., 'Expedition nach Neu-Guinea', *ZGEB* (1907) pp. 121, 405, 82,.

Louis, W.R., 'Australian and German Colonies in the Pacific, 1914–1919', *Journal of Modern History, (=JMH)* 38 (1966) pp. 407ff.

MacGregor, W., 'British New Guinea: Administration', *Proceeding of the Royal Colonial Institute,* vol. xxvi (1894–95)

Maiden, P., 'The Tragedy of the New Guinea Prospecting Expedition', *Australian Heritage* (2006).

Märker, 'Gutachten über die Phosphate auf den Purdy-Inseln', *NKWL* (1888) pp. 237–44.

Marquardsen, H. & Danckelman, A. v., 'Berichte über das Meteorologische Beobachtungswesen im Schutzgebiet Deutsch-Neuguinea', *Mitteilungen aus den Deutschen Schutzgebieten,* vols. 3-27 (1890-1914).

Merrett, D.T. 'Australian Banking Practice and the Crisis of 1893' *Australian. Economic History Review (=AEHR), 29, 1* (1990) pp. 60ff.

Mayo, J., 'The Protectorate of British New Guinea 1884–1888', *Second Waigani Seminar* (1968).

McKillop, R.F. 'Tramways and Oxen: The New Guinea Kompagnie Tramways of Astrolabe Bay', *Light Railways,* 81 (1883)

Meeker, R., 'History of Shipping Subsidies', *American Economic Association,* 6 (1905) p. 171.

Meier, H., 'Bericht über eine von Simbang aus Unternommene Inlandexpedition', *ABl-R* (1911).

Mende, W., 'Zur Übernahme der Verwaltung des Schutzgebiets von Neu Guinea durch das Reich', *Koloniales Jahrbuch* (1897) pp. 270-9.

Molesworth, B.H. 'Kanaka Labour in Queensland', *Royal Historical Society of Queensland* (1916).

Morren, F.W., 'Ein Holländischer Pflanzer über Deutsch-Neu-Guinea', *DKZ* (1895) pp. 106–8.

Mortensen, R., 'Slaving in Australian Courts: Blackbirding Cases, 1869–1871', *Journal of South Pacific Law,* 4 (2000).

Moses, J.A., 'The German Empire in Melanesia 1884–1914', *Second Waigani Seminar* (1968).

——, 'Australia and the Reich, 1870–1942: Deutschtumpolitik in Australia from Kaiserreich to the Third Reich', *Chauvel Seminar Series, No. 1* (University of New England, 2000).

Müller, G., 'Arbeitspflicht und Arbeitszwang der Eingeborenen', *Die Deutschen Kolonien* (1902).

Murray, J.H.P., 'Three Power Rule in New Guinea', Parliamentary Report (1919).

——, 'Indirect Rule in Papua', *Australian Association for the Advancement of Science* (1928) pp. 329ff

Nelson, H.N., 'The Swinging Index: Capital Punishment and British and Australian Administration in Papua New Guinea, 1888–1945', *JPH,* 13 (1978) pp. 130–52.

Neubauer, P., 'Die Wirtschaftliche Bedeutung der Deutschen Kolonien', *Marine Rundschau,* 12 (1895).

Neuhauß, R., 'Wirtschaftliches aus Deutsch-Neu-Guinea', *KR* (1911) pp. 348–58.

——, 'Die Erforschung von Neuguinea mit dem Luftballon', *DKZ* (1913) p. 22.

——, 'Die Wirtschaftliche Ausnutzung von Kaiser-Wilhelmsland', *Deutsche Erde* (1913) p. 185.

Neumayer, 'Bestimmungen der Magnetischen Deklination, Ausgeführt von S.M.S. *Möwe* auf den Salomon-Inseln und Neu Guinea', *Hydrographien und Maritimen Meteorologie* (1897) p. 308.

Oldörp, R. & Dammköhler, W., 'Bericht über eine Reise in DNG 1908–09', *ABl-R* (1909) pp. 135–6.

Osborne, D.H. 'Gira and Yodda Goldfields: Early Discoveries in North-East Papua', *PIM,* xiii (1943)

Overlack, P., 'Australian Defence Awareness and German Naval Planning in the Pacific', *War & Society-Australian Defence Force Academy* (1992) pp. 37-51.

——, 'German Commerce Warfare for the Australian Stations 1900–1914', *War & Society,* 14 (1992)

——, 'Bless the Queen and Curse the Colonial Office; Australian Reaction to German Consolidation in the Pacific, 1871–99', *JPH,* 33 (1998) p. 133 ff.

Pauli, C., 'Gelbe Konkurrenz im Schutzgebiete von Deutsch-Neu-Guinea', *Koloniale Zeitschrift* (1904) pp. 199-200.

Penck, A., 'Die Erforschung des Kaiserin-Augusta-Flusses durch Leonardt Schultze', *ZGEB* (1911)

Pfannenschmidt, 'Wirtschaftliche Ausblicke aus der Südsee', *TP* (1904) pp. 667–73.

Pfeil, J. v., 'Expedition nach Neu-Mecklenburg', *NKWL* (1888) pp. 153–4.

——, 'Der Bismarck-Archipel im Deutschen Schutzgebiet der Südsee.' Internationaler Geographischer Congress (1892).

——, 'Der Etat für Neu-Guinea', *DKZ* (1901) pp. 2–3, 1902) pp. 111–12.

——, 'Die Wirtschaftliche Entwicklung des Bismarckarchipels', *DKZ*, 6 (1902) pp. 30ff

Pflüger, A., 'Einige Geologische Bemerkungen über den Bismarck-Archipel', *Mitteilungen aus den Schutzgebieten, Wissenschaftliches Beiheft zum Deutschen Kolonialblatt* (1901) pp. 131–8.

Pöch, R., 'Berichte von Meiner Reise nach Neu-Guinea', Akademie der Wissenschaften, Sitzungsbericht Mathematisch-Naturwissenschaft (1905) pp. 437ff.

——, 'Meine Reisen in Deutsch-, Britisch- und Niederländisch-Neu Guinea', *ZGEB* (1907) pp. 149-65.

Pogge v. Strandmann, H., 'Domestic Origins of Germany's Colonial Expansion under Bismarck', *PP*, 42 (1969)

Poschinger, H. v., 'Aus der Denkwürdigkeit Heinrich von Kusserow', *Deutsche Revue,* I (1908).

Preuß, P., 'Die Pflanzlichenausfuhrprodukte Neu-Guineas', *Tropenpflanzer (=TP)* 1909 pp. 327-31.

——, 'Wirtschaftliche Werte in den Deutschen Südseekolonien', *TP,* 8 & 10 (1916) pp. 441ff.

Price, C. & Baker, E., 'Origins of Pacific Island Labourers in Queensland, 1863—1904', *JPH*, 2 (1976)

Range, P., 'Die Metallerze der Deutschen Schutzgebiete', *Zeitschrift der deutschen Geologischen Gesellschaft* (1939).

——, 'Petroleum im Kaiser-Wilhelms-Land', *TP* (1942) pp. 77–80.

Reiber, J., 'Eine Geologische Expedition in das Toricelligebirge im Kaiser Wilhelmsland', *PGM*, 56 (1910) pp. 78ff

Reiber, J. & Richarz, S., 'Vorläufiger Bericht über Geologische Untersuchungen in Kaiser-Wilhelmsland', *PGM,* 53 (1907) pp. 285-6.

Reinecke, F., 'Die Entwicklung der Südsee-Schutzgebiete.' *DKZ* (1907) pp. 136–7.

Richarz, S., 'Geologischer Bau von Kaiser-Wilhelms-Land', *Neues Jahrbuch für Mineralogie*, 29 (1910) pp. 406–536.

Riedel, O. ,Die Wirtschaftliche Leistungsfähigkeit der Deutschen Südsee-Besitzungen', *Zukunft der Deutschen Kolonien* (Berlin, 1918) pp. 59-63.

Risely, H.H., 'The Idea of a Greater Germany', *Asiatic Quarterly Review* (Sep. 1890).

Rowley, C.D., 'Native Officials and Magistrates of German New Guinea 1897–1921', *South Pacific* (1954).

——, 'The Promotion of Native Health in German New Guinea', *South Pacific* ix (1957) pp. 391-9.

Runge, R., 'Beriberifälle in Käwieng', *ABl-NG* (1909) pp. 138–40.

Rüdiger, H., 'Bericht über den Verlauf der Ehlersschen Expedition', *DKBl,* 1896, pp. 448–53

Sack, P.G., 'A History of German New Guinea: A Debate about Evidence and Judgements', *JPH*, 20 (1985) pp. 84–94.

——, 'Protectorates and Twists: Law, History and the Annexation of German New Guinea', *Australian Year Book of International Law* (1986)

Salisbury, R.F., 'Early Stages of Economic Development in New Guinea', *Journal of the Polynesia Society,* IXXI (1962).

Sapper, K., 'Bevölkerungsabnahme und Arbeiteranwerbung auf Neumecklenburg', *ABl-R* (1909)

——, 'Wissenschaftliche Ergebnisse einer amtlichen Forschungsreise nach dem Bismarck-Archipel im Jahre 1908.' *Mitteilungen Aus den Schutzgebieten, Wissenschaftliches Beiheft DKBl* (1910).

Schellong, O., 'Tropenhygenische Betrachtungen unter Spezieller Berücksichtigung der für Kaiser-Wilhelmsland in Betrachtkommenden Verhältnisse', *DKZ*, 5 (1888) pp. 341 ff.

——, 'Der Deutsche in Kaiser-Wilhelmsland in seiner Stellungnahme zum Landeseingeborenen', *DKZ*, 6 (1889) pp. 69 ff.

——, 'Das Tropenklima und sein Einfluß auf das Leben und die Lebensweise des Europäers', *Koloniales Jahrbuch,* 5 (1892) pp. 58 ff.

Schlechter, R., 'Reisebericht der Guttapercha- und Kautschuk-Expedition nach den Südsee-Kolonien', 1901-1903, *TP* (1903) pp. 211ff

——, 'Über Eine Reise in Neu-Guinea und Neu-Guinea-Guttapercha', *DKBl* (1904) p. 296.

——, 'Gutta- und Kautschuk-Stationen auf Neu-Guinea', *TP,* Beilage (1911) pp. 256ff.

Schlechter, R. & Hahl, A., 'Fortführung des Guttapercha- und Kautschuk-Unternehmens und Reisbauversuche in Neu Guinea', *Kolonial-Wirtschaftliches Komitee* (1910) pp. 8-21.

Schleinitz, G. v., 'Beschreibung der Nordküste von Kaiser Wilhelms-Land', *NKWL* (1889) pp. 48–87.

——, 'Begleitworte zur Karte der Nordküste des Westlichen Theiles der Insel Neu-Pommern', *ZGEB* (1896) pp. 137–54.

——, 'Was Gibt uns der Fall Wehlan zu Denken und zu Lernen', *DKZ.* (1896) pp. 65–7.

Shlomowitz, R. 'Mortality and the Pacific Labour Trade', *JHP* 22 (1987) p. 48

——, 'Mortality and Indentured Labour in Papua (1885–1914)', *JPH* 23 (1988) pp. 70–7

Schmeisser, 'Über Geologische Untersuchungen in den Deutschen Kolonien in der Südsee', *OAL* (1906) p. 548.

——, 'Bodenschätze in den Deutschen Schutzgebieten des Fernen Ostens', *OAL*(1908) p. 451.

Schmiele, G., 'Characteristik des Schutzgebietes der NGC', *DKBl* (1892) pp. 469–73.

Schott, G., 'Kapitänleutnant Lebahn und die Forschungsreise S.M.S. *Planet*', *Annalen der Hydrographien und Maritimen Meteorologie* (1907) p. 145.

Schrader, C., 'Erforschung des Gebietes Nördlich von Finschhafen', *NKWL* (1886) pp. 119–21.

Schultze, L., 'Forschungsreise im Inneren der Insel Neu-Guinea', *Geographische Gesellschaft München* (1912) p. 296.

——, 'Forschungen im Innern der Insel Neu-Guinea', *Mitteilungen aus den Schutzgebieten, DKBl* (1914).

Sieben, F.M., 'Über die Aussichten von Tropischen Kulturen in Ost-Afrika und Neu Guinea', *Koloniales Jahrbuch* (1893)

Singelmann, 'Prof. Dr. Finschs Anteil an der Erwerbung des Deutschen Südsee-Schutzgebietes', *DKZ* (1909)

Snelling, R.C., 'Peacemaking, 1919: Australia, New Zealand and the British Empire Delegation at Versailles', *The Journal of Imperial and Commonwealth History,* 4 (1975-76) pp. 15-28.

Spennemann, D., 'An Officer, Yes; but a Gentleman? A Biographical Sketch of Eugen Brandeis', *PSM,* 21 (1998).

St Julian, C., 'The Latent Resources of Polynesia', *Australian Era* (1851).

Stollé, A., 'Berichte des Leiters der Kaiserin-Augusta-Strom-Expedition bis zum 2. Mai 1912', *DKZ,* 29 (1912) pp. 469–70.

Stollé, A. & Behrmann, W., 'Expedition zur Erforschung des Kaiserin-Augusta-Stromes', *DKZ* (1912)

——, 'Berichte, Bilder und Ergebnisse aus Kaiser-Wilhelmsland vom Kaiserin-Augustafluß und seinen Nebenflüssen', *DKZ,* 30 (1913) pp. 6ff

Strantz, V. v., 'Deutschlands Wirtschaftliche Position in der Süd-See', *Deutsche Rundschau,* 10 (1888)

Tappenbeck, E., 'Die Arbeiterverhältnisse in Kaiser Wilhelmsland', *DKZ* (1894) pp. 131–2.

——, 'Die Chinesengefahr in Den Deutschen Kolonien', *DKZ* (1894).

——, 'Kaiser-Wilhelmsland-Expedition', *DKZ* (1897) pp. 21–4.

——, 'Stephansort und Erima', *DKZ* (1897) pp. 256ff.

——, 'Bericht über die Ramu-Expedition', *NKWL* (1898) pp. 52–9.

Tate, M., 'The Australian Monroe Doctrine', *Political Science Quarterly,* 76 (1961) pp. 264–84.

Taylour, H.H. & Morley, I., 'The Development of Gold Mining in Morobe, New Guinea',*The Australian Institute of Mining & Metallurgy,* 89 (1933) p. 5

Thiel, F., 'Johann Stanislaus Kubary die unermüdliche Erforscher der Südsee', *DKZ,* 31 (1899).

Thilenius, G., 'Die Arbeiterfrage in der Südsee', *Globus,* 77 (1900) pp. 69-72.

——, 'Geologische Notizen aus dem Bismarck-Archipel', *Globus,* 78 (1900) p. 201.

——, 'Eine Durchquerung des Gebietes zwischen dem Kaiserin-Augusta-Fluß und der Küste von Neuguinea', *Mitteilungen aus den Deutschen Schutzgebieten* (1913) pp. 357-63.

Thurnwald, R., 'Die Eingeborenen Arbeitskräfte im Südsee-Schutzgebiet', *KR* (1910)

——, 'Entdeckungen im Becken des Oberen Sepik', *Mitteilungen aus den Deutschen Schutzgebieten* (1914) pp. 338ff.

——, 'Nachrichten von der Deutschen Neu-Guinea Expedition', *ZGEB* (1914) pp. 54–6 & 791–8.

——, 'Der Wert von New Guinea als Deutsche Kolonie', *KR* (1918) pp. 43–56.

——, 'Detzners Forschungen in Neuguinea während des Krieges.' *PGM* (1920).

Treue, W., 'Die Jaluit-Gesellschaft', *Tradition Zeitschrift für Firmengeschichte und Unternehmer,* vii (1962)

Truppel, G., 'Die Aussichten im Bismarck-Archipel', *DKZ* (1888) pp. 287–90.

Verbeck, P., 'Die Entdeckung des Bismarckarchipels vor 200 Jahren durch William Dampier', *ZKPKW* (1899/1900) p. 389.

Vetter, K., 'Papuanische Rechtsverhältnisse der Jabim Eingeborenen', *NKWL* (1897) pp. 86–102.

Vogelsang, T.W., 'Zur Frage der Einführung von Chinesen in Neu-Guinea', *DKZ* (1900) p. 164.

Volkens, G., 'Der Jahresbericht über die Entwicklung des Schutzgebietes von Deutsch-Neu-Guinea 1899/1900', *DKZ* (1901)

Vollmer, A., 'Die Wirtschaftlichen Fortschritte der Südsee-Inseln 1890–91', *Globus,* 61 (1892) p. 291.

——, 'Goldsucher in Neuguinea', *PGM,* 43 (1897) pp. 138-9.

Ward, S.N. & Day, S., 'Ritter Island Volcano - Lateral Collapse and the Tsunami of 1888', *Geographical Journal International,* 154 (2003) pp. 891-902.

Warnack, Supf, M. & Matthiesen, W., 'Unsere Kolonialwirtschaft in ihrer Bedeutung für Industrie, Handel und Landwirtschaft', KWK (1914) p. 136.

Warnack, M., 'Der Handel Neuguineas 1912', *DKZ* (1913) pp. 608–9.

Wehler, H.U., 'Bismarck's Imperialism 1862–1890', *PP* (1970) pp. 119-55.

Wendland, W., 'Über das Auftreten der Beri-Beri Krankheit in Kaiser-Wilhelmsland', *AfSuTH* (1897)

Werner, B. v., 'Die Erste Kreuzung Deutscher und Amerikanischer Interessen auf Samoa', *Unsere Zeit, Deutsche Revue der Gegenwart,* I (1889) pp. 162–76.

Wernicke, W., 'Die Waria-Expedition', *DKBl* (1908) pp. 948–9.

West, F.J., 'The Beginning of Australian Ruler in Papua', *Political Science* (1957) pp. 38–50.

Weule, K. ,Die Erforschung von Kaiser-Wilhelms-Land', in, *KVZ* (Köln, 1897).

Weyhmann, H., 'Eduard Hernsheim', *Südsee Bote* (1918).

Wichmann, A., 'Deutsch-Niederländische Grenzkommission in Neu Guinea', *PGM,* 57 (1911)

Wick, W., 'Physiologische Studien zur Akklimatisation an die Tropen', *AfSuTH* (1910)

Wiese, G., 'Wirtschaftliches und Ethnographisches aus Kaiser-Wilhelms-Land', *DKG* (1912Winkler, C., 'Handel und Verkehr von Deutsch-Neuguinea im Jahre 1909', *DKZ* (1911) pp. 357–61.

Wolff-Posen, E., 'Der Farbige Obervorsteher im Schutzgebiet Deutsch Neuguinea', *Zeitschrift der Deutchen Kolonialgesellschaft für Kolonialpolitik und Kolonialwirtschaft* (1904) pp. 850–8.

Young, M.W., 'The Best Workmen in Papua: Goodenough Islanders and the Labour Trade, 1900–1960', *JPH,* 18 (1983)

Zöller, H., 'Meine Untersuchungen in das Finisterre-Gebirge', *PGM,* 36 (1890) pp. 233ff.

——, 'Untersuchungen von 24 Sprachen aus dem Schutzgebiet der Neu-Guinea-Kompagnie', *PGM,* 36 (1890) pp. 122–8 & 45–52.

——, 'Die Deutschen Salomo-Inseln Buka und Bougainville', *PGM,* 37 (1891).

——, 'Meine Expedition in das Innere von Deutsch-Neuguinea', *Geographische Gesellschaft München* (1891) pp. 1–19.

Disastrous Ventures

CHARTS

Disastrous Ventures

Chart 1

European and Japanese population trend in German New Guinea and The Island Territory, 1886–1913
1 April to 30 March from 1886 to 1899, calendar year thereafter
Males (age ≥ 15 years)
Females
Children
Kaiser Wilhelmsland and Bismarck Archipelago
Total European
Population
1,800
1,600
1,400
1,200
1,000
800
600
400
200
0
1886/87
1887/88
1888/89
1889/90
1890/91
1891/92
1892/93
1893/94
1894/95
1895/96
1896/97
1897/98
1898/99
1899
1900
1901
1902
1903
1904
1905
1906
1907
1908
1909
1910
1911
1912
1913

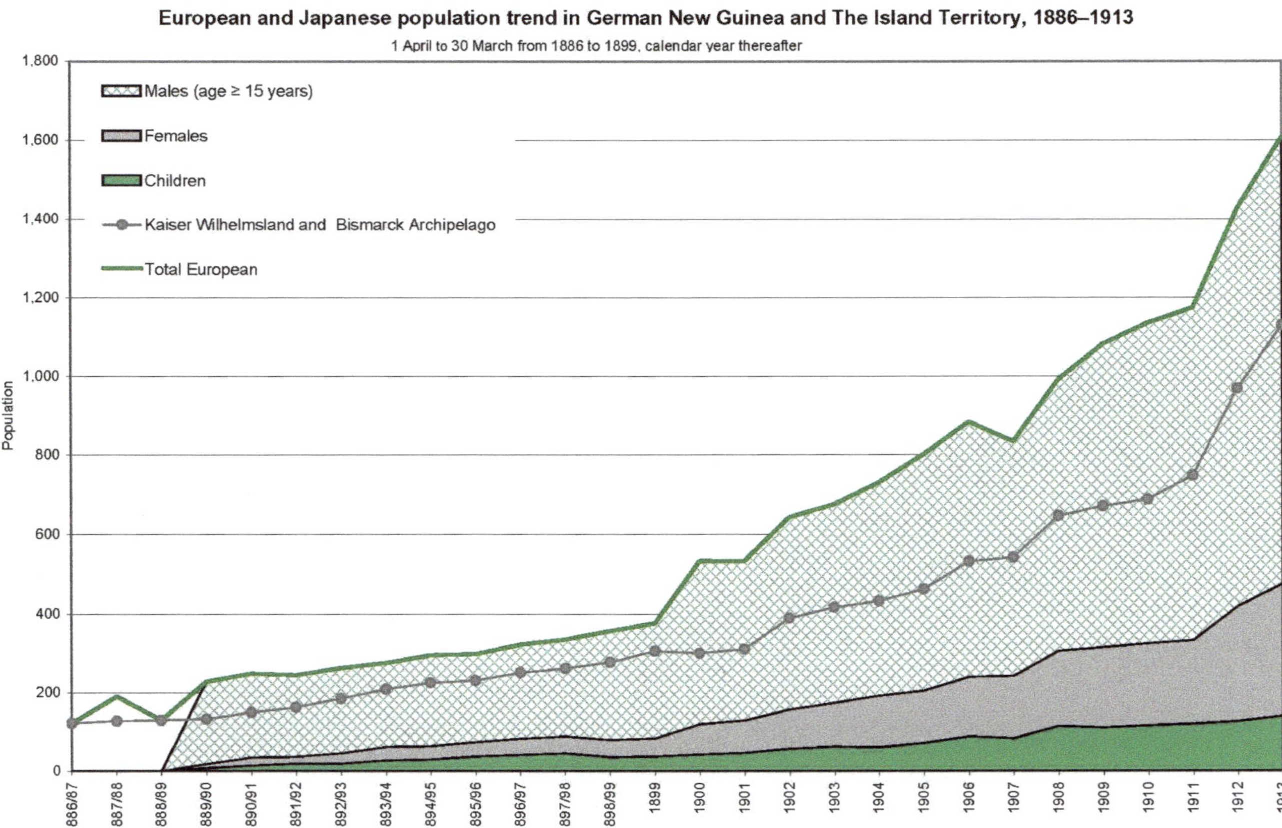

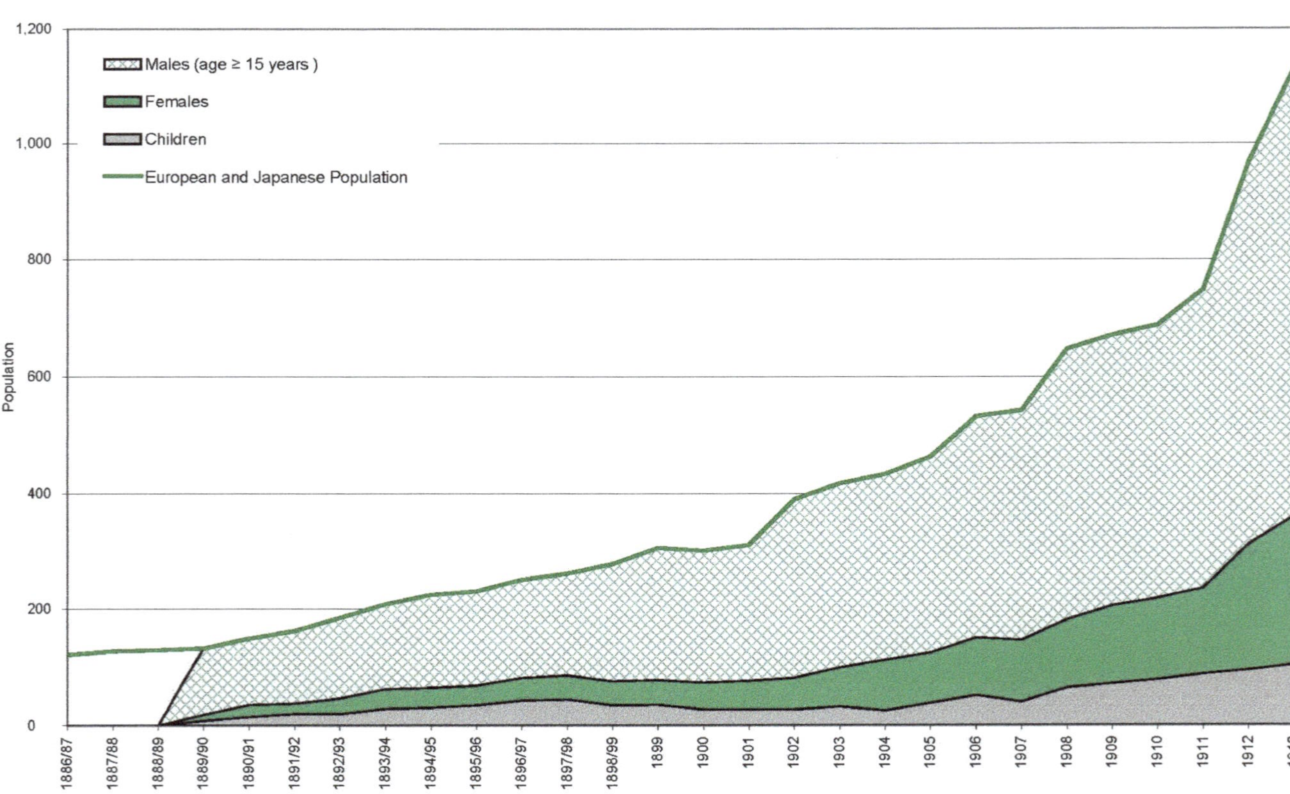

Chart 2
European and Japanese population in German New Guinea, 1886–1913
Males (age ≥ 15 years)
Females
Children
European and Japanese Population
Population
1,200
1,000
800
600
400
200
0
1886/87
1887/88
1888/89
1889/90
1890/91
1891/92
1892/93
1893/94
1894/95
1895/96
1896/97
1897/98
1898/99
1899
1900
1901
1902
1903
1904
1905
1906
1907
1908
1909
1910
1911
1912
1913

Chart 3

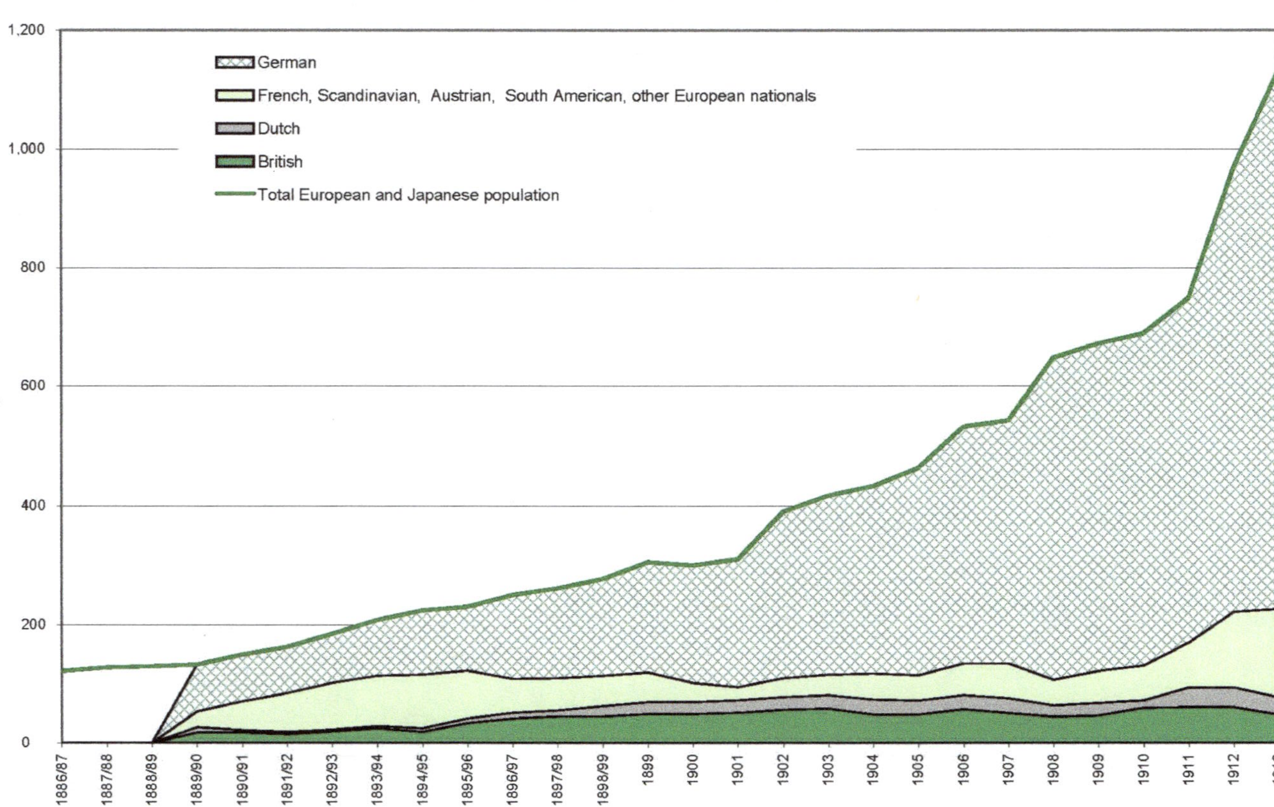

Chart 4

European and Japanese population by citizenship in German New Guinea and The Island Territory, 1888–1913
German
Dutch, French, Scandinavian, Austrian and South American
Japanese
Spanish and Portuguese
British and Australian
North American
European and Japanese
Population
600
500
400
300
200
100
0
1888
1889
1890
1891
1892
1893
1894
1895
1896
1897
1898
1899
1900
1901
1902
1903
1904
1905
1906
1907
1908
1909
1910
1911
1912
1913

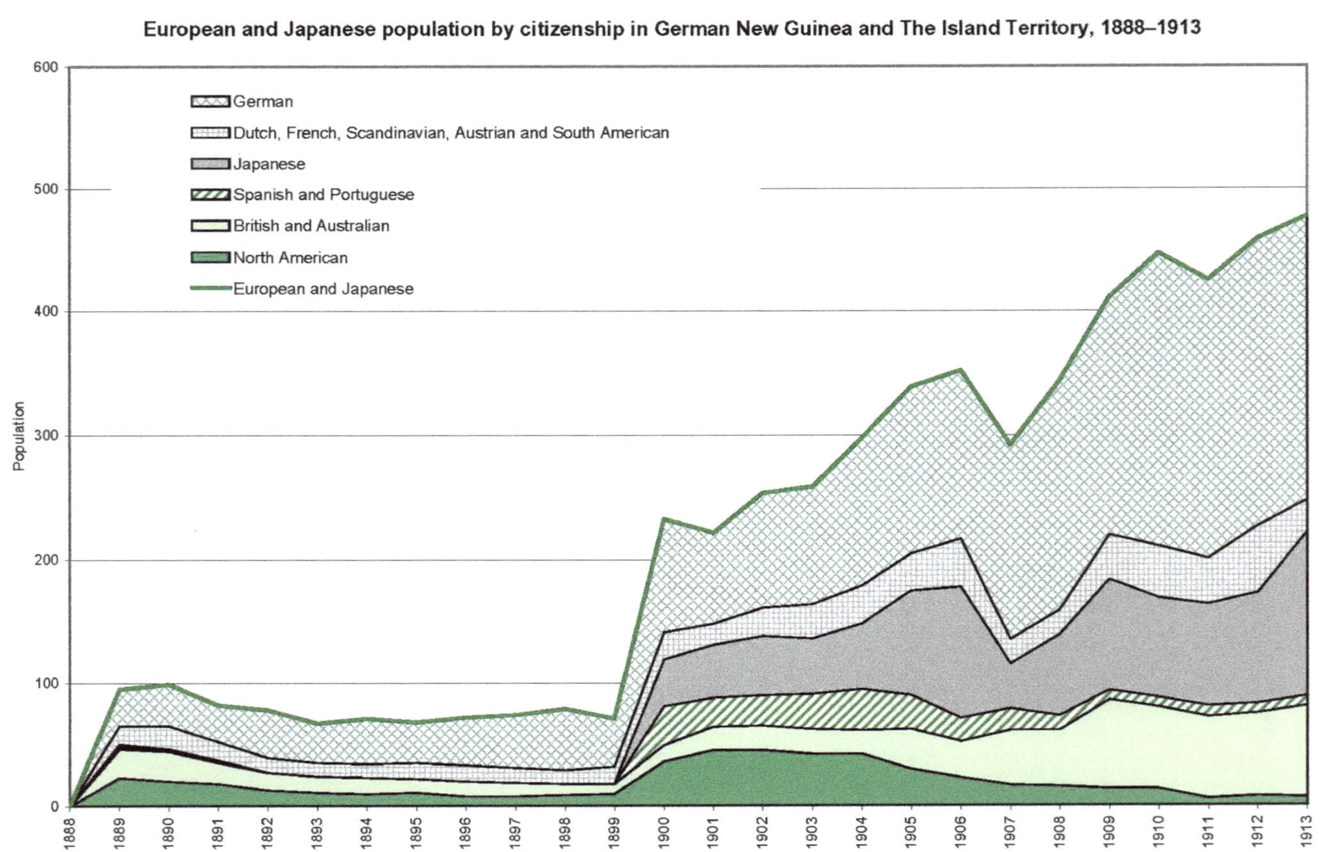

Chart 5

European population by profession in German New Guinea, 1886–1913

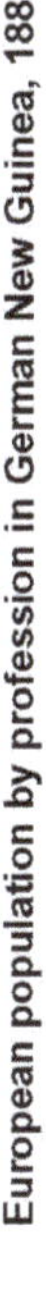

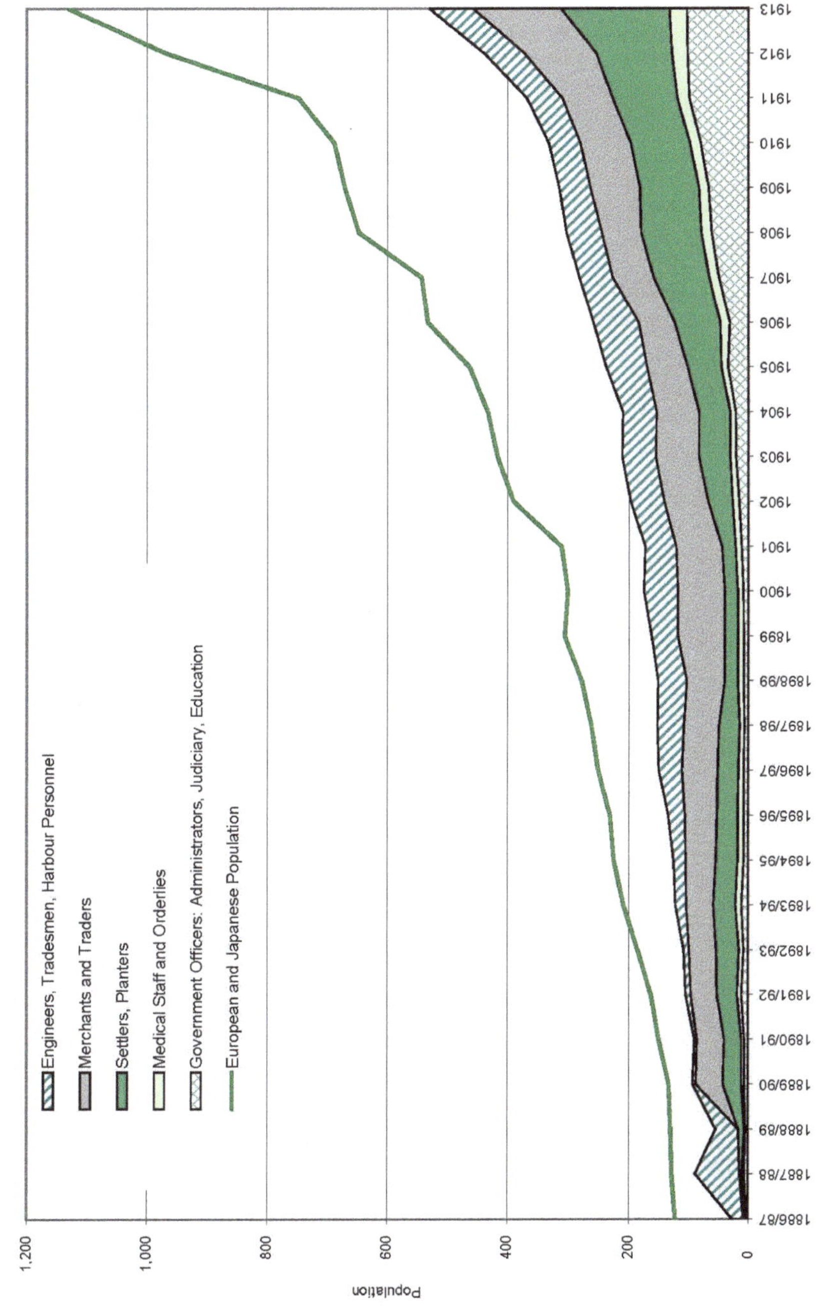

Chart 6

European population by profession in German New Guinea and The Island Territory, 1886–1913
Engineers, Tradesmen, Sailors, Fishermen, Artisans
Settlers, Planters, Gardeners
Merchants and Traders
Medical Staff and Orderlies
Government Officers: Administrators, Justice, Education
Kaiser Wilhelms-Land and Bismarck-Archipel Population
European and Japanese Population
Population
1,800
1,600
1,400
1,200
1,000
800
600
400
200
0
1886/87
1887/88
1888/89
1889/90
1890/91
1891/92
1892/93
1893/94
1894/95
1895/96
1896/97
1897/98
1898/99
1899
1900
1901
1902
1903
1904
1905
1906
1907
1908
1909
1910
1911
1912
1913

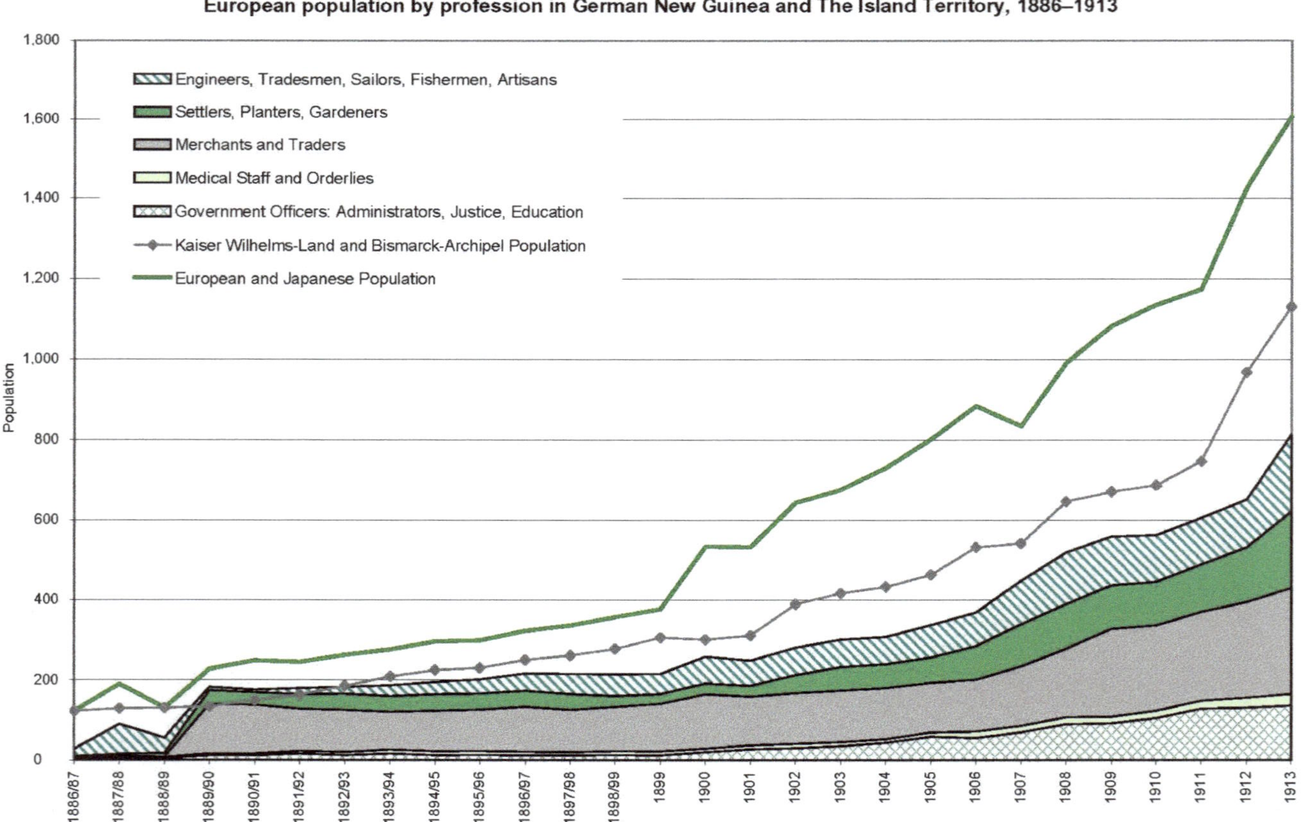

Chart 7

European population in British New Guinea and Papua, 1888–1914

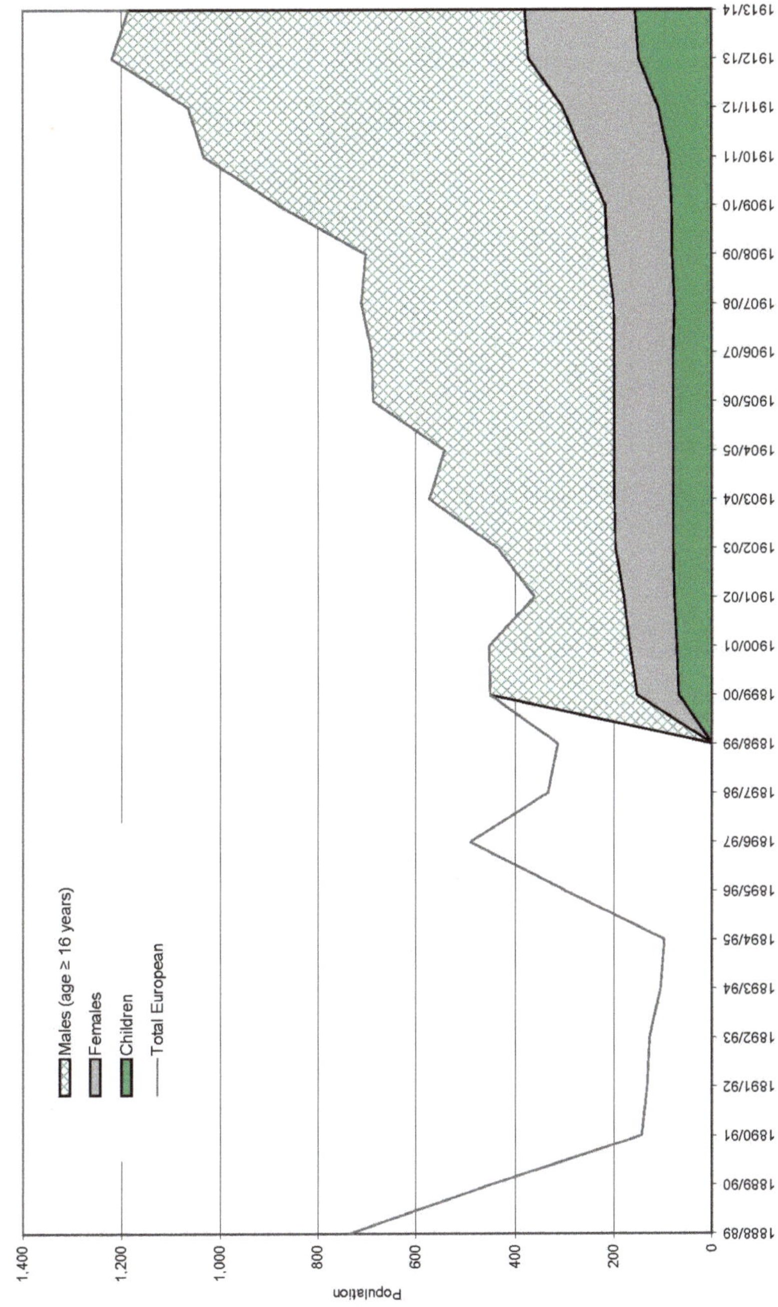

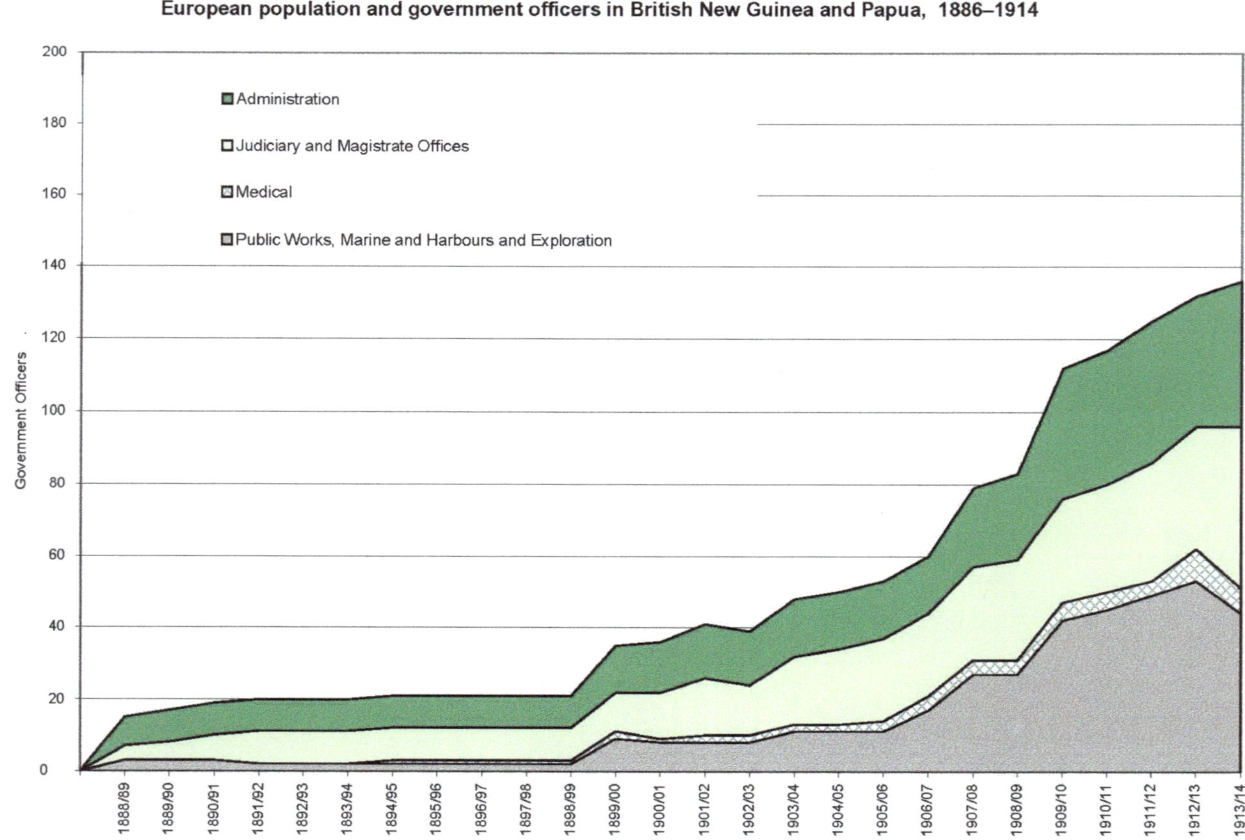

Chart 8
European population and government officers in British New Guinea and Papua, 1886–1914
Government Officers
200
180
160
140
120
100
80
60
40
20
0
Administration
Judiciary and Magistrate Offices
Medical
Public Works, Marine and Harbours and Exploration
1888/89
1889/90
1890/91
1891/92
1892/93
1893/94
1894/95
1895/96
1896/97
1897/98
1898/99
1899/00
1900/01
1901/02
1902/03
1903/04
1904/05
1905/06
1906/07
1907/08
1908/09
1909/10
1910/11
1911/12
1912/13
1913/14

Chart 9

European population in British New Guinea, Papua, German New Guinea and The Island Territory, 1903–1914
German New Guinea from April to March, from 1900 calendar year; British New Guinea and Papua from 1 July t o 30 June
1903/04
1904/05
1905/06
1906/07
1907/08
1908/09
1909/10
1910/11
1911/12
1912/13
1913/14
1,800
1,600
1,400
1,200
1,000
800
600
400
200
0
Population
Island Territory European+Japanese
GNG European+Japanese
Papua European
1903
1904
1905
1906
1907
1908
1909
1910
1911
1912
1913

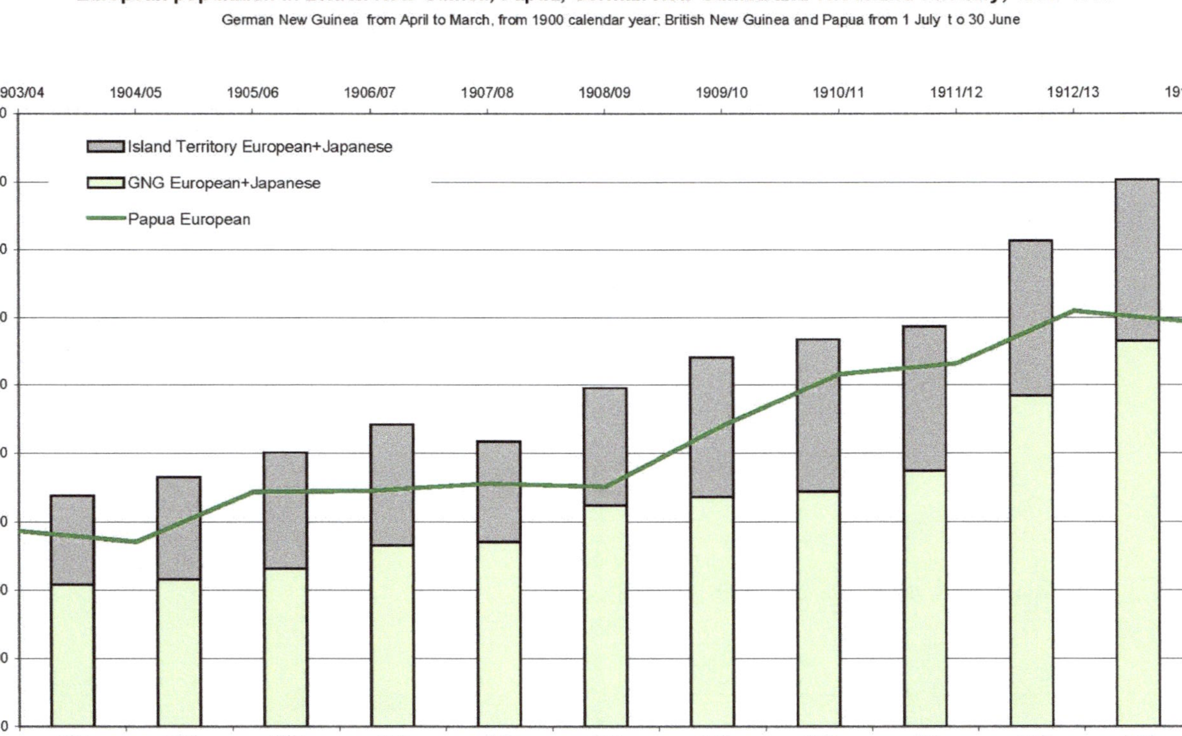

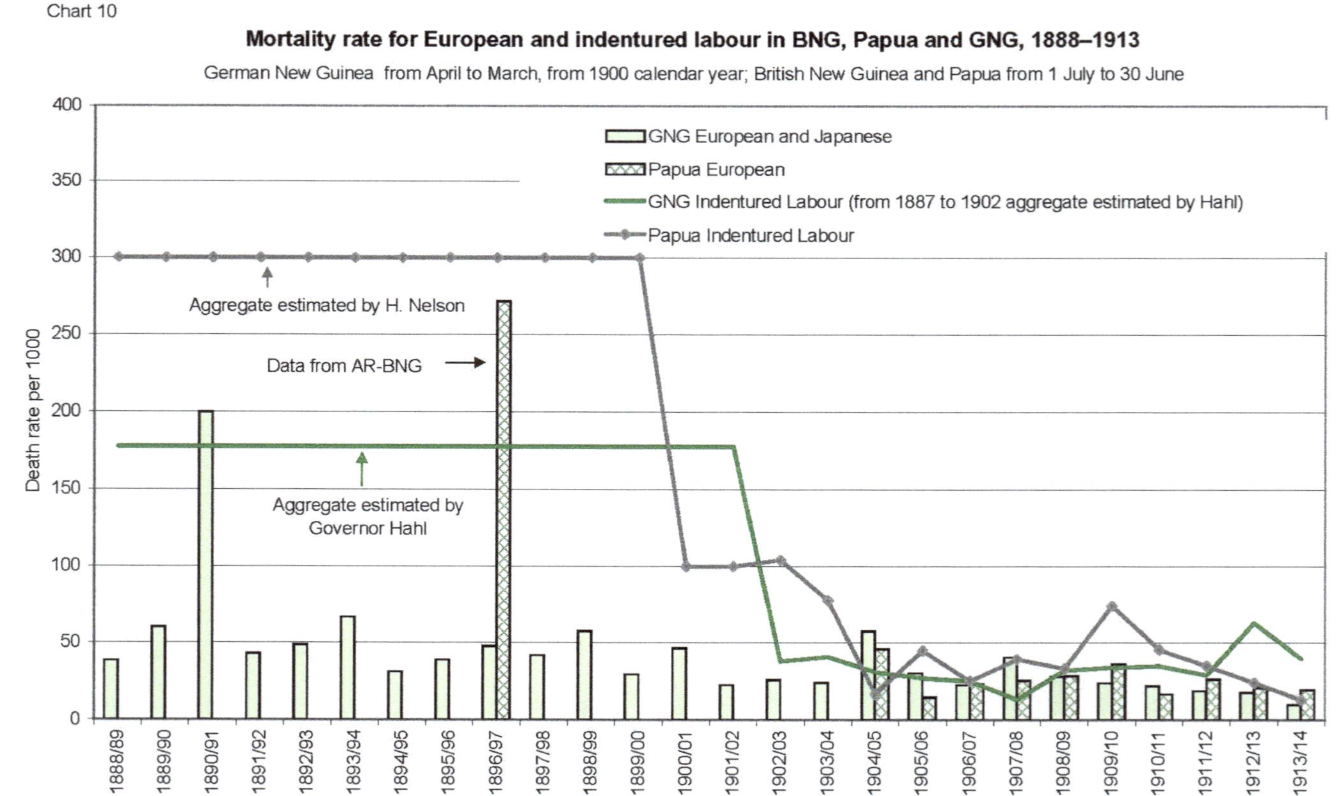
Chart 10
Mortality rate for European and indentured labour in BNG, Papua and GNG, 1888–1913
German New Guinea from April to March, from 1900 calendar year; British New Guinea and Papua from 1 July to 30 June
GNG European and Japanese
Papua European
GNG Indentured Labour (from 1887 to 1902 aggregate estimated by Hahl)
Papua Indentured Labour
Aggregate estimated by H. Nelson
Data from AR-BNG
Aggregate estimated by Governor Hahl
Death rate per 1000
400
350
300
250
200
150
100
50
0
1888/89
1889/90
1890/91
1891/92
1892/93
1893/94
1894/95
1895/96
1896/97
1897/98
1898/99
1899/00
1900/01
1901/02
1902/03
1903/04
1904/05
1905/06
1906/07
1907/08
1908/09
1909/10
1910/11
1911/12
1912/13
1913/14

Chart 11

Medical expenditures in German New Guinea, 1899–1913
Health expenditure per head of European/Japanese Population and Indentured Labour Force
GNG European and Japanese
GNG Indentured Labour (from 1887 to 1902 aggregate estimated by Hahl)
Expenditure per head (RM)
Mortality Rate per 1000
Hahl estmated a mean mortality rate of 17.7% during 1887 - 1902
14
12
10
8
6
4
2
0
200
180
160
140
120
100
80
60
40
20
0
1899
1900
1901
1902
1903
1904
1905
1906
1907
1908
1909
1910
1911
1912
1913

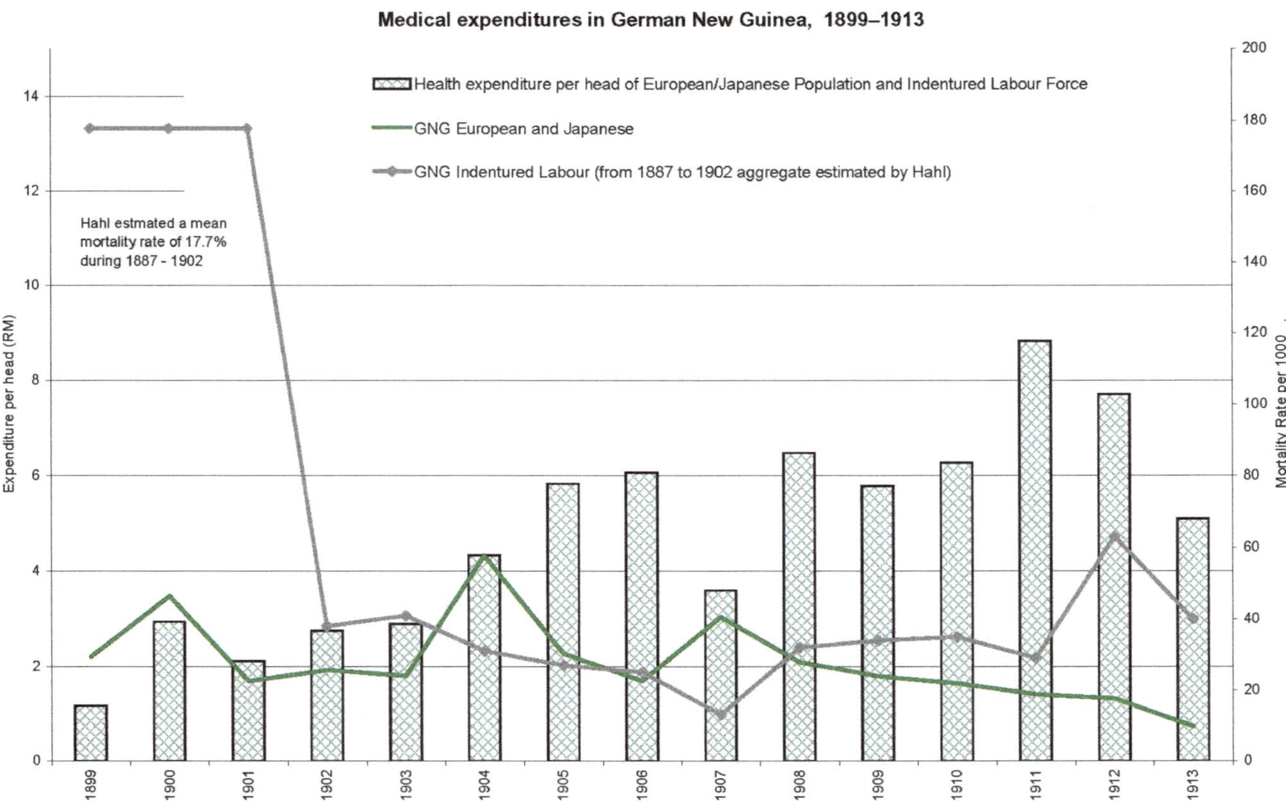

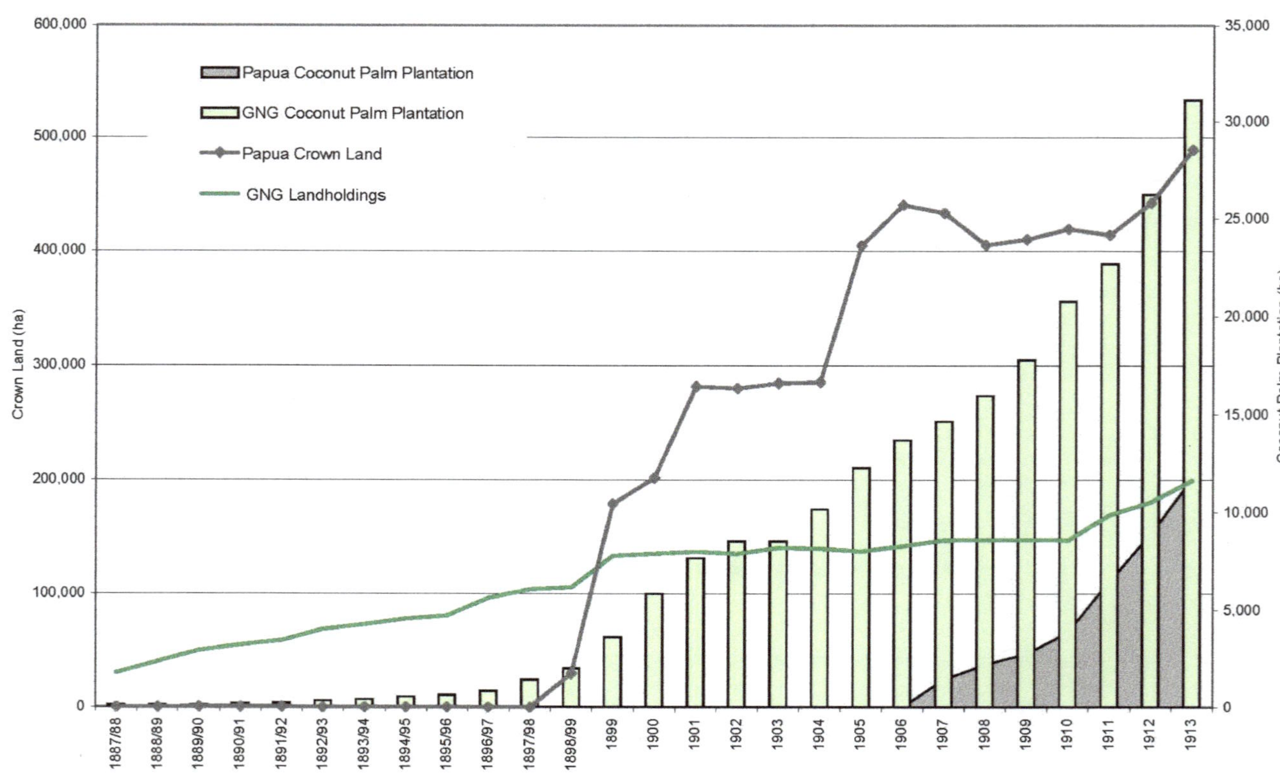

Chart 12
Land and plantations in British, Papua and German New Guinea, 1887–1913
Crown Land (ha)
600,000
500,000
400,000
300,000
200,000
100,000
0
Coconut Palm Plantation (ha)
35,000
30,000
25,000
20,000
15,000
10,000
5,000
0
Papua Coconut Palm Plantation
GNG Coconut Palm Plantation
Papua Crown Land
GNG Landholdings
1887/88
1888/89
1889/90
1890/91
1891/92
1892/93
1893/94
1894/95
1895/96
1896/97
1897/98
1898/99
1899
1900
1901
1902
1903
1904
1905
1906
1907
1908
1909
1910
1911
1912
1913

Chart 13

Plantation area in German New Guinea, 1886–1913
Cotton
Kapok, Hemp and Sisal
Coconut Palm Plantation
Tobacco (number of fields x 0.25 ha)
Coffee
Cocoa
Caoutchouc and Gutta-percha
Maize, Rice and Millet
Other Cereals and Tropical Fruit
Planted Area – NGC
Area under cultivation
(ha)
40,000
35,000
30,000
25,000
20,000
15,000
10,000
5,000
0
1886/87
1887/88
1888/89
1889/90
1890/91
1891/92
1892/93
1893/94
1894/95
1895/96
1896/97
1897/98
1898/99
1899
1900
1901
1902
1903
1904
1905
1906
1907
1908
1909
1910
1911
1912
1913

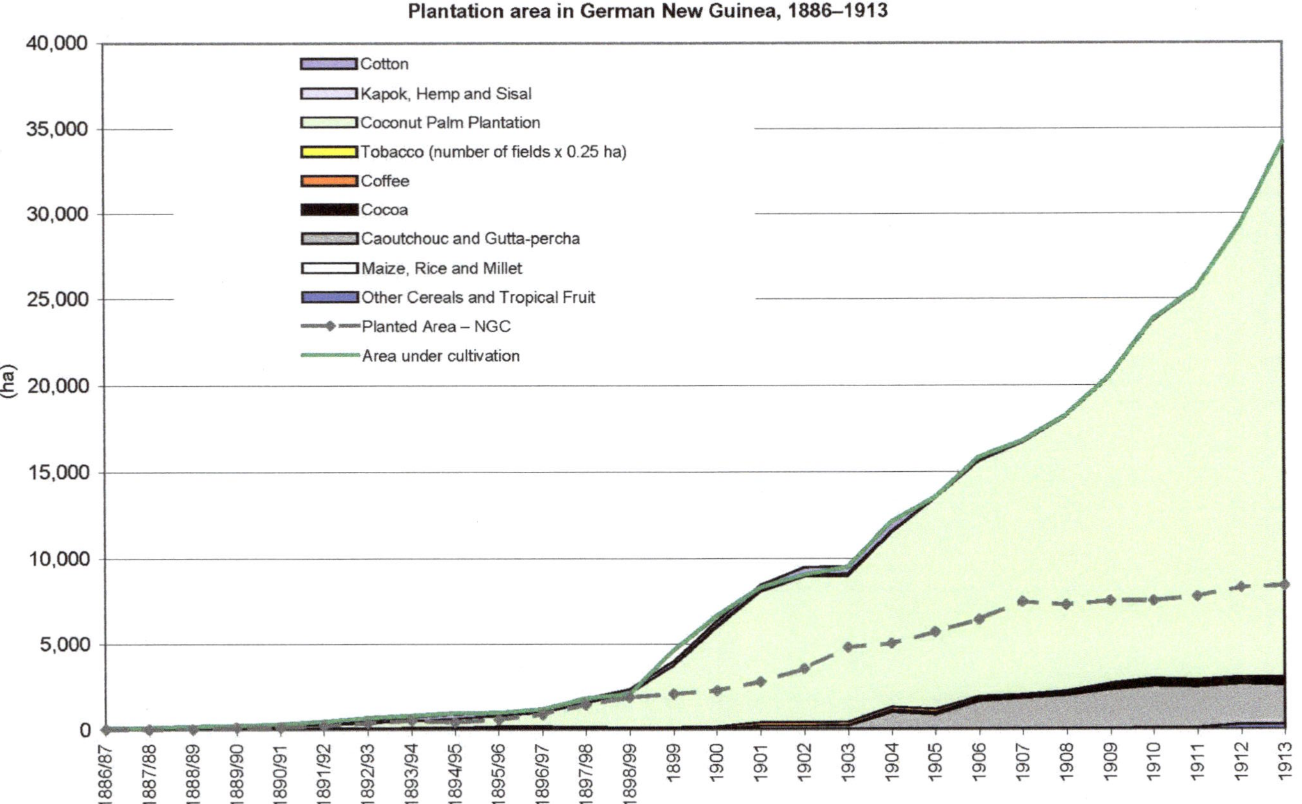

Disastrous Ventures

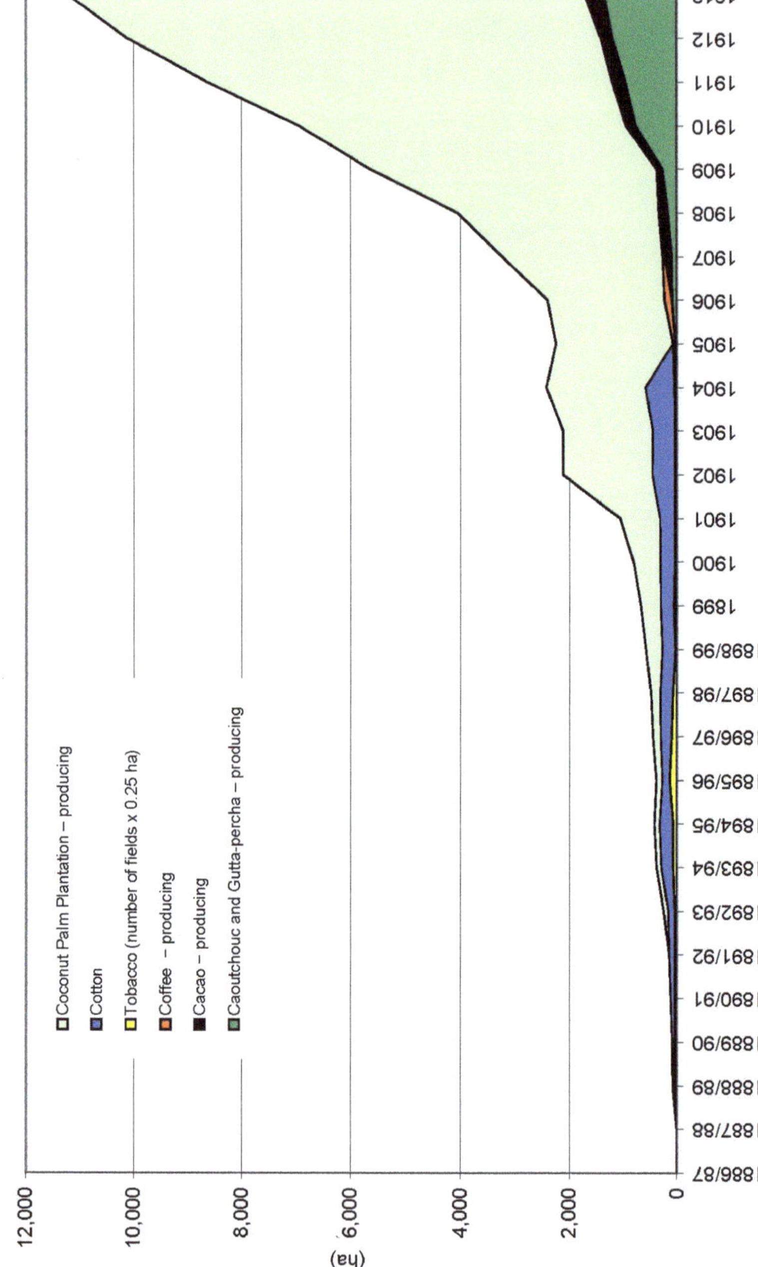

Chart 15

Development and administration expenditures in German New Guinea and The Island Territory, 1886–1914
Government Subsidy
Operating costs (excl. NGC instalment)
Capital Expenditure post NGC
Operating Surplus
Net Fiscal Cost to GNG
Revenue
NGC Instalment
NGC Capitalised Expenditure
Cashflow (after capex)
Neu Guinea Compagnie administration
German government administration
Cost to administer the Protectorate
(£)
(RM)
200000
150000
100000
50000
0
-50000
-100000
-150000
4.000.000
3.000.000
2.000.000
1.000.000
0
-1.000.000
-2.000.000
-3.000.000
1886/87
1887/88
1888/89
1889/90
1890/91
1891/92
1892/93
1893/94
1894/95
1895/96
1896/97
1897/98
1898/99
1899
1900
1901
1902
1903
1904
1905
1906
1907
1908
1909
1910
1911
1912
1913

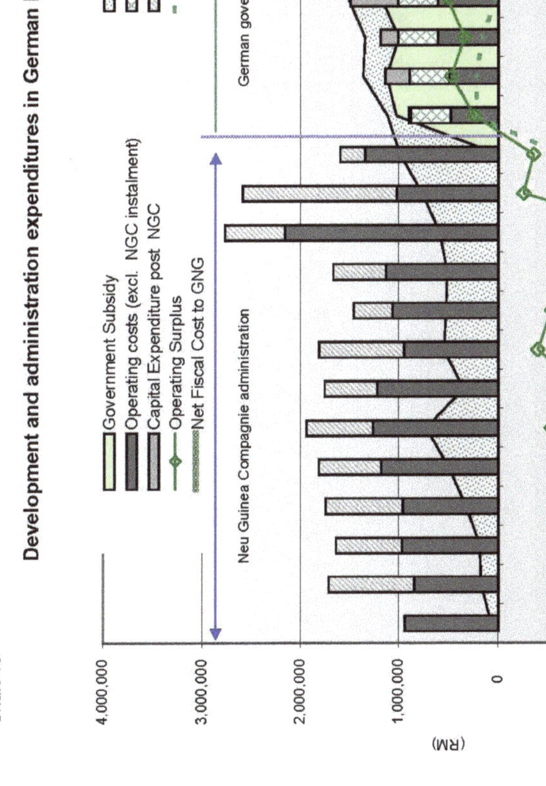

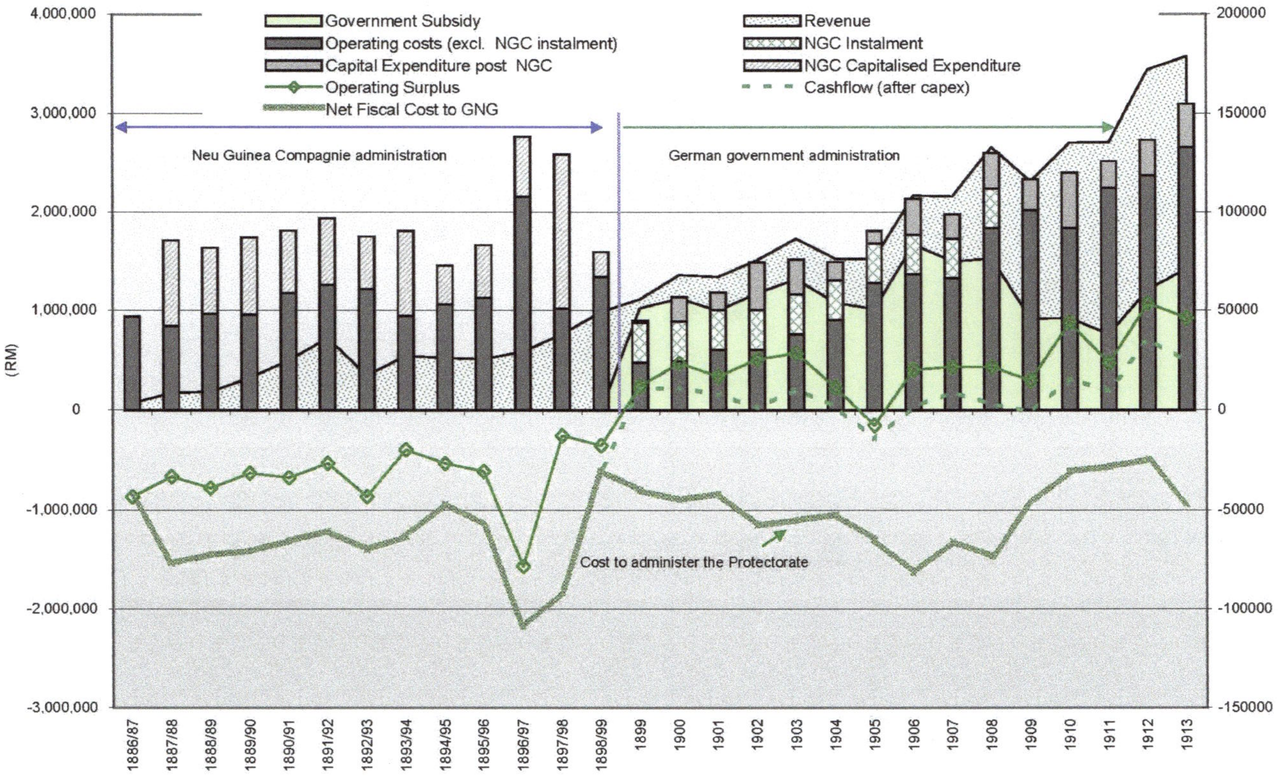

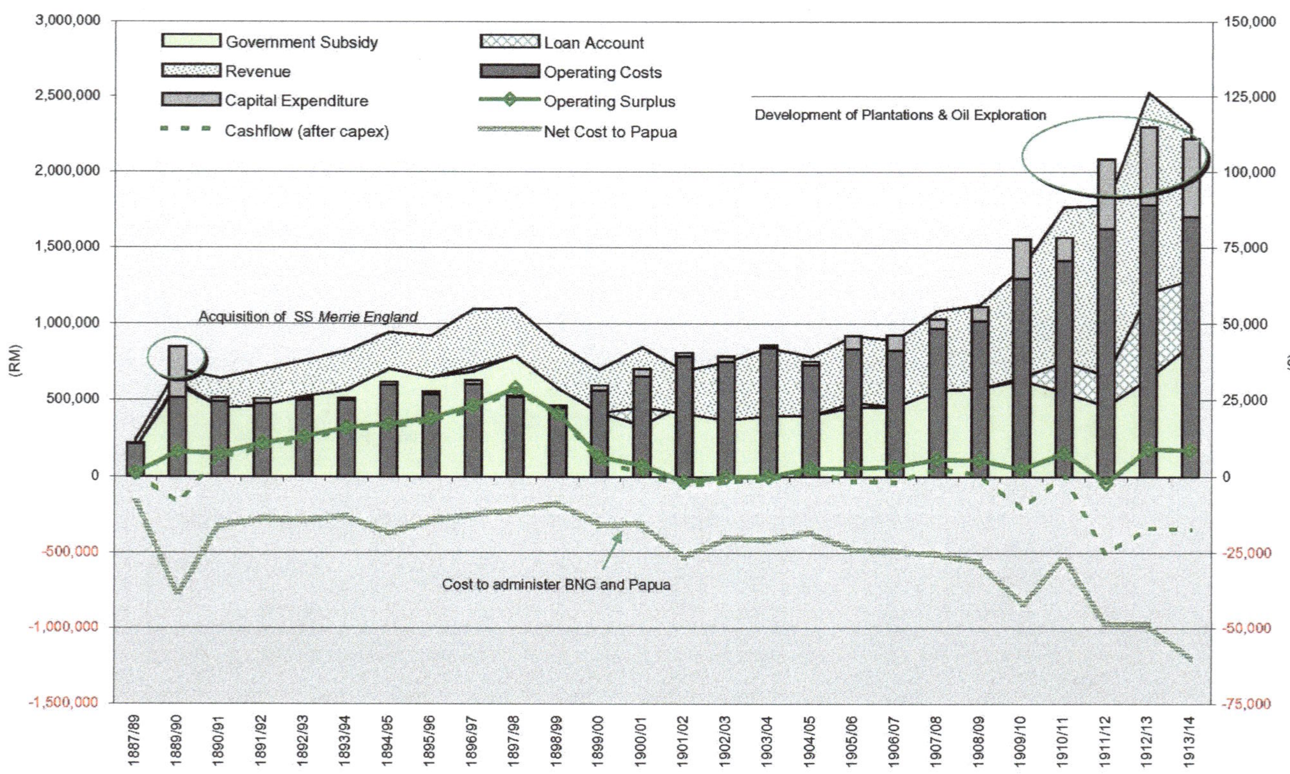

Chart 16
Development and administration expenditures in British New Guinea and Papua , 1887–1914
(RM)
3,000,000
2,500,000
2,000,000
1,500,000
1,000,000
500,000
0
-500,000
-1,000,000
-1,500,000
(£)
150,000
125,000
100,000
75,000
50,000
25,000
0
-25,000
-50,000
-75,000
Government Subsidy
Loan Account
Revenue
Operating Costs
Capital Expenditure
Operating Surplus
Cashflow (after capex)
Net Cost to Papua
Development of Plantations & Oil Exploration
Acquisition of SS Merrie England
Cost to administer BNG and Papua
1887/89
1889/90
1890/91
1891/92
1892/93
1893/94
1894/95
1895/96
1896/97
1897/98
1898/99
1899/00
1900/01
1901/02
1902/03
1903/04
1904/05
1905/06
1906/07
1907/08
1908/09
1909/10
1910/11
1911/12
1912/13
1913/14

Chart 17

Annual running cost per head of European population in Papua and German New Guinea, 1886–1913

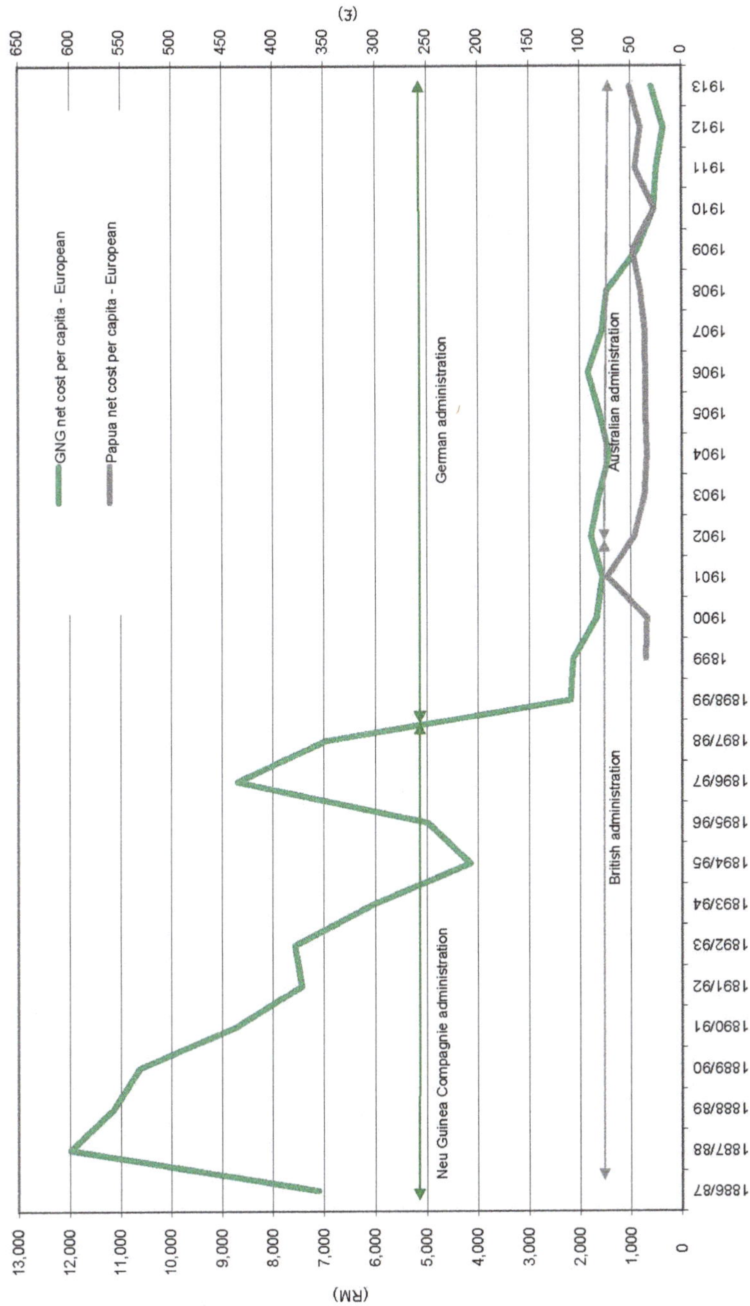

Chart 18

Annual running cost per head of indentured labour in British New Guinea, Papua and German New Guinea, 1897–1913
GNG net cost per indentured & casual labour
Papua net cost per indentured & casual labour
(RM)
(£)
420
400
380
360
340
320
300
280
260
240
220
200
180
160
140
120
100
80
60
40
20
0
21
20
19
18
17
16
15
14
13
12
11
10
9
8
7
6
5
4
3
2
1
0
Papua data before 1902/03 for goldfields
1897/98
1898/99
1899
1900
1901
1902
1903
1904
1905
1906
1907
1908
1909
1910
1911
1912
1913

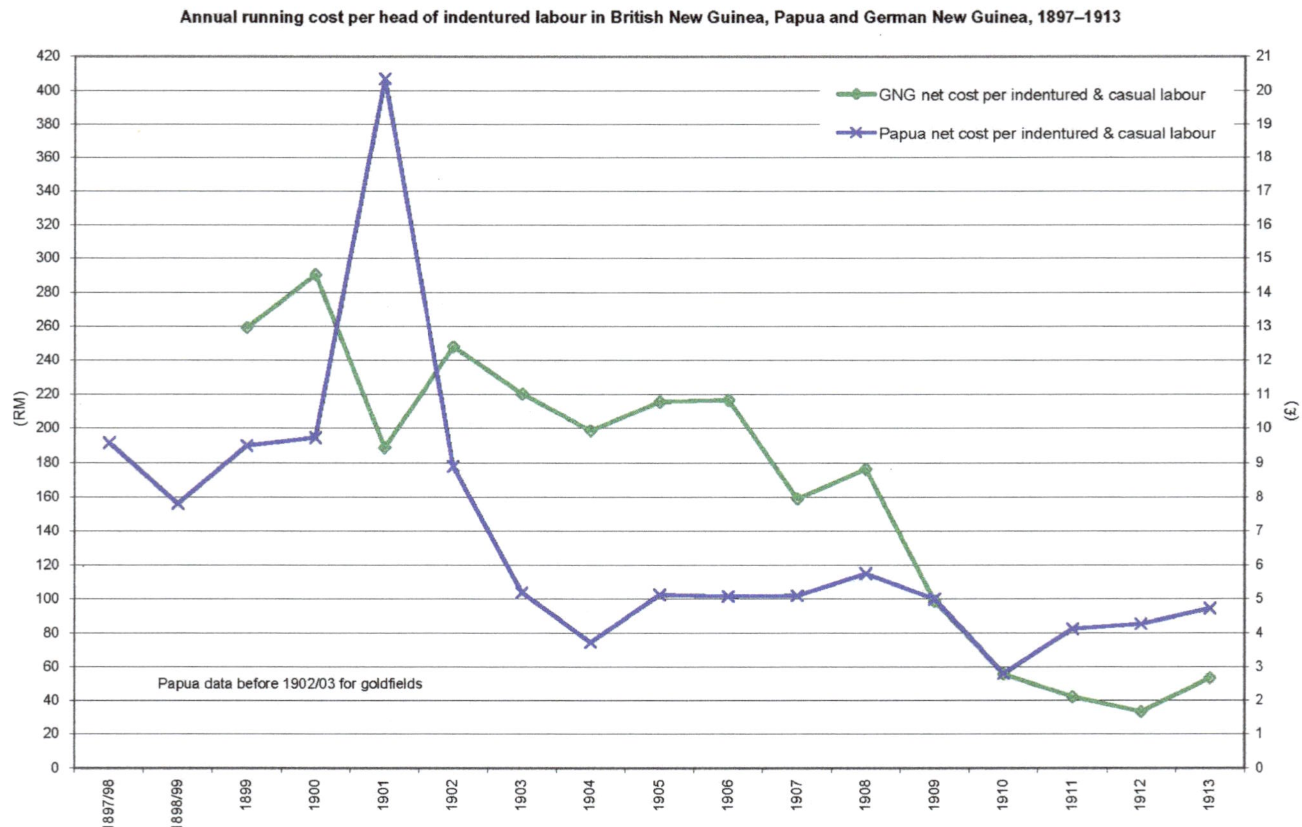

Chart 19

Import and Export Trade Data for German New Guinea and The Island Territory, 1886–1913

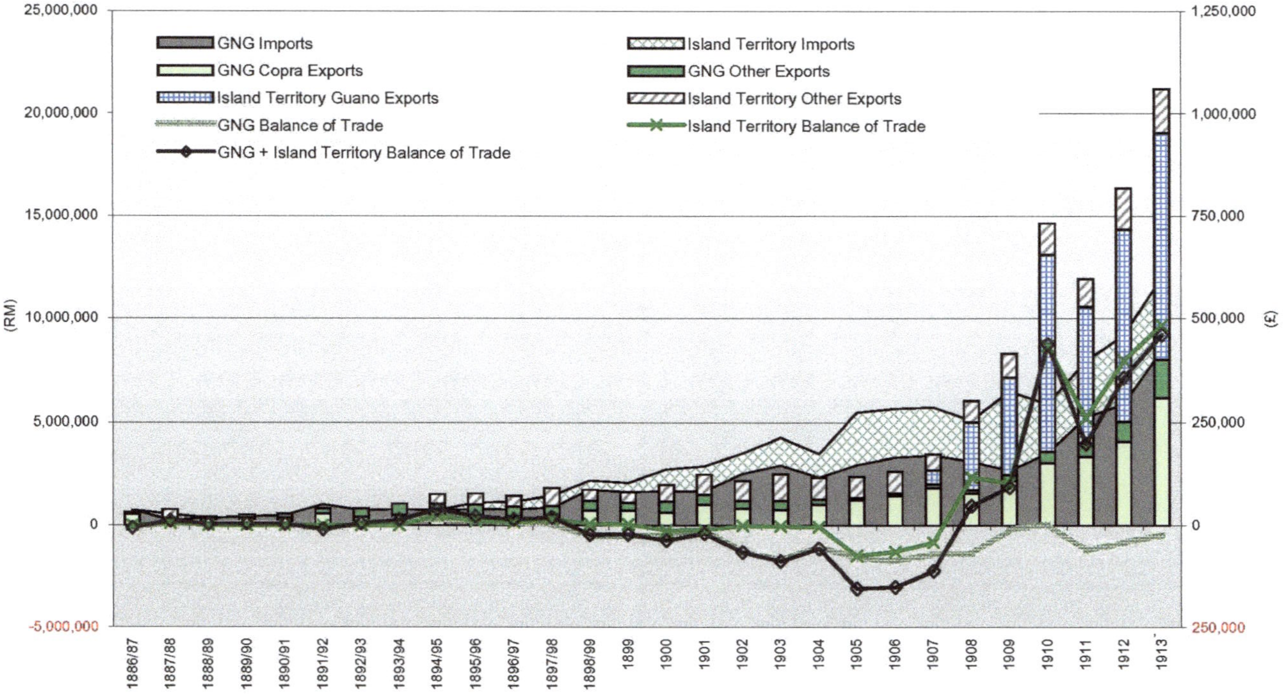

Disastrous Ventures

Chart 20

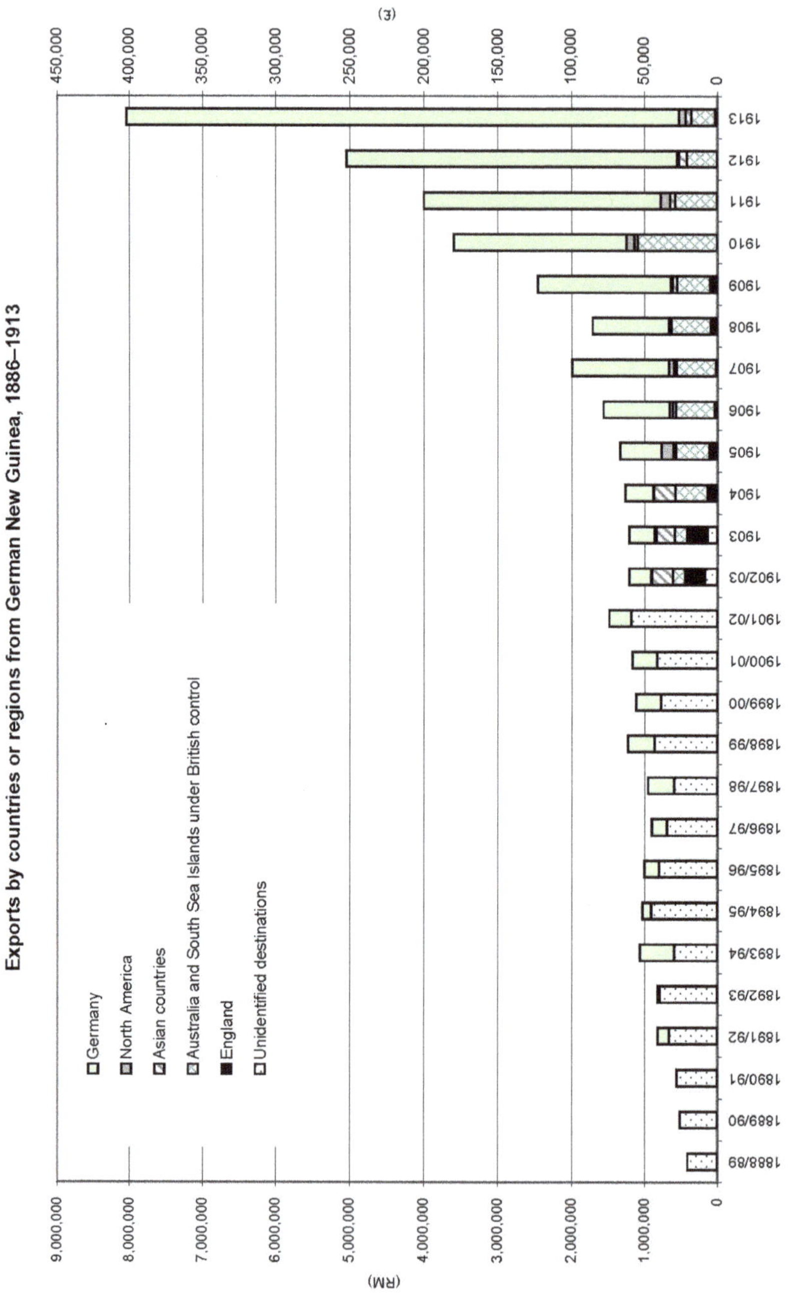

Exports by countries or regions from German New Guinea, 1886–1913

(£)

450,000
400,000
350,000
300,000
250,000
200,000
150,000
100,000
50,000
0

(RM)

9,000,000
8,000,000
7,000,000
6,000,000
5,000,000
4,000,000
3,000,000
2,000,000
1,000,000
0

Germany
North America
Asian countries
Australia and South Sea Islands under British control
England
Unidentified destinations

1913
1912
1911
1910
1909
1908
1907
1906
1905
1904
1903
1902/03
1901/02
1900/01
1899/00
1898/99
1897/98
1896/97
1895/96
1894/95
1893/94
1892/93
1891/92
1890/91
1889/90
1888/89

454

Chart 21

Imports by countries or regions to German New Guinea, 1885–1913
(£)
(RM)
450,000
400,000
350,000
300,000
250,000
200,000
150,000
100,000
50,000
0
9,000,000
8,000,000
7,000,000
6,000,000
5,000,000
4,000,000
3,000,000
2,000,000
1,000,000
0
Unidentified destinations
Germany
America and other countries
Asian countries
Australia and South Sea Islands under British control
Great Britain
1913
1912
1911
1910
1909
1908
1907
1906
1905
1904
1903
1902/03
1901/02
1900/01
1899/00
1898/99
1897/98
1896/97
1895/96
1894/95
1893/94
1892/93
1891/92
1890/91
1889/90
1888/89
1887/88
1885/87

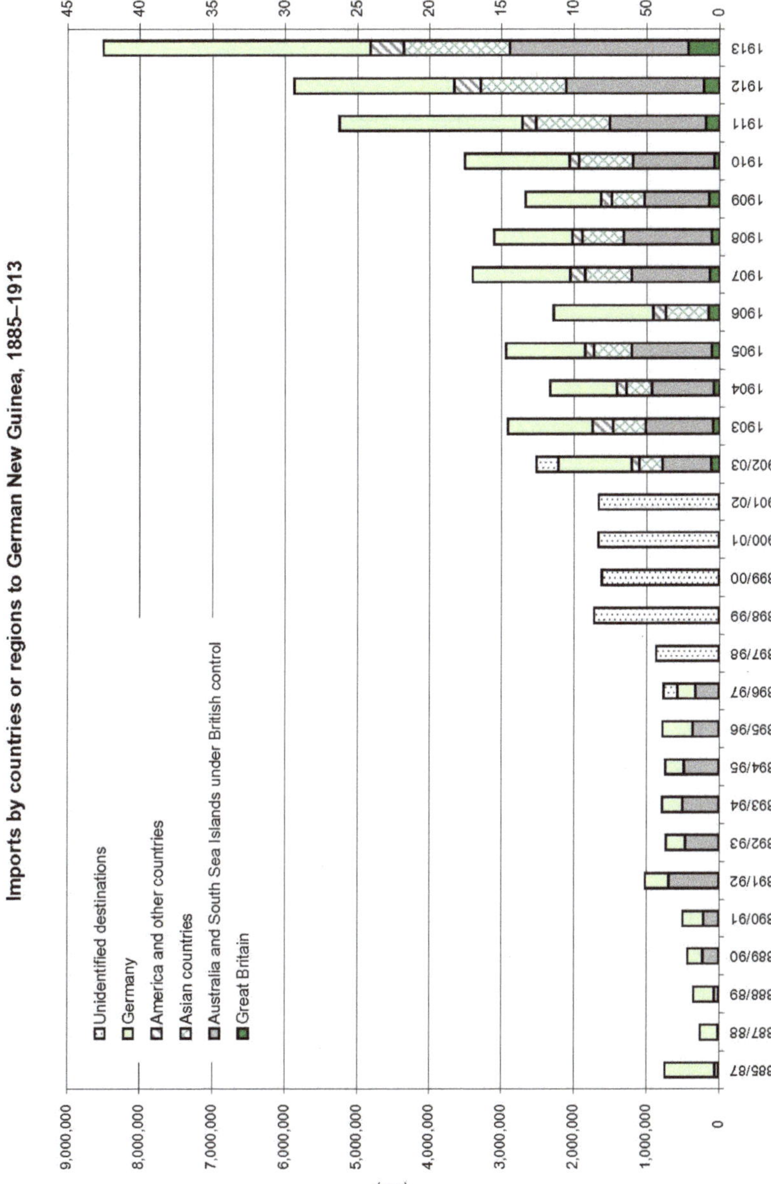

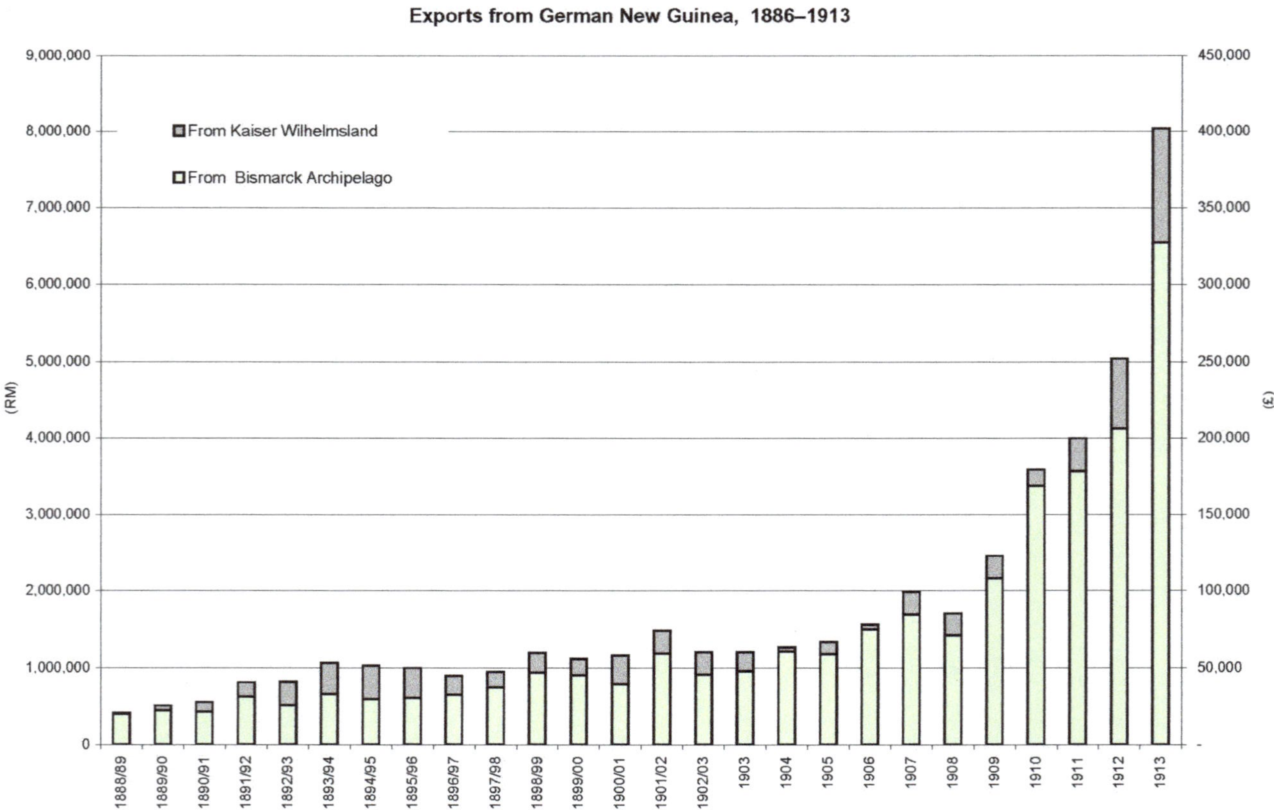

Chart 22
Exports from German New Guinea, 1886–1913
From Kaiser Wilhelmsland
From Bismarck Archipelago
(RM)
9,000,000
8,000,000
7,000,000
6,000,000
5,000,000
4,000,000
3,000,000
2,000,000
1,000,000
0
(£)
450,000
400,000
350,000
300,000
250,000
200,000
150,000
100,000
50,000
1888/89
1889/90
1890/91
1891/92
1892/93
1893/94
1894/95
1895/96
1896/97
1897/98
1898/99
1899/00
1900/01
1901/02
1902/03
1903
1904
1905
1906
1907
1908
1909
1910
1911
1912
1913

Chart 23

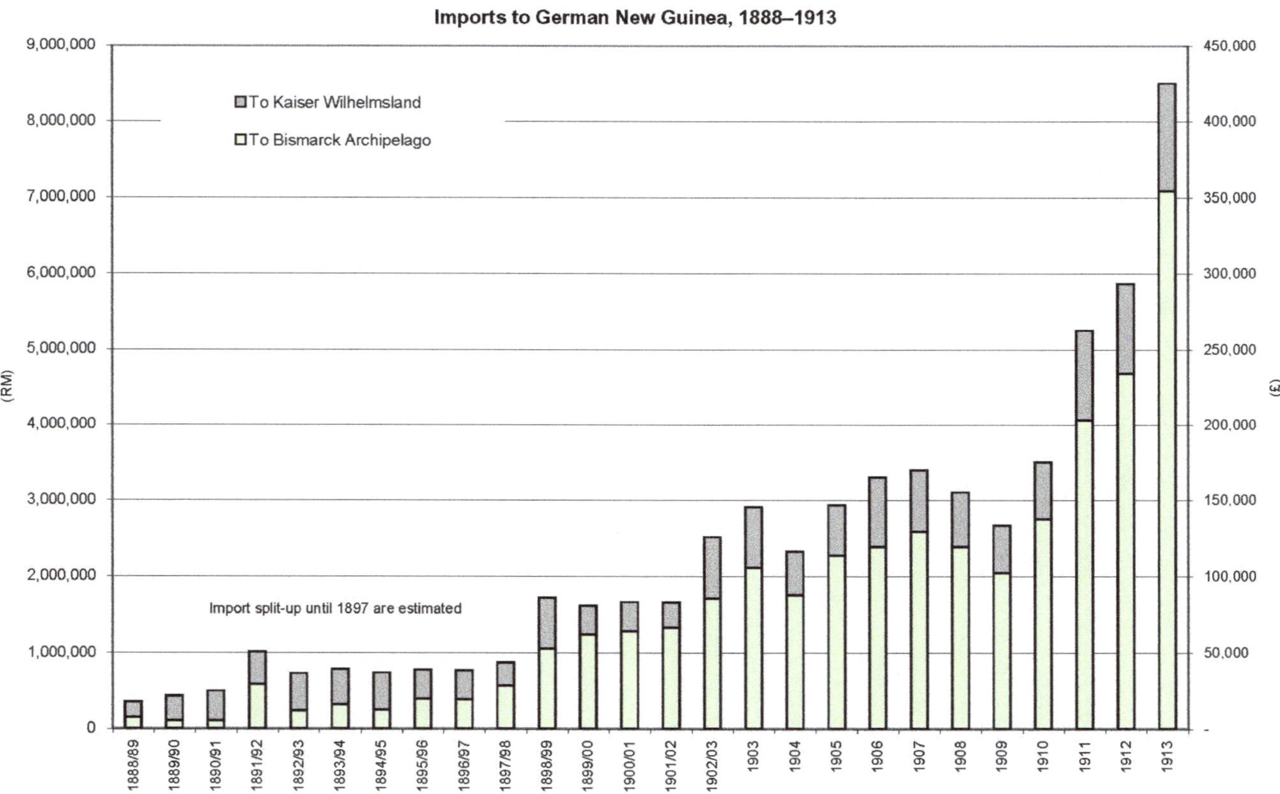

Disastrous Ventures

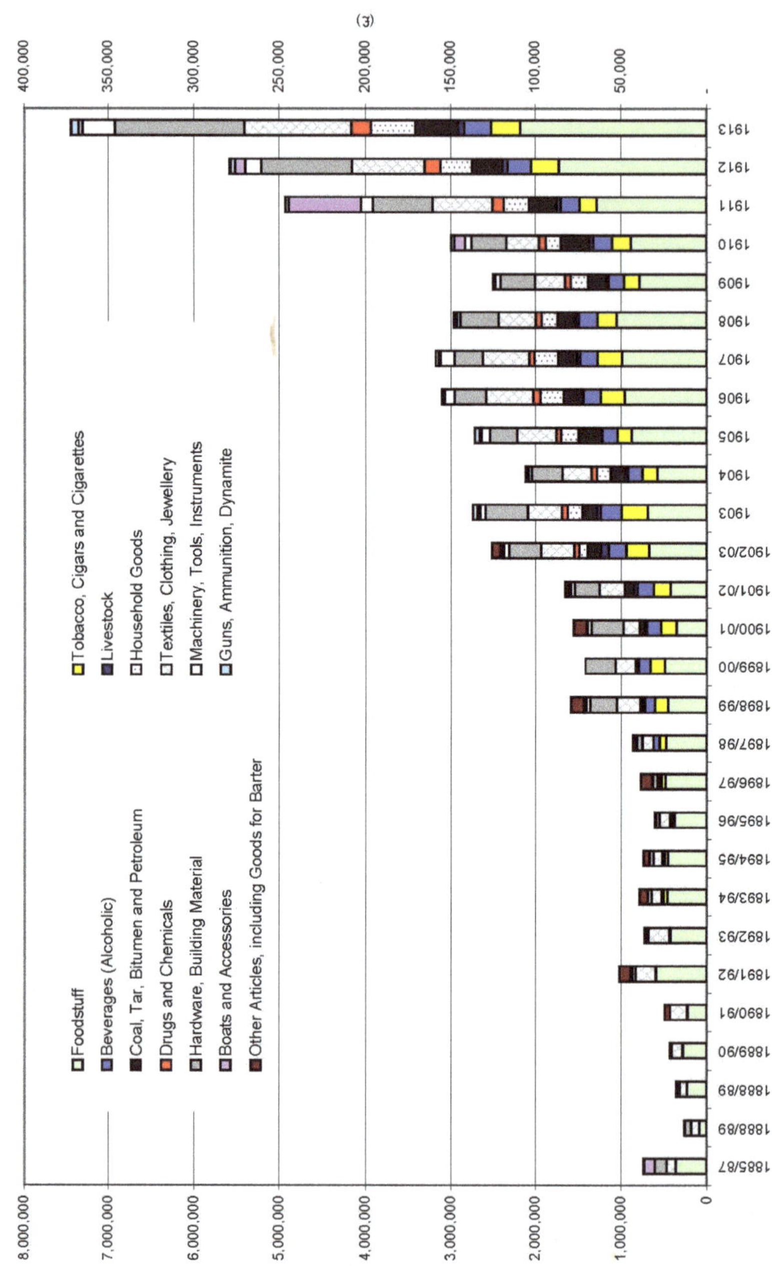

Chart 25

Exports by countries or regions from The Island Territory, 1897–1912

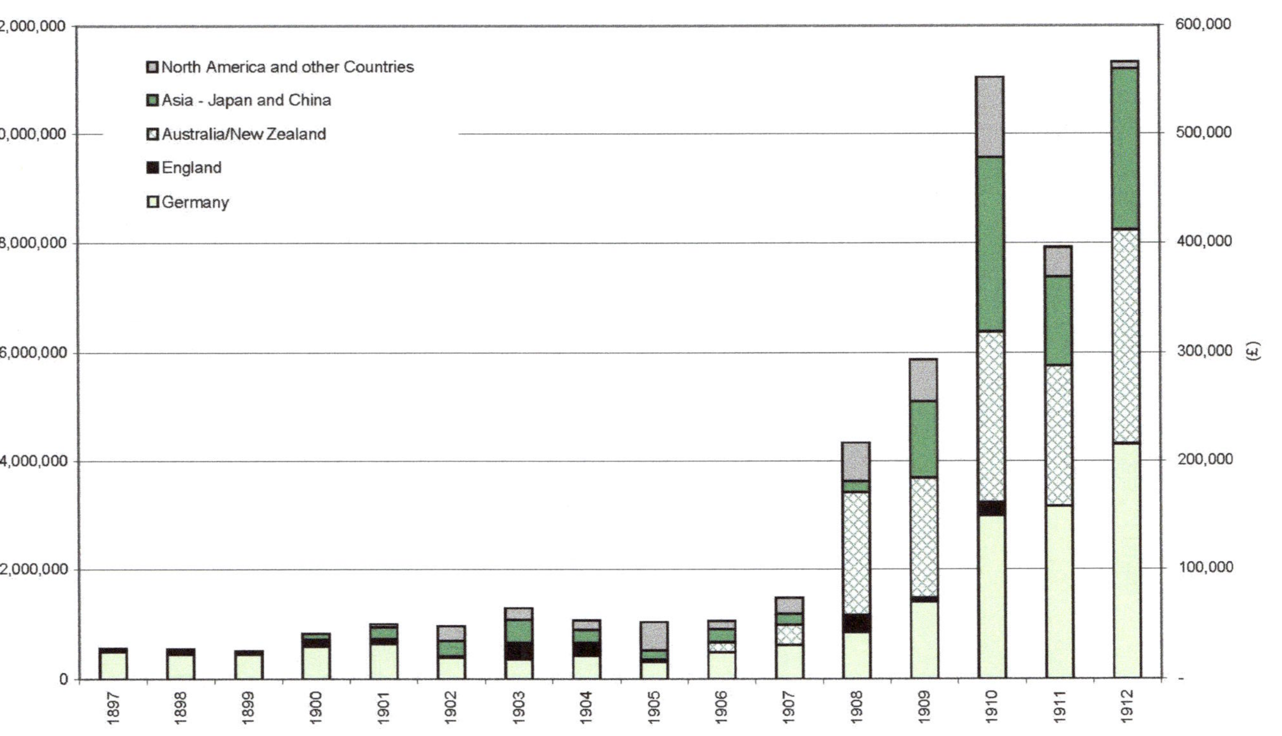

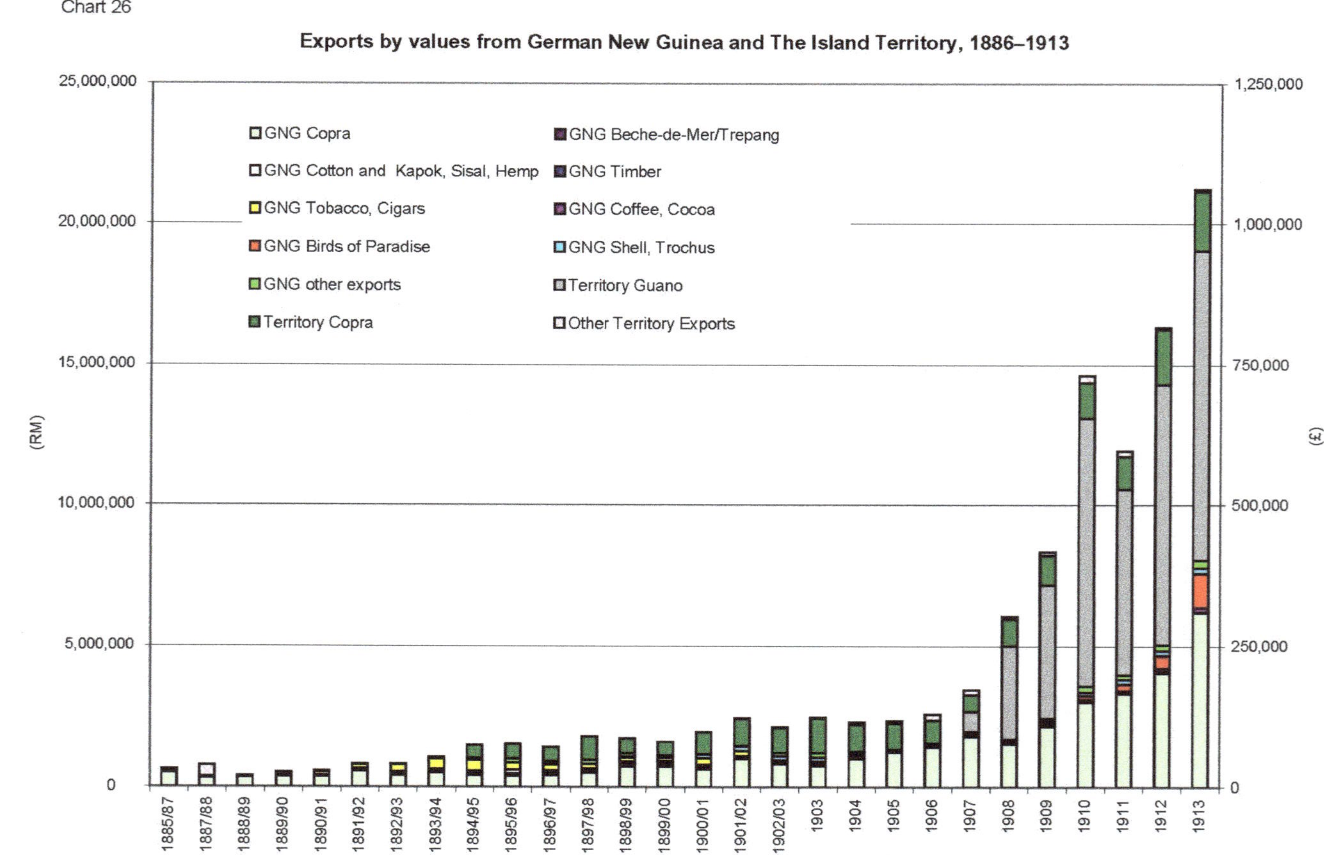

Chart 26
Exports by values from German New Guinea and The Island Territory, 1886–1913
(RM)
25,000,000
20,000,000
15,000,000
10,000,000
5,000,000
0
(£)
1,250,000
1,000,000
750,000
500,000
250,000
0
GNG Copra
GNG Cotton and Kapok, Sisal, Hemp
GNG Tobacco, Cigars
GNG Birds of Paradise
GNG other exports
Territory Copra
GNG Beche-de-Mer/Trepang
GNG Timber
GNG Coffee, Cocoa
GNG Shell, Trochus
Territory Guano
Other Territory Exports
1885/87
1887/88
1888/89
1889/90
1890/91
1891/92
1892/93
1893/94
1894/95
1895/96
1896/97
1897/98
1898/99
1899/00
1900/01
1901/02
1902/03
1903
1904
1905
1906
1907
1908
1909
1910
1911
1912
1913

Chart 27

Imports by countries or regions to The Island Territory, 1897–1912
(£)
225,000
200,000
175,000
150,000
125,000
100,000
75,000
50,000
25,000
0
(RM)
4,500,000
4,000,000
3,500,000
3,000,000
2,500,000
2,000,000
1,500,000
1,000,000
500,000
0
North America and other Countries
Japan and China
Australia/New Zealand
England
Germany
1897
1898
1899
1900
1901
1902
1903
1904
1905
1906
1907
1908
1909
1910
1911
1912

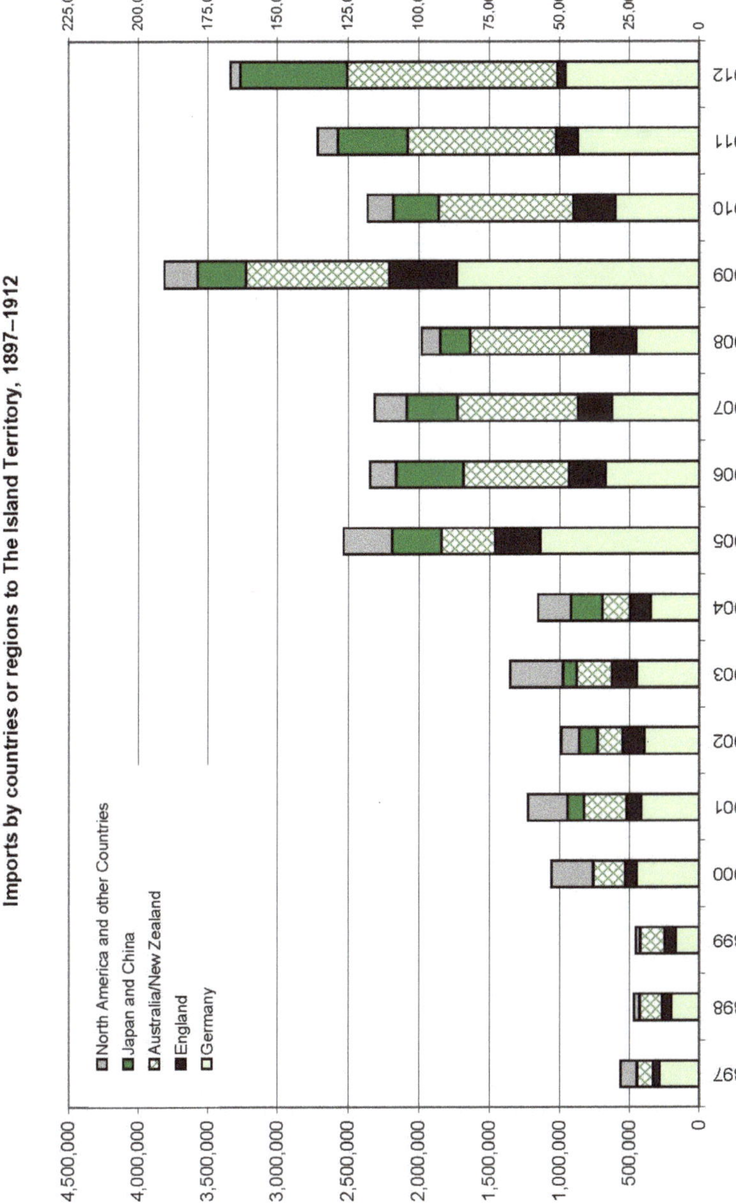

Disastrous Ventures

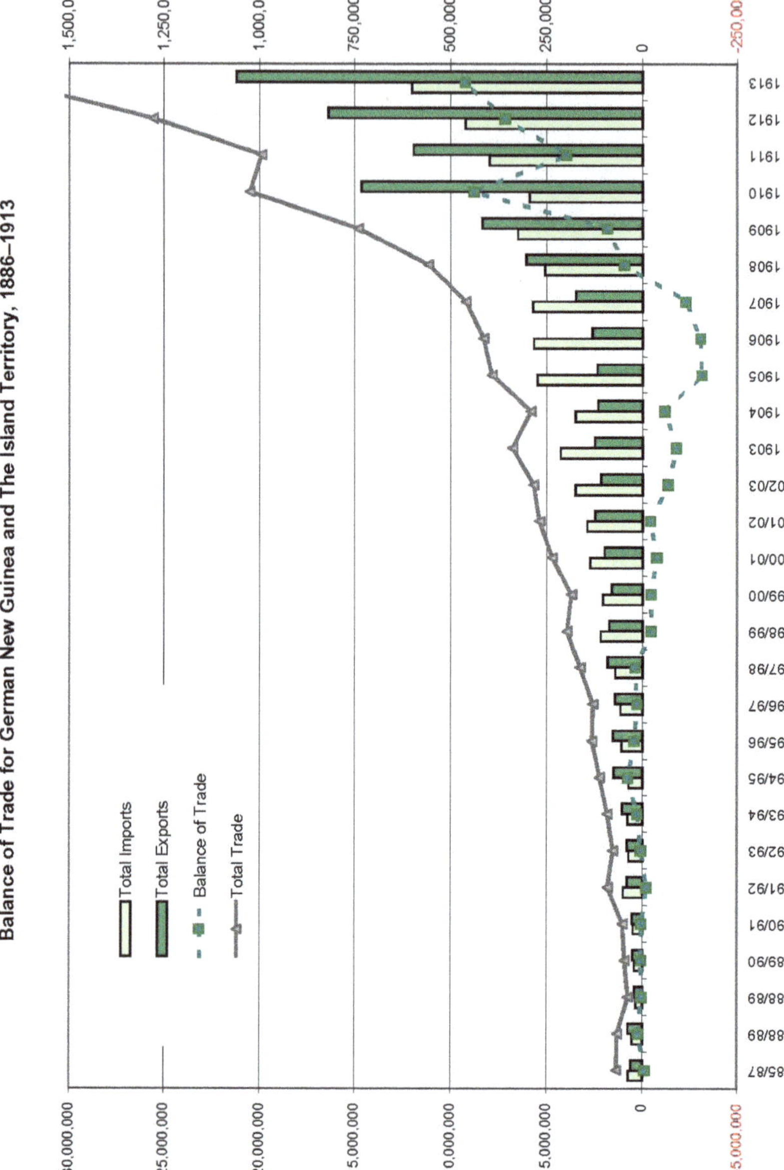

Chart 29

Balance of Trade for British New Guinea and Papua, 1887–1914
(£)
(RM)
250,000
200,000
150,000
100,000
50,000
0
-50,000
-100,000
-150,000
5,000,000
4,000,000
3,000,000
2,000,000
1,000,000
0
-1,000,000
-2,000,000
-3,000,000
Papua Gold Exports (estimate)
Papua Gold Exports (recorded)
Papua non-gold Exports
Papua Imports
Papua Balance of Trade
1887/89
1889/90
1890/91
1891/92
1892/93
1893/94
1894/95
1895/96
1896/97
1897/98
1898/99
1899/00
1900/01
1901/02
1902/03
1903/04
1904/05
1905/06
1906/07
1907/08
1908/09
1909/10
1910/11
1911/12
1912/13
1913/14

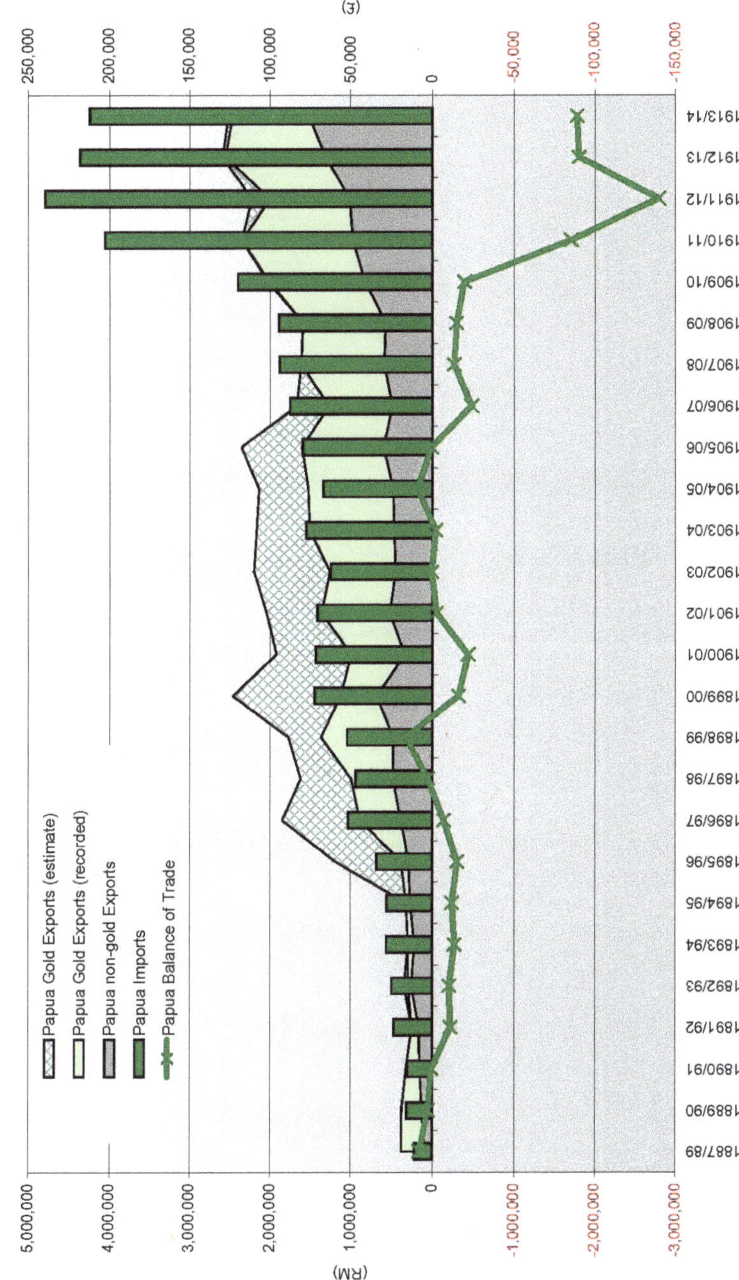

Chart 30

Exports by values from British New Guinea and Papua, 1886–1914

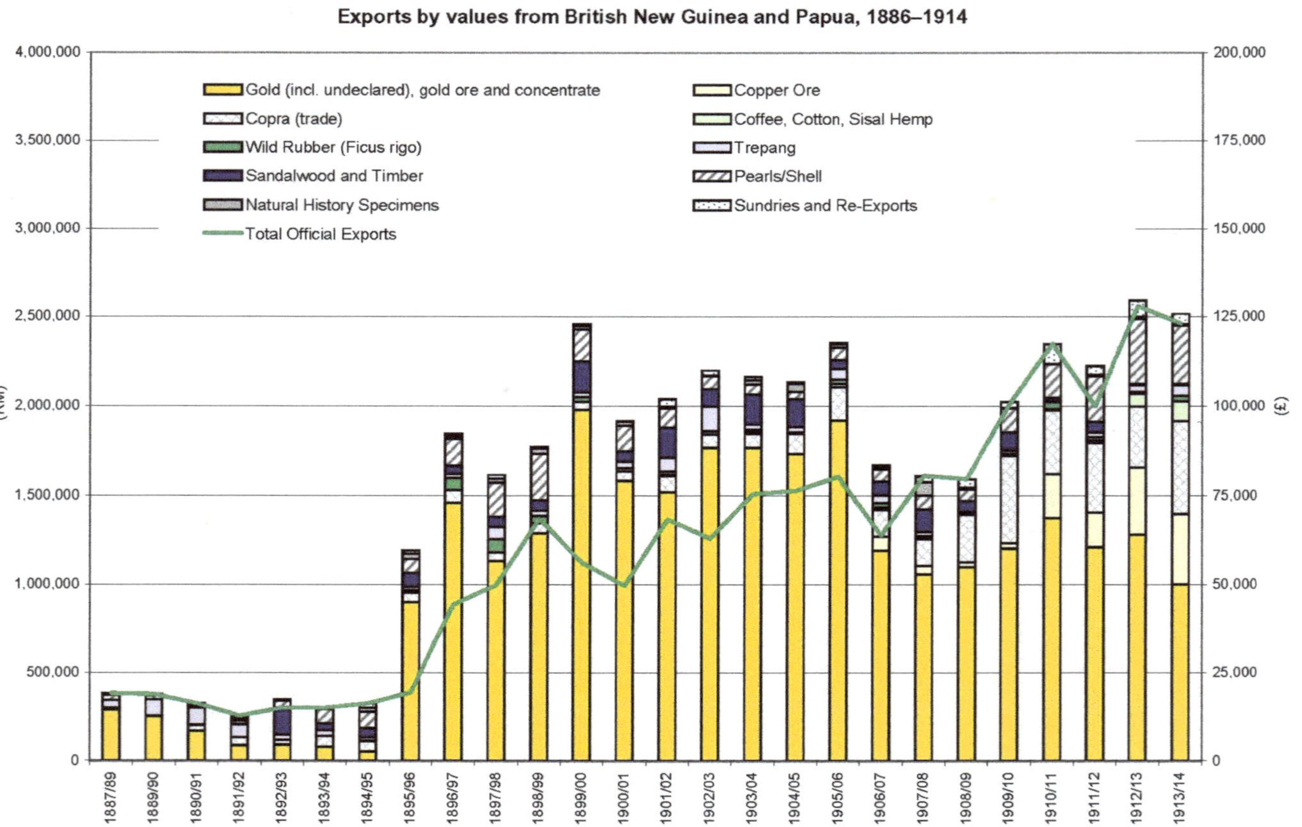

Chart 31

Imports by values to British New Guinea and Papua, 1886–1914
(RM)
6,000,000
5,000,000
4,000,000
3,000,000
2,000,000
1,000,000
0
(£)
300,000
250,000
200,000
150,000
100,000
50,000
0
Miscellaneous
Government Stores
Coal
Oil and Kerosene (Paints and Varnish from 1912)
Beverages (alcoholic)
Drugs and Chemicals
Tobacco Trading (including personal consumption)
Guns, Ammunition, Dynamite
Livestock
Boats and Oars, Launches
Machinery, Mining, Agriculture, Tools
Hardware, Building Material
Textiles and Household Goods
Foodstuff and Agricultural Products
Total
1887/89
1889/90
1890/91
1891/92
1892/93
1893/94
1894/95
1895/96
1896/97
1897/98
1898/99
1899/00
1900/01
1901/02
1902/03
1903/04
1904/05
1905/06
1906/07
1907/08
1908/09
1909/10
1910/11
1911/12
1912/13
1913/14

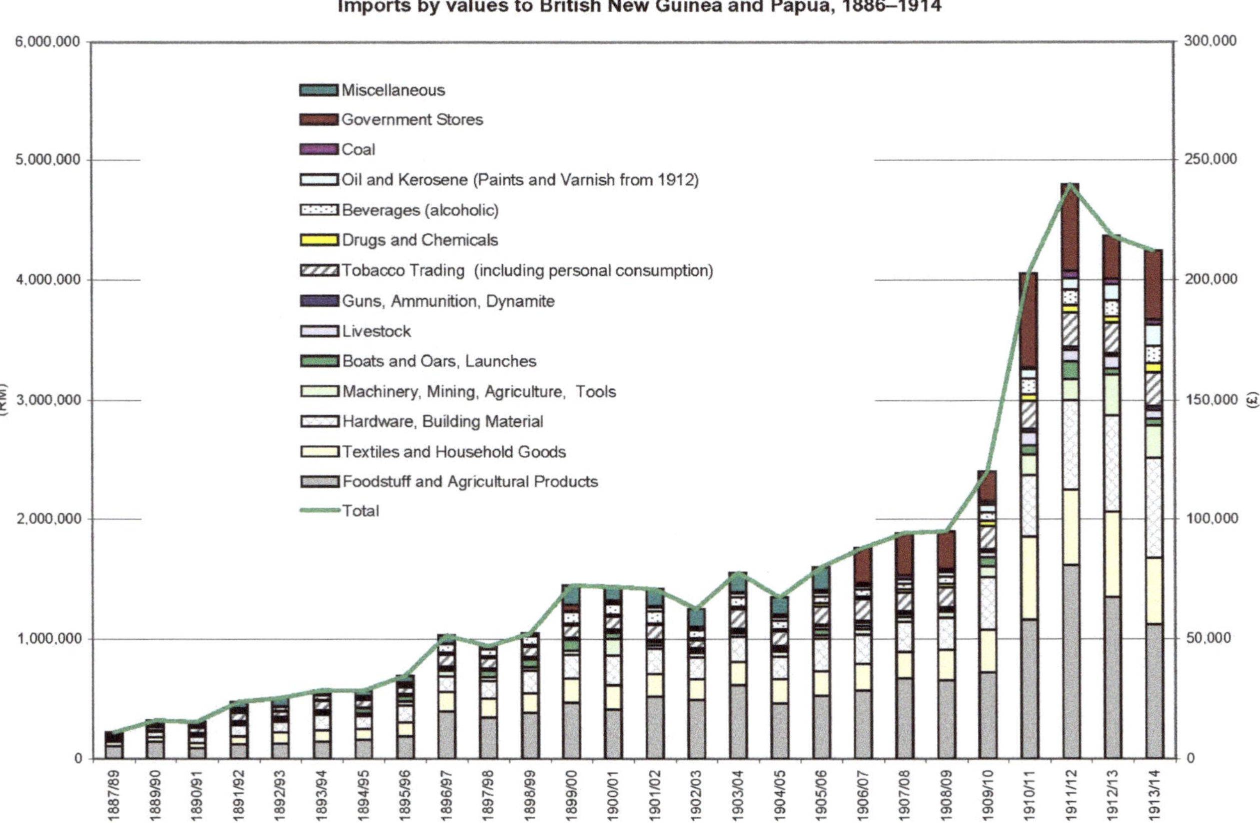

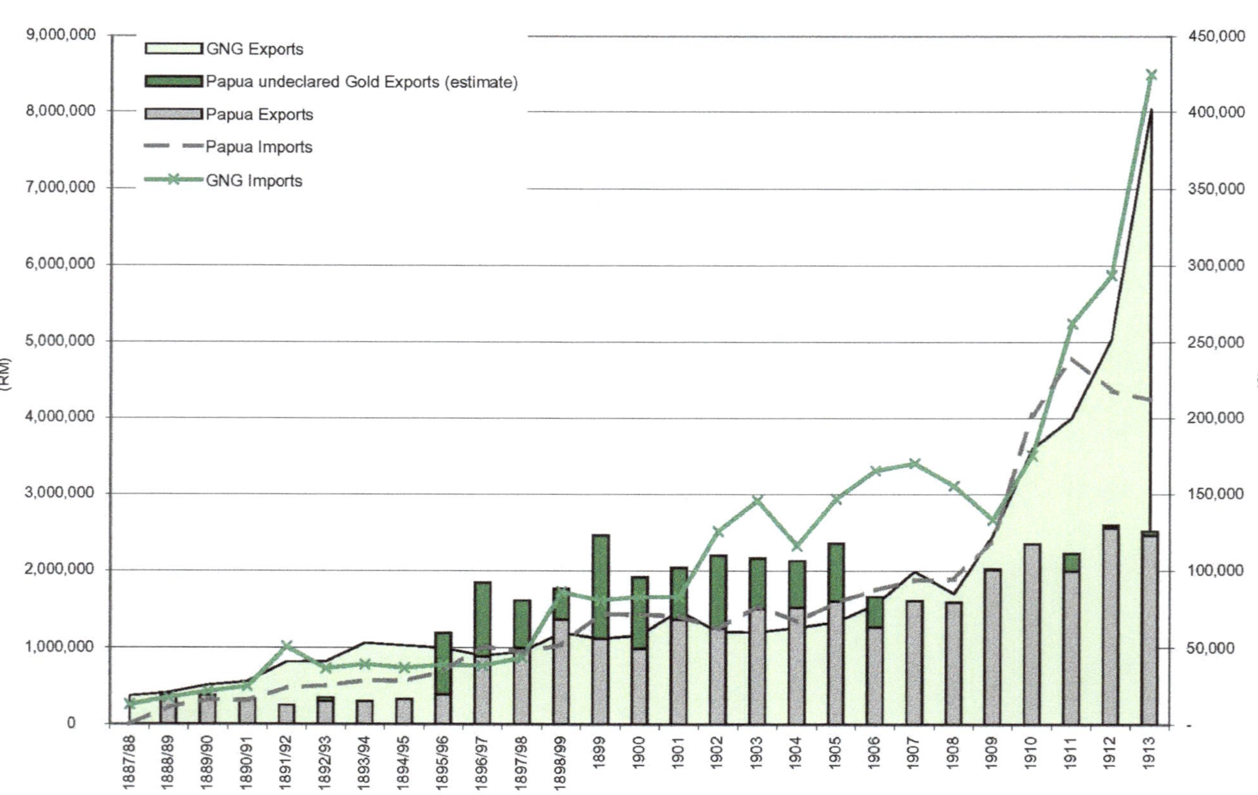
Chart 32
Trade comparison between British New Guinea, Papua and German New Guinea, 1887–1913
GNG Exports
Papua undeclared Gold Exports (estimate)
Papua Exports
Papua Imports
GNG Imports
(RM)
(£)
9,000,000
8,000,000
7,000,000
6,000,000
5,000,000
4,000,000
3,000,000
2,000,000
1,000,000
0
450,000
400,000
350,000
300,000
250,000
200,000
150,000
100,000
50,000
1887/88
1888/89
1889/90
1890/91
1891/92
1892/93
1893/94
1894/95
1895/96
1896/97
1897/98
1898/99
1899
1900
1901
1902
1903
1904
1905
1906
1907
1908
1909
1910
1911
1912
1913

Chart 33

Major export commodities for Papua and German New Guinea, 1888–1913

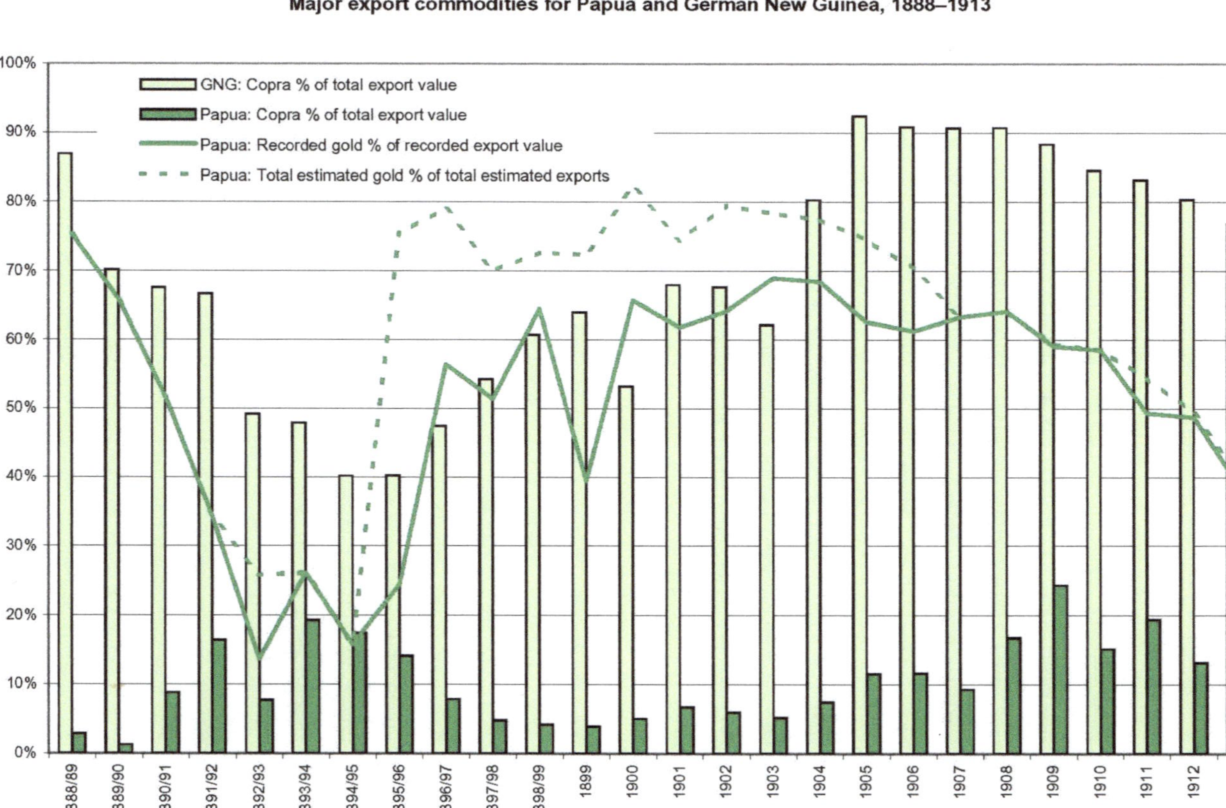

Disastrous Ventures

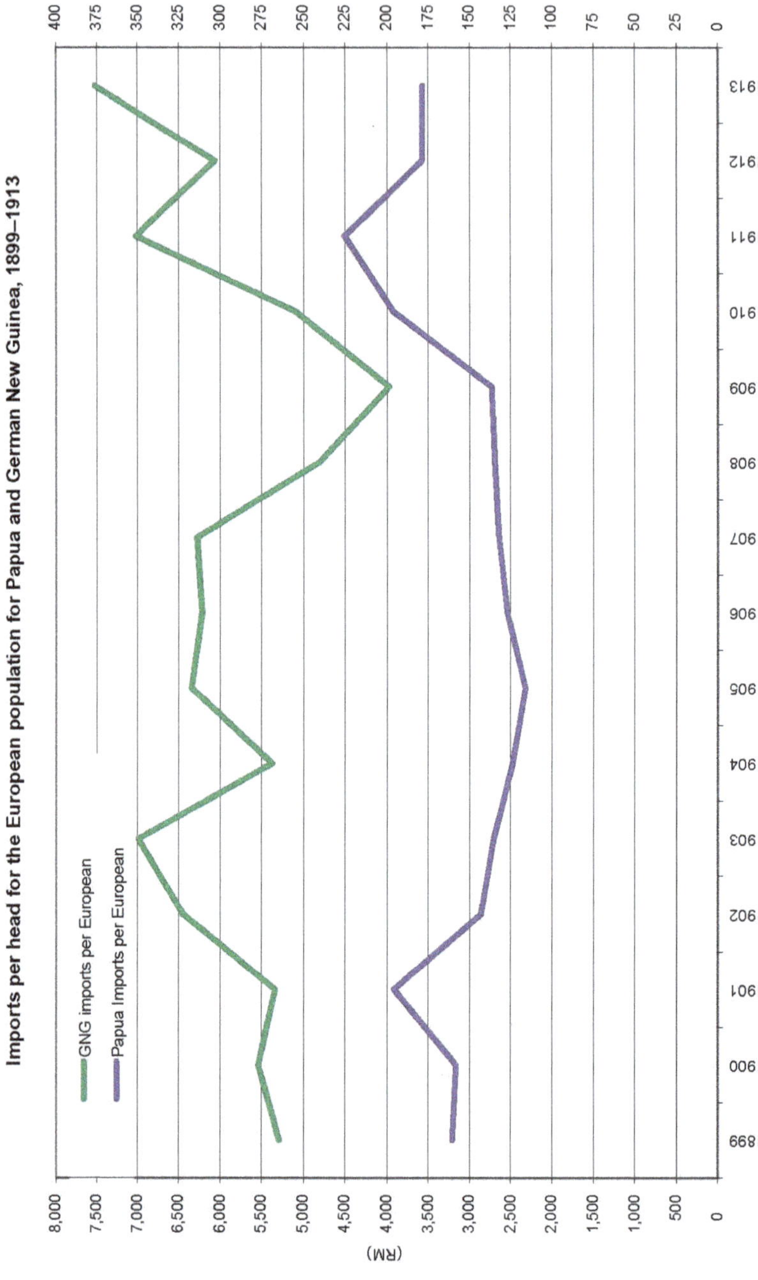

Chart 35

Annual rainfall for British New Guinea and Papua, 1891–1914

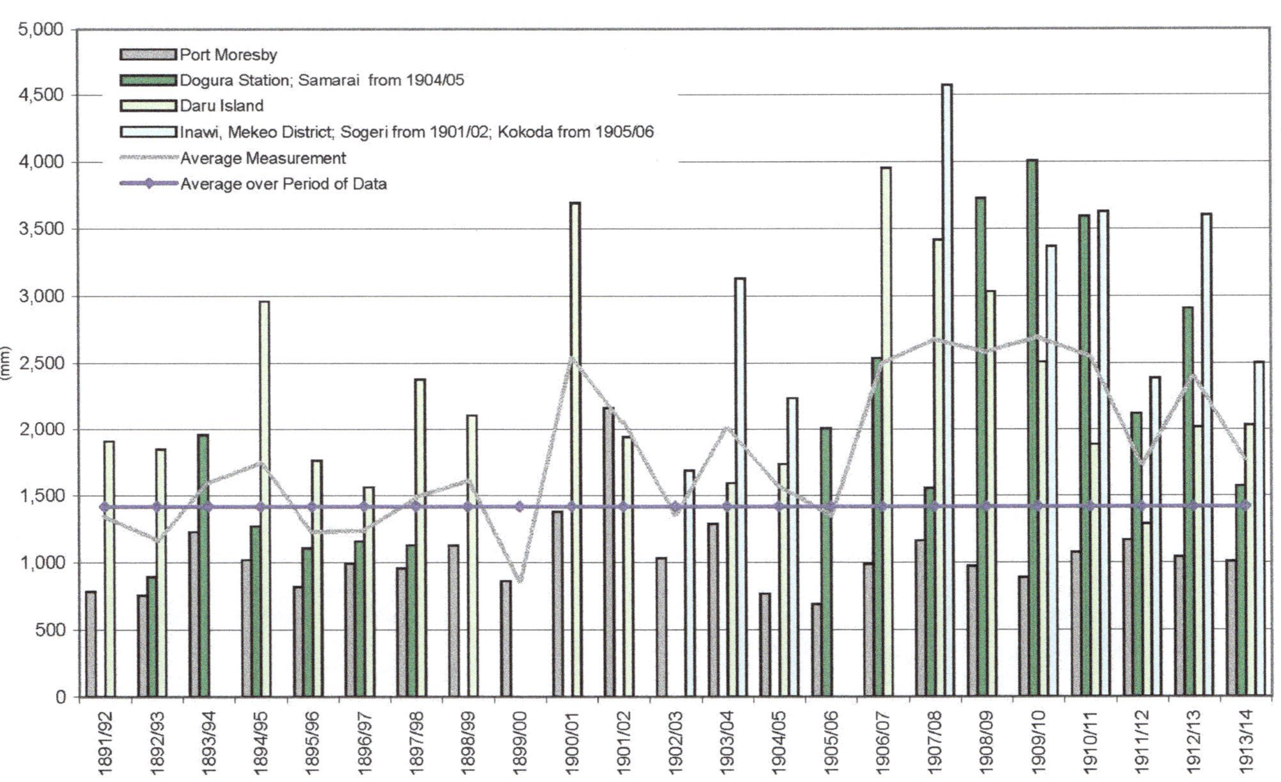

Chart 36

Annual rainfall for German New Guinea, 1886–1913
Friedrich Wilhelmshafen; Modillion Station from 1905
Hatzfeldthafen (1886-1890); Seleo/Aitape from 1902
Constantinhafen
Finschhafen (1886-1891); Simbang from 1895; Wareo from 1905
Average Measurement
Kieta
Stephansort
Erima until 1901; Erimahafen thereafter
Herbertshöhe
Period Average
(mm)
7,000
6,000
5,000
4,000
3,000
2,000
1,000
0
1886/87
1887
1888
1889
1890
1891
1892
1893
1894
1895
1896
1897
1898
1899
1900
1901
1902
1903
1904
1905
1906
1907
1908
1909
1910
1911
1912
1913

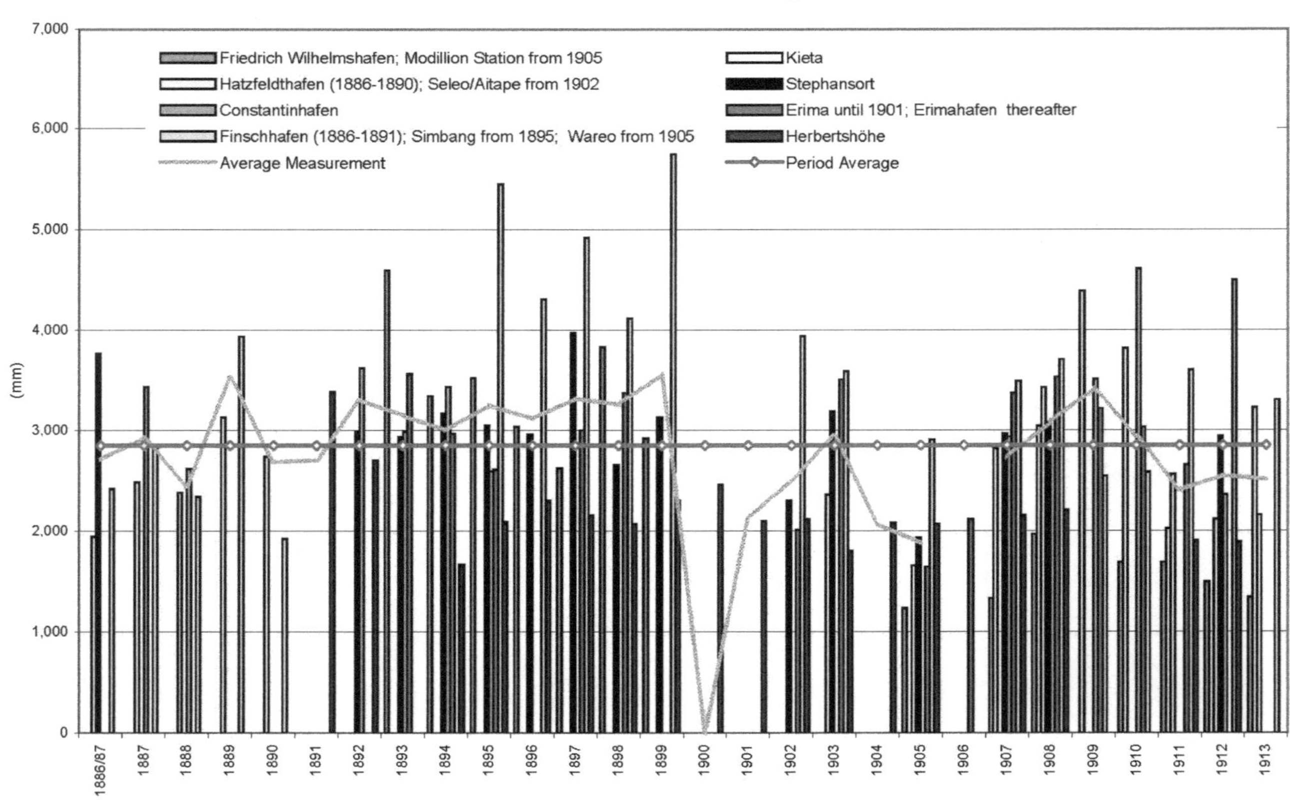

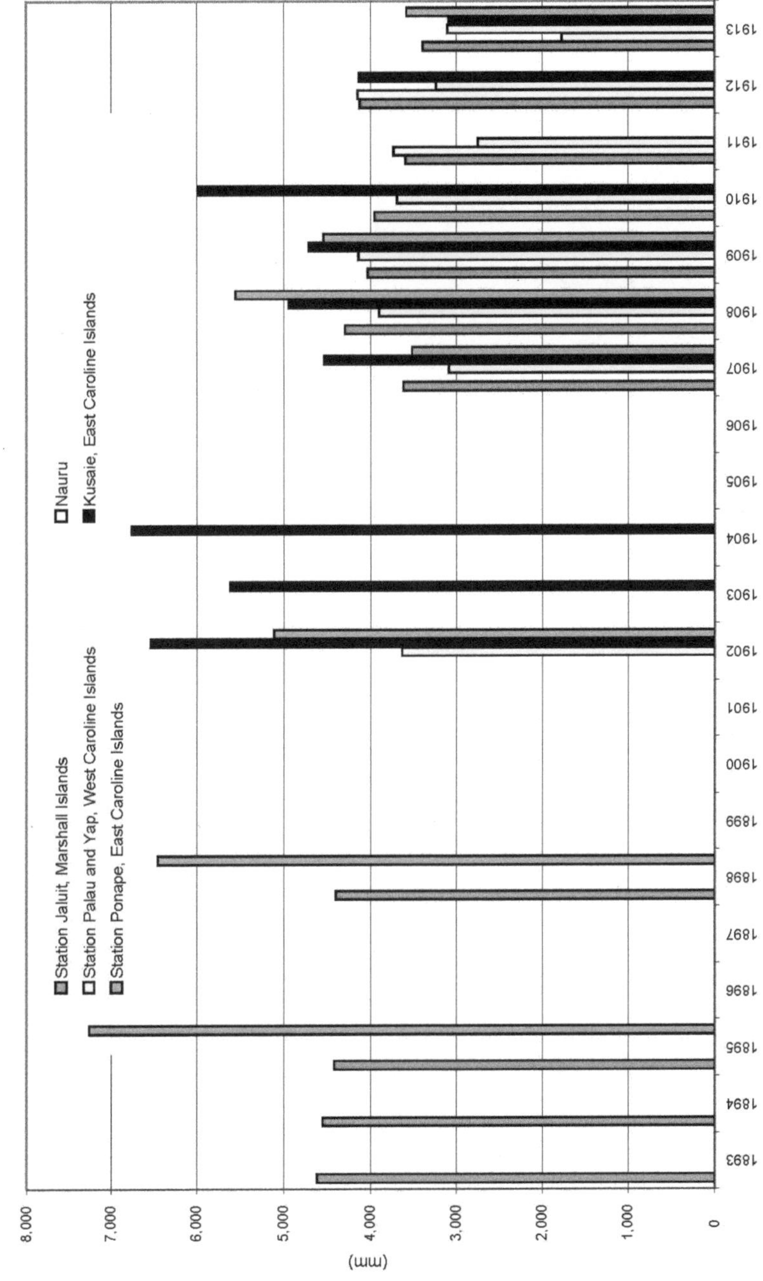
Chart 37
Annual rainfall for The Island Territory, 1893–1913
Station Jaluit, Marshall Islands
Station Palau and Yap, West Caroline Islands
Station Ponape, East Caroline Islands
Nauru
Kusaie, East Caroline Islands
(mm)
8.000
7.000
6.000
5.000
4.000
3.000
2.000
1.000
0
1893
1894
1895
1896
1897
1898
1899
1900
1901
1902
1903
1904
1905
1906
1907
1908
1909
1910
1911
1912
1913

Disastrous Ventures

472

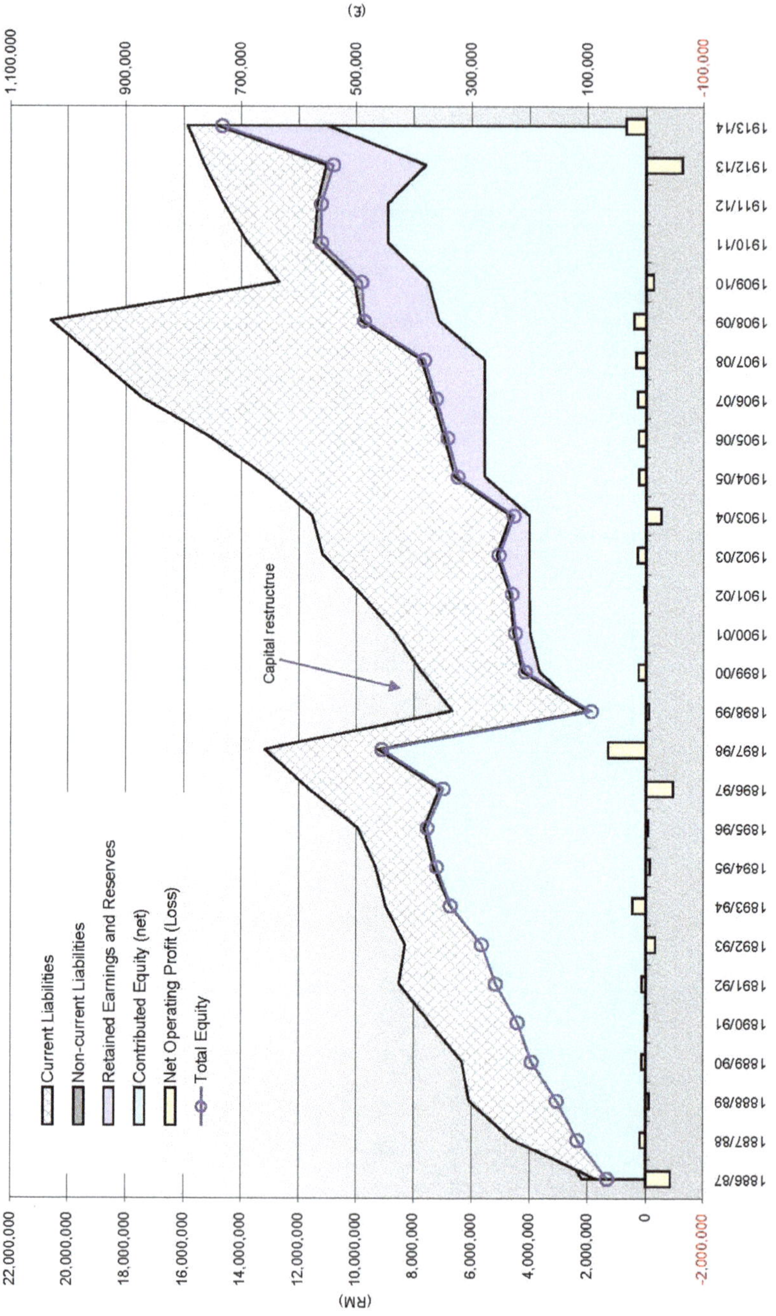

Chart 1

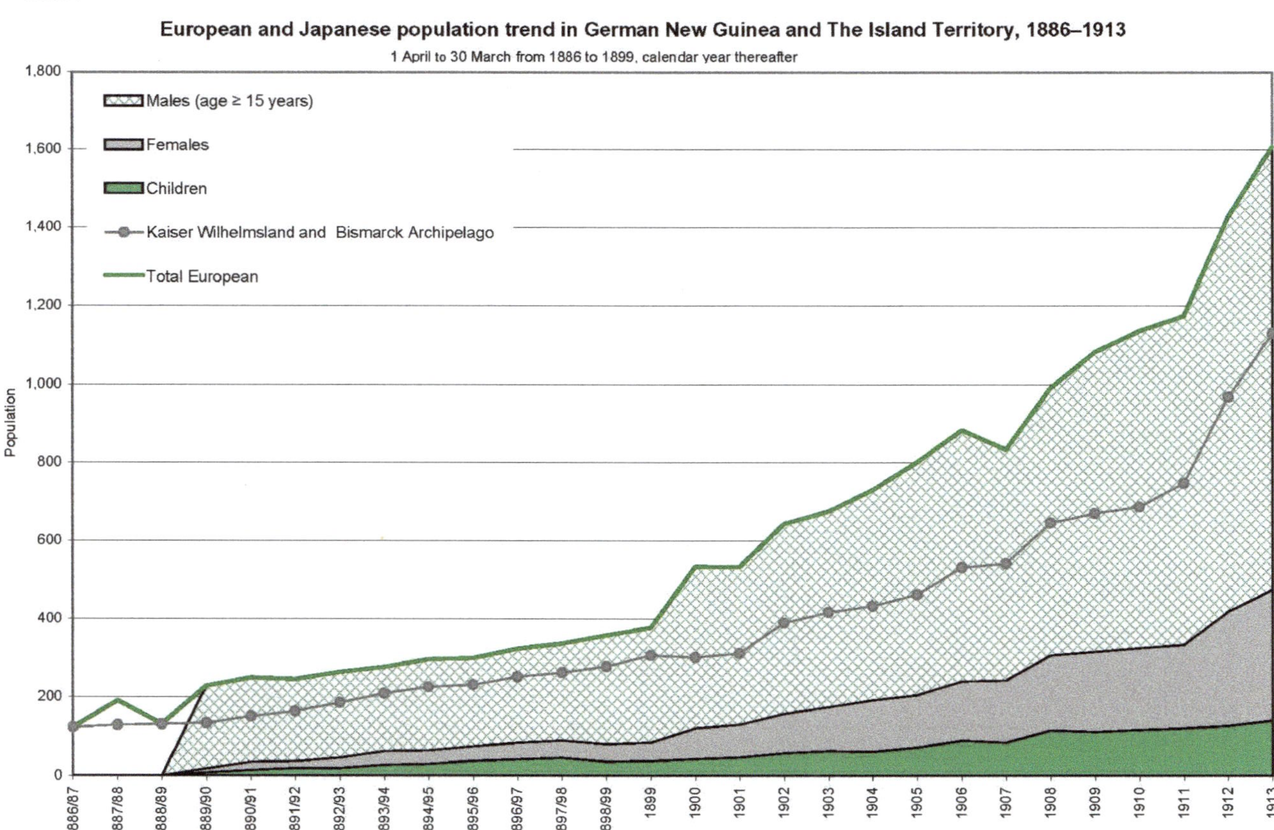

Disastrous Ventures

INDEX

C